Programming ASP.NET

Other Microsoft .NET resources from O'Reilly

Related titles	ASP.NET 2.0: A Developer's Notebook™	Programming Visual Basic 2005
	Programming C#	Visual Basic 2005: A Developer's Notebook™
	ASP.NET Cookbook™	
	C# Cookbook™	Visual C# 2005: A Developer's Notebook™

.NET Books Resource Center
dotnet.oreilly.com is a complete catalog of O'Reilly's books on .NET and related technologies, including sample chapters and code examples.

ONDotnet.com provides independent coverage of fundamental, interoperable, and emerging Microsoft .NET programming and web services technologies.

Conferences
O'Reilly brings diverse innovators together to nurture the ideas that spark revolutionary industries. We specialize in documenting the latest tools and systems, translating the innovator's knowledge into useful skills for those in the trenches. Visit *conferences.oreilly.com* for our upcoming events.

Safari Bookshelf (*safari.oreilly.com*) is the premier online reference library for programmers and IT professionals. Conduct searches across more than 1,000 books. Subscribers can zero in on answers to time-critical questions in a matter of seconds. Read the books on your Bookshelf from cover to cover or simply flip to the page you need. Try it today for free.

THIRD EDITION

Programming ASP.NET

Jesse Liberty and Dan Hurwitz

Beijing · Cambridge · Farnham · Köln · Paris · Sebastopol · Taipei · Tokyo

Programming ASP.NET, Third Edition

by Jesse Liberty and Dan Hurwitz

Published by O'Reilly Media, Inc., 1005 Gravenstein Highway North, Sebastopol, CA 95472.

O'Reilly books may be purchased for educational, business, or sales promotional use. Online editions are also available for most titles (*safari.oreilly.com*). For more information, contact our corporate/institutional sales department: (800) 998-9938 or *corporate@oreilly.com*.

Editor:	John Osborn
Developmental Editor:	Brian MacDonald
Production Editor:	Matt Hutchinson
Production Services:	GEX, Inc.
Cover Designer:	Emma Colby
Interior Designer:	David Futato

Printing History:

October 2005:	Third Edition.
September 2003:	Second Edition.
February 2002:	First Edition.

ISBN-10: 0-596-00916-X
ISBN-13: 978-0-596-00916-8
[M]

This book is dedicated to my family:
strong women with strong values.

—Jesse Liberty

I dedicate this book to my parents, who taught me
to work hard and do a good job.

—Dan Hurwitz

Table of Contents

Preface

ASP.NET 2.0 is arguably the fastest, most efficient, most reliable and best supported way to create interactive web applications available today. It has some of the best development tools on the market, and Microsoft has created new controls with Version 2 you can drag onto your web form that take care of nearly all the "plumbing" (security, data access, layout, and so on) you would normally write for yourself; this allows you to concentrate on your specific application.

About This Book

This book will teach you all you need to know to build professional quality, interactive, robust data-driven web applications.

ASP.NET is not difficult. All of the concepts are straightforward, and the Visual Studio 2005 environment simplifies the process of building powerful web applications. The difficulty in ASP.NET is only that it is so complete and flexible that there are many pieces that must be woven together to build a robust, scalable, and efficient application.

We assume you have some background with C# or sufficient programming experience to pick up what you need to know from the examples shown.

Since there are two authors' names on this book, you might be concerned that the tone will be uneven. Every possible measure has been taken to avoid this. Though each chapter was initially written by one author, all chapters were edited by both. Then every chapter was extensively edited and rewritten by Jesse Liberty to give the book a single voice. And if that weren't enough, the chapters were subsequently edited by O'Reilly editors as well as independent tech editors, and again by the authors. The bottom line is that while two authors wrote this book, you should find that it reads as if written by a single author.

How This Book Is Organized

Chapter 1, *ASP.NET 2.0*, is an introduction to ASP.NET and the .NET platform. There are also notes in this first chapter on the major improvements made in ASP.NET 2.0 over ASP.NET 1.x.

Chapter 2, *Visual Studio 2005*, explores the Visual Studio 2005 Integrated Development Environment and shows how you can use it most efficiently to create ASP.NET applications.

The next three chapters (Chapter 3, *Controls: Fundamental Concepts*, Chapter 4, *Basic Controls*, and Chapter 5, *Advanced Controls*) provide complete coverage of ASP.NET Server Controls.

Chapter 6, *Web Site Fundamentals*, goes beyond the controls to show you how to use code-behind effectively, and how to manage state in the otherwise stateless Web and describes the lifecycle of a Web page in detail and, finally shows you how to take advantage of advanced *directives*.

Chapter 7 examines *Tracing, Debugging, and Error Handling* in ASP.NET.

Chapter 8 looks at *Validation*. ASP.NET provides extensive support for data validation, including ensuring that a choice has been made, checking that values are within a range, and matching regular expressions. The ASP.NET Framework will automatically and invisibly take advantage of the capabilities of up-level browsers (such as IE6) to do the data validation at the client, while still providing server-based validation for down-level browsers and to protect against spoofing.

Chapter 9 looks at *Web Data Access*, and explores the new controls in ASP.NET 2.0 that make interacting with data sources such as databases and XML files far easier than ever before. With these new controls you can reduce the amount of code you write by over 75 percent.

Chapter 10, *ADO.NET*, shows you the technology underlying the controls described in Chapter 9, so you understand fully how it all works and so you can take precise control when necessary.

Chapter 11, *Forms-Based Security*, describes in detail how to implement forms-based security to constrain user access to your web site over the Internet. New controls in ASP.NET 2.0 integrate with SQLExpress, SQL Server, or your own data store to create users and roles (groups) and to facilitate authentication and authorization.

Chapter 12, *Master Pages and Navigation*, describes features that help you build professional-quality Web Applications. Master Pages allow you to create a uniform look and feel throughout your application, and the Navigation controls allow you to build site maps, menus, and breadcrumbs quickly and easily to facilitate navigation of large applications.

Chapter 13, *Personalization*, shows you how to allow your users to tailor the look and feel of your site to their own requirements and how to store that information so when the user returns, the site remembers the user's preferences and state. New ASP.NET controls and technology make this surprisingly easy and facilitate the creation of advanced professional web sites.

Chapter 14, *Custom and User Controls*, covers the powerful, yet easy to use, technology that allows you to extend ASP.NET to create controls customized for your specific problem domain.

Chapter 15, *Creating Web Services*, shows you how to create web services that allow other applications to interact with your application programmatically, and Chapter 16, *Consuming Web Services*, shows you how to create client applications that present data retrieved from Web Services.

Chapter 17 looks at *Caching and Performance*, focusing on issues related to building fast, scalable applications.

Chapter 18 covers *Application Logic and Configuration,* and Chapter 19 focuses on *Deployment*. The .NET platform simplifies building ASP.NET applications, with text file configuration and XCOPY deployment, but often you want to go beyond the fundamentals to create self-deploying applications that can be used on web farms and that facilitate easy installation.

Appendix A provides the Visual Studio 2005 keyboard shortcuts, while Appendix B provides a crash course in *Relational Database Technology*.

Who This Book Is For

This book was written for programmers and web developers who want to build web applications using Microsoft's powerful new ASP.NET 2.0 platform. Many readers will have experience with "classic" ASP or ASP.NET 1.x, though that is not required. Many developers will have read a primer on C# (and if not, you may want to take a look at *Programming C#* or *Learning C#* both by Jesse Liberty and published by O'Reilly.) Other experienced VB, Java, or C++ developers may decide they can pick up what they need to know about the languages by working through the exercises in this book.

Conventions Used in This Book

The following font conventions are used in this book:

Italic
> Used for pathnames, filenames, program names, Internet addresses, such as domain names and URLs, and new terms where they are defined.

Constant Width

> Used for command lines and options that should be typed verbatim, and names and keywords in program examples. Also used for parameters, attributes, expressions, statements, and values.

Constant Width Italic

> Used for replaceable items, such as variables or optional elements, within syntax lines or code.

Constant Width Bold

> Used for emphasis within program code examples.

Pay special attention to notes set apart from the text with the following icons:

> This is a tip. It contains useful supplementary information about the topic at hand.

> This is a warning. It helps you solve and avoid annoying problems.

Support: A Note from Jesse Liberty

I provide ongoing support for my books through my web site. You can obtain the source code for all of the examples in Programming ASP.NET at:

> *http://www.LibertyAssociates.com*

You'll find access to a book support discussion group which has a section set aside for questions about *Programming ASP.NET*. Before you post a question, however, please check my web site to see if there is a Frequently Asked Questions (FAQ) list or an errata file. If you check these files and still have a question, then please go ahead and post to the discussion center. The most effective way to get help is to ask a precise question or to create a small program that illustrates your area of concern or confusion, and be sure to mention which edition of the book you have (this is the third edition).

We have tested and verified the information in this book to the best of our ability, but you may find that features have changed (or that we have made mistakes). Please let us know about any errors you find, as well as your suggestions for future editions, by sending email to *jliberty@libertyassociates.com*.

Using Code Examples

This book is here to help you get your job done. In general, you may use the code in this book in your programs and documentation. You do not need to contact us for permission unless you're reproducing a significant portion of the code. For example, writing a program that uses several chunks of code from this book does not require permission. Selling or distributing a CD-ROM of examples from O'Reilly books *does* require permission. Answering a question by citing this book and quoting example code does not require permission. Incorporating a significant amount of example code from this book into your product's documentation *does* require permission.

We appreciate, but do not require, attribution. An attribution usually includes the title, author, publisher, and ISBN. For example: "*Programming ASP.NET*, Third Edition, by Jesse Liberty and Dan Hurwitz. Copyright 2006 O'Reilly Media, Inc., 0-596-00916-X."

If you feel your use of code examples falls outside fair use or the permission given above, feel free to contact us at *permissions@oreilly.com*.

We'd Like to Hear from You

Please address comments and questions concerning this book to the publisher:

O'Reilly Media, Inc.
1005 Gravenstein Highway North
Sebastopol, CA 95472
(800) 998-9938 (in the United States or Canada)
(707) 829-0515 (international or local)
(707) 829-0104 (fax)

We have a web page for this book, where we list errata, examples, and any additional information. You can access this page at:

http://www.oreilly.com/catalog/progaspdotnet3

To comment or ask technical questions about this book, send email to:

bookquestions@oreilly.com

For more information about our books, conferences, Resource Centers, and the O'Reilly Network, see the web site:

http://www.oreilly.com

Visit the O'Reilly .NET DevCenter:

http://www.oreillynet.com/dotnet

Safari Enabled

 When you see a Safari® enabled icon on the cover of your favorite technology book, that means the book is available online through the O'Reilly Network Safari Bookshelf.

Safari offers a solution that's better than e-books. It's a virtual library that lets you easily search thousands of top tech books, cut and paste code samples, download chapters, and find quick answers when you need the most accurate, current information. Try it free at *http://safari.oreilly.com*.

Acknowledgments

From Jesse Liberty

I am particularly grateful to John Osborn who has shepherded all my work through O'Reilly, and to Brian MacDonald who is an extraordinary editor. I would like to thank Jason Alexander, Ron Buckton, and David Mercer, who were among the best technical editors I've ever worked with.

Kevin Shafer, Ron Petrusha, Claire Cloutier, and Tatiana Diaz helped make this book better than what we'd written. Rob Romano created a number of the illustrations and improved the others. Kevin Shafer of Kevin Shafer and Associates coordinated our preproduction work.

From Dan Hurwitz

In addition to the people mentioned by Jesse, as always I especially want to thank my wife and family for being so supportive of this project and making it possible.

CHAPTER 1

ASP.NET 2.0

The White Rabbit put on his spectacles. "Where shall I
begin, please, your Majesty?"
"Begin at the beginning" the King said gravely, "and
go on till you come to the end, then stop."
—Lewis Carroll
Alice's Adventures in Wonderland, Chapter XII

ASP.NET 2.0 is the successor to ASP.NET 1.x, which was the successor, in turn to
Active Server Pages (ASP) and is now, arguably, the most popular and powerful way
to write interactive Web Applications. Along with the development of ASP.NET has
come the rapid evolution of Visual Studio 2005 (VS2005), once again arguably the
most powerful and flexible tool for creating interactive web applications. VS2005
does not excel at laying out web pages (there are better tools for that, such as Dream-
weaver) but nothing comes close for building interactive web sites, especially data-
driven sites that interact with a server-side database.

Microsoft first announced ASP.NET 1.0 (then called ASP+) and the .NET Framework in July, 2000. In essence, .NET was a new development framework that provided a fresh application programming interface to the services and APIs of classic
Windows operating systems, especially Windows 2000, while bringing together a
number of disparate technologies that emerged from Microsoft during the late 1990s.
Among the latter are COM+ component services, a commitment to XML and object-
oriented design, support for new web services protocols such as Simple Object
Access Protocol (SOAP), Web Service Description Language (WSDL), and Universal
Description, Discovery, and Integration (UDDI), and a focus on the Internet.

With more than five years of experience and developer feedback, Microsoft has
released the .NET Framework 2.0, VS2005, and most important for you, ASP.NET
2.0. The goal of ASP.NET 2.0 was to reduce the coding required to build ASP.NET
applications by 70 percent compared with ASP.NET 1.x; an amazing achievement.
With the latest tools, you can focus on the business logic of your application and
drag and drop controls that provide virtually all the plumbing for you.

"Begin at the Beginning"

There are two ways to read this book. The first way is to read its chapters in sequence, beginning with Chapter 1, which explains the .NET Framework and the new features of ASP.NET 2.0, and then Chapter 2, which provides a rapid tour of Visual Studio 2005. These chapters will equip you with the concepts and tools you need to get started. You can proceed through the remaining chapters, working your way through their exercises, we hope, and building more complex skills as you go.

The second way is put this book down, open VS2005, create a new web site (File → New Web Site) and start building an application by dragging and dropping controls onto forms, diving into the appropriate chapter when (and if) you need help or deeper understanding of a topic.

Either approach is fine with us. We didn't write the book to be a step-by-step tutorial and there is no law saying you have to read the chapters in order, but we did try to avoid forward references, so you may be better off reading the book in the traditional manner after all.

.NET Framework 2.0

The .NET Framework sits on top of the operating system, which can be any recently released version of Windows, including Windows 2000, Windows XP, or Windows Server 2003. Currently, the .NET Framework consists of:

- Compilers for five official languages (C#, Visual Basic, Managed C++, J#, and the Jscript scripting language).
- A number of related class libraries, collectively known as the Framework Class Library (FCL), that include support for Windows and web applications, data access, web services, and more.
- The Common Language Runtime (CLR), the object-oriented engine at the heart of the Framework that translates the intermediate code generated by the language compilers into the native code required to execute the application.

The .NET Framework is an integral part of Windows Server 2003 but must be downloaded and installed to run on Windows 2000 or Windows XP.

 Because the CLR translates all code to a common interactive language that is later complied to native code, .NET can, in principle, be implemented on Unix, Linux, Mac OS X, or any other operating system.

Figure 1-1 breaks down the .NET Framework into its architectural components.

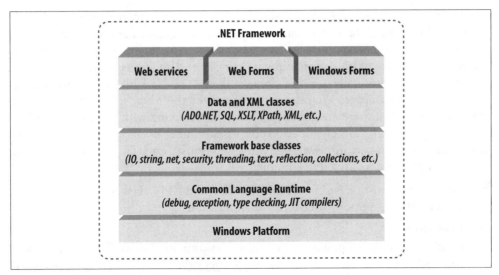

Figure 1-1. .NET Framework architecture

The CLR executes your program on your web server. The CLR activates objects, performs security checks on them, lays them out in memory, executes them, and handles garbage collection.

In Figure 1-1, the layer on top of the CLR is a set of framework base classes, followed by an additional layer of data and XML classes, plus another layer of classes intended for web services, web sites, and Windows forms. Collectively, these classes are known as the FCL. With more than 5,000 classes, the FCL facilitates rapid development of ASP.NET applications.

 This same class library is used for all .NET applications, including console, desktop, and mobile devices, as well as ASP.NET.

The .NET Framework supports a Common Language Specification (CLS), which allows you to choose the syntax with which you are most comfortable. You can write classes in C# and derive from them in Visual Basic 2005 (VB2005). You can throw an exception in VB2005 and catch it in a C# class. Suddenly the choice of language is a personal preference rather than a limiting factor in your application's development.

The set of Framework base classes supports rudimentary input and output, string manipulation, security management, network communication, thread management, text manipulation, reflection, and collections functionality, and so on.

Above the base class level are classes that support data management and XML manipulation. The data classes support persistent management of data that are maintained on backend databases. These classes include the Structured Query Language (SQL) classes to let you manipulate persistent data stores through a standard SQL interface. Additionally, a set of classes called ADO.NET allows you to manipulate persistent data. There are classes optimized for the Microsoft SQL Server relational database, and there are generic classes for interacting with OLE DB compliant databases. The .NET Framework also supports a number of classes to let you manipulate XML data and perform XML searching and translations. Chapter 10 discuss the data-handling aspects of the .NET Framework.

Beyond the Framework base classes and the data and XML classes is yet another tier of classes geared to support three types of application:

Windows forms
> Facilitates the development of Windows desktop and Smart Client applications with rich and flexible user interfaces. These "traditional" desktop applications can interact with other computers on the local network or over the Internet through the use of web services. Windows application are not the subject of this book.

Web sites
> Supports the development of robust, scalable web pages and web sites, especially ASP.NET applications. Server controls enable many new features, such as validation, event-driven programmatic manipulation of the web pages, state maintenance, and more. Chapters 6 through 8 discuss web sites in detail.

Web services
> Supports the development of applications that can process RPC-style method calls or XML messages over the Internet. Web services include a number of classes that support the development of lightweight distributed components, which will work even in the face of firewalls and Network Address Translation (NAT) software. Because web services employ standard Hypertext Transfer Protocol (HTTP) and SOAP as underlying communications protocols, these components support plug-and-play across cyberspace. Chapters 15 and 16 discuss web services specifically.

ASP.NET 2.0

ASP.NET 2.0 is the umbrella term for the combination of two web development technologies: web sites and web services. Using ASP.NET 2.0, it is easier than ever to create web sites that are dynamic and data-driven, that scale well, and that work well across a broad range of browsers without any custom coding by the developer.

VS2005 allows you to apply Rapid Application Development (RAD) techniques to building web applications: Drag and drop controls onto your form, double-click on a control, and write the code to respond to the associated event.

Generally, web services are web applications without a user interface that allow you to provide services to other web sites or applications. As you'll see in later chapters, ASP.NET 2.0 has classes to facilitate the creation of standards-compliant web services and web clients, and tools incorporated into Visual Studio 2005 help enforce conformance.

New Features

ASP.NET 2.0 includes a new Web Site Administration Tool that provides a wizard interface for web-site maintenance, as shown in Figure 1-2.

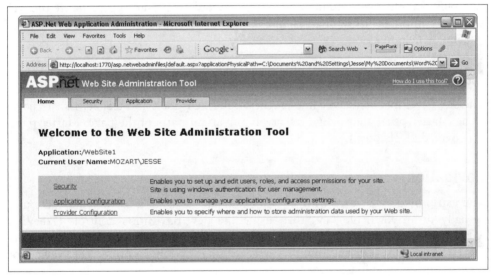

Figure 1-2. Web Site Application Administration Tool

From within this tool you can establish the database provider both for security and for role management, and you can manage your Application, SMTP, and other site management settings. The web site configuration tool is described fully in Chapter 18.

Special Folders Make Integration Easier

Web sites can now include an *App_Code* folder immediately below the application root. You may put source code into this folder and it will be compiled automatically every time the web app is run. In addition, an *App_Data* folder is reserved for databases, and there are additional special folders for XML files, for localization, and for skins and themes (see Chapter 13).

ASP.NET 2.0 takes advantage of the new language feature of "partial classes." In short, this allows VS2005 to separate the tool-generated code from your code, simplifying your tasks and making your code easier to read and maintain.

Security

ASP.NET 2.0 includes a number of controls and scripts that make implementing web-based security far simpler than in previous versions of ASP.NET. The login and related controls are covered in detail in Chapter 11.

Personalization

ASP.NET 2.0 includes a number of controls that allow a user to personalize the web site's user interface, using themes and skins and related controls. These are covered in detail in Chapter 13.

Master Pages

The site developer can easily implement a consistent look and feel across site pages using Master pages that define (relatively) invariant parts of the page. Master pages are covered in Chapter 12.

Navigation

You can provide your user with sophisticated site navigation by defining a site map (usually in an XML file) and then using the new navigation controls (TreeView, SiteMapPath, and so on) to create menus and treeviews. Breadcrumbs can be displayed to help the user see how they reached their current location. The Navigation controls are covered in Chapter 12.

Web Sites Without IIS

When you're working in VS2005, you do not need to have IIS installed, and you can store your entire web site in a folder hierarchy separate from *inetpub*. This makes sharing development of web sites far easier, and is the technique we use to provide working examples on our support web site that you can download and run or debug immediately.

Improved Controls

All the ASP.NET controls now generate XHTML1.1-compliant markup and support adaptive rendering.

The new datasource controls provide a far simplified interface to data, though you are still free to use the traditional ADO.NET objects. Accessing data is covered in Chapter 9.

You can now group your validation controls to allow different parts of a page to be validated based on state that can be managed programmatically. These new validation features are covered in Chapter 8.

New Controls

ASP.NET 2.0 includes a host of new controls to simplify your coding experience. These controls will be explored in depth throughout this book, but here is a quick overview:

- Data Access Controls may represent the most significant improvement between ASP.NET 1.x and ASP.NET 2.0. You can bind data to controls on web pages using data source controls that encapsulate connections, commands, and parameters. The source for these controls can be a database, a web service, a business object, a site map, or an XML file. In addition, the ObjectDataSource control allows you to add data access to a page based on an n-tier business object.

- Complementing the Data Access Controls are a suite of new or improved Data Display Controls, including the GridView, DetailsView, and FormView. Hierarchical data can be displayed in the TreeVew and navigation is supported in the SiteMapPath control.

- ASP.NET 2.0 provides a complete suite of controls to create web-based security for your application. These include login controls (that prompt the user for credentials and validate them) and the LoginStatus control that manages different views based on if the user is logged in. The LoginView control allows you to constrain access to data and controls to logged in users, and the PasswordRecovery control provides options for helping users recover lost or forgotten passwords.

- Working closely with the Security controls are the personalization controls that allow you to provide individually personalized views (themes, skins, etc.) to your users. In addition, anonymous personalization is supported to allow you to create, for example, a shopping cart for an anonymous user that is then ported to the user's account when the user does sign in.

Visual Studio 2005 (VS2005)

VS2005 offers numerous improvements over previous versions, including the ability to share configurations across a team, Intellisense in all code windows, including page content files, drag and drop onto code pages as well as design views, support for refactoring and code snippets to speed development, and visualizers to examine complex data in the debugger.

VS2005 sports a new modern tabbed document interface and improved interaction and synchronization between the design and the source view. Code completion has been beefed up considerably as has the context-sensitive help. In addition, many compile errors are flagged immediately even before you try to compile the application. Further, VS2005 will often propose a solution to your compile error, and if you agree, it will implement the fix for you.

Perhaps most important, in VS2005 all .NET languages use the same source code editor, making it far easier to move between C# and Visual Basic and to learn each language.

Mobile Devices

At a recent industry event, it was predicted that by the end of this decade, something like 90 percent of all web traffic would be to small-screen devices, such as wireless PDAs and cell phones. Whether or not you believe this prediction to be accurate, mobile devices comprise a significant part of the web world, and their role will increase.

ASP.NET 1.x did not have any inherent facility for dealing with web sites displayed on mobile devices, as opposed to desktop browsers, other than many classes that supported the .NET Compact Framework for Windows CE .NET. However, none of the classes with a visual component, such as Button and TextBox, supported the Compact Framework.

Many of the visual controls, such as TextBox and Calendar, to name only two, did have equivalent controls in the System.Web.UI.MobileControls namespace. However, this meant that if you wanted to target a conventional desktop browser and a mobile device with the same web site, you had to create two different versions (at least) of the web site, detect which type of device was making the request, then serve the appropriate version.

The previous editions of this book did not include a chapter on mobile devices because the topic seemed more to warrant its own book, of which there are many, rather than a chapter.

Originally ASP.NET 2.0 set out to change all of that. It was going to include a new Display Adapter Architecture, in which there would be only a single set of controls. The Framework would take care of figuring out what type of device or browser was making the request, and render appropriate output. An uplevel desktop browser, such as IE 5 or higher, would get DHTML and script, a downlevel browser would get its appropriate level of HTML and script (as before), and a mobile device would get the correct version of whatever rendering language it preferred, such as WAP. A display adapter layer would intervene between the control and the output rendering, and essentially all visual controls would incorporate this display adapter.

However, Microsoft could not get this new architecture working to their satisfaction in time for the initial release of ASP.NET 2.0 and, to their credit, pulled the mobile rendering adaptors rather than ship substandard software. To develop web sites for mobile devices, you still need to use the controls of the `MobileControls` namespace. Consequently, this book does not have a chapter on mobile controls.

If Microsoft releases a new version of ASP.NET which incorporates mobile controls more integrally, we will write an additional chapter and post it for download.

On to VS2005

It always shocks me that developers spend so much of their time working in Visual Studio but invest so little time learning all its tricks and traps. Investing your time in learning to use VS2005 well pays off many times over, because the VS2005 is the single point of development, testing, and deployment for your entire web application. The next chapter delves into VS2005 in depth.

CHAPTER 2
Visual Studio 2005

Visual Studio 2005 (VS2005) is an invaluable tool for creating robust and elegant applications with few bugs in a minimum amount of time. VS2005 offers many advantages to the .NET developer, including:

- A modern interface, using a tabbed document metaphor for code and layout screens, and dockable toolbars and information windows.
- Convenient access to multiple design and code windows.
- What You See Is What You Get (WYSIWYG) visual design of Windows and Web Forms.
- Code completion, which allows you to enter code with fewer errors and less typing.
- Intellisense, which displays tips for every method, providing the return type and the types of all the parameters.
- Dynamic, context-sensitive help, which allows you to view topics and samples relevant to the code you are writing at the moment. You also can search the complete SDK library from within the IDE.
- Immediate flagging of syntax errors, which allows you to fix problems as they are entered.
- A Start Page, which provides easy access to new and existing projects.
- The same code editor for all .NET languages, which shortens the learning curve. Each language can have specialized aspects, but all languages benefit from shared features, such as incremental search, code outlining, collapsing text, line numbering, color-coded keywords, etc.
- An HTML editor, which provides Design and HTML views that update each other in real time.
- A Solution Explorer, which displays in outline form all the files comprising your solution.

- An integrated Debugger, which allows you to step through code, observe program runtime behavior, and set breakpoints, even across multiple languages and multiple processes.
- Integrated support for source control software, such as Visual Source Safe.
- Ability to modify your controls' properties declaratively or through a properties window.
- Ability to integrate custom controls that you create or purchase from a third party.

Features that are new or significantly improved in VS2005 include:

- Support for all three coding models: in-line, code-behind, mixed.
- Access to web sites through the filesystem, File Transfer Protocol (FTP), or Internet Information Services (IIS). (IIS no longer has to be installed on the developer's machine since a built-in web server is provided.)
- Full support for look-and-feel features, such as skins, themes, and master pages.
- An improved Server Explorer, which allows you to log on to servers to which you have network access, access the data and services on those servers, drag and drop data sources onto controls, and perform various other chores.
- Ability to import and export user preferences.
- Ability to drag and drop controls onto your web page in Design mode or in Source mode (looking at the control declarations and other content of the page).
- Code refactoring capabilities.

VS2005 is a useful tool that can save you hours of repetitive tasks. It is a large and complex program, so this chapter cannot explore every nook and cranny. Instead, this chapter will lay the foundation for understanding and using VS2005, and we'll point out some of the nastier traps you might run into along the way.

 For a thorough coverage of VS2005, see *Mastering Visual Studio 2005*, by Jon Flanders, Ian Griffiths, and Chris Sells (O'Reilly).

Start Page

When you open VS2005 for the first time (unless you configure it otherwise), you'll find yourself looking at the VS2005 application window, as shown in Figure 2-1.

Along the top of the application window is a typical collection of Windows menu items and buttons, plus several that are specific to the VS2005 Integrated Development Environment (IDE). Specialized tabs that provide access to tools and controls, and to other servers and databases in the development environment, appear on the left side of the application window, labeled Toolbox and Server Explorer, respectively. The

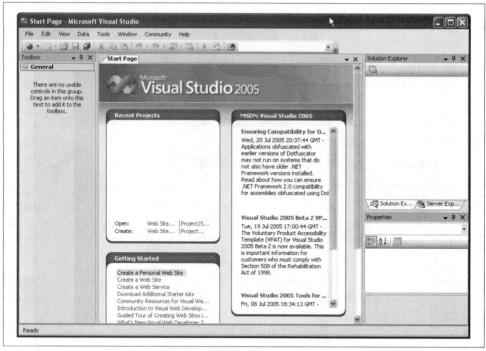

Figure 2-1. Visual Studio 2005 Start Page

Solution Explorer, for exploring the files and classes associated with a particular project, appears on the right side. More windows are available through the VS2005 menu bar (see "The Integrated Development Environment (IDE)").

At the center of the application window is the Start Page, which contains links for creating new projects and web sites or opening existing ones. It also contains several windows with links to helpful topics for getting started and up-to-date news items.

In a tradition that goes back to the early days of computing, our first program will be a web site that displays the words "Hello World." We'll jazz it up a bit by adding a button that changes the text to "Hello Visual Studio 2005."

To begin, start VS2005 and from the Start Page click on New Web Site… or from the menu choose File → New Web Site…. The New Web Site dialog opens, offering a number of options, as shown in Figure 2-2.

In the Templates window, chose ASP.NET Web Site.

Below the list of templates are a set of controls for setting the location and language for your web site.

The first drop-down, Location, allows you to work on web apps in three different manners, from three different locations: File System, HTTP, and FTP. The choice

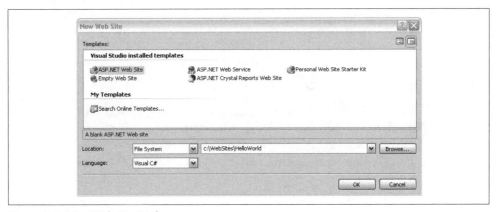

Figure 2-2. New Web Site Dialog

here controls much more than just a physical location, as will be described in the following sections.

File System

File System is the default; it causes the new web site folder to be created somewhere on the physical filesystem accessible to this PC and this user, either on the local machine or the network.

The Browse… button and associated drop-down allow you to browse the filesystem, such as Windows Explorer, and select any desired folder.

Choosing File System causes VS2005 to run the web app using its own internal web server and not IIS. A persistent virtual directory for the web app is not created and IIS is not part of the picture. In fact, you don't even need to have IIS installed on the development machine. (Of course, IIS is required on any deployment servers.)

The downside to using File System as the Location is that web pages created this way cannot be run from a browser, only through VS2005 (since there is no virtual directory to reference after "localhost" in the browser address box). This is true even when redirecting users to another page programatically with the Response.Redirect or Server.Response methods.

```
http://localhost/myWebApp/default.aspx
```

The above URL references the target web site and will not work unless you manually create a virtual directory called myWebApp in Computer Management on the local machine. To do this, right-click on My Computer and select Manage, then drill down to Services and Applications → Internet Information Services → Web Sites → Default Web Site, then right-click and select New → Virtual Directory….

The advantage, however, is that sharing file-based solutions is easy: You just copy the entire directory to the new machine and open it in Visual Studio. This will be the preferred approach for this book.

HTTP

The second selection is HTTP, which indicates that IIS will be serving the pages. As such, it requires that the web app be located in an IIS virtual directory. VS2005 will automatically create this virtual directory. This is evident when you open a browser on the local machine and enter a URL such as `http://localhost/myWebApp/default.aspx`, which will work fine.

The Browse... button and associated drop-down allow you to browse and select from the contents, especially the virtual directories, on IIS running locally or remotely. Use the buttons on the left side of the dialog box to choose.

You can also see any virtual directories created by VS2005 by opening Computer Management and looking under Default Web Site.

FTP

FTP allows you to develop your web site on a remote location accessible via the FTP protocol.

The Browse... button and associated drop-down allows you to enter the information necessary to log in to an FTP site. You will be presented with an FTP Log On dialog box with a checkbox to allow Anonymous Log in and textboxes for login user name and password if necessary.

 The first time you run a new web site, you will see a dialog box entitled *Debugging Not Enabled.*, asking if VS2005 should create a file named *web.config* to enable debugging. *web.config* will be described in detail in Chapter 18. For now just click OK to create the file and enable debugging.

Creating Your First Web Page

When you click OK, VS2005 creates a new web site in the file location you've designated and creates your first web page, named *Default.aspx*, and puts you into the Source View for that page, as shown in Figure 2-3.

Before we go into the details of the myriad capabilities of VS2005, let's get this simple program up and running. Drag a Label from the toolbox right into the source code between the opening and closing `<div>` tags. Your label will be given the default ID of `Label1` and the default Text of `Label1`. Change the text to "Hello World."

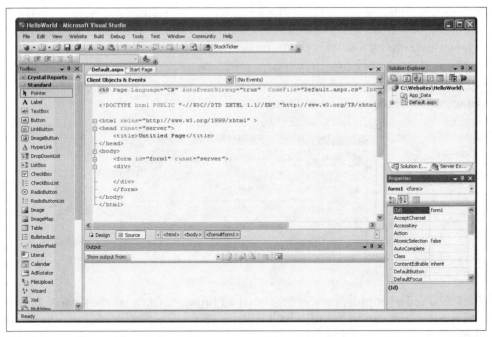

Figure 2-3. Hello World created

Switch to Design View by clicking on the tab at the bottom of the screen, and there's your label.

Drag a Button from the toolbox onto the form, next to the label. Click on the button and look at the properties in the Properties window. Scroll down the Properties window and set the text for the button to "Change." The text on the button changes immediately. Switch back to Source view and you can see that the button has been added after the label:

```
<div>
    <asp:Label ID="Label1" runat="server" Text="Hello World"></asp:Label>
    <asp:Button ID="Button1" runat="server" Text="Change" />
</div>
```

Return to Design view and double click on the Button. All sorts of things just happened. VS2005 took your double-click as an instruction to create an event handler for the "default" event of the button (all of this is explained in detail below and in later chapters). You are now in the code-behind file (the file containing the programming logic, explained in detail in Chapter 6) in the event handler. Type in the one line of code needed to change the label's Text property to "Hello Visual Studio 2005":

```
protected void Button1_Click(object sender, EventArgs e)
{
    Label1.Text = "Hello Visual Studio 2005";
}
```

As you type, Intellisense will try to help you locate the control you want (Label1). It will then provide all the properties and methods of that control for you to set or invoke. Just keep typing; we'll get to Intellisense later on.

Run the application by choosing Debug → Start Debugging. VS2005 will notice that you do not have debugging enabled and will offer to create a new *web.config* file with debugging enabled, as shown in Figure 2-4.

Figure 2-4. Enable Debugging

Click OK and your program will come up in a browser. Click on the Change button and your event handler runs, changing the text as expected and, as shown in Figure 2-5.

Figure 2-5. Running Hello World

You have just created a fully functional web site, with controls and an event handler that responds to user action by changing the property of one of the controls. Though this is admittedly a very simple web site, it is still notable how little typing you had to do. VS2005 does its best to make your job easier.

Projects and Solutions

A typical .NET web application consists of many items: content files (such as *.aspx* files), source files (such as *.cs* files), assemblies (such as *.exe* and *.dll* files) and assembly information files, data sources (such as *.mdb* files), references, and icons, as well as miscellaneous other files and folders. VS2005 organizes these items into a folder that represents the web site. All the files that make up the web site are contained in a *solution*. When you create a new web site, VS2005 automatically creates the solution and displays it in the Solution Explorer. Additional projects (described below) can also be added to the web site.

In addition to web sites, VS2005 can create *projects*. These projects can be added to the solution or placed in their own solution. Many types of projects can be built in VS2005, including among others:

- Windows Application
- Windows Service
- Windows Control Libary
- Web Control Library
- Class Library
- Pocket PC Application, Class Library, Control Library, or Empty Project
- SmartPhone Application, Class Library, or Empty Project
- Windows CE Application, Class Library, Control Library, or Empty Project
- SQL Server Project
- Empty Project

Notable in its absence from the above list are Web Applications. Web applications are not contained within projects, just solutions and, as you saw above, you open new web sites directly, using File → New Web Site... rather than File → New Project. You can, however, add a project to a web application solution. You will see this demonstrated in Chapter 19 when you learn how to create setup projects for deploying your finished web site.

Solutions

Solutions typically contain one or more projects and/or web sites. They may contain other, independent items as well. These independent *solution items,* such as business case presentations, specification documents, or timelines, are not specific to any particular project but apply, or *scope*, to the entire solution. The solution items are not an integral part of the application because they can be removed without changing the compiled output. They display in Solution Explorer (described later in this chapter) in a Solution Items folder and can be managed with source control.

Miscellaneous files are independent of the solution or project, but they may be useful to have handy. They are not included in any build or compile but will display in the Solution Explorer and may be edited from there. Typical miscellaneous files include project notes, database schemas, or sample code files. To display the Miscellaneous Files folder as part of the solution, go to Tools → Options → Environment → Documents, and check the checkbox for Show Miscellaneous files in Solution Explorer.

You can have a solution that does not contain any projects but contains only solution items or miscellaneous files, which can be edited using VS2005. This might be handy just to take advantage of the editing, organizational, and (with additional software such as Visual Source Safe) source control capabilities.

Solutions are defined by a *solution file*, created by VS2005 and named for the solution with a *.sln* extension. The *.sln* file contains a list of the projects that comprise the solution, the location of any solution-scoped items, and any solution-scoped build configurations. VS2005 also creates a *.suo* file with the same name as the *.sln* file (e.g., *mySolution.sln* and *mySolution.suo*). The *.suo* file contains data used to customize the IDE on a per-user and per-solution basis.

> In previous versions of Visual Studio, the *.suo* file was maintained only on a per-solution and not a per-developer basis.

The solution file is placed in the Visual Studio projects location. By default, it will look like this (with your user name substituted):

```
c:\Documents and Settings\dhurwitz\My Documents\Visual Studio\Projects
```

You can change it to something a little easier to navigate, such as this:

```
c:\vsProjects
```

Go to Tools → Options → Projects and Solutions → General and change the default Visual Studio projects location.

You can open a solution in VS2005 by double-clicking the *.sln* file in Windows Explorer. Even if the *.sln* file is missing, you can still open a project in VS2005. A new *.sln* file will be created when you save.

> Let's be clear here: there is no project file, but there is a project folder. There are no solution folders, but there is a solution file that lives in a project folder. A solution file may reference multiple projects, including projects from other project folders. Okay, maybe "clear" wasn't the right word.
>
> Furthermore, the Solution Explorer in VS2005 (described below) displays projects as though they are contained within solutions even though the physical directory structure does not support this interpretation.
>
> This can be a bit confusing, but it all comes together and works well enough once you get used to it. It makes it much easier to work with projects since they can easily be opened up wherever they happen to be located. Project files from previous versions of Visual Studio .NET are still supported.

Projects and Files

A project contains content files, source files, and other files such as data sources and graphics. Typically, the contents of a project are compiled into an assembly, such as an executable file (.*exe*) or a dynamic link library (DLL) file, which can be identified by its .*dll* extension.

Most of the content of a web page or user control (user controls are described in Chapter 14) consists of server control declarations and HTML. This content, along with any necessary directives (directives are described in Chapter 6) and script comprise the *content file* for the page or user control. Content files for web pages have an extension of .*aspx* and for user controls have an extension of .*ascx*. There are other types of content files in ASP.NET, listed in Table 2-1.

Table 2-1. Content file types

File type	Extension
Page	.*aspx*
User Control	.*ascx*
Web Service	.*asmx*
Master Page	.*master*

The script contained within content files can be contained in script blocks delimited by <script> tags or in-line with HTML delimited by <% %> tags. The script can be run client-side or server-side. If the script is written in JavaScript or VBScript, as indicated by a language attribute in the script block, it is sent to the browser and run client-side. If the script block contains a runat="server" attribute, then the code it contains, written in the .Net language specified in the Language attribute of the Page directive, is compiled and run server-side.

ASP.NET supports code separation, where the server-side source code, (the C# or VS2005) is contained in a *code-behind* file separate from the content file. The code behind file typically has an extension indicating the programming language, such as .cs.

Server-side script and code contained in code-behind files are all compiled into a single class. Code separation and code-behind files are discussed in detail in Chapter 6.

Code-behind is the default coding model used by VS2005. When a new web site is created, VS2005 automatically creates two files: the content file, with a default name, such as *Default.aspx*, and a code-behind file with a matching name, such as *Default. aspx.cs* (assuming you are using C# as your programming language). If you change the name of the content file (highly recommended), the code-behind file will automatically assume the new name.

To see this at work, right-click on *Default.aspx* in the Solution Explorer and choose View Code. The file *Default.aspx.cs* will open with a partial class definition of the class used to support your page (_Default) that inherits from the System.Web.UI.Page class. To get you started, a skeleton Page_Load event handler is provided (this event handler is explained in Chapter 6.

For more on partial classes, see *Programming C#* or *Visual C# 2005: A Developer's Notebook,* both by Jesse Liberty (O'Reilly).

Templates

When you create a new project by clicking the New Project… link on the Start Page (shown in Figure 2-1) or File → New Project…, you will get the New Project dialog box, as shown in Figure 2-6.

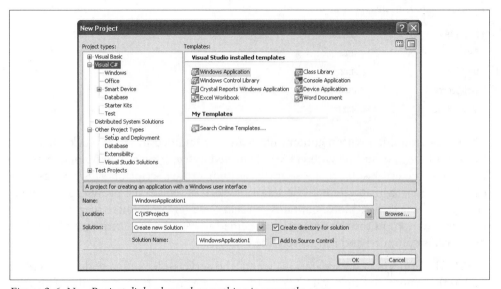

Figure 2-6. New Project dialog box when nothing is currently open

As described previously, web applications are not created by creating a new project but by creating a new web site.

To create a new project, you select a project type and a template. Various templates exist for each project type. For example, the templates for Visual C# Projects, shown in Figure 2-6, are different from the templates available in the Other Project Types/ Setup and Deployment section. You can create an empty solution, ready to receive whatever items you want to add.

The template controls what items will be created automatically and included in the project, as well as default project settings. For example, if your project is a C# Class

Library, a language-specific *.cs* file will be created as part of the project. If the project is a VS2005 project, the corresponding *.vb* file will be created instead. If a different template were selected, an entirely different set of files would be created.

Project Names

Project names may consist of any standard ASCII characters except for the following:

- Pound (#)
- Percent (%)
- Ampersand (&)
- Asterisk (*)
- Vertical bar (|)
- Backslash (\)
- Colon (:)
- Double quotation mark (")
- Less than (<)
- Greater than (>)
- Question mark (?)
- Forward slash (/)
- Leading or trailing spaces
- Windows or DOS keywords, such as "nul," "aux," "con," "com1," and "lpt1"

The Integrated Development Environment (IDE)

The VS2005 Integrated Development Environment (IDE) consists of windows for visual design of forms, code-editing windows, menus, and toolbars providing access to commands and features, toolboxes containing controls for use on the forms, and windows providing properties and information about forms, controls, projects, and the solution.

But more important than the physical layout of the IDE is the productivity boost it provides to you, the developer. You can visually drag controls from the toolbox onto a design window or a code window. In code editing windows, Intellisense automatically pops up a list of all the available members for any given situation. Syntax errors are highlighted in code windows, signalling a problem even before you try to compile the project. The list goes on: a little time invested getting familiar with the IDE will reap tremendous payback.

Layout

VS2005 consists of a single parent window, which contains multiple windows. All the menus, toolbars, design and editing windows, and miscellaneous other windows are associated with the single parent window.

A typical layout of the IDE is shown in Figure 2-7. Basically, it consists of a menu and toolbar arrangement across the top and a work surface below, flanked by other toolbars and windows.

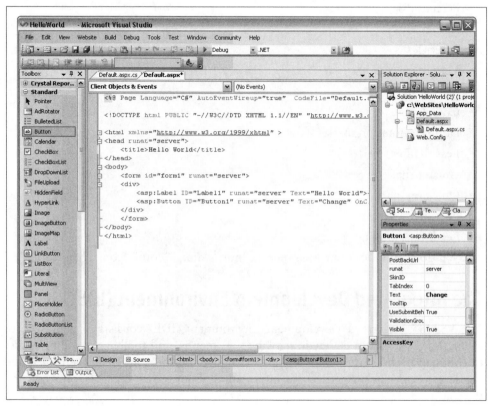

Figure 2-7. Typical IDE layout

When working on content files, such as page, user control, or master page files, which all have visual content, you have your choice of two different views, selectable by tabs at the bottom of the screen. *Design view* shows the content in a WYSIWYG mode. *Source view* shows the source code for the content, that is, the server control declarations, any HTML and static content, and any script blocks on the page.

Users of previous versions of Visual Studio will notice that the IDE now opens by default in Source view rather than Design view. Also, new web pages start out in flow layout mode (like a word processor) rather than grid layout mode (absolute positioning).

VS2005 has a title bar across the top with menus below. Under the menus are toolbars with buttons that duplicate many of the common menu commands. Nearly everything that can be done through menus can also be done with context-sensitive pop-up menus, as described in the discussion that follows. You can easily customize the menu and toolbars by clicking on Tools → Customize.

The toolbars are docked along the top of the window by default. As with many Windows applications, they can be undocked and moved to other locations, either free-floating or docked along other window edges. You move the toolbars by grabbing them with the mouse and dragging them where you want.

Figure 2-7 shows a Source view of a web form, with the Source window occupying the work surface in the center of the screen. When you click the Design button at the bottom of the window, the work surface will display a visual representation of the page. In either Design or Source view, you can drag and drop controls, components, or data sources from the Toolbox or Server Explorer onto the page. In Design view, this puts an accurate visual representation on the page. In Source view, it puts the control or component declaration in the source code. You can work in either mode, switching to whatever is most convenient at the moment, editing in either mode and seeing those results in either mode.

 The ability to drag and drop from the Toolbox onto the Source view, as well as onto the Design view, is new to VS2005.

Along the right side of the screen are two windows, both of which will be covered in more detail later in this chapter. The upper window is the Solution Explorer. Below that is the Properties window. Many other similar windows are available to you as will be described.

Right-clicking on the title bar of a dockable window pops up a menu with five mutually exclusive check items:

Floating
> The window will not dock when dragged against the edge of the VS2005 window. The floating window can be placed anywhere on the desktop, even outside the VS2005 window.

Dockable
> The window can be dragged and docked along any side of the VS2005 window.

While dragging a window to be docked, two sets of blue docking icons will appear in the window. One icon will be located at each edge of the application window and a set of five icons will be located in the center of the current window. Dragging and releasing the window to be docked over one of these docking icons will cause it to dock against the indicated edge. The center docking icon of the set of five will cause the window to be one of the tabbed windows on the central work surface.

You can double-click on the title bar or the tab to dock and undock the window. Double-clicking on the title when docked undocks the entire group. Double-clicking on the tab just undocks the one window, leaving the rest of the group docked.

Tabbed Document

The window occupies the work surface, with a tab for navigation, the same as the code and design windows.

Auto Hide

The window will disappear, indicated only by a tab, when the cursor is not over the window. It will reappear when the cursor is over the tab. A pushpin in the upper-right corner of the window will be pointing down when Auto Hide is turned off and pointing sideways when it is turned on.

Hide

The window disappears. To see the window again (unhide it), use the View menu.

In the upper-right corner of the window are two buttons: a pushpin and an X. The pushpin toggles the AutoHide property of the window. The X is the standard close window button. The work surface uses a tabbed metaphor, meaning the tabs along the top edge of that window indicate there are other windows below it. You can change to a Multiple Document Interface (MDI) style, if you prefer, in Tools → Options → Environment → General.

You will find navigational aids along the bottom of the work surface. Depending on the context, there may be one or more buttons. When you're looking at a web page, for example, as shown in Figures 2-7 and 2-8, two buttons labeled Design and Source allow switching between the design view and underlying source code. Buttons represent the HTML hierarchy of the page, seen as <body> and <div> buttons in Figure 2-8. The cursor in the code window or the focus in Design view dictates which objects will be represented as buttons: one button for the current level and one more for each parent level. Clicking on any of the buttons highlights that level of code in the code window.

When you switch from a design window to a code window, the menu items, toolbars, and toolbox change in a context-sensitive manner.

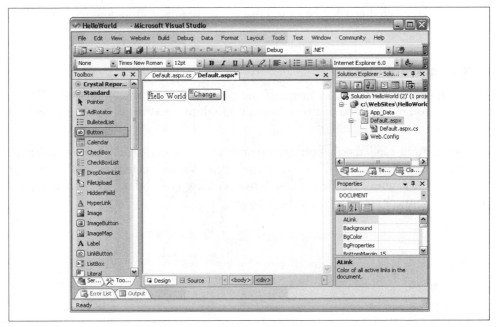

Figure 2-8. Design view window in IDE

The code window has context-sensitive drop-down lists at the top of the screen for navigating around the application. In the HTML editor, the left drop-down lists Client Objects & Events and Client Script, and the right drop-down lists event handlers. In the C# code editor, the left drop-down contains a list of all the classes in the code, and the right drop-down has a list of all the objects in the current class.

The left margin of a code window shows a yellow bar next to lines that have been changed and a green bar next to lines that have been saved. This color coding is per session; it resets when the project is first loaded.

Along the bottom edge of the IDE window is a status bar, which shows such information as the current cursor position (when a code window is visible), the status of the Insert key, and any pending shortcut key combinations.

Building and Running

You can run your application at any time by selecting either Start or Start Without Debugging from the Debug menu, or you can accomplish the same results by pressing F5 or Ctrl-F5, respectively. In addition, you can start the program by clicking the Start icon (▶) on the Standard toolbar.

The program can be built (i.e., *.exe* and *.dll* files generated) by selecting a command under the Build menu. You have the option of building the entire solution or only the currently selected project. For a full discussion of application deployment, please see Chapter 19.

Menus and Toolbars

The menus provide access to many of the commands and capabilities of VS2005. The more commonly used menu commands are duplicated with toolbar buttons for ease of use.

The menus and toolbars are context-sensitive (i.e., the available selection is dependent on what part of the IDE is currently selected and what activities are expected or allowed). For example, if the current active window is a code-editing window, the top-level menu commands will be the following:

- File
- Edit
- View
- Website
- Build
- Debug
- Tools
- Window
- Community
- Help

If the current window is a design window, the Data, Format, and Layout menu commands will also become available, for example.

Many of the menu items have keyboard shortcuts, listed adjacent to the menu item itself. Look over the list of shortcut keys in Appendix A; many of them will become indispensible to your daily development effort.

The following sections describe some of the menu items and their submenus, focusing on those aspects that are interesting and different from common Windows commands.

File Menu

The File menu provides access to a number of file-related, project-related, and solution-related commands. Many of these commands are context sensitive. Below are descriptions of those commands that are not self-explanatory.

There are many different editions of VS2005 available. Each may have a slightly different menu structure.

New

As in most Windows applications, the New menu item creates new items that you can work on in the application. In VS2005, the New menu item has four submenu items, to handle the different possibilities:

Project… (Ctrl-Shift-N)
> The New Project command brings up the New Project dialog shown in Figure 2-6.

Web Site…
> The New Web Site command brings up the New Web Site dialog box shown in Figure 2-2.

File… (Ctrl-N)
> The File command brings up the Add New Item dialog box shown in Figure 2-9. It offers a range of template files, including Web Form, for adding web pages to a pre-existing project. Files created this way are located in the project directory.

Project From Existing Code…
> This command brings up a wizard which walks you through the steps necessary to copy existing files to a new project.

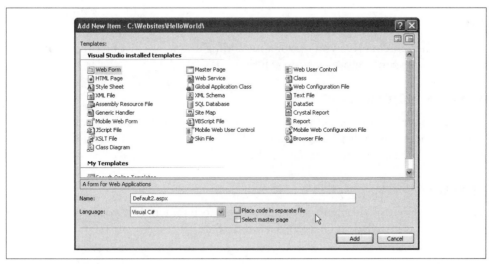

Figure 2-9. Add New Item dialog box

The New command has an equivalent button in the Standard toolbar, which exposes the New Project and New Web Site commands.

Open

The Open menu item is used to open preexisting items. It has four submenu items:

Project/Solution... (Ctrl-Shift-O)
> Opens a previously existing project. Radio buttons give you a choice of adding this project to the current solution or closing the current solution before opening the project.

Web Site...
> An Open Web Site dialog box is presented. Buttons down the left side of the dialog box give you the choice of opening a web site from the filesystem, local IIS, an FTP site, or a remote web site. As described back in the section on Projects and Files, these buttons dictate the type of access to the web site, e.g., through the filesystem versus a virtual directory.

File... (Ctrl-O)
> Presents a standard Open File dialog box, allowing you to browse to and open any file accessible on your network. Files opened are visible and editable in VS2005, but are not part of the project. To make a file part of the project, use one of the Add menu commands described later in this chapter. The Open File command has an equivalent button on the Standard toolbar.

Convert
> The Convert dialog box displays a list of converters to convert from one type of project to another, e.g. VB 6.0 to VS2005, and radio buttons to add the converted project to the current solution or create a new solution.

Add

The Add menu item gives you options for adding a new or existing project or a new or existing web site to a pre-existing solution.

Advanced Save Options...

Advanced Save Options is a context-sensitive submenu that is only visible when editing in a code window. It presents a dialog box, which allows you to set the encoding option and line ending character(s) for the file.

Source Control

The Source Control submenu item allows you to interact with your source control program if it is installed, such as Visual Source Safe.

Edit Menu

The Edit menu contains the text editing and searching commands that one would expect but also includes commands useful in editing code. The most useful are discussed in this section.

Cycle Clipboard Ring (Ctrl-Shift-V)

The Clipboard Ring is like copy and paste on steroids. You can copy a number of different selections to the Windows clipboard, using the Edit → Cut (Ctrl X) or Edit → Copy (Ctrl-C) commands. Then, you can use Ctrl-Shift-V to cycle through all the selections, allowing you to paste the correct one when it comes around.

This submenu item is context-sensitive and is visible only when editing a code window.

Finding and replacing

VS2005 offers a number of useful options for finding and replacing text, both in the current file and in a range of files.

Quick Find (Ctrl-F) / Quick Replace (Ctrl-H). These slightly jazzed names are for slightly jazzed versions of the typical Find and Replace. Both commands call essentially the same dialog boxes, switchable by a tab at the top of the dialog box, as shown in Figures 2-10 and 2-11.

Figure 2-10. Find and Replace dialog box: Quick Find tab

The search string defaults to the text currently selected in the code window or, if nothing is selected, to the text immediately after the current cursor location.

The Look in drop-down offers the choice of the Current Document, All Open Documents, the Current Project, and the current method.

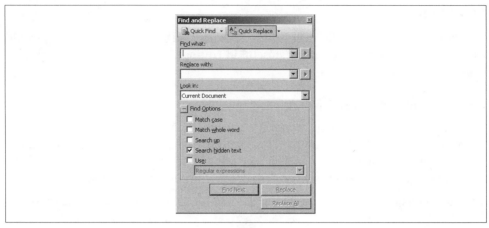

Figure 2-11. Find and Replace dialog box: Quick Replace tab

You can expand or collapse the search options by clicking on the plus/minus button next to Find Options. By default, Search hidden text is checked, which allows the search to include code sections currently collapsed in the code window. The Use checkbox allows the use of regular expressions (see the sidebar) or wildcards. If the Use checkbox is checked, the Expression Builder button to the right of the Find what textbox will become enabled, providing a handy way to insert valid regular expression or wildcard characters.

Once a search string has been entered in the Find what textbox, the Find Next button becomes enabled. In Quick Find mode is a Bookmark All button, which finds all occurrences of the search string and places a bookmark (described in the Bookmarks section later in this chapter) next to the code.

In Quick Replace mode, there is also a Replace with text box, and buttons for replacing either a single or all occurrences of the search string.

Find in Files (Ctrl-Shift-F). Find in Files is a powerful search utility that finds text strings anywhere in a directory or in subdirectories (subfolders). It presents the dialog box shown in Figure 2-12. Checkboxes present several self-explanatory options, including the ability to search using wildcards or regular expressions.

Replace in Files (Ctrl-Shift-H). Replace in Files is identical to the Find in Files command, described in the previous section, except that it allows you to replace the target text string with a replacement text string.

If you click on the Replace in Files tab at the top of the Find and Replace dialog box shown in Figure 2-12, you will get the Replace in Files dialog box shown in Figure 2-13.

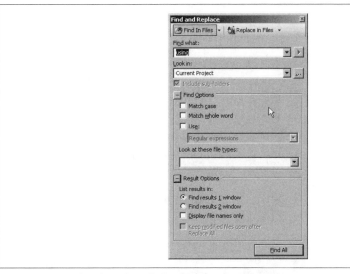

Figure 2-12. Find and Replace dialog box: Find in Files tab

Regular Expressions

Regular expressions are a language unto themselves, expressly designed for incredibly powerful and sophisticated searches. A full explanation of regular expressions is beyond the scope of this book. For a complete discussion of regular expressions, see the SDK documentation or *Mastering Regular Expressions*, Second Edition, by Jeffrey E. F. Friedl (O'Reilly, 2002).

This command is useful for renaming forms, classes, namespaces, projects and so on. Renaming objects is a common requirement because you don't want to be saddled with the default names assigned by VS2005.

Renaming should not be difficult, but it can be. Object names are spread throughout a project, often hidden in obscure locations such as solution files, and throughout source code files. Though all of these files are text files and can be searched and edited, it can be a tedious and error-prone task. The Replace in Files command makes it simple, thorough, and reasonably safe. Of course, you can always undo a Find and Replace operation if you make a mistake.

Find Symbol (Alt-F12). Clicking on this command will bring up the Find Symbol dialog box shown in Figure 2-14. This allows you to search for symbols (such as namespaces, classes, and interfaces) and their members (such as properties, methods, events, and variables). It also allows you to search in external components for which the source code is unavailable.

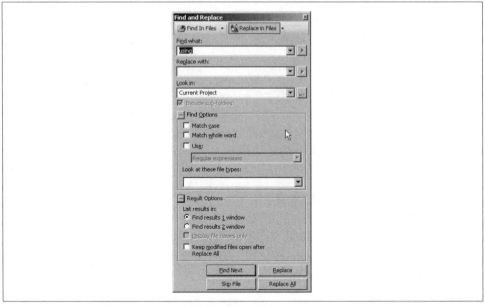

Figure 2-13. Find and Replace dialog box: Replace in Files tab

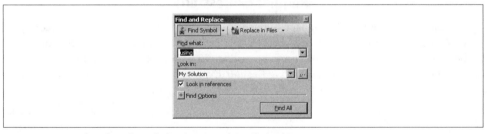

Figure 2-14. Find and Replace dialog box: Find Symbol tab

The search results will be displayed in a window labeled Find Symbol Results. From there, you can move to each location in the code by double-clicking on each result.

Go To...

This command brings up the Go To Line dialog box, which allows you to enter a line number and immediately go to that line. It is context-sensitive and is visible only when editing a text window.

Insert File As Text...

This command allows you to insert the contents of any file into your source code, as though you had typed it in. It is context-sensitive and is visible only when editing a text window.

A standard file browsing dialog box is presented for searching for the file to be inserted. The default file extension will correspond to the project language, but you can search for any file with any extension.

Advanced

The context-sensitive Advanced command is visible only when editing a code window. It has many submenu items. These include commands for the following:

- Creating or removing tabs in a selection (converting spaces to tabs and vice versa)
- Forcing selected text to uppercase or lowercase
- Deleting horizontal white space
- Viewing white space (making tabs and space characters visible on the screen)
- Toggling word wrap
- Commenting and uncommenting blocks of text
- Increasing and decreasing line indenting
- Searching incrementally (described next)

Incremental search (Ctrl-I)

Incremental search allows you to search an editing window by entering the search string character by character. As each character is entered, the cursor moves to the first occurrence of matching text.

To use incremental search in a window, select the command on the Advanced submenu or press Ctrl-I. The cursor icon will change to a binocular with an arrow indicating the direction of search. Begin typing the text string to search for.

The case sensitivity of an incremental search will come from the previous Find, Replace, Find in Files, or Replace in Files search (described earlier).

The search will proceed downward and left to right from the current location. To search backward, use Ctrl-Shift-I.

The key combinations listed in Table 2-2 apply to incremental searching.

Table 2-2. Incremental searching

Key combination	Description
Esc	Stop the search
Backspace	Remove a character from the search text
Ctrl-Shift-I	Change the direction of the search
Ctrl-I	Move to the next occurrence in the file for the current search text

Bookmarks

Bookmarks are useful for marking spots in your code and easily navigating to them later. Several context-sensitive commands are on the Bookmarks submenu (listed in Table 2-3, along with their shortcut key combinations). Unless you add the item to the task list, bookmarks are lost when you close the file though they are saved when you close the solution (as long the file was still open).

Table 2-3. Bookmark commands

Command	Key combination	Description
Toggle Bookmark	Ctrl-K, Ctrl-K	Place or remove a bookmark at the current line. When a bookmark is set, a blue rectangular icon will appear in the column along the left edge of the code window.
Previous Bookmark	Ctrl-B, P	Move to the previous bookmark.
Next Bookmark	Ctrl-B, N	Move to the next bookmark.
Previous Bookmark in Folder	Ctrl-Shift-K, Ctrl-Shift-P	Move to the previous bookmark in the folder.
Next Bookmark in Folder	Ctrl-Shift-K, Ctrl-Shift-N	Move to the next bookmark in the folder.
Clear Bookmarks	Ctrl-B, Ctrl-C	Clear all the bookmarks.
Previous Bookmark in Document	None	Move to the previous bookmark in the current document.
Next Bookmark in Document	None	Move to the next bookmark in the current document.
Add Task List Shortcut	Ctrl-K, Ctrl-H	Add an entry to the Task List (described later in the "View Menu" section) for the current line. When a task list entry is set, a curved arrow icon (▮) appears in the column along the left edge of the code window.

This menu item only appears when a code window is the current window.

Outlining

VS2005 allows you to *outline*, or collapse and expand, sections of your code to make it easier to view the overall structure. When a section is collapsed, it appears with a plus sign in a box along the left edge of the code window (⊞ . . .). Clicking on the plus sign expands the region.

You can nest the outlined regions, so one section can contain one or more other collapsed sections. Several commands facilitate outlining shown in Table 2-4.

Table 2-4. Outlining commands

Command	Key combination	Description
Hide Selection	Ctrl-M, Ctrl-H	Collapses currently selected text. In C# only, this command is visible only when automatic outlining is turned off or the Stop Outlining command is selected.
Toggle Outlining Expansion	Ctrl-M, Ctrl-M	Reverses the current outlining state of the innermost section in which the cursor lies.

Table 2-4. Outlining commands (continued)

Command	Key combination	Description
Toggle All Outlining	Ctrl-M, Ctrl-L	Sets all sections to the same outlining state. If some sections are expanded and some collapsed, all will become collapsed.
Stop Outlining	Ctrl-M, Ctrl-P	Expands all sections. Removes the outlining symbols from view.
Stop Hiding Current	Ctrl-M, Ctrl-U	Removes outlining information for currently selected section. In C#, this command is visible when automatic outlining is turned off or the Stop Outlining command is selected.
Collapse to Definitions	Ctrl-M, Ctrl-O	Automatically creates sections for each procedure in the code window and collapses them all.
Start Automatic Outlining	None	Restarts automatic outlining after it has been stopped.

You can set the default behavior for outlining with the Tools → Options menu item. Go to Text Editor and then the specific language for which you want to set the options. The outlining options can be set for VS2005 under Basic → VB Specific and for C# under C# → Advanced.

IntelliSense

Microsoft Intellisense technology makes the lives of programmers much easier. It has real-time, context-sensitive help available, which appears under your cursor. Code completion automatically completes words for you, reducing your typing. Drop-down-lists provide all methods and properties possible in the current context, available at a keystroke or mouse click.

Unlike previous versions of Visual Studio, Intellisense works in all code windows, including the C# code-behind files, but also within server-side (script) and client-side (HTML) code in content files, i.e., in *.aspx* and *.ascx* files.

The default Intellisense features can be configured by going to Tools → Options and then the language-specific pages under Text Editor.

Most of the Intellisense features appear as you type inside a code window, or allow the mouse to hover over a portion of the code. In addition, the Edit → Intellisense menu item offers the commands shown in Table 2-5.

Table 2-5. Intellisense commands

Command	Key combination	Description
List Members	Ctrl-J	Displays a list of all possible members available for the current context. As you enter keystrokes, the list is incrementally searched. Press any key to insert the highlighted selection into your code; that key becomes the next character after the inserted name. Use the Tab key to select without entering any additional characters.
		This can be accessed by right-clicking and selecting List Member from the context-sensitive menu.

Table 2-5. Intellisense commands (continued)

Command	Key combination	Description
Parameter Info	Ctrl-Shift-Space	Displays a list of number, names, and types of parameters required for a method, sub, function, or attribute.
Quick Info	Ctrl-K, Ctrl-I	Displays the complete declaration for any identifier (such as a variable name or class name) in your code. This is also enabled by hovering the mouse cursor over any identifier.
Complete Word	Alt-Right Arrow or Ctrl-Space	Automatically completes the typing of any identifier once you type in enough characters to uniquely identify it. This only works if the identifier is being entered in a valid location in the code.
Insert Snippet	Ctrl-K, Ctrl-X	Displays a selection of code snippets to insert, such as the complete syntax for a `switch case` block or an `if` block.
Surround With	Ctrl-K, Ctrl-S	Displays a selection of code snippets to surround a block of code, such as a class declaration.
Generate Method Stub	Ctrl-K,M	With cursor over a method call, will automatically generate a code skeleton for that method.
Implement Interface Implicitly	Ctrl-K, Ctrl-I	With cursor over an inherited interface, will automatically generate implicit interface member declarations, meaning that member calls will not include the interface name in their declarations.
Implement Interface Explicitly	Ctrl-K, Ctrl-E	With cursor over an inherited interface, will automatically generate explicit interface member declarations, meaning that member calls will include the interface name in their declarations.
Implement Abstract Class	Ctrl-K, Ctrl-T	With cursor over an inherited abstract class, will automatically generate class member declarations.

The *member list* presents itself when you type the dot following any class or member name.

Every member of the class is listed, and each member's type is indicated by an icon. There are icons for methods, fields, properties, events, etc. In addition, each icon may have a second icon overlaid to indicate the accessibility of the member: public, private, protected, and so on. If there is no accessibility icon, then the member is public.

 If the member list does not appear, ensure you have added all the necessary using statements. You'll also want to remember that Intellisense is case-sensitive in C#. Occasionally C# needs a rebuild before it will reflect the most recent changes.

Table 2-6 lists all the different icons used in the member lists and other windows throughout the IDE. The accessibility icons are listed in Table 2-7.

Table 2-6. Object icons

Icon	Member type
	Class
	Constant
	Delegate
	Enum
	Enum item
	Event
	Exception
	Global
	Interface
	Intrinsic
	Macro
	Map
	Map item
	Method or Function
	Module
	Namespace
	Operator
	Property
	Structure
	Template
	Typedef
	Union
	Unknown or Error
	Variable or Field

Table 2-7. Object accessibility icons

Icon	Accessibility type
	Shortcut
	Internal
	Private
	Protected

Two of the subcommands under the Intellisense menu item, Insert Snippet… and Surround With…, tap into a great feature to reduce typing and minimize errors: *code snippets*. A code snippet is a chunk of code that replaces an alias. For example, the alias switch would be replaced with the following:

```
switch (switch_on)
{
   default:
}
```

After the replacement, the switch expression switch_on is highlighted in yellow and the cursor is in place, ready to type in your own expression. In fact, all the editable fields will be highlighted, and you can use the Tab key to navigate through them or Shift-Tab to go backward. Any changes made to the editable field are immediately propagated to all the instances of that field in the code snippet. Press Enter or Esc to end the field editing and return to normal editing.

To do a straight alias replacement, select Insert Snippet from the menu or, more easily, press Ctrl-K, Ctrl-X. Alternatively, type an alias in the code window and an Intellisense menu will pop up with a list of aliases, with the current one highlighted. Press the Tab key to insert that code snippet.

Alternatively, a code snippet can surround highlighted lines of code, say with a for construct. To surround lines of code with a code snippet construct, highlight the code and then select Surround With from the menu or press Ctrl-K, Ctrl-S.

View Menu

The View menu provides access to the myriad windows available in the VS2005 IDE. You will probably keep many of these windows open all the time; others you will use rarely, if at all.

When the application is running, a number of other windows, primarily used for debugging, become visible or available. You can access these windows via the Debug → Windows menu item, not from the View menu item.

VS2005 can store several different window layouts. In particular, it remembers a completely different set of open windows during debug sessions than it does during normal editing. These layouts are stored per-user, not per-project or per-solution.

This section discusses those areas that may not be self-explanatory.

Solution Explorer (Ctrl-Alt-L)

You use the Solution Explorer to manage projects and solutions. Solution Explorer presents the solution and projects and all the files, folders, and items contained within them in a hierarchical, visual manner. The Solution Explorer is typically visible in a window along the upper right side of the VS2005 screen though the Solution Explorer window can be closed or undocked and moved to other locations, like all the windows accessible from the View menu. A typical Solution Explorer is shown in Figure 2-15.

Figure 2-15. Solution Explorer

You will find several menu buttons along the top of the Solution Explorer window. These buttons are context-sensitive, meaning they may or may not appear, depending on the currently selected item in the Solution Explorer.

Table 2-8 details the purpose of each button.

Table 2-8. Solution Explorer buttons

Button	Name	Shortcut keys	Description
	Properties	F4	If the currently highlighted item is a solution or a project, this button displays the Properties page for that item. Otherwise, it moves the cursor to the Properties window for that item.
	Refresh	None	Refreshes the Solution Explorer display.
	Nest Related Files	None	Toggles between nested and non-nested view of related files, such as Default.aspx and Default.aspx.cs.
	View Code	None	Displays source code on the work surface. Only visible for page and user control files.
	View Designer	None	Displays visual designer on the work surface. Only visible for items with visual components.
	Copy Web Site	None	Puts the copy web site dialog, described fully under the Website menu item, on the work surface.
	ASP.NET Configuration	None	Opens the ASP.NET Configuration utility, described fully in Chapter 18.

You can display miscellaneous files in the Solution Explorer: Go to Tools → Options..., then go to Environment → Documents. Check the checkbox labeled Show Miscellaneous files in Solution Explorer.

Most of the functionality of the Solution Explorer is redundant with the VS2005 menu items, though performing a given chore in Solution Explorer rather than in the menus is often easier and more intuitive. Right-clicking on any item in the Solution Explorer will pop up a context-sensitive menu. Three different pop-up menus from Solution Explorer are shown in Figure 2-16. From left to right, they are for a solution, a web page, and a source code file.

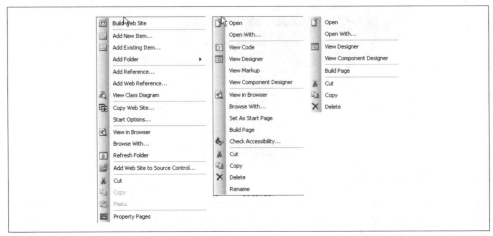

Figure 2-16. Solution Explorer context-sensitive menus for solutions, web pages, and source files

Some of the context-sensitive menus are not redundant with any of the menu commands:

View Code / View Designer / View Markup

Code and Markup are only available when looking at a content file, i.e., files with extensions of *.aspx* or *.ascx*. The Code menu item displays the C# code-behind file on the work surface, i.e., a file with an extension of *.cs*. The Markup menu item has the same effect as clicking on the Source button at the bottom of the work surface, displaying the underlying HTML and script of the content file.

The Designer menu item is available whenever a design view is available. It has the same effect as clicking on the Design button at the bottom of the work surface, switching to a WYSIWYG design view.

Add Reference...

The Add Reference command brings up the Add Reference dialog box shown in Figure 2-17. This allows you to reference assemblies or DLLs external to your application, making the public classes, methods, and members contained in the referenced resource available to your application.

Add Web Reference...

The Add Web Reference command, available in the Solution Explorer by right-clicking a project, allows you to add a web reference to your project, thereby becoming a consuming application of a web service.

Web services and distributed applications are covered in Chapters 15 and 16.

Server Explorer (Ctrl-Alt-S)

The Server Explorer allows you to access any server to which you have network access. If you have sufficient permissions, you can log on, access system services,

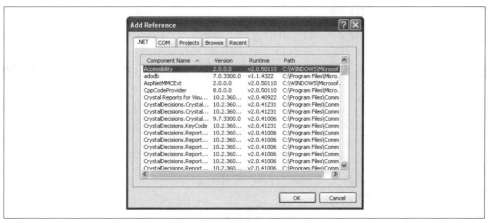

Figure 2-17. Add Reference dialog box

open data connections, access and edit database information, access message queues and performance counters, and more.

A typical Server Explorer is shown in Figure 2-18. It is a hierarchical view of the available servers. In this figure, two servers available are: sony290 (on which resides the Northwind database) and virt-sony290 (which is the local machine). The figure shows a drill-down into a data connection, showing the tables in the Northwind database. These tables, and all other objects in this tree view, are directly accessible and editable from the window.

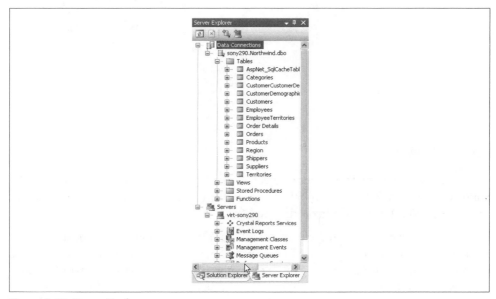

Figure 2-18. Server Explorer

Properties Windows (F4)

The Properties window displays all the properties for the currently selected item. Some of the properties (such as Font) may have subproperties, indicated by a plus sign next to their entries in the window. The property values on the right side of the window are editable.

One thing that can be confusing is that certain items have more than one set of properties. For example, a Form content file can show two different sets of properties, depending on if you select the source file in the Solution Explorer or the form, as shown in the Design view.

A typical Properties window while in Design view is shown in Figure 2-19.

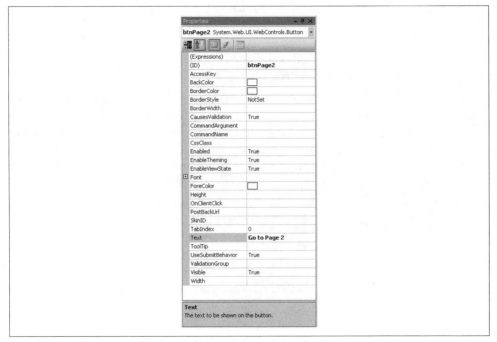

Figure 2-19. Properties window

The name and type of the current object is displayed in the field at the top of the window. In Figure 2-19, it is an object named btnPage2 of type Button, contained in the System.Web.UI.WebControls namespace.

Most properties can be edited either in the Properties window or declaratively (that is, manually) in the Source view. The Font property has subproperties that may be set directly in the Properties window by clicking on the plus sign to expand its subproperties and then editing the subproperties in place.

The Properties window has several buttons below the name and type of the object. The first two buttons on the left toggle the list by category or alphabetically. The next two buttons from the left (visible only in Design view) toggle between displaying properties for the selected item and displaying events for the selected item. The right-most button displays property pages for the object if there are any.

 Some objects have both a Properties window and Property Pages. The Property Pages display additional properties other than those shown in the Properties window.

The box below the list of properties displays a brief description of the selected property.

Visible Borders (Ctrl-Q)

This menu item is only available in Design view and toggles the display of borders around controls on the page or user control.

Details (Ctrl- Shift-Q)

This menu item is only available in Design view and toggles the display of items such as HTML breaks, spans and divs.

Non Visual Controls (Ctrl- Shift-N)

This menu item is only available in Design view and toggles the display of non visual controls, such as data source controls (described in Chapter 9) and Web Parts controls (described in Chapter 13).

Object Browser (Ctrl-Alt-J)

The Object Browser is a tool for examining objects (such as namespaces, classes, and interfaces) and their members (such as methods, properties, variables, and events). A typical Object Browser window is shown in Figure 2-20.

The objects are listed in the pane on the left side of the window, and members of the object, if any, are listed in the right pane. The objects are listed hierarchically, with the ability to drill down through the tree structure. The icons used in this window are listed in Tables 2-6 and 2-7.

Right-clicking on an object or a member brings up a context-sensitive pop-up menu with various menu options.

Document Outline (Ctrl- Alt-T)

The Document Outline menu item is available in either Design or Source view when a page or user control is visible on the work surface.

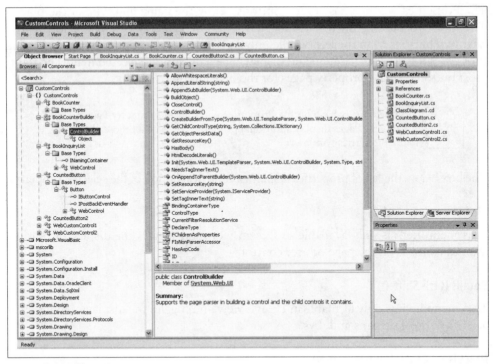

Figure 2-20. Object Browser

The Document Outline displays the hierarchical structure of a web page or user control, including directives, script blocks, HTML elements, and server controls, as shown in Figure 2-21. Clicking on any item in the Document Outline will immediately select that item on the work surface but not vice versa.

Error List (Ctrl-W, Ctrl-E)

Available in all editor views, the Error List window displays errors, warnings, and messages generated as you edit and compile your project. Syntax errors flagged by Intellisense are displayed here, as well as deployment errors. Double-clicking on an error in this list will open the offending file and move the cursor to the error location.

Task List (Ctrl-W, Ctrl-T)

In large applications, keeping a to-do list can help. VS2005 provides this functionality with the Task List window. You can provide shortcuts to comments in the Task List along with token strings, such as TODO, HACK, or UNDONE. Also, the compiler populates the Task List with any compile errors. Clicking on a line in the Task List will take you to the relevant line of code in the code editor.

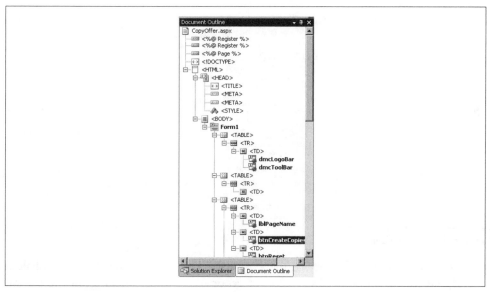

Figure 2-21. Document Outline

Toolbox (Ctrl-Alt-X)

Displays the toolbox if it is not currently displayed. If it is currently displayed, nothing happens, and it does not toggle the display. To undisplay the toolbox, click on the X in the toolbox title bar.

Command window (Ctrl-Alt-A)

The Command window is used to enter commands directly, bypassing the menu system or executing commands that are not contained in the menu system. (You can add any command to the menu or a toolbar button using Tools → Customize.)

For a complete discussion of command window usage, consult the SDK documentation.

Other windows

Several other windows have been relegated to a submenu called Other Windows:

Class View (Ctrl-Shift-C)
> The Class View shows all the classes in the solution in a hierarchical manner. A typical Class View, somewhat expanded, is shown in Figure 2-22. The icons used in this window are listed in Tables 2-6 and 2-7.
>
> As with the Solution Explorer, any item in the class view can be right-clicked, which exposes a pop-up menu with a number of context-sensitive menu items. This can provide a convenient way to sort the display of classes in a project or solution or to add a method, property, or field to a class.

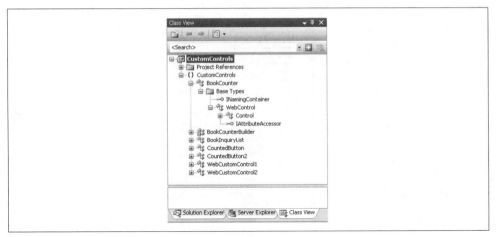

Figure 2-22. Class View

The button on the left above the class list allows for sorting the classes listed, alphabetically, by type, by access, or grouped by type. Clicking on the button sorts by the current sort mode, while clicking on the down arrow next to it presents the other sort buttons and changes the sort mode.

The button on the right above the class list allows you to create virtual folders for organizing the classes listed. These folders are saved as part of the solution in the *.suo* file.

These folders are virtual; they are only used for viewing the list. As such, they have no effect on the actual items. Items copied to the folder are not physically moved, and if the folders are deleted, the items in them will not be lost. If you rename or delete an object from the code that is in a folder, you may need to drag the item manually into the folder again to clear the error node.

Resource View (Ctrl-Shift-E)

This window displays the resource files included in the project. *Resources* are nonexecutable data deployed with an application, such as icons and graphics, culture-specific text messages, and persisted data objects.

Macro Explorer (Alt-F8)

VS2005 offers the ability to automate repetitive chores with macros. A macro is a set of instructions written in VS2005, either created manually or recorded by the IDE, and saved in a file. The Macro Explorer is the one of the main tools for viewing, managing, and executing macros. It provides access into the Macro IDE.

Macros are described further in the section "Tools Menu."

Output (Ctrl-Alt-O)

The Output window displays status messages from the IDE, such as build progress. You can set the Output window to display by default when a build starts by going to Tools → Options → Projects and Solutions → General and checking "Show Output window when build starts."

This window is available in all editor views.

Refactor Menu

Refactoring, to quote the Microsoft MSDN Library for VS2005, "is the process of improving your code after it has been written, by changing the internal structure of the code without changing the external behavior of the code."

What this means in English is that after you write your code, you may make code changes to enhance readability and maintainability. VS2005 makes this easy.

 For details on refactoring, we recommend the book *Refactoring: Improving the Design of Existing Code* by Fowler et al. (Addison Wesley).

The Refactor menu item is available when you're looking at a code window for a web page, user control, or language source code file. It is also available from context menus when you right-click on an identifier in a Class View, Object Browser, or Solution Explorer window.

The refactoring menu items will modify your code, for example, extracting common code to a method and then calling that method in the place from which it was extracted. Refactoring can also be used to rename methods, and all references to the renamed method will automatically be updated as well across all files in the project and across all projects of the same language. Before any changes are committed, an optional Preview Changes dialog box will appear, giving you the opportunity to accept or cancel the changes. A project that is unable to build successfully can still be refactored, though ambiguous references might not update properly.

The following functions are available under the Refactor menu item:

Rename...(Ctrl-R, Ctrl-R)

To rename a code symbol such as a method, class, namespace, field, local variable, property, or type, click on the symbol in your code and select the Rename menu item, press F2, or right-click on the symbol and select Refactor → Rename... from the popup menu.

The Rename dialog box will appear with a textbox for the new name to be entered. A read-only textbox will show the current cursor location. Several context-sensitive checkboxes will present options. "Preview reference changes" will be checked by default. Other options might include "Search in comments," "Search in strings," and "Rename overloads."

After you click OK, the program will process for a bit before displaying the Preview Changes dialog box, if that option was left checked. The top pane will list all the files and lines of code where the symbol is to be renamed. Clicking any of the lines will show the source code in context in the bottom pane of the dialog box.

Click Apply to apply the changes or Cancel to cancel the operation.

Alternatively, type a new name and then click the smart tag that appears at the end of the name and choose the Rename option.

Extract Method... (Ctrl-R,Ctrl-M)

As described above, the extract method extracts duplicate code and turns it into a method, leaving a call to that new method in place of the old (duplicate) code.

The new method is inserted into the source file in the same class immediately following the current method. If no instance data is referenced by the new method, the method will be declared a static method.

The Extract Method dialog box will preview the new method signature. You can click OK to create the new method or click Cancel to cancel. If you wish to revert back after creating the new method, use Edit → Undo (Ctrl-Z).

Encapsulate Field... (Ctrl-R,Ctrl-F)

A public member variable can be accessed externally and its value altered without the knowledge or consent of its class, breaking encapsulation. A better practice is to declare private fields and use properties with get and/or set accessors to control external access to the field.

The Encapsulate Field function creates a property from an existing public field and updates the code to refer to the new property rather than the field. The previously public field is converted to private, and the get and set accessors are created. If the original field had been declared as read-only, the set accessor will not be created.

Extract Interface

If multiple classes, structs, or interfaces use a common set of members, it can be beneficial to extract those common members into an interface, which is then implemented by the original classes, structs or interfaces.

This menu item is only available when the cursor is in the class, struct, or interface containing the members to extract into an interface. The new interface is created in a new file. The Extract Interface dialog lets you enter the name of the new interface, the new file name, and which public members to include in the new interface.

Promote Local Variable to Parameter (Ctrl-R,Ctrl-P)

This function converts a local variable to a parameter of a method, indexer, constructor, or delegate. It also updates all the calls to that local variable.

Remove Parameters... (Ctrl-R,Ctrl-V)

This function removes parameters from methods, indexers, constructors, or delegates. It updates all the calls to the now defunct parameter. The easiest way to invoke this function is to right-click anywhere within the declaration of the object (e.g., method, struct, property) where you want to remove the parameter(s), then select Refactor → Remove Parameters... from the context menu.

Reorder Parameters... (Ctrl-R,Ctrl-O)

Similar to the Remove Parameters function, this menu item allows you to change the order of parameters in methods, indexers, constructors, or delegates. It updates all the calls to the modified objects to reflect the new order of parameters.

Website Menu

This menu item mostly provides redundancy with, and works in conjunction with, the Solution Explorer. It allows you to add new or existing items, references, or web references, all affecting the current selection in the Solution Explorer. These menu items have been described previously in this chapter.

In addition, it provides other menu items, some of which are redundant with the Solution Explorer, some of which are not.

Start Options

Opens the Property Pages dialog box with the Start Options for the current web site shown in Figure 2-23. This allows you to specify settings such as the start page or URL, the server to use, and the debugger to use. This menu item is unavailable on the Solution Explorer.

Copy Web Site

This menu item, which is also available as an icon at the top of the Solution Explorer, allows you to easily copy all or part of a web site to a new web site. If the new web site does not exist, it will create it. It brings up the window shown in Figure 2-24.

To copy a web site, click on the Connections drop down at the top of the window. Then navigate to the target location. If the target location does not exist, you will be prompted to create it. Highlight the files and folders on the left you wish to copy and then click the rightward-facing arrow in the middle to copy those selected items.

A number of other self-explanatory controls exist, such as buttons for refreshing the list, deleting items, synchronizing the directories, and viewing the log.

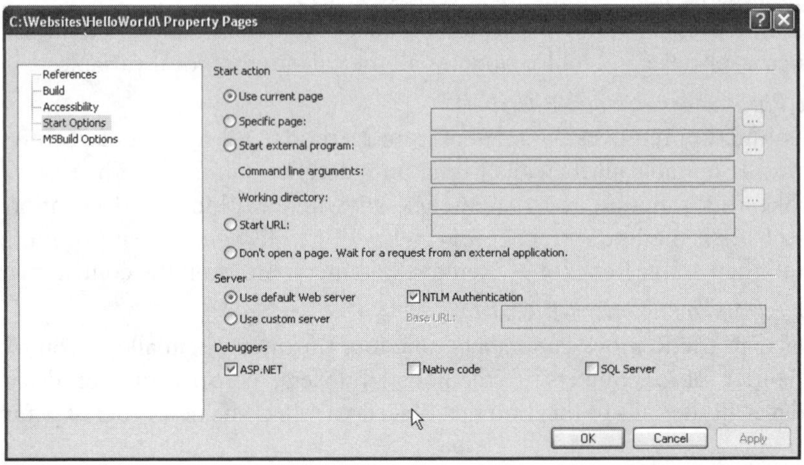

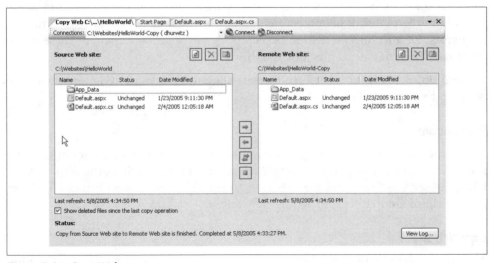

Figure 2-23. Start Options

Figure 2-24. Copy Web site

This process does not create an IIS virtual directory for the new web site, so if you are using virtual directories (necessary for deployment, for example), you will have to make the virtual directory manually. To do so, right-click on My Computer or go to Control Panel → Administrative Tools → Computer Management and drill down through Services and Applications → Internet Information Services → Web Sites to Default Web Site. Then right-click and select New → Virtual Directory and follow the wizard.

ASP.NET Configuration

This menu item is also available as an icon at the top of the Solution Explorer. It brings up the ASP.NET Web Site Administration Tool, which will be covered in detail in Chapter 18.

Project Menu

The Project menu provides functionality related to project management. It is only visible when the solution is selected in the Solution Explorer. All of the functionality exposed by the Project menu is available in the Solution Explorer by right-clicking on the solution. Accomplishing your goals in Solution Explorer is often easier and more intuitive, but the menus lend themselves to keyboard use.

Each of the commands under this menu pertain to the object currently highlighted in the Solution Explorer.

Add New Item... (Ctrl-Shift-A)

This command brings up the Add New Solution dialog box, which lets you add new items based on templates, such as a text file, style sheet, class file, etc. This command is *not* for adding a new project to the solution; that is done with the File → New → New Project command.

Add Existing Item... (Shift-Alt-A)

This command brings up the Add Existing Item - Solution Items dialog box, which allows you to browse your filesystem for existing items to add to the solution.

Add New Solution Folder

Solution folders are used to organize solution items within a solution. This command lets you add a folder to the solution. These solution folders are virtual, meaning no corresponding physical folder is on your filesystem. Instead, the solution folders are remembered within the solution file (*.sln*). Any solution items added to the solution folder are physically stored in the project file along with the *.sln* file and other solution items.

Set StartUp Projects...

Visual Studio must know which project, or projects, in a solution will be the startup project(s). This command brings up the Solution Properties Pages dialog box, with the Startup Project page displayed. You can either select the current project as the startup project, any specified project from the solution, or multiple projects. By default, the first project created in a solution becomes the startup project.

If multiple projects are selected, the startup page for each project will execute sequentially, so multiple browser windows will be opened.

Project Dependencies... / Project Build Order...

These commands, visible only when a solution contains multiple projects, present the Project Dependiencies dialog box that allows you to control the dependencies and build order of the projects in a solution. You can also access this dialog from the Solution Explorer by right-clicking a solution. The dialog box has two tabs, one for Dependencies and one for Build Order.

For each project in a solution, the Project Dependencies tab allows you to specify which projects it depends upon. The dependent projects will be built first.

The Project Build Order tab presents a list of all the projects in the order in which they will be built. You can't change the Build Order from this tab. It is inferred from the dependencies.

Build Menu

The Build menu offers menu items for building the current project (highlighted in Solution Explorer) or the solution. It also exposes the Configuration Manager for configuring the build process. The Build menu will be covered in detail in Chapter 19.

Debug Menu

The Debug menu allows you to start an application with or without debugging, set breakpoints in the code, and control the debugging session. The Debug menu will be covered along with the topic of debugging in Chapter 7.

Data Menu

This context-sensitive menu is visible only when in design mode. It is not available when editing code pages. The commands under it are available when appropriate data controls are on the form. Data controls and data binding will be covered in Chapters 9 and 10.

Format Menu

The Format menu is visible only in design mode, and the commands under it are context-sensitive to the control(s) currently selected. This menu offers the ability to control the size and layout of controls, though many of the menu options are grayed out for certain web form controls. You can:

- Align controls with a grid or with other controls six different ways
- Change the size of one or more controls to be bigger, smaller, or all be the same
- Control the spacing horizontally and vertically
- Move controls forward or backward in the vertical plane (Z order) of the form

To operate on more than one control, select the controls in one of several ways:

- Hold down the Shift or Ctrl key while clicking on controls to be selected.
- Use the mouse to click and drag a selection box around all the controls to be selected. If any part of a control falls within the selection box, that control will be included.
- To unselect one control, hold down the Shift or Ctrl key while clicking that control.
- To unselect all the controls, select a different control or press the Esc key.

When you operate on more than one control, the last control selected will be the baseline. In other words, if you are making all the controls the same size, they will all become the same size as the last control selected. Likewise, if aligning a group of controls, they will all align with the last control selected.

As controls are selected, they will display eight resizing handles. These resizing handles will be black for all the selected controls except the baseline, or last control, which will have white handles.

With that in mind, all of the commands under the Format menu are fairly self-explanatory.

Tools Menu

The Tools menu presents commands accessing a wide range of functionality, ranging from connecting to databases to accessing external tools to setting IDE options. Some of the more useful commands are described in the following sections.

Connect to Device...

Brings up a dialog box that allows you to connect to either a physical mobile device or an emulator.

Connect to Database...

The Connect to Database command default brings up the dialog box that allows you to select a server, log in to that server, and connect to the database on the server. Microsoft SQL Server is the default database (surprise!), but the Change... button allows you to connect to any number of other databases, including any for which there are Oracle or ODBC providers.

Code Snippets Manager (Ctrl-K, Ctrl-B)

This command brings up the Code Snippets Manager dialog box, which allows you to maintain the code snippets, described above in the Intellisense section. This dialog box allows you to add or remove code snippets for any of the supported languages. You can import code snippets and search online for code snippets.

Choose Toolbox Items...

This command brings up the Choose Toolbox dialog box shown in Figure 2-25. The dialog box has two tabs: one for adding (legacy) COM components and one for adding .NET CLR-compliant components. All the components available on your machine (which include registered COM components and .NET components in specific directories—you can browse for .NET components if they are not listed) are listed in one or the other. In either case, check or uncheck the box in front of the component to include or not include the desired component.

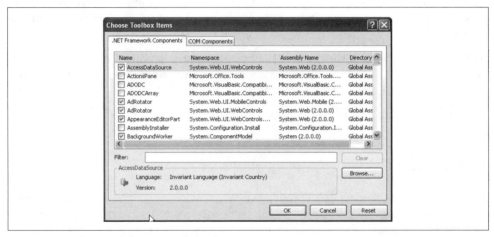

Figure 2-25. Choose Toolbox Items dialog box

 When you want to add a .NET component to the toolbox, it is generally easier to just drag it from Windows Explorer onto the toolbox.

You can sort the components listed in the dialog box by clicking on the column head that you wish to sort by.

Macros

Macros are a wonderful feature that allow you to automate tasks in the IDE. Macros can either be coded by hand using VS2005 or recorded as you perform the desired task. If you allow the IDE to record the macro for you, you can subsequently examine and edit the macro code it creates. This is similar to the macro functionality provided as part of Microsoft Word or Microsoft Excel.

 Macro recording doesn't work for anything inside a dialog box. For example, if you record the changing of some property in a project's Property Pages, the recorded macro will open the Property Pages but won't do anything in there.

You can easily record a temporary macro by using the Macros → Record Temporary-Macro command or by pressing Ctrl-Shift-R. This temporary macro can then be played back using the Macros → Run TemporaryMacro command or by pressing Ctrl-Shift-P. You can save the macro with the Macros → Save TemporaryMacro command, which will automatically bring up the Macro Explorer, described next.

You manage macros with the Macro Explorer window, accessed via a submenu of the Macros command or by pressing Alt-F8, shown in Figure 2-26 after recording a temporary macro.

Figure 2-26. Macro Explorer

Right-clicking on a macro in the Macro Explorer pops up a menu with four items:

Run
Runs the highlighted macro. The macro can also be run by double-clicking on the macro name.

Edit
Brings up the macro editing IDE, where all the macros for the user can be edited. The macro language is VS2005, irrespective of the language used for the project. You can also invoke the macro editing IDE using the Macros → Macro IDE command, or by pressing Alt-F11.

Rename
Allows you to rename the macro.

Delete
Deletes the macro from the macro file.

All the macros are contained in a *macro project* called, by default, MyMacros. This project is comprised of a binary file called *MyMacros.vsmacros* (unless you have elected to convert it to the multiple files format), which is physically located in a folder called VSMacros80 in the current projects directory for each user. You can create a new macro project by using the Macros → New Macro Project command or by right-clicking on the root object in the Macro Explorer and selecting New Macro Project. In either case, you will get the New Macro Project dialog box, which will allow you to specify the name and location of the new macro project file.

Macro projects contain modules, which are units of code. Each module contains subroutines, which correspond to the macros. So, for example, the macro called TemporaryMacro shown in Figure 2-26 is the TemporaryMacro subroutine contained in the module named RecordingModule, which is part of the MyMacros project.

External Tools...

Depending on the options selected at the time VS2005 was installed on your machine, you may have one or more external tools available on the Tools menu. These might include tools such as Create GUID or Dotfuscator Community Edition. (Use of these tools is beyond the scope of this book.)

The Tools → External Tools... command allows you to add additional external tools to the Tools menu. When you select it, you are presented with the External Tools dialog box. This dialog box has fields for the tool title, the command to execute the tool, any arguments and the initial directory, and several checkboxes for different behaviors.

Import and Export Settings...

This command brings up the Import and Export Settings dialog box, which is a wizard for importing and exporting IDE environment settings. With this wizard, you can transfer your carefully wrought IDE settings from one machine to the next.

Customize...

The Customize... command allows you to customize many aspects of the IDE user interface. (The Options... command, described in the following section, allows you to set other program options.) It brings up the Customize dialog box, which has two different tabs plus one additional button, allowing customization in three different areas.

Toolbars

This tab presents a checkbox list of all the available toolbars, with checkmarks indicating those toolbars currently visible. You can control the visibility of specific toolbars by checking or unchecking them in this list or, alternatively, use the View → Toolbars command.

You can also create new toolbars, rename or delete existing toolbars, or reset all the toolbars back to the original installation version on this tab. Checkboxes allow you to control tooltips and icons.

Commands

The Commands tab allows you to add or remove commands from a toolbar or modify buttons on the toolbar.

To add a command to a toolbar, select the category and command from the lists in the dialog box and then use the mouse to drag the command to the desired toolbar.

To remove a command from a toolbar, drag it from the toolbar to anywhere in the IDE while the Customize Commands dialog is showing.

The Modify Selection button is only active when a button on an existing toolbar is selected. It allows you to perform such chores as renaming or deleting the button, changing the image displayed on the button, changing the display style of the button (e.g., image only, text only), and organizing buttons into groups.

Keyboard...

The Keyboard... button brings up the Environment → Keyboard page, also accessible under the Tools → Options command described below. This page allows you to define and change keyboard shortcuts for commands.

Options...

The Options... command brings up the Options dialog box. This dialog box allows setting a wide range of options, ranging from the number of items to display in lists of recently used items to HTML Designer options.

The dialog box displays a hierarchical list of categories on the left side. Selecting any category allows you to drill down through the tree structure. Clicking on a detail item brings up the available properties on the right side of the dialog box.

Most of the available options are fairly self-explanatory. If you have any questions about specific settings, clicking on the Help button at the bottom of the Options dialog box will bring up context-sensitive help about all the properties relevant to the current detail item.

Window Menu

The Window menu is a standard Windows application Window command. It displays a list of all the currently open windows, allowing you to bring any window to the foreground by clicking on it. All the file windows currently displayed in the IDE have tabs along the top edge of the work surface, below the toolbars (unless you have selected MDI mode in Tools → Options → Environment → General), and windows can be selected by clicking on a tab.

This is a context-sensitive menu. The menu items available for different circumstances are listed in Table 2-9.

Table 2-9. Window menu item commands

Current window	Description of available commands
Design	Auto Hide All hides all dockable windows. Clicking on a window's pushpin icon turns AutoHide off for that window.
	New Horizontal/Vertical Tab Group creates another set of windows with it own set of tabs.
	Close All Documents is self-explanatory.
Code	Same as for a design window plus the following: New Window creates a new window containing the same file as the current window (use this to open two windows to the same source file); Split creates a second window in the current window for two different views of the same file; and Remove Split removes a split window.
Dockable	This category of window includes the Solution Explorer, the Properties window, the Class View window, the toolboxes, etc. These windows are dockable, as indicated by the pushpin icon in the upper right corner of each.
	Available menu items are the same as for a design window, with the addition of commands to dock, hide, or float a window.

Help Menu

The Help menu provides access to a number of submenus. Those that are not self-explanatory are described here.

Dynamic Help (Ctrl-Alt-F4)

If you are developing on a machine with enough horsepower, Dynamic Help is a wonderful thing. Otherwise, it is quite a performance hog. (You can disable it by unchecking all the checkboxes under Tools → Options → Environment → Dynamic Help) Alternatively, closing the window is sufficient to prevent the performance hit, and that way it is available when you need it.

That said, using Dynamic Help is simple. Open a Dynamic Help window by clicking on this menu item or pressing Ctrl-F1. Then, wherever the focus is, whether in a design, code, or dockable window, the context-sensitive hyperlinks will appear in the Dynamic Help window. Click on any of these links to bring up the relevant help topic in a separate window.

Contents... (Ctrl-Alt-F1) / Index... (Ctrl-Alt-F2) / Search... (Ctrl-Alt-F3)

These three commands provide different views into the SDK help system, allowing you to search by a (pseudo) table of contents, an incremental index, or a search phrase, respectively. The first type of search is an indexed search, while the latter two are full text searches, so you may get different results using the different search types using the same phrase.

The Help system exposed by these commands is the exact same Help system exposed in two other places by the Start button:

- Programs → Microsoft Visual Studio 2005 → Microsoft Visual Studio 2005 Documentation
- Programs → Microsoft .NET Framework SDK v2.0 → Documentation

This Help tool uses a browser-type interface, with Forward and Back navigation and Favorites. The list of topics is displayed in the lefthand pane, and the help topic itself, including hyperlinks, is displayed on the right.

Index Results... (Shift-Alt-F2)

When you're searching for Help topics by Index, many topics are often for a given index entry. In these cases, the multiple topics are listed in an Index Results window. This window will display automatically if this is the case. This command allows you to view the Index Results window if it has been closed.

Check for Updates

This command will check for service releases for your currently installed version of VS2005. In order for this command to work, your machine must be connected to the Internet. If there is an update available, you will be prompted to close the IDE before the service release is installed.

CHAPTER 3
Controls: Fundamental Concepts

Controls are the building blocks of a graphical user interface (GUI). Some controls you're probably familiar with include buttons, checkboxes, and list boxes. Controls provide a means for a user to indicate a preference, enter data, or make selections. They can also provide infrastructure support in areas such as validation, data manipulation, master pages, and security.

There are four types of web controls (each but the first will be covered in detail in this and subsequent chapters):

HTML controls
> The original controls available to any HTML page. These all work in ASP.NET as they work in other web pages. HTML controls will be used where appropriate in this book but will not be discussed in detail. For a good resource on HTML controls, see *HTML and XHTML: The Definitive Guide*, Fifth Edition, by Chuck Musciano and Bill Kennedy (O'Reilly).

HTML server controls
> These are based on the original HTML controls but are enhanced to enable server-side processing.

ASP.NET server controls
> These rich and flexible server-side controls are integrated into the ASP.NET programming model. These controls are rendered to the client as HTML and provide the same functionality as HTML server controls and more.

User controls and custom controls
> Controls created by the developer. Chapter 14 discusses user and custom controls.

ASP.NET server controls (sometimes called ASP controls because of the way they are coded in content files) are at the heart of ASP.NET, replacing classic client-side HTML controls with a server-side implementation that integrates with and follows the object-oriented programming model of the .NET Framework. Most important, ASP.NET server controls remove all the inconsistencies of how attributes are set in HTML controls: ASP.NET server controls are predictable.

ASP.NET server controls can be either declared in a content file (a page file, user control file, or master page file) similar to classic HTML elements, or they can be programmatically instantiated and manipulated in C# (or other .NET language) assemblies.

In addition to straightforward form elements such as text boxes, labels, buttons, and checkboxes, ASP.NET server controls include several broad categories that provide rich functionality with little developer coding. These include the following:

Validation controls

These controls provide a full range of built-in form validation capability. Chapter 8 discusses validation controls.

Data source controls

These controls provide data binding to various data stores, including Microsoft SQL Server and Access and other relational databases, XML files, and classes implemented in code. Data source controls are covered in Chapter 9.

Data view controls

These controls are various lists and tables that can bind to a data source for display and editing. Data view controls are covered in Chapter 9.

Personalization controls

These controls allow users to personalize their view of a site, including rearrangement of the page itself. User information can be saved automatically and transparently and can be persisted from one session to the next. Personalization is covered in Chapter 13.

Login & Security controls

These controls handle the common chores of logging in to a site and maintaining user passwords. Login and Security controls are covered in Chapter 12.

Master pages

Help create web sites with a consistent layout and user interface. Master Pages are covered in Chapter 11.

Rich controls

Controls to implement features such as menus, tree views, and wizards, among others.

Version 1 of ASP.NET introduced server-side controls, both the HTML and the ASP.NET server variety. The latter gave a taste of the rich potential with the Validation, AdRotator, and Calendar controls. Version 2 expands this with new and expanded classes of controls to handle data binding, security, log in, etc.

A design goal of Version 2 was to reduce coding by 70 percent over ASP.NET 1.1. To accomplish this, they have moved a lot of functionality into controls you can just drag and drop onto your form; the control takes care of the plumbing. As part of this, ASP.NET server controls are more declarative than ever, meaning that more of their properties and events can be declared in the content file (*.aspx* or *.ascx*) rather than manipulated programmatically (though that latter technique remains available).

ASP.NET server controls offer significant improvements over the old-style HTML controls. These include the following:

- The ability to have the page automatically maintain the state of the control, discussed in detail in Chapter 6.

- ASP.NET detects the level of the target browser. "Uplevel" DHTML-enabled browsers are sent script for client-side processing. On "downlevel" old-fashioned browsers, all processing is done on the server. The appropriate HTML is generated for each browser.

- The use of a compiled language instead of an interpreted script, resulting in better performance.

- The ability to bind to a data source (as discussed in Chapter 9).

- Events can be raised by controls on the browser and easily handled by code on the server.

Each web page and server control is represented by a class derived from the System. Web.UI.Control class. For example, the ASP.NET Button control is represented by the Button class, and the HTML Button control is represented by the HtmlButton class. In addition, the Page class is derived from the Control class. As such, all pages and controls share all of the properties, methods and events which are members of the Control class. These will be covered later in this chapter in the section "ASP.NET Server Control Class Hierarchy."

Events

The two models of program execution (which are not necessarily mutually exclusive) are *linear* and *event-driven*. The key to understanding ASP.NET is that it is event-driven.

Linear programs move from step 1, to step 2, and so on, to the end of all the steps. Flow control structures within the code (such as loops, if statements, or method calls) may redirect the flow of the program, but essentially, once the program execution begins, it runs its course unaffected by anything the user or system may do. Before GUI environments, most computer programs were linear.

In contrast, event-driven programming responds to something happening (such as a button being pressed). Most often, events are generated by user action, but events can be raised by the system. For example, the system might raise an event when a file that you open for reading has been read into memory or when your battery's power is running low.

In ASP.NET, objects may raise events and other objects may have assigned event handlers. For example, a button may raise the Click event, and the page may have a method to handle the button's click event (such as Button1_Click). Your code in the event handler then responds to the button's being clicked in whatever way is appropriate for your application.

The main point to remember here is that server controls are objects that can raise events. Any action a user takes with a server control on the browser raises an event. Your server-side code responds to that event, running the code you have placed in the event handler method.

ASP.NET Events

ASP.NET has thousands of events. The application has events (such as Start and End), each session has events (again, such as Start and End), and the page and most of the server controls can raise events. All ASP.NET events are handled on the server. Some events cause an immediate posting to the server, and other events are stored until the next time the page is posted back to the server.

Because they are handled on the server, ASP.NET events are somewhat different from events in traditional client applications, in which both the event itself and the event handler are on the client. In ASP.NET applications, an event is typically raised on the client (such as by the user clicking a button displayed in the browser) but handled on the server.

Consider an ASP.NET web page with a button control. A Click event is raised when the button is clicked. Unlike an HTML button control, the ASP.NET button has an attribute, runat=server, that adds server-side processing to all the normal functionality of an HTML button.

When the Click event is raised once again, the browser handles the client-side event by posting the page to the server. This time, however, an event message is transmitted to the server. The server determines if the Click event has an event handler associated with it, and if it does, the event handler will be executed on the server.

An event message is transmitted to the server via an HTTP POST. ASP.NET automagically (that's a technical term) handles all the mechanics of capturing the event, transmitting it to the server, and processing the event. As the programmer, all you have to do is create your event handlers.

Many events, such as MouseOver, are ineligible for server-side processing because they kill performance. All server-side processing requires a postback (a round trip to the server and back), and you do not want to post the page every time there is a MouseOver event. If these events are handled at all, it is on the client side (using script) and outside the scope of ASP.NET.

> It is possible, and often useful, to endow server controls with client-side processing, as described later in this chapter. However, this is essentially an end run around the fundamental nature of ASP.NET.

Event Arguments

Events are implemented with *delegates*. A delegate is an object that encapsulates the description of a method to which you may assign responsibility for handling the event.

> For a complete discussion of delegates, see *Programming C#*, Fourth Edition, by Jesse Liberty (O'Reilly).

By convention, all ASP.NET event handlers take two parameters and return void. The first parameter represents the object raising the event. By convention, it is called sender, though that is not a requirement. Using the sending object will be covered later in this chapter in the section on Programmatic Access to Controls.

The second parameter, called the *event argument*, contains information specific to the event if there is any. For most events, the event argument is of type EventArgs, which does not expose any properties. So, the general prototype for an event is the following:

```
private void EventName (object sender, EventArgs e)
```

For some controls, the event argument may be of a type derived from EventArgs and may expose properties specific to that event type. For example, the AdRotator control's AdCreated event handler receives an argument of type AdCreatedEventArgs, which has the properties AdProperties, AlternateText, ImageUrl, and NavigateUrl. The specifics of the event arguments for each control are detailed in the chapters describing each control.

Application and Session Events

ASP.NET supports the Application and Session events familiar to classic ASP programmers. An Application_Start event is raised when the application starts. This is a good time to initialize resources that will be used throughout the application, such as database connection strings (but not the database connection itself). An Application_End event is raised when the application ends. This is the time to close resources and do any other housekeeping that may be necessary. Garbage collection will automatically take care of freeing up memory, but if you allocated unmanaged resources, such as components created with languages that are noncompliant with the .NET Framework, you must clean them up yourself.

Likewise, there are session events. A session starts when a user first requests a page from your application and ends when the application closes the session or the session times out. A Session_Start event is raised when the session starts, at which time you can initialize resources that will be session-specific, such as opening a database connection, though it is probably better to open a database connection when it is needed and close it immediately when finished with it. When the session ends, there will be a Session_End event.

Page and Control Events

The page and controls all have events that are inherited from the Control class (or the TemplateControl class in the case of the Error event). All of these events pass an event argument of type EventArgs that exposes no properties. The most common of these events are listed in Table 3-1. (A complete list of all properties, methods, and events for every class can be found in the documentation.)

Table 3-1. Some common page and control events

Event name	Description
DataBinding	Occurs when the control binds to a data source
Disposed	Occurs when the control is released from memory
Error	For the page only; occurs when an unhandled exception is thrown
Init	Occurs when the control is initialized
Load	Occurs when the control is loaded to the Page object
PreRender	Occurs when the control is about to be rendered
Unload	Occurs when the control is unloaded from memory

Binding a control to a data source means that the control and the data source are tied together so that the control knows to use that data source for populating itself. Chapters 9 and 10 provide a complete description of data controls and data binding.

Postback Versus Non-Postback Events

Postback events cause the form to be posted back to the server immediately. These include click-type events, such as Button.Click. In contrast, many events (typically change events such as TextBox.TextChanged, or selection events, such as CheckBox. CheckedChanged) are considered *non-postback* because the event is not posted back to the server immediately. Instead, these events are cached by the control until the next time a post occurs. Controls with non-postback events can be forced to behave in a postback manner by setting their AutoPostBack property to true.

Table 3-2 summarizes the controls with postback and non-postback events.

Table 3-2. Postback and non-postback controls

Postback	Non-postback
Button	BulletedList
Calendar	CheckBox
DataGrid	CheckBoxList
DataList	DropDownList
FileUpload	ListBox
GridView	RadioButtonList
ImageButton	RadioButton
ImageMap	TextBox
LinkButton	
Menu	
Repeater	

IsPostBack

The Page object exposes the IsPostBack property. This is a read-only Boolean property that indicates if the page is being loaded for the first time or if it is being loaded in response to a client postback. There are many expensive operations (such as getting data from a database or populating ListItems) you will want to perform only the first time the page is loaded. If the page is posted to the server and then reloaded, there will be no need to repeat the operation, since any data entered or populated is retained (using view state, described in Chapter 6) on subsequent posts. By testing the value of IsPostBack, you can skip the expensive operation, as in the following code snippet:

```
protected void Page_Load(Object sender, EventArgs e)
{
    if (! IsPostBack)
    {
```

```
        // Do the expensive operations only the
        // first time the page is loaded.
    }
}
```

Events in Visual Studio 2005

The Visual Studio 2005 (VS2005) IDE can automatically handle much of the work required to implement events in ASP.NET. For example, it offers a list of all the possible events for each control. If you choose to implement an event, you can type in a name for the event handler. The IDE will create the boilerplate code necessary and will wire up the associated delegate.

When you create a new web application, VS2005 automatically includes the following code snippet to handle the Page Load event:

```
protected void Page_Load(object sender, EventArgs e)
{
}
```

Every page has a number of events for which you may create handlers, similar to the Page_Load event handler. These predefined event handler names are created by concatenating Page_ with the name of the event. So, the following event handlers will automatically be hooked to their corresponding event:

Page_Load	Page_AbortTransaction
Page_CommitTransaction	Page_DataBinding
Page_Disposed	Page_Error
Page_Init	Page_InitComplete
Page_Load	Page_LoadComplete
Page_PreInit	Page_PreLoad
Page_PreRender	Page_PreRenderComplete
Page_SaveStateComplete	Page_Unload

In addition, controls placed on the page will have their own events that you may handle as well. When you add the control, you can see its events by clicking on the control in Design view and then clicking on the events button (the lightning bolt) in the Properties window. For example, the events for a Button control placed on the page are shown in Figure 3-1, with the events button indicated.

You can type the name of a method in the space next to any event or double-click in that space, and VS2005 will create an event handler for you. In either case, you'll be placed in the event handler, ready to type your code to implement the event, as shown in Figure 3-2.

In this case, I double-clicked in the space next to the Click event. VS2005 named the event Button1_Click (ControlName_EventName), created the skeleton of the event handler, and placed the cursor within that event handler.

Figure 3-1. Button events

```
Default.aspx.cs*   Default.aspx*                                    ▾ × 
_Default                              ▾   Button1_Click(object sender, EventArgs e)   ▾

using System;
using System.Data;
using System.Configuration;
using System.Web;
using System.Web.Security;
using System.Web.UI;
using System.Web.UI.WebControls;
using System.Web.UI.WebControls.WebParts;
using System.Web.UI.HtmlControls;

public partial class _Default : System.Web.UI.Page
{
    protected void Page_Load(object sender, EventArgs e)
    {

    }
    protected void Button1_Click(object sender, EventArgs e)
    {
        |
    }
}
```

Figure 3-2. Button event handler

Every control has a default event, presumably the event most commonly implemented for that control. Predictably, the default event for the Button class is the
Click event. You can create the default event handler just by double-clicking on the
control in Design view. Thus, had you not created the Button1_Click event handler,
as shown above, you could open Design view and double-click on the button. The
effect would be identical: an event handler named Button1_Click would be created,
and you'd be placed in the event handler ready to type your code to implement the
method.

The default event for some of the most common web controls are listed in Table 3-3.

Table 3-3. Default events for some ASP.NET controls

Control	Default event
AdRotator	AdCreated
BulletedList	Click

Table 3-3. Default events for some ASP.NET controls (continued)

Control	Default event
Button	Click
Calendar	SelectionChanged
CheckBox	CheckedChanged
CheckBoxList	SelectedIndexChanged
DataGrid	SelectedIndexChanged
DataList	SelectedIndexChanged
DropDownList	SelectedIndexChanged
HyperLink	Click
ImageButton	Click
ImageMap	Click
Label	None
LinkButton	Click
ListBox	SelectedIndexChanged
Menu	MenuItemClick
RadioButton	CheckedChanged
RadioButtonList	SelectedIndexChanged
Repeater	ItemCommand

Multiple Controls to One Event Handler

A single event handler can handle events from several different controls. For example, you may have a generic button click event handler that handles all the buttons on your form. The button that raised the event can be determined by testing the value of the sender parameter. In the following code snippet, a button click event handler casts the sender object (that is, the control that raised the event) to the Button type and then assigns the ID property of that button to a string variable.

```
private void BtnClick(object sender, System.EventArgs e)
{
   Button b = sender as Button;
   String buttonID = b.ID;
   switch (buttonID)
   {
      case "btnDoThis":
         //  code to do this
      case "btnDoThat":
         //  code to do that
   }
   //  code to do stuff common to all the buttons
}
```

This can eliminate a great deal of duplicate code and can make your program easier to read and maintain.

ASP.NET Server Controls

The primary control type used in ASP.NET is the *ASP.NET server control*. Server controls may have methods and event handlers associated with them, and this code is processed on the server. (Some server controls provide client-side script as well, but even then the processing is done, again, on the server.)

If the control has a visual component (e.g., labels, buttons, and tables), ASP.NET renders classic HTML to the browser, taking the target browser capabilities into account. If the ASP.NET server control requires client-side script to implement its functionality as, for example, with the validation controls described in Chapter 8, then browser-appropriate script is generated and sent to the browser. However, server-side validation will be performed as well.

 This is a key point and bears repeating: What is sent to the client is plain vanilla HTML, so ASP.NET programs can be run on any browser by any manufacturer. All processing is done on the server, and all ASP.NET server controls are presented to the browser as standard HTML. Sending script is an optimization and is never required.

ASP.NET server controls offer a consistent programming model. For example, in HTML, the input tag (`<input>`) is used for buttons, single-line text fields, checkboxes, hidden fields, and passwords. For multiline text fields, you must use the `<textarea>` tag. With ASP.NET server controls, each different type of functionality corresponds to a specific control. For example, all text is entered using the TextBox control; the number of lines is specified using a property. In fact, for ASP.NET server controls in general, all the declared attributes correspond to properties of the class that represents the control.

The ASP.NET server controls include all the functionality provided by HTML controls and much more. This includes basic controls such as buttons, labels, checkboxes, and tables, advanced data controls (such as data sources, lists, data grids, and grid views), validation controls, security and login controls, and rich controls (such as the Calendar, AdRotator, Menu and DynamicImage controls).

In the content file, the syntax used to implement ASP.NET server controls is of this form:

```
<asp:controlType
    id="ControlID"
    runat="server"
    thisProperty="this value"
    thatProperty="that value"/>
```

Because of the leading asp, these controls are sometimes known as ASP controls.

Here, the control tag always begins with asp:, known as the *tag prefix*. The controlType is the type, or class, of the control, such as Button, CheckBoxList, or GridView. An id attribute allows you to refer to this instance of the control programmatically. The runat attribute tells the server this control is to be processed on the server.

You might think that the runat="server" attribute would be the default and unnecessary to include with every control, since the most common scenario is for server controls to be processed on the server. However, that is not the case: you must include this attribute with every declaration of every server control. If you omit it, there will be no errors, but the control will be ignored and will not be rendered.

The control will render properly if you omit the ID attribute, but the control cannot be referenced and manipulated elsewhere in code.

You can declare additional attributes within the angle brackets. For example, you can declare Text and Width attributes for a TextBox like this:

```
<asp:TextBox ID="txtBookName"
             runat="server"
             Width="250px"
             Text="Enter a book name."/>
```

ASP.NET server controls use well-formed XHTML syntax, though ASP.NET is tolerant of missing quotation marks around attribute values. (See the sidebar for a description of well-formed XHTML.) Specifically, the angle brackets must be self-closing, as shown above, or have closing elements. So, the above TextBox could equivalently be written this way:

```
<asp:TextBox ID="txtBookName"
             runat="server"
             Width="250px"
             Text="Enter a book name."></asp:TextBox>
```

In addition, many ASP.NET server controls can make use of *inner HTML*, which is content between the opening tag and the closing tag. In the case of a TextBox control, for example, the Text property can be specified as inner HTML rather than an attribute of the opening element. So, the above control could again be equivalently written this way:

```
<asp:TextBox ID="txtBookName"
             runat="server"
             Width="250px">Enter a book name.</asp:TextBox>
```

Well-Formed XHTML

XHTML is a World Wide Web Consortium (W3C) standard, of which the current version is 1.1. It defines HTML as a well-formed XML document. Many web browsers are very forgiving, and ill-formed HTML will work fine, but the world is moving toward a stricter syntax to increase the robustness of the Web. Well-formed code has a huge benefit for authoring tools and is worthwhile when hand coding since it decreases confusion and ambiguity.

Among the rules of well-formed HTML are these:

Close all tags

Several HTML tags, such as <p>, <tr>, and <td>, are routinely left unclosed. In well-formed HTML, there will always be a closing tag, such as </td>. Many tags, such as <br>, <hr>, <input>, and <img>, can be made self-closing by putting the closing forward slash within the tag itself. This makes it well-formed, as in this example:

```
<input type="submit"
id="btnBookName"
value="Book Name"
onServerClick="btnBookName_Click"
runat="server" />
```

No overlapping tags

Some browsers are tolerant of overlapping tags, but well-formed HTML requires that tags do not overlap. For example, consider the overlapping tags in the following line of HTML:

```
<b>This is <i>the year</b>for the Red Sox.</i>
```

This can, instead, be expressed this way:

```
<b>This is</b> <i><b>the year</b>for the Red Sox.</i>
```

Case-sensitivity

Like all HTML and ASP pages, ASP.NET is generally not case-sensitive. The one glaring exception is that C# is always case-sensitive. That said, it should be noted script components, i.e., code intended to be rendered to the browser as executable script, are XML files, and as such should follow XML conventions. According to these conventions, element types and attributes are case-sensitive. This will usually only matter if you use an XML editing tool to work with the script components or if you are creating an XML file (such as an advertisement file for use with the AdRotator control, described in Chapter 5). However, it is good practice to follow the XML guidelines. Element types and attributes are usually lowercase, except multipart names (such as onServerClick), which use camel notation with initial lowercase. For other HTML tags, being well-formed requires that start and end tags have matching case. This book will generally use lowercase for all HTML tags.

—continued—

Quotation marks
> In well-formed HTML, all attributes are enclosed in quotation marks.

Single root
> The top-level element in a page must be <html>. Remember to close it at the end with </html>.

Reserved characters
> There are only five built-in character entities in XML:

> | | |
> |---|---|
> | < | < |
> | > | > |
> | & | & |
> | " | " |
> | ' | ' |

If any of these characters are used in script, then it must be "escaped" by using the above character entity or by enclosing the entire script block in a CDATA section. (CDATA is an XML type.)

HTML controls are divided into two categories: *input* and *container*. HTML input controls do not require a closing tag (though to be well formed, they should be made self-closing with a trailing /) and have Name, Value, and Type attributes, which may be accessed and controlled programmatically.

HTML container controls, on the other hand, must have a trailing / or a closing tag. They do not have Name, Value, or Type attributes. Instead, the content found between opening and closing tags may be accessed programmatically using the InnerHtml or InnerText property. The difference between these two properties is that InnerText provides automatic HTML encoding and decoding of special characters, such as < or >. If you use the InnerHtml property, these characters will be interpreted as being part of the HTML and will not display in the final output.

You implement ASP.NET server control attributes as properties of the server control class, and you can access them programmatically. Once a control has been declared, or otherwise instantiated in code, you can retrieve or set its properties programmatically. Using this example, your code could set or change the Text property with the following line of code:

```
txtBookName.Text = "Programming ASP.NET";
```

Most ASP.NET server controls expose events. Event handling in general is explained previously in this chapter, and each control's events are covered in the chapter where that control is discussed.

The following example will demonstrate many of the features provided by VS2005 to minimize typing and errors when using controls, including:

- Dragging and dropping controls onto either the Design or Source views of the web page
- Intellisense to display and auto-complete properties declaratively in Source view of the web page
- Using a Properties window for entering properties in either the Design or Source view of the web page

Open VS2005 and click New Web Site. Click ASP.NET Web Site, ensuring the language is set to C#. Call the new web site *ASPNETServerControls*.

This will create a new web application with a page called *Default.aspx*. The IDE will show the Source view of *Default.aspx* on the work surface, with the Toolbox on the left side of the screen and the Solution Explorer and Properties windows on the right. The code shown in Example 3-1 (reformatted slightly for better readability on this page) will be inserted by default.

Example 3-1. Default boilerplate code

```
<%@ Page Language="C#" AutoEventWireup="true" CodeFile="Default.aspx.cs"
    Inherits="_Default" %>

<!DOCTYPE html PUBLIC "-//W3C//DTD XHTML 1.1//EN"
    "http://www.w3.org/TR/xhtml11/DTD/xhtml11.dtd">

<html xmlns="http://www.w3.org/1999/xhtml" >
<head runat="server">
    <title>Untitled Page</title>
</head>
<body>
    <form id="form1" runat="server">
    <div>

    </div>
    </form>
</body>
</html>
```

Replace the default title text with something more meaningful, such as *ASP.NET Server Controls*. Inside the <div> element, type in a header element:

```
<h1>ASP.NET Server Controls</h1>
```

Though many of the commonly used HTML controls are available for drag and drop from the Toolbox, header controls are not. However, as soon as you type an opening angle bracket, Intellisense will drop down a complete list of all the possible HTML and web server controls.

You can enter the first few characters of the control's name to get to the control or use the mouse to slide down and select the control. Pressing the Tab key will insert the currently selected control. Type the closing angle bracket and the closing tag will automatically pop into place with the cursor positioned between the opening and closing tags, ready for typing.

In Design view, a formatting drop-down allows you to apply an HTML style to selected text.

Immediately following the first header, enter a second header control, as follows:

```
<h2>The date and time is <% =DateTime.Now.ToString( ) %>.</h2>
```

Intellisense is continually helpful here. It automatically provides the closing h2 element, and as soon as you enter the <% characters, indicating the beginning of server-side code, it automatically provides the closing %> characters. As soon as you enter each successive period in the DateTime expression, it provides a drop-down with all the possible members available next.

Remember that C# is case sensitive. If you are not using the correct case, the code will not work, and Intellisense will not display anything.

You can place server-side code in-line (without being wrapped within a <script> block) in a content file by enclosing the code within the <% %> characters as was done in the previous code snippet. This works because the browser ignores anything between the script block characters, not rendering it to the page. The ASP.NET runtime, however, recognizes that content as it processes the page. When the runtime sees valid Framework code, it processes it. In this case, that code returns a text string containing the current date and time, which then gets incorporated directly into the rendered output.

Switch to the Design view of the page by clicking the Design button at the bottom of the work surface. The cursor should be at the end of the h2 header you entered. That header will display the following:

```
The date and time is .
```

It does this since the script that provides the date and time will not run until the page is run.

Commenting Your Code

Commenting ASP.NET is particularly difficult. As an ASP.NET developer, you may be working with HTML, C#, VS2005, JavaScript, VBScript, and TransactSQL, among others. Each language has its own unique syntax for comments, and one language can overlap another.

Here is a summary of the different ways to comment:

HTML

```
<!-- text to be commented goes in here -->
```

JavaScipt

```
// commented text follows //
/* multiline
comment */
```

C#

```
// commented text follows //
/* multiline
comment */
```

VS2005 and VBScript

```
' commented text follows a single quotation mark
REM  comments can also follow the REM keyword
```

Transact SQL

```
-- commented text follows two dashes
/* multiline
comment */
```

XML Commenting

VS2005 can automatically convert XML comments placed in the code-behind file into well-formatted documentation:

```
/// In C#, the XML comments follow three slashes.
''' In VS2005, comments follow three single quotes.
```

Page (.aspx) or user control (.ascx) file

These characters actually indicate server-side code, but behave as comments since they do not render unless there is valid code.

```
<% The comments go here. %>
```

ASP.NET controls: There is no comment within an ASP.NET control. Since any unrecognized attributes are ignored, some developers prepend any attributes they wish to comment out with XX.

Ensure the cursor is at the end of that header line and press the Enter key a few times to space out the content. Drag a TextBox control from the Toolbox (under the Standard category) onto the form. A TextBox control will appear on the work surface.

In the Properties window on the right side of the window, change the ID property from the default value, TextBox1, to txtBookName. At the same time, change the Text property from the blank default to Enter a book name., and change the Width property to 250. The Width property will display 250px, for pixels.

 It is always good practice to assign a meaningful name to any controls that will be referenced in code.

Before proceeding any further, click the Source button at the bottom of the work surface to see the code generated by VS2005. Between the div tags, you should see something similar to the following (reformatted to fit on this page):

```
<h1>ASP.NET Server Controls</h1>
<h2>The date and time is <% =DateTime.Now.ToString( ) %>.</h2>
<p>
     </p>
<p>
    <asp:TextBox ID="txtBookName" runat="server" Width="250px">
        Enter a book name.</asp:TextBox>
     </p>
```

VS2005 inserted paragraph elements with enclosed non-breaking spaces where you pressed the Enter key. More significantly, it inserted a TextBox ASP.NET server control with the Width property set and the Text property contained in the inner HTML.

You can edit the generated HTML and ASP.NET server control declarations directly in the Source window, edit the design in the Design window, or change the properties in the Properties window. In any case, all other views of the page will immediately reflect those changes.

Moving on, drag a Button control from the Toolbox (again, under the Standard category) onto the work surface after the TextBox, either in the Design or Source view. Change its ID to btnBookName and its Text property to Book Name.

If you're on the Design view, press Enter after the button to insert a new line. If you're in Source view, enter a <p> HTML element after the button control. Then drag a Label control onto the page in either case. Change its ID to lblBookName and set its Text property to blank.

The goal here is to enable the user to type a book name into the text box, click the button, and have that book name display as the Text property of the label.

To accomplish this, you need to hook up the click event of the button to an event handler as described previously in this chapter. Switch to the Design view of the page and double-click the button. Double-clicking a control tells VS2005 you want to implement the "default" event for that control; for buttons, the default event is Click.

The code-behind file, *Default.aspx.cs*, will open with a code snippet for the click event handler method in place and the cursor inside the method, ready to accept your typing. Enter the highlighted line of code below:

```
protected void btnBookName_Click(object sender, EventArgs e)
{
    lblBookName.Text = txtBookName.Text;
}
```

Switch back to the content file, *Default.aspx*, by clicking on the tab at the top of the work surface. Go to Source view by clicking the Source button at the bottom of the work surface. The OnClick attribute has been added to the button control, with its value set to the name of the event handler method to which you added the line of text.

Run your web page by pressing F5 or clicking the Debug → Start menu item. If this is the first time you have run the page, you will be prompted to create a configuration file to enable debugging. Click Yes in that dialog box.

The page will appear in a browser with the current date and time displayed in the second header you entered. Change the text in the text box and click the button. The text you entered will display in the label below the button. The page will look something like that shown in Figure 3-3.

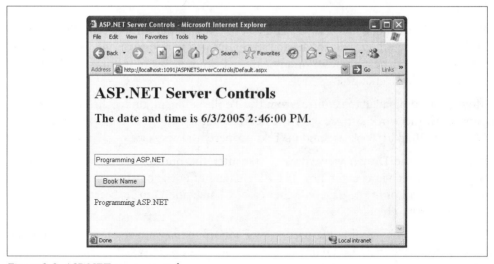

Figure 3-3. ASP.NET server controls

ASP.NET and Browsers

Let's say it just one more time: *The browser never sees the ASP.NET server control.* The *server* processes the ASP.NET server control and sends standard HTML to the browser.

ASP.NET considers browsers to be *either uplevel* or *downlevel*. Uplevel browsers support script Versions 1.2 (ECMA Script, JavaScript, JScript), Cascading Style Sheets (CSS) and HTML 4.0; typical uplevel browsers would include Internet Explorer 4.0 and later releases. Downlevel browsers, on the other hand, support only HTML 3.2.

ASP.NET can tell you which browser is being used to display the page. This information is made available via the `HttpRequest.Browser` property. `HttpRequest.Browser` returns a `HttpBrowserCapabilities` object whose many properties include a number of Booleans, such as whether the browser supports cookies, frames, and so forth.

You will find that you don't often need to check the `HttpBrowserCapabilities` object because the server will automatically convert your HTML to reflect the capabilities of the client browser. For example, validation controls (considered in Chapter 8) can be used to validate customer data entry. If the user's browser supports client-side JavaScript, the validation will happen on the client (and then again on the server to prevent spoofing). However, if the browser does not support client-side scripting, the validation will be done server side only.

From within your browser, view the source for the web page displayed in Figure 3-3. This source is shown in Example 3-2. No server controls exist; all the controls have been converted to traditional HTML tags, and a hidden field with the name `__VIEWSTATE` has been inserted into the output. This is how ASP.NET maintains the state of the controls. When a page is submitted to the server and then redisplayed, the controls are not reset to their default values. Chapter 6 discusses *state*.

Example 3-2. Output HTML from WebServerControls.aspx

```
<!DOCTYPE html PUBLIC "-//W3C//DTD XHTML 1.1//EN"
    "http://www.w3.org/TR/xhtml11/DTD/xhtml11.dtd">

<html xmlns="http://www.w3.org/1999/xhtml" >
<head><title>
    ASP.NET Server Controls
</title></head>
<body>
    <form method="post" action="Default.aspx" id="form1">
<div>
<input type="hidden" name="__VIEWSTATE"
    value="/wEPDwUKLTk1NTc5MjE0OQ9kFgICAw9kFgICAg8PFgIeBFRleHQFE1Byb2dy
    YW1taW5nIEFTUC5ORVRkZGTO9m86wvDVg2RbAlzO/3UYSr36Yg==" />
</div>
```

Example 3-2. Output HTML from WebServerControls.aspx (continued)

```
  <div>
    <h1>ASP.NET Server Controls</h1>
    <h2>The date and time is 6/3/2005 2:46:00 PM.</h2>
     <p>
         </p>
     <p>
        <input name="txtBookName" type="text"
          value="Programming ASP.NET" id="txtBookName"
          style="width:250px;" />
         </p>
     <p>
        <input type="submit" name="btnBookName" value="Book Name"
             id="btnBookName" /> </p>
     <p>
        <span id="lblBookName">Programming ASP.NET</span>
         </p>

  </div>
  </form>
</body>
</html>
```

ASP.NET Server Control Class Hierarchy

All the ASP.NET server controls that have a visual aspect when rendered to the browser are derived from the WebControl class. This class provides the properties, methods, and events common to all these controls. Among these are common properties, such as BorderColor, BorderStyle, and BorderWidth, and the RenderBeginTag and RenderEndTag methods.

The WebControl class and several other ASP.NET server controls (e.g., Literal, PlaceHolder, Repeater, and XML) derive from System.Web.UI.Control, which derives from System.Object. The Control class provides base properties such as ID, EnableViewState, Parent, and Visible; base methods such as Dispose, Focus, and RenderControl; and life cycle events such as Init, Load, PreRender, and Unload.

The WebControl class and the controls derived from Control are in the System.Web.UI. WebControls namespace. These relationships are shown in Figures 3-4a and 3-4b.

All of the properties, events, and methods of WebControl and System.Web.UI.Control are inherited by the ASP.NET server controls. Table 3-4 lists many of the commonly used properties inherited by all the ASP.NET server controls from the Control or the WebControl classes. Where applicable, default values are indicated.

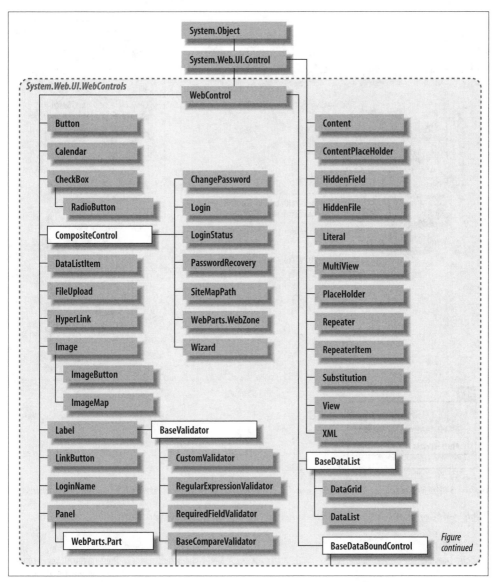

Figure 3-4a. Relationships of controls in the System.Web.UI.WebControls namespace

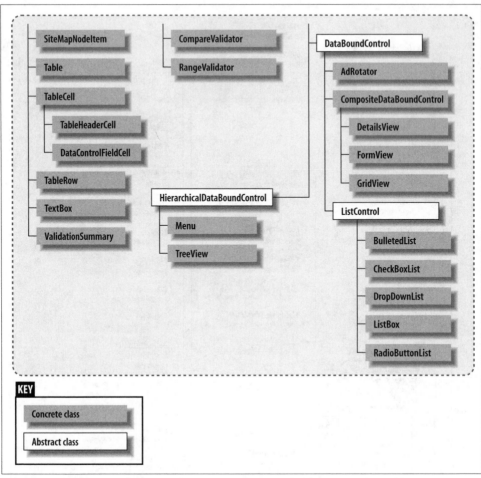

Figure 3-4b. Relationships of controls in the System. Web.UI.WebControls namespace (continued)

Table 3-4. Commonly used properties inherited by all ASP.NET server controls

Name	Type	Get	Set	Values	Description
AccessKey	String	✗	✗	Single-character string	Pressing the Alt key in combination with this value moves focus to the control.
BackColor	Color	✗	✗	Azure, Green, Blue, and so on	Background color.
BorderColor	Color	✗	✗	Fuchsia, Aqua, Coral, and so on	Border color.
BorderStyle	BorderStyle	✗	✗	Dashed, Dotted, Double, NotSet, and so on	Border style. Default is NotSet.

Table 3-4. Commonly used properties inherited by all ASP.NET server controls (continued)

Name	Type	Get	Set	Values	Description
BorderWidth	Unit	✗	✗	nn, nnpt	Width of the border. If of the form nn, where nn is an integer, then in units of pixels. If of the form nnpt, where nn is an integer, then in units of points.
CausesValidation	Boolean	✗	✗	true, false	Indicates if entering control causes validation for controls that require validation. Default is true.
Controls	ControlCollection	✗			A collection of all the control objects contained by this control.
CssClass	String	✗	✗		CSS class. See the "CSS Styles" section that follows.
Enabled	Boolean	✗	✗	true, false	If disabled, control is visible but grayed out and not operative. Contents are still selectable for copy and paste. Default is true.
EnableTheming	Boolean	✗	✗	true, false	Indicates if theming applies to this control.
EnableViewState	Boolean	✗	✗	true, false	Indicates if this control persists its view state. Default is true.
Font	FontInfo	✗	✗		See Table 4-1.
ForeColor	Color	✗	✗	Lavender, LightBlue, Blue, and so on	Foreground color.
Height	Unit	✗	✗	nn, nn%	If of the form nn, where nn is an integer, then in units of pixels. If of the form nn%, then it is a percentage of the height of the container. For downlevel browsers, will not render for Label, HyperLink, LinkButton, any validator controls, or for CheckBoxList, RadioButtonList, or DataList when their RepeatLayout property is Flow.
ID	String	✗	✗		Programmatic identifier for the control.

Name	Type	Get	Set	Values	Description
Parent	Control	✗		Control on the page	Returns a reference to this control's parent control in the page control hierarchy.
SkinID	String	✗	✗	Skin filename	Specifies which skin file from a theme directory to apply to this control.
ToolTip	String	✗	✗		Text string displayed when the mouse hovers over the control; not rendered in downlevel browsers.
Visible	Boolean	✗	✗	true, false	If false, then control is not rendered; the default is true.
Width	Unit	✗	✗	nn, nn%	If of the form *nn*, where *nn* is an integer, then in units of pixels. If of the form *nn%*, where *nn* is an integer, then it is a percentage of the width of the container. For downlevel browsers, will not render for Label, HyperLink, LinkButton, any validator controls, or for CheckBoxList, RadioButtonList, or DataList when their RepeatLayout property is Flow.

CSS Styles

Cascading Style Sheets (CSS) provide a means to apply uniform and consistent styles across an entire web site. It is a World Wide Web Consortium (W3C) standard, first supported in IE 4.0 and Netscape 4.0.

> For a complete discussion of CSS, see the following books: *HTML & XHTML: The Definitive Guide*, by Chuck Musciano and Bill Kennedy, or *Cascading Style Sheets: The Definitive Guide*, by Eric Meyer, both published by O'Reilly.

To see how ASP.NET and VS2005 support CSS, create a new web site called Styles. Right-click on the application root in the Solution Explorer and click Add New Item. Select Style Sheet from the list of templates and leave the default name. (You could change the name if you want.)

This will add the new stylesheet file to the web site and display the contents on the work surface, including two lines of boilerplate code:

```
body {
}
```

Replace that code with the contents of Example 3-3. No period precedes the body class name, but a period is before the other two class names, indicating they are *generic* classes.

Example 3-3. StyleSheet.css

```
body {
   FONT-SIZE: 12px;
   COLOR: blue;
   FONT-FAMILY: arial, helvetica, verdana, sans-serif;
   TEXT-DECORATION: underline
}
.button
{
   FONT-WEIGHT: bold;
   FONT-SIZE: 14px;
   COLOR: red;
   background-color:Yellow;
   FONT-FAMILY: arial, helvetica, verdana, sans-serif;
   TEXT-DECORATION: none
}
.label
{
   FONT-WEIGHT: bold;
   FONT-SIZE: 11px;
   COLOR: black;
   FONT-FAMILY: arial, helvetica, verdana, sans-serif;
   TEXT-DECORATION: none
}
```

Go to the Source view of the page file. Add the following <style> element inside the <head> element.

```
<style>@import url(StyleSheet.css ); </style>
```

Now add two ASP.NET server controls to the page: a Button and a Label. Set the CssClass property of the Button to button and of the Label to label. (They are case-sensitive.) Add some text to the Label control. The declaration of the two controls within the page file should look something like that listed in Example 3-4.

Example 3-4. CssStyles demonstration

```
<asp:Button  ID="Button1" runat="server" Text="Button"
           CssClass="button"></asp:Button>
<asp:Label ID="Label1" runat="server"
           CssClass="body">
   This is some sample text.
</asp:Label>
```

When the page displays, the two controls will reflect the styles set in the stylesheet file, *StyleSheet.css*.

HTML Server Controls

This book focuses on using ASP.NET server controls. However, understanding and using HTML and HTML server controls can be useful in real-life applications.

Normal HTML controls such as <h1>, <a>, and <input> are not processed by the server but are sent directly to the browser for display. Standard HTML controls can be exposed to the server and made available for server-side processing by turning them into HTML server controls.

To convert an HTML control to an HTML server control, simply add the attribute runat="server". In addition, you will probably want to add an id attribute, so the control contents can be accessed and controlled programmatically. For example, start with a simple input control:

```
<input type="text" size="40">
```

You can convert it to an HTML server control by adding the id and runat attributes, as follows:

```
<input type="text" id="BookTitle" size="40" runat="server">
```

There are two main reasons for using HTML server controls rather than ASP.NET server controls:

Converting existing HTML pages to run under ASP.NET
> To convert an HTML file to run under ASP.NET, all you need to do is change the extension of the file to *.aspx*. However, the HTML controls will run client side, not server side. To take advantage of server-side processing, including automatic maintenance of state (see Chapter 6), you must add the runat attribute.

Using HTML tables for page layout
> Server-side controls consume server resources. For static tables commonly used to lay out the page, server-side processing is unnecessary unless you need to refer to one or more of the table elements in your code. The following example illustrates this point.

Create a new web site in VS2005. Call it *HtmlServerControls*. Drag an HTML table control from the Toolbox onto the Design surface. Give it two columns and six rows. Drag an HTML button onto the page below the table. Give the button ID and runat="server" attributes.

For the first row in the table, enter the text string Name in the first column and an Input (text) control in the second column. Give that input control an ID of txtName. The next three rows should be similar, with input controls named txtStreet, txtCity, and txtState. Leave the fifth row in the table as an empty spacer. Leave the second column in the last row empty but give it an `ID` of `tdInnerHtml`. The design should look something like that shown in Figure 3-5, where the controls are named as indicated.

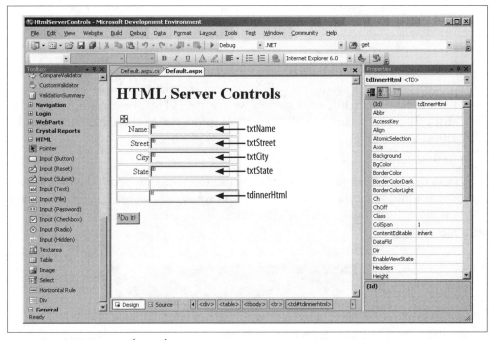

Figure 3-5. HTML control page layout

Be certain that all the named controls also have the `runat="server"` attribute as well. However, all the other table elements on the page need neither an `ID` nor a `runat` attribute since they are used for static display and will not be processed on the server.

Double-click the button in Design view to bring up the event handler method in the code-behind page. Enter the following highlighted lines of code:

```
protected void btnDoIt_ServerClick(object sender, EventArgs e)
{
    string strHtml = "";
    strHtml += txtName.Value + "<br/>";
    strHtml += txtStreet.Value + "<br/>";
    strHtml += txtCity.Value + ", " + txtState.Value;
    tdInnerHtml.InnerHtml = strHtml;
}
```

If you look at the HTML for the button on the Source view of *Default.aspx*, you will see that rather than the traditional `onClick` attribute used in conventional HTML or ASP pages, the button has an `onServerClick` attribute, telling the server what function to call when the `Click` event occurs:

```
onServerClick="btnDoIt_ServerClick"
```

If you want the control to handle the event on the client side, you should use the traditional `onClick` attribute. In this case, you must provide client-side scripting to handle the event.

You can have an `onClick` and an `onServerClick` attribute for the same control, in which case the client-side code will be run first, followed by the server-side code. This is demonstrated later in this chapter.

If you take a look at the `Click` event handler, which is executed every time the Do It! button is clicked, you'll see that an HTML string is constructed containing the values of the input text fields, interspersed with some HTML to control line breaks. This string is then assigned to the `InnerHtml` property of the table cell with the `tdInnerHtml` id attribute:

```
tdInnerHtml.InnerHtml = strHtml
```

If you use the `InnerText` property instead of the `InnerHtml` property, then the resulting page would display the < and > symbols. As written, however, the resulting page will look something like Figure 3-6, after values are entered in the text fields and the button is clicked.

Figure 3-6. HTML Server Controls with InnerHtml populated

Table 3-5 lists HTML tags and the category to which they belong. In the example shown in Figures 3-5 and 3-6, the two types of input controls are text fields and a button. Both happen to use the `<input>` HTML tag, though as you can see in Table 3-5, other input controls do not use those tags.

Table 3-5. HTML tags and their categories

HTML tag	Category	HTML server control name	Description
`<head>`	Container	`HtmlHead`	`<head>` element. Other elements can be added to its `Controls` collection.
`<input>`	Input	`HtmlInputButton` `HtmlInputCheckbox` `HtmlInputFile` `HtmlInputHidden` `HtmlInputImage` `HtmlInputPassword` `HtmlInputRadioButton` `HtmlInputReset` `HtmlInputSubmit` `HtmlInputText`	`<input type=button	submit	reset>` `<input type=checkbox>` `<input type=file>` `<input type=hidden>` `<input type=image>` `<input type=password>` `<input type=radio>` `<input type=reset>` `<input type=submit>` `<input type=text	password>`
`<img>`	n.a.	`HtmlImage`	Image.
`<link>`	n.a.	`HtmlLink`	Href property gets/sets the URL target.
`<textarea>`	Input	`HtmlTextArea`	Multiline text entry.
`<a>`	Container	`HtmlAnchor`	Anchor.
`<button>`	Container	`HtmlButton`	Customizable output format, usable with IE 4.0 and above browsers.
`<form>`	Container	`HtmlForm`	Maximum of one `HtmlForm` control per page; default method is POST.
`<table>`	Container	`HtmlTable`	Table, which can contain rows, which can contain cells.
`<td> <th>`	Container	`HtmlTableCell`	Table cell; Table header cell.
`<tr>`	Container	`HtmlTableRow`	Table row.
`<title>`	Container	`HtmlTitle`	Title element.
`<select>`	Container	`HtmlSelect`	Pull-down menu of choices.
	Container	`HtmlGenericControl`	Any HTML control not listed here.

 You never actually use the name of the HTML server control shown in Table 3-5 in a content file such as a page, user control, or master page. What goes in your HTML code is the HTML tag with the addition of the `runat="server"` attribute and usually with the addition of an `id` attribute.

Any HTML control can be converted to server-side processing with the addition of the `runat="server"` attribute. Those not listed in Table 3-5 will be treated as an `HtmlGenericControl`. As with any other container control, this allows programmatic access to the control's inner HTML.

All the HTML server controls derive from the `System.Web.UI.Control` class and are contained in the `System.Web.UI.HTMLControls` namespace. Figure 3-7 shows the HTML server control hierarchy.

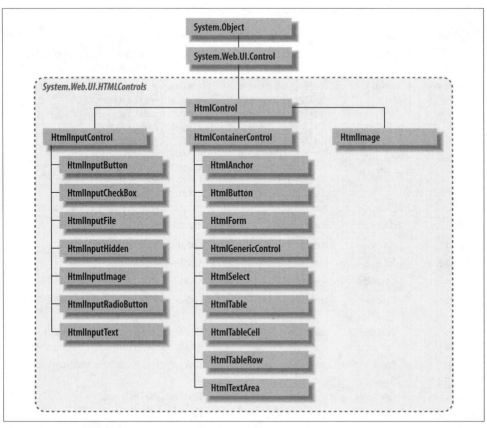

Figure 3-7. The HTML server control object hierarchy

Client-Side Processing

Server-side processing is at the heart of ASP.NET. However, this approach does have some shortcomings. The main problem is that a postback to the server is required before any processing can occur. Even for intranet applications connected to the server with a high-speed local network connection, this introduces a noticeable delay often unacceptable to the user experience. For Internet applications, even those connected via high-speed broadband, the delays can seem interminable.

Client-side processing can greatly enhance the user experience, providing nearly instantaneous response to user actions. This is accomplished using scripting languages such as JavaScript or VBScript.

Some ASP.NET server controls use client-side scripting to provide responses to user actions without posting back to the server. For example, validation controls typically download script to the browser so invalid data are caught and flagged to the user without requiring a round trip to the server. However, in these cases, this client-side script is provided by ASP.NET and you, the developer, do not have to write or manage that script.

As you will see, calling client-side code from any ASP.NET server control is possible. In addition, the ASP.NET Button server control has a property, `OnClientClick`, that lets you specify client-side script to execute when the button is clicked.

Conventional and server HTML controls expose a number of events that can execute script when they are raised. This script can be contained in a script block in the content file or contained in-line with the attributes in the control declaration. Previously, you saw the `onclick` and `onserverclick` attributes for the HTML Button control for handling click events. Table 3-6 lists a few of the commonly used events available to HTML controls.

Table 3-6. Commonly used HTML events

Event	Description
onblur	Fires when the control loses input focus
onfocus	Fires when the control receives focus
onclick	Fires when the control is clicked
onchange	Fires when the value of the control changes
onkeydown	Fires when the user presses a key
onkeypress	Fires when the user presses an alphanumeric key
onkeyup	Fires when the user releases a key
onmouseover	Fires when the mouse pointer is moved over the control
onserverclick	Raises the `ServerClick` event when the control is clicked

To see client-side script in action, create a new web site called *ClientSideProcessing*. In the Source view of the content file, add the following script block between the closing `</head>` tag and the opening `<body>` tag:

```
<script language=javascript>
    function ButtonTest( )
    {
        alert("Button clicked - client side processing");
    }

    function DoChange( )
    {
        document.getElementById("btnSave").disabled=false;
    }
</script>
```

The language is specified with the `language` attribute in the opening `<script>` tag, in this case JavaScript. In this example, two different functions are implemented. `ButtonTest` uses the alert method to pop up a dialog box. `DoChange` enables a Save button. This addresses the scenario where you want a Save button to be disabled until the user makes a change to some data, at which point the Save button should become enabled.

 Learning JavaScript is beyond the scope of this book. See *JavaScript: The Definitive Guide*, Fourth Edition, by David Flanagan (O'Reilly).

Add the following controls to the form: an HTML button, two ASP.NET buttons, an HTML input text box, and an ASP.NET TextBox. You can drag the controls onto the form, rename the button controls, and add the attributes shown in Example 3-5. The two HTML controls have ID and runat attributes, making them server controls. btnServer has the OnClientClick property set, and that btnSave has its Enabled property set to false.

Example 3-5. Controls in Default.aspx for ClientSideProcessing

```
<h1>Client-Side Processing</h1>
<input id="btnHTML" runat=server type="button"
      value="HTML Button"
      onclick="javascript:ButtonTest();"
      onserverclick="btnHTML_ServerClick"/>
<asp:Button ID="btnServer" runat="server"
          Text="ASP.NET Button"
          OnClientClick="javascript:ButtonTest();" />
<br />
<input id="txtHTML" type="text" runat="server"
      onchange="javascript:DoChange();" /><br />
<br />
<asp:TextBox ID="TextBox1" runat="server"
            onchange="javascript:DoChange();"></asp:TextBox>
<br />
<asp:Button ID="btnSave" runat="server"
          Text="Save" Enabled=false />
```

Double-click btnHTML in Design view to create an event handler in the code-behind file. Add the following highlighted line of code:

```
protected void btnHTML_ServerClick(object sender, EventArgs e)
{
    txtHTML.Value = "An HTML server control";
}
```

Double-click btnServer in Design view to create an event handler for that button and add the following highlighted line of code in the code-behind file:

```
protected void btnServer_Click(object sender, EventArgs e)
{
    txtHTML.Value = "An ASP.NET server control";
}
```

Now run the page. Initially, the Save button will be disabled (grayed out). Clicking the HTML button will cause the JavaScript function ButtonTest to execute, popping up a dialog box with the message "Button clicked - client side processing." Once that dialog is cleared, then the server-side code will run, populating the HTML input box with the string "An HTML server control." Similarly, clicking on the ASP.NET Server button will pop up the same dialog box, then populate the HTML input box with the string "An ASP.NET server control." Changing the contents of either text box and tabbing out of the text box will enable the Save button.

The ability to call client-side script from an ASP.NET server control, other than using the Button.OnClientClick property, is essentially an undocumented feature. It works by taking advantage of the fact that any attributes declared with the control, that are unrecognized by ASP.NET are passed unchanged to the browser.

You can see this by viewing the source for the page in the browser. The ASP.NET TextBox from the code snippet above is rendered to the browser this way:

```
<input name="TextBox1" type="text" id="TextBox1"
    onchange="javascript:DoChange( );" />
```

Since onchange is a valid event for an HTML input control, it correctly processes the JavaScript function.

CHAPTER 4
Basic Controls

Chapter 3 introduced controls. Though it briefly mentioned both server and classic HTML controls, most of the coverage was on ASP.NET server controls, the heart of ASP.NET.

 As noted previously, server controls are known variously as "ASP controls," "ASP.NET controls," "ASP.NET server controls," "Web controls," and "Web server controls." In this book, we will use "ASP.NET server control" or "server control." When referring to "server control," it should be clear from the context if this means only ASP.NET server controls or includes HTML server controls as well.

Topics common to all ASP.NET server controls were covered, such as events, syntax, programmatic access to controls during runtime (using the ID property), and the use of VS2005 to build your web site using controls. However, it did not go into significant detail about any specific controls.

This chapter provides a wealth of detail about many of the basic ASP.NET controls, including the TextBox, Button, CheckBox, and RadioButton controls, lists, tables, and images. It discusses the features and properties common to many controls and surveys the specific details of the basic ASP.NET server controls included with the .NET Framework.

The next chapter will cover many of the advanced server controls included as part of ASP.NET, such as view controls, and the Wizard, FileUpload, AdRotator, and Calendar controls. Other chapters will focus on data controls, validation controls, login and security controls, and so on.

The Basics

In this section, you will create a simple web page two different ways: once using a generic text editor (Notepad) and then again using VS2005. The purpose of this exercise is to show you how to create a web site using any text editor and to show you how much easier it is to use VS2005.

 This is the only time in the entire book you will create a web site without using VS2005.

Using either technique, the resulting web page should look something like that shown in Figure 4-1. This page will demonstrate some of the properties, events, and methods common to all ASP.NET server controls.

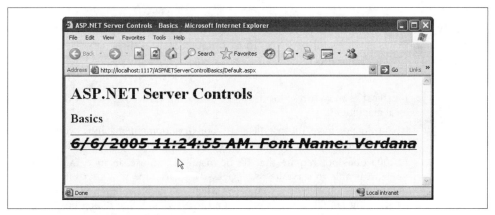

Figure 4-1. ASP.NET server controls: Basics

To create this web page without benefit of VS2005, open Notepad or your favorite editor capable of creating a flat text file (not Microsoft Word, for example, unless you want to jump through hoops). Enter the code in Example 4-1 into the file.

Example 4-1. ASPNETServerControlBasics-TextEditor.aspx

```
<%@ Page Language="C#" %>
<script runat="server">
   void lblTime_Init(object sender, EventArgs e)
   {
      lblTime.Font.Name = "Verdana";
      lblTime.Font.Size = 20;
      lblTime.Font.Underline = true;
      lblTime.Font.Bold = true;
      lblTime.Font.Italic = true;
      lblTime.Font.Overline = true;
      lblTime.Font.Strikeout = true;
      lblTime.Text = DateTime.Now.ToString() +
         ". Font Name: " +
         lblTime.Font.Name;
   }
</script>
```

Example 4-1. ASPNETServerControlBasics-TextEditor.aspx (continued)

```
<html>
   <body>
      <form id="form1" runat="server">
         <h2>Basics</h2>
         <asp:Label ID="lblTime" runat="server"
                    OnInit="lblTime_Init" />
      </form>
   </body>
</html>
```

Save the file as *ASPNETServerControlBasics-TextEditor.aspx* in any folder you want, say *c:\websites*.

To easily see your page processed by ASP.NET on a web server, you need to access the page in a browser via localhost. You must create a virtual directory for the folder that contains the web page file.

> localhost is the address for browsers to find an IIS web server on the local machine.
>
> If you do not have IIS installed on your development machine, you will not be able to see this page run from a browser outside of VS2005.
>
> VS2005 does not require that IIS be installed because, in its default mode, it is able to serve its own pages. You can force VS2005 to use the IIS mode of accessing web pages when you create a new web site by selecting HTTP as the Location on the New Web Site dialog box. In this case, VS2005 will automatically create the necessary virtual directory for you.
>
> For a complete description of the different ways that VS2005 can access web pages, see Chapter 2.

Open Computer Management by right-clicking My Computer and selecting Manage from the menu. (Alternatively, open Start → Control Panel → Administrative Tools → Computer Management.) Drill down to Services and Applications → Internet Information Services → Web Sites → Default Web Site and right-click on Default Web Site. From the drop-down, select New → Virtual Directory. Follow the wizard, using websites for the alias and browsing to the folder location where you put the *.aspx* file.

Now open a browser and give it the following URL:

```
http://localhost/websites/ASPNETServerControlBasics-TextEditor.aspx
```

The browser will cook a moment while the ASP.NET runtime processes the page and returns the rendered HTML.

Now you'll create the exact equivalent web page using VS2005. Open the IDE and create a new web site called *ASPNETServerControlBasics*. Enter a few HTML header elements and drag and drop a Label control onto the page so that the finished *default.aspx* file looks something like the code shown in Example 4-2. Notice how the combination of drag and drop and Intellisense makes for so much less tedious and error-prone typing.

Example 4-2. Content of Default.aspx in ASPNETServerControlBasics

```
<%@ Page Language="C#" AutoEventWireup="true"
    CodeFile="Default.aspx.cs" Inherits="_Default" %>

<!DOCTYPE html PUBLIC "-//W3C//DTD XHTML 1.1//EN"
    "http://www.w3.org/TR/xhtml11/DTD/xhtml11.dtd">

<html xmlns="http://www.w3.org/1999/xhtml" >
<head runat="server">
    <title>ASP.NET Server Controls - Basics</title>
</head>
<body>
    <form id="form1" runat="server">
    <div>
      <h1>ASP.NET Server Controls</h1>
      <h2>Basics</h2>
      <asp:Label ID="lblTime" runat="server"
                OnInit="lblTime_Init"></asp:Label>
    </div>
    </form>
</body>
</html>
```

 For step-by-step directions on how to create this web page using VS2005 with drag and drop and Intellisense, see the sidebar "From ASPX to Drag and Drop."

Once the controls are in place, you now want to create an event handler for the Init event of the label control lblTime. Switch to Design view if you are not there. Select the label lblTime. The lightning bolt icon will appear along the top of the Properties window.

Clicking on the lightning bolt will display all the possible events for this control. Double-click on the cell next to the Init event. The code-behind file, *default.aspx.cs*, will open on the work surface with a code skeleton in place for the event handler, named lblTime_Init, and the cursor inside the curly braces, ready for you to start typing your C# code. Enter the highlighted code from Example 4-3.

From ASPX to Drag and Drop

When you develop with VS2005, the goal is to use Intellisense and drag and drop as much as possible, rather than manually typing your code. On the other hand, rather than us giving you laborious, step-by-step instructions on building each page, it is more efficient, more flexible for you, and less error prone to just show you the finished product as a screenshot and/or an .aspx page.

The goal is not for you to type in the entire .aspx page, but rather for you to read through the content presented here and recreate it on your own machine, using whatever combination of drag and drop and manual editing works best for you. Let's walk through the steps of how you can create your application by looking at Figure 4-1 and by reading Example 4-2.

The first thing you notice is that the name of the web site (shown in the URL in Figure 4-1) is ASPNETServerControlBasics. Open a new web site and name it ASPNETServerControlBasics. Open that web site's *default.aspx* page.

Notice in Example 4-2 that the title is set (ASP.NET Server Controls - Basics). Set that in your *default.aspx* by typing directly into the file.

Next, notice the two HTML header elements: an h1 and an h2. Those, too, are typed directly into the Source view of *default.aspx* since the HTML section of the Toolbox does not include any header controls. Here, however, Intellisense helps as soon as you type the opening angle bracket by dropping down a list of all the possible elements that can legally go inside a pair of angle brackets. This list dynamically reflects all the possibilities as you enter each character.

Next, drag a Label control onto the page from the Standard section of the Toolbox, onto either the Source or Design views. The advantage of doing this in Design view is that it is a bit easier to generate the event handlers.

With the cursor on this Label button on the page, again in either Source or Design view, the Properties window will show the current properties of the control. Change the ID from the default Label1 to lblTime. Delete the contents of the Text property.

Alternatively, you can type the control declarations directly on the Source view, without using the Properties window. Intellisense will help by popping up lists of all the possible attributes (properties) and events. If you change any view or Properties window, all the other views and windows will immediately reflect the change.

The advantage of presenting the *.aspx* to you in this way is that it is clear what your code should look like when you are done, and you can build that code by hand or by using drag and drop and/or the Properties window—your choice. In fact, if you prefer not to do any of that work, you can download the completed source code from the Liberty Associates web site as described in the Preface.

Example 4-3. lblTime Init event handler code for WebServerControlBasics1

```
using System;
using System.Data;
using System.Configuration;
using System.Web;
using System.Web.Security;
using System.Web.UI;
using System.Web.UI.WebControls;
using System.Web.UI.WebControls.WebParts;
using System.Web.UI.HtmlControls;

public partial class _Default : System.Web.UI.Page
{
    protected void Page_Load(object sender, EventArgs e)
    {
    }

    protected void lblTime_Init(object sender, EventArgs e)
    {
        lblTime.Font.Name = "Verdana";
        lblTime.Font.Size = 20;
        lblTime.Font.Underline = true;
        lblTime.Font.Bold = true;
        lblTime.Font.Italic = true;
        lblTime.Font.Overline = true;
        lblTime.Font.Strikeout = true;
        lblTime.Text = DateTime.Now.ToString( ) +
            ". Font Name: " +
            lblTime.Font.Name;
    }
}
```

Run the page either by pressing F5 or selecting the Debug → Start menu item. You will see something similar to that shown in Figure 4-1.

These two examples demonstrate a Label control, an event handler, and properties being set for a control.

This simple web page has static text and a web server Label control. The Label control has been assigned an id of lblTime, which allows the control to be referred to elsewhere in the code.

Of more interest is the onInit attribute, which defines an event handler for the Init event. The Init event, a member of the Control class, is called when a control is initialized. It is the first step in each control's life cycle. All WebControls, since they are derived from Control, have an Init event.

In Examples 4-1 and 4-3, the Init event is handled by a method called lblTime_Init, defined in the code block at the top of the *.aspx* file or in the code-behind file, respectively. The lblTime_Init method sets several properties of the label's font (Name, Size, and so on) and sets the value of the Text property. The Text property value is a concatenation of the current date and time, a literal string, and the name of the font used. Because DateTime.Now is of type DateTime, it must be converted to a string in the C# code.

The results, shown in Figure 4-1, are not pretty, but they are instructive. The figure shows how several text attributes—bold, italic, overline, underline, and strikeout—can be applied to a label.

Fonts deserve special mention. Fonts contain *subproperties*, which are listed in Table 4-1. When used in HTML, subproperties are accessed declaratively in code in the form:

```
Font-Italic
```

Table 4-1. Subproperties of the Font object

SubProperty	Type	Values	Description
Bold	Boolean	true, false	Makes the text bold; the default is false.
Italic	Boolean	true, false	Italicizes the text; the default is false.
Name	String	Verdana, Courier, and so on	Automatically updates first item in Names property. Font must be installed and available to the client browser.
Names	String	Times and so on	Ordered array of font names. Stores list of available font names. Name property automatically updated with first item in array.
Strikeout	Boolean	true, false	Puts a line through the text; the default is false.
Underline	Boolean	true, false	Puts a line under the text; the default is false.
Overline	Boolean	true, false	Puts a line over the text; the default is false. Will not render on downlevel browsers.
Size	FontUnit or String	Small, Smaller, Large, Larger, or an integer representing point size	Uses named sizes or integer point size. Named sizes only work declaratively as control attributes.

When used in code blocks, subproperties are accessed programmatically in this form:

```
Font.Italic
```

If you use points rather than named sizes for the font size, then it is worth noting that the C# version of FontUnit provides an implicit conversion operator that takes an int and creates a FontUnit. Thus, you can write the following:

```
lblTime.Font.Size = 20;
```

You can do this without having to explicitly instantiate a FontUnit object (as is required in VS2005, for example).

For the remainder of this chapter, we're going to discuss the various controls available to you. We'll explain how to use each one and give you examples to work with.

Label Control

You use a Label control to display text. The Label control's Text property contains the text string to be displayed. Text is the only Label control property that is not inherited from the Control or WebControl classes. The Label control has no events or methods that are not derived from Control or WebControl.

You have seen the Label control used in code examples in previous chapters. You can set the Text and Font properties of the Label control programmatically (as shown in Examples 4-1 and 4-3) or declaratively.

TextBox Control

The TextBox control can be used for both user input and read-only text display. You can configure it to be single line or multiline or to accept passwords. If you set it to multiline, it automatically wraps unless the Wrap property is set to false. The text it contains can exceed the length of the control displayed on the page. The TextBox, DropDownList, Label, and other text-friendly controls implement the ITextControl interface, which is new to Version 2.0 of ASP.NET. This interface has a single property, Text, which is the visual content of the control.

Table 4-2 lists many of the common properties specific to the TextBox control. If any of these attributes are omitted from the control, then the default value will apply.

Table 4-2. Some properties specific to the TextBox control

Name	Type	Get	Set	Values	Description
AutoPostBack	Boolean	✗	✗	true, false	Determines if automatic postback to server will occur if user changes contents of control. If false, postback to server will not occur until the page is posted, either by a button or another control with AutoPostBack set to true. Default is false.
Columns	Int32	✗	✗	0, 1, 2, and so on	Width of the text box in characters. Default is 0, which indicates the property is not set.
MaxLength	Int32	✗	✗	0, 1, 2, and so on	Maximum number of characters allowed. If MaxLength is greater than Columns, then only a portion of the string will display without using the Home, End, or arrow keys. Its default value is 0, which does not impose a limit on the number of characters entered into the text box.

Table 4-2. Some properties specific to the TextBox control (continued)

Name	Type	Get	Set	Values	Description
ReadOnly	Boolean	✗	✗	true, false	If true, content cannot be changed by user though it can still be changed programmatically. Default is false.
Rows	Int32	✗	✗	0, 1, 2, and so on	Number of lines of text in a multiline text box. The default is 0, which imposes no limit on the number of lines.
Text	string	✗	✗		Content of the TextBox.
TextMode	TextBoxMode	✗	✗	SingleLine, MultiLine, Password	SingleLine The default value displays a single line of text. MultiLine Allows multiple lines of text and displays a vertical scrollbar, even for Rows = 1. The text wraps automatically to fit the width of the box. The Enter key enters a carriage return/line feed. The mouse or Tab key causes focus to leave the box and initiates postback if AutoPostBack is true. Password Displays content in asterisks, then clears the text box on posting. The value is not case-sensitive.
ValidationGroup	String	✗	✗		Specifies which validation group, if any, this control is a member of. See Chapter 8 for a discussion of validation.
Wrap	Boolean	✗	✗	true, false	Indicates if text within a multiline text box should wrap. If false, then the text box will have a horizontal scrollbar. Default is true.

In addition to the events inherited from the WebControl class, such as Init, Load, and PreRender, the TextBox control raises the TextChanged event when the contents of the text box have changed and the control loses focus. This is not a postback event unless the AutoPostBack property is set to true.

When a TextBox control is declared in a content file (*.aspx* or *.ascx*), the TextChanged event handler method is specified with the OnTextChanged attribute. TextChanged is the default event handler created by VS2005 when you double-click on a TextBox in Design view. This event handler is passed a standard EventArgs argument.

The following example demonstrates the basic use of a TextBox, including handling of the TextChanged event. This example has two text boxes: one to input text, and a second, read-only control, to echo the contents of the first box. The finished web page should look something like that shown in Figure 4-2, after changing the text in the input box.

Figure 4-2. TextBoxDemo

Create a new web site in VS2005 called *TextBoxDemo*. Drag two TextBox controls onto the page. Set the ID property of the first to txtInput and the second to txtEcho. Set the AutoPostBack property of txtInput to true, so that the form will automatically post back whenever the contents of the control changes. Set the BackColor property of txtEcho to LightGray and the ReadOnly property to true.

The content file is shown in Example 4-4, after the OnTextChanged attribute is added, as described in the next paragraph.

Example 4-4. Default.aspx for TextBoxDemo

```
<%@ Page Language="C#" AutoEventWireup="true"
   CodeFile="Default.aspx.cs" Inherits="_Default" %>

<!DOCTYPE html PUBLIC "-//W3C//DTD XHTML 1.1//EN"
   "http://www.w3.org/TR/xhtml11/DTD/xhtml11.dtd">

<html xmlns="http://www.w3.org/1999/xhtml" >
<head runat="server">
    <title>TextBox Demo</title>
</head>
<body>
    <form id="form1" runat="server">
    <div>
        <h1>TextBox Demo</h1>
        <asp:TextBox ID="txtInput" runat="server"
                    AutoPostBack="true"
                    OnTextChanged="txtInput_TextChanged" >
            Enter some text
        </asp:TextBox>
```

Example 4-4. Default.aspx for TextBoxDemo (continued)

```
        <br />
        <asp:TextBox ID="txtEcho" runat="server"
                     BackColor="LightGray"
                     ReadOnly="True">
        </asp:TextBox>
    </div>
    </form>
</body>
</html>
```

To easily create the default event handler for txtInput, switch to Design view and double-click on the TextBox. The OnTextChanged attribute will be added to the txtInput declaration in the content file, and the code-behind file will open with a code skeleton in place for the event handler. Enter the highlighted line of code from Example 4-5.

Example 4-5. TextChanged event handler for TextBoxDemo

```
protected void txtInput_TextChanged(object sender, EventArgs e)
{
    txtEcho.Text = txtInput.Text;
}
```

When the application is first run, txtInput will contain "Enter some text." When you change the contents of the control and tab out of the text box, the TextChanged event will fire and the event handler specified in the OnTextChanged attribute, txtInput_TextChanged, will execute, populating txtEcho.

HiddenField Control

Hidden fields were a common trick of the HTML web developer's trade for carrying information within a page when you did not want that information to be visible to the user.

An easier and more elegant way of accomplishing this task is to use one of the state mechanisms provided by the .NET Framework (see Chapter 6 for a complete discussion of state). However, sometimes this is impossible, perhaps for performance, bandwidth, or security reasons. (Performance and bandwidth are really two sides of the same coin.)

In classic HTML pages, you might use something such as the following code snippet to implement a hidden field:

```
<input type="hidden" value="foo">
```

ASP.NET uses a hidden field to implement view state. You can see this by examining the source that is rendered to the browser, via the View → Source menu command in Internet Explorer. (Other browsers have analogous commands.) You will see something similar to the following, where the value attribute encodes all the information saved in view state.

```
<input type="hidden" name="__VIEWSTATE"
    value="/wEPDwUJLOCHlBR...YfL+BDX7xhMw=" />
```

To reap the benefits of server-side processing, you can convert this into an HTML server control with the addition of id and runat attributes:

```
<input type="hidden" value="foo" id="myHiddenControl" runat="server">
```

An ASP.NET HiddenField control is best of all these options (assuming there is some compelling reason not to use ASP.NET's state capabilities) because it adds the following features:

- Programming consistency
- Easy access to the Value property, which holds the value being maintained by the control
- The ClientID property, inherited from Control, which provides the ID attribute of the control itself
- Access to the ValueChanged event (the default event for the HiddenField control in VS2005)

The HiddenField control is new to Version 2.0 of ASP.NET.

The ValueChanged event is raised on postback when the Value property of the control is different from the previous posting. The event does not cause a postback itself, and unlike most non-postback controls, the HiddenField does not expose an AutoPostBack property to force an instantaneous postback. As with all non-postback controls (explained in the previous chapter), the event will be cached until the form is posted back by some other control, at which point it will be handled by the server.

These features will be demonstrated in Example 4-6, called HiddenFieldDemo. The content file is also listed in this example. In addition to some display HTML, including an <h2> header to tell you when the page has been posted, it contains a TextBox for entering a new value for the HiddenField control, an HTML button (used to execute a client-side function without causing a postback to the server), and an ASP.NET Button (to force a postback to the server). A Label displays the contents of the hidden field.

Example 4-6. Default.aspx in HiddenFieldDemo web site

```
<%@ Page Language="C#" AutoEventWireup="true" CodeFile="Default.aspx.cs"
        Inherits="_Default" %>

<!DOCTYPE html PUBLIC "-//W3C//DTD XHTML 1.1//EN"
    "http://www.w3.org/TR/xhtml11/DTD/xhtml11.dtd">

<html xmlns="http://www.w3.org/1999/xhtml" >
<head runat="server">
    <title>HiddenField Control</title>
</head>

<script language=javascript>
    function ChangeHiddenValue( )
    {
        alert('Entering ChangeHiddenValue');

        var hdnId = '<%=hdnSecretValue.ClientID%>'
        var hdn = document.getElementById(hdnId);

        var txt = document.getElementById('txtSecretValue');

        hdn.value = txt.value;
        alert('Value changed');
    }
</script>

<body>
    <form id="form1" runat="server">
    <div>
        <h1>HiddenField Control</h1>
        <h2>This page was posted at <% =DateTime.Now.ToString( ) %>.</h2>
        <asp:HiddenField ID="hdnSecretValue" runat="server"
                         OnValueChanged="hdnSecretValue_ValueChanged" />
        Enter secret value:
        <asp:TextBox ID="txtSecretValue" runat="server" />
        <br />
        <br />
        <input type=button value="Change hidden value"
                         onclick="ChangeHiddenValue( )" />
        <asp:Button ID="btnPost" runat="server" Text="Post" />
        <br />
        <br />
        <asp:Label ID="lblMessage" runat="server" Text=""/>
    </div>
    </form>
</body>
</html>
```

The HTML button calls a function, ChangeHiddenValue, which is contained in the Java-
Script script block highlighted in the code listing. This function has two alert methods helpful in debugging; they can be omitted or commented out.

ChangeHiddenValue demonstrates two equivalent ways of getting a reference to a control on the page, both using the JavaScript getElementById method. This method returns a reference to the first object it finds on the page with the specified ID attribute.

In the first technique, a reference is obtained to the HiddenField control via the ClientID property of the HiddenField control. Since this property is derived from Control, it is available to all ASP.NET server controls. That bit of server-side code is called from within the JavaScript function by enclosing it within the <%= %> tags.

In the second technique, the ID attribute of the TextBox control is passed to the getElementById method.

The HiddenField ValueChanged event is handled by a server-side method, hdnSecretValue_ValueChanged, as indicated by the highlighted OnValueChanged attribute in Example 4-6. The event handler from the code-behind file, *default.aspx.cs*, is shown in Example 4-7. The remainder of the code-behind file, not shown here, is just standard boilerplate inserted by VS2005.

Example 4-7. Excerpt from default.aspx.cs for HiddenFieldDemo

```
protected void hdnSecretValue_ValueChanged(object sender, EventArgs e)
{
   HiddenField hdn = (HiddenField)sender;
   lblMessage.Text = "The new value is " + hdn.Value + ".";
}
```

The first line in hdnSecretValue_ValueChanged obtains a reference to the control that raised the event, carried in the sender argument. It casts sender as type HiddenField. Then the Value property of the HiddenField object is used to set the Text property of lblMessage.

After you enter a secret value and press the Post button, you'll see a web page much like Figure 4-3. The Post button does not have an event handler because we don't need it to perform any function other than to cause a postback to the server.

Button Controls

Buttons are controls that post the form back to the server, enabling server-side processing to commence. There are three types of ASP.NET Button controls, all members of the System.Web.UI.WebControls namespace:

Button
> This is the standard button.

LinkButton
> The LinkButton control is sort of a cross between a standard button and a HyperLink control (described in the next section). A LinkButton appears to the user as a hyperlink (i.e., the text is colored and underlined).

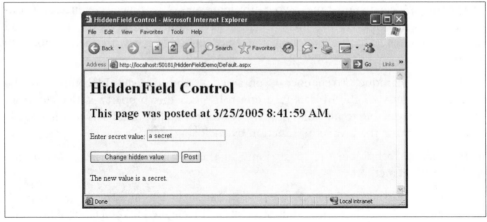

Figure 4-3. HiddenFieldDemo

ImageButton

> The ImageButton control performs the same function as the standard button, except that an image bitmap takes the place of the button on the browser UI. For the ImageButton control, there is no Text attribute but there is an AlternateText attribute, which specifies what text to display on non-graphical browsers.

> In addition, the event handler uses an ImageClickEventArgs event argument, which is different than the event handlers for the Button and LinkButton controls. This event argument exposes two fields (not used in this example) containing the X and Y coordinates of the location where the user clicked on the image. These fields could be used to implement your own image map type of functionality.

In addition to all the properties, methods, and events inherited from WebControl, all three button types have the following two events:

Click

> This event is raised when the control is clicked and no command name is associated with the button (that is, no value has been assigned to the Button control's CommandName property). The method is passed an argument of type EventArgs.

Command

> This event is raised when the control is clicked and a command name is associated with the button (that is, a command name has been assigned to the Button control's CommandName property). The event is passed an argument of type CommandEventArgs, which has the following two members:

CommandName

> The name of the command

CommandArgument

> An optional argument for the command

All three types of Button controls implement the IButtonControl interface, new to Version 2.0 of ASP.NET. This interface requires the Click and Command events, plus properties such as Text and CausesValidation, among others, which will be described shortly. It is the IButtonControl interface that causes a control to act like a button.

This next example, ButtonDemo, creates a web page containing a Button, a LinkButton, and an ImageButton. Each button performs the same task: transferring control to another web page. The content file is shown in Example 4-8.

Example 4-8. Default.aspx for ButtonDemo web site

```
<%@ Page Language="C#" AutoEventWireup="true" CodeFile="Default.aspx.cs"
        Inherits="_Default" %>

<!DOCTYPE html PUBLIC "-//W3C//DTD XHTML 1.1//EN"
    "http://www.w3.org/TR/xhtml11/DTD/xhtml11.dtd">

<html xmlns="http://www.w3.org/1999/xhtml" >
<head runat="server">
    <title>Buttons</title>
</head>
<body>
    <form id="form1" runat="server">
    <div>
      <h1>Button Controls</h1>
        <asp:Button ID="btnLink" runat="server"
                Text="Link To Target Page"
                ToolTip="Click here to go to the target page."
                OnClick="btnLink_Click" />
        <asp:ImageButton ID="imgLink" runat="server"
                AlternateText="Link to Target Page"
                ImageUrl="Dan at Vernal Pool.jpg"
                ToolTip="Click here to go to the target page."
                OnClick="imgLink_Click" />
        <asp:LinkButton ID="lnkLink" runat="server"
                ToolTip="Click here to go to the target page."
                Font-Name="Comic Sans MS Bold"
                Font-Size="16pt"
                OnClick="btnLink_Click">
            LinkButton To Target Page
        </asp:LinkButton>
    </div>
    </form>
</body>
</html>
```

The button Click event handlers from the code-behind file are shown in Example 4-9.

Example 4-9. Click event handlers for ButtonDemo web site

```
protected void btnLink_Click(object sender, EventArgs e)
{
    Response.Redirect("//localhost/websites/TargetPage.aspx");
}
```

Example 4-9. Click event handlers for ButtonDemo web site (continued)

```
protected void imgLink_Click(object sender, ImageClickEventArgs e)
{
    Response.Redirect("//localhost/websites/TargetPage.aspx");
}
```

File Locations

Whenever a file location is required in ASP.NET, as with the argument to the Redirect method, or properties such as `ImageButton.ImageUrl`, there are four ways to represent a URL:

Relative

> The location is specified with respect to the application root directory. It starts with period (.) or the name itself, but not with a slash (/).

Application Relative

> The location is relative to the application root. It uses the ~ (tilde) operator, which resolves to the application root directory as in this example:

> `BackImageUrl="~/images/Sunflower Bkgrd.jpg"`

> This would refer to a file in the *images* folder off the application root.

> The advantage to using relative or application relative addressing is it makes deployment easier. For a complete discussion of deployment issues, see Chapter 19.

Absolute

> A path on the local machine that starts with a slash (/), indicating a folder on the current hard drive or a drive, indicator plus a path.

> If the application is deployed to a machine with a different directory structure, the code may have to be changed to prevent errors.

Fully Qualified

> This can be one of several types. A Universal Naming Convention (UNC) formatted name specifies a location anywhere on the network. It is of the following form:

> `\\server-name\shared-resource-pathname`

> It can be a URL to a page on the Internet, of the form:

> `http://www.SomeDomainName.com`

> It can be a location served from the local machine, as in:

> `//localhost/websites/TargetPage.aspx`

The resulting web page is shown in Figure 4-4.

Figure 4-4. ButtonDemo web site

 For the code in the ButtonDemo web site to work correctly, you must have a target web page to which to link. This can be any valid *.htm*, *.asp*, or *.aspx* file. In this example, the target page is hard-coded as *TargetPage.aspx*, located in the *Websites* virtual directory. In addition, you will need an image file for the ImageButton control. This example uses a file called *Dan at vernal pool.jpg*, located in the web site directory, but you can use any image file you want.

The big difference between a LinkButton control and a standard Button control is that the LinkButton's functionality is implemented using client-side scripting. This is readily apparent if you look at the source code rendered to your browser resulting from the ButtonDemo web page, an excerpt of which is shown in Example 4-10. Remember, this source code is output by ASP.NET, not written by you.

Example 4-10. Browser source excerpt from ButtonDemo web page

```
<script type="text/javascript">
<!--
var theForm = document.forms['form1'];
function __doPostBack(eventTarget, eventArgument) {
    if (theForm.onsubmit == null || theForm.onsubmit()) {
        theForm.__EVENTTARGET.value = eventTarget;
        theForm.__EVENTARGUMENT.value = eventArgument;
        theForm.submit();
    }
}
```

Example 4-10. Browser source excerpt from ButtonDemo web page (continued)

```
// --->
</script>

<input type="submit" name="btnLink" value="Link to Target Page"
   id="btnLink" title="Click here to go to Target Page." />

<input type="image" name="imgLink" id="imgLink"
   title="Click here to go to Target Page."
   src="Dan%20at%20Vernal%20Pool.jpg" alt="Link to Target Page"
   style="border-width:0px;"/>

<a id="lnkLink" title="Click here to go to Target Page."
   href="javascript:__doPostBack('lnkLink','')"
   style="font-family:Comic Sans MS Bold;font-size:16pt;">
   Link to Target Page</a>
```

HyperLink Control

A HyperLink control looks similar to a LinkButton control with a fundamental difference: the HyperLink control immediately navigates to the target URL without a postback, while the LinkButton control posts the form. If the LinkButton event handler chooses, it will navigate to the target URL. A HyperLink control behaves very similarly to an HTML control.

The HyperLink control has four specific attributes:

ImageUrl

The path to an image (rather than text) to display. If this attribute is used, the control appears to the user as identical to an ImageButton control, though the ImageButton control still posts the form and the HyperLink control only navigates.

NavigateUrl

The target URL to navigate to.

Text

The text string that will be displayed on the browser as the link. If the Text and ImageUrl properties are both set, the ImageUrl takes precedence. The text will be displayed if the image is unavailable.

If the browser supports tool tips and the ToolTip property (inherited from the WebControl class) has not been set, the Text value will display as a tool tip. If the ToolTip property has been set, the ToolTip text string will display as a tool tip.

Target

Defines the target window or frame that will load the linked page. The value is case-insensitive and must begin with a character in the range of a to z, except for the special values shown in Table 4-3, all of which begin with an underscore.

Table 4-3. Special values of the Target attribute

Target value	Description
_blank	Renders the content in a new unnamed window without frames.
_new	Not documented, but behaves the same as _blank.
_parent	Renders the content in the parent window or frameset of the window or frame with the hyperlink. If the child container is a window or top-level frame, it behaves the same as _self.
_self	Renders the content in the current frame or window with focus. This is the default value.
_top	Renders the content in the current full window without frames.

The following example, HyperLinkDemo, demonstrates a HyperLink control. The content file is shown in Example 4-11. Since the HyperLink control does not post back to the server, there is no code-behind file in this example.

Example 4-11. Default.aspx from HyperLinkDemo

```
<%@ Page Language="C#" AutoEventWireup="true"  CodeFile="Default.aspx.cs"
        Inherits="_Default" %>

<!DOCTYPE html PUBLIC "-//W3C//DTD XHTML 1.1//EN"
   "http://www.w3.org/TR/xhtml11/DTD/xhtml11.dtd">

<html xmlns="http://www.w3.org/1999/xhtml" >
<head runat="server">
    <title>HyperLink Control</title>
</head>
<body>
    <form id="form1" runat="server">
    <div>
      <h1>HyperLink Control</h1>
      <asp:HyperLink ID="hypLink" runat="server"
                    NavigateUrl="//localhost/websites/TargetPage.aspx"
                    Target="_self"
                    Font-Names="Impact"
                    Font-Size="16"
                    ToolTip="Click here to go to target page.">
          HyperLink to Target Page
      </asp:HyperLink>
    </div>
    </form>
</body>
</html>
```

When the HyperLinkDemo page is run, it looks like Figure 4-5. For this page to work correctly as written, there must be a page called *TargetPage.aspx* located in the physical directory that corresponds to the *websites* virtual directory on your local machine.

Figure 4-5. HyperLinkDemo

The HyperLink control is rendered on the client browser as an HTML anchor tag (that is, <a>). You can verify this by examining the source code for the web page on your browser.

Selecting Values

Several ASP.NET server controls allow the user to select a value or values:

CheckBox
> Allows selection of Boolean data

CheckBoxList
> Group of CheckBox controls that can be dynamically created and bound to a data source

RadioButton
> Allows only a single option to be selected from a group

RadioButtonList
> Group of RadioButton controls that can be dynamically created and bound to a data source

ListBox
> Allows selection of one or more items from a predefined list

DropDownList
> Similar to a ListBox but allows only a single selection

BulletedList
> Formatted with bullets and can be simple text or a link

All of these controls derive from the WebControl class. The RadioButton derives further from the CheckBox class, and the list controls all derive from the abstract ListControl class. Each of these controls is considered in detail in upcoming sections.

CheckBox Control

A CheckBox control provides a means for a user to select Boolean data (i.e., Yes/No or True/False). If you have several checkboxes arranged together (not to be confused with a CheckBoxList, discussed next), you can select multiple options. No option is mutually exclusive of another.

The CheckBox and RadioButton controls implement the ICheckBoxControl interface, which is new to ASP.NET Version 2.0. This interface provides for a single property called Checked, and a single event called CheckedChanged, both of which are described next.

The following example, CheckBoxDemo, shown in Figure 4-6, demonstrates the use of three independent CheckBoxes to control the appearance of a Label. Clicking any of the checkboxes in this example—Underline, Overline, or Strikeout—imposes that font attribute on the text string in the Label control.

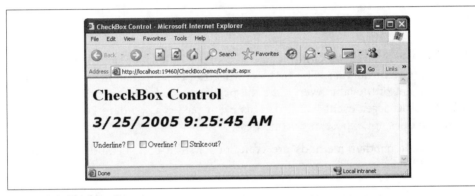

Figure 4-6. CheckBoxDemo

The content file is shown in Example 4-12.

Example 4-12. Default.aspx from CheckBoxDemo

```
<%@ Page Language="C#" AutoEventWireup="true"  CodeFile="Default.aspx.cs"
        Inherits="_Default" %>

<!DOCTYPE html PUBLIC "-//W3C//DTD XHTML 1.1//EN"
   "http://www.w3.org/TR/xhtml11/DTD/xhtml11.dtd">

<html xmlns="http://www.w3.org/1999/xhtml" >
<head runat="server">
    <title>CheckBox Control</title>
</head>
<body>
    <form id="form1" runat="server">
    <div>
      <h1>CheckBox Control</h1>
        <asp:Label ID="lblTime" runat="server"
```

Example 4-12. Default.aspx from CheckBoxDemo (continued)

```
                    OnInit="lblTime_Init" />
      <br />
      <br />
      <asp:CheckBox ID="chkUnderLine" runat="server"
                    AutoPostBack="True"
                    Text="Underline?"
                    TextAlign="Left"
                    OnCheckedChanged="chkUnderLine_CheckedChanged" />
      <asp:CheckBox ID="chkOverLine" runat="server"
                    AutoPostBack="True"
                    Text="Overline?"
                    OnCheckedChanged="chkOverLine_CheckedChanged" />
      <asp:CheckBox ID="chkStrikeout" runat="server"
                    AutoPostBack="True"
                    Text="Strikeout?"
                    OnCheckedChanged="chkStrikeout_CheckedChanged" />
    </div>
    </form>
</body>
</html>
```

Each of the ASP.NET server controls in this example, the label and the three check-boxes, has an event handler. The Init event for the Label is handled to set the format and content of the label every time the page is posted. The CheckBoxes have the default CheckedChanged event handled. This event passes a standard EventArgs argument, which does not expose any properties.

All these event handler methods are contained in the code-behind file, listed in Example 4-13.

Example 4-13. Event handlers in Default.aspx.cs code-behind file for CheckBoxDemo

```
protected void lblTime_Init(object sender, EventArgs e)
{
    lblTime.Font.Name = "Verdana";
    lblTime.Font.Size = 20;
    lblTime.Font.Bold = true;
    lblTime.Font.Italic = true;
    lblTime.Text = DateTime.Now.ToString( );
}

protected void chkUnderLine_CheckedChanged(object sender, EventArgs e)
{
    if (chkUnderLine.Checked)
        lblTime.Font.Underline = true;
    else
        lblTime.Font.Underline = false;
}

protected void chkOverLine_CheckedChanged(object sender, EventArgs e)
{
```

```
    if (chkOverLine.Checked)
        lblTime.Font.Overline = true;
    else
        lblTime.Font.Overline = false;
}

protected void chkStrikeout_CheckedChanged(object sender, EventArgs e)
{
    if (chkStrikeout.Checked)
        lblTime.Font.Strikeout = true;
    else
        lblTime.Font.Strikeout = false;
}
```

Like all controls derived from WebControl, CheckBoxes have an ID property. But as the sample code in Example 4-12 shows, there are several other properties and methods that are not inherited from WebControl. These members are listed in Table 4-4. However, some of these properties, such as AutoPostBack and Text, are common to several other controls.

Table 4-4. Members of the CheckBox class not inherited from WebControl control class

Name	Type	Get	Set	Values	Description
AutoPostBack	Boolean	✗	✗	true, false	Determines if automatic postback to the server will occur if the user changes the contents of the control. If false (the default), postback to the server will not occur until the page is posted, either by a button or other postback control or a control with AutoPostBack set to true.
Checked	Boolean	✗	✗	true, false	Indicates if the CheckBox is checked. Default is false.
Text	String	✗	✗		The text label associated with the CheckBox.
TextAlign	TextAlign	✗	✗	Left, Right	Dictates if the text label is on the left or right of the CheckBox. Default is Right.
CheckedChanged	Event			EventArgs	This event is raised when the Checked property is changed. This event will not immediately post back to the server unless AutoPostBack is set to true.

RadioButton Control

A RadioButton control is very similar to, and in fact is derived from, a CheckBox control. The essential difference between the two classes is that RadioButtons are typically grouped using the GroupName property, and only one RadioButton in the group can be checked (i.e., its Checked property is true) at one time. Changing the Checked property of one RadioButton control in the group to true changes the Checked property of all other controls in the group to false. In addition, radio buttons typically display as round, as opposed to the square checkboxes.

The next example, RadioButtonDemo, contains three RadioButton controls to set the font size of a label. Each of the radio buttons in RadioButtonDemo are part of the group grpSize.

The content file for this example is shown in Example 4-14, and the event handlers in the code-behind file are in Example 4-15. The result of running it is shown in Figure 4-7.

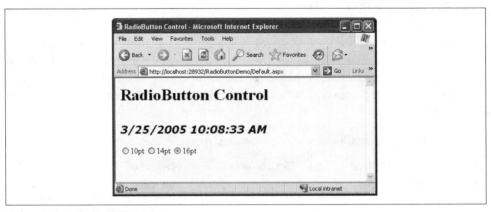

Figure 4-7. RadioButtonDemo

Example 4-14. Default.aspx for RadioButtonDemo web site

```
<%@ Page Language="C#" AutoEventWireup="true"  CodeFile="Default.aspx.cs"
        Inherits="_Default" %>

<!DOCTYPE html PUBLIC "-//W3C//DTD XHTML 1.1//EN"
   "http://www.w3.org/TR/xhtml11/DTD/xhtml11.dtd">

<html xmlns="http://www.w3.org/1999/xhtml" >
<head runat="server">
    <title>RadioButton Control</title>
</head>
<body>
    <form id="form1" runat="server">
    <div>
      <h1>RadioButton Control</h1>
        <br />
        <asp:Label ID="lblTime" runat="server"
                 OnInit="lblTime_Init"></asp:Label>
        <br />
        <br />
        <asp:RadioButton ID="rdoSize10" runat="server"
                 GroupName="grpSize"
                 AutoPostBack="True"
```

Example 4-14. Default.aspx for RadioButtonDemo web site (continued)

```
                        Text="10pt"
                        OnCheckedChanged="grpSize_CheckedChanged" />
        <asp:RadioButton ID="rdoSize14" runat="server"
                        GroupName="grpSize"
                        AutoPostBack="True"
                        Text="14pt"
                        OnCheckedChanged="grpSize_CheckedChanged" />
        <asp:RadioButton ID="rdoSize16" runat="server"
                        GroupName="grpSize"
                        AutoPostBack="True"
                        Text="16pt"
                        OnCheckedChanged="grpSize_CheckedChanged" />
    </div>
    </form>
</body>
</html>
```

Example 4-15. Event handlers in Default.aspx.cs code-behind file for RadioButtonDemo

```
protected void grpSize_CheckedChanged(object sender, EventArgs e)
{
    if (rdoSize10.Checked)
        lblTime.Font.Size = 10;
    else if (rdoSize14.Checked)
        lblTime.Font.Size = 14;
    else lblTime.Font.Size = 16;
}

protected void lblTime_Init(object sender, EventArgs e)
{
    lblTime.Font.Name = "Verdana";
    lblTime.Font.Size = 20;
    lblTime.Font.Bold = true;
    lblTime.Font.Italic = true;
    lblTime.Text = DateTime.Now.ToString( );
}
```

The `CheckedChanged` event, which is derived from `CheckBox`, is handled by the `onCheckedChanged` event handler, which points to the `grpSize_CheckedChanged` method. That method is an `if..else` block that changes the text size depending on which button is selected. In practice, it would probably be better to use a C# `switch` statement to make it easier to add additional radio buttons in the future.

Selecting from a List

ASP.NET provides five server controls for selecting single or multiple items from a list:

- `BulletedList`
- `CheckBoxList`

- `DropDownList`
- `ListBox`
- `RadioButtonList`

All of these controls are derived from `ListControl` and have much in common:

- `ListItem` (the information displayed by the list) works exactly the same way for all the `ListControls`, with a `Value` property and a `Text` property.
- The `Items` property of the control contains the collection of all the `ListItems`.
- `ListItems` can be added to the Items collection either statically, i.e., declaratively in the content file, programmatically through the `Add` method, or from a data source.

  The Data Source Configuration Wizard or the ListItem Collection Editor can be easily accessed by clicking the control's smart tag, the little icon in the upper-right corner of the control.
- The `SelectedIndex` and `SelectedItem` properties of the control point to the selected item with the lowest index. For single select controls, such as the `DropDownList`, the `RadioButtonList`, and the `ListBox` (if the `SelectionMode` property is set to `ListSelectionMode.Single`, the default value), the selected index is by definition, the lowest index. For multi-select controls, such as `CheckBoxList` and the `ListBox` with the `SelectionMode` property set to `ListSelectionMode.Multiple`, these properties will refer to the selected item with the lowest index.
- The `SelectedValue` property of the control retrieves or specifies the value of the selected item.
- The `AppendDataBoundItems` property of the control (new to Version 2 of ASP.NET) allows items added through data binding (described in Chapter 9) to be added to the Items collection, rather than replace the Items collection, the default behavior.
- All five controls raise and respond to the `SelectedIndexChanged` event.

The `ListBox` and `DropDownList` controls differ from the other list controls (`BulletedList`, `CheckBoxList`, and `RadionButtonList`) in that they appear to the user to be a single control (a list box or a drop-down list) rather than a collection of links, buttons or checkboxes. The `ListBox` and `DropDownList` controls lend themselves to longer lists because they scroll.

Table 4-5 summarizes the differences among the five list controls.

Table 4-5. Differences among the five list controls

Characteristic	BulletedList	CheckBoxList	RadioButtonList	DropDownList	ListBox
Single selection only	✗		✗	✗	
Able to select more than one item		✗			✗

Table 4-5. Differences among the five list controls (continued)

Characteristic	BulletedList	CheckBoxList	RadioButtonList	DropDownList	ListBox
Displays the entire list	✗	✗	✗		
Displays single item at a time, along with a button for seeing the entire list, using vertical scrollbar if necessary				✗	
Displays multiple items, using vertical scrollbar if necessary					✗
Best for short lists	✗	✗	✗		
Best for long lists				✗	✗

The following sections describe the controls and objects related to selecting items from a list.

ListItem Object

Five server controls allow you to select from a list, all derived from the `ListControl` class. A `ListControl` control consists of a collection of `ListItem` objects. Each `ListItem` object has four properties, detailed in Table 4-6.

Table 4-6. Properties of the ListItem object

Name	Type	Get	Set	Description
`Enabled`	Boolean	✗	✗	If set to `false`, allows an item to be dormant and invisible when the list is displayed, yet remain in the Items collection.
`Selected`	Boolean	✗	✗	A value indicating that the item has been selected.
`Text`	String	✗	✗	The text string displayed for a `ListItem`.
`Value`	String	✗	✗	A value associated with a `ListItem`. The value is not displayed, but is available programmatically.

When dealing with lists, displaying one thing to the user but passing something different to your code is common. For example, if presenting your users with a list of states, the list might display state names, such as Massachusetts. But when they select an item, the program will pass the selected item as ma. Massachusetts would be the `ListItem` object's Text property, and ma would be the Value property.

The Text property can be specified in one of two ways:

Inner HTML content
    Text contained between the opening and closing tags of any control

Text *attribute*
    An attribute within the opening tag of the `ListItem` control

There can be either a closing tag with no inner HTML, or the opening tag can be self-closing. All three of the following lines are equivalent:

```
<asp:ListItem>Item 7</asp:ListItem>
<asp:ListItem text="Item 7"></asp:ListItem>
<asp:ListItem text="Item 7"/>
```

If both a Text property and inner HTML content are specified, the inner HTML content will be displayed. For example, consider the following line:

```
<asp:ListItem text="Item 7">Item 8</asp:ListItem>
```

If you used that line, "Item 8" would be displayed on the web page.

The Value property can be set similarly to the Text property. So, for example, you could modify the lines of code presented previously to also set the value, as follows:

```
<asp:ListItem value="7">Item 7</asp:ListItem>
<asp:ListItem text="Item 7" value="7"></asp:ListItem>
<asp:ListItem text="Item 7" value="7"/>
```

CheckBoxList Control

The CheckBoxList is a parent control containing a collection of CheckBox items. It is very similar to the group of CheckBox controls shown previously in CheckBoxDemo in Figure 4-6, except that all the child checkboxes are handled as a group. The CheckBoxList control derives from ListControl rather than directly from WebControl.

The CheckBoxList control is better suited than individual checkboxes for creating a series of checkboxes out of data in a database, although either type of control can be bound to data. Chapter 9 discusses data binding.

There are three ways to add items to the Items collection of a CheckBoxList:

- Declaratively using the <asp:ListItem> control tag
- Programmatically from an array
- Dynamically from a data source such as a database

Adding items declaratively

The web site shown in Figure 4-8, CheckBoxList-DeclarativeItems, demonstrates many of the properties of the CheckBoxList control. The list items are added declaratively in the content file, *Default.aspx*. Attributes in the CheckBoxList control declaration, corresponding to properties of the CheckBoxList class, specify the appearance and behavior of the control.

The content file for this web site is shown in Example 4-16. Since there are no events handled in this web application and hence no event handlers, there is no code-behind file.

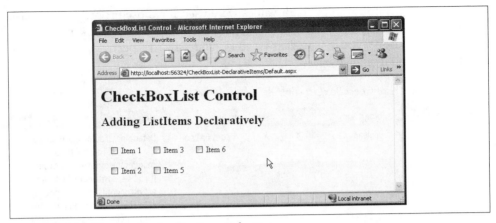

Figure 4-8. CheckBoxList-DeclarativeItems web site

Example 4-16. Default.aspx for CheckBoxList-DeclarativeItems web site

```
<%@ Page Language="C#" AutoEventWireup="true"  CodeFile="Default.aspx.cs"
        Inherits="_Default" %>

<!DOCTYPE html PUBLIC "-//W3C//DTD XHTML 1.1//EN"
    "http://www.w3.org/TR/xhtml11/DTD/xhtml11.dtd">

<html xmlns="http://www.w3.org/1999/xhtml" >
<head runat="server">
    <title>CheckBoxList Control</title>
</head>
<body>
    <form id="form1" runat="server">
    <div>
      <h1>CheckBoxList Control</h1>
      <h2>Adding ListItems Declaratively</h2>
       <asp:CheckBoxList ID="cblItems" runat="server"
                         AutoPostBack="True"
                         CellPadding="5"
                         CellSpacing="10"
                         RepeatColumns="3">
         <asp:ListItem> Item 1 </asp:ListItem>
         <asp:ListItem> Item 2 </asp:ListItem>
         <asp:ListItem> Item 3 </asp:ListItem>
         <asp:ListItem> Item 5 </asp:ListItem>
         <asp:ListItem> Item 6 </asp:ListItem>
      </asp:CheckBoxList>
    </div>
    </form>
</body>
</html>
```

In the code in Example 4-16, default values were used for those properties that have defaults, as indicated in Table 4-7. By changing the RepeatDirection, RepeatLayout, and TextAlign properties to Horizontal, Flow, and Left, respectively, you get the results shown in Figure 4-9.

Table 4-7. Properties of CheckBoxList control

Name	Type	Get	Set	Values	Description
AutoPostBack	Boolean	✗	✗	true, false	Determines if automatic postback to the server will occur if the user changes the contents of the control. If false, postback to the server will not occur until the page is posted, either by a button or another control with AutoPostBack set to true. Its default value is false.
CellPadding	integer	✗	✗	Integers	Distance in pixels between the border and contents of a cell. The default is -1, which indicates the property is not set.
CellSpacing	integer	✗	✗	Integers	Distance in pixels between the border and contents of a cell. The default is -1, which indicates the property is not set.
DataSource	Object	✗	✗		Source that populates the control.
RepeatColumns	Integer	✗	✗	Integers	Number of columns to display.
RepeatDirection	RepeatDirection	✗	✗	Horizontal, Vertical	Horizontal Specifies that items are loaded from left to right, then top to bottom. Vertical Specifies that items are loaded top to bottom, then left to right. The default value is Vertical.
RepeatLayout	RepeatLayout	✗	✗	Flow, Table	Flow Specifies that items are displayed without a table structure. Table Specifies that items are displayed in a table structure. Default is Table.
Selected	Boolean	✗	✗	true, false	Indicates an item has been selected. Default is false.
TextAlign	TextAlign	✗	✗	Left, Right	Dictates if the text label is on the left or right of the checkboxes. Default is Right.

Figure 4-9. Static CheckBoxList-DeclarativeItems modified to use non-default property values

The ListItems can be manually typed into the content file (Intellisense will help minimize the typing), or you can use the Collection Editor. To use the Collection Editor, select the CheckBoxList in Design view, click on the smart tag (the little icon in the upper-right corner of the control in Design view) and select Edit Items... from the smart tag menu. The dialog box shown in Figure 4-10 will appear. Use this dialog box to add or remove ListItems and change their properties.

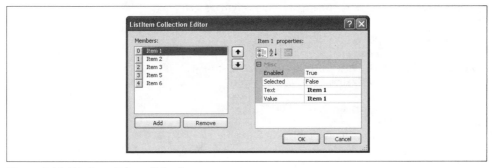

Figure 4-10. ListItem Editor dialog box

Adding items programmatically from an array

There are times when you do not know at compile time what checkboxes you want to create. For example, you may want your program to populate the list dependent on the value of other controls on the page. In these cases, you need to be able to add items to the Items collection programmatically.

In this next example, CheckBoxList-ArrayItems, shown in Figure 4-11, ListItem objects are added both programmatically and also are hardcoded within the CheckBoxList tags for purposes of illustration.

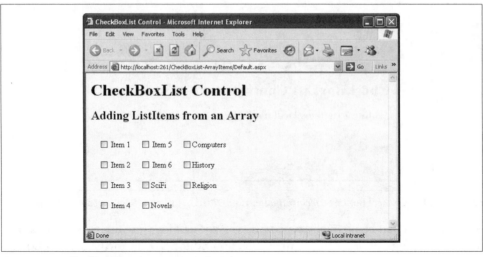

Figure 4-11. CheckBoxList-ArrayItems web site

The content file for this web site is shown in Example 4-17, and the code-behind file is listed in Example 4-18.

Example 4-17. Default.aspx for CheckBoxList-ArrayItems web site

```
<%@ Page Language="C#" AutoEventWireup="true"  CodeFile="Default.aspx.cs"
    Inherits="_Default" %>

<!DOCTYPE html PUBLIC "-//W3C//DTD XHTML 1.1//EN"
    "http://www.w3.org/TR/xhtml11/DTD/xhtml11.dtd">

<html xmlns="http://www.w3.org/1999/xhtml" >
<head runat="server">
    <title>CheckBoxList Control</title>
</head>
<body>
    <form id="form1" runat="server">
    <div>
      <h1>CheckBoxList Control</h1>
      <h2>Adding ListItems from an Array</h2>
      <asp:CheckBoxList ID="cblGenre" runat="server"
                      AutoPostBack="True"
                      CellPadding="5"
                      CellSpacing="10"
                      RepeatColumns="3"
                      OnInit="cblGenre_Init">
        <asp:ListItem> Item 1 </asp:ListItem>
        <asp:ListItem> Item 2 </asp:ListItem>
```

Example 4-17. Default.aspx for CheckBoxList-ArrayItems web site (continued)

```
        <asp:ListItem> Item 3 </asp:ListItem>
        <asp:ListItem> Item 4 </asp:ListItem>
        <asp:ListItem> Item 5 </asp:ListItem>
        <asp:ListItem> Item 6 </asp:ListItem>
    </asp:CheckBoxList>

  </div>
  </form>
</body>
</html>
```

Example 4-18. Event handler in code-behind file for CheckBoxList-ArrayItems web site

```
protected void cblGenre_Init(object sender, EventArgs e)
{
   // create an array of items to add
   string[] Genre = { "SciFi", "Novels", "Computers", "History",
                    "Religion" };
   for (int i = 0; i < Genre.Length; i++)
   {
      this.cblGenre.Items.Add(new ListItem(Genre[i]));
   }
}
```

The remainder of the code-behind file for this example is just boilerplate inserted by VS2005.

You add an attribute to the control tag that implements an event handler for control initialization:

```
    onInit="cblGenre_Init"
```

Then you add the cblGenre_Init method, called by onInit, to the code-behind file, *default.aspx.cs*. This method creates a string array of genres to add to the list of checkboxes. Then, a for loop is used to iterate through the array, calling the Add method on each item to add a new ListItem object to the Items collection of the CheckBoxList control.

You can modify the code in Examples 4-17 and 4-18 to add Value properties for some of the ListItems created in the CheckBoxList declaration, as well as in all the ListItem objects created in the cblGenre_Init event procedure. This is demonstrated in the new web site CheckBoxList-ArrayItemsAndValues, copied from CheckBoxList-ArrayItems and modified. The resulting web page is shown in Figure 4-12. The *default.aspx* content file for the web site is listed in Example 4-19, with lines of code highlighted which differ from Example 4-17.

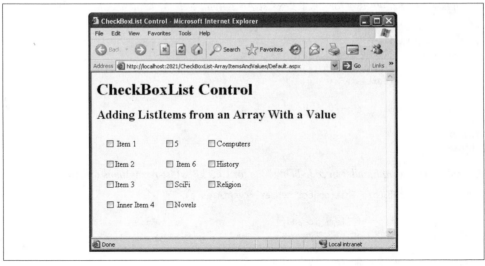

Figure 4-12. CheckBoxList-ArrayItemsAndValues web site

Example 4-19. Default.aspx for CheckBoxList-ArrayItemsAndValues web site

```
<%@ Page Language="C#" AutoEventWireup="true"  CodeFile="Default.aspx.cs"
        Inherits="_Default" %>

<!DOCTYPE html PUBLIC "-//W3C//DTD XHTML 1.1//EN"
   "http://www.w3.org/TR/xhtml11/DTD/xhtml11.dtd">

<html xmlns="http://www.w3.org/1999/xhtml" >
<head runat="server">
    <title>CheckBoxList Control</title>
</head>
<body>
    <form id="form1" runat="server">
    <div>
      <h1>CheckBoxList Control</h1>
      <h2>Adding ListItems from an Array With a Value</h2>
      <asp:CheckBoxList ID="cblGenre" runat="server"
                        AutoPostBack="True"
                        CellPadding="5"
                        CellSpacing="10"
                        RepeatColumns="3"
                        OnInit="cblGenre_Init">
        <asp:ListItem value="1"> Item 1 </asp:ListItem>
        <asp:ListItem text="Item 2" value="2"></asp:ListItem>
        <asp:ListItem text="Item 3"/>
        <asp:ListItem text="Item 4"> Inner Item 4 </asp:ListItem>
        <asp:ListItem value="5"></asp:ListItem>
        <asp:ListItem> Item 6 </asp:ListItem>
      </asp:CheckBoxList>
```

```
      </div>
      </form>
</body>
</html>
```

In the `Init` event handler in the code-behind file, shown in Example 4-20, the difference from the previous example is highlighted.

Example 4-20. Event handler in code-behind file for CheckBoxList-ArrayItemsAndValues web site

```
protected void cblGenre_Init(object sender, EventArgs e)
{
    // create an array of items to add
    string[] Genre = { "SciFi", "Novels", "Computers", "History",
                       "Religion" };
    string[] Code = { "sf", "nvl", "cmp", "his", "rel" };

    for (int i = 0; i < Genre.Length; i++)
    {
        //  Add both Text and Value
        this.cblGenre.Items.Add(new ListItem(Genre[i], Code[i]));
    }
}
```

In `cblGenre_Init`, listed in Example 4-20, where you previously created a single string array to hold the `Text` properties, there are now two string arrays: one for the `Text` properties and one for the `Value` properties. You now use the overloaded `Add` method, passing in a single argument consisting of a `ListItem` object:

```
    this.cblGenre.Items.Add(new ListItem(Genre[i],Code[i]));
```

 An object may *overload* its methods, which means it may declare two or more methods with the same name. The compiler differentiates among these methods based on the number and type of parameters provided.

For example, the `ListItemCollection` class overloads the `Add` method. One version takes a string, and the second version takes a `ListItem` object.

Finally, in creating the static `ListItems`, you used several different methods of creating `Values` and `Text`, including instances of missing `Text` (Item 5), missing `Value` (Item 3, Item 4, Item 6), and divergent `Text` property from inner HTML content (Item 4). The differences between Figures 4-11 and 4-12 can be seen in Items 4 and 5.

You can see that if the `Value` is missing, then the `Text` is displayed. If the `Text` is missing, the `Value` will be displayed. If the `Text` is different from the inner HTML content, the inner HTML content will be displayed.

Adding items from a data source

The real power of adding items programmatically comes when you can use a data source to populate the items in a CheckBoxList control. The ultimate data source, obviously, is a database. This will be covered in Chapter 9. However, you can use the array just created to demonstrate binding to a data source.

Copy the previous example to a new web site, called CheckBoxList-ArrayItemsData-Bind. Modify only the cblGenre_Init event handler method in the code-behind file. By replacing the for loop in cblGenre_Init in Example 4-18 with two lines of code (which specify the data source and then bind to it), the method now appears, as shown in Example 4-21.

Example 4-21. Modified code-behind for CheckBoxList-ArrayItemsDataBind web site

```
protected void cblGenre_Init(object sender, EventArgs e)
{
   // create an array of items to add
   string[] Genre = { "SciFi", "Novels", "Computers", "History",
                      "Religion" };

   cblGenre.DataSource = Genre;
   cblGenre.DataBind( );
}
```

You might expect the results to be unchanged from Figure 4-12, but that is not the case. Instead, you get the results shown in Figure 4-13.

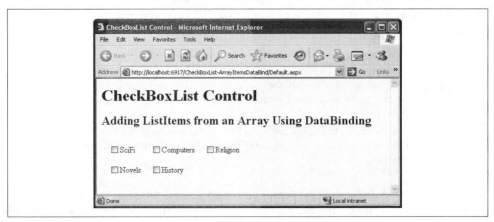

Figure 4-13. CheckBoxList with items added using DataBinding

In the previous example, using the `for` loop, `ListItems` were added by the `Init` method after the control was created. In this example, the preexisting `ListItem` objects were replaced by the new data source because the `ListControl.Items` collection is initialized by the data source, so any previously defined `ListItem` objects are lost.

That is the default behavior when data binding to a `ListControl` object. Alternatively, you can set the `AppendDataBoundItems` property (new to Version 2.0 of ASP. NET) of the control to true, in which case the data-bound items will be added to the existing `Items` collection, rather than replacing the existing `Items` collection.

Responding to user selections

When a user checks or unchecks one of the checkboxes in a `CheckBoxList`, the `SelectedIndexChanged` event is raised. This event passes an argument of type `EventArgs`, which does not expose any properties. By setting an attribute for handling this event and putting code in the event handler method, you can respond to the user clicking on one of the checkboxes. If `AutoPostBack` is set to `true`, the response occurs immediately. Otherwise, the response occurs the next time the form is posted to the server.

To see this, copy the previous example to a new web site, CheckBoxList-RespondingToEvents, and add the highlighted code from the content file in Example 4-22 and the code-behind file shown in Example 4-23. The resulting web page, after selecting a few checkboxes, is shown in Figure 4-14.

Example 4-22. default.aspx in CheckBoxList-RespondingToEvents web site

```
<%@ Page Language="C#" AutoEventWireup="true"  CodeFile="Default.aspx.cs"
        Inherits="_Default" %>

<!DOCTYPE html PUBLIC "-//W3C//DTD XHTML 1.1//EN"
   "http://www.w3.org/TR/xhtml11/DTD/xhtml11.dtd">

<html xmlns="http://www.w3.org/1999/xhtml" >
<head runat="server">
    <title>CheckBoxList Control</title>
</head>
<body>
    <form id="form1" runat="server">
    <div>
      <h1>CheckBoxList Control</h1>
      <h2>Responding To Events</h2>
      <asp:CheckBoxList ID="cblGenre" runat="server"
                        AutoPostBack="True"
                        CellPadding="5"
```

```
                              CellSpacing="10"
                              RepeatColumns="3"
                              OnInit="cblGenre_Init"
                   OnSelectedIndexChanged="cblGenre_SelectedIndexChanged">
         <asp:ListItem value="1"> Item 1 </asp:ListItem>
         <asp:ListItem text="Item 2" value="2"></asp:ListItem>
         <asp:ListItem text="Item 3"/>
         <asp:ListItem text="Item 4"> Inner Item 4 </asp:ListItem>
         <asp:ListItem value="5"></asp:ListItem>
         <asp:ListItem> Item 6 </asp:ListItem>
      </asp:CheckBoxList>
      <asp:Label ID="lblGenre" runat="server" Text="Label"></asp:Label>
   </div>
   </form>
</body>
</html>
```

Example 4-23. Modified event handlers in CheckBoxList-RespondingToEvents web site

```
protected void cblGenre_Init(object sender, EventArgs e)
{
    string[] Genre = { "SciFi", "Novels", "Computers", "History",
                       "Religion" };
    string[] Code = { "sf", "nvl", "cmp", "his", "rel" };

    for (int i = 0; i < Genre.Length; i++)
    {
        // Add both Text and Value
        this.cblGenre.Items.Add(new ListItem(Genre[i], Code[i]));
    }
}
protected void cblGenre_SelectedIndexChanged(object sender, EventArgs e)
{
    StringBuilder sb = new StringBuilder();
    foreach (ListItem li in cblGenre.Items)
    {
        if (li.Selected == true)
        {
            sb.Append("<br/>" + li.Value + " - " + li.Text);
        }
    }

    if (sb.Length == 0)
        lblGenre.Text = "No genres selected.";
    else
        lblGenre.Text = sb.ToString();

}
```

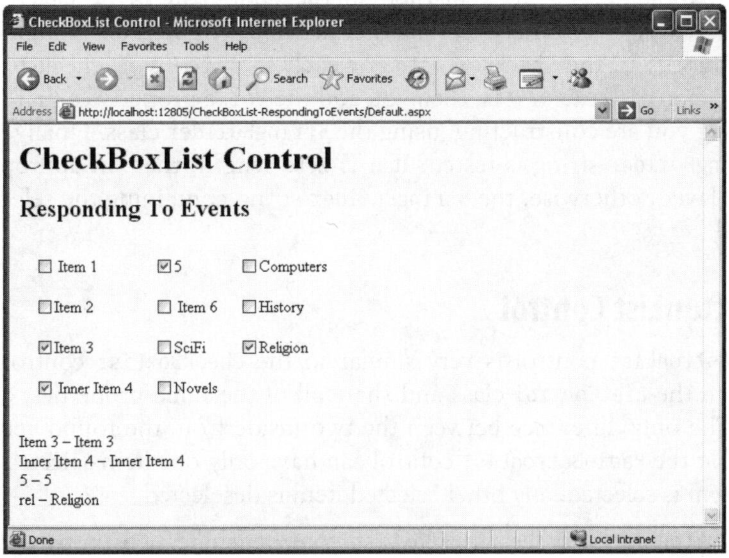

Figure 4-14. CheckBoxList-RespondingToEvents web site after selecting several checkboxes

Notice how the StringBuilder class is used in the method cblGenre_ SelectedIndexChanged to create the string, rather than concatenating each string value onto the previous value, as in this line of C# code:

```
str += "<br/>" + li.Value + " - " + li.Text;
```

Strings are immutable. When you write :

```
String firstString = "Hello";
string firstString += " world";
```

it appears as if you are concatenating the second part of the string onto firstString. What is actually happening, however, is that a second string is being allocated and assigned to your string reference, and the first string is being destroyed. If you do this a lot (in a tight loop, for example) it is very inefficient since creating and destroying the string objects are time-consuming operations.

The StringBuilder class provides a more efficient way of constructing strings, since it does not require that a new string be created with every modification.

The additional code added to the previous examples, shown highlighted in Examples 4-22 and 4-23, demonstrates responding to SelectedIndexChanged.

In the code in Examples 4-22 and 4-23, you add an attribute named OnSelectedIndexChanged to identify the event handler for the SelectedIndexChanged event. Like all event handlers, the attribute name comes from prepending the word "On" to the event name. Add a Label control to the form, lblGenre, to display the selected items.

The event handler points to a method in the code-behind file called cblGenre_ SelectedIndexChanged. In this event handler method, you iterate through the collection of ListItems in the CheckBoxList. For each ListItem, you check to see if the Selected property is true. If it is, then you add the Value property of that item to the HTML string you are constructing, using the StringBuilder class. Finally, the length of the StringBuilder string is tested. If it is zero length, then an appropriate message is displayed; otherwise, the StringBuilder string containing the selected values is displayed.

RadioButtonList Control

The RadioButtonList control is very similar to the CheckBoxList control. Both are derived from the ListControl class and share all of the same properties, events, and methods. The only difference between the two (aside from the round versus square shape) is that the RadioButtonList control can have only one item selected at a time. When an item is selected, any other selected item is deselected.

The RadioButtonList and the CheckBoxList controls share two properties inherited from ListControl, shown in Table 4-8.

Table 4-8. Selection properties inherited from the ListControl class

Name	Type	Get	Set	Description
SelectedIndex	Integer	✗	✗	The lowest index of the selected items in the list. If equal to −1, then nothing will have been selected.
SelectedItem	ListItem	✗		Returns the selected item with the lowest index.

To demonstrate how these properties are useful, copy the web site used to demonstrate radio buttons, RadioButtonDemo, to a new web site, called RadioButtonList-Demo. Replace the three radio buttons controlling the font size with a single RadioButtonList, calling it rblSize, as shown in Example 4-24. The final page is shown in Figure 4-15 after selecting a font size. It looks similar to the individual radio buttons, but it is easier to populate from a data source.

Example 4-24. default.aspx for RadioButtonListDemo web site

```
<%@ Page Language="C#" AutoEventWireup="true"  CodeFile="Default.aspx.cs"
        Inherits="_Default" %>

<!DOCTYPE html PUBLIC "-//W3C//DTD XHTML 1.1//EN"
   "http://www.w3.org/TR/xhtml11/DTD/xhtml11.dtd">

<html xmlns="http://www.w3.org/1999/xhtml" >
<head runat="server">
    <title>RadioButtonList Control</title>
</head>
<body>
```

Example 4-24. default.aspx for RadioButtonListDemo web site (continued)

```
    <form id="form1" runat="server">
    <div>
      <h1>RadioButtonList Control</h1>
      <br />
      <asp:Label ID="lblTime" runat="server"
                 OnInit="lblTime_Init"></asp:Label>

      <br />
      <br />
      <asp:radioButtonList
         id="rblSize" runat="server"
         autoPostBack="true"
         cellSpacing="20"
         repeatColumns="3"
         repeatDirection="horizontal"
         RepeatLayout="table"
         textAlign="right"
         OnSelectedIndexChanged="rblSize_SelectedIndexChanged">

         <asp:ListItem text="10pt" value="10"/>
         <asp:ListItem text="14pt" value="14"/>
         <asp:ListItem text="16pt" value="16"/>
      </asp:radioButtonList>

    </div>
    </form>
</body>
</html>
```

Figure 4-15. RadioButtonListDemo

The event handlers in the code-behind file for this page are shown in Example 4-25.

Example 4-25. Event handlers in default.aspx.cs for RadioButtonListDemo web site

```
protected void lblTime_Init(object sender, EventArgs e)
{
```

```
        lblTime.Font.Name = "Verdana";
        lblTime.Font.Size = 20;
        lblTime.Font.Bold = true;
        lblTime.Font.Italic = true;
        lblTime.Text = DateTime.Now.ToString( );
}
protected void rblSize_SelectedIndexChanged(object sender, EventArgs e)
{
    //  Check to verify that something has been selected.
    if (rblSize.SelectedIndex != -1)
    {
        int size = Convert.ToInt32(rblSize.SelectedItem.Value);
        lblTime.Font.Size = size;
    }
}
```

In RadioButtonListDemo, the original separate radio buttons are replaced by a
RadioButtonList control. Each ListItem object has a Text property and a Value property. The event handler, rblSize_SelectedIndexChanged, sets the Font.Size property,
requiring an integer value to do so, which it gets from the SelectedItem.Value property of the radio button list:

```
        int size = Convert.ToInt32(rblSize.SelectedItem.Value);
        lblTime.Font.Size = size;
```

> This works because C# provides an implicit conversion operator to
> convert the Int32 to a new FontUnit instance.

The event handler method makes use of the SelectedIndex and SelectedItem properties mentioned previously. The SelectedIndex property represents the lowest integer
value index of all the selected items. The SelectedItem property returns the Text
property of the item pointed to by SelectedIndex. Since a RadioButtonList, by definition, can have at most a single selected item, then SelectedIndex and SelectedItem
will tell us which item is selected. These properties are more ambiguous when
applied to a CheckBoxList control or other multi-select ListControl control.

RadioButtonListDemo verifies that at least one of the values has been selected. If no
item has been selected, then the SelectedIndex property is equal to –1. If an item has
been selected, you set the Font.Size property by converting the SelectedItem.Value
property to an integer. Note the following two lines of C# code in Example 4-25:

```
        int size = Convert.ToInt32(rblSize.SelectedItem.Value);
        lblTime.Font.Size = size;
```

They could have been written as a single line:

```
        lblTime.Font.Size = Convert.ToInt32(rblSize.SelectedItem.Value);
```

However, I often use the more verbose version to enhance readability and make the code easier to debug.

DropDownList Control

DropDownList controls display a single item at a time with a button for dropping the list to display more selections. Only a single item can be selected.

This next example, DropDownListDemo, demonstrates a DropDownList control. A two-dimensional string array is used in the Page_Load event handler to hold the Text and Value properties. The array is then used to add the ListItem objects to the Items collection. The result can be seen in Figure 4-16. The content file to accomplish this page is listed in Example 4-26, and the code-behind file is shown in Example 4-27.

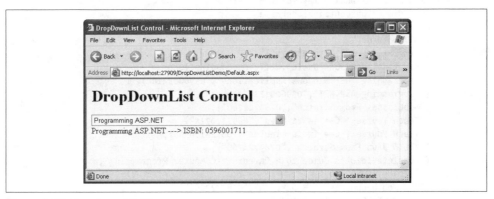

Figure 4-16. DropDownListDemo

Example 4-26. default.aspx for DropDownListDemo

```
<%@ Page Language="C#" AutoEventWireup="true"  CodeFile="Default.aspx.cs"
    Inherits="_Default" %>

<!DOCTYPE html PUBLIC "-//W3C//DTD XHTML 1.1//EN"
    "http://www.w3.org/TR/xhtml11/DTD/xhtml11.dtd">

<html xmlns="http://www.w3.org/1999/xhtml" >
<head runat="server">
    <title>DropDownList Control</title>
</head>
<body>
    <form id="form1" runat="server">
    <div>
      <h1>DropDownList Control</h1>

        <asp:DropDownList ID="ddl" runat="server"
                    AutoPostBack="True"
                    OnSelectedIndexChanged="ddl_SelectedIndexChanged">
        </asp:DropDownList>
```

Example 4-26. default.aspx for DropDownListDemo (continued)

```
        <br />
        <asp:Label ID="lblDdl" runat="server" ></asp:Label>


    </div>
    </form>
</body>
</html>
```

Example 4-27. Event handlers in code-behind file for DropDownListDemo

```
protected void Page_Load(object sender, EventArgs e)
{
    if (!IsPostBack)
    {
        //  Build 2 dimensional array for the lists
        //  First dimension contains bookname
        //  2nd dimension contains ISBN number
        string[,] books = {
            {"Programming C#","0596001177"},
            {"Programming Visual Basic .NET","0596004389"},
            {"Programming .NET Windows Applications","0596003218"},
            {"Programming ASP.NET","0596001711"},
            {"WebClasses From Scratch","0789721260"},
            {"Teach Yourself C++ in 21 Days","067232072X"},
            {"Teach Yourself C++ in 10 Minutes","067231603X"},
            {"XML & Java From Scratch","0789724766"},
            {"Complete Idiot's Guide to a Career in Computer Programming",
                "0789719959"},
            {"XML Web Documents From Scratch","0789723166"},
            {"Clouds To Code","1861000952"},
            {"C++ Unleashed","0672312395"}
          };

        //  Now populate the list.
        for (int i = 0; i < books.GetLength(0); i++)
        {
            //  Add both Text and Value
            ddl.Items.Add(new ListItem(books[i, 0], books[i, 1]));
        }
    }
}

protected void ddl_SelectedIndexChanged(object sender, EventArgs e)
{
    //  Check to verify that something has been selected.
    if (ddl.SelectedIndex != -1)
    {
        lblDdl.Text = ddl.SelectedItem.Text + " --->ISBN: " +
            ddl.SelectedValue;
    }
}
```

In Example 4-26, a `DropDownList` with the `ID` of `ddl` is added. This control is populated when the page is first loaded in the `Page_Load` event handler method.

To prevent this code from running every time the page is reloaded, you test to see if the `IsPostBack` property is `true`. The `IsPostBack` property is `false` when the page is first loaded but is set to `true` whenever the form is posted back to the server as a result of user action on one of the controls. In many applications, the contents of controls are filled from a database, which can be an expensive operation. Hitting the database only when necessary makes the implementation more efficient. In the CheckBoxList-ArrayItemsAndValues example, you used two arrays to populate a `CheckBoxList` with both the `Text` and `Value` properties. In this example, you use a single two-dimensional array to accomplish the same thing. As before, you call the `Items.Add` method to add the `ListItems` to the control. In Chapter 9, you will see how to populate a `ListControl` from a database.

As with the other `ListControls`, the `OnSelectedIndexChanged` attribute points to the event handler method, `ddl_SelectedIndexChanged`. In that method, as with the `RadioButtonList` control, you first check to see if something is selected by testing if the `SelectedIndex` property is not equal to –1. If an item has been selected, you display a concatenation of `SelectedItem.Text` and `SelectedValue` in the `Label` called `lblDdl`.

ListBox Control

`ListBox` controls are very similar to `DropDownList` controls, except that all the list items are visible, with the aid of a vertical scrollbar if necessary. By changing the `SelectionMode` property from the default value of `Single` to `Multiple`, the `ListBox` control can be used to select multiple items.

This next example, ListBoxDemo, shown in Figure 4-17, demonstrates two different `ListBoxes`: one using single selection and one allowing multiple selection. As you will see, the two `ListBoxes` are almost identical in implementation, the significant difference between them being the technique used to identify the selected item(s).

The significant differences between this example and the previous example, DropDownListDemo, are highlighted in Example 4-28, the content file for ListBoxDemo, and Example 4-29, the event handlers in the code-behind file for ListBoxDemo. These differences include the addition of the two `DropDownList` controls, modification to the `Page_Load` method to populate those controls, and the addition of event handlers for those two controls.

Figure 4-17. ListBoxDemo

Example 4-28. default.aspx for ListBoxDemo

```
<%@ Page Language="C#" AutoEventWireup="true"  CodeFile="Default.aspx.cs"
        Inherits="_Default" %>

<!DOCTYPE html PUBLIC "-//W3C//DTD XHTML 1.1//EN"
   "http://www.w3.org/TR/xhtml11/DTD/xhtml11.dtd">

<html xmlns="http://www.w3.org/1999/xhtml" >
<head runat="server">
   <title>ListBox Control</title>
</head>
<body>
   <form id="form1" runat="server">
   <div>
      <h1>ListBox Control</h1>
      <h2>ListBox - Single Selection</h2>
      <asp:ListBox ID="lbSingle" runat="server"
                   AutoPostBack="True"
                   Rows="6"
                   OnSelectedIndexChanged="lbSingle_SelectedIndexChanged">
      </asp:ListBox>
      <br />
      <asp:Label ID="lblSingle" runat="server"></asp:Label>
      <br />
      <h2>ListBox - Multiple Selection</h2>
```

Example 4-28. default.aspx for ListBoxDemo (continued)

```
      <asp:ListBox ID="lbMulti" runat="server"
                   AutoPostBack="True"
                   SelectionMode="Multiple"
                   OnSelectedIndexChanged="lbMulti_SelectedIndexChanged">
      </asp:ListBox>
      <br />
      <asp:Label ID="lblMulti" runat="server"></asp:Label>
  </div>
  </form>
</body>
</html>
```

Example 4-29. Event handlers in code-behind file for ListBoxDemo

```
protected void Page_Load(object sender, EventArgs e)
{
    if (!IsPostBack)
    {
        // Build 2 dimensional array for the lists
        // First dimension contains bookname
        // 2nd dimension contains ISBN number
        string[,] books = {
            {"Programming C#","0596001177"},
            {"Programming Visual Basic .NET","0596004389"},
            {"Programming .NET Windows Applications","0596003218"},
            {"Programming ASP.NET","0596001711"},
            {"WebClasses From Scratch","0789721260"},
            {"Teach Yourself C++ in 21 Days","067232072X"},
            {"Teach Yourself C++ in 10 Minutes","067231603X"},
            {"XML & Java From Scratch","0789724766"},
            {"Complete Idiot's Guide to a Career in Computer Programming",
                "0789719959"},
            {"XML Web Documents From Scratch","0789723166"},
            {"Clouds To Code","1861000952"},
            {"C++ Unleashed","0672312395"}
          };

        // Now populate the list.
        for (int i = 0; i < books.GetLength(0); i++)
        {
            // Add both Text and Value
            lbSingle.Items.Add(new ListItem(books[i, 0], books[i, 1]));
            lbMulti.Items.Add(new ListItem(books[i, 0], books[i, 1]));
        }
    }
}

protected void lbSingle_SelectedIndexChanged(object sender, EventArgs e)
{
    // Check to verify that something has been selected.
    if (lbSingle.SelectedIndex != -1)
    {
```

```
        lblSingle.Text = lbSingle.SelectedItem.Text + " ---> ISBN: " +
            lbSingle.SelectedItem.Value;
    }
}

protected void lbMulti_SelectedIndexChanged(object sender, EventArgs e)
{
    string str = "";
    foreach (ListItem li in lbMulti.Items)
    {
        if (li.Selected == true)
        {
            str += "<br/>" + li.Text + " ---> ISBN: " + li.Value;
        }
    }

//   Alternative technique
//      foreach (int i in lbMulti.GetSelectedIndices())
//      {
//          ListItem li = lbMulti.Items[i];
//          str += "<br/>" + li.Text + " ---> ISBN: " + li.Value;
//      }

    if (str.Length == 0)
        lblMulti.Text = "No books selected.";
    else
        lblMulti.Text = str;
}
```

ListBox controls have two properties in addition to those inherited from ListControl. These properties are shown in Table 4-9.

Table 4-9. Properties of ListBox control not inherited from ListControl

Name	Type	Get	Set	Values	Description
SelectionMode	ListSelectionMode	✗	✗	Single, Multiple	Determines if a ListBox is in single selection mode or multiple selection mode. Default is Single.
Rows	Integer	✗	✗		Number of rows displayed. Default is 4.

The first ListBox added in ListBoxDemo, with an ID of lbSingle, is a single-selection list box. The Rows property has been set to 6, and six items are displayed. Since the control has been populated with more than six items, a vertical scrollbar automatically appears. If a second item is selected, the first item is deselected. As with most of the examples in this chapter, AutoPostBack has been set to true so the effects of the change are visible immediately.

The second `ListBox` control, with an ID of `lbMulti`, is a multiple selection list box. The `Rows` property has not been set, so the default four rows are visible. Since it is multiselect, the standard Windows techniques of multi-selection can be used.

Windows Multi-Selection Techniques

Most Windows applications use the same techniques for selecting multiple items.

To add a *range of items* to the selected list, click on the first item to be selected, then hold down the Shift key while clicking on the last item to be selected. All the items between the two are highlighted for selection.

You can also multi-select a range of items by clicking the left mouse button on an item and holding it down while dragging the mouse to the last item in the range, then releasing the mouse button.

To add *non-contiguous items* to the selection, hold down the Ctrl key while clicking on items.

To deselect single items that have already been selected, hold down the Ctrl key while clicking on each item to toggle its selection status.

The event handlers for processing the selections of the two list boxes are very different. The event handler for the single selection list box is similar to the one for the `DropDownList` control or any other single select `ListControl`, such as the `RadioButtonList` control.

The event handler listed in Example 4-29 for the multi-select list box shows two different techniques for building up the string of selected items. The first technique is like that used for the `CheckBoxList` control. It iterates through the collection of `ListItem` objects, checking each to see if the `Selected` property is `true`. If it is `true`, then the `Text` and `Value` properties will be added to the string for output to a label. The second technique, commented out in Example 4-29, uses the `ListBox` `GetSelectedIndices` method (new to Version 2.0 of ASP.NET) to return an integer array of indices of all the selected items. That array is iterated, with each selected `ListItem` being instantiated to get its `Text` and `Value` properties.

BulletedList Control

The `BulletedList` control (new to Version 2.0 of ASP.NET) provides an ASP.NET server control analog to the HTML ordered (`<ol>`) and unordered lists (`<ul>`). The appearance and functionality of the list is controlled with properties of the `BulletedList` control. Like the other controls derived from `ListControl`, the `BulletedList` has an `Items` property, which is a collection of `ListItem` objects.

The style of the bullet is specified with the BulletStyle property. The valid values are contained within the BulletStyle enumeration, with values such as Circle, Disc, Numbered, LowerAlpha, UpperAlpha, LowerRoman, and UpperRoman. If the BulletStyle property is not set, a value of NotSet is the default, in which case the browser determines what style of bullet to use, typically the same as Disc.

If the BulletStyle property is set to a numeric or alphabetic style, such as Numbered, LowerAlpha, UpperAlpha, LowerRoman, or UpperRoman, then the starting value can be set using the FirstBulletNumber property. The default value is 1. Numeric bullet styles (Numbered, LowerRoman, UpperRoman) display numbers, and alphabetic types display the alphabetical equivalent.

The DisplayMode property determines appearance and functionality. It can be any one of the three values of the BulletedListDisplayMode enumeration:

Text

> The default value; causes the list content to display as text. No events will be associated with the control if this value is used, that is, there is no user interaction with this control, other than eyeballing it on the page.

HyperLink

> Each ListItem is displayed as an underlined link. When clicked, no server-side events are raised, and the form is *not* posted back to the server. Rather, like the HyperLink control itself, the user is navigated directly to the URL specified in the Value property of the ListItem that was clicked.

> The Target property of the BulletedList control works in conjunction with the DisplayMode set to HyperLink, dictating the browser window in which the target page will be displayed. The values of the Target property are the same as those listed in Table 4-3 for the HyperLink control.

LinkButton

> Each ListItem is displayed as an underlined link, exactly like the HyperLink. However, when the user clicks an item, the BulletedList.Click event is raised and immediately posted back to the server. A server-side event handler, specified by the OnClick attribute of the BulletedList control, is executed.

The example shown in Figure 4-18, BulletedListDemo, demonstrates the different bullet styles, starting numbers and display modes, as well as event handling with the BulletedList control. The content file for the example is shown in Example 4-30, and the event handler methods from the code-behind file are shown in Example 4-31.

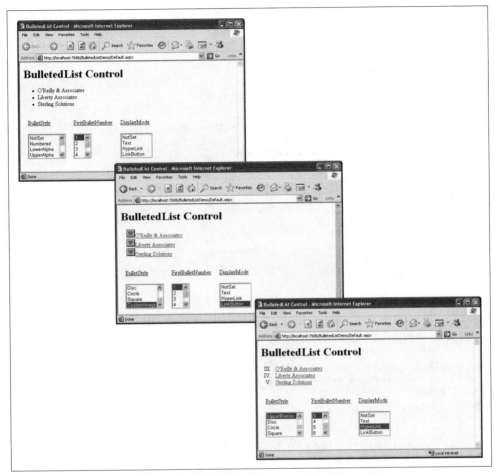

Figure 4-18. BulletedListDemo with all default values

Example 4-30. Default.aspx for BulletedListDemo

```
<%@ Page Language="C#" AutoEventWireup="true"  CodeFile="Default.aspx.cs"
        Inherits="_Default" %>

<!DOCTYPE html PUBLIC "-//W3C//DTD XHTML 1.1//EN"
   "http://www.w3.org/TR/xhtml11/DTD/xhtml11.dtd">

<html xmlns="http://www.w3.org/1999/xhtml" >
<head runat="server">
   <title>BulletedList Control</title>
</head>
<body>
<form id="form1" runat="server">
```

Example 4-30. Default.aspx for BulletedListDemo (continued)

```
<div>
    <h1>BulletedList Control</h1>
    <asp:BulletedList ID="bltList" runat="server"
                      OnClick="bltList_Click"
                      Target="_blank">
        <asp:ListItem Value="http://www.oreilly.com/">
            O'Reilly & Associates</asp:ListItem>
        <asp:ListItem Value="http://www.LibertyAssociates.com">
            Liberty Associates</asp:ListItem>
        <asp:ListItem Value="http://www.stersol.com"
                      Text="Sterling Solutions"></asp:ListItem>
    </asp:BulletedList>

    <table cellpadding=10>
        <tr>
            <td colspan=3 id="tdMessage" runat="server">
            </td>
        </tr>
        <tr>
            <td>
                <u>BulletStyle</u>
            </td>
            <td>
                <u>FirstBulletNumber</u>
            </td>
            <td>
                <u>DisplayMode</u>
            </td>
        </tr>
        <tr>
            <td>
                <asp:ListBox ID="lbBulletStyle" runat="server"
                        AutoPostBack=true
                        OnSelectedIndexChanged="lb_SelectedIndexChanged">
                    <asp:ListItem>NotSet</asp:ListItem>
                    <asp:ListItem>Numbered</asp:ListItem>
                    <asp:ListItem>LowerAlpha</asp:ListItem>
                    <asp:ListItem>UpperAlpha</asp:ListItem>
                    <asp:ListItem>LowerRoman</asp:ListItem>
                    <asp:ListItem>UpperRoman</asp:ListItem>
                    <asp:ListItem>Disc</asp:ListItem>
                    <asp:ListItem>Circle</asp:ListItem>
                    <asp:ListItem>Square</asp:ListItem>
                    <asp:ListItem>CustomImage</asp:ListItem>
                </asp:ListBox>
            </td>
            <td>
                <asp:ListBox ID="lbFirstBulletNumber" runat="server"
                        AutoPostBack=true
                        Width=50
                        OnSelectedIndexChanged="lb_SelectedIndexChanged">
                    <asp:ListItem selected="true">1</asp:ListItem>
```

Example 4-30. Default.aspx for BulletedListDemo (continued)

```
                <asp:ListItem>2</asp:ListItem>
                <asp:ListItem>3</asp:ListItem>
                <asp:ListItem>4</asp:ListItem>
                <asp:ListItem>5</asp:ListItem>
                <asp:ListItem>6</asp:ListItem>
            </asp:ListBox>
        </td>
        <td>
            <asp:ListBox ID="lbDisplayMode" runat="server"
                AutoPostBack=true
                OnSelectedIndexChanged="lb_SelectedIndexChanged">
                <asp:ListItem>NotSet</asp:ListItem>
                <asp:ListItem>Text</asp:ListItem>
                <asp:ListItem>HyperLink</asp:ListItem>
                <asp:ListItem>LinkButton</asp:ListItem>
            </asp:ListBox>
        </td>
    </tr>
  </table>
</div>
</form>
</body>
</html>
```

Example 4-31. Event handler methods from default.aspx.cs for BulletedListDemo

```csharp
protected void lb_SelectedIndexChanged(object sender, EventArgs e)
{
    ListBox lb = (ListBox)sender;
    string strID = lb.ID;
    string strValue = lb.SelectedValue;

    switch (strID)
    {
        case "lbBulletStyle":
            BulletStyle style =
                (BulletStyle)Enum.Parse(typeof(BulletStyle), strValue);
            bltList.BulletStyle = style;

            //  Special case the CustomImage
            if (style == BulletStyle.CustomImage)
            {
                bltList.BulletImageUrl = "heart.bmp";
            }
            break;

        case "lbFirstBulletNumber":
            bltList.FirstBulletNumber = Convert.ToInt32(strValue);
            break;

        case "lbDisplayMode":
            BulletedListDisplayMode displayMode =
```

Example 4-31. Event handler methods from default.aspx.cs for BulletedListDemo (continued)

```
            (BulletedListDisplayMode)Enum.Parse(
                typeof(BulletedListDisplayMode),
                strValue);

            bltList.DisplayMode = displayMode;
            break;

        default:
            break;
    }
}       // close for lb_SelectedIndexChanged

protected void bltList_Click(object sender, BulletedListEventArgs e)
{
    BulletedList b = (BulletedList)sender;
    tdMessage.InnerHtml = "Selected index: " + e.Index.ToString() +
        "<br>" +
        "Selected value: " + b.Items[e.Index].Value +
        "<br>";
}
```

In Example 4-30, the BulletedList control has three ListItems in its Items collection, all added statically. It so happens that all the list items represent web sites. In anticipation of the HyperLink DisplayMode being applied, each ListItem has its Value property set, which supplies the URL to navigate to. The Target property of the BulletedList control is set to _blank, so according to Table 4-3, this will cause the new page to open in a new, unnamed browser window.

The OnClick attribute of the BulletedList control hooks the Click event to the bltList_Click method in the code-behind file, shown highlighted in Example 4-31.

The event handler for this Click event will concatenate the Index and the Value properties of the clicked ListItem, along with some HTML elements, and assign that string to the InnerHtml property of an HTML server-side control. This event handler method requires an event argument of type BulletedListEventArgs, which exposes a single property, Index. This property returns the zero-based index of the clicked ListItem in the Items collection.

However, to retrieve either the actual Text or Value of the clicked ListItem, you must have a reference to the specific BulletedList control that raised the event. In this example, there is only a single BulletedList control and the ID is known to us: bltList. However, a more generic technique is used here where a single event handler will work with any number of controls. You first cast the object that raised the event, encapsulated in sender, to an object of type BulletedList, then index into the

`ListItems` collection represented by the `Items` property of that `BulletedList` object. This is accomplished in the following line of code from Example 4-31:

```
"Selected value: " + b.Items[e.Index].Value +
```

Though not directly related to the `BulletedList` control, some interesting techniques are used with all three of the `ListBox` controls on the page.

All the `ListBoxes` have `AutoPostBack` set to `true` so you will see the results of changing a value immediately. Also, all three controls use the same event handler method, `lb_SelectedIndexChanged`, for the `SelectedIndexChanged` event. The following two attributes in each of the `ListControl` declarations implements this:

```
AutoPostBack=true
OnSelectedIndexChanged="lb_SelectedIndexChanged">
```

Looking at the `lb_SelectedIndexChanged` method in the code-behind file in Example 4-31, the first line of code gets a reference to the control that raised the event by casting sender to a `ListBox` object:

```
ListBox lb = (ListBox)sender;
```

Then the `ID` and `SelectedValue` properties of the list box can be retrieved.

A switch block is used to take action appropriate for each list box. The `ListBox` that sets the `FirstBulletNumber` property is straightforward, converting the `SelectedValue`, contained in the string variable `strValue`, to an integer and assigning that integer to the `FirstBulletNumber` property:

```
bltList.FirstBulletNumber = Convert.ToInt32(strValue);
```

The case blocks for the other two `ListBoxes` are a bit more interesting. The goal is to determine the item selected, either a `BulletStyle` or a `DisplayMode`, and apply that to the `BulletedList`. In both cases, this is accomplished using the static `Enum.Parse` method. This method converts a name or value of an enumerated constant into its equivalent enumerated object. You must pass it the type of the enumerated constant and the value of the constant.

So, looking at the case for `lbBulletStyle` (`lbDisplayMode` is exactly equivalent), the Type of the enumeration is obtained from the `typeof` operator, which returns a `System.Type` object. The value of the selected constant is contained in `strValue`. Given these two arguments, `Enum.Parse` returns an object, which you then cast to the desired type and assign to a variable:

```
BulletStyle style =
    (BulletStyle)Enum.Parse(typeof(BulletStyle), strValue);
```

This variable can then be used to set the appropriate property:

```
bltList.BulletStyle = style;
```

In the case of `lbBulletStyle`, you must special case the `CustomImage` to assign the `BulletImageUrl` property. Here you can compare `BulletStyle` directly with the enumerated constants to see if there is a match:

```
if (style == BulletStyle.CustomImage)
{
    bltList.BulletImageUrl = "heart.bmp";
}
```

Tables

Tables are very important in web page design as they are one of the primary means of controlling the layout on the page. In pure HTML, several tags create and format tables, and many of those have analogs in ASP.NET server controls. If you don't need server-side capabilities, then you will be fine using the static HTML tags. But when you need to control the table at runtime, then server controls are the way to go. (You could also use HTML server controls, described in the previous chapter, but they don't offer the consistency of implementation and object model offered by ASP.NET controls.)

Table 4-10 summarizes the ASP.NET server controls used to create tables in web pages.

Table 4-10. ASP.NET server controls used to create tables in web pages

ASP.NET server control	HTML Analog	Description
Table	\<table\>	Parent control for `TableRow` controls. The `Rows` property of the `Table` object is a collection of `TableRow` objects.
TableRow	\<tr\>	Parent control for `TableCell` controls. The `Cells` property of the `TableRow` object contains a collection of `TableCell` objects.
TableCell	\<td\>	Contains content to be displayed. The `Text` property contains HTML text. The `Controls` collection can contain other controls.
TableHeaderCell	\<th\>	Derived from the `TableCell` class. Controls the display of heading cell(s).
TableHeaderRow	\<thead\>	Creates header row element.
TableFooterRow	\<tfoot\>	Creates footer row element.

There is some overlap in the functionality of `Table` controls and the `Data` controls. These controls, covered in detail in Chapter 9, including the `GridView`, `Repeater`, `DataList`, and `DataGrid` controls, are primarily used to display data from a data source, such as a database, XML file, or array. Both the `Table` control and the `Data` controls can be used to display data in a table or list-formatted layout. In fact, all of these controls render to a desktop browser (or have the option to render) as HTML tables. (You can verify this by going to your browser and viewing the source of the page displayed.) Table 4-11 summarizes the differences between these five controls.

Table 4-11. Differences between the Table control and DataList controls

Control	Usage	Description
Table	General layout	• Can contain any combination of text, HTML, and other controls, including other tables • Uses `TableCell` rather than templates to control appearance • Not data bound but can contain data-bound controls
Repeater	Read-only data	• Read-only • Uses templates for the look • Data bound • No paging
DataList	List output with editing	• Default layout is a table • Can be extensively customized using templates and styles • Editable • Data bound • No paging
DataGrid	List output with editing	• Default look is a grid (that is, a customizable table) • Optionally may use templates • Editable • Data bound • Supports paging and sorting
GridView	List output with editing	Similar to `DataGrid` but with more capabilities, and much less code to write.

TableDemo, shown in Figure 4-19, demonstrates most of the basic table functionality of the Table control. This example uses a CheckBoxList control and a RadioButtonList control to set attributes of the font samples displayed in the table. Then a table is created that contains a sample of every font installed on your system.

The content file shown in Example 4-32, uses a static HTML table to position the font style and size selection controls. After some opening headers, there is a standard, plain vanilla HTML table. This uses the familiar <table> tags enclosing table rows (<tr>), which enclose table cells (<td>). There is nothing dynamic going on here, just the common technique of using a table to control the layout of the page.

The second cell of the first row contains a CheckBoxList server control, and the second cell of the second row contains a RadioButtonList server control, both of which have been discussed earlier in this chapter. Both of these controls have several things in common: an id attribute, the all-important runat attribute, and AutoPostBack set to true, so any changes will take effect immediately. Both controls also have various other attributes to give the desired layout.

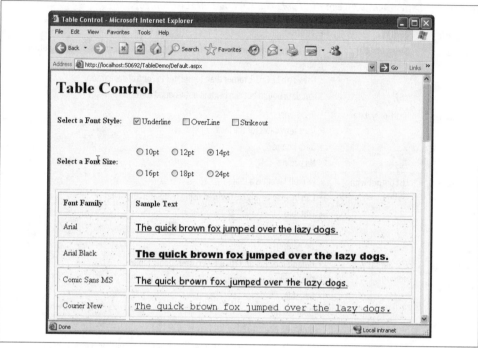

Figure 4-19. TableDemo

Example 4-32. default.aspx for TableDemo

```
<%@ Page Language="C#" AutoEventWireup="true"  CodeFile="Default.aspx.cs"
        Inherits="_Default" %>

<!DOCTYPE html PUBLIC "-//W3C//DTD XHTML 1.1//EN"
   "http://www.w3.org/TR/xhtml11/DTD/xhtml11.dtd">

<html xmlns="http://www.w3.org/1999/xhtml" >
<head runat="server">
    <title>Table Control</title>
</head>
<body>
    <form id="form1" runat="server">
    <div>
        <h1>Table Control</h1>
        <table>
           <tr>
             <td>
                <strong>Select a Font Style:</strong>
             </td>
             <td>
                <asp:CheckBoxList ID="cblFontStyle" runat="server"
                                  AutoPostBack="True"
                                  CellPadding="5"
                                  CellSpacing="10"
```

Example 4-32. default.aspx for TableDemo (continued)

```
                                RepeatColumns="3"
                                OnInit="cblFontStyle_Init">
            </asp:CheckBoxList>
          </td>
        </tr>
        <tr>
          <td>
            <strong>Select a Font Size:</strong>
          </td>
          <td>
            <asp:RadioButtonList ID="rblSize" runat="server"
                                 AutoPostBack="True"
                                 CellSpacing="20"
                                 RepeatColumns="3"
                                 RepeatDirection="Horizontal">
              <asp:ListItem text="10pt" value="10"/>
              <asp:ListItem text="12pt" value="12" selected = "true"/>
              <asp:ListItem text="14pt" value="14"/>
              <asp:ListItem text="16pt" value="16"/>
              <asp:ListItem text="18pt" value="18"/>
              <asp:ListItem text="24pt" value="24"/>
            </asp:RadioButtonList>
          </td>
        </tr>
      </table>

      <asp:Table ID="tbl" runat="server"
                 BackImageUrl="Sunflower Bkgrd.jpg"
                 Font-Names="Times New Roman"
                 Font-Size="12"
                 GridLines="Both"
                 CellPadding="10"
                 CellSpacing="5"
                 HorizontalAlign="Left"
                 Width="100%">
        <asp:TableHeaderRow HorizontalAlign="Left">
          <asp:TableHeaderCell>Font Family</asp:TableHeaderCell>
          <asp:TableHeaderCell Width="80%">
            Sample Text
          </asp:TableHeaderCell>
        </asp:TableHeaderRow>
      </asp:Table>
    </div>
    </form>
</body>
</html>
```

The CheckBoxList control has an event handler defined for initialization, onInit (highlighted in Example 4-32), which points to the method cblFontStyle_Init, which is contained in the code behind file, shown in Example 4-33.

Example 4-33. default.aspx.cs for TableDemo

```csharp
using System;
using System.Data;
using System.Configuration;
using System.Web;
using System.Web.Security;
using System.Web.UI;
using System.Web.UI.WebControls;
using System.Web.UI.WebControls.WebParts;
using System.Web.UI.HtmlControls;
using System.Drawing;              //  necessary for FontFamily
using System.Drawing.Text;         //  necessary for Fonts

public partial class _Default : System.Web.UI.Page
{
    protected void Page_Load(object sender, EventArgs e)
    {
      string str = "The quick brown fox jumped over the lazy dogs.";
      int i = 0;

      //  Get the style checkboxes.
      bool boolUnder = false;
      bool boolOver = false;
      bool boolStrike = false;

      foreach(ListItem li in cblFontStyle.Items)
      {
        if (li.Selected == true)
        {
          switch (li.Value)
          {
            case "u":
                boolUnder = true;
                break;
            case "o":
                boolOver = true;
                break;
            case "s":
                boolStrike = true;
                break;
          }
        }
      }

      //  Get the font size.
      int size = Convert.ToInt32(rblSize.SelectedItem.Value);

      //  Get a list of all the fonts installed on the system
      //  Populate the table with the fonts and sample text.
      InstalledFontCollection ifc = new InstalledFontCollection( );
      foreach( FontFamily ff in ifc.Families )
      {
        TableRow r = new TableRow( );
```

Example 4-33. default.aspx.cs for TableDemo (continued)

```
            TableCell cFont = new TableCell( );
            cFont.Controls.Add(new LiteralControl(ff.Name));
            r.Cells.Add(cFont);

            TableCell cText = new TableCell( );
            Label lbl = new Label( );
            lbl.Text = str;

            //  ID not necessary here. This just to show it can be set.
            i++;
            lbl.ID = "lbl" + i.ToString( );

            //  Set the font name
            lbl.Font.Name = ff.Name;

            //  Set the font style
            if (boolUnder)
                lbl.Font.Underline = true;
            if (boolOver)
                lbl.Font.Overline = true;
            if (boolStrike)
                lbl.Font.Strikeout = true;

            //  Set the font size.
            lbl.Font.Size = size;

            cText.Controls.Add(lbl);
            r.Cells.Add(cText);

            tbl.Rows.Add(r);
        }
    }

    protected void  cblFontStyle_Init(object sender, EventArgs e)
    {
        // create arrays of items to add
        string[] FontStyle = {"Underline","OverLine", "Strikeout"};
        string[] Code = {"u","o","s"};

        for (int i = 0; i < FontStyle.GetLength(0); i++)
        {
            //  Add both Text and Value
            this.cblFontStyle.Items.Add(new ListItem(FontStyle[i],Code[i]));
        }
    }
}
```

This code is very similar to the code shown in Example 4-18 for filling a CheckBoxList from an array. Here you create two string arrays, FontStyle and Code, to fill the ListItem properties Text and Value, respectively.

The RadioButtonList control, on the other hand, does not have an onInit event handler, but rather the ListItems it contains are defined right within the control itself. This example uses self-closing ListItem tags with attributes specifying both the Text property and the Value property. In the case of the 12-point radio button, the Selected property is set to true, which makes this the default value on initialization.

Neither of these controls has any other event handler. Specifically, no event handler exists for OnSelectedIndexChanged, as there are in previous examples in this chapter. Yet, AutoPostBack is true. As you will see, the ASP.NET Table control is rebuilt every time the page is loaded, which occurs every time the CheckBoxList or the RadioButtonList control is changed. The current value for the font style is obtained from the CheckBoxList control, and the current font size is obtained from the RadioButtonList control.

Notice the two using statements (highlighted in Example 4-33) in the code-behind file, in addition to those inserted by default by VS2005. These are necessary to enable usage of the Font and FontFamily classes without typing fully qualified member names.

The Table control is the heart of this page:

```
<asp:Table ID="tbl" runat="server"
           BackImageUrl="Sunflower Bkgrd.jpg"
           Font-Names="Times New Roman"
           Font-Size="12"
           GridLines="Both"
           CellPadding="10"
           CellSpacing="5"
           HorizontalAlign="Left"
           Width="100%">
    <asp:TableHeaderRow HorizontalAlign="Left">
       <asp:TableHeaderCell>Font Family</asp:TableHeaderCell>
       <asp:TableHeaderCell Width="80%">
          Sample Text
       </asp:TableHeaderCell>
    </asp:TableHeaderRow>
</asp:Table>
```

Like all ASP.NET server controls, the Table control inherits from WebControl and therefore has the standard set of properties, methods, and events from that class and the classes above it in the hierarchy. In addition, the Table control has properties of its own, which are listed in Table 4-12. Most of these properties are demonstrated in TableDemo.

Table 4-12. Properties of the Table control not derived from other classes

Name	Type	Get	Set	Values	Description
BackImageUrl	String	✗	✗		The URL of an image to display behind the table. If the image is smaller than the table, it will be tiled.
Caption	String	✗	✗		The text to render to an HTML caption element. Use of this property makes the control more accessible to Assistive Technology device users.
CaptionAlign	TableCaptionAlign	✗	✗	NotSet, Top, Bottom, Left, Right	Specifies the formatting of the HTML caption element.
CellPadding	Integer	✗	✗		Distance, in pixels, between the border and the contents of a table cell.
CellSpacing	Integer	✗	✗		Distance, in pixels, between adjacent table cells.
GridLines	GridLines	✗	✗	Both, Horizontal, None, Vertical	Determines which, if any, grid-lines will be drawn in the table. Default is None.
HorizontalAlign	HorizontalAlign	✗	✗	Center, Justify, Left, NotSet, Right	Specifies the horizontal alignment of the table within the page. Default is NotSet.

Note the following information about the Table control in TableDemo:

- The BackImageUrl attribute in the Table control points to an image file located in the same directory as the *.aspx* file itself, so the URL does not need to be fully qualified. In these code examples we used *SunflowerBkgrd.jpg*, which was copied from the *c:\ProgramFiles\CommonFiles\MicrosoftShared\Stationery* directory. You can use any *.jpg* file you want or simply omit the BackImageUrl attribute. For a complete discussion of relative and absolute addressing, see the sidebar "File Locations" in the section "Button Controls."

- The syntax for font name and size attributes is Font-Name and Font-Size when declared as part of the ASP.NET server control using its declarative syntax, but Font.Name and Font.Size when used in the code-behind file.

- If the Width attribute is set as an integer with no units, it causes the table to be the specified number of pixels in width, irrespective of the width of the browser window. The table can be made wider than the browser window.

- If the Width attribute is not specified, then the table will automatically be as wide as necessary to display the contents of the cells. If the browser window is not wide enough, the cell contents will wrap. Once the browser window is made wide enough that all the cells can display without wrapping, the table will not get any wider.

Nested inside the Table control is a single TableHeaderRow control. This row contains the header cells, indicated by TableHeaderCell controls.

Table Rows

The TableRow control is used to represent a single row in a Table control. It is derived from the WebControl class like the Table control. As Table 4-13 shows, it has several properties not shared with all its other sibling controls.

Table 4-13. Properties of the TableRow control not shared by other ASP.NET server controls

Name	Type	Get	Set	Values	Description
HorizontalAlign	HorizontalAlign	✗	✗	Center, Justify, Right, NotSet, Left	Specifies the horizontal alignment of the contents of all the cells in the row. Default is NotSet.
VerticalAlign	VerticalAlign	✗	✗	Bottom, Middle, NotSet, Top	Specifies the vertical alignment of the contents of all the cells in the row. Default is NotSet.
Cells	TableCellCollection	✗			Collection of TableCell objects comprising the row.
TableSection	TableRowSection	✗	✗	TableBody, TableFooter, TableHeader	Specifies where the row is placed in a table.

The TableRow class has six other controls, or classes, derived from it as described in Table 4-14.

Table 4-14. Controls derived from TableRow

Derived control	Description
DataGridItem	A row in a DataGrid control
DetailsViewRow	A row within a DetailsView control
FormViewRow	A row within a FormView control
GridViewRow	A row within a GridView control

Table 4-14. Controls derived from TableRow (continued)

Derived control	Description
TableFooterRow	A footer row in a Table control.
TableHeaderRow	A header row in a Table control.

 All of the controls derived from TableRow are new for ASP.NET Version 2, except for the DataGridItem.

Table Cells

There are two types of table cell controls: a TableCell control for the body of the table and a TableHeaderCell for header cells. Both are used in TableDemo.

The TableHeaderCell control represents a heading cell in a Table control. It is derived from the TableCell control class. In fact, all of its properties, events, and methods are exactly the same as for the TableCell control. The single difference between the TableCell and TableHeaderCell controls is that the TableHeaderCell control renders to the browser as a <th> element rather than a <td>. Most browsers display <th> cells in a centered, bold font. As can be seen in Figure 4-19, the header cells are bold, but the HorizontalAlign attribute in the TableRow declaration in Example 4-32 overrides the default text alignment. Perhaps more fundamentally, TableHeaderCells are a distinctly different type of control in the Controls collection of the page.

None of the nested TableHeaderCell controls in this example have an id or a runat attribute. These attributes are unnecessary here since these controls are not accessed programmatically elsewhere in the code.

Only a single row is defined statically. The rest of the rows are defined dynamically in the Page_Load method in the code-behind file shown in Example 4-33.

In Example 4-32, the content of the header cells is the literal text strings between the opening and closing control tags. Alternatively, you may use self-closing tags and specify the content as a Text property:

```
<asp:TableHeaderCell text="Font Family"/>
```

The TableCell control is used to contain the actual content of the table. Like the Table and TableRow controls, it is derived from the WebControl class. The TableCell and the TableHeaderCell controls have the properties shown in Table 4-15, which are not shared with its siblings.

Table 4-15. Properties of the TableCell and TableHeaderCell controls not shared with other table controls

Name	Type	Get	Set	Values	Description
AssociatedHeaderCellID	String	✗	✗		A comma-separated list of table header cells associated with a cell, used by non-visual browsers to aid in navigation.
ColumnSpan	Integer	✗	✗		Number of columns in the table that the cell spans.
HorizontalAlign	HorizontalAlign	✗	✗	Center, Justify, Left, NotSet, Right	Specifies the horizontal alignment of the content of the cell. Default is NotSet.
RowSpan	Integer	✗	✗		Number of rows in the Table that the cell spans.
Text	String	✗	✗		The text content of the cell.
VerticalAlign	VerticalAlign	✗	✗	Bottom, Middle, NotSet, Top	Specifies the vertical alignment of the contents of the cell. Default is NotSet.
Wrap	Boolean	✗	✗	true, false	If true (the default), the contents of the cell wraps. If false, contents do not wrap. There is an interaction between the Wrap property and cell width.

In TableDemo, you have a Table control containing a single TableRow object that contains a pair of TableHeaderCell objects. The Page_Load method in the code-behind file, which is run every time the page is loaded, creates the balance of the table rows dynamically.

Often times, the Page_Load method will examine the IsPostBack property to test if the page is being loaded for the first time. If the load is the result of a postback, you may not want certain code to execute, either because it is unnecessary and expensive, or because you will lose or change state information. (See Chapter 3 for a full discussion of the IsPostBack property.)

In this example, however, you want the code to run every time the page loads. In fact, the CheckBoxList and the RadioButtonList controls have their AutoPostBack properties set to true to force the page to post. This forces the table to be regenerated. Each time the table is regenerated, the font styles are obtained from the CheckBoxList control, and the font size is obtained from the RadioButtonList control.

The Page_Load method begins by initializing a couple of variables:

```
string str = "The quick brown fox jumped over the lazy dogs.";
int i = 0;
```

str is the text displayed in the table, and i is a counter used later on.

You get the style or styles from the CheckBoxList control. To do so, you initialize three Boolean variables to use as flags, one for each style:

```
bool boolUnder = false;
bool boolOver = false;
bool boolStrike = false;
```

Then, using a foreach loop to test each of the ListItem objects in the cblFontStyle CheckBoxList in turn, you set the Boolean variable for each font style to true if that checkbox has been selected. That is done by testing to see if the Selected property of the ListItem object is true:

```
foreach(ListItem li in cblFontStyle.Items)
{
    if (li.Selected == true)
    {
        switch (li.Value)
        {
            case "u":
                boolUnder = true;
                break;
            case "o":
                boolOver = true;
                break;
            case "s":
                boolStrike = true;
                break;
        }
    }
}
```

Getting the font size selected in the RadioButtonList rblSize is much simpler since all you have to do is get the Value property of the ListItem object returned by the SelectedItem property. You put that integer into the size variable:

```
int size = Convert.ToInt32(rblSize.SelectedItem.Value);
```

Now comes the meat of the method. You need to get a list of all the fonts installed on the machine. To do this, instantiate a new InstalledFontCollection object:

```
InstalledFontCollection ifc = new InstalledFontCollection();
```

Iterate over that collection, using a foreach loop, looking at each of the FontFamily objects in turn:

```
foreach( FontFamily ff in ifc.Families )
```

For each font family in the collection of FontFamilies, you create a new TableRow object:

```
TableRow r = new TableRow( );
```

Within that TableRow object, you create two TableCell objects: one called cFont to hold the font name and a second called cText to hold the sample text string defined earlier. The following code implements the cFont cell:

```
TableCell cFont = new TableCell( );
cFont.Controls.Add(new LiteralControl(ff.Name));
r.Cells.Add(cFont);
```

The cFont TableCell object makes use of an ASP.NET server control called the LiteralControl. This control is used to insert text and HTML elements into the page. The only property of the LiteralControl, other than those inherited from Control, is the Text property.

For the cell containing the sample text, you will use a slightly different technique, because you want to be able to manipulate the font and size properties of the text string. After instantiating a new TableCell object named cText, you will instantiate a Label control and assign the variable str, defined earlier, to its Text property:

```
TableCell cText = new TableCell( );
Label lbl = new Label( );
lbl.Text = str;
```

You increment the counter defined earlier and use it by assigning an ID property to the Label control:

```
i++;
lbl.ID = "lbl" + i.ToString( );
```

Actually, this step is unnecessary because nowhere in this example do you need to refer back to any specific cell, but it was added to demonstrate how it can be done.

You now assign the font name:

```
lbl.Font.Name = ff.Name;
```

The syntax used here differs from the syntax for setting the font name within the tags of a ASP.NET server control (Font.Name versus Font-Name).

Use the flags set earlier to set the font styles:

```
if (boolUnder)
    lbl.Font.Underline = true;
if (boolOver)
    lbl.Font.Overline = true;
if (boolStrike)
    lbl.Font.Strikeout = true;
```

Since the table is being recreated from scratch each time the page is loaded and the defaults for each of these styles is no style (i.e., false), there is no need to set the properties explicitly to false.

Set the font size, add the Label object to the `TableCell` object, add the `TableCell` object to the `TableRow` object, and add the `TableRow` object t the `Table` object:

```
lbl.Font.Size = size;
cText.Controls.Add(lbl);
r.Cells.Add(cText);
tbl.Rows.Add(r);
```

There you have it.

Cell Width

Controlling the width of the cells merits special mention. It is similar to controlling table width but different enough to cause some confusion. Looking at the HTML in Example 4-32, you can see that the second cell in the header row has a `Width` attribute set to 80%:

```
<asp:TableHeaderCell Width="80%">
    Sample text
</asp:TableHeaderCell>
```

Browsers make all the cells in a column the same width. If none of the cells have any width specification, the column will automatically size to best accommodate all the cells, taking into account any width specifications for the table and the size of the browser window.

If multiple cells in a column have a width specification, then the widest cell specification is used. For easiest readability, include a width specification in only one row, generally the first row of the table. Hence, the `Width` attribute appears in the header row of this example.

When the width is specified declaratively as part of a ASP.NET server control tag, it can be given either as a percentage of the entire table, as was done in this example, or it can be given as a fixed number of pixels, as in the following:

```
Width="400"
```

Cell width can also be specified programmatically, in which case the syntax is somewhat different. In C#, the code is the following:

```
TableCell cText = new TableCell();
```

The variable cText, of type `TableCell`, is assigned to the new cell instance. The Width property can be applied to this `TableCell` instance, either as pixels or as a percentage of the table width. To specify the Width property as 80 percent of the table width, use the following line of code:

```
cText.Width = Unit.Percentage(80);
```

To specify a fixed number of pixels, use *either* of the following lines of code:

```
cText.Width = Unit.Pixel(400);
cText.Width = 400;
```

There is an interaction between the cell `Width` property and the `Wrap` property. The default value for the `Wrap` property is `true`. If the `Wrap` property is set to `false`, one of the following situations will occur:

- If there is no `Width` property specified, then the contents of the cell will not wrap and the column width expands to accommodate the largest cell.
- If the `Width` property is set to a pixel value, the `Wrap` property will be overridden and the cell contents wrap to honor the `Width` property.
- If the `Width` property is set to a percentage value, it will be overridden and the column will be made wide enough to preclude any wrapping.

Panel Control

The `Panel` control is used as a container for other controls. It serves several functions:

- To control the visibility of the controls it contains
- To control the appearance of the controls it contains
- To make it easier to generate controls programmatically

The `Panel` control is derived from `WebControl` and adds the properties shown in Table 4-16. The `Panel` control has no methods or events not inherited from the `Control` or `WebControl` classes. Specifically, there are no events raised by user interaction.

Table 4-16. Properties of the Panel control not inherited from Control or WebControl

Name	Type	Get	Set	Values	Description
BackImageUrl	String	✗	✗		The URL of an image to display as background of the panel. If the image is smaller than the panel, it will be tiled.
Direction	ContentDirection	✗	✗	LeftToRight, RightToLeft, NotSet	Direction to display text in a container control. Default is NotSet.
GroupingText	string	✗	✗		Causes the Panel to render to the browser as `<fieldset>` element rather than `<div>` element. Value of this property is used for the `<legend>` element.
HorizontalAlign	HorizontalAlign	✗	✗	Center, Justify, Left, NotSet, Right	Specifies the horizontal alignment of the contents. Default is NotSet. Note there is no VerticalAlign property.

Table 4-16. Properties of the Panel control not inherited from Control or WebControl (continued)

Name	Type	Get	Set	Values	Description
`ScrollBars`	ScrollBars	✗	✗	`Auto`, `Both`, `Horizontal`, `None`, `Vertical`	Specifies the visibility and location of scrollbars. The default value is `None`.
`Wrap`	Boolean	✗	✗	`true`, `false`	If `true` (the default), the contents of the panel will wrap. If `false`, contents will not wrap.

The next example, PanelDemo, shown in Figure 4-20, contains two `Panel` controls. The first demonstrates how to control the appearance and visibility of child controls and how to add controls programmatically. The second panel demonstrates the use of the `GroupingText`, `ScrollBars`, and `Wrap` properties to control the appearance of the control.

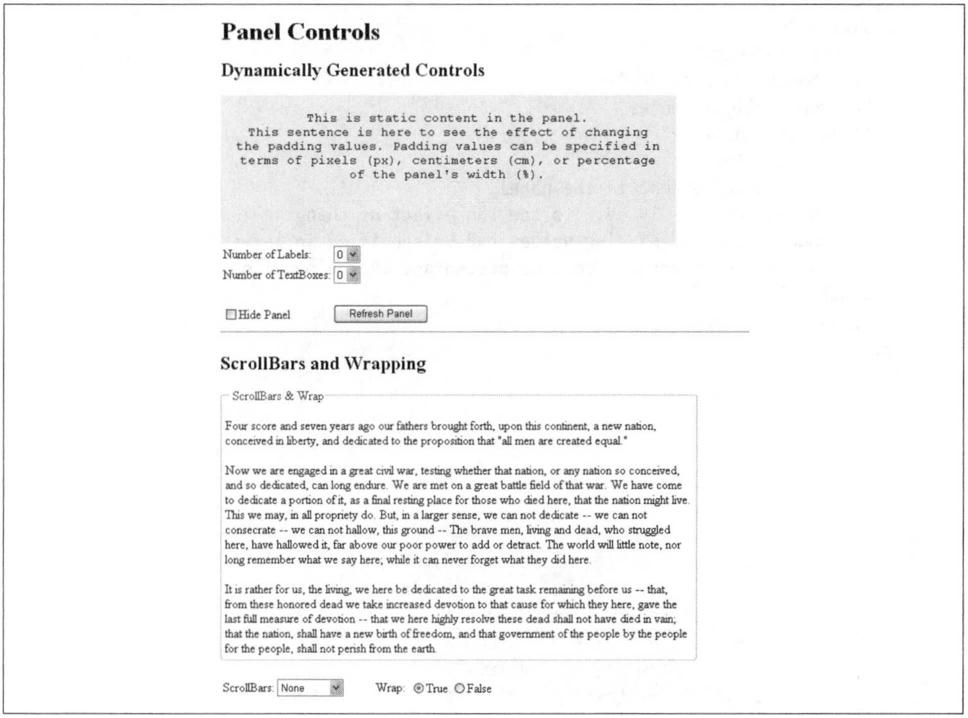

Figure 4-20. PanelDemo

The two `Panel` declarations in this example are highlighted in Example 4-34. The first one, with an ID of `pnlDynamic`, has some static content between the opening and closing `Panel` tags. The remainder of the content of this panel is added dynamically, depending on the values selected in the two drop-downs, `ddlLabels`, and `ddlBoxes`.

Example 4-34. default.aspx for PanelDemo

```
<%@ Page Language="C#" AutoEventWireup="true"  CodeFile="Default.aspx.cs"
        Inherits="_Default" %>

<!DOCTYPE html PUBLIC "-//W3C//DTD XHTML 1.1//EN"
    "http://www.w3.org/TR/xhtml11/DTD/xhtml11.dtd">

<html xmlns="http://www.w3.org/1999/xhtml" >
<head runat="server">
    <title>Panel Control</title>
</head>
<body>
    <form id="form1" runat="server">
    <div>
        <h1>Panel Controls</h1>
        <h2>Dynamically Generated Controls</h2>
        <asp:Panel ID="pnlDynamic" runat="server"
            Height="150"
            Width="80%"
            BackColor="Beige"
            Font-Names="Courier New"
            HorizontalAlign="Center"
            Style="padding:20px"
            ScrollBars="Auto">
            This is static content in the panel.
            <br />This sentence is here to see the effect of changing
            the padding values. Padding values can be specified in terms of
            pixels (px), centimeters (cm), or percentage of the panel's
            width (%).
            <p />          <p />
        </asp:Panel>

        <table>
            <tr>
                <td>
                    Number of Labels:
                </td>
                <td>
                    <asp:DropDownList id=ddlLabels runat="server">
                        <asp:ListItem text="0" value="0" />
                        <asp:ListItem text="1" value="1" />
                        <asp:ListItem text="2" value="2" />
                        <asp:ListItem text="3" value="3" />
                        <asp:ListItem text="4" value="4" />
                    </asp:DropDownList>
                </td>
            </tr>
            <tr>
                <td>
                    Number of TextBoxes:
                </td>
                <td>
                    <asp:DropDownList id=ddlBoxes runat="server">
```

Example 4-34. default.aspx for PanelDemo (continued)

```
            <asp:ListItem text="0" value="0" />
            <asp:ListItem text="1" value="1" />
            <asp:ListItem text="2" value="2" />
            <asp:ListItem text="3" value="3" />
            <asp:ListItem text="4" value="4" />
        </asp:DropDownList>
    </td>
</tr>
<tr>
    <td colspan=2>
         
    </td>
</tr>
<tr>
    <td>
        <asp:CheckBox id="chkHide" runat="server"
                    text="Hide Panel" />
    </td>
    <td>
        <asp:Button ID="Button1" runat="server"
            text="Refresh Panel" />
    </td>
</tr>
</table>

<hr/>
<h2>ScrollBars and Wrapping</h2>

<asp:Panel ID="pnlScroll" runat="server"
            Height="200px"
            Width="90%"
            GroupingText="ScrollBars & Wrap">
    <asp:Label ID="lblPanelContent" runat="server"></asp:Label>
</asp:Panel>
    <br />
<table >
    <tr>
        <td align=right>
            ScrollBars:
        </td>
        <td>
            <asp:DropDownList id=ddlScrollBars runat="server"
                        AutoPostback=true
                        OnSelectedIndexChanged=
                            "ddlScrollBars_SelectedIndexChanged">
            <asp:ListItem text="None"  Selected=True/>
            <asp:ListItem text="Auto" />
            <asp:ListItem text="Both" />
            <asp:ListItem text="Horizontal" />
            <asp:ListItem text="Vertical" />
        </asp:DropDownList>
    </td>
```

Example 4-34. default.aspx for PanelDemo (continued)

```
              <td align=right width=75>
                Wrap:
              </td>
              <td>
                <asp:RadioButtonList ID="rblWrap" runat="server"
                                     AutoPostBack=true
                                     RepeatDirection=Horizontal
                                     OnSelectedIndexChanged=
                                        "rblWrap_SelectedIndexChanged">
                    <asp:ListItem Text="True" Value="true" Selected=True/>
                    <asp:ListItem Text="False" Value="false" />
                </asp:RadioButtonList>
              </td>
            </tr>
        </table>
      </div>
      </form>
  </body>
  </html>
```

This first panel has several attributes defined, including BackColor, Height (in pixels), Width (in percentage of the browser window), the font name (Font-Name), and the horizontal alignment (HorizontalAlign). (Note that this control does not have a property for vertical alignment.)

The Style attribute sets the padding to 20 pixels along each of the four sides. Alternatively, you can specify the padding along each side by including multiple values in the Style attribute, according to Table 4-17. So, for example, the following attribute would set the top, right, bottom, and left padding values to 20, 40, 60, and 20 pixels, respectively.

```
Style="padding:20px 40px 60px 20px"
```

The padding shortcuts from Table 4-17 work equivalently in Style attributes setting the border and margin values as well.

Table 4-17. Effect of multiple Padding values

Number of values	Effect
1	All four sides
2	First value sets top and bottom, second value sets left and right
3	First value sets top, second sets left and right, third sets bottom
4	First value sets top, second sets right, third sets bottom, fourth sets left

The Scrollbars attribute is set to Auto, which causes a horizontal or vertical scrollbar, or both, to be present only if necessary. Since the Wrap property is true by default, the static text will wrap within the space available; hence this first panel control will never require a horizontal scrollbar. However, as you add enough labels and/or text boxes to the panel, a vertical scrollbar will appear as necessary.

The value for the `Height` attribute is an integer representing the number of pixels. The `px` as part of the value is optional but does serve to self-document. For example, the following two lines are equivalent:

```
Height="250px"
Height="250"
```

Alternatively, the `Height` can be expressed as a percentage, if it is contained within a fixed-size container, such as another `Panel` control. If it is not within a fixed-size container and it has no content, the panel will only be a single line high, no matter what percentage value is used.

If the `Height` attribute is missing, then the `Panel` control automatically sizes itself vertically to contain all of its children controls.

The `Width` attribute can be either an integer number of pixels or a percentage of the browser window. The latter is shown in this example. If the `Width` attribute is missing, the `Panel` control will default to a width of 100 percent.

Two static HTML tables are defined in PanelDemo to lay out the controls that will control the two panels. The first table, associated with the first panel control, contains two `DropDownList` controls, a `CheckBox` control, and a `Button` control.

None of the controls in the table associated with the first panel have its `AutoPostBack` property set. Therefore, to see any of the changes take effect, you need to click the button, which posts the form. When the form is posted, the `Page_Load` method, contained in Example 4-35, is run.

Example 4-35. Default.aspx.cs for PanelDemo

```
using System;
using System.Data;
using System.Configuration;
using System.Web;
using System.Web.Security;
using System.Web.UI;
using System.Web.UI.WebControls;
using System.Web.UI.WebControls.WebParts;
using System.Web.UI.HtmlControls;

public partial class _Default : System.Web.UI.Page
{
    protected void Page_Load(object sender, EventArgs e)
    {
        // First do the panel w/ the dynamically generated controls
        // Show/Hide Panel Contents
        if (chkHide.Checked)
        {
            pnlDynamic.Visible = false;
```

Example 4-35. Default.aspx.cs for PanelDemo (continued)

```
        }
        else
        {
            pnlDynamic.Visible = true;
        }

        // Generate label controls
        int numlabels = Int32.Parse(ddlLabels.SelectedItem.Value);
        for (int i = 1; i <= numlabels; i++)
        {
            Label lbl = new Label();
            lbl.Text = "Label" + (i).ToString();
            lbl.ID = "Label" + (i).ToString();
            pnlDynamic.Controls.Add(lbl);
            pnlDynamic.Controls.Add(new LiteralControl("<br />"));
        }

        // Generate textbox controls
        int numBoxes = Int32.Parse(ddlBoxes.SelectedItem.Value);
        for (int i = 1; i <= numBoxes; i++)
        {
            TextBox txt = new TextBox();
            txt.Text = "TextBox" + (i).ToString();
            txt.ID = "TextBox" + (i).ToString();
            pnlDynamic.Controls.Add(txt);
            pnlDynamic.Controls.Add(new LiteralControl("<br />"));
        }

        // Next take care of the Scrollbar panel.
        string strText = "<p>Four score and seven years ago our fathers brought forth, upon
this continent, a new nation, conceived in liberty, and dedicated to the proposition that
\"all men are created equal.\"</p>";
        strText += "<p>Now we are engaged in a great civil war, testing whether that nation,
or any nation so conceived, and so dedicated, can long endure. We are met on a great
battle field of that war. We have come to dedicate a portion of it, as a final resting
place for those who died here, that the nation might live. This we may, in all propriety
do. But, in a larger sense, we can not dedicate -- we can not consecrate -- we can not
hallow, this ground -- The brave men, living and dead, who struggled here, have hallowed
it, far above our poor power to add or detract. The world will little note, nor long
remember what we say here; while it can never forget what they did here.</p>";
        strText += "<p>It is rather for us, the living, we here be dedicated to the great
task remaining before us -- that, from these honored dead we take increased devotion to
that cause for which they here, gave the last full measure of devotion -- that we here
highly resolve these dead shall not have died in vain; that the nation, shall have a new
birth of freedom, and that government of the people by the people for the people, shall
not perish from the earth.</p>";

        lblPanelContent.Text = strText;
    }

    protected void ddlScrollBars_SelectedIndexChanged(object sender,
                                                         EventArgs e)
```

Example 4-35. Default.aspx.cs for PanelDemo (continued)

```
    {
        DropDownList ddl= (DropDownList)sender;
        string strValue = ddl.SelectedValue;


        ScrollBars scrollBar =
            (ScrollBars)Enum.Parse(typeof(ScrollBars), strValue);
        pnlScroll.ScrollBars = scrollBar;
    }

    protected void rblWrap_SelectedIndexChanged(object sender, EventArgs e)
    {
        RadioButtonList rbl = (RadioButtonList)sender;
        pnlScroll.Wrap = Convert.ToBoolean(rbl.SelectedValue);
    }
}
```

The first half of the Page_Load method takes care of the first panel control, and the second half deals with the second panel control. Still focusing on the first panel, an if-else block turns on or off the visibility of the panel. When the panel is not visible, it contents are not visible either. Likewise, when the panel is visible, all of its contents are visible.

There are two for loops, one each for labels and text boxes, which generate the contained controls. After converting the entry in the appropriate DropDownList control to an integer, the for loop iterates through the procedure the specified number of times.

The procedure is similar in each of the two cases. A new control is instantiated, then the Text and ID properties are assigned. The control is added to the Controls collection of the panel, and finally a LiteralControl containing some HTML is added to the collection as well.

The font name specified inside the Panel tags affected the static text and labels in the panel but not the contents of the text boxes.

The second panel, pnlScroll, has only three attributes declared (other than ID and runat): Height, Width, and GroupingText. The first two were described previously. GroupingText has the effect of putting a border around the panel with the string value of the GroupingText property as a caption within the border.

In this panel, the only content is a Label control, lblPanelContent. The Text property of lblPanelContent is set in the Page_Load method to the rather lengthy text string contained in the variable strText. This text string contains some HTML paragraph elements to force line breaks.

The two controls associated with this panel are a drop-down list setting the value of the Scrollbars property, and a radio button list setting the Wrap property. AutoPostback is set to true for both of these, so no further user action is required to see them take effect.

In the event handler for the SelectedIndexChanged event of the drop-down list, ddlScrollBars_SelectedIndexChanged, highlighted in Example 4-35, the Scrollbars property of the panel is set. The technique of setting the value from the ScrollBars enumeration is exactly as described previously in Example 4-31 for the BulletedListDemo example.

In the event handler method for the SelectedIndexChanged event of the radio button list, also highlighted in Example 4-35, a reference to the radio button list is obtained by casting sender to a variable of type RadioButtonList. Then the Wrap property of pnlScroll is set appropriately by converting the SelectedValue of the control to a Boolean.

If the text string in strText did not have any HTML tags in it, then it would display a single, very long line if Wrap is set to false. As it is, with each "line" enclosed in the paragraph tags, when Wrap is set to false, it displays as three separate lines.

Images

Images are an important aspect of most web sites. ASP.NET provides several ASP.NET server controls for displaying images. Two of them, the Image and the ImageMap controls, are covered in this section. The AdRotator control will be covered in the next chapter.

Image Control

The Image control has limited functionality: it is used for displaying an image on a web page or, alternatively, displaying some text if the image is unavailable. It raises no events for user interaction, other than those inherited from Control, such as Init and Load. If you need to have button functionality (i.e., to capture mouse clicks), you should use the ImageButton control, described earlier in this chapter.

In addition to the properties inherited from the WebControl class, the Image control has the properties shown in Table 4-18.

Table 4-18. Properties of the Image control

Name	Type	Get	Set	Values	Description
AlternateText	String	x	x		The text displayed in the control if the image is unavailable. In browsers that support the ToolTips feature, this text is also displayed as a ToolTip.
ImageAlign	ImageAlign	x	x	See Table 4-19.	Alignment options relative to the text of the web page. See Table 4-19.
ImageUrl	String	x	x		The URL pointing to the location of an image to display.

The `ImageUrl` property can be either *relative* or *absolute*, as described fully in the sidebar "File Locations" in the section "Button Controls."

There are ten possible values for the `ImageAlign` property, as shown in Table 4-19. If you need better control of image and text placement, you will probably want to put the Image control in a table.

Table 4-19. Members of the ImageAlign enumeration

Values	Description
NotSet	Not set. This is the default value.
AbsBottom	Aligns the lower edge of the image with the lower edge of the largest element on the same line.
AbsMiddle	Aligns the middle of the image with the middle of the largest element on the same line.
Top	Aligns the upper edge of the image with the upper edge of the highest element on the same line.
Bottom	Aligns the lower edge of the image with the lower edge of the first line of text. Same as `Baseline`.
Baseline	Aligns the lower edge of the image with the lower edge of the first line of text. Same as `Bottom`.
Middle	Aligns the middle of the image with the lower edge of the first line of text.
TextTop	Aligns the upper edge of the image with the upper edge of the highest text on the same line.
Left	Aligns the image on the left edge of the page with text wrapping on the right.
Right	Aligns the image on the right edge of the page with the text wrapping on the left.

In Example 4-36, ImageDemo, shown in Figure 4-21, you will see how the various ImageAlign values affect the appearance of a web page. The code-behind for this example is listed in Example 4-37.

Example 4-36. default.aspx for ImageDemo

```
<%@ Page Language="C#" AutoEventWireup="true"  CodeFile="Default.aspx.cs"
        Inherits="_Default" %>

<!DOCTYPE html PUBLIC "-//W3C//DTD XHTML 1.1//EN"
    "http://www.w3.org/TR/xhtml11/DTD/xhtml11.dtd">

<html xmlns="http://www.w3.org/1999/xhtml" >
<head runat="server">
    <title>Image Control</title>
</head>
<body>
    <form id="form1" runat="server">
    <div>
        <h1>Image Control</h1>

        <font name="Garamond" size ="4">
        This is a sample paragraph which is being used
        to demonstrate the effects of various values
        of ImageAlign. As you will see, the effects
        are sometimes difficult to pin down, and vary
        depending on the width of the browser window.
        </font>
```

Example 4-36. default.aspx for ImageDemo (continued)

```
    <asp:Image ID="img1" runat="server"
            AlternateText="Dan"
            ImageUrl="Dan at vernal pool.jpg" />
    <hr />
    <asp:Button runat="server" Text="Sample Button" />
    <asp:Image ID="img2" runat="server"
            AlternateText="Dan" ImageUrl="Dan at Vernal pool.jpg" />
    <hr />
    <asp:DropDownList ID="ddl" runat="server" AutoPostBack="True">
        <asp:ListItem text="NotSet" />
        <asp:ListItem text="AbsBottom" />
        <asp:ListItem text="AbsMiddle" />
        <asp:ListItem text="Top" />
        <asp:ListItem text="Bottom" />
        <asp:ListItem text="BaseLine" />
        <asp:ListItem text="TextTop" />
        <asp:ListItem text="Left" />
        <asp:ListItem text="Right" />
    </asp:DropDownList>
    </div>
    </form>
</body>
</html>
```

Image Control

This is a sample paragraph which is being used to demonstrate the effects of various values of ImageAlign. As you will see, the effects are sometimes difficult to pin down, and vary depending on

the width of the browser window.

Sample Button

NotSet

Figure 4-21. ImageDemo

Example 4-37. default.aspx.cs for ImageDemo

```
using System;
using System.Data;
using System.Configuration;
using System.Web;
using System.Web.Security;
using System.Web.UI;
```

Example 4-37. default.aspx.cs for ImageDemo (continued)

```
using System.Web.UI.WebControls;
using System.Web.UI.WebControls.WebParts;
using System.Web.UI.HtmlControls;

public partial class _Default : System.Web.UI.Page
{
    protected void Page_Load(object sender, EventArgs e)
    {
        switch (ddl.SelectedIndex)
        {
            case 0:
                img1.ImageAlign = ImageAlign.NotSet;
                img2.ImageAlign = ImageAlign.NotSet;
                break;
            case 1:
                img1.ImageAlign = ImageAlign.AbsBottom;
                img2.ImageAlign = ImageAlign.AbsBottom;
                break;
            case 2:
                img1.ImageAlign = ImageAlign.AbsMiddle;
                img2.ImageAlign = ImageAlign.AbsMiddle;
                break;
            case 3:
                img1.ImageAlign = ImageAlign.Top;
                img2.ImageAlign = ImageAlign.Top;
                break;
            case 4:
                img1.ImageAlign = ImageAlign.Bottom;
                img2.ImageAlign = ImageAlign.Bottom;
                break;
            case 5:
                img1.ImageAlign = ImageAlign.Baseline;
                img2.ImageAlign = ImageAlign.Baseline;
                break;
            case 6:
                img1.ImageAlign = ImageAlign.Middle;
                img2.ImageAlign = ImageAlign.Middle;
                break;
            case 7:
                img1.ImageAlign = ImageAlign.TextTop;
                img2.ImageAlign = ImageAlign.TextTop;
                break;
            case 8:
                img1.ImageAlign = ImageAlign.Left;
                img2.ImageAlign = ImageAlign.Left;
                break;
            case 9:
                img1.ImageAlign = ImageAlign.Right;
                img2.ImageAlign = ImageAlign.Right;
                break;
            default:
                img1.ImageAlign = ImageAlign.NotSet;
```

Example 4-37. default.aspx.cs for ImageDemo (continued)

```
            img2.ImageAlign = ImageAlign.NotSet;
            break;
        }
    }
}
```

 For the code in ImageDemo to work correctly, you will need an image file for the `ImageUrl`. These examples use *Dan at vernal pool.jpg*, located in the web site directory. You can use any image file you want.

ImageMap Control

HTML provides the <map> element to implement images with multiple hyperlinks. These are known as *image maps*. The `ImageMap` server control provides this functionality in ASP.NET.

The `ImageMap` control derives from the `Image` class, and adds a number of properties and a single event, `Click`, to that class to provide the image map functionality. These properties are listed in Table 4-20.

Table 4-20. Properties of the ImageMap control

Name	Type	Get	Set	Values	Description
AlternateText	String	✗	✗		The text will be displayed in the control if the image is unavailable. In browsers that support the ToolTips feature, this text is also displayed as a ToolTip.
GenerateEmptyAlternateText	Boolean	✗	✗	true, false	If `true`, forces an empty `alt` attribute in the rendered HTML even if the `AlternateText` property is empty ("") or not specified. The default is `false`. This property is provided to support the web pages compatible with assistive technology devices, such as screen readers.

Table 4-20. Properties of the ImageMap control (continued)

Name	Type	Get	Set	Values	Description
HotSpotMode	HotSpotMode	✗	✗	Inactive, Navigate, NotSet, PostBack	Specifies the default hotspot mode, or action taken when a hotspot is clicked, for the control. Individual hotspots may specify different modes. Navigate immediately navigates to the URL specified by the NavigateUrl property, while PostBack causes a postback to the server.
HotSpots	HotSpotCollection	✗			A collection of HotSpot objects contained by the ImageMap control.

Each ImageMap control contains a collection of HotSpots: clickable regions of the image corresponding to HTML <area> tags within the image map. HotSpots will either raise a Click event on the server, if the HotSpotMode is set to PostBack, or will immediately navigate to the URL specified by the NavigateUrl property, if the HotSpotMode is set to Navigate.

There are three types of hotspots:

RectangleHotSpot
> Defines a rectangular region of the image with Top, Bottom, Left, and Right properties, all in pixels relative to the upper-left corner of the image.

CircleHotSpot
> Defines a circular region of the image with X and Y properties specifying the center of the circle, in pixels relative to the upper-left corner of the image, and the Radius property, specifying the radius of the circle in pixels.

PolygonHotSpot
> Defines a many-sided region of the image with a comma-separated list of X and Y coordinates of endpoints of line segments outlining the region, in pixels relative to the upper left corner of the image.

All of the HotSpot objects have in common the properties listed in Table 4-21.

Table 4-21. Properties of the HotSpot object

Name	Type	Get	Set	Values	Description
AlternateText	String	✗	✗		The text displayed in the control if the image is unavailable. In browsers that support the ToolTips feature, this text is also displayed as a ToolTip.
HotSpotMode	HotSpotMode	✗	✗	Inactive, Navigate, NotSet, PostBack	Specifies the default hotspot mode, or action taken when a hotspot is clicked, for the control. Individual hotspots may specify different modes. Navigate immediately navigates to the URL specified by the NavigateUrl property, while PostBack causes a postback to the server.
NavigateUrl	String	✗	✗		Specifies the URL to navigate to when a hotspot with a HotSpotMode set to Navigate is clicked. Allows either relative or absolute references, as described in the sidebar, "File Locations" in the section, "Button Controls".
PostBackValue	String	✗	✗		The value of the clicked HotSpot object passed by the ImageMapEventArgs event argument. Only relevant if the HotSpotMode is set to PostBack.
Target	String	✗	✗		Specifies the browser window in which the target page will be displayed. The values of the Target property are the same as those listed in Table 4-3 for the HyperLink control. Only relevant if the HotSpotMode is set to Navigate.

All of these properties and the Click event are demonstrated in the next example, ImageMapDemo. This web page is shown in Figure 4-22 after the Yes hotspot has been clicked. This example has two image maps. The one at the top of the page contains three rectangular hotspots and a circular hotspot. The second image map has three polygonal hotspots defined: one above the band, one below, and the band itself.

The content file for this example is shown in Example 4-38 and the code-behind file is shown in Example 4-39. The only code of interest in the latter is the event handler method, imgmapYesNoMaybe_Click (highlighted), which is executed whenever a hotspot with a HotSpotMode set to PostBack is clicked.

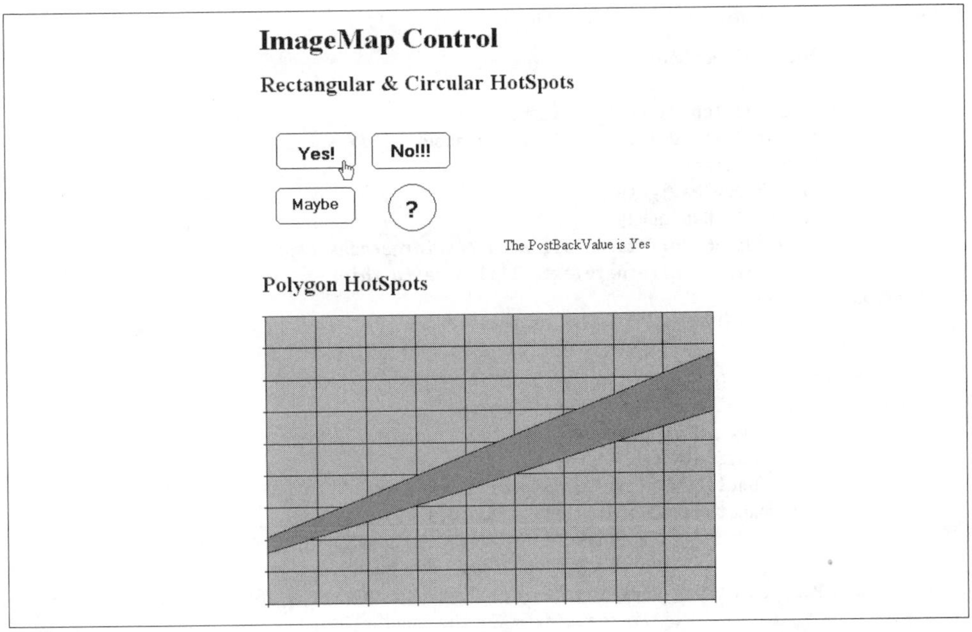

Figure 4-22. ImageMapDemo

Example 4-38. default.aspx for ImageMapDemo

```
<%@ Page Language="C#" AutoEventWireup="true"  CodeFile="Default.aspx.cs"
        Inherits="_Default" %>

<!DOCTYPE html PUBLIC "-//W3C//DTD XHTML 1.1//EN"
   "http://www.w3.org/TR/xhtml11/DTD/xhtml11.dtd">

<html xmlns="http://www.w3.org/1999/xhtml" >
<head runat="server">
   <title>ImageMapDemo</title>
</head>
<body>
   <form id="form1" runat="server">
   <div>
      <h1>ImageMap Control</h1>
      <h2>Rectangular &amp; Circular HotSpots</h2>
      <asp:ImageMap ID="imgmapYesNoMaybe" runat="server"
         ImageUrl="YesNoMaybe.gif"
         HotSpotMode="Postback" OnClick="imgmapYesNoMaybe_Click">
         <asp:RectangleHotSpot
           PostBackValue="Yes"
           Bottom="60" Top="21" Left="17" Right="103"
           AlternateText="Damn right" />
         <asp:RectangleHotSpot
           HotSpotMode=PostBack
           PostBackValue="No"
           Bottom=60 Top=21 Left=122 Right=208
           AlternateText="Hell no"/>
```

Example 4-38. default.aspx for ImageMapDemo (continued)

```
            <asp:RectangleHotSpot
               PostBackValue="Maybe"
               Bottom=122 Top=83 Left=16 Right=101
               AlternateText="Well..., I'll think about it"/>
            <asp:CircleHotSpot
               HotSpotMode="Navigate"
               X=165 Y=106 Radius=25
               NavigateUrl=http://localhost/websites/targetpage.aspx
               Target=_blank  AlternateText="I'll have to think about it."/>
         </asp:ImageMap>
         <asp:Label ID="lblMessage" runat="server" />

         <h2>Polygon HotSpots</h2>
         <asp:ImageMap ID="imgmapPlot" runat="server"
                    ImageUrl="plot.gif"
                    HotSpotMode="PostBack"
                    OnClick="imgmapYesNoMaybe_Click">
            <asp:PolygonHotSpot Coordinates="4,245,4,3,495,3,495,45,"
                             AlternateText="Above the band"
                             PostBackValue="Above the band" />
            <asp:PolygonHotSpot Coordinates="4,245,495,45,495,112,3,264"
                             AlternateText="In the band"
                             PostBackValue="In the band" />
            <asp:PolygonHotSpot Coordinates="495,45,495,112,495,320,4,320"
                             AlternateText="Below the band"
                             PostBackValue="Below the band" />
         </asp:ImageMap>
      </div>
      </form>
</body>
</html>
```

Example 4-39. default.aspx.cs for ImageMapDemo

```
using System;
using System.Data;
using System.Configuration;
using System.Web;
using System.Web.Security;
using System.Web.UI;
using System.Web.UI.WebControls;
using System.Web.UI.WebControls.WebParts;
using System.Web.UI.HtmlControls;

public partial class _Default : System.Web.UI.Page
{
    protected void Page_Load(object sender, EventArgs e)
    {
    }
    protected void imgmapYesNoMaybe_Click(object sender,
                                    ImageMapEventArgs e)
```

Example 4-39. default.aspx.cs for ImageMapDemo (continued)

```
    {
        lblMessage.Text = "The PostBackValue is " + e.PostBackValue;
    }
}
```

In the declaration of the first image map, imgMapYesNoMaybe, an image file is specified, *YesNoMaybe.gif*, which is located in the same directory as the page itself. Alternatively, a relative directory path could be specified, such as:

```
ImageUrl="images\YesNoMaybe.gif"
```

or an absolute directory path, such as:

```
ImageUrl="c:\websites\images\YesNoMaybe.gif"
```

or an Internet or intranet location, such as the following:

```
ImageUrl="HTTP://www.SomeWebSite.com/images/YesNoMaybe.gif"
```

The default HotSpotMode for this image map is set to PostBack. The Yes and Maybe hotspots assumes this value, the No hotspot explicitly specifies the same value, and the question mark hotspot uses a different HotSpotMode of Navigate. In this latter case, the NavigateUrl and Target properties provide direction as to where and how to navigate. For the postback hotspots, the OnClick attribute of the image map hooks the Click event to the imgmapYesNoMaybe_Click method contained in the code-behind file, shown highlighted in Example 4-39.

The second image map, imgmapPlot, defines three irregularly shaped hotspots, defined by a set of X,Y coordinates. In this example, the hotspots are simple, with only four straight sides each. In a more typical usage, say a map of the United States with each state defined as a hotspot, you might have many dozens of nodes specified. The more nodes, the finer and more accurate the hotspot. However, don't go too crazy trying to make the outline perfect because most users click near the middle of the hotspot, and if they are too close to the edge of the region and get the adjoining region by mistake, they will just hit the Back button and try again a little more carefully.

The Click event argument is of type ImageMapEventArgs. It exposes a single public property. PostBackValue. This corresponds to the HotSpot property of the same name declared with each HotSpot in the example. This property is retrieved in the Click event handler in Example 4-39 and used to populate the Text property of the Label control on the page.

CHAPTER 5

Advanced Controls

In previous chapters, you've seen the standard ASP.NET server controls that provide functionality that is more or less analogous to traditional HTML controls. In addition, however, ASP.NET provides a number of controls that provide a much richer level of functionality. These richer controls include, among others:

MultiView and View
> Work together to create a navigable series of page sections.

Wizard
> Creates the familiar set of dialogs used for walking through a well-defined set of steps to accomplish some task.

FileUpload
> Provides a file browser for selecting a file to upload, and the infrastructure for doing so.

AdRotator
> Presents an image randomly selected from a list every time the page reloads.

Calendar
> A fully featured control for displaying and picking dates.

All of these controls will be covered in this chapter. In addition, ASP.NET includes various specialized rich controls, providing functionality such as validation, data access and display, security and log on, personalization, and navigation. Each of these topics have their own chapter in the book.

MultiView and View Controls

Sometimes you might want to break a web page into different chunks, displaying only a single chunk at a time, with easy navigation from chunk to chunk. The classic use of this technique would be to step a user through a number of process steps within the context of a static page, such as the checkout procedure from an online store or the procedure to transfer funds from one account to another. You might also use these controls to create wizard-like applications, although there is now a Wizard control, described shortly, for this exact purpose.

ASP.NET provides the View control to manage the chunks—i.e., the content in a section of the page: one View control per chunk. All of the View objects are contained together within a MultiView object, which makes one View object, called the active view, visible at a time.

As seen in Figure 3-4a both the View and Multiview controls derive not from Web-Control, but directly from System.Web.UI.Control.

The MultiView control has a read-only property called Views, of type ViewCollection, which is a collection of the View controls contained within the MultiView. As with all .NET collections, the elements in the collection are indexed. Hence, the MultiView control has a property called ActiveViewIndex, which gets or sets the zero-based index of the currently active view. If no view is active, then ActiveViewIndex will be 1, which is the default value.

The MultiView control has four properties, listed in Table 5-1, that correspond to the four CommandName attributes which you can assign to buttons for automated navigation of the views.

Table 5-1. MultiView CommandNames

Field	Default CommandName	Description
NextViewCommandName	NextView	Navigates to the next higher ActiveViewIndex. If currently at the last view, sets ActiveViewIndex to -1 and nothing is displayed.
PreviousViewCommandName	PrevView	Navigates to the next lower ActiveViewIndex. If currently at the first view, sets ActiveViewIndex to -1 and nothing is displayed.
SwitchViewByIDCommandName	SwitchViewByID	Navigates to the View with the ID specified. Can use the CommandArgument attribute to specify the ID.
SwitchViewByIndexCommandName	SwitchViewByIndex	Navigates to the View with the index specified. Can use the CommandArgument attribute to specify the index.

For example, a Button, ImageButton, or LinkButton with the CommandName NextView will automatically navigate the MultiView control to the next View when that button is clicked, with no additional code required. The developer (that's you) does not have to write a Click event handler for the button.

You can also set or retrieve the active view by calling the SetActiveView or GetActiveView methods of the MultiView control. SetActiveView takes a reference to a View object as an argument, and GetActiveView returns a reference to a View object.

 An important point to remember is that all the controls on all the Views, even those Views not currently visible, are available to the app and server-side processing. Not only are they available to code, but they participate in View state and are part of the Controls collection of the page.

Every time a view is changed, the page is posted back to the server and a number of events are raised by both the MultiView and the View controls.

Whenever the active view changes, the ActiveViewChanged event is raised by the MultiView control. At the same time, the ViewControl that is now active raises the Activate event, and the ViewControl that is now inactive raises the Deactivate event.

All of these events have an event argument of type EventArgs, which you will remember is a placeholder and provides no additional information about the event. However, as with all event handlers, a reference to the sender is passed to the event handler as will be demonstrated.

The View control has a Visible property of type Boolean, which can be set to control the visibility of specific View objects or retrieved to determine programmatically which View is visible.

Neither the MultiView nor the View controls have any style properties. That is not too surprising for the MultiView, since it is just a container for the Views. In the case of the View control, if you want to impose style properties, you must apply them to each of the controls contained within the View. Another technique would be to embed a Panel control in the View and set the style properties of the Panel.

The following example, *MultiViewDemo*, demonstrates many of the features of the MultiView and View controls. The web page, after some navigation has occurred, is shown in Figure 5-1.

Figure 5-1. MultiViewDemo

MultiViewDemo, shown in Design view in Figure 5-2, consists of a single web page with a MultiView control, MultiView1. MultiView1 contains four View controls (vwFirst, vwSecond, vwThird, and vwLast), along with other controls for navigating the MultiView. The page also contains controls for displaying data from and about the MultiView and its contained Views.

Each of the four Views contain buttons for navigation. In addition, the first two Views contain a TextBox for demonstrating how controls on a View are accessible to the application even when that View is not visible.

To create this example, create a new web site in VS2005 called *MultiViewDemo*. The complete content file for this example is listed in Example 5-1, with the MultiView and View controls highlighted. We will look first at the MultiView and View controls in this source file and then look at the other controls on the page.

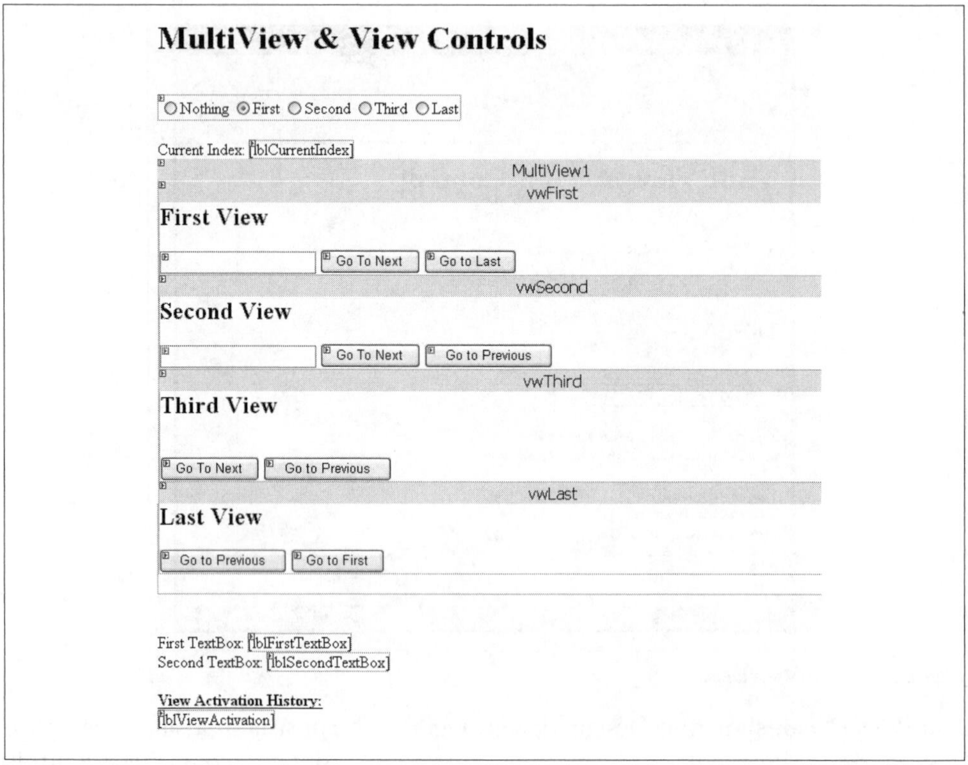

Figure 5-2. MultiViewDemo in Design view

Example 5-1. Default.aspx for MultiViewDemo

```
<%@ Page Language="C#" AutoEventWireup="true"  CodeFile="Default.aspx.cs"
    Inherits="_Default" %>

<!DOCTYPE html PUBLIC "-//W3C//DTD XHTML 1.1//EN"
    "http://www.w3.org/TR/xhtml11/DTD/xhtml11.dtd">

<html xmlns="http://www.w3.org/1999/xhtml" >
<head runat="server">
    <title>MultiView & View Controls</title>
</head>
<body>
    <form id="form1" runat="server">
    <div>
        <h1>MultiView & View Controls</h1>
        <br />
            <asp:RadioButtonList ID="rblView" runat="server"
                    AutoPostBack="True"
                    OnSelectedIndexChanged="rblView_SelectedIndexChanged"
                    RepeatDirection="Horizontal" >
                <asp:ListItem Value="-1">Nothing</asp:ListItem>
                <asp:ListItem Selected="True" Value="0">First</asp:ListItem>
```

Example 5-1. Default.aspx for MultiViewDemo (continued)

```
            <asp:ListItem Value="1">Second</asp:ListItem>
            <asp:ListItem Value="2">Third</asp:ListItem>
            <asp:ListItem Value="3">Last</asp:ListItem>
    </asp:RadioButtonList>
    <br />
    Current Index:
    <asp:Label ID="lblCurrentIndex" runat="server"></asp:Label>
    <br/>
    <asp:MultiView ID="MultiView1" runat="server"
        ActiveViewIndex="0"
        OnActiveViewChanged="MultiView1_ActiveViewChanged">
        <asp:View ID="vwFirst" runat="server"
            OnActivate="ActivateView"
            OnDeactivate="DeactivateView">
            <h2>First View</h2>
            <asp:TextBox ID="txtFirstView" runat="server" />
            <asp:Button ID="btnNext1" runat="server"
                CommandName="NextView"
                Text="Go To Next" />
            <asp:Button ID="btnLast" runat="server"
                CommandName="SwitchViewByID"
                CommandArgument="vwLast"
                Text="Go to Last" />
        </asp:View>
        <asp:View ID="vwSecond" runat="server"
            OnActivate="ActivateView"
            OnDeactivate="DeactivateView">
            <h2>Second View</h2>
            <asp:TextBox ID="txtSecondView" runat="server" />
            <asp:Button ID="btnNext2" runat="server"
                CommandName="NextView"
                Text="Go To Next" />
            <asp:Button ID="btnPrevious2" runat="server"
                CommandName="PrevView"
                Text="Go to Previous" />
        </asp:View>
        <asp:View ID="vwThird" runat="server"
            OnActivate="ActivateView"
            OnDeactivate="DeactivateView">
            <h2>Third View</h2>
            <br />
            <asp:Button ID="btnNext3" runat="server"
                CommandName="NextView"
                Text="Go To Next" />
            <asp:Button ID="btnPrevious3" runat="server"
                CommandName="PrevView"
                Text="Go to Previous" />
        </asp:View>
        <asp:View ID="vwLast" runat="server"
            OnActivate="ActivateView"
            OnDeactivate="DeactivateView">
            <h2>Last View</h2>
```

Example 5-1. Default.aspx for MultiViewDemo (continued)

```
                <asp:Button ID="btnPrevious4" runat="server"
                    CommandName="PrevView"
                    Text="Go to Previous" />
                <asp:Button ID="btnFirst" runat="server"
                    CommandArgument="0"
                    CommandName="SwitchViewByIndex"
                    Text="Go to First" />
            </asp:View>
        </asp:MultiView>
    <br />
    <br />
    First TextBox:
    <asp:Label ID="lblFirstTextBox" runat="server" />
    <br />
    Second TextBox:
    <asp:Label ID="lblSecondTextBox" runat="server" />
    <br />
    <br />
    <strong><span style="text-decoration: underline">
        View Activation History:
    </span></strong>
    <br />
    <asp:Label ID="lblViewActivation" runat="server" />
    </div>
    </form>
</body>
</html>
```

The MultiView control highlighted in Example 5-1 is declared with a MultiView1 ID. The ActiveViewIndex attribute is set to 0, so the first view in the Views collection will display. If this property is not set, it will default to -1 and none of the Views will display.

The OnActiveViewChanged attribute points to an event handler method in the code-behind file, MultiView1_ActiveViewChanged (listed in Example 5-2), which will fire every time the active index changes.

Example 5-2. ActiveViewChanged event handler for MultiViewDemo

```
protected void MultiView1_ActiveViewChanged(object sender, EventArgs e)
{
    lblFirstTextBox.Text = txtFirstView.Text;
    lblSecondTextBox.Text = txtSecondView.Text;
    rblView.SelectedIndex = MultiView1.ActiveViewIndex + 1;
}
```

This event handler does two things: it retrieves the values of the two textboxes on the first two Views and displays them on the page in the labels that were placed there for that purpose. Second, it sets the `RadioButtonList` at the top of the page, `rblView`, to the proper value. This code is relatively straightforward because the `RadioButtonList.SelectedIndex` and the `MultiView.ActiveViewIndex` properties are of type integer, however you must compensate for the fact that the lowest value of the `ActiveViewIndex` property is `-1`, while the lowest index of the `RadioButtonList` is 0. That is, they are offset by one.

There are four `View` instances declared: `vwFirst`, `vwSecond`, `vwThird`, and `vwLast`. Each has both `OnActivate` and `OnDeactivate` event handlers declared:

```
OnActivate="ActivateView"
OnDeactivate="DeactivateView">
```

The Activate event is handled by a method called `ActivateView` and the Deactivate event by `DeactivateView`. Those two event handlers are listed in Example 5-3. They retrieve the contents of the `Label` holding the activation history, append the ID and action of the current `View`, and assign the string back to the `Label`.

Example 5-3. Activate and Deactivate event handlers

```
protected void ActivateView(object sender, EventArgs e)
{
    string str = lblViewActivation.Text;
    View v = (View)sender;
    str += "View " + v.ID + " activated <br/>";
    lblViewActivation.Text = str;
}

protected void DeactivateView(object sender, EventArgs e)
{
    string str = lblViewActivation.Text;
    View v = (View)sender;
    str += "View " + v.ID + " deactivated <br/>";
    lblViewActivation.Text = str;
}
```

 Because sender is of type object, it must first be cast to type `View` before assigning it to a reference to `View` and obtaining properties of the `View` object such as the ID property.

Each `View` object contains navigation buttons. The .NET Framework makes it particularly easy to set them up. (It's harder to explain in words than to actually do it.) As enumerated in Table 5-1, if a button has its `CommandName` attribute set to one of the default values, the corresponding action will automatically occur. So, the first `View` object, `vwFirst`, will have buttons labeled "Go To Next" and "Go To Last," with `CommandNames` of `NextView` and `SwitchViewByID`, respectively. The first is easy, it just navigates to the next `View`.

The `SwitchByViewID` action requires an ID to switch to, so the `CommandArgument` attribute is used to pass in that argument.

```
CommandName="SwitchViewByID"
CommandArgument="vwLast"
```

Each of the `Views` contains content in addition to navigation buttons. This content includes standard HTML elements and ASP.NET server controls. As you have seen, these server controls are accessible to the application even when their `View` is not displayed.

The next step is to update the `RadioButtonList` at the top of the page. As you have seen, the `SelectedIndex` property is set by the code in `MultiView1_ActiveViewChanged` every time the active view changes. When the `SelectedIndex` changes due to user action, the `SelectedIndexChanged` event is fired, which calls `rblView_SelectedIndexChanged`.

```
OnSelectedIndexChanged="rblView_SelectedIndexChanged"
```

This method, listed in Example 5-4, consists of a single line that sets the `ActiveViewIndex` property of the `MultiView` to the `SelectedValue` of the `RadioButtonList`.

Example 5-4. RadioButtonList SelectedIndexChanged event handler

```
protected void rblView_SelectedIndexChanged(object sender, EventArgs e)
{
    MultiView1.ActiveViewIndex = Convert.ToInt32(rblView.SelectedValue);
}
```

The final bit of interesting code is contained in the event handler for the `PreRender` event of the `Page` (listed in Example 5-5), where `lblCurrentIndex` is populated with the index of the currently active view. This code cannot be run in `Page_Load` because `Page_Load` is called before the label is updated.

 See Chapter 6 for complete coverage of the Page lifecycle.

Example 5-5. Page PreRender event handler

```
protected void Page_PreRender(object sender, EventArgs e)
{
    lblCurrentIndex.Text = MultiView1.ActiveViewIndex.ToString( );
}
```

Now that you've seen how to use the `MultiView` class to create a simple paged application, you can expand it to more complex uses. Sometimes, though, you want a traditional Windows-style wizard on your page. In that case, you can use the `Wizard` control, discussed next.

Wizard Control

Users expect modern applications to provide wizards to walk them through multistep processes. These UIs are distinguished by the use of magic. Sorry, just kidding.

Wizards provide the infrastructure to present the user with successive steps in a process, providing access to all the data collected in all the steps, with easy forward and backward navigation.

Similar to the MultiView control, the Wizard control contains a collection of WizardStep objects. These WizardSteps derive from the View class as can be seen in Figure 5-3, and the relationship between WizardSteps and the Wizard control is analogous to the relation between the View and MultiView.

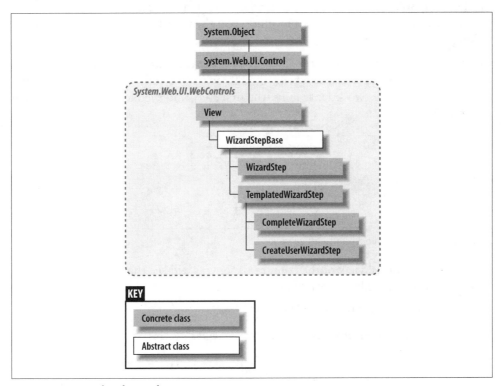

Figure 5-3. View class hierarchy

As with the MultiView control, all the controls on all the WizardSteps are part of the page's control hierarchy and are accessible via code at runtime regardless of which specific WizardStep is currently visible. Every time a user clicks on a navigation button or link, the page posts back to the server. Cross-page posting, described in Chapter 6, is not supported.

The Wizard control takes care of all the plumbing required to implement navigation, both linear (going from one step to the next or back) and non-linear (going from any step to any other step). It automatically creates the appropriate buttons, such as Next, Previous, and Finish (on the very last step). The first step does not have a Previous button, and the last step does not have a Next button. It also makes provisions for steps that can only be navigated to a single time. In addition, by default, the Wizard displays a toolbar with navigation links, enabling the user to go to any step from any other step.

Almost every aspect of the look and feel of the Wizard can be customized with styles and templates. This includes all the various buttons and links, the header and footer, the sidebar, and the WizardSteps.

The best way to explore the Wizard control is to look at an example. In this example, you will create a whimsical wizard to guide you through the steps you follow when waking up in the morning.

Create a new web site called WizardDemo. Drag a Wizard control onto the page. It creates a default two-step wizard, which, though sparse, is fully functional. In Design view, you will see the two sidebar links, the first step, and the Next button, as shown in Figure 5-4.

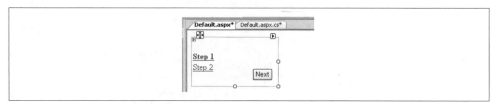

Figure 5-4. The Wizard control in Design view

Looking at the Source view of the content page, you will see that the Wizard declaration looks something like the following:

```
<asp:Wizard ID="Wizard1" runat="server">
   <WizardSteps>
      <asp:WizardStep ID="WizardStep1" runat="server" Title="Step 1">
      </asp:WizardStep>
      <asp:WizardStep ID="WizardStep2" runat="server" Title="Step 2">
      </asp:WizardStep>
   </WizardSteps>
</asp:Wizard>
```

Within the <asp:Wizard> tags are a pair of <WizardSteps> tags. The WizardStep controls are declared within those tags.

If you run this page, you will see the web page shown in Figure 5-5. Since this is the first step, only the Next button is displayed, but the sidebar shows links for both steps.

Figure 5-5. Default Wizard control

Now let's spiff this example up a bit. Click on the content area of the WizardStep and type in some text, for example, an <h2> heading that says "Wake Up," as shown in Figure 5-6.

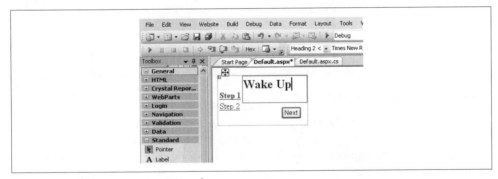

Figure 5-6. Adding content to a Wizard step

Next, click the smart tag of the Wizard control and select Add/Remove WizardSteps. This will bring up the WizardStep Collection Editor, as shown in Figure 5-7. Add five more steps so there are a total of seven. For each (including the first two), enter a value for the Title and for the ID, as listed in Table 5-2.

Table 5-2. WizardSteps for WizardDemo

ID	Title
stpWakeUp	Step 1
stpShower	Step 2
stpTakeMeds	Step 3
stpBrushTeeth	Step 4

Table 5-2. WizardSteps for WizardDemo (continued)

ID	Title
stpGetDressed	Step 5
stpEatBreakfast	Step 6
stpFinish	Step 7

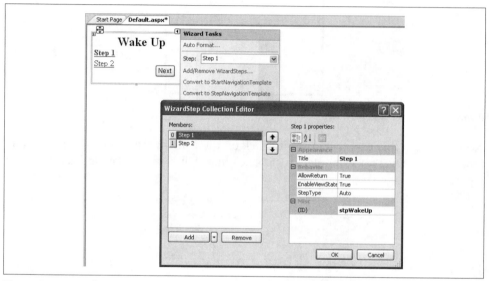

Figure 5-7. WizardStep Collection Editor

Though you can click on the smart tag, select each step in turn and add content to each step as you did above with Step 1; it is easier to switch to Source view and edit the WizardStep declarations directly. When you are done, the Wizard control declaration should look something like that shown in Example 5-6.

Example 5-6. Wizard declaration after adding steps

```
<asp:Wizard ID="wzrdMorning" runat="server">
    <WizardSteps>
        <asp:WizardStep ID="stpWakeUp" runat="server" Title="Step 1">
            <h2>Wake Up</h2>
        </asp:WizardStep>
        <asp:WizardStep ID="stpShower" runat="server" Title="Step 2">
            <h2>Shower</h2>
        </asp:WizardStep>
        <asp:WizardStep ID="stpTakeMeds" runat="server" Title="Step 3">
            <h2>Take Medicine</h2>
        </asp:WizardStep>
        <asp:WizardStep ID="stpBrushTeeth" runat="server" Title="Step 4">
            <h2>Brush Teeth</h2>
        </asp:WizardStep>
        <asp:WizardStep ID="stpGetDressed" runat="server" Title="Step 5">
```

Example 5-6. Wizard declaration after adding steps (continued)

```
      <h2>Get Dressed</h2>
    </asp:WizardStep>
    <asp:WizardStep ID="stpEatBreakfast" runat="server" Title="Step 6">
        <h2>Eat Breakfast</h2>
    </asp:WizardStep>
    <asp:WizardStep ID="stpFinish" runat="server" Title="Step 7">
        <h2>Out the Door</h2>
    </asp:WizardStep>
  </WizardSteps>
</asp:Wizard>
```

The Wizard control has many properties for controlling appearance and behavior. Table 5-3 lists some of the most important Wizard properties other than those relating to the appearance of the buttons. The button-related properties are listed in Table 5-4. You'll see many of these properties as you continue with this example, *WizardDemo*.

Table 5-3. Wizard Properties not related to style or button display

Name	Type	Get	Set	Description
ActiveStep	WizardStepBase	✗		The currently displayed step in the WizardsSteps collection.
ActiveStepIndex	Integer	✗	✗	The zero-based index of the currently displayed step in the WizardsSteps collection.
CancelDestinationPageUrl	String	✗	✗	The URL the user navigates to when clicking the Cancel button.
CellPadding	Integer	✗	✗	Number of pixels between the cell's contents and border. Defaults to 0.
CellSpacing	Integer	✗	✗	Number of pixels betweens cells. The default is 0.
DisplayCancelButton	Boolean	✗	✗	If true, a Cancel button will be displayed. Default is false.
DisplaySideBar	Boolean	✗	✗	If true, the default, the sidebar area will be displayed.
FinishDestinationPageUrl	String	✗	✗	The URL the user navigates to when clicking the Finish button.
FinishNavigationTemplate	ITemplate	✗	✗	The template used to specify content and styles for the navigation area of the Finish step, either the last step or the step with StepType = Finish.
HeaderStyle	TableItemStyle	✗		Style properties for the header area.
HeaderTemplate	ITemplate	✗	✗	The template used to specify content and styles for the header area displayed at the top of every step.

Name	Type	Get	Set	Description
HeaderText	string	✗	✗	Text displayed in the header area.
NavigationButtonStyle	Style	✗		The style properties that specify the appearance of the buttons in the navigation area.
NavigationStyle	TableItemStyle	✗		Style properties for the navigation area.
SideBarButtonStyle	Style	✗		The style properties that specify the appearance of the buttons in the sidebar area.
SideBarStyle	TableItemStyle	✗		Style properties for the sidebar area.
SideBarTemplate	ITemplate	✗	✗	The template used to specify content and styles for the sidebar area.
SkipLinkText	string	✗	✗	Rendered as alternate text with an invisible image to work with assistive technologies. Default is "Skip Navigation Links", localized for server locale.
StartNavigationTemplate	ITemplate	✗	✗	The template used to specify content and styles for the navigation area of the Start step, either the first step or the step with StepType = Start.
StepNavigationTemplate	ITemplate	✗	✗	The template used to specify content and styles for the navigation area of all the steps other than Start, Finish, or Complete.
StepStyle	TableItemStyle	✗		Style properties for the WizardStep objects.
WizardSteps	WizardStepCollection	✗		Collection of WizardStep objects.

Table 5-4. Wizard Properties related to button displays

Property	Type	Get	Set	Values	Description
CancelButtonImageUrl FinishStepButtonImageUrl FinishStepPreviousButtonImageUrl NextStepButtonImageUrl PreviousStepButtonImageUrl StartStepNextButtonImageUrl	string	✗	✗		The URL of the image displayed for the button.
CancelButtonStyle FinishStepButtonStyle FinishStepPreviousButtonStyle NextStepButtonStyle PreviousStepButtonStyle StartStepNextButtonStyle	Style	✗			The style properties that specify the appearance of the button.

Table 5-4. Wizard Properties related to button displays (continued)

Property	Type	Get	Set	Values	Description
CancelButtonText FinishStepButtonText FinishStepPreviousButtonText NextStepButtonText PreviousStepButtonText StartStepNextButtonText	string	✗	✗		The text displayed on the button.
CancelButtonType FinishStepButtonType FinishStepPreviousButtonType NextStepButtonType PreviousStepButtonType StartStepNextButtonType	ButtonType	✗	✗	Button, Image, Link	The type of button rendered as the button.

Many of the properties are of type TableItemStyle. This class, which derives from System.Web.UI.WebControls.Style, contains properties used to format the table rows and cells that make up the Wizard control. The TableItemStyle class has many properties, including BackColor, BorderColor, BorderStyle, BorderWidth, CssClass, Font, ForeColor, Height, HorizonalAlign, VerticalAlign, Width, and Wrap.

When setting the properties of a Wizard control in VS2005 in Design view, the properties that are of type TableItemStyle appear in the Properties window with a plus sign next to them. Clicking on the plus sign expands the list to display the TableItemStyle properties as subproperties, as seen in Figure 5-8. Properties set in this manner will be contained in separate elements within the Wizard control declaration in the content file, as in the highlighted code in the following snippet:

```
<asp:Wizard ID="Wizard1" runat="server" ActiveStepIndex="0">
   <WizardSteps>
      <asp:WizardStep ID="stpWakeUp" runat="server" Title="Step 1">
         <h2>
            Wake Up</h2>
      </asp:WizardStep>
      <asp:WizardStep ID="WizardStep2" runat="server" Title="Step 2">
      </asp:WizardStep>
   </WizardSteps>
   <HeaderStyle
      BackColor="Gray"
      BorderColor="Black"
      BorderStyle="Solid"
      BorderWidth="2px"
      Font-Size="0.9em"
      ForeColor="White"
      HorizontalAlign="Center" />
</asp:Wizard>
```

Figure 5-8. TableItemStyle type properties in Design view

When working in Source view, however, the `TableItemStyle` type properties are listed and inserted directly into the `Wizard` control declaration in the format shown in Figure 5-9 and shown in the highlighted code in the snippet below:

```
<asp:Wizard ID="Wizard1" runat="server"
    ActiveStepIndex="0"
    SideBarStyle-BackColor="Yellow"
    SideBarStyle-BorderStyle="Dashed"
    SideBarStyle-Font-Bold="true"
    SideBarStyle-ForeColor="Black">
    <WizardSteps>
        <asp:WizardStep ID="stpWakeUp" runat="server" Title="Step 1">
          <h2>
              Wake Up</h2>
        </asp:WizardStep>
        <asp:WizardStep ID="WizardStep2" runat="server" Title="Step 2">
        </asp:WizardStep>
    </WizardSteps>
</asp:Wizard>
```

The `WizardStep` has a `StepType` property, which has one of the values of the `WizardStepType` enumeration listed in Table 5-5. By default, the `StepType` is `Auto`, in which the navigation UI is determined by the order of the steps in the `WizardSteps` collection. The first step has only a Next button, the last step has only a Previous button, and all the other steps of `StepType` `Auto` have both Previous and Next buttons.

Alternatively, you can assign a different value to the `StepType` property to modify the default behavior, as described in Table 5-5. For example, you can create a confirmation page, with no navigation buttons at all, by changing the `StepType` to `Complete`.

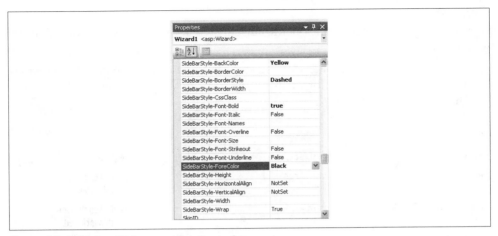

Figure 5-9. TableItemStyle type properties in Source view

Table 5-5. WizardStepType enumeration members

Member	Description
Auto	Navigation UI determined automatically by the order in which the step is declared. The default value.
Complete	The last step to display. No navigation buttons rendered.
Finish	The final data collection step. Renders only Finish and Previous buttons.
Start	The first step. Renders only a Next button.
Step	Any step other than Start, Finish, or Complete. Renders Previous and Next buttons.

The WizardStep class has one additional property of particular interest: AllowReturn. This property enforces linear navigation. It is impossible to navigate to a step with AllowReturn set to false more than once. If the DisplaySideBar property is true (the default) so the sidebar is displayed, then any step with AllowReturn set to false will still display in the navigation links, but clicking on that link will have no effect.

 The AllowReturn property only disallows user interaction; program code can force a return to a step even if the AllowReturn property is false.

The Wizard control has six events, listed in Table 5-6. One is the ActiveStepChanged event, raised when the current step is changed. The other five events are all raised in response to button clicks. As noted in Table 5-6, all the button click events other than CancelButtonClick have an event argument of type WizardNavigationEventArgs, which exposes three properties:

Cancel
> Boolean value is true if the navigation to the next step should be canceled. The default is false.

CurrentStepIndex

The zero-based integer index of the current step in the WizardSteps collection.

NextStepIndex

The zero-based integer index of the step that will display next. If the Previous button has been clicked, for example, the value of NextStepIndex will be one less than the CurrentStepIndex.

Table 5-6. Wizard events

Event	Event Argument	Description
ActiveStepChanged	EventArgs	Raised when a new step is displayed.
CancelButtonClick	EventArgs	Raised when the Cancel button is clicked.
FinishButtonClick	WizardNavigationEventArgs	Raised when the Finish button is clicked.
NextButtonClick	WizardNavigationEventArgs	Raised when the Next button is clicked.
PreviousButtonClick	WizardNavigationEventArgs	Raised when the Previous button is clicked.
SideBarButtonClick	WizardNavigationEventArgs	Raised when a sidebar button is clicked.

The Wizard control has three methods of particular interest, listed in Table 5-7.

Table 5-7. Wizard methods

Method Name	Return Type	Description
GetHistory	ICollection	Returns a collection of WizardStepBase objects in the order they were accessed, where index 0 is the most recent step.
GetStepType	WizardStepType	The type of step, as listed in Table 5-5.
MoveTo	void	Moves to the WizardStep object passed in as a parameter.

Now, let's return to the *WizardDemo* example, where you will apply many of the properties, methods, and events that we just listed and discussed.

First, add a bit of text to each of the WizardSteps. The content of each step can include text and HTML, other ASP.NET server controls, and user controls, enabling the easy reuse of UI and code.

Next, set the StepType of the first step to Start and Step 7 to Finish. Set the AllowReturn property of Step 3 to False, so you can only access that step a single time. Finally, add one additional WizardStep to the WizardSteps collection, with a StepType of Complete. The new <WizardSteps> section of the Wizard declaration will now look like Example 5-7, with the modified code highlighted (except for the added text content).

Example 5-7. WizardSteps declaration

```
<WizardSteps>
    <asp:WizardStep ID="stpWakeUp" runat="server"
        Title="Step 1"
        StepType="Start">
        <h2>Wake Up</h2>
        Rise and shine sleepy head.
    </asp:WizardStep>
    <asp:WizardStep ID="stpShower" runat="server"
        Title="Step 2">
        <h2>Shower</h2>
        Make it cold!
    </asp:WizardStep>
    <asp:WizardStep ID="stpTakeMeds" runat="server"
        Title="Step 3"
        AllowReturn="False">
        <h2>Take Medicine</h2>
        Only do this once.
    </asp:WizardStep>
    <asp:WizardStep ID="stpBrushTeeth" runat="server"
        Title="Step 4">
        <h2>Brush Teeth</h2>
        Don't forget to floss.
    </asp:WizardStep>
    <asp:WizardStep ID="stpGetDressed" runat="server"
        Title="Step 5">
        <h2>Get Dressed</h2>
        Got to look good.
    </asp:WizardStep>
    <asp:WizardStep ID="stpEatBreakfast" runat="server"
        Title="Step 6">
        <h2>Eat Breakfast</h2>
        The most important meal of the day.
    </asp:WizardStep>
    <asp:WizardStep ID="stpFinish" runat="server"
        Title="Step 7"
        StepType="Finish">
        <h2>Out the Door</h2>
        Meet the world!
    </asp:WizardStep>
    <asp:WizardStep ID="stpComplete" runat="server"
        StepType="Complete"
        Title="Complete">
        <h2>Complete!</h2>
        Your morning routine is now complete.
    </asp:WizardStep>
</WizardSteps>
```

Next, add a drop-down along with several labels to the page. The labels will be used to display various information and the drop-down will be used to demonstrate how step navigation can occur programmatically outside the Wizard control. The code snippet from the content file shown in Example 5-8 declares these additional controls.

Example 5-8. Additional controls in WizardDemo

```
<br />
Select a step: 
<asp:DropDownList ID="DropDownList1" runat="server"
    AutoPostBack="True"
    OnSelectedIndexChanged="DropDownList1_SelectedIndexChanged" >
    <asp:ListItem>1</asp:ListItem>
    <asp:ListItem>2</asp:ListItem>
    <asp:ListItem>3</asp:ListItem>
    <asp:ListItem>4</asp:ListItem>
    <asp:ListItem>5</asp:ListItem>
    <asp:ListItem>6</asp:ListItem>
    <asp:ListItem>7</asp:ListItem>
</asp:DropDownList>
<br />
<br />
Active Step: 
<asp:Label ID="lblActiveStep" runat="server" />
<br />
ActiveStepIndex: 
<asp:Label ID="lblActiveStepIndex" runat="server" />
<br />
StepType: 
<asp:Label ID="lblStepType" runat="server" />
<br />
Button Info: 
<asp:Label ID="lblButtonInfo" runat="server" />
<br />
<br />
<u>History</u>
<br />
<asp:Label ID="lblHistory" runat="server" />
```

Go back to the Design view, click the smart tag of the Wizard control and select Auto Format. Select one of the format schemes presented; in this example, we use Simple. This will automatically apply a number of formatting properties, as you will see momentarily.

In the Properties window for the Wizard control, set the DisplayCancelButton to true.

While in Design view with the Wizard control selected, click the Events icon (the lightning bolt) in the Properties window. Double-click the cell next to ActiveStepChanged to insert an event handler with the default name (wzrdMorning_ActiveStepChanged) for that event. Do the same for the CancelButtonClick event. For the FinishButtonClick event, enter the name Button_Click, which will insert a skeleton event handler with that name in the code-behind file. Finally, enter Button_Click for each of the NextButtonClick, PreviousButtonClick, and SideBarButtonClick events.

Switch over to the code-behind file, *Default.aspx.cs*. Add the following using statement to the top of the file:

```
using System.Collections;
```

This is necessary so you can use the ICollection object returned by the GetHistory method of the Wizard control without typing in full namespace qualification.

Add the highlighted code from Example 5-9 to all the event handler code skeletons already inserted by VS2005.

Example 5-9. Event handlers in Default.aspx.cs for WizardDemo

```
protected void wzrdMorning_ActiveStepChanged(object sender, EventArgs e)
{
    lblActiveStep.Text = wzrdMorning.ActiveStep.Title;
    lblActiveStepIndex.Text = wzrdMorning.ActiveStepIndex.ToString();
    lblStepType.Text = wzrdMorning.ActiveStep.StepType.ToString();

    // get the history
    ICollection steps = wzrdMorning.GetHistory();
    string str = "";
    foreach(WizardStep step in steps)
    {
        str += step.Title + "<br/>";
    }
    lblHistory.Text = str;
}

protected void Button_Click(object sender, WizardNavigationEventArgs e)
{
    string str = "Current Index: " +
        e.CurrentStepIndex.ToString() +
        ".   Next Step: " + e.NextStepIndex.ToString();
    lblButtonInfo.Text = str;
}

protected void wzrdMorning_CancelButtonClick(object sender, EventArgs e)
{
    lblActiveStep.Text = "";
    lblActiveStepIndex.Text = "";
    lblStepType.Text = "";
    lblButtonInfo.Text = "Canceled";
    wzrdMorning.Visible = false;
}

protected void DropDownList1_SelectedIndexChanged(object sender,
                                                  EventArgs e)
{
    DropDownList ddl = (DropDownList)sender;
    int index = ddl.SelectedIndex;
    WizardStepBase step = wzrdMorning.WizardSteps[index];
    wzrdMorning.MoveTo(step);
}
```

The ActiveStepChanged event handler, wzrdMorning_ActiveStepChanged, is fired every time the current step changes, whether through user interaction or programmatically.

This method gathers three pieces of information, populates the labels, and displays a history of the steps accessed.

The first label displays the currently active step. The ActiveStep property of the Wizard control returns a WizardStep object. The Title property of that object gives you the information you want. The second label is filled with the ActiveStepIndex property value. Since it is of type integer, it must be converted to a string. The third label displays the StepType property of the WizardStep class, which is of type WizardStepType and, therefore, must be converted to a string for assignment to the Text property of the TextBox.

Second, the wzrdMorning_ActiveStepChanged method calls the GetHistory method of the Wizard class, which returns a collection of WizardStep objects (strictly speaking it returns a collection of WizardStepBase objects, from which WizardStep derives). The collection is iterated and the Title property of each step is appended to a text string which is then assigned to the lblHistory label. The most recent step accessed has an index of 0, the subsequent step has an index of 1, and so on.

All the buttons and links, other than the Cancel button, use the same event handler method: Button_Click. This method fills lblButtonInfo with the current step index and the next step index, both of which are properties of the event argument.

The Cancel button click event handler, wzrdMorning_CancelButtonClick, clears all the labels and hides the Wizard control.

The DropDownList on this page lets the user move to any of the wizardsteps. It casts the sender object to type DropDownList, then extracts the SelectedIndex property. This value is used as an index into the WizardSteps collection to get a reference to the desired WizardStep object (actually a WizardStepBase object, from which WizardStep is derived). Then the MoveTo method of the Wizard is called to move programmatically to that step. The really interesting thing here is that it is possible to move multiple times to a step, such as Step 3, which has the AllowReturn property set to false.

As a result of setting the event handlers and the Auto Formatting, the Wizard declaration will now look something like that shown in Example 5-10.

Example 5-10. Wizard declaration after adding event handlers and formatting

```
<asp:Wizard ID="wzrdMorning" runat="server"
    DisplayCancelButton="True"
    OnCancelButtonClick="wzrdMorning_CancelButtonClick"
    OnActiveStepChanged="wzrdMorning_ActiveStepChanged"
    OnFinishButtonClick="Button_Click"
    OnNextButtonClick="Button_Click"
    OnPreviousButtonClick="Button_Click"
    OnSideBarButtonClick="Button_Click"
    BackColor="#E6E2D8" BorderColor="#999999" BorderWidth="1px"
    Font-Names="Verdana" Font-Size="0.8em" >
    <WizardSteps>
        <!--  unchanged from Example 5-7  -- >
```

```
    </WizardSteps>
    <StepStyle BackColor="#F7F6F3" BorderColor="#E6E2D8"
        BorderStyle="Solid" BorderWidth="2px" />
    <SideBarStyle BackColor="#1C5E55" Font-Size="0.9em"
        VerticalAlign="Top" />
    <NavigationButtonStyle BackColor="White" BorderColor="#C5BBAF"
        BorderStyle="Solid"
        BorderWidth="1px" Font-Names="Verdana"
        Font-Size="0.8em" ForeColor="#1C5E55" />
    <SideBarButtonStyle ForeColor="White" />
    <HeaderStyle BackColor="#666666" BorderColor="#E6E2D8"
        BorderStyle="Solid" BorderWidth="2px"
        Font-Bold="True" Font-Size="0.9em" ForeColor="White"
        HorizontalAlign="Center" />
</asp:Wizard>
```

Running the web page and navigating through several of the steps will yield something similar to Figure 5-10.

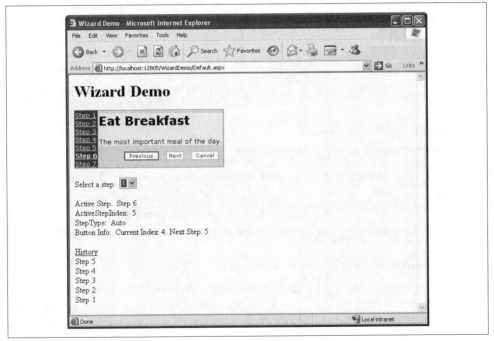

Figure 5-10. WizardDemo after some navigation

The Wizard control is a fairly well-defined control, with obvious uses. You could walk your user through entering their preferences or setting up a stock sale. Any time you want a clearly defined series of steps for the user to follow, the Wizard control is useful.

FileUpload Control

Often an application finds the need to allow users to upload files to the web server. Although it was possible to do this in ASP.NET Version 1.x, it is made much easier in ASP.NET Version 2 with the introduction of the FileUpload control.

This control makes it easy for the user to browse for and select the file to transfer, providing a Browse button and a text box for entering the file name. Once the user has entered a fully-qualified file name in the text box, either by typing it directly or using the Browse button, the SaveAs method of the FileUpload control can be called to save the file to disk.

In addition to the normal complement of members inherited from the WebControl class, the FileUpload control also exposes several read-only properties of particular interest, listed in Tables 5-8 and 5-9.

Table 5-8. FileUpload properties

Name	Type	Get	Set	Description
FileContent	Stream	✗		Returns a Stream object that points to the file to upload.
FileName	string	✗		Returns the name of the file to be uploaded, without any qualifying path information.
HasFile	Boolean	✗		If true, indicates that the control has a file to upload.
PostedFile	HttpPostedFile	✗		Returns a reference to the file which has been uploaded. Exposes the read-only properties listed in Table 5-9.

Table 5-9. HttpPostedFile properties

Name	Type	Get	Set	Description
ContentLength	integer	✗		Returns the size of the file, in bytes, of an uploaded file.
ContentType	string	✗		Returns the MIME content type of the uploaded file.
FileName	string	✗		Returns the fully qualified file name on the client computer.
InputStream	Stream	✗		Returns a Stream object that points to the uploaded file.

All of these properties will be demonstrated in the following example.

To see a FileUpload control in action, create a new web site called *FileUploadDemo*. Drag a FileUpload control onto the page. Add two ASP.NET Button controls, with Text properties set to Save and Display, and ID properties set to btnSave and btnDisplay, respectively. Add two Label controls with ID's set to lblMessage and lblDisplay. Sprinkle a few
 HTML elements to space things out. Switch to Design view and double-click on each of the buttons to create default-named Click event handlers for each button in the code-behind file. When you are done, the content file should look something like that shown in Example 5-11.

Example 5-11. default.aspx for FileUploadDemo

```
<%@ Page Language="C#" AutoEventWireup="true"  CodeFile="Default.aspx.cs"
    Inherits="_Default" %>

<!DOCTYPE html PUBLIC "-//W3C//DTD XHTML 1.1//EN"
    "http://www.w3.org/TR/xhtml11/DTD/xhtml11.dtd">

<html xmlns="http://www.w3.org/1999/xhtml" >
<head runat="server">
    <title>FileUpload Control</title>
</head>
<body>
    <form id="form1" runat="server">
    <div>
      <h1>FileUpload Control</h1>
      <asp:FileUpload ID="FileUpload1" runat="server" />
      <br />
      <asp:Button ID="btnSave" runat="server"
                  Text="Save"
                  OnClick="btnSave_Click" />
      <asp:Button ID="btnDisplay" runat="server"
                  Text="Display"
                  OnClick="btnDisplay_Click" />
      <br />
      <br />
      <asp:Label ID="lblMessage" runat="server" />
      <asp:Label ID="lblDisplay" runat="server" />
    </div>
    </form>
</body>
</html>
```

In the code-behind file, add the highlighted code from Example 5-12. The non-highlighted code was put in place by VS2005.

Example 5-12. Default.aspx.cs for FileUploadDemo

```
using System;
using System.Data;
using System.Configuration;
using System.Web;
using System.Web.Security;
using System.Web.UI;
using System.Web.UI.WebControls;
using System.Web.UI.WebControls.WebParts;
using System.Web.UI.HtmlControls;
using System.IO;        // necessary for Stream

public partial class _Default : System.Web.UI.Page
{
    protected void Page_Load(object sender, EventArgs e)
    {
    }
```

Example 5-12. Default.aspx.cs for FileUploadDemo (continued)

```csharp
protected void btnSave_Click(object sender, EventArgs e)
{
    string str = "";
    if (FileUpload1.HasFile)
    {
        try
        {
            str += "Uploading file: " + FileUpload1.FileName;

            //  Save the file
            FileUpload1.SaveAs("c:\\websites\\uploads\\" +
                                    FileUpload1.FileName);

            //  show info about the file
            str += "<br/>Saved As: " + FileUpload1.PostedFile.FileName;
            str += "<br/>File Type: " +
                FileUpload1.PostedFile.ContentType;
            str += "<br/>File Length (bytes): " +
                FileUpload1.PostedFile.ContentLength;
            str += "<br/>PostedFile File Name: " +
                FileUpload1.PostedFile.FileName;
        }
        catch (Exception ex)
        {
            str += "<br/><b>Error</b><br/>Unable to save
                    c:\\websites\\uploads\\" + FileUpload1.FileName +
                "<br/>" + ex.Message;
        }
    }
    else
    {
        str = "No file uploaded.";
    }
    lblMessage.Text = str;
    lblDisplay.Text = "";
}

protected void btnDisplay_Click(object sender, EventArgs e)
{
    string str = "<u>File:  " + FileUpload1.FileName + "</u><br/>";
    if (FileUpload1.HasFile)
    {
        try
        {
            Stream stream = FileUpload1.FileContent;
            StreamReader reader = new StreamReader(stream);
            string strLine = "";
            do
            {
                strLine = reader.ReadLine( );
                str += strLine;
            } while (strLine != null);
```

Example 5-12. Default.aspx.cs for FileUploadDemo (continued)

```
        }
        catch (Exception ex)
        {
            str += "<br/><b>Error</b><br/>Unable to display " +
                        FileUpload1.FileName +
                    "<br/>" + ex.Message;
        }
    }
    else
    {
        str = "No file uploaded.";
    }
    lblDisplay.Text = str;
    lblMessage.Text = "";
    }
}
```

The highlighted using statement is necessary to use the Stream object without having to type fully qualified namespaces.

In btnSave_Click, the event handler for the Save button, the HasFile property of the FileUpload control is used to test if a valid, fully qualified filename is entered in the control text box. If the text box is blank or the filename entered is not a valid file, this test will fail and lblMessage will display "No file uploaded."

Assuming there is a valid file to upload, the code in the try block is executed. The key statement here calls the SaveAs method of the FileUpload control, using a hard-coded path along with the FileName property to pass in a fully qualified file name. This statement may fail for any number of reasons, including insufficient disk space, an invalid path, or security issues (more on that in a moment).

If the SaveAs fails, then the catch block will come into play, displaying an error message in lblMessage, including ex.Message, the Exception Message property.

If the SaveAs is successful, then a number of pieces of information about the uploaded file are displayed in lblMessage, retrieved from properties of the FileUpload.PostedFile property (which is of type HttpPostedFile).

After saving a file, the page will look something like that shown in Figure 5-11.

The event handler for the Display button Click event is similar except that, instead of displaying information about the file, it displays contents of the file itself. It does this by using the FileContent property to retrieve the contents of the uploaded file as a Stream object, which is then used to instantiate a StreamReader object. The ReadLine method of the StreamReader class is then used to step through the file, line by line, concatenating the lines to display in lblDisplay.

After displaying a file, in this case a text file containing the Gettysburg Address, the page will look something like that shown in Figure 5-12.

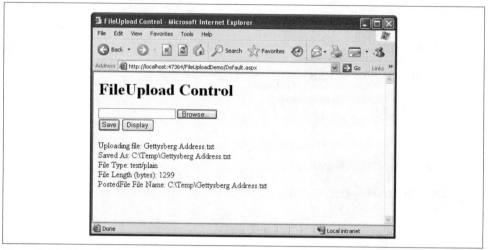

Figure 5-11. FileUploadDemo after saving a file

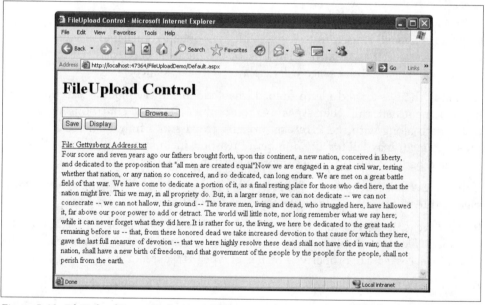

Figure 5-12. FileUploadDemo displaying a file

Whenever you talk about uploading a file to a web server from clients, security is a big concern. There are two considerations. First, opening up your web server in this way can present a huge security hole, and should be done only with care and careful consideration. Not only can uploaded files contain viruses, Trojan horses, and other malicious software, but it would be dangerous to allow the client to browse the directory structure of the web server itself. For that reason, you will almost always want to either hard-code the target directory or at least severely circumscribe where the uploaded files can be saved.

The other consideration is the permissions necessary to allow a process to write a file to disk. When developing a web application, the development computer is typically its own web server, especially when using the default mode of VS2005, in which an internal web server is used and the access to the web site is via the filesystem rather than IIS. In this situation, you will probably never run into any permissions problems.

However, when the web site is deployed to a production web server and the web site is accessed via IIS and a virtual directory, problems will arise. This is because the account that ASP.NET runs under must have write permission for the directory in which the uploaded files are to be saved. In Windows 2000/XP, this account is named ASPNET. In Windows Server 2003, write permission must given to the IIS_WPG account group.

With a FileUpload control, and good security precautions in place, your users will be able to send their own files to your site, increasing your site's versatility.

AdRotator Control

This control is called an AdRotator because it is most often used to display advertisements on web pages. It displays an image randomly selected from a list stored either in a separate XML file or a data-bound data source. In either case, the list contains image attributes, including the path to the image and a URL to link to when the image is clicked. The image changes every time the page is loaded.

In addition to the properties inherited from WebControl, the AdRotator control has the properties and events listed in Table 5-10.

Table 5-10. Properties and events of the AdRotator control

Name	Type	Get	Set	Description
AdvertisementFile	String	X	X	The path to an XML file that contains the list of advertisements and their attributes. This file is described in detail below.
AlternateTextField	String	X	X	Element name from the Advertisement file or data field from which the alternate text is stored. Default is AlternateText.
DataMember	String	X	X	The name of the specific list of data the control will bind to.
DataSource	Object	X	X	An object from which the control can retrieve data.
DataSourceID	String	X	X	The ID of the control from which the AdRotator can retrieve data.
ImageUrlField	String	X	X	Element name from the Advertisement file or data field from which the URL for the image is stored. Default is ImageUrl.

Table 5-10. Properties and events of the AdRotator control (continued)

Name	Type	Get	Set	Description
KeywordFilter	String	✗	✗	Filters ads displayed to include only those with the specified keyword in the `AdvertisementFile`.
NavigateUrlField	String	✗	✗	Element name from the Advertisement file or data field in which the URL to `navigate` to is stored. Default is `NavigateUrl`.
Target	String	✗	✗	The browser window or frame that displays the contents of the page linked to when the `AdRotator` is clicked.
AdCreated	Event			Occurs once per round trip to the server after creation of the control, but before the page is rendered.

The Target property is used to specify which browser window or frame is used to display the results of clicking on the `AdRotator` control. It dictates if the resulting page displaces the current contents in the current browser window or frame, opens a new browser window, or does something else. The values of the `Target` property must begin with any letter in the range of a to z, case insensitive, except for the special values shown in Table 5-11, which begin with an underscore. These are the same special values recognized by the `Target` property of the `HyperLink` control.

Table 5-11. Special values of the Target property

Value	Description
_blank	Renders the content in a new, unnamed window without frames.
_new	Not documented. Behaves the same as `_blank` the first time the control is clicked, but subsequent clicks will render to that same window, rather than open another blank window.
_parent	Renders the content in the parent window or frameset of the window or frame with the hyperlink. If the child container is a window or top-level frame, it behaves the same as `_self`.
_self	Renders the content in the current frame or window with focus. This is the default behavior.
_top	Renders the content in the current full window without frames.

Advertisement File

The *advertisement file* is an XML file that contains information about the advertisements to be displayed by the `AdRotator` control. Its location and filename is specified by the `AdvertisementFile` property of the control.

The location of the advertisement file can be relative to the web site root directory or can be absolute. If its location is other than the web root, you will need to ensure that the application has sufficient rights to access the file, especially after deployment. For this and other security reasons, it is usually best to locate the file directly in the web root.

The `AdvertisementFile` property cannot be set simultaneously with the `DataSource`, `DataMember`, or `DataSourceID` properties. In other words, if the data is coming from an advertisement file, then it cannot simultaneously come from a data source, and vice versa.

The advertisement file and the `AdvertisementFile` property are optional. If you want to create an advertisement programmatically, without the use of an advertisement file, put the code to display the desired elements in the `AdCreated` event.

As an XML file, the advertisement file is a structured text file with well-defined tags delineating the data. Table 5-12 lists the standard tags, which are enclosed in angle brackets (< >) and require matching closing tags.

Table 5-12. XML tags used in the advertisement file

Tag	Description
Advertisements	Encloses the entire advertisement file.
Ad	Delineates each separate ad.
ImageUrl	The URL of the image to display. Required.
NavigateUrl	The URL of the page to navigate to when the control is clicked.
AlternateText	The text displayed in the control if the image is unavailable. In browsers that support the ToolTips feature, this text is also displayed as a ToolTip.
Keyword	The advertisement category. The keyword can be used to filter the advertisements displayed by the control by setting the AdRotator KeywordFilter property.
Impressions	A value indicating how often the ad is displayed relative to the other ads in the file.

 Since this is XML and not HTML, it is much less forgiving of files that are not well-formed. These tags are case-sensitive: `ImageUrl` will work; `ImageURL` will not.

For a complete description of well-formed XML, see the sidebar, "Well-Formed XHTML," in Chapter 3.

In addition to the tags listed in Table 5-12, you can include your own custom tags to have custom attributes. The sample advertisement file in Example 5-13, contains a custom attribute called `Animal`, which will hold the animal pictured on the cover of each book. (No, the authors have no say in selecting the animal that goes on our books.)

Example 5-13. ads.XML, sample advertisement file

```
<Advertisements>
   <Ad>
      <ImageUrl>ProgAspNet.gif</ImageUrl>
      <NavigateUrl>
         http://www.oreilly.com/catalog/progaspdotnet2/index.html
      </NavigateUrl>
      <AlternateText>Programming ASP.NET</AlternateText>
      <Keyword>Web</Keyword>
```

Example 5-13. ads.XML, sample advertisement file (continued)

```
      <Impressions>50</Impressions>
      <Animal>stingray</Animal>
   </Ad>

   <Ad>
      <ImageUrl>WinApps.gif</ImageUrl>
      <NavigateUrl>
         http://www.oreilly.com/catalog/pnetwinaps/index.html
      </NavigateUrl>
      <AlternateText>Programming .NET Windows Applications</AlternateText>
      <Keyword>Windows</Keyword>
      <Impressions>40</Impressions>
      <Animal>darter</Animal>
   </Ad>

   <Ad>
      <ImageUrl>ProgCSharp.gif</ImageUrl>
      <NavigateUrl>
         http://www.oreilly.com/catalog/progcsharp4/
      </NavigateUrl>
      <AlternateText>Programming C#</AlternateText>
      <Keyword>Language</Keyword>
      <Impressions>40</Impressions>
      <Animal>African Crowned Crane</Animal>
   </Ad>

   <Ad>
      <ImageUrl>ProgVB.gif</ImageUrl>
      <NavigateUrl>
         http://www.oreilly.com/catalog/progvb2005/
      </NavigateUrl>
      <AlternateText>Programming Visual Basic 2005</AlternateText>
      <Keyword>Language</Keyword>
      <Impressions>30</Impressions>
      <Animal>catfish</Animal>
   </Ad>

</Advertisements>
```

All the attribute tags in the advertisement file are parsed and placed in the adProperties dictionary. This dictionary can be used programmatically to access attributes, either standard or custom, by placing code in the AdCreated event handler.

Example 5-13 shows a sample advertisement file that contains references to books and web sites for several excellent programming books.

Using AdRotator

Now all you need is a web page with an AdRotator control to use this advertisement file, as shown in the next example, AdRotatorDemo. After creating a new web site by that name, drag an AdRotator control onto the page, along with a Label control to display the animal. The content file should look something like Example 5-14.

Example 5-14. Default.aspx for AdRotatoDemo

```
<%@ Page Language="C#" AutoEventWireup="true"  CodeFile="Default.aspx.cs"
    Inherits="_Default" %>

<!DOCTYPE html PUBLIC "-//W3C//DTD XHTML 1.1//EN"
    "http://www.w3.org/TR/xhtml11/DTD/xhtml11.dtd">

<html xmlns="http://www.w3.org/1999/xhtml" >
<head runat="server">
    <title>AdRotator</title>
</head>
<body>
    <form id="form1" runat="server">
    <div>
      <h1>AdRotator Control</h1>
      <asp:AdRotator ID="ad" runat="server"
          Target="_blank"
          AdvertisementFile="ads.xml"
          OnAdCreated="ad_AdCreated" />
      <br />
      Animal:
      <asp:Label id="lblAnimal" runat="server"/>
    </div>
    </form>
</body>
</html>
```

The event handler, ad_AdCreated, is highlighted in the code-behind file listed in Example 5-15.

Example 5-15. Default.aspx.cs for AdRotatorDemo

```
using System;
using System.Data;
using System.Configuration;
using System.Web;
using System.Web.Security;
using System.Web.UI;
using System.Web.UI.WebControls;
using System.Web.UI.WebControls.WebParts;
using System.Web.UI.HtmlControls;

public partial class _Default : System.Web.UI.Page
{
    protected void Page_Load(object sender, EventArgs e)
    {
    }
```

Example 5-15. Default.aspx.cs for AdRotatorDemo (continued)

```
    protected void ad_AdCreated(object sender, AdCreatedEventArgs e)
    {
        if ((string)e.AdProperties["Animal"] != "")
            lblAnimal.Text = (string)e.AdProperties["Animal"];
        else
            lblAnimal.Text = "n.a.";
    }
}
```

Make certain that the advertisement file called *ads.xml*, listed in Example 5-13, is located in the web site root directory, along with the image files specified within that file: *ProgAspNet.gif, ProgCSharp.gif, ProgVB.gif, and WinApps.gif.*

The results of running `AdRotatorDemo` are shown in Figure 5-13. To see the images cycle through, refresh the view on your browser.

Figure 5-13. AdRotatorDemo

This control raises an `AdCreated` event, which occurs on every round trip to the server after the control is created but before the page is rendered. An attribute in the control declaration called `OnAdCreated` specifies the event handler to execute whenever the event fires. The event handler is passed an argument of type `AdCreatedEventArgs`, which has the properties listed in Table 5-13.

Table 5-13. Properties of the AdCreateEventArgs class

Property	Description
AdProperties	Gets a dictionary object that contains all the advertisement properties contained in the advertisement file.
AlternateText	The alternate text displayed by the browser when the advertisement image is unavailable. If the browser supports ToolTips, then this text will be displayed as a ToolTip.
ImageUrl	The URL of an image to display.
NavigateUrl	URL of the web page to display when the control is clicked.

Every time the ad is changed (i.e., every time the page is reloaded), the event handler, ad_AdCreated, fires and updates lblAnimal contained on the page. ad_AdCreated first tests to be certain a value is in the Animal attribute. If not, then "n.a." (for "not available") is displayed.

AdProperties returns a Dictionary object. When the AdProperties property is invoked, it implicitly calls the Item method of the Dictionary object, which returns the value corresponding to the dictionary entry whose key is Animal. This value is then cast, or converted, to a string. In C#, this is done with the following syntax:

```
(string)e.AdProperties["Animal"]
```

Calendar

The ASP Calendar control is a rich web control that provides several capabilities:

- Displays a calendar showing a single month
- Allows the user to select a day, week, or month
- Allows the user to select a range of days
- Allows the user to move to the next or previous month
- Programmatically controls the display of specific days

The Calendar control is customizable, with various properties and events. Before digging into all the detail, look at a bare bones *.aspx* file showing a simple Calendar control, along with the resulting web page. Create a new web site called *Calendar-Simple*, and drag a Calendar control onto the page.

Example 5-16 contains the code with the Calendar declaration highlighted, and Figure 5-14 shows the results. There is no code-behind file with this example other than the default boilerplate created by VS2005.

Example 5-16. Default.aspx for Calendar-Simple

```
<%@ Page Language="C#" AutoEventWireup="true"  CodeFile="Default.aspx.cs"
   Inherits="_Default" %>

<!DOCTYPE html PUBLIC "-//W3C//DTD XHTML 1.1//EN"
   "http://www.w3.org/TR/xhtml11/DTD/xhtml11.dtd">

<html xmlns="http://www.w3.org/1999/xhtml" >
<head runat="server">
    <title>Calendar - Simple</title>
</head>
<body>
    <form id="form1" runat="server">
    <div>
      <h1>Calendar Control</h1>
      <h2>Default Calendar</h2>
        <asp:Calendar ID="Calendar1" runat="server"></asp:Calendar>
    </div>
    </form>
</body>
</html>
```

Figure 5-14. A default Calendar control

Pretty spiffy. Zero manual coding yields a web page with a working calendar that displays the current month. The user can select a single day (though at this point nothing happens when a day is selected, other than it being highlighted) and move through the months by clicking on the   and   navigation symbols on either side of the month name.

As you see in Table 5-14, these navigation symbols are specified by the NextMonthText and PrevMonthText properties as > and <, respectively. These HTML character entities normally display as the greater than (>) and less than (<) symbols. However, in the Calendar control, these symbols are displayed as underlined. This is because all the selectable elements in the Calendar control are rendered to the browser as hyperlinks, hence the underlines.

Table 5-14. Properties of the Calendar control

Name	Type	Get	Set	Values	Description
Caption	String	✗	✗		Text to display on the page above the calendar.
CaptionAlign	TableCaption-Align	✗	✗	Bottom, Left, NotSet, Right, Top	Specifies horizontal and vertical alignment of the Caption.
CellPadding	Integer	✗	✗	0, 1, 2, and so on	Distance in pixels between the border and contents of a cell. Applies to all the cells in the calendar and to all four sides of each cell. Default is 2.
CellSpacing	Integer	✗	✗	0, 1, 2, and so on	Distance in pixels between cells. Applies to all the cells in the calendar. Default is 0.
DayNameFormat	DayName-Format	✗	✗	Full, Short, FirstLetter, FirstTwoLetters	Format of days of the week. Values are self-explanatory, except Short, which is the first three letters. Default is Short.
FirstDayOfWeek	FirstDayOfWeek	✗	✗	Default, Sunday, Monday, ... Saturday	Day of week to display in the first column. Default (the default) specifies system setting.
NextMonthText	String	✗	✗		Text for next month navigation control. The default is >, which renders as the greater than sign (>). Only applies if ShowNextPrevMonth property is true.
NextPrevFormat	NextPrevFormat	✗	✗	CustomText, FullMonth, ShortMonth	To use CustomText, set this property and specify the actual text to use in NextMonthText and PrevMonthText.

Table 5-14. Properties of the Calendar control (continued)

Name	Type	Get	Set	Values	Description
PrevMonthText	String	✗	✗		Text for previous month navigation control. Default is `&lt;`, which renders as less than sign (<). Only applies if `ShowNextPrevMonth` property is `true`.
SelectedDate	DateTime	✗	✗		A single selected date. Only the date is stored; the time is set to null.
SelectedDates	DateTime	✗	✗		Collection of `DateTime` objects when multiple dates are selected. Only the date is stored; the time is set to null.
SelectionMode	Calendar-Selection-Mode	✗	✗		Described later in this section.
SelectMonth-Text	String	✗	✗		Text for month selection element in the selector column. Default is `&gt;&gt;`, which renders as two greater than signs (>>). Only applies if `SelectionMode` property is set to `DayWeekMonth`.
ShowDayHeader	Boolean	✗	✗	`true`, `false`	If `true`, the default, the days of week headings are shown.
ShowGridLines	Boolean	✗	✗	`true`, `false`	If `true`, grid lines between cells are displayed. Default is `false`.
ShowNextPrev-Month	Boolean	✗	✗	`true`, `false`	Indicates if next and previous month navigation elements are shown. Default is `true`.
ShowTitle	Boolean	✗	✗	`true`, `false`	Indicates if the title is shown. If `false`, then next and previous month navigation elements will be hidden. Default is `true`.
TitleFormat	Title-Format	✗	✗	`Month`, `MonthYear`	Indicates if title is month only or month and year. Default is `MonthYear`.
TodaysDate	DateTime	✗	✗		Today's date.
UseAccessible-Header	Boolean	✗	✗	`true`, `false`	Specifies if a header accessible to assistive technologies is to be used.
VisibleDate	DateTime	✗	✗		Any date in the month to display.

In addition to the properties inherited by all the ASP.NET server controls that derive from WebControl, the Calendar has many properties of its own. The most important ones are listed in Table 5-14.

Selecting Dates in the Calendar

If you want to give the user the ability to select either a single day, an entire week, or an entire month, then you must set the SelectionMode property. Table 5-15 lists the legal values for the SelectionMode property.

Table 5-15. Members of the CalendarSelectionMode enumeration

	Description
Day	Allows the user to select a single day. This is the default value.
DayWeek	Allows user to select a single day or an entire week.
DayWeekMonth	Allows user to select a single day, an entire week, or an entire month.
None	Nothing on the Calendar can be selected.

To see the effects of setting the SelectionMode property, copy *Calendar-Simple* to a new web site, called *Calendar-SelectionMode*. The content file will be nearly identical to Example 5-16, with the addition of a single attribute to the Calendar declaration:

```
SelectionMode="DayWeekMonth"
```

The resulting calendar, with the entire month selected, looks like Figure 5-15.

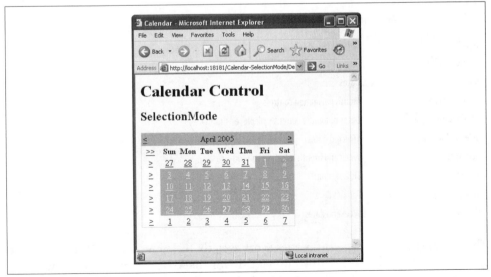

Figure 5-15. Calendar-SelectionMode with a month selected

When the SelectionMode property is set to DayWeek, an extra column containing the ≥ symbol is added to the left side of the calendar. Clicking on one of those symbols selects that entire week.

Similarly, when the SelectionMode property is set to DayWeekMonth, in addition to the week selection column, a ≥≥ symbol (two greater than or equal symbols) is added to the left of the day names row. Clicking on that symbol selects the entire month, as is shown in Figure 5-15.

Controlling the Calendar's Appearance

A number of read/write properties, all of type TableItemStyle, control the style for each part of the calendar. These TableItemStyle type properties are listed in Table 5-16 and demonstrated in the next example, *Calendar-Styles*, shown in finished form in Figure 5-16.

Table 5-16. Calendar control properties of type TableItemStyle

Name	Sets style for...
DayHeaderStyle	Days of the week
DayStyle	Dates
NextPrevStyle	Month navigation controls
OtherMonthDayStyle	Dates not in the currently displayed month
SelectedDayStyle	Selected dates
SelectorStyle	Week and month selection column
TitleStyle	Title section
TodayDayStyle	Today's date
WeekendDayStyle	Weekend dates

These TableItemStyle type properties work exactly the same way in VS2005 for the Calendar control as was described previously for the Wizard control. When working in Design view, the properties appear as in Figure 5-8, and when working in Source

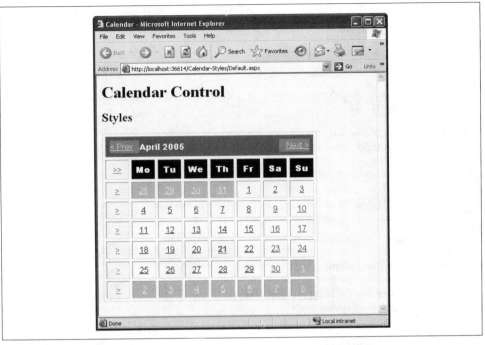

Figure 5-16. Calendar-Styles

view, the properties appear as in Figure 5-9. The format of the declaration also follows the same pattern described for the Wizard control.

In addition to the TableItemStyle type properties, there are four read/write Boolean properties that control various aspects of the calendar, shown in Table 5-17.

Table 5-17. Boolean properties controlling various aspects of the Calendar control's appearance

Property	Default	Controls visibility of...
ShowDayHeader	true	Names of the days of the week
ShowGridLines	false	Grid lines between the days of the month
ShowNextPrevMonth	true	Month navigation controls
ShowTitle	true	Title section

You could click on the Calendar control smart tag in Design view and select one of the Auto Format formats, but in this example, you will choose your own styles. You can do this in the Properties window after selecting the Calendar control in either Design or Source view.

To see how these style properties are used, copy the previous example, *Calendar-SelectionMode*, to a new web site, *Calendar-Styles*, and open the new web site. The complete content file for this latest example is listed in Example 5-17, with the

Calendar declaration highlighted, and the finished page is shown in Figure 5-16. You can see what styles to set for this example by looking at the declarations in Example 5-17.

Example 5-17. Default.aspx for Calendar-Styles

```
<%@ Page Language="C#" AutoEventWireup="true"  CodeFile="Default.aspx.cs"
    Inherits="_Default" %>

<!DOCTYPE html PUBLIC "-//W3C//DTD XHTML 1.1//EN"
    "http://www.w3.org/TR/xhtml11/DTD/xhtml11.dtd">

<html xmlns="http://www.w3.org/1999/xhtml" >
<head runat="server">
    <title>Calendar</title>
</head>
<body>
    <form id="form1" runat="server">
    <div>
      <h1>Calendar Control</h1>
      <h2>Styles</h2>
       <asp:Calendar ID="Calendar1" runat="server"
         SelectionMode="DayWeekMonth"
         CellPadding="7"
         CellSpacing="5"
         DayNameFormat="FirstTwoLetters"
         FirstDayOfWeek="Monday"
         NextMonthText="Next >"
         PrevMonthText="< Prev"
         ShowGridLines="True"
         DayStyle-BackColor="White"
         DayStyle-ForeColor="Black"
         DayStyle-Font-Names="Arial">
          <DayHeaderStyle
            BackColor="Black"
            Font-Names="Arial Black"
            ForeColor="White" />
          <SelectedDayStyle
            BackColor="Cornsilk"
            Font-Bold="True"
            Font-Italic="True"
            Font-Names="Arial"
            ForeColor="Blue" />
          <SelectorStyle
            BackColor="Cornsilk"
            Font-Names="Arial"
            ForeColor="Red" />
          <WeekendDayStyle
            BackColor="LavenderBlush"
            Font-Names="Arial"
            ForeColor="Purple" />
          <OtherMonthDayStyle
            BackColor="LightGray"
```

Example 5-17. Default.aspx for Calendar-Styles (continued)

```
                Font-Names="Arial"
                ForeColor="White" />
            <TodayDayStyle
               BackColor="Cornsilk"
               Font-Bold="True"
               Font-Names="Arial"
               ForeColor="Green" />
            <NextPrevStyle
               BackColor="DarkGray"
               Font-Names="Arial"
               ForeColor="Yellow" />
            <TitleStyle
               BackColor="Gray"
               Font-Names="Arial Black"
               ForeColor="White"
               HorizontalAlign="Left" />
        </asp:Calendar>
    </div>
    </form>
</body>
</html>
```

Programming the Calendar Control

The Calendar control provides three events that are not inherited from other control classes and are of particular interest. By providing event handlers for the events, you can exercise considerable control over how the calendar behaves. These events are:

- *SelectionChanged*
- *DayRender*
- *VisibleMonthChanged*

The following sections describe each of these in detail.

SelectionChanged Event

The SelectionChanged event fires when the user makes a selection—either a day, a week, or an entire month—in the Calendar control. The event is not fired if the selection is changed programmatically. The event handler is passed an argument of type EventArgs.

The next example, *Calendar-SelectionChanged*, demonstrates handling the SelectionChanged event. Whenever you select a new date, it displays text strings with today's date, the selected date, and number of days selected.

To create this example, copy the previous example, *Calendar-Styles*, to a new web site called *Calendar-SelectionChanged*. Add the default named event handler for the SelectionChanged event by selecting the Calendar control in Design view, clicking on the Events icon (the lightning bolt) in the Properties window, and double-clicking on the space next to the SelectionChanged event.

This will add the OnSelectionChanged attribute to the Calendar declaration in the content file and open the code-behind file with the event handler skeleton in place, ready to accept your typing. In the Calendar1_SelectionChanged method, type in the highlighted code from Example 5-18, as well as the highlighted helper method lblCountUpdate.

Example 5-18. Default.aspx.cs from Calendar-SelectionChanged

```
using System;
using System.Data;
using System.Configuration;
using System.Web;
using System.Web.Security;
using System.Web.UI;
using System.Web.UI.WebControls;
using System.Web.UI.WebControls.WebParts;
using System.Web.UI.HtmlControls;

public partial class _Default : System.Web.UI.Page
{
    protected void Page_Load(object sender, EventArgs e)
    {

    }

    protected void Calendar1_SelectionChanged(object sender, EventArgs e)
    {
        lblTodaysDate.Text = "Today's Date is " +
            Calendar1.TodaysDate.ToShortDateString();

        if (Calendar1.SelectedDate != DateTime.MinValue)
            lblSelected.Text = "The date selected is " +
                Calendar1.SelectedDate.ToShortDateString();

        lblCountUpdate();
    }

    private void lblCountUpdate()
    {
        lblCount.Text = "Count of Days Selected:  " +
            Calendar1.SelectedDates.Count.ToString();
    }
}
```

You must also add three Label controls to the bottom of the page to display the information from the calendar. The content file is listed in Example 5-19, with the style attributes of the Calendar control omitted since they are the same as the previous example. The code changed since the previous example is highlighted.

Example 5-19. Truncated default.aspx.cs from Calendar-SelectionChanged (Calendar style attributes not shown)

```
<%@ Page Language="C#" AutoEventWireup="true"  CodeFile="Default.aspx.cs"
    Inherits="_Default" %>

<!DOCTYPE html PUBLIC "-//W3C//DTD XHTML 1.1//EN"
    "http://www.w3.org/TR/xhtml11/DTD/xhtml11.dtd">

<html xmlns="http://www.w3.org/1999/xhtml" >
<head runat="server">
    <title>Calendar</title>
</head>
<body>
    <form id="form1" runat="server">
    <div>
      <h1>Calendar Control</h1>
      <h2>SelectionChanged</h2>
      <asp:Calendar ID="Calendar1" runat="server"
        OnSelectionChanged="Calendar1_SelectionChanged">
      </asp:Calendar>

      <br/>
      <asp:Label id="lblCount" runat="server" />
      <br/>
      <asp:Label id="lblTodaysDate" runat="server" />
      <br/>
      <asp:Label id="lblSelected" runat="server" />
    </div>
    </form>
</body>
</html>
```

Running the page and selecting a date will result in the screen shown in Figure 5-17.

Looking at Example 5-19, you can see that this example adds the OnSelection-Changed event handler to the Calendar control. This event handler points to the Calendar1_SelectionChanged method in the code-behind file, shown in Example 5-18. Three Label controls have been added after the Calendar control. The first of these, lblCount, is used to display the number of days selected. The other two labels, named lblTodaysDate and lblSelected, are used to display today's date and the currently selected date, respectively.

All three of these labels have their Text property set in the SelectionChanged event handler method. Looking at that method in Example 5-18, you can see that lblTodaysDate is filled by getting the Calendar control's TodaysDate property, with the following line of code:

```
lblTodaysDate.Text = "Today's Date is " +
    Calendar1.TodaysDate.ToShortDateString( );
```

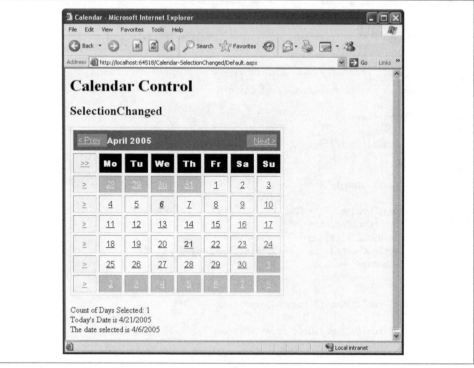

Figure 5-17. Calendar-SelectionChanged with date selected

The ID of the Calendar control is Calendar1. TodaysDate is a property of the Calendar control that returns an object of type System.DateTime. To assign this to a Text property (which is an object of type String), you must convert the DateTime to a String. This is done with the ToShortDateString method.

The DateTime structure has various methods for converting a DateTime object to other formats, including those shown in Table 5-18.

Table 5-18. Methods for converting a DateTime object to a string

Method name	Description
ToFileTime	Converts to the format of the local filesystem
ToLongDateString	Converts to a long date string
ToLongTimeString	Converts to a long time string
ToShortTimeString	Converts to a short time string
ToString	Converts to a string

Though not specific to ASP.NET, the DateTime structure is useful for obtaining all sorts of date and time information. Some of the read-only properties available from this structure include those listed in Table 5-19.

Table 5-19. DateTime read-only properties

Property name	Type	Description
Date	DateTime	Returns the date component
Day	Integer	Returns the day of the month
DayOfWeek	DayOfWeek	Returns the day of the week, e.g., Friday, Saturday, and so on
DayOfYear	Integer	Returns the day of the year
Hour	Integer	Returns the hour component
Millisecond	Integer	Returns the millisecond component
Minute	Integer	Returns the minute component
Month	Integer	Returns the month component
Second	Integer	Returns the second component
Ticks	Long	Returns the number of 100 nanosecond ticks representing the date and time
TimeOfDay	TimeSpan	Returns the time of day
Year	Integer	Returns the year component

lblSelected is filled by the following line of code:

```
if (Calendar1.SelectedDate != DateTime.MinValue)
    lblSelected.Text = "The date selected is " +
        Calendar1.SelectedDate.ToShortDateString( );
```

To detect if any date has been selected, you test to see if the currently selected date, Calendar1.SelectedDate, is equal to DateTime.MinValue. DateTime.MinValue is a constant representing the smallest possible value of DateTime and is the default value for the SelectedDate property if nothing has been selected yet. MinValue has the literal value of 12:00:00 AM, 1/1/0001 CE. There is also a MaxValue that has the literal value of 11:59:59 PM, 12/31/9999 CE.

 CE, which stands for the Common Era, is the scientific notation for the span of years referred to as AD (Anno Domini) on the Gregorian calendar. BCE (Before Common Era) is the scientific equivalent to BC (Before Christ).

If a date has been selected by the user, the Text property of lblSelected will be set to the string value of the SelectedDate property.

The Label control lblCount displays the number of days selected. The SelectionChanged event handler calls the lblCountUpdate method, which sets the Text property of lblCount. To set that control, you must determine how many dates were selected. The Calendar control has a SelectedDates property that returns a SelectedDates collection. SelectedDates is a collection of DateTime objects representing all the dates selected in the Calendar control. Count is a property of the SelectedDatesCollection object that returns an integer containing the number of dates in the collection. Since the Count property is an integer, you must use the `ToString` method to convert it to a string so that it can be assigned to the Text property.

```
Calendar1.SelectedDates.Count.ToString()
```

Though `SelectedDates` (the collection of selected dates) and `SelectedDate` (the single selected date) both contain `DateTime` objects, only the `Date` value is stored. The time value for these objects is set to a `null` reference in C#.

The range of dates in the `SelectedDates` collection is sorted in ascending order by date. When the `SelectedDates` collection is updated, the `SelectedDate` property is automatically updated to contain the first object in the `SelectedDates` collection.

The user can navigate from month to month by clicking on the month navigation controls to either side of the month title. The user can also select a single day by clicking on that day, an entire week by clicking on the week selector control, or the entire month by clicking on the month selector control.

However, you can give the user much more flexibility than this. To demonstrate, you must add several controls and methods. Copy the current example, *Calendar-SelectionChanged,* to a new web site called *Calendar-MoreSelections*.

To enable the user to navigate directly to any month in the current year, add a `DropDownList` containing all the months of the year and a button, labeled `TGIF`, which selects all the Fridays in the currently viewed month.

The `Calendar` control also allows the user to select a range of dates. You might expect to be able to use the standard Windows techniques of holding down the Ctrl or Shift keys while clicking on dates, but this does not work. However, you can put controls on the page to select a starting day and ending day. In *Calendar-MoreSelections,* you will add a pair of `TextBox` controls to accept a starting day and an ending day for a range of dates. A `Button` control can force the selection of the range of dates.

The content file to accomplish this is listed in Example 5-20. Again, all the style-related attributes for the `Calendar` control have been omitted for the sake of brevity; they are identical to those shown back in Example 5-17. The code which has changed from the previous example, representing the added controls, is highlighted.

Example 5-20. Default.aspx for Calendar-MoreSelections, omitting Calendar style attributes

```
<%@ Page Language="C#" AutoEventWireup="true"  CodeFile="Default.aspx.cs"
    Inherits="_Default" %>

<!DOCTYPE html PUBLIC "-//W3C//DTD XHTML 1.1//EN"
    "http://www.w3.org/TR/xhtml11/DTD/xhtml11.dtd">

<html xmlns="http://www.w3.org/1999/xhtml" >
<head runat="server">
    <title>Calendar</title>
</head>
```

Example 5-20. Default.aspx for Calendar-MoreSelections, omitting Calendar style attributes (continued)

```
<body>
    <form id="form1" runat="server">
    <div>
       <h1>Calendar Control</h1>
       <h2>More Selections</h2>
        <asp:Calendar ID="Calendar1" runat="server"
          OnSelectionChanged="Calendar1_SelectionChanged">
        </asp:Calendar>

       <br/>
       <asp:Label id="lblCount" runat="server" />
       <br/>
       <asp:Label id="lblTodaysDate" runat="server" />
       <br/>
       <asp:Label id="lblSelected" runat="server" />
       <br/>
       <table>
          <tr>
             <td>
                Select a month:
             </td>
             <td>
                <asp:DropDownList id= "ddl" runat="server"
                   AutoPostBack="true"
                   onSelectedIndexChanged = "ddl_SelectedIndexChanged">
                   <asp:ListItem text="January" value="1" />
                   <asp:ListItem text="February" value="2" />
                   <asp:ListItem text="March" value="3" />
                   <asp:ListItem text="April" value="4" />
                   <asp:ListItem text="May" value="5" />
                   <asp:ListItem text="June" value="6" />
                   <asp:ListItem text="July" value="7" />
                   <asp:ListItem text="August" value="8" />
                   <asp:ListItem text="September" value="9" />
                   <asp:ListItem text="October" value="10" />
                   <asp:ListItem text="November" value="11" />
                   <asp:ListItem text="December" value="12" />
                </asp:DropDownList>
             </td>
             <td>
                <asp:Button id="btnTgif" runat="server"
                   text="TGIF"
                   onClick="btnTgif_Click"/>
             </td>
          </tr>
          <tr>
             <td colspan="2"> </td>
          </tr>
          <tr>
             <td colspan="2"><b>Day Range</b></td>
          </tr>
```

Example 5-20. Default.aspx for Calendar-MoreSelections, omitting Calendar style attributes (continued)

```
            <tr>
               <td>Starting Day</td>
               <td>Ending Day</td>
            </tr>
            <tr>
               <td>
                  <asp:TextBox id= "txtStart" runat="server"
                     Width="25"
                     MaxLength="2" />
               </td>
               <td>
                  <asp:TextBox id= "txtEnd" runat="server"
                     Width="25"
                     MaxLength="2" />
               </td>
               <td>
                  <asp:Button id="btnRange" runat="server"
                     text="Apply"
                     onClick="btnRange_Click" />
               </td>
            </tr>
         </table>
      </div>
      </form>
</body>
</html>
```

The complete code-behind file for this example is listed in Example 5-21. Code changed from the previous example is highlighted.

Example 5-21. Default.aspx.cs for Calendar-MoreSelections

```
using System;
using System.Data;
using System.Configuration;
using System.Web;
using System.Web.Security;
using System.Web.UI;
using System.Web.UI.WebControls;
using System.Web.UI.WebControls.WebParts;
using System.Web.UI.HtmlControls;

public partial class _Default : System.Web.UI.Page
{
    /// <summary>
    /// This Page_Load makes the selected days visible first time
    ///  the TGIF button is clicked by initializing the VisibleDate
    ///  property.
    /// </summary>
    /// <param name="sender"></param>
    /// <param name="e"></param>
```

Example 5-21. Default.aspx.cs for Calendar-MoreSelections (continued)

```
    protected void Page_Load(object sender, EventArgs e)
    {
        if (!IsPostBack)
        {
            Calendar1.VisibleDate = Calendar1.TodaysDate;
            ddl.SelectedIndex = Calendar1.VisibleDate.Month - 1;
        }
        lblTodaysDate.Text = "Today's Date is " +
                Calendar1.TodaysDate.ToShortDateString( );
    }

    protected void Calendar1_SelectionChanged(object sender, EventArgs e)
    {
        lblSelectedUpdate( );
        lblCountUpdate( );
        txtClear( );
    }

    private void lblSelectedUpdate( )
    {
        if (Calendar1.SelectedDate != DateTime.MinValue)
            lblSelected.Text = "The date selected is " +
            Calendar1.SelectedDate.ToShortDateString( );
    }

    private void lblCountUpdate( )
    {
        lblCount.Text = "Count of Days Selected:  " +
            Calendar1.SelectedDates.Count.ToString( );
    }

    protected void ddl_SelectedIndexChanged(Object sender, EventArgs e)
    {
        Calendar1.SelectedDates.Clear( );
        lblSelectedUpdate( );
        lblCountUpdate( );
        Calendar1.VisibleDate = new DateTime(Calendar1.VisibleDate.Year,
                        Int32.Parse(ddl.SelectedItem.Value), 1);
        txtClear( );
    }

    protected void btnTgif_Click(Object sender, EventArgs e)
    {
        int currentMonth = Calendar1.VisibleDate.Month;
        int currentYear = Calendar1.VisibleDate.Year;

        Calendar1.SelectedDates.Clear( );

        for (int i = 1;
                i <= System.DateTime.DaysInMonth(currentYear,
                                                 currentMonth);
                i++)
```

Example 5-21. Default.aspx.cs for Calendar-MoreSelections (continued)

```
    {
        DateTime date = new DateTime(currentYear, currentMonth, i);
        if (date.DayOfWeek == DayOfWeek.Friday)
            Calendar1.SelectedDates.Add(date);
    }

    lblSelectedUpdate( );
    lblCountUpdate( );
    txtClear( );
}

protected void btnRange_Click(Object sender, EventArgs e)
{
    int currentMonth = Calendar1.VisibleDate.Month;
    int currentYear = Calendar1.VisibleDate.Year;
    DateTime StartDate = new DateTime(currentYear, currentMonth,
                            Int32.Parse(txtStart.Text));
    DateTime EndDate = new DateTime(currentYear, currentMonth,
                            Int32.Parse(txtEnd.Text));

    Calendar1.SelectedDates.Clear( );
    Calendar1.SelectedDates.SelectRange(StartDate, EndDate);

    lblSelectedUpdate( );
    lblCountUpdate( );
}

private void txtClear( )
{
    txtStart.Text = "";
    txtEnd.Text = "";
}
}
```

The result of running *Calendar-MoreSelections* is shown in Figure 5-18 after selecting a range of days.

The selection controls are all in a static HTML table so you can control the layout of the page.

The ListItem objects in the DropDownList contain the names of the months for the Text properties and the number of the months for the Value properties.

The Calendar1_SelectionChanged method has been modified by having the bulk of its code refactored into a separate method named lblSelectedUpdate, which updates the Text property of the lblSelected label. This method is then called from Calendar1_SelectionChanged, as well as several other places throughout the code. In addition, another helper method, txtClear, is called to clear the Start and End Day text boxes.

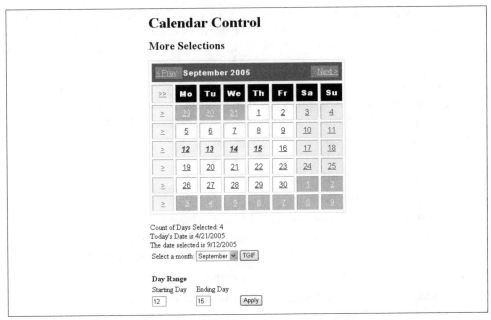

Figure 5-18. Calendar-MoreSelections with a range of days selected

The `ddl_SelectedIndexChanged` event handler method begins by clearing the `SelectedDates` collection:

```
Calendar1.SelectedDates.Clear( );
```

A call is made to the `lblSelectedUpdate` method to clear the `Label` control containing the first selected date and to the `lblCountUpdate` method to clear the `Label` control containing the count of selected dates. Then the `VisibleDate` property of the Calendar control is set to the first day of the newly selected month:

```
Calendar1.VisibleDate = new DateTime(Calendar1.VisibleDate.Year,
                Int32.Parse(ddl.SelectedItem.Value), 1);
```

The `VisibleDate` property is of type `DateTime`; a new `DateTime` is instantiated. The `DateTime` structure, like many objects in the .NET Framework, uses an *overloaded constructor*. An object may have more than one constructor; each must be differentiated by having different types of arguments or a different number of arguments.

In this case, you want to instantiate a `DateTime` object that contains only the date. To do so requires three integer parameters: year, month, and day. The first parameter, `cal.VisibleDate.Year`, and the last parameter, `1`, are inherently integers. However, the month parameter comes from the `Value` property of the selected item in the `DropDownList` control. The `Value` property is a string, not an integer, though the characters it contains *look* like an integer. Therefore, it must be converted to an integer using the statement:

```
Int32.Parse(ddl.SelectedItem.Value)
```

The TGIF button is named btnTgif and has an event handler for the Click event, btnTgif_Click. This method iterates over all the days of the currently visible month and tests to see if it is Friday. If so, it will add that date to the collection of SelectedDates.

First, the btnTgif_Click method gets the month and year of the currently visible month, using the VisibleDate property of the Calendar control, which is a DateTime object, and gets the Month and Year properties of the DateTime object:

```
int currentMonth = Calendar1.VisibleDate.Month;
int currentYear = Calendar1.VisibleDate.Year;
```

Then, it clears all the currently selected dates:

```
Calendar1.SelectedDates.Clear( );
```

Now, it does the iteration. The limit part of the for loop is the number of days in the month as determined by the DaysInMonth property of the DateTime object. The month in question is specified by the currentYear and currentMonth arguments:

```
System.DateTime.DaysInMonth(currentYear, currentMonth)
```

Once inside the for loop, a DateTime variable called date is assigned to each day. Again, the DateTime object is instantiated with parameters for year, month, and day. The crucial question becomes, "Is the day of the week for this day a Friday?" If so, then TGIF and add it to the collection of SelectedDates:

```
DateTime date = new DateTime(currentYear, currentMonth, i);
if (date.DayOfWeek == DayOfWeek.Friday)
    cal.SelectedDates.Add(date);
```

Finally, after iterating over all the days of the month, call the lblSelectedUpdate method to update the label showing the first selected date, call the lblCountUpdate method to update the label showing the number of days selected, and call txtClear to clear the Start and End day text boxes.

You will notice a Page_Load method in the code-behind file. As the comment in the code explains, this makes the page behave correctly the first time the TGIF button is clicked even before the month is changed. Without this Page_Load event procedure, the page behaves correctly for the TGIF button only after the month has been changed at least once. The btnTgif_Click method uses the VisibleDate property to set the current month and year variables. If that property is not initialized during the initial page load, then the values assigned to those variables will not correspond to the visible month.

In addition, the code to update the label displaying today's data, lblTodaysDate, has been moved from the SelectionChanged method to the Page_Load method because it makes more sense to have it there.

The controls for selecting the range are in the same static HTML table as the controls for selecting the month and all the Fridays. There are two text boxes, one named `txtStart` for the start day and one named `txtEnd` for the end day. In this example, the `TextBox` controls' `Width` and `MaxLength` attributes provide limited control over the user input. In a production application you will want to add validation controls, as described in Chapter 8, to avoid getting all sorts of nasty error messages if the user enters invalid characters or numbers out of range.

The UI provided in *Calendar-MoreSelections* for selecting a range of dates is admittedly limiting because you cannot span multiple months. You could almost as easily provide three independent `Calendar` controls: one for the start date, one for the end date, and one for the range. Also, the day range does not apply after the month changes without reapplying the selection because the `VisibleMonthChanged` event is not trapped. (See the section "VisibleMonthChanged event" later in this chapter.)

A helper method, `txtClear`, is provided to clear the day range selection boxes. This method is called at appropriate points in the other methods.

The Apply button is named `btnRange`, with the `Click` event handled by the method `btnRange_Click`. In `btnRange_Click`, you set integer variables to hold the current month and year:

```
int currentMonth = Calendar1.VisibleDate.Month;
int currentYear = Calendar1.VisibleDate.Year;
```

Set two `DateTime` variables to hold the start date and the end date:

```
DateTime StartDate = new DateTime(currentYear, currentMonth,
                                  Int32.Parse(txtStart.Text));
DateTime EndDate = new DateTime(currentYear, currentMonth, Int32.Parse(txtEnd.Text));
```

Similarly to the month `DropDownList` described previously, the `DateTime` object requires the year, month, and day. You have the year and month as integers; all you need is the day. You get the day by converting the text entered in the appropriate text box to an integer.

 This is not very robust code. If the user enters non-numeric data in one of the text boxes, or a value greater than the number of days in the month, an ugly error will result. If the start date is later than the end date, no error message will result, but neither will anything be selected. In a real application, you will want to use validation controls as described in Chapter 8.

Once the method has the start and end dates as `DateTime` objects, it clears any currently selected dates and uses the `SelectRange` method of the `SelectedDatesCollection` class to add the range of dates to the `SelectedDates` collection:

```
Calendar1.SelectedDates.Clear( );
Calendar1.SelectedDates.SelectRange(StartDate, EndDate);
```

The `SelectRange` method requires two parameters: the start date and the end date.

DayRender Event

Data binding is not supported directly for the Calendar control. However, you can modify the content and formatting of individual date cells. This allows you to retrieve values from a database, process those values in some manner, and place them in specific cells.

Before the Calendar control is rendered to the client browser, all of the components that comprise the control are created. As each date cell is created, it raises the DayRender event. This event can be handled.

The DayRender event handler receives an argument of type DayRenderEventArgs. This object has two properties that may be programmatically read:

Cell
> TableCell object that represents the cell being rendered

Day
> CalendarDay object that represents the day being rendered in that cell

This next example, *Calendar-Events*, will demonstrate the DayRender event. (The following section on the VisibleMonthChanged event will build on this same example.) All the weekend days will have their background color changed and a New Year's greeting will be displayed for January 1.

Copy the previous example, *Calendar-MoreSelections*, to a new web site called *Calendar-Events*. In this section, you will make the changes to handle the DayRender event. There are only two changes.

First, go into Design view, select Calendar1, click on the Events icon in the Properties window (the lightning bolt), and double-click on the text box next to DayRender. This will add the following attribute to the Calendar1 declaration in the content file:

```
OnDayRender="Calendar1_DayRender"
```

This will also create a default event handler code skeleton in the code-behind file, with the cursor placed ready to type. Enter the code highlighted in Example 5-22 to this code skeleton.

Example 5-22. DayRender event handler in Calendar-Events

```
protected void Calendar1_DayRender(object sender, DayRenderEventArgs e)
{
    // Notice that this overrides the WeekendDayStyle.
    if (!e.Day.IsOtherMonth && e.Day.IsWeekend)
        e.Cell.BackColor = System.Drawing.Color.LightGreen;

    // Happy New Year!
    if (e.Day.Date.Month == 1 && e.Day.Date.Day == 1)
        e.Cell.Controls.Add(new LiteralControl("<br/>Happy New Year!"));
}
```

The first thing the Calendar1_DayRender method does is color the weekends LightGreen. Recall that there is a WeekendDayStyle property set for this control that colors the weekends LavenderBlush. The DayRender method overrides the WeekendDayStyle. (The distinction may not be apparent in the printed book, but you will see the colors when you run the web page in a browser.)

The event handler method is passed two parameters:

```
void DayRender(Object sender, DayRenderEventArgs e)
```

DayRenderEventArgs contains properties for the Day and the Cell. The Day is tested to see if it is both the current month and also a weekend day:

```
(!e.Day.IsOtherMonth && e.Day.IsWeekend)
```

The Day property is a member of the CalendarDay class, which has the properties shown in Table 5-20 (all of which are read-only except IsSelectable).

Table 5-20. Properties of the CalendarDay class

Property	Type	Description
Date	DateTime	Date represented by this Day. Read-only.
DayNumberText	String	String representation of the day number of this Day. Read-only.
IsOtherMonth	Boolean	Indicates this Day is in a different month than the month currently displayed by the Calendar. Read-only.
IsSelectable	Boolean	Indicates if Day can be selected. Not read-only.
IsSelected	Boolean	Indicates if Day is selected.
IsToday	Boolean	Indicates if Day is today's date.
IsWeekend	Boolean	Indicates if Day is a weekend date.

If the date is both in the current month and is also a weekend day, then the Cell. BackColor property is assigned a color:

```
e.Cell.BackColor=System.Drawing.Color.LightGreen;
```

Calendar1_DayRender then tests to see if the selected date is New Year's Day. Again, the Day property of the DayRenderEventArgs object is tested to see if the Month of the Date is 1 and the Day of the Date is 1:

```
if (e.Day.Date.Month == 1 && e.Day.Date.Day == 1)
```

If so, a LiteralControl is added to the cell that adds an HTML break tag and a greeting:

```
e.Cell.Controls.Add(new LiteralControl("<br/>Happy New Year!"));
```

The thing to remember here is that, like all ASP.NET server controls, what is actually sent to the browser is HTML. Thus, a calendar is rendered on the browser as an HTML table. Each of the selectable components of the calendar has an anchor tag associated with it, along with some JavaScript that accomplishes the postback. (This is evident when you hover the cursor over any clickable element of the calendar: the status line of the browser will display the name of the JavaScript function that will be executed if the link is clicked.) Using a `LiteralControl` inserts the text in its argument as a control into the HTML cell as is. A look at a snippet from the source code visible on the browser confirms this:

```
<td align="Center" style="color:Black;background-color:White;
                          font-family:Arial;width:12%;">
    <a href="javascript:__doPostBack('cal','selectDay7')" style="color:Black">
    1
    </a>
    <br/>Happy New Year!
</td>
```

When the *Calendar-Events* example is run and the month navigated to January, you will see something like that shown in Figure 5-19.

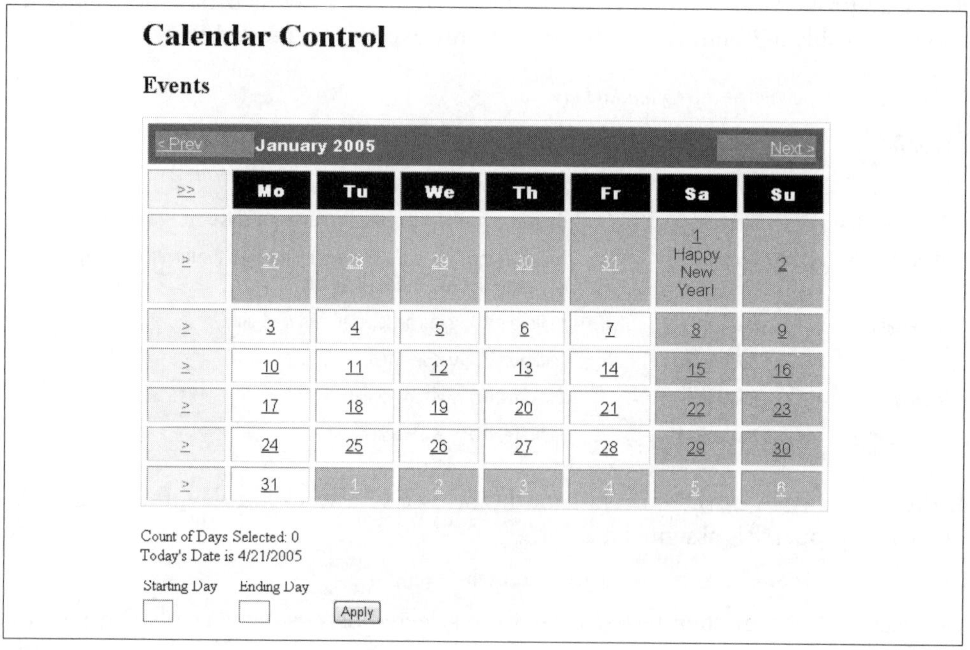

Calendar Control

Events

>>	Mo	Tu	We	Th	Fr	Sa	Su
≥	27	28	29	30	31	1 Happy New Year!	2
≥	3	4	5	6	7	8	9
≥	10	11	12	13	14	15	16
≥	17	18	19	20	21	22	23
≥	24	25	26	27	28	29	30
≥	31	1	2	3	4	5	6

< Prev   **January 2005**   Next >

Count of Days Selected: 0
Today's Date is 4/21/2005

Starting Day   Ending Day   [Apply]

Figure 5-19. Calendar-Events showing results of DayRender event

VisibleMonthChanged event

The `Calendar` control also provides an event to indicate that the user has changed months. You will extend the current example, *Calendar-Events*, to handle this event.

In the same manner as you added an event handler to `Calendar1` for the `DayRender` event, add a hander for the `VisibleMonthChanged` event. This will add the following attribute to the `Calendar1` declaration in the content file:

```
OnVisibleMonthChanged="Calendar1_VisibleMonthChanged">
```

and create a default event handler code skeleton in the code-behind file, with the cursor placed ready to type. Enter the code highlighted in Example 5-23 to this code skeleton.

Example 5-23. VisibleMonthChanged event handler in Calendar-Events

```
protected void Calendar1_VisibleMonthChanged(object sender,
                                       MonthChangedEventArgs e)
{
   if ((e.NewDate.Year > e.PreviousDate.Year) ||
      ((e.NewDate.Year == e.PreviousDate.Year) &&
      (e.NewDate.Month > e.PreviousDate.Month)))
      lblMonthChanged.Text = "My future's so bright...";
   else
      lblMonthChanged.Text = "Back to the future!";

   Calendar1.SelectedDates.Clear();
   lblSelectedUpdate();
   lblCountUpdate();
   txtClear();
}
```

You will also need to add a Label control, named lblMonthChanged, to the content file just before the Calendar control:

```
<asp:Label id="lblMonthChanged" runat="server" />
```

The Calendar1_VisibleMonthChanged event handler method receives an argument of type MonthChangedEventArgs. This argument contains two properties that may be read programmatically:

NewDate
    Represents the month currently displayed by the Calendar

PreviousDate
    Represents the month previously displayed by the Calendar

These values are tested in the Calendar1_VisibleMonthChanged method to see which came first. Depending on the results, one of two text strings is assigned to the Text property of lblMonthChanged.

Finally, the selected dates are cleared from the calendar, the text strings below the calendar are updated, and the day range edit boxes are cleared with the following lines of code:

```
Calendar1.SelectedDates.Clear()
lblSelectedUpdate()
lblCountUpdate()
txtClear()
```

The results of running *Calendar-Events* and navigating a month can be seen in Figure 5-20.

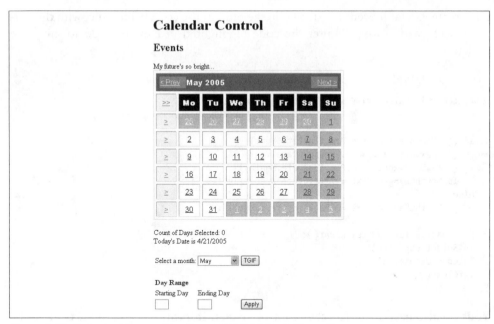

Figure 5-20. Calendar-Events with effects of VisibleMonthChanged event

CHAPTER 6

Web Site Fundamentals

In Chapters 3, 4, and 5, you learned many of the details about using ASP.NET server controls in web pages. In this chapter, you will learn techniques to help you utilize the full power of ASP.NET in creating web sites, including the following:

- Understanding the Page class, posting, and cross-page posting
- Using code-behind to segregate the presentation code from the logic
- Understanding the life cycle of a web page and controls
- Managing state in ASP.NET

The Page

An ASP.NET page consists of, at the minimum, a single file with an extension of *.aspx* though, typically, other files will be associated with the page, as we will describe. In the parlance of VS2005, this *.aspx* file is called the *content* file because it contains primarily the visual content of the page, i.e., HTML, text, and ASP.NET server controls.

Any content in the content file that is not part of a server control or server-side code is treated as a normal HTML file. It is passed from the server to the browser exactly as is, so the browser can deal with as it would any other HTML.

The *.aspx* file can contain script blocks. These are written in a scripting (non-compiled) language, such as JavaScript or VBScript, which will execute client side, meaning on the browser. It may also contain server-side code blocks, written in any .NET supported language, such as C# or VB2005, though these code blocks are more commonly contained in a separate *code-behind* file, as will be described in the next section.

When a browser requests the *.aspx* file from a web server, the server processes the page. If it is the first time that the page has been requested since the web application started, the ASP.NET runtime will compile from the page a Page class that derives from the base System.Web.UI.Page class. The compiled class contains all the control declarations and code that make up the page, including properties, event handlers, and other methods.

 Everyone knows what an application is, more or less. Still, an ASP. NET application is defined more rigorously in Chapter 18.

The class is then compiled into an assembly, which is what is actually run by the Framework runtime to render output to the client. That assembly is cached in server memory, so subsequent calls to the page do not require the compilation step, and the request can be serviced more quickly.

 You will notice this lag time the first time a page is viewed. It can be significant for complex pages. ASP.NET Version 2.0 adds the ability to pre-compile all the pages of a web site to avoid this problem after deployment. Deployment will be covered in Chapter 19.

The name of the compiled class is derived from the name of the *.aspx* file. If you keep the default name for a VS2005 content page, *default.aspx*, the class name will be _default. For any other page name, the class name will be same as the page name minus the extension, so *SomePage.aspx* will inherit from a class called SomePage.

For an *.aspx* file to be processed by the ASP.NET runtime, it must have a *page directive* as the first line in the file. Directives will be covered in detail later in this chapter, but for now the important point is that they provide information to the compiler, such as the language in use, the name of the code-behind file, if any, and the name of the Page class.

The class hierarchy for the Page class is shown in Figure 6-1. Since the Page class derives from Control, as do all the ASP.NET server controls, it shares all of the members of the Control class, including properties such as Controls, EnableTheming, EnableViewState, ID, SkinID, and Visible, all of which are described in Table 3-1. It also has a number of properties of its own, the most commonly used of which are listed in Table 6-1.

Table 6-1. Commonly used Page class properties

Name	Type	Get	Set	Description
Application	Application	✗		Retrieves a reference to the Application object for the current request.
Cache	Cache	✗		Retrieves the Cache object of the application.
ClientQueryString	string	✗		Retrieves the query string portion of the URL.

Table 6-1. Commonly used Page class properties (continued)

Name	Type	Get	Set	Description
Controls	ControlCollection	✗		Retrieves a reference to the collection of Controls on the page. Inherited from Control.
ErrorPage	string	✗	✗	The name of the page to redirect the browser to when there is an error. See Chapter 7 for coverage of error handling.
IsCrossPagePostBack	Boolean	✗		If true, this page has called another page.
IsPostBack	Boolean	✗		If true, this page is being loaded in response to a client post. If false, it is being loaded for the first time.
IsValid	Boolean	✗		If true, validation succeeded for all the controls on the page.
MaintainScrollPositionOnPostback	Boolean	✗		If true, the browser positioning of the page will be preserved across postbacks. The default is false.
Master	MasterPage	✗		Retrieves a reference to the master page for this page. See Chapter 11 for coverage of master pages.
MasterPageFile	string	✗	✗	The filename of the master page.
PreviousPage	Page	✗		Retrieves a reference to the previous page.

Code-Behind

You can interweave content, such as HTML, text, server controls, and program code in a single file, as was done with traditional ASP. This is known, cleverly, as the *single-file model*.

To see an example of the single-file model, look at *CodeSingleFile.aspx*, listed in Example 6-1. If you place this file in a folder on your machine, (such as *c:\websites*), create a virtual directory pointing to that folder, named, for example, *Websites*, and then enter the following URL in your browser:

```
http://localhost/websites/CodeSingleFile.aspx
```

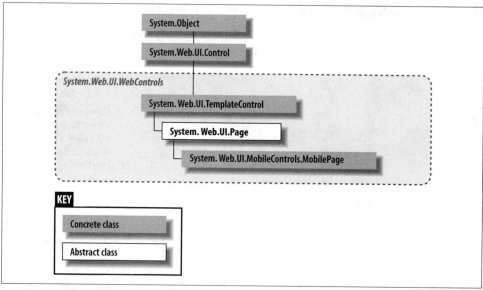

Figure 6-1. Page class hierarchy

Example 6-1. CodeSingleFile.aspx

```
<%@ Page Language="C#" %>

<script runat="server">
    protected void btnHello_Click(object sender, EventArgs e)
    {
       lblMessage.Text = "Hello. The time is " +
           DateTime.Now.ToLongTimeString( );
    }
</script>

<html>
<head runat="server">
    <title>Code-Beside</title>
</head>
<body>
    <form id="form1" runat="server">
    <div>
      <h1>Code-Beside</h1>
      <asp:Button ID="btnHello" runat="server"
                  Text="Hello"
                  OnClick="btnHello_Click" />
      <br />
      <asp:Label ID="lblMessage" runat="server"  />
    </div>
    </form>
</body>
</html>
```

The page will appear, containing a button that will display a text string every time it is clicked.

 Unlike previous versions of Visual Studio, Intellisense now works in content files in VS2005. This is true in code blocks as well as with the HTML and server controls.

The single file still requires a `Page` directive, and any compiled server-code is contained within `<script>` tags (highlighted in Example 6-1). For this web page, the name of the generated `Page` class would be `CodeSingleFile`.

The single-file model can produce source control nightmares and difficult-to-maintain pages. ASP.NET addresses these problems by giving developers the ability to separate the executable code from the presentation code. You write the content in a content file, and you write the program logic in the *code-behind* file (with a *.cs* or *.vb* extension, depending on your language choice). The term "code-behind" refers to the "code file behind the form."

 The nomenclature "content file," as used in this context, should not be confused with the use of the same term when talking about master pages, where the content file is replaceable content that is inserted onto a master page. Where the meaning is unclear or ambiguous in this book, it will be pointed out. Master pages are covered in Chapter 11.

There are other types of content files in the ASP.NET Framework besides page files. These are listed in Table 6-2.

Table 6-2. Content file types

File type	Extension
Page	*.aspx*
User Control	*.ascx*
Web Service	*.asmx*
Master Page	*.master*

The code-behind model is the default way that VS2005 operates, automatically creating both a content file and a code-behind file whenever you create a new page (or other item as appropriate).

To better understand the code-behind model, look at a simple web site. In VS2005, create a new web site called CodeBehind. Drag a `Button` and `Label` control onto the page, along with any other HTML adornment you like.

Name the Label control lblMessage and delete the Text property so it initially has nothing to display.

Name the Button btnHello, set its Text property to Hello, and give it a default (Click) event handler by going to Design view and double-clicking on the button. The code-behind file will open with the cursor placed for typing in the Click event handler method. Enter the highlighted text listed in Example 6-2.

Example 6-2. Code-behind file (Default.aspx.cs) for CodeBehind example

```
using System;
using System.Data;
using System.Configuration;
using System.Web;
using System.Web.Security;
using System.Web.UI;
using System.Web.UI.WebControls;
using System.Web.UI.WebControls.WebParts;
using System.Web.UI.HtmlControls;

public partial class _Default: System.Web.UI.Page
{
    protected void Page_Load(object sender, EventArgs e)
    {
    }

    protected void btnHello_Click(object sender, EventArgs e)
    {
        lblMessage.Text = "Hello. The time is " +
            DateTime.Now.ToLongTimeString();
    }
}
```

The complete content file is listed in Example 6-3. The two server control declarations are highlighted.

Example 6-3. Content file (Default.aspx) for CodeBehind example

```
<%@ Page Language="C#" AutoEventWireup="true"
    CodeFile="Default.aspx.cs"
    Inherits="_Default " %>

<!DOCTYPE html PUBLIC "-//W3C//DTD XHTML 1.1//EN"
    "http://www.w3.org/TR/xhtml11/DTD/xhtml11.dtd">

<html xmlns="http://www.w3.org/1999/xhtml" >
<head runat="server">
    <title>Code-Behind</title>
</head>
<body>
    <form id="form1" runat="server">
    <div>
      <h1>Code-Behind</h1>
```

```
        <asp:Button ID="btnHello" runat="server"
                    Text="Hello"
                    OnClick="btnHello_Click" />
        <br />
        <asp:Label ID="lblMessage" runat="server"  />
    </div>
    </form>
</body>
</html>
```

The name of the class created from the content file is specified in the `Page` directive with the `Inherits` attribute. VS2005 defaults this to the *original* name of the content file. The name of the code-behind file for this content file is specified in the `CodeFile` attribute.

 If you rename the content file in Solution Explorer in VS2005, the code-behind file will automatically be renamed identically. However, the class name specified in the `Page` directive and in the class declaration in the code-behind file will be unchanged. If this is important to you, manually change the class name in those lines of code.

In the code-behind file, a partial class is declared that inherits from `System.Web.UI.Page`.

```
    public partial class _Default : System.Web.UI.Page
```

Partial classes, new to Version 2.0 of ASP.NET, allow the definition of a class to be split across two or more source files. In the case of code-behind files, this allows VS2005 to hide the details of initializing the controls on the page and allows you to focus on the event handlers and other methods that you created in your *.aspx.cs* file.

Access Modifiers

The keywords `public`, `protected`, `private`, and `internal` are access modifiers. An access modifier determines which class methods can see and use a member variable or method. Table 6-3 summarizes the access modifiers.

The default accessibility of members of a class is `private`. Thus, if there is no access modifier provided for a class member, it will be a private member. Regardless of this circumstance, it is always a good idea to specify the access modifier explicitly to enhance the readability of the code.

Table 6-3. Access modifiers

Access modifier	Restrictions
public	No restrictions. Members marked `public` are visible to any method of any class.
private	The members in class A that are marked `private` are accessible only to methods of class A.
protected	The members in class A that are marked `protected` are accessible to methods of class A and to methods of classes derived from class A.
internal	The members in class A that are marked `internal` are accessible to methods of any class in A's assembly.
protected internal	The members in class A that are marked `protected internal` are accessible only to methods of class A, to methods of classes derived from class A, and to any class in A's assembly. This is effectively `protected` or `internal`.

Moving to Another Page

By default, when a page is submitted to the server, it is posted back to itself. However, there are many situations in a web application where you need to direct the application flow to another page, either directly or after posting to the server. There are four different ways to do this: `HyperLink`, `Server.Transfer`, `Response.Redirect`, and cross-page posting.

HyperLink

The `Hyperlink` control navigates directly to the location contained in the `NavigateUrl` property of the control without a postback to the server. This control is covered in Chapter 4.

Server.Transfer

The `Transfer` method of the `HttpServerUtility` class takes a URL of an *.aspx* or *.htm* page (but not *.asp*) as a string argument and posts back to the server. Execution of the current page is terminated and execution of the new page begins.

Because the `HttpResponse.End` method is called on the current page, it always raises a `ThreadAbortException`. This is usually not an issue, but if the `Server.Transfer` occurs as part of a connection-based database transaction (see Chapter 10 for details on connection-based database transactions) inside a `try` block, where the `Rollback` method is called in a `catch` block, the transaction will never commit because the transaction `Commit` method will be negated by the `ThreadAbortException`, unless you specifically catch the `ThreadAbortException`, as in the following code snippet:

```
try
{
    // do database stuff,then Commit the transaction
    transaction.Commit( );
```

```
      // Navigate to another page assuming a successful Commit.
      // This will raise a ThreadAbortException every time.
      Server.Transfer("OrderDetails.aspx?OrderID=" + strOrderID);
}
catch (ThreadAbortException ex)
{
      // placeholder to catch the routine exception
}
catch (Exception ex)
{
      // there was a problem w/ the Commit, so roll back
      transaction.Rollback();
}
finally
{
      // always close the connection
      connection.Close();
}
```

The original and target pages must be part of the same application. The target page can access public members of the control page, as will be demonstrated.

`Server.Transfer` does not verify that the current user is authorized to view the target page. If this is important for your application, you will need to use one of the other techniques described here.

After the transfer to the new page, the browser will continue to display the URL of the original page in its address box and not the current page. The browser's history does not reflect the transfer, so clicking the browser's Back button generally will not yield the desired results.

An overloaded form of the method takes a Boolean argument, which, if `true`, will indicate that the `QueryString` and `Form` collections of the original page will be preserved. The default is `false`.

This overload is particularly useful when you truly need to transfer complete control to another page. For example, if you were creating a multi-step web-based setup wizard and you needed the order of the various steps to be conditional based on the user's selections on previous answers, you could use this `Server.Transfer` overload to pass complete control to the pertinent page and preserve any `QueryString` and `Form` collections from previous pages or steps in the setup wizard.

Keep in mind that view state will not be preserved from page to page even though view state is stored within a hidden form variable. View state is page-scoped and invalidates when transferred to another page via `Server.Transfer`.

Response.Redirect

The `Redirect` method of the `HttpResponse` class is the programmatic equivalent of a HyperLink. It takes a URL of an *.aspx* or *.htm* page (but not *.asp*) as a string argument and performs a client-side redirect without posting back to the server. Consequently, it is faster than `Server.Transfer`. Since it is a completely new server request, it forces complete authentication and authorization.

Data from the original page is unavailable to the target page unless they are both in the same application, in which case data can be transferred using Session or Application state.

An overloaded form of this method takes a Boolean argument, which if `true`, indicates that the current page execution will be terminated.

Cross-Page Posting

A page can be submitted to the server and post directly back to another page. This is implemented via the `PostBackUrl` property of specific controls. It can only transfer to another *.aspx* page, not *.asp* or *.htm*. Controls from the previous page are available by using the `Page.PreviousPage` property.

If the original page and target page are both within the same application, then like all pages in an application, they can share Session and Application state as well as public members of the original page. A page can cross-post to a page outside the application, but data from the originating page is not available to the target page.

If the `PreviousPage` property of the target page is accessed, the original page is instantiated again and the stored View state from the original page is restored. Consequently, the performance penalty from using the `PreviousPage` property is directly affected by the amount of information stored in View state in the previous page. (View state is covered in more detail later in this chapter.)

 Cross-page posting is new to Version 2.0 of ASP.NET.

To see how these three techniques work, create a new web site in VS2005 called CrossPagePostingSimple. Drag three `Button` controls onto the default content page and name them `btnServerTransfer`, `btnRedirect`, and `btnCrossPage`. In Design view, double-click each of the first two buttons to give them default `Click` event handlers. `btnCrossPage` does not have any event handler code. However, for that button, set the `PostBackUrl` property to `TargetPage.aspx`. The complete code listing for the content file, *Default.aspx*, is shown in Example 6-4, with the three `Button` declarations highlighted.

Example 6-4. Default.aspx for CrossPagePostingSimple

```
<%@ Page Language="C#" AutoEventWireup="true" CodeFile="Default.aspx.cs"
    Inherits="_Default" %>
```

Example 6-4. Default.aspx for CrossPagePostingSimple (continued)

```
<!DOCTYPE html PUBLIC "-//W3C//DTD XHTML 1.1//EN"
    "http://www.w3.org/TR/xhtml11/DTD/xhtml11.dtd">

<html xmlns="http://www.w3.org/1999/xhtml" >
<head runat="server">
    <title>Cross-Page Posting</title>
</head>
<body>
    <form id="form1" runat="server">
    <div>
        <h1>Cross-Page Posting</h1>
        <asp:Button ID="btnServerTransfer" runat="server"
          Text="Server.Transfer"
          OnClick="btnServerTransfer_Click" />
        <asp:Button ID="btnRedirect" runat="server"
          Text="Response.Redirect"
          OnClick="btnRedirect_Click" />
        <asp:Button ID="btnCrossPage" runat="server"
          Text="Cross-Page Post"
          PostBackUrl="TargetPage.aspx" />
    </div>
    </form>
</body>
</html>
```

In the code-behind file, enter the event handlers shown in Example 6-5.

Example 6-5. Event handlers in Default.aspx.cs for CrossPageSimple

```
protected void btnServerTransfer_Click(object sender, EventArgs e)
{
    Server.Transfer("TargetPage.aspx");
}

protected void btnRedirect_Click(object sender, EventArgs e)
{
    Response.Redirect("TargetPage.aspx");
}
```

Now add a new web page to the project and call it TargetPage.aspx. For now, this is a simple page with only an HTML header element, as shown in Example 6-6. There is no code behind page for the target page at this point (other than the boilerplate created by VS2005).

Example 6-6. TargetPage.aspx for CrossPageSimple

```
<%@ Page Language="C#" AutoEventWireup="true"
    CodeFile="TargetPage.aspx.cs" Inherits="TargetPage_aspx" %>

<!DOCTYPE html PUBLIC "-//W3C//DTD XHTML 1.1//EN"
    "http://www.w3.org/TR/xhtml11/DTD/xhtml11.dtd">
```

Example 6-6. TargetPage.aspx for CrossPageSimple (continued)

```html
<html xmlns="http://www.w3.org/1999/xhtml" >
<head runat="server">
    <title>Target Page</title>
</head>
<body>
    <form id="form1" runat="server">
    <div>
      <h1>Target Page</h1>
    </div>
    </form>
</body>
</html>
```

Set *Default.aspx* as the Start page and run the application. You will get something like that shown in Figure 6-2.

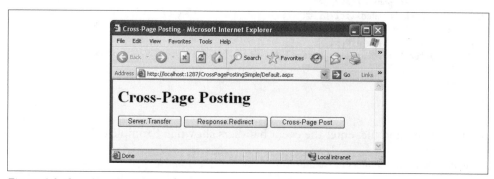

Figure 6-2. CrossPagePostingSimple

Clicking on the Server.Transfer button will bring up the page shown in Figure 6-3.

Figure 6-3. TargetPage via Server.Transfer

The URL in the address bar still points to the original page, *Default.aspx*.

Now click on the browser Back button to get back to the original page and click on either the Response.Redirect or Cross-Page Post buttons. The result will be almost the same, shown in Figure 6-4.

Figure 6-4. TargetPage via Response.Redirect or Cross-Page Post

Notice, however, that the URL now points to the current page, *TargetPage.aspx*. Though the end result of the Response.Redirect and the cross-page post appears the same, there is a fundamental difference. Response.Redirect does not post to the server, and so no server-side code can execute. Cross-page posting does post to the server, as does Server.Transfer, so you can handle the Click event and run server-side code.

The cross-page post was accomplished simply by setting the PostBackUrl property of the button.

```
PostBackUrl="TargetPage.aspx" />
```

PostBackUrl is a property of all controls that implement the IButtonControl interface. This includes the Button, ImageButton, and LinkButton ASP.NET server controls. Since cross-page posting is implemented on a control-by-control basis, rather than a page basis, it gives great flexibility in directing where a page will post back to.

Retrieving data from the previous page

When posting to a different page, a typical requirement is to access controls and objects from the previous page. You could stash cross-page data in session state (described later in this chapter), but that consumes server resources and should be used cautiously with large objects.

The Page class exposes the PreviousPage property to provide a reference to the previous page object. There are two different ways of retrieving data from this Page reference, both of which will be demonstrated shortly. The technique you can use is dependent upon whether or not the Page object is strongly typed.

A *strongly typed* object has a very specific collection of public members, with each member being of a specific type. Under these circumstances, you could retrieve a public member of a Page, say a property called Password, of type string, with the following line of code:

```
string str = PreviousPage.Password;
```

Under normal circumstances, i.e., by default, the Page object returned by the PreviousPage property is *not* strongly typed. In this case, to retrieve the contents of a control, you must use late-binding, i.e., use reflection to determine what controls are in the Page's Controls collection at runtime and find a specific control using the FindControl method of the Page. However, late-binding imposes a performance penalty, and so should be avoided if possible.

In order to strongly type the PreviousPage Page object, the content file of the target page (i.e., the page being transferred to) must have an additional directive, PreviousPageType, added at the top of the file. The PreviousPageType directive has two possible attributes, of which only one may be used at a time on a page:

TypeName
    A string representing the type of the previous page

VirtualPath
    A string representing the relative URL of the previous page

To see this in action, copy the previous example, CrossPagePostingSimple, to a new web site, CrossPagePostingAccessingPrevious. To *default.aspx*, add a DropDownList named ddlFavoriteActivity populated with a number of your favorite activities, along with some <br/> elements to space things out. *Default.aspx* is listed in Example 6-7, with the new code highlighted. Set the AutoPostback property of the DropDownList to true so you can see the that when the form is posted normally, it comes back to itself.

Example 6-7. Default.aspx for CrossPagePostingAccessingPrevious

```
<%@ Page Language="C#" AutoEventWireup="true"
   CodeFile="Default.aspx.cs" Inherits="_Default" %>

<!DOCTYPE html PUBLIC "-//W3C//DTD XHTML 1.1//EN"
   "http://www.w3.org/TR/xhtml11/DTD/xhtml11.dtd">

<html xmlns="http://www.w3.org/1999/xhtml" >
<head runat="server">
    <title>Cross-Page Posting</title>
</head>
<body>
    <form id="form1" runat="server">
    <div>
      <h1>Cross-Page Posting</h1>
      Select your favorite activity: 
      <asp:DropDownList ID="ddlFavoriteActivity" runat="server"
        AutoPostBack="true">
        <asp:ListItem Text="Eating" />
        <asp:ListItem Text="Sleeping" />
        <asp:ListItem Text="Programming" />
        <asp:ListItem Text="Watching TV" />
        <asp:ListItem Text="Sex" />
        <asp:ListItem Text="Skiing" />
```

```
        <asp:ListItem Text="Bicycling" />
      </asp:DropDownList>
      <br />
      <br />
      <br />
      <asp:Button ID="btnServerTransfer" runat="server"
        Text="Server.Transfer"
        OnClick="btnServerTransfer_Click" />
      <asp:Button ID="btnRedirect" runat="server"
        Text="Response.Redirect"
        OnClick="btnRedirect_Click" />
      <asp:Button ID="btnCrossPage" runat="server"
        Text="Cross-Page Post"
        PostBackUrl="TargetPage.aspx" />
    </div>
    </form>
</body>
</html>
```

Since the Page object returned by the PreviousPage property can only access public members, you must publicly expose ddlFavoriteActivity. The best way to do this is to create in the Page class a public, read-only property of type DropDownList. To do that, edit *Default.aspx.cs* to add the code highlighted in Example 6-8.

Example 6-8. Default.aspx.cs for CrossPagePostingAccessingPrevious

```
using System;
using System.Data;
using System.Configuration;
using System.Web;
using System.Web.Security;
using System.Web.UI;
using System.Web.UI.WebControls;
using System.Web.UI.WebControls.WebParts;
using System.Web.UI.HtmlControls;
using System.Threading;          //  necessary for ThreadAbortException

public partial class _Default : System.Web.UI.Page
{
    protected void Page_Load(object sender, EventArgs e)
    {
    }

    public DropDownList FavoriteActivity
    {
        get { return ddlFavoriteActivity; }
    }

    protected void btnServerTransfer_Click(object sender, EventArgs e)
    {
        Server.Transfer("TargetPage.aspx");
    }
```

```
    protected void btnRedirect_Click(object sender, EventArgs e)
    {
        Response.Redirect("TargetPage.aspx");
    }
}
```

There is no inherent reason why this property must be read-only. By adding a set accessor, you could make it read/write. However, in this type of scenario, read-only is usually adequate.

Now that you have exposed a public property that returns an instance of a DropDownList, you must prepare the target page to retrieve it. Modify the content page of the Target page, *TargetPage.aspx*, adding the code highlighted in Example 6-9.

Example 6-9. TargetPage.aspx in CrossPagePostingAccessingPrevious

```
<%@ Page Language="C#" AutoEventWireup="true"
   CodeFile="TargetPage.aspx.cs" Inherits="TargetPage_aspx" %>
<%@ PreviousPageType  VirtualPath="~/Default.aspx" %>

<!DOCTYPE html PUBLIC "-//W3C//DTD XHTML 1.1//EN"
   "http://www.w3.org/TR/xhtml11/DTD/xhtml11.dtd">

<html xmlns="http://www.w3.org/1999/xhtml" >
<head runat="server">
    <title>Target Page</title>
</head>
<body>
    <form id="form1" runat="server">
    <div>
      <h1>Target Page.</h1>

      Your favorite activity is
        <asp:Label ID="lblActivity" runat="server" Text="unknown" />
    </div>
    </form>
</body>
</html>
```

You added a PreviousPageType directive, with the VirtualPath attribute set to the URL of the original page. (The ~/ preceding the filename is not required but is put there by Intellisense in the VS2005 editor. It resolves to the root of the application.) You also added a Label server control to display the value retrieved from the DropDownList on the previous page.

The final step in this process is to add the highlighted lines of code from Example 6-10 to the *TargetPage* code-behind file.

Example 6-10. TargetPage.aspx.cs for CrossPagePostingAccessingPrevious

```
using System;
using System.Data;
using System.Configuration;
using System.Collections;
using System.Web;
using System.Web.Security;
using System.Web.UI;
using System.Web.UI.WebControls;
using System.Web.UI.WebControls.WebParts;
using System.Web.UI.HtmlControls;

public partial class TargetPage_aspx : System.Web.UI.Page
{
    protected void Page_Load(object sender, EventArgs e)
    {
        if (Page.PreviousPage != null)
        {
            lblActivity.Text =
                PreviousPage.FavoriteActivity.SelectedItem.ToString( );
        }
    }
}
```

This code in the Page_Load event handler first tests to see if the PreviousPage property has been set. If it hasn't, for example if you arrive here by clicking on the Response.Redirect button on the Default page, then the initially declared (i.e., declared in *TargetPage.aspx*) Text property of lblActivityText will be displayed.

If the PreviousPage property has been set, by posting the request to the server using either Server.Transfer or cross-page posting, then lblActivity will be populated by retrieving the SelectedItem property of ddlFavoriteActivity via the FavoriteActivity property.

The implication of this entire process is that any page can only be transferred to by a single other page since the previous page name is hardcoded in the PreviousPageType directive if you are to use strongly typed Page objects and the PreviousPage property. However, this is not the case. You can transfer or post from any page as long as they all have the same *signature*, i.e., the specific list of public members and types.

If all the pages you need to transfer from do not have the same signature, or if you cannot know at design time the name of a page to specify the types, you will have to use late-binding techniques (or, more likely, session state). Once again, this technique incurs a significant performance penalty versus the early-bound, strongly typed method.

To see late-binding at work, copy the previous example, CrossPagePostingAccessing-Previous, to a new web site called CrossPagePostingAccessingPreviousLateBound. *Default.aspx* is unchanged from before, but there is no longer any need for the public property FavoriteActivity, so that can be deleted from *Default.aspx.cs*. In

TargetPage.aspx, delete the `PreviousPageType` directive. Then, in *TargetPage.aspx.cs*, replace the `Page_Load` method with the highlighted code from Example 6-11.

Example 6-11. TargetPage.aspx.cs for CrossPagePostingAccessingPreviousLateBound

```
using System;
using System.Data;
using System.Configuration;
using System.Collections;
using System.Web;
using System.Web.Security;
using System.Web.UI;
using System.Web.UI.WebControls;
using System.Web.UI.WebControls.WebParts;
using System.Web.UI.HtmlControls;

public partial class TargetPage_aspx : System.Web.UI.Page
{
    protected void Page_Load(object sender, EventArgs e)
    {
        if (Page.PreviousPage != null)
        {
            DropDownList ddl =
                (DropDownList)Page.PreviousPage.FindControl(
                    "ddlFavoriteActivity");
            if (ddl != null)
                lblActivity.Text = ddl.SelectedItem.ToString() +
                                    " (late-bound)";
        }
    }
}
```

By removing the public property `FavoriteActivity` from the *default.aspx.cs* listed in Example 6-8, the Text assignment line of code in Example 6-10 fails. Instead, `Page_Load` in Example 6-11 uses the `FindControl` method of the `Page`class to get a reference directly to the `DropDownList`. The `PreviousPageType` directive was removed because it no longer serves any purpose.

Note well that the `PreviousPage` property is still defined but only if the page was navigated to via a server post. If you click the Response.Redirect button, which redirects to the target page from client-side code, not server code, then `lblActivity` will never be populated in `Page_Load` and the initial value will be used again.

How did I get here?

It is often helpful to know if a page has been opened directly or as the result of a transfer or cross-page post. Two read-only `Page` properties of type Boolean, `IsPostBack` and `IsCrossPagePostBack`, allow this to be determined.

Though the IsCrossPagePostBack property is new to Version 2.0 of ASP.NET, the usage of these two properties is such that Version 1.x behavior is unchanged.

The values that these properties assume is not always what you might expect at first glance. To follow this, copy the previous example, CrossPagePostingAccessingPreviousLateBound, to a new web site called CrossPagePostingPostBackProperties. You will add Label controls to each of the two content pages to display the values of the various properties, and you will modify the two Page_Load methods to populate those labels. All four files are listed, with the new code highlighted, in Examples 6-12 through 6-15.

Example 6-12. Default.aspx for CrossPagePostingPostBackProperties

```
<%@ Page Language="C#" AutoEventWireup="true" CodeFile="Default.aspx.cs"
   Inherits="_Default" %>

<!DOCTYPE html PUBLIC "-//W3C//DTD XHTML 1.1//EN"
   "http://www.w3.org/TR/xhtml11/DTD/xhtml11.dtd">

<html xmlns="http://www.w3.org/1999/xhtml" >
<head runat="server">
    <title>Cross-Page Posting</title>
</head>
<body>
    <form id="form1" runat="server">
    <div>
      <h1>Cross-Page Posting</h1>
      Select your favorite activity: 
      <asp:DropDownList ID="ddlFavoriteActivity" runat="server"
        AutoPostBack="true">
        <asp:ListItem Text="Eating" />
        <asp:ListItem Text="Sleeping" />
        <asp:ListItem Text="Programming" />
        <asp:ListItem Text="Watching TV" />
        <asp:ListItem Text="Sex" />
        <asp:ListItem Text="Skiing" />
        <asp:ListItem Text="Bicycling" />
      </asp:DropDownList>
      <br />
      <br />
      <br />
      <asp:Button ID="btnServerTransfer" runat="server"
        Text="Server.Transfer"
        OnClick="btnServerTransfer_Click" />
      <asp:Button ID="btnRedirect" runat="server"
        Text="Response.Redirect"
        OnClick="btnRedirect_Click" />
      <asp:Button ID="btnCrossPage" runat="server"
        Text="Cross-Page Post"
```

```
        PostBackUrl="TargetPage.aspx" />
    <br />
    <br />
    IsPostBack:
    <asp:Label ID="lblIsPostBack" runat="server" Text="not defined" />
    <br />
    IsCrossPagePostBack:
    <asp:Label ID="lblIsCrossPagePostBack" runat="server"
               Text="not defined" />
    <br />
    PreviousPage:
    <asp:Label ID="lblPreviousPage" runat="server" Text="not defined" />
  </div>
  </form>
</body>
</html>
```

Example 6-13. Default.aspx.cs for CrossPagePostingPostBackProperties

```csharp
using System;
using System.Data;
using System.Configuration;
using System.Web;
using System.Web.Security;
using System.Web.UI;
using System.Web.UI.WebControls;
using System.Web.UI.WebControls.WebParts;
using System.Web.UI.HtmlControls;
using System.Threading;          //  necessary for ThreadAbortException

public partial class _Default : System.Web.UI.Page
{
    protected void Page_Load(object sender, EventArgs e)
    {
        lblIsPostBack.Text = IsPostBack.ToString();
        lblIsCrossPagePostBack.Text = IsCrossPagePostBack.ToString();
        if (Page.PreviousPage != null)
            lblPreviousPage.Text = Page.PreviousPage.Title;
    }

    protected void btnServerTransfer_Click(object sender, EventArgs e)
    {
        Server.Transfer("TargetPage.aspx");
    }

    protected void btnRedirect_Click(object sender, EventArgs e)
    {
        Response.Redirect("TargetPage.aspx");
    }
}
```

Example 6-14. TargetPage.aspx for CrossPagePostingPostBackProperties

```
<%@ Page Language="C#" AutoEventWireup="true"
   CodeFile="TargetPage.aspx.cs" Inherits="TargetPage_aspx" %>

<!DOCTYPE html PUBLIC "-//W3C//DTD XHTML 1.1//EN"
   "http://www.w3.org/TR/xhtml11/DTD/xhtml11.dtd">

<html xmlns="http://www.w3.org/1999/xhtml" >
<head runat="server">
    <title>Target Page</title>
</head>
<body>
    <form id="form1" runat="server">
    <div>
        <h1>Target Page.</h1>
        Your favorite activity is
        <asp:Label ID="lblActivity" runat="server" Text="unknown" />
        <br />
        <br />
        IsPostBack:
        <asp:Label ID="lblIsPostBack" runat="server" Text="not defined" />
        <br />
        IsCrossPagePostBack:
        <asp:Label ID="lblIsCrossPagePostBack" runat="server"
                Text="not defined" />

        <br />
        PreviousPage:
        <asp:Label ID="lblPreviousPage" runat="server"
                Text="not defined" />

        <br />
        Previous Page IsPostBack:
        <asp:Label ID="lblPreviousPageIsPostBack" runat="server"
                Text="not defined" />

        <br />
        Previous Page IsCrossPagePostBack:
        <asp:Label ID="lblPreviousPageIsCrossPagePostBack" runat="server"
                Text="not defined" />
    </div>
    </form>
</body>
</html>
```

Example 6-15. TargetPage.aspx.cs for CrossPagePostingPostBackProperties

```
using System;
using System.Data;
using System.Configuration;
using System.Collections;
using System.Web;
using System.Web.Security;
using System.Web.UI;
using System.Web.UI.WebControls;
using System.Web.UI.WebControls.WebParts;
using System.Web.UI.HtmlControls;
```

Example 6-15. TargetPage.aspx.cs for CrossPagePostingPostBackProperties (continued)

```
public partial class TargetPage_aspx : System.Web.UI.Page
{
    protected void Page_Load(object sender, EventArgs e)
    {
        if (Page.PreviousPage != null)
        {
            DropDownList ddl =
                (DropDownList)Page.PreviousPage.FindControl(
                    "ddlFavoriteActivity");
            if (ddl != null)
                lblActivity.Text = ddl.SelectedItem.ToString() +
                    " (late-bound)";
        }

        lblIsPostBack.Text = IsPostBack.ToString();
        lblIsCrossPagePostBack.Text = IsCrossPagePostBack.ToString();
        if (Page.PreviousPage != null)
        {
            lblPreviousPage.Text = Page.PreviousPage.Title;
            lblPreviousPageIsPostBack.Text =
                Page.PreviousPage.IsPostBack.ToString();
            lblPreviousPageIsCrossPagePostBack.Text =
                Page.PreviousPage.IsCrossPagePostBack.ToString();
        }
    }
}
```

Running CrossPagePostingPostBackProperties through the various scenarios reveals the matrix shown in Table 6-4.

Table 6-4. PostBack property values

Action	Page	Property	Value
default.aspx posting itself	*default.aspx*	IsPostBack	true
	default.aspx	IsCrossPagePostBack	false
	default.aspx	PreviousPage	null
default.aspx to TargetPage.aspxPage via Server.Transfer	*TargetPage.aspx*	IsPostBack	false
	TargetPage.aspx	IsCrossPagePostBack	false
	TargetPage.aspx	PreviousPage	Default
	default.aspx	IsPostBack	true
	default.aspx	IsCrossPagePostBack	false
default.aspx to TargetPage.aspxPage via cross-page posting	*TargetPage.aspx*	IsPostBack	false
	TargetPage.aspx	IsCrossPagePostBack	false
	TargetPage.aspx	PreviousPage	Default
	default.aspx	IsPostBack	true
	default.aspx	IsCrossPagePostBack	true

You can see the effects of default.apx posting back to itself by selecting a new value from the DropDownList since the AutoPostBack property is set to true for that control. The only difference between posting to a new page via Server.Transfer and cross-page posting is in the value of the original page's IsCrossPagePostBack property, which is false for the former and true for the latter.

State

State is the current value of all the controls and variables for the current user in the current session. The web is inherently a *stateless* environment, which means that every time a page is posted to the server and then sent back to the browser, the page is re-created from scratch. Unless the state of all the controls is explicitly preserved before the page is posted, the state is lost and all the controls are created with default values. One of the great strengths of ASP.NET is that it automatically maintains state for server controls—both HTML and ASP.NET—so you do not have to write any code to accomplish this. This section will explore how this is done and how you can make use of the ASP.NET state management capabilities.

ASP.NET manages four types of state:

- View state (which is saved in the state bag)
- Control state
- Application state
- Session state

Control state, (described below in conjunction with View state), cannot be modified, accessed directly, or disabled. Table 6-5 compares the other kinds of state management.

Table 6-5. Comparison of types of state

Feature	View state	Application state	Session state
Uses server resources	No	Yes	Yes
Uses bandwidth	Yes	No	No
Times out	No	No	Yes
Security exposure	Yes	No	Depends
Optimized for non-primitive types	No	Yes	Yes
Available for arbitrary data	Yes	Yes	Yes
Programmatically accessible	Yes	Yes	Yes
Scope	Page	Application	Session
Survives restart	Yes	No	Depends on configuration

The following sections will examine each type of state in turn.

Session State

When you connect to an ASP.NET web site, you create a session. The session imposes state on the otherwise stateless Web and allows the web site to recognize that subsequent page requests are from the same browser that started the session. This allows you to maintain state across pages until you consciously end the session or the session times out. (The default timeout is 20 minutes.)

While an application is running, there will be many *sessions*, essentially, one for each user interacting with the web site.

ASP.NET provides session state with the following features:

- Works with browsers that have had cookies disabled.
- Identifies if a request is part of an existing session.
- Stores session-scoped data for use across multiple requests. This data can be configured to persist across IIS restarts and work in multi-processor (web garden) and multi-machine (web farm) environments, as well as in single-processor, single-server situations.
- Raises session events such as Session_Start and Session_End, which can be handled either in the *global.asax* file or in other application code.
- Automatically releases session resources if the session ends or times out.

By default, session state is stored in server memory as part of the ASP.NET process. However, as will be shown shortly, it can be configured to be stored separately from the ASP.NET process, either on a separate state server or in a SQL Server database, in which case it will survive a crash or restart of the ASP.NET process.

Sessions are identified and tracked with a 120-bit SessionID that is passed from client to server and back using an HTTP cookie or a modified URL, depending on how the application is configured. The SessionID is handled automatically by the .NET Framework; there is no need to manipulate it programmatically. The SessionID consists of URL-legal ASCII characters that have two important characteristics:

- They are globally unique so there is no chance of two different sessions having the same SessionID.
- They are random so it is difficult to guess the value of another session's SessionID after learning the value of an existing session's SessionID.

Session state is implemented using the Contents collection property of the HttpSessionState class. This collection is a key-value (non-generic) dictionary containing all the session state dictionary objects that have been directly added programatically. The dictionary objects are set and retrieved using the Session keyword, as shown in the following example, SessionStateDemo.

This example presents a set of radio buttons. Selecting one of the radio buttons and clicking the Submit button sets three session dictionary objects—two strings and a string array. These session dictionary objects are then used to populate a label control and a drop-down list control.

To create this example, drag a RadioButtonList, a Button, a Label, and an invisible DropDownList control onto the page, along with some HTML to spread things out a bit. The content file is listed in Example 6-16.

Example 6-16. Default.aspx for SessionStateDemo

```
<%@ Page Language="C#" AutoEventWireup="true"  CodeFile="Default.aspx.cs"
    Inherits="_Default" %>

<!DOCTYPE html PUBLIC "-//W3C//DTD XHTML 1.1//EN"
    "http://www.w3.org/TR/xhtml11/DTD/xhtml11.dtd">

<html xmlns="http://www.w3.org/1999/xhtml" >
<head runat="server">
    <title>Session State</title>
</head>
<body>
    <form id="form1" runat="server">
    <div>
      <h1>Session State</h1>
      <h3>Select a book category</h3>
      <asp:RadioButtonList ID="rbl" runat="server"
            CellSpacing="20"
            RepeatColumns="3"
            RepeatDirection="Horizontal"
            OnSelectedIndexChanged="rbl_SelectedIndexChanged">
        <asp:ListItem Value="n">.NET</asp:ListItem>
        <asp:ListItem Value="d">Databases</asp:ListItem>
        <asp:ListItem Value="h">Hardware</asp:ListItem>
      </asp:RadioButtonList>
      <asp:Button ID="btn" runat="server"
            Text="Submit"
            OnClick="btn_Click" />
      <br />
      <br />
      <asp:Label ID="lblMessage" runat="server"></asp:Label>
      <br />
      <br />
      <asp:DropDownList ID="ddl" runat="server" Visible="False">
      </asp:DropDownList>
    </div>
    </form>
</body>
</html>
```

In the code-behind file are two event handlers, one for the SelectedIndexChanged event of the RadioButtonList and one for the Click event of the Button. A using System.Text statement is required at the beginning of the file to enable use of the StringBuilder. The complete code-behind file is shown in Example 6-17.

Example 6-17. Default.aspx.cs for SessionStateDemo

```
using System;
using System.Data;
using System.Configuration;
using System.Web;
using System.Web.Security;
using System.Web.UI;
using System.Web.UI.WebControls;
using System.Web.UI.WebControls.WebParts;
using System.Web.UI.HtmlControls;
using System.Text;          //  necessary for StringBuilder

public partial class _Default : System.Web.UI.Page
{
    protected void Page_Load(object sender, EventArgs e)
    {
    }

    protected void rbl_SelectedIndexChanged(object sender, EventArgs e)
    {
        if (rbl.SelectedIndex != -1)
        {
            string[] Books = new string[3];

            Session["cattext"] = rbl.SelectedItem.Text;
            Session["catcode"] = rbl.SelectedItem.Value;

            switch (rbl.SelectedItem.Value)
            {
                case "n":
                    Books[0] = "Programming C#";
                    Books[1] = "Programming ASP.NET";
                    Books[2] = "C# Essentials";
                    break;
                case "d":
                    Books[0] = "Oracle & Open Source";
                    Books[1] = "SQL in a Nutshell";
                    Books[2] = "Transact-SQL Programming";
                    break;
                case "h":
                    Books[0] = "PC Hardware in a Nutshell";
                    Books[1] = "Dictionary of PC Hardware and Data
                                Communications Terms";
                    Books[2] = "Linux Device Drivers";
                    break;
            }
            Session["books"] = Books;
        }
    }

    protected void btn_Click(object sender, EventArgs e)
    {
        if (rbl.SelectedIndex == -1)
```

Example 6-17. Default.aspx.cs for SessionStateDemo (continued)

```
        {
            lblMessage.Text = "You must select a book category.";
        }
        else
        {
            StringBuilder sb = new StringBuilder( );
            sb.Append("You have selected the category ");
            sb.Append((string)Session["cattext"]);
            sb.Append(" with code \"");
            sb.Append((string)Session["catcode"]);
            sb.Append("\".");
            lblMessage.Text = sb.ToString( );

            ddl.Visible = true;
            string[] CatBooks = (string[])Session["books"];

            // Populate the DropDownList.
            int i;
            ddl.Items.Clear( );
            for (i = 0; i < CatBooks.GetLength(0); i++)
            {
                ddl.Items.Add(new ListItem(CatBooks[i]));
            }
        }
    }
}
```

Look first at `rbl_SelectedIndexChanged`, the `RadioButtonList` event handler in Example 6-17. This method populates the `Session` dictionary objects whenever the user selects a different radio button.

After testing to ensure that something is selected, `rbl_SelectedIndexChanged` defines a string array to hold the lists of books in each category. Then it assigns the selected item Text and Value properties to two `Session` dictionary objects.

```
    Session["cattext"] = rbl.SelectedItem.Text;
    Session["catcode"] = rbl.SelectedItem.Value;
```

`rblSelectedIndexChanged` next uses a `switch` statement to fill the previously declared string array with a list of books, depending on the book category selected.

Finally, the method assigns the string array to a `Session` dictionary object.

```
    Session["books"] = Books;
```

This example stores only strings and an array in the `Session` dictionary objects. However, you can store any object that inherits from `ISerializable`. These include all the primitive data types and arrays comprised of primitive data types, as well as the `DataSet`, `DataTable`, `HashTable`, and `Image` objects, and any user-created classes that implement the interface. This allows you to store query results, for example, or a collection of items in a user's shopping cart.

The other event handler method, btn_Click, is called whenever the user clicks the Submit button. It tests to verify that a radio button has been selected. If not, the Label will be filled with a warning message.

```
if (rbl.SelectedIndex == -1)
{
    lblMsg.Text = "You must select a book category.";
}
```

The else clause of the if statement is the meat of this page. It retrieves the Session dictionary objects and uses the StringBuilder class to concatenate the strings together to make a single string for display in the Label control.

```
StringBuilder sb = new StringBuilder( );
sb.Append("You have selected the category ");
sb.Append((string)Session["cattext"]);
sb.Append(" with code \"");
sb.Append((string)Session["catcode"]);
sb.Append("\".");

lblMsg.Text = sb.ToString( );
```

The btn_Click method unhides the DropDownList that was created and made invisible in the content file of the page. The method then retrieves the string array from the Session dictionary object and populates the DropDownList:

```
ddl.Visible = true;
string[] CatBooks = (string[])Session["books"];

// Populate the DropDownList.
int i;
ddl.Items.Clear( );
for (i = 0; i < CatBooks.GetLength(0); i++)
{
    ddl.Items.Add(new ListItem(CatBooks[i]));
}
```

As you examine this example, you might wonder what advantage is gained here by using session state, rather than using the programmatically accessible control values. In this trivial example, no advantage is gained. However, in a real-life application with many different pages, session state provides an easy method for values and objects to be passed from one page to the next, with all the advantages listed at the beginning of this section.

Session state configuration

The configuration of session state is controlled on a page-by-page basis by entries in the Page directive at the top of the page. On an application-wide basis, it is controlled by the *web.config* configuration file, typically located in the virtual root directory of the application. (Page directives will be covered in detail later in this chapter, and configuration files will be covered in detail in Chapter 18.)

Session state is enabled by default. You can explicitly enable session state for a specific page by adding the EnableSessionState attribute to the Page directive, as in the following:

```
<%@ Page Language="C#" AutoEventWireup="true" CodeFile="Default.aspx.cs"
    Inherits="_Default" EnableSessionState="True"%>
```

To disable session state for the page, you would use the following:

```
<%@ Page Language="C#" AutoEventWireup="true" CodeFile="Default.aspx.cs"
    Inherits="_Default" EnableSessionState="False"%>
```

To enable session state in a read-only mode—i.e., values can be read but not changed—use the ReadOnly value of EnableSessionState, as in the following:

```
<%@ Page Language="C#" AutoEventWireup="true" CodeFile="Default.aspx.cs"
    Inherits="_Default" EnableSessionState="ReadOnly"%>
```

(All of the values for EnableSessionState are case-insensitive.) The reason for disabling session state or making it read-only is to enhance performance. If you know that you will not be using session state on a page, you can gain a small performance boost and conserve server resources at the same time by disabling session state.

By default, session state is stored in server memory as part of the ASP.NET process. However, using the mode attribute of the sessionState tag in *web.config*, it can be configured to be stored separately from the ASP.NET process, either on a separate state server or in a SQL Server database, in which case it will survive a crash or restart of the ASP.NET process. In addition to unplanned outages, ASP.NET can be configured to perform a preventative restart periodically of each process after a specified number of requests or after a specified length of time, improving availability and stability. (This is configurable in *machine.config* and/or *web.config*. See Chapter 18 for a complete discussion of configuration.) Session state is preserved even across these restarts.

> Keep in mind that *web.config* is an XML file, and as such, it must be well formed. (Well-formed XML files are described in the sidebar "Well-Formed XHTML" in Chapter 3.) The values are case-sensitive, and the file consists of sections delimited by tags.

Within *web.config*, the session state configuration information is contained in the <system.web> section, which itself is contained within the <configuration> section. Thus, a typical session state configuration snippet will look something like Example 6-18.

Example 6-18. Session State code snippet from web.config

```
<?xml version="1.0" encoding="utf-8" ?>
<configuration>
```

Example 6-18. Session State code snippet from web.config (continued)

```
<system.web>
    .
    .
    .

    <sessionState
            mode="InProc"
            cookieless="false"
            timeout="20"
            stateConnectionString="tcpip=127.0.0.1:42424"
            sqlConnectionString="data source=127.0.0.1;userid=sa;password="
    />
```

There are several possible attributes, all optional, for the `sessionState` section:

allowCustomSqlDatabase

> If `true`, the SQL database storing session data can be a custom database. The default is `false`, in which case the default database is ASPState and an Initial Catalog cannot be specified in the connection string.

mode

> Specifies whether the session state is disabled for all the pages controlled by this copy of *web.config*, and, if enabled, where the session state is stored. Table 6-6 lists the permissible values.

> Storing the session state `Inproc` is the fastest method and is well-suited to small amounts of volatile data. However, it is susceptible to crashes and is unsuitable for web farms (multiple servers) or web gardens (multiple processors on a single machine). For these cases, you should use either `StateServer` or `SqlServer`. `SqlServer` is the most robust for surviving crashes and restarts.

cookieless

> Cookies are used with session state to store the `SessionID` so the server knows which session the request is connected to. The permissible values of `cookieless` are `AutoDetect`, `UseCookies`, `UseDeviceProfile`, and `UseUri`, with `UseCookies` being the default.

> `AutoDetect` will check to see if the requesting client supports cookies. `UseDeviceProfile` will determine if cookies are supported based on `HttpBrowserCapabilities`. If either of these determine that cookies are unsupported or if `UseUri` is specified, then the `SessionID` will be persisted by adding a value to the URL, as shown in the address bar in Figure 6-5. A value of `cookieless` that forces the `SessionID` to be added to the URL will not work within the VS2005 environment if using File System access but will work outside VS2005 using a virtual directory.

cookieName

The name of the cookie that stores the `SessionID`. The default is `ASP.NET_SessionId`.

customProvider

The name of the custom session state provider.

regenerateExpiredSessionId

For use with cookieless sessions. If `true`, expired `SessionID`'s are replaced with a new identifier. The default is `false`.

sqlCommandTimeout

The number of seconds a SQL command is idle before being canceled. The default value is 30.

sqlConnectionString

Specifies a connection string to a running instance of SQL Server. It must be set if `mode` is set to `SqlServer`. Similar to `stateConnectionString` in that it lends itself to use with web farms and gardens; it will persist despite crashes and shutdowns. The session state is saved in SQL tables indexed by `SessionID`.

stateConnectionString

Specifies the server and port used to save the session state. It is required if `mode` is set to `StateServer`. Use of a specific server for saving state enables easy and effective session state management in web farm or web garden scenarios. Here is an example of a `stateConnectionString`:

```
stateConnectionString="tcpip=127.0.0.1:42424"
```

In this example, a server with an IP address of `127.0.0.1` would be used. This happens to be `localhost` (the local machine). The port is `42424`. For this to work, the server being specified must have the ASP.NET State service started (accessible via Control Panel → Administrative Tools → Services) and must have the specified port available for communications (i.e., not disabled or blocked by a firewall or other security measure).

stateNetworkTimeout

Used when the `mode` is set to `StateServer`, the number of seconds the TCP/IP network connection can be idle before the request is canceled. The default is 10.

timeout

Specifies the number of minutes of inactivity before a session times out and is abandoned by the server. The default value is 20.

useHostingIdentity

If `true`, which is the default, the ASP.NET process identity will be impersonated.

Table 6-6. Possible values for the mode attribute

Values	Description
Off	Session state is disabled.
InProc	Session state is stored in process on the local server. This is the default value.
StateServer	Session state is stored on a remote server. If this attribute is used, then an entry must exist for stateConnectionString, which specifies which server to use to store the session state.
SqlServer	Session state is stored on a SQL Server. If this attribute is used, then an entry must exist for sqlConnectionString, which specifies how to connect to the SQL Server. The SQL Server used can be on the local or a remote machine.
Custom	Allows you to specify a custom provider.

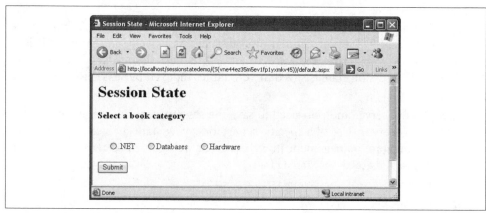

Figure 6-5. SessionStateDemo with cookieless=UseUri

Session scoped application objects

One additional way of providing information across the session is through the use of static objects, which are declared in the *global.asax* file (described in Chapter 18). Once declared with the Scope attribute set to Session, the objects are accessible by name to the session anywhere within the application code.

View State

The *view state* is the state of the page and all its controls. The view state is automatically maintained across posts by the ASP.NET Framework. When a page is posted to the server, the view state is read. Just before the page is sent back to the browser, the view state is restored.

The view state is saved in the state bag (described in the next section) in a hidden field on the page that contains the state encoded in a string variable. Since the view state is maintained via form fields, this technique works with all browsers.

If there is no need to maintain the view state for a page, you can boost performance by disabling view state for that page. For example, if the page does not post back to itself or if the only control on a page that might need to have its state maintained is populated from a database with every round trip to the server, then there will be no need to maintain the view state for that page. To disable view state for a page, add the EnableViewState attribute with a value of false to the Page directive:

```
<%@ Page Language="C#"  EnableViewState="false" %>
```

The default value for EnableViewState is true.

Alternatively, omit the server-side form tag (<form runat="server">), but note carefully that doing so will disable all server-side processing and controls.

The view state can be disabled for an entire application by setting the EnableViewState property to false in the <pages> section of the *web.config* configuration file, or for all applications in the *machine.config* configuration file (described in Chapter 18).

Maintaining or disabling the view state for specific controls is possible. This is done with the Control.EnableViewState property, which is a Boolean value with a default of true. Disabling view state for a control, just as for the page, will improve performance. This would be appropriate, for example, in a situation where a GridView is populated from a database every time the page is loaded. In this case, the contents of the control would be overridden by the database query, so there is no point in maintaining view state for that control. If the GridView in question were named gv, the following line of code would disable its view state:

```
gv.EnableViewState = false;
```

There are some situations where view state is not the best place to store data. If a large amount of data must be stored, view state is not an efficient mechanism since the data is transferred back and forth to the server with every page post. If security concerns exist about the data and the data is not being displayed on the page, then including the data in view state increases the security exposure. Finally, view state is optimized only for strings, integers, Booleans, arrays, ArrayLists, and hashtables. Other .NET types may be serialized and persisted in view state but will result in degraded performance and a larger view state footprint.

In some of these instances, session state might be a better alternative; on the other hand, view state does not consume any server resources and does not time out, as does session state.

In Version 2.0 of ASP.NET, the serialization format for view state has been reformulated, cutting the size of the hidden field that is embedded in the page by as much as 50 percent compared to ASP.NET 1.x.

The second change is perhaps more useful. In Version 1.x, many controls used view state to store data required for functionality as well as data display. For example, sorting and paging of the DataGrid required that view state be enabled. If you disabled view state, you disabled that functionality. Version 2.0 separates out the functional data from the display data and stores the former in a new category called *control state*. Control state cannot be disabled, so even if view state is disabled, the control will still function correctly.

State Bag

If values are not associated with any control and you wish to preserve these values across round trips, you can store these values in the page's *state bag*. The *state bag* is a data structure containing attribute/value pairs, stored as strings associated with objects. The valid objects are the primitive data types—integers, bytes, strings, Booleans, and so on. The state bag is implemented using the StateBag class, which is a (non-type-safe) dictionary object. You add or remove items from the state bag as with any dictionary object. For a complete discussion of dictionary objects in C#, see *Programming C#*, Fourth Edition, by Jesse Liberty (O'Reilly).

The state bag is maintained using the same hidden field as view state. You can set and retrieve values of things in the state bag using the ViewState keyword, as shown in the following example, StateBagDemo.

This example sets up a counter that is maintained as long as the page is current. Every time the Increment Counter button is clicked, the page is reloaded, which causes the counter to increment.

Create StateBagDemo by creating a new web site in VS2005. Drag a Label control, named lblCounter, and a Button control, named btn, onto the page. The listing for the content file is shown in Example 6-19.

Example 6-19. default.as for StateBagDemo

```
<%@ Page Language="C#" AutoEventWireup="true"  CodeFile="Default.aspx.cs"
    Inherits="_Default" %>

<!DOCTYPE html PUBLIC "-//W3C//DTD XHTML 1.1//EN"
    "http://www.w3.org/TR/xhtml11/DTD/xhtml11.dtd">

<html xmlns="http://www.w3.org/1999/xhtml" >
<head runat="server">
    <title>State Bag</title>
</head>
```

Example 6-19. default.as for StateBagDemo (continued)

```
<body>
    <form id="form1" runat="server">
    <div>
      <h1>State Bag</h1>
      Counter:
       <asp:Label ID="lblCounter" runat="server" />
       <asp:Button ID="btn" runat="server" Text="Increment Counter" />
    </div>
    </form>
</body>
</html>
```

The code-behind creates a property of type integer, called Counter. The contents of Counter is stored in the state bag using the ViewState property of the Page class. In the Page_Load method, the Counter property is assigned to the Label and then incremented. Since all the button is doing is submitting the form, it does not require an event handler. The complete code-behind is shown in Example 6-20, with the Counter property highlighted.

Example 6-20. Default.aspx.cs for StateBagDemo

```
using System;
using System.Data;
using System.Configuration;
using System.Web;
using System.Web.Security;
using System.Web.UI;
using System.Web.UI.WebControls;
using System.Web.UI.WebControls.WebParts;
using System.Web.UI.HtmlControls;

public partial class _Default : System.Web.UI.Page
{
    protected void Page_Load(object sender, EventArgs e)
    {
        lblCounter.Text = Counter.ToString();
        Counter++;
    }

    public int Counter
    {
      get
      {
        if (ViewState["intCounter"] != null)
        {
            return ((int)ViewState["intCounter"]);
        }
        return 0;
      }
      set
```

Example 6-20. Default.aspx.cs for StateBagDemo (continued)

```
        {
            ViewState["intCounter"] = value;
        }
    }
}
```

In the get block of the `Counter` property, the contents of the state bag named `intCounter` are tested to see if anything is there.

```
if (ViewState["intCounter"] != null )
```

If the `intCounter` state bag is empty, then zero is returned. Otherwise, the value is retrieved and returned. The state bag returns an object that is not implicitly recognized as an integer so it must be cast as an integer before the method returns the value.

```
return ((int)ViewState["intCounter"]);
```

In the set block, the `intCounter` value is set.

```
ViewState["intCounter"] = value;
```

In this code, value is a keyword used in the property set block to represent the implicit variable containing the value being passed in.

Then, in the `Page_Load`, `Counter` is called twice: once to retrieve the counter value to set the value of the `Label` control's `Text` property and once to increment itself.

```
lblCounter.Text = Counter.ToString( );
Counter++;
```

Application State

A web *application* consists of all the web pages, files, components, code, and images that reside in a virtual directory or its subdirectories.

The file *global.asax* contains global code for the web application. The *global.asax* file resides in the virtual root directory of the application. Chapter 18 discusses this file in detail. For now, only the aspects relating to application state and session state will be covered.

Among other things, the *global.asax* file contains event handlers for the `Application_Start`, `Application_End`, `Application_Error`, `Session_Start`, and `Session_End` events. When the application receives the first user request, the `Application_Start` event is fired. If the *global.asax* file is edited and the changes are saved, then all current pending requests will be completed, the `Application_End` event will be fired, and the application will be restarted. This sequence effectively *reboots* the application, flushing all state information. However, the rebooting of the application is transparent to all users since it occurs only after satisfying any pending requests and before any new requests are accepted. When the next request is received, the application starts over again, raising another `Application_Start` event.

Information can be shared *globally* across your application via a dictionary of objects, each object associated with a key value. This is implemented using the intrinsic `Application` property of the `HttpApplication` class. The `Application` property allows access to the `Contents` collection, whose contents have been added to the `Application` state directly through code.

To add a *global.asax* file to a project, click Website → Add New Item… (or right-click the project root directory in the Solution Explorer and select Add New Item…). From the Add New Item dialog box, select Global Application Class and accept the default name of *Global.asax*. The file will be created with empty event handler methods for the application and session events mentioned above.

Create a new web site in VS2005 and add a *global.asax* file to a project. To this file, add the highlighted code listed in Example 6-21.

Example 6-21. global.asax file in C#

```
<%@ Application Language="C#" %>
<script runat="server">
    void Application_Start(Object sender, EventArgs e) {
        // Code that runs on application startup
        Application["strStartMsg"] = "The application has started.";
        Application["strConnectionString"] =
                "SERVER=Zeus;DATABASE=Pubs;UID=sa;PWD=secret;";
        string[] Books = {"SciFi","Novels", "Computers",
                    "History", "Religion"};
        Application["arBooks"] = Books;
        WriteFile("Application Starting");
    }

    void Application_End(Object sender, EventArgs e) {
        //  Code that runs on application shutdown
        Application["strEndMsg"] = "The application is ending.";
        WriteFile("Application Ending");
    }

    void Application_Error(Object sender, EventArgs e) {
        // Code that runs when an unhandled error occurs
    }

    void Session_Start(Object sender, EventArgs e) {
        // Code that runs when a new session is started
    }

    void Session_End(Object sender, EventArgs e) {
        // Code that runs when a session ends.
        // Note: The Session_End event is raised only when the sessionstate mode
        // is set to InProc in the Web.config file. If session mode is set to StateServer
        // or SQLServer, the event is not raised.
    }
```

Example 6-21. global.asax file in C# (continued)

```
    void WriteFile(string strText)
    {
        System.IO.StreamWriter writer = new
                        System.IO.StreamWriter(@"C:\test.txt", true);
        string str;
        str = DateTime.Now.ToString() + "   " + strText;
        writer.WriteLine(str);
        writer.Close();
    }
</script>
```

A *global.asax* file is similar to a normal *.aspx* file in that a directive is on the first line followed by a script block in the language specified in the directive. In this case, the directive is not the `Page` directive of a normal page, but an `Application` directive. In C#, these two lines look like this:

```
<%@ Application  Language="C#"%>
<script runat="server">
```

You can see that the *global.asax* file has two event handlers that actually have code to do something: one each for `Application_Start` and `Application_End`. In addition, it has a method called `WriteFile`, which uses a `StreamWriter` to write a simple log to a text file hardcoded to be in the root of the C drive.

 There can only be one *global.asax* file in any application virtual directory.

As mentioned previously, every time the *global.asax* file is modified, the .NET Framework detects this and automatically stops and restarts the application.

You could copy this *global.asax* file into the virtual root of any web site and see it in action. However, for now, you will use ApplicationStateDemo, which you just created. The content page has no controls other than perhaps a heading. The content file is shown in Example 6-22.

Example 6-22. Default.aspx for ApplicationStateDemo

```
<%@ Page Language="C#" AutoEventWireup="true"  CodeFile="Default.aspx.cs"
    Inherits="_Default" %>

<!DOCTYPE html PUBLIC "-//W3C//DTD XHTML 1.1//EN"
    "http://www.w3.org/TR/xhtml11/DTD/xhtml11.dtd">

<html xmlns="http://www.w3.org/1999/xhtml" >
<head runat="server">
    <title>Application State</title>
</head>
<body>
```

Example 6-22. Default.aspx for ApplicationStateDemo (continued)

```
    <form id="form1" runat="server">
    <div>
        <h1>Application State</h1>
    </div>
    </form>
</body>
</html>
```

In the `Page_Load` of the code-behind file, you will retrieve values from Application state and write them to the page using `Response.Write`. To do this, add the highlighted lines of code from Example 6-23 to the code-behind file.

Example 6-23. Default.aspx.cs from ApplicationStateDemo

```
using System;
using System.Data;
using System.Configuration;
using System.Web;
using System.Web.Security;
using System.Web.UI;
using System.Web.UI.WebControls;
using System.Web.UI.WebControls.WebParts;
using System.Web.UI.HtmlControls;

public partial class _Default : System.Web.UI.Page
{
    protected void Page_Load(object sender, EventArgs e)
    {
        Response.Write((string)Application["strStartMsg"] + "<br/>");
        Response.Write((string)Application["strConnectionString"] + "<br/>");
        Response.Write((string)Application["strEndMsg"]);

        string[] arTest = (string[])Application["arBooks"];
        Response.Write(arTest[1].ToString( ));
    }
}
```

The `Application` dictionary objects are retrieved by using the key value as an indexer into the dictionary, then casting the object returned to the appropriate type for use in the `Response.Write` method.

Run the application and you will see something like the screen shown in Figure 6-6.

At the instant the server receives and begins to process the page request, the application starts and the `Application_Start` event handler is called.

If you now open another browser and call some other *.aspx* file located in the same virtual directory, the application doesn't start again because it is already running. In fact, closing all your browsers and then opening a page will still not fire the `Application_Start` event. The application must first be ended, as described in the explanation for Example 6-24.

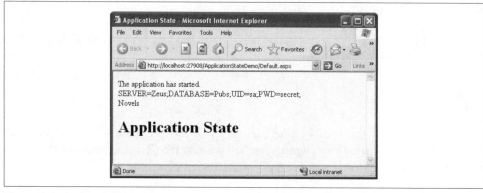

Figure 6-6. ApplicationStateDemo

Example 6-24. Test.txt

```
5/25/2006 11:09:59 AM  Application Starting
5/25/2006 11:10:41 AM  Application Starting
5/25/2006 11:10:57 AM  Application Ending
5/25/2006 11:11:22 AM  Application Starting
5/25/2006 11:13:32 AM  Application Ending
5/25/2006 11:13:47 AM  Application Starting
5/25/2006 2:37:18 PM  Application Ending
5/25/2006 2:53:23 PM  Application Starting
5/25/2006 2:55:51 PM  Application Ending
5/25/2006 2:55:54 PM  Application Starting
5/25/2006 3:27:13 PM  Application Ending
5/25/2006 3:35:14 PM  Application Starting
5/25/2006 3:37:05 PM  Application Ending
```

The Application property exposes a dictionary of objects linked to keys. In the Application_Start event handler, in Example 6-21, three objects are entered in the Application dictionary: two strings and one string array. Then a call is made to the WriteFile method, which is coded further down in the file. WriteFile writes a text log to the root of the C drive. If the file does not exist it will be created, and if it does exist the strings will be appended to the end of the file.

> For WriteFile to work, the ASP.NET user must have sufficient permissions to write a file to the specified location. See the description of the FileUpload control in Chapter 5 for a discussion of this issue.

Finally, the Application_End event handler of *global.asax* puts another string object in the Application dictionary and makes a log entry.

ApplicationStateDemo shows how these Application dictionary entries are used as global variables. Though the *global.asax* file is an excellent place to initialize global Application objects, it is not the only place. Application objects can be set from anywhere in the application, including any web page or code-behind file. The benefit of using the *global.asax* file is that you can be certain the global Application objects will be set when the application first starts, regardless of which component of the application is accessed first. On the other hand, if the application design is such that a specific web page is always accessed first, then it will be perfectly reasonable to have that web page, or its associated code-behind file, perform any initialization.

For backward compatibility with traditional ASP, you can refer to the Contents sub-property of the Application object. Thus, the following two lines of C# code are equivalent:

```
Response.Write((string)Application["strConnectionString"] + "<br/>");
Response.Write((string)Application.Contents["strConnectionString"] + "<br/>");
```

The application ends whenever *global.asax* is edited. (It also ends when IIS or the physical server is restarted or when one of the application configuration files, such as *web.config*, is edited. Chapter 18 discusses the use of these configuration files.) Furthermore, the results of this effective rebooting of the application is invisible to the end users since all pending requests are filled before the application shuts down. This can be seen if you force the application to end by making a minor change to *global.asax* and saving the file, then looking at the resulting log file, *c:\test.txt*, in Notepad, as shown in Example 6-24.

As soon as any page in the virtual directory is requested by a browser, another line appends itself to the log, containing the words Application Starting. However, you will *never* see the contents of the strEndMsg Application property (which was set in the Application_End event handler of *global.asax*, as shown in Example 6-21) displayed in your browser because the application always ends between browser requests.

When using the application state, keep in mind the following considerations:

Concurrency and application locking

Concurrency refers to two or more pages accessing the same Application dictionary object simultaneously. As long as an Application dictionary object is read-only, this is not a problem. However, if you are going to allow clients to modify objects held in application state, exercise great care (you'll see why in a moment). You must use the Lock and Unlock methods of the HttpApplicationState class to control access to the application state objects. If you fail to lock the application state object, one client may corrupt the data used by a second client. For example, consider the following code snippet, which increments an Application dictionary object called Counter:

```
int iCtr = (int)Application["Counter"];
iCtr++;
Application["Counter"] = iCtr
```

Two clients could possibly call this code at about the same time. This code works by reading the Application["Counter"] value, adding 1 to it, and writing it back. Suppose that clients A and B read the counter when its value is 5. Client A increments and writes back 6. Client B increments and writes back 6, which is not what you want, and you've lost track of Client A's increment. If you were keeping track of inventory, that would be a serious bug. You can solve this problem by locking and unlocking the critical code:

```
Application.Lock( );
Application.Unlock( );
```

Now when Application A reads the counter, it locks it. When Application B comes along, it is blocked by the lock until A unlocks. Thus, the value is properly incremented at the cost of a potential performance bottleneck.

You should always call the Unlock method as soon as possible to prevent blocking other users. If you forget to call Unlock, the lock will be automatically removed by .NET when the request completes or times out, or when an unhandled error occurs that causes the request to fail, thus minimizing prolonged deadlocks.

Simple locks like this are fraught with danger. For example, suppose that you have two resources controlled by locks: Counter and ItemsOnHand. Application A locks Counter and then tries to lock ItemsOnHand. Unfortunately, ItemsOnHand is locked, so A must wait, holding its lock on Counter. It turns out that Application B is holding the lock on ItemsOnHand waiting to get the lock on Counter. Application B must block waiting for A to let go of Counter, and A waits for B to let go of ItemsOnHand. This is called a *deadlock* or a *deadly embrace*. It is deadly to your application, which grinds to a halt.

Locks are particularly dangerous with web applications that have to scale up quickly. Use application locking with extreme caution. By extension, you should also use read-write application state with extreme caution.

Scalability

The issue of concurrency has a direct effect on scalability. Unless all the Application dictionary objects are read-only, you are liable to run into severe performance issues as the number of simultaneous requests increases, due to locks blocking other processes from proceeding.

Memory

This is a consideration for scalability also, since every Application dictionary object takes up memory. Whether you have a million short string objects or a single DataSet that takes up 50MB, you must be cognizant of the potential memory usage of Application state.

Persistence and survivability

Application state objects will not survive if the application is halted, whether intentionally because of updates to *global.asax* or a planned shutdown, or because of unanticipated system crashes. (When is a crash ever anticipated?) If it is important to persist global application state, then you must take some measure to save it, perhaps to a database or other permanent file on disk.

Expandability to web farms and web gardens

> The Application state is specific to a single process on a single processor. There-fore, if you are running a *web farm* (multiple servers) or a *web garden* (multiple processors in a single server), any global values in the Application state will not be global across all the servers or processors and so will not be global. As with persistence and survivability, if this is an issue, then you should get and set the value(s) from a central store accessible to all the processes, such as a database or data file.

One additional way of providing information globally across the application is through the use of static objects. These objects are declared in the *global.asax* file, described more fully in Chapter 18. Once declared with the Scope attribute set to Application, the objects are accessible by name anywhere within the application code.

Lifecycle

A user sits at her browser and types in a URL. A web page appears, with text and images and buttons and so forth. She fills in a text box and clicks a button. What is going on behind the scenes?

Every request made of the web server initiates a sequence of steps. These steps, from beginning to end, constitute the *lifecycle* of the page.

When a page is requested from the server, it is loaded into server memory, pro-cessed, sent to the user, and unloaded from memory. From one end of the lifecycle to the other, the goal of the page is to render appropriate HTML to the requesting browser. At each step, methods and events are available to let you override the default behavior or add your own programmatic enhancements.

To understand the lifecycle of the page and its controls, you must recognize that the Page class creates a hierarchical tree of all the controls on the page. All the compo-nents on the page, except for directives, are part of this *control tree.* You can see the control tree for any page by adding trace="true" to the Page directive. (Directives are described in the next section of this chapter. Chapter 7 discusses tracing in detail.)

The Page itself is at the root of the tree. All the named controls are included in the tree, referenced by control ID. Static text, including whitespace, newlines, and HTML tags, are represented in the tree as LiteralControls. The order of controls in the tree is strictly hierarchical. Within a given level of the hierarchy, the controls are in the order in which they appear in the content file.

Web components, including the Page, go through the entire lifecycle every time the page is loaded. (This involves a fair amount of performance overhead, which you can reduce somewhat by caching. Caching and performance are covered in

Chapter 17.) Events fire first on the Page, then recursively on every object in the control tree.

The following is a detailed description of each of the phases of the component lifecycle in a web form. There are two slightly different sequences of events in the lifecycle: on the first loading of the page and on subsequent postbacks. This lifecycle is shown schematically in Figure 6-7.

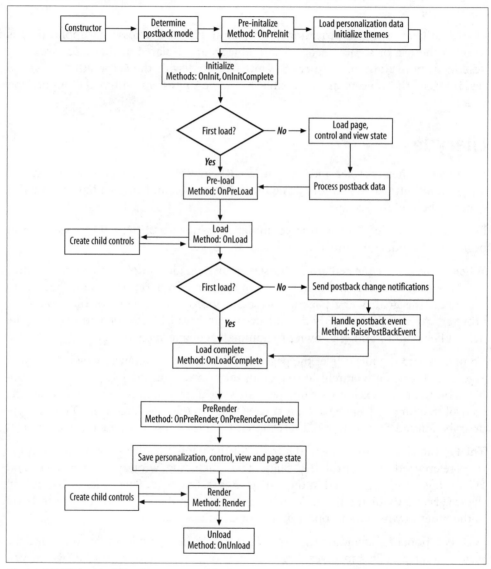

Figure 6-7. Web page lifecycle

During the first page load, the lifecycle is composed of the following steps:

1. The constructor is run. This is the first step in the lifecycle for the Page or any control on the page.

2. Determine the PostBack mode. Is this the first load, a self-postback, or a cross-page post?

3. Pre-initialization. This step is necessary to determine the target device before the page is initialized. PreInit is the first event in the lifecycle that can be trapped and handled, using the OnPreInit method.

4. Personalization and themes are loaded and initialized.

5. Initialization. The *initialization* phase is when the control tree is built. In this phase, you can initialize any values needed for the duration of the request.

   The initialize phase is modified by handling the Init event with the OnInit method.

6. Pre-load. Occurs before postback data is loaded in the controls. This phase can be modified by handling the PreLoad event with OnPreLoad method.

7. Load. User code runs and the form controls show client-side data. View state information is available and controls in the Page's control hierarchy can be accessed.

   The load phase can be modified by handling the Load event with the OnLoad method.

8. Load complete. The load process is completed. The LoadComplete event can be handled by the OnLoadComplete method.

9. Pre-render. This is the phase just before the output is rendered. Modifications are made via the PreRender event, using the OnPreRender method.

10. Save state. Personalization, Control, View and Page state information is saved.

11. Render. The page and its controls are rendered as HTML. You can override using the Render method. Within Render, CreateChildControls is called, if necessary, to create and initialize server controls in the control tree.

12. Unload. This is the last phase of the lifecycle. It gives you an opportunity to do any final cleanup and release references to any expensive resources, such as database connections. This is important for scalability. It can be modified using the OnUnload method.

During postback, the lifecycle is the same as during the first load, except for the following:

1. Load State. After initialization is complete, the Page and Control state is loaded and the ViewState is loaded from a hidden variable on the page as described in "View State" earlier in this chapter.

2. Postback data is processed. During this phase, the data sent to the server via the `Post` method is processed. Any updates to the view state necessitated by the postback are performed via the `LoadPostData` method.

3. Pre-load and load. Same as on first load.

4. Send postback change notifications. If any state changes between the current state and the previous state occur, change events are raised via the `RaiseChangedEvents` method. The events are raised for the controls in the order in which the controls appear in the control tree.

5. Handle postback events. Exactly one user action caused the postback. That user action is handled now, after all the change events have been handled. The original client-side event that instigated the postback is handled in the `RaisePostBackEvent` method.

6. Load complete. From here on out, it is the same as on first load.

Directives

Directives are used to pass optional settings to the ASP.NET pages and compilers. They typically have the following syntax:

```
<%@ directive attribute=value [attribute=value] %>
```

The many valid types of directives will be described in detail in the following sections. Each directive can have one or more attribute/value pairs unless otherwise noted. Attribute/value pairs are separated by a space character. These pairs do *not* have any space characters surrounding the equals sign (=) between the attribute and its value.

Directives are typically located at the top of the appropriate file though that is not a strict requirement. For example, `Application` directives are at the top of the *global.asax* file, and `Page` directives are at the top of the *.aspx* files.

Application Directive

The `Application` directive is used to define application-specific attributes. It is typically the first line in the *global.asax* file, which is described fully in Chapter 18.

Here is a sample `Application` directive:

```
<%@ Application Language="C#" %>
```

There are three possible attributes for use in the `Application` directive, which are outlined in Table 6-7.

Table 6-7. Application directive attributes

Attribute	Description
Inherits	The name of the class to inherit from.
Description	Text description of the application. This is ignored by the parser and compiler.
Language	Identifies the language used in any code blocks. Valid values are "C#", "VB", and "JS". As other languages adopt support for the .NET Framework, this list will be expanded.

Assembly Directive

The Assembly directive links an assembly to the application or page at parse-time. It is analogous to the /reference: command-line switch used by the C# command-line compiler.

The Assembly directive is contained in the *global.asax* file for application-wide linking, or in a page (*.aspx*) or user control (*.ascx*) file for linking to a specific page or user control. There can be multiple Assembly directives in any file. Each Assembly directive can have multiple attribute/value pairs.

Assemblies located in the *bin* subdirectory under the application's virtual root are automatically linked to the application and do not need to be included in an Assembly directive.

Two permissible attributes are listed in Table 6-8.

Table 6-8. Assembly directive attributes

Attribute	Description
Name	The name of the assembly to link to the application or page. Does not include a filename extension. Assemblies usually have a .dll extension.
Src	Path to a source file to dynamically compile and link.

For example, the following Assembly directives link to the assembly or assemblies contained in the *MyAssembly.dll* file, and compile and link to a C# source code file named *SomeSource.cs*:

```
<%@ Assembly Name="MyAssembly" %>
<%@ Assembly Src="SomeSource.cs" %>
```

This directive is often used in conjunction with the Import directive, described later in this chapter.

Control Directive

The Control directive is used only with user controls and is contained in user control files (*.ascx*). There can only be one Control directive per *.ascx* file. Here is an example:

```
<%@ Control Language="C#" EnableViewState="false" %>
```

The `Control` directive has many possible attributes. Some of the more common attributes appear in Table 6-9.

Table 6-9. Common Control directive attributes

Attribute	Values	Description
AutoEventWireup	true, false	Enables or disables event autowiring. Default is true.
ClassName	Any valid class name	The class name for the page that will be compiled dynamically.
Debug	true, false	Enables or disables compiling with debug symbols. Default is false.
Description	string	Text description of the page, ignored by the parser.
EnableViewState	true, false	Indicates if view state is maintained across page requests. Default is true.
Explicit	true, false	If language is VB, tells compiler to use Option Explicit mode. Default is false.
Inherits	Class name	Name of code-behind or other class for the page to inherit.
Language	VB, C#, JS	Programming language used for in-line code and script blocks. As other languages adopt support for the .NET Framework this list will be expanded.
Src	Filename	Relative or fully qualified filename containing code-behind class.
Strict	true, false	If language is VB, tells compiler to use Option Strict mode. Default is false.

Implements Directive

The `Implements` directive is used in page (*.aspx*) and user control (*.ascx*) files or associated code-behind files. It specifies an a COM interface that the current page implements. This allows a page or user control to declare the interface's events, methods, and properties.

For example, the following `Implements` directive allows access to a custom `IDataAccess` interface contained in a custom `ProgrammingASPNET` namespace:

```
<%@ Implements Interface="ProgrammingASPNET.IDataAccess" %>
```

Import Directive

The `Import` directive imports a namespace into a page, user control, or application, making all the classes and namespaces of the imported namespace available. Imported namespaces can be part of the .NET Framework Class Library or can be custom.

If the `Import` directive is contained in *global.asax*, then it will apply to the entire application. If it is in a page (*.aspx*) or user control (*.ascx*) file, then it only applies to that page or user control.

Each `Import` directive can have only a single namespace attribute. If you need to import multiple namespaces, use multiple `Import` directives.

The following namespaces are automatically imported into all pages and user controls and do not need to be included in `Import` directives:

- System
- System.Collections
- System.Collections.Specialized
- System.Configuration
- System.IO
- System.Text
- System.Text.RegularExpressions
- System.Web
- System.Web.Caching
- System.Web.Security
- System.Web.SessionState
- System.Web.UI
- System.Web.UI.HtmlControls
- System.Web.UI.WebControls

The following two lines import the `System.Drawing` namespace from the .NET Base Class Library and a custom namespace:

```
<%@ import namespace="System.Drawing" %>
<%@ import namespace="ProgrammingASPNET" %>
```

Master Directive

Identifies a page file as being a master page. Master pages are covered in Chapter 11.

MasterType Directive

Assigns a class name to the `Master` property of a page so the page can be strongly typed.

OutputCache Directive

The `OutputCache` directive controls output caching for a page or user control. Chapter 17 discusses caching and the use of the `OutputCache` directive.

Page Directive

The Page directive is used to define attributes for the page parser and compiler specific to the page (.aspx) file. No more than one Page directive can exist for each page file. Each Page directive can have multiple attributes.

The Page directive has many possible attributes. Some of the more common attributes of the Page directive are listed in Table 6-10.

Table 6-10. Common Page directive attributes

Attribute	Values	Description
AutoEventWireup	true, false	Enables or disables Page events being automatically bound to methods that follow the naming convention Page_*event*, e.g. Page_Load. Default is true.
Buffer	true, false	Enables or disables HTTP response buffering. Default is true.
ClassName	Any valid class name	The class name for the page that will be compiled dynamically.
ClientTarget	Any valid user-agent value or alias	Targets user agent that server controls should render content for.
CodeFile	Filename	Used by VS2005 to indicate the name of the code-behind file.
Debug	true, false	Enables or disables compiling with debug symbols. Default is false.
Description	string	Text description of the page; ignored by the parser.
EnableSessionState	true, false, ReadOnly	Enables, disables, or makes SessionState read-only. Default is true.
EnableViewState	true, false	Enables or disables maintenance of view state across page requests. Default is true.
ErrorPage	Any valid URL	Targets URL for redirection if an unhandled page exception occurs.
Inherits	Class name	Name of code-behind or other class.
Language	VB, C#, JS	Programming language used for in-line code.
SmartNavigation	true, false	Indicates support for smart navigation by the browser, which enables scroll position on a page to survive postbacks. Default is false.
Src	Filename	Relative or fully qualified filename containing code behind class.
Trace	true, false	Enables or disables tracing. Default is false.
TraceMode	SortByTime, SortByCategory	Indicates how trace messages are to be displayed. Default is SortByTime.

Table 6-10. Common Page directive attributes (continued)

Attribute	Values	Description
Transaction	NotSupported, Supported, Required, RequiresNew	Indicates if transactions supported on this page. Default is NotSupported.
ValidateRequest	true, false	If true (the default) all input data is validated against a hard-coded list of potentially dangerous values, to reduce the risk of cross-site scripting and SQL injection attacks.

The following code snippet is a sample Page directive

```
<%@ Page Language="C#" AutoEventWireup="true" CodeFile="Default.aspx.cs"
    Inherits="_Default" Trace="true"%>
```

Reference Directive

The Reference directive can be included in a page file (*.aspx*). It indicates that another page or user control should be compiled and linked to the current page, giving you access to the controls on the linked page or user control as part of the ControlCollection object.

There are two permissible attributes: Page and Control. For either, the allowable value is a relative or fully qualified filename. For example:

```
<%@ Reference Page="AnotherPage.aspx" %>
```

Register Directive

The Register directive is used in custom server controls and user controls to associate aliases with namespaces. Chapter 14 discusses custom server controls and user controls.

CHAPTER 7

Tracing, Debugging, and Error Handling

Every computer programmer has run into bugs. It comes with the territory. Many bugs are found during the coding process. Others pop up only when an end user performs a specific and unusual sequence of steps or the program receives unexpected data. It is highly desirable to find bugs early in the development process and very important to avoid having end users find your bugs for you. Countless studies have shown that the earlier you find a bug, the easier and less expensive it is to fix.

In the event that your program does run into a problem, you will want to recover quickly and invisibly, or, at worst, fail gracefully. ASP.NET provides tools and features to help reach these goals:

Tracing
> You can trace program execution at either the page or application level. ASP. NET provides an extensible trace log with program lifecycle information.

Symbolic debugging
> You can step through your program, set breakpoints, examine and modify variables and expressions, and step into and out of classes, even those written in other languages.

Error handling
> You can handle standard or custom errors at the application or page level. You can also show different error pages for different errors.

To get started exploring the ASP.NET debugging tools, you should first create a simple web site to which you will add tracing code. You will then introduce bugs into the program and use the debugger to find and fix the bugs.

Creating the Sample Application

To start, create a new web site in VS2005 and name it *DebuggingApp*. This will consist of a single web page containing a header label, a DropDownList with a label below it to display the selected item, and a hyperlink.

Drag a Label control to the top of the page and set its Text property to:

    Tracing, Debugging & Error Handling Demo

Change its Font.Name property to Arial Black, its Font.Size property to Large, and its Font.Bold property to true.

Place a DropDownList control on the form. Name it ddlBooks. Change its AutoPostBack property to true. The drop-down list's event handling code needs to be added. In Design view, click on the lightning bolt Events icon at the top of the Properties window, and double-click on the field next to SelectedIndexChanged. The code-behind file, *Default.aspx.cs*, will open, and the cursor will be located in the event handler method ddlBooks_SelectedIndexChanged. Type in the highlighted code from Example 7-1.

Example 7-1. SelectedIndexChanged event handler

```
protected void ddlBooks_SelectedIndexChanged(object sender,
                                             System.EventArgs e)
{
    //  Check to verify that something has been selected.
    if (ddlBooks.SelectedIndex != -1)
    {
        lblDdl.Text=ddlBooks.SelectedItem.Text + " ---> ISBN: " +
                ddlBooks.SelectedItem.Value;
    }
}
```

Add a label below the DropDownList called lblDdl. Set the Text property so it is empty.

In the Page_Load method in the code-behind file, add the code from Example 7-2.

Example 7-2. Page_Load event handler

```
private void Page_Load(object sender, System.EventArgs e)
{
    // Put user code to initialize the page here
    if (! IsPostBack)
    {
        //  Build 2 dimensional array for the lists
        //  First dimension contains bookname
        //  2nd dimension contains ISBN number
```

Example 7-2. Page_Load event handler (continued)

```
    string[,] books = {
            {"Programming C#","0596006993"},
            {"Programming .NET Windows Applications","0596003218"},
            {"Programming ASP.NET","0596004877"},
            {"WebClasses From Scratch","0789721260"},
            {"Teach Yourself C++ in 21 Days","067232072X"},
            {"Teach Yourself C++ in 10 Minutes","067231603X"},
            {"XML & Java From Scratch","0789724766"},
            {"Complete Idiot's Guide to a Career in Computer
                    Programming","0789719959"},
            {"XML Web Documents From Scratch","0789723166"},
            {"Clouds To Code","1861000952"},
            {"C++ Unleashed","0672312395"}
        };

    //  Now populate the lists.
    int i;
    for (i = 0; i < books.GetLength(0); i++)
    {
        //  Add both Text and Value
        ddlBooks.Items.Add(new ListItem(books[i,0],books[i,1]));
    }
  }
}
```

Finally, add a HyperLink control below lblDdl. Name it hplTest. Change the Text property to Link To and change the NavigateUrl property to *TestLink.aspx*. No page with this name exists. This is an intentional error to demonstrate error handling later in the chapter.

Run the web page and select one of the items in the drop-down list; you should see something like Figure 7-1.

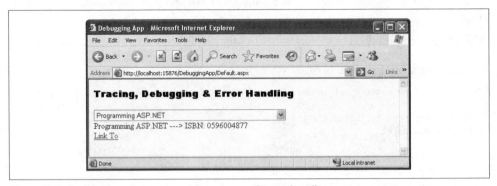

Figure 7-1. Sample page for tracing, debugging, and error handling

You will use this application through the rest of this chapter to demonstrate various techniques for analyzing and debugging code in ASP.NET and for handling errors in your application.

Tracing

Tracing is an easy way to determine what is going on in your program. Back in the days of classic ASP, the only way to trace what was happening in your code was to insert Response.Write statements in strategic places. This allowed you to see that you had reached a known point in the code and, perhaps, to display the value of some variables. The big problem with this hand-tracing technique, aside from the amount of work involved, was that you had to laboriously remove or comment out all those statements before the program went into production.

ASP.NET provides better ways of gathering the trace information. You can add tracing at the application level or at the page level. With *application-level tracing*, every page is traced, and with *page-level tracing*, you choose the pages to which to add tracing.

Page-Level Tracing

To add page-level tracing, modify the Page directive at the top of the *.aspx* page, by adding a Trace attribute and setting its value to true, as follows:

```
<%@ Page Language="C#" AutoEventWireup="true"  CodeFile="Default.aspx.cs"
    Inherits="_Default"  Trace="true" %>
```

When you view this page, there will now be tables at the bottom that contain a wealth of information about your web application. Select a book from the drop-down list and you will see something like Figure 7-2.

The top section, labeled Request Details, shows basic information, including the SessionID, the Time of Request, Request Type, and Status Code (see Table 7-1). Every time the page is posted to the server, this information is updated. If you change the selection (remember that AutoPostBack is set to true), you will see that the Time of Request is updated, but the SessionID remains constant.

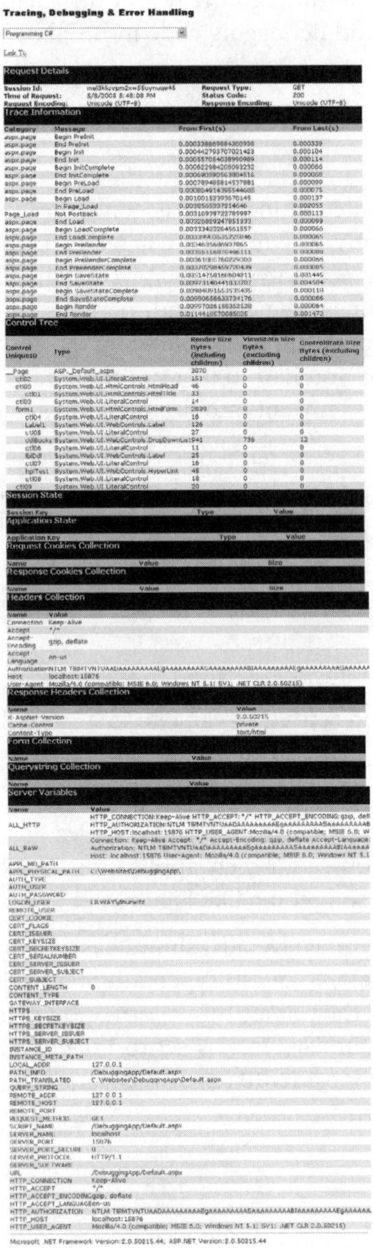

Figure 7-2. Trace results

Table 7-1. Status codes

Category	Number	Description
Informational (100–199)	100	Continue
	101	Switching protocols
Successful (200–299)	200	OK
	204	No content
Redirection (300–399)	301	Moved permanently
	305	Use proxy
	307	Temporary redirect
Client Errors (400–499)	400	Bad request
	402	Payment required
	404	Not found
	408	Request timeout
	417	Expectation failed
Server Errors (500–599)	500	Internal server error
	503	Service unavailable
	505	HTTP version not supported

The next section, labeled Trace Information, is the *trace log*, which provides lifecycle information. This includes elapsed times, in seconds, since the page was initialized (the From First(s) column) and since the previous event in the lifecycle (the From Last(s) column). You can add custom trace information to the trace log as explained later in the chapter.

The next section in the trace, under the heading Control Tree, lists all the controls on the page in a hierarchical manner, including the name of the control, its type, and its size in bytes, both on the page and in the ViewState state bag.

This is followed by Session and Application State summaries, and itemizations of the Cookies and Headers collections. Finally, there is a list of all the server variables.

Inserting into the Trace Log

You can add custom information to the trace output by writing to the Trace object. This object, encapsulated in the TraceContext class, exposes two methods for putting your own statements into the trace log: Write and Warn. The only difference between the two methods is that Warn writes to the log in red. The Warn and Write methods are overloaded to take either a single argument, two arguments, or two strings and an exception object, as the following cases illustrate:

```
Trace.Warn("Warning Message")
```
Inserts a record into the trace log with the message passed in as a string

```
Trace.Warn("Category","Warning Message")
```
Inserts a record into the trace log with the category and message you pass in

```
Trace.Warn("Category","Warning Message", excp)
```
Inserts a record into the trace log with a category, warning message, and exception

To see this in action, add the highlighted code from Example 7-3 to the code-behind file in your sample web site, *DebuggingApp*.

Example 7-3. Writing to the Trace object

```
protected void Page_Load(object sender, System.EventArgs e)
{
    // Put user code to initialize the page here
    Trace.Write("In Page_Load");
    if (! IsPostBack)
    {
        Trace.Write("Page_Load", "Not Postback.");
        //  Build 2 dimensional array for the lists
        //  First dimension contains bookname
        //  2nd dimension contains ISBN number
        string[,] books = {
          {"Programming C#","0596001177"},
          {"Programming ASP.NET","1234567890"},
          {"WebClasses From Scratch","0789721260"},
          {"Teach Yourself C++ in 21 Days","067232072X"},
          {"Teach Yourself C++ in 10 Minutes","067231603X"},
          {"XML & Java From Scratch","0789724766"},
          {"Complete Idiot's Guide to a Career in Computer Programming","0789719959"},
          {"XML Web Documents From Scratch","0789723166"},
          {"Clouds To Code","1861000952"},
          {"C++: An Introduction to Programming","1575760614"},
          {"C++ Unleashed","0672312395"}
                          };

        //  Now populate the lists.
        int i;
        for (i = 0; i < books.GetLength(0); i++)
        {
            //  Add both Text and Value
            ddlBooks.Items.Add(new ListItem(books[i,0],books[i,1]));
        }
    }
}

protected void ddlBooks_SelectedIndexChanged(object sender, System.EventArgs e)
{
    // Force an exception
    try
    {
        int a = 0;
        int b = 5/a;
    }
    catch (System.Exception ex)
    {
        Trace.Warn("UserAction","Calling b=5/a",ex);
    }
```

Example 7-3. Writing to the Trace object (continued)

```
//  Check to verify that something has been selected.
if (ddlBooks.SelectedIndex != -1)
{
    lblDdl.Text=ddlBooks.SelectedItem.Text + " ---> ISBN: " +
        ddlBooks.SelectedItem.Value;
}
}
```

The first message is added in the `Page_Load` method to signal that you've entered that method:

```
Trace.Write("In Page_Load");
```

The second message is added if the page is not a postback:

```
if (! IsPostBack)
{
    Trace.Write("Page_Load", "Not Postback.");
```

This second message is categorized as `Page_Load`; using a category can help you organize the trace output. The effect of these two `Write` statements is shown in Figure 7-3.

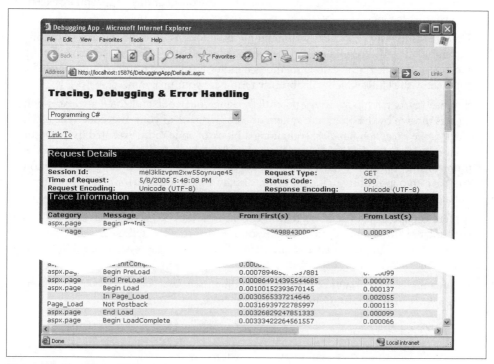

Figure 7-3. Two Trace.Write outputs

The third message is added to demonstrate the process of inserting an exception into the error log. The ddlBooks_SelectedIndexChanged event handler now contains code to force an exception by dividing by zero. The code catches that exception and logs the exception with a Trace statement, as shown by the following code fragment:

```
try
{
    int a = 0;
    int b = 5/a;
}
catch (System.Exception ex)
{
    Trace.Warn("UserAction","Calling b=5/a",ex);
}
```

Exception Handling

Like many object-oriented languages, C# handles predictable but abnormal conditions (lost network connections, files missing, and so on) with exceptions. When your program encounters an exceptional circumstance, it "throws" an exception and execution of the current method halts, and the stack is unwound until an appropriate exception handler is found.

This means that if the currently running method does not handle the exception, the current method will terminate and the calling method will get a chance to handle the exception. If none of the calling methods handles it, the exception will ultimately be handled by the CLR, which will abruptly terminate your program.

You use try/catch blocks to *try* potentially dangerous code and *catch* any exception objects thrown by the operating system or by other parts of your own code. The catch block is the *exception handler*, containing a block of code to be executed in the event of an exception. Ideally, if the exception is caught and handled, the program can fix the problem and continue. Even if your program can't continue, by catching the exception you have an opportunity to log the error, display a meaningful error message, and terminate gracefully.

If there is code in your method that must run regardless of whether an exception is encountered (for example, to release resources you've allocated, such as closing an open file), you can place that code in a finally block, where it is guaranteed to run, even in the presence of exceptions.

For a complete discussion of exception handling, see Jesse Liberty's book *Programming C#*, Fourth Edition (O'Reilly).

The output from this Trace statement is shown in Figure 7-4.

Because this Trace statement was written calling the Warn method rather than the Write method, the trace output appears in red onscreen (though not in your copy of

Trace Information

Category Message	From First(s)	From Last(s)
aspx.page Begin PreInit		
aspx.page End PreInit	0.0001458285899464880	.000146
aspx.page Begin Init	0.0002447238405998530	.000099
aspx.page End Init	0.0004670984720125040	.000222
aspx.page Begin InitComplete	0.0005344254646889480	.000067
aspx.page End InitComplete	0.0006031492829395910	.000069
aspx.page Begin LoadState	0.00101018425525149	0.000407
aspx.page End LoadState	0.00153622876650524	0.000526
aspx.page Begin ProcessPostData	0.00162171449164628	0.000085
aspx.page End ProcessPostData	0.00173960657010877	0.000118
aspx.page Begin PreLoad	0.00180553673721101	0.000066
aspx.page End PreLoad	0.0018815240484475	0.000076
aspx.page Begin Load	0.00194633675509038	0.000065
In Page_Load	0.00203657168718371	0.000090
aspx.page End Load	0.00211283836353503	0.000076
aspx.page Begin ProcessPostData Second Try	0.00218826694454183	0.000075
aspx.page End ProcessPostData Second Try	0.00228213362312808	0.000094
aspx.page Begin Raise ChangedEvents	0.00234778442511548	0.000066
Calling b=5/a		
Attempted to divide by zero.		
UserAction at Default_aspx.ddlBooks_SelectedIndexChanged(Object sender, EventArgs e) in c:\Websites\DebuggingApp\Default.asp:.cs:line 62	0.053010927366467	0.050663
aspx.page End Raise ChangedEvents	0.0563057595308901	0.003295

Figure 7-4. Trace.Warn output

this book). Notice that string you passed in, Calling b=5/a, is displayed, followed by an error message extracted automatically from the exception object.

Implementing Trace statements is easy, and when it is time to put your page into production, all these statements can remain in place. The only modification you need to make is to change the Trace attribute in the Page directive from true to false.

Application-Level Tracing

Application-level tracing applies to all the pages in a given web site. It is configured through the *web.config* file, which will be described more fully in Chapter 18.

The *web.config* file is typically located in the root directory of the web site. If there is a *web.config* file in a subdirectory of the application root, then that copy will apply only to the pages in that subdirectory and in the subdirectories under it. If tracing is enabled application-wide from the root directory, tracing will be applied across the application uniformly. The exception is when a specific page has a contradictory page directive, which supersedes the application directive.

Web.config is an XML file that consists of sections delimited by tags. The trace configuration information is contained in the <trace> section within the <system.web> section, which is contained within the <configuration> section.

> *Web.config*, like all XML documents, must consist of well-formed XML. The elements of a well-formed XML file are discussed in a sidebar in Chapter 3. Note that XML is case-sensitive.

A typical trace configuration snippet will look something like Example 7-4.

Example 7-4. Trace code snippet from web.config

```
<?xml version="1.0"?>
<configuration xmlns="http://schemas.microsoft.com/.NetConfiguration/v2.0" >

  <system.web>
.
.
.
    <trace
        enabled="true"
        requestLimit="10"
        pageOutput="false"
        traceMode="SortByTime"
        localOnly="true"
    />
```

You can edit the *web.config* file using the ASP.NET Configuration Tool, available by clicking the Website → ASP.NET Configuration menu item or the ASP.NET configuration iron at the top of the Solution Explorer in VS2005. Alternatively, you can edit *web.config* manually by double-clicking on the file in the Solution Explorer. (If the Solution Explorer is not visible, click on the View → Solution Explorer menu item.) Alternatively, this file can be edited in any text editor.

There are seven possible properties in the <trace> section. These properties appear in Table 7-2. Several of these properties affect the trace viewer, which will be described in the following section.

Table 7-2. Trace section properties

Property	Values	Description
enabled	true, false	Enables or disables application-level tracing. Default is false. If enabled, then all pages in the application will display trace information unless a specific page has Trace=false in the Page directive.
localOnly	true, false	Indicates if the trace viewer is available only on the host web server. Default is true.
mostRecent	true, false	If true, will discard older requests when the value of the RequestLimit property is exceeded. If false, the default, the trace service will be disabled when the RequestLimit is reached.
pageOutput	true, false	Dictates if trace information is displayed on both the application pages and in the trace viewer. Default is false. Pages with tracing enabled are not affected by this setting.
requestLimit	Integer	Number of trace requests that will be stored on the server and visible in the trace viewer. Default is 10.

Table 7-2. Trace section properties (continued)

Property	Values	Description
traceMode	SortByTime, SortByCategory	Dictates if the trace log is sorted by Time or Category. Default is TraceMode.SortByTime.
writeToDiagnosticsTrace	true, false	If true, messages from the trace log are forwarded to the Trace class. The default is false.

Trace Viewer

If application-level tracing is enabled, you can view the trace log directly from your browser for any application, even across multiple page requests. The trace facility provides a *trace viewer*, called *trace.axd*. Aim your browser toward *trace.axd* as though it were a page in the application, with the following URL, for example:

```
http://localhost/DebuggingApp/trace.axd
```

You will see a summary of all the entries in the trace log, as shown in Figure 7-5.

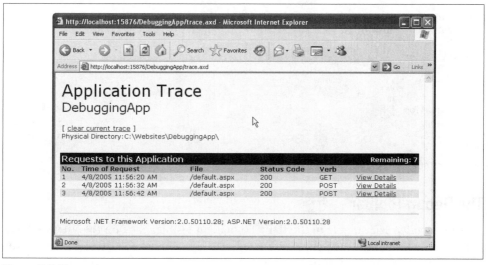

Figure 7-5. Trace viewer

Clicking on any of the View Details links will bring you to the same page as would be seen in page-level tracing for that page.

Debugging

Tracing provides you with a snapshot of the steps your code has taken after the code has run. At times, however, you'd like to monitor your code while it is running. What you want is more of a CAT scan than an autopsy. The code equivalent of a CAT scan is a symbolic debugger.

When you run your code in the debugger, you can watch your code work, step by step. As you walk through the code, you can see the variables change values, and you can watch as objects are created and destroyed.

This section will provide a brief introduction to the most important parts of the debugger that accompanies the VS2005 IDE. For complete coverage of how to use the debugger, we urge you to spend time with the documentation and to experiment freely. The debugger is one of the most powerful tools at your disposal for learning ASP.NET.

An application can be configured to either enable or disable debugging. This is done through the configuration file, *web.config*, which is described more fully in Chapter 18. The debugging configuration information is contained within the <compilation> section, within the <system.web> section, which in turn is contained within the <configuration> section. So, a typical compilation configuration snippet will look something like Example 7-5.

Example 7-5. Debug configuration code snippet from web.config

```
<?xml version="1.0" encoding="utf-8" ?>
<configuration xmlns="http://schemas.microsoft.com/.NetConfiguration/v2.0" >

    <system.web>
    .
    .
    .
    <compilation
        debug="true"
    />
```

Setting debug to false improves the runtime performance of the application.

The Debug Toolbar

A *Debug toolbar* is available in the IDE. To make it visible, click on the View → Toolbars menu commands, then click on Debug, if it is not checked. Table 7-3 shows the icons that appear on the Debug toolbar.

Table 7-3. Debug toolbar icons

Icon	Debug menu equivalent	Keyboard shortcut	Description
			Toolbar handle. Click and drag to move the toolbar to a new location.
	Start / Continue	F5	Starts or continues executing the program.
	Break All	Ctrl-Alt-Break	Stops program execution at the currently executing line.

Table 7-3. Debug toolbar icons (continued)

Icon	Debug menu equivalent	Keyboard shortcut	Description
■	Stop Debugging	Shift-F5	Stops debugging.
	Restart	Ctrl-Shift-F5	Stops the run currently being debugged and immediately begins a new run.
⇨			Shows next statement.
Statement ▼	Step Into	F11	If the current line contains a call to a method or function, this icon will single-step the debugger into that method or function.
	Step Over	F10	If the current line contains a call to a method or function, this icon will not step into that method or function but will go to the next line after the call.
	Step Out	Shift-F11	If the current line is in a method or function, that method or function will complete and the debugger will stop on the line after the method or function call.
Hex			Hexadecimal display toggle.
	Windows		Debug window selector.
▾			Toolbar options. Offers options for adding and removing buttons from all toolbars (Debug, Text Editor, and so on).

Breakpoints

> *"The crux of the biscuit is the apostrophe."*
> —Frank Zappa, "Apostrophe(')"

Breakpoints are at the heart of debugging. A breakpoint is an instruction to .NET to run to a specific line in your code and to stop and wait for you to examine the current state of the application. As the execution is paused, you can do the following:

- Examine and modify values of variables and expressions.
- Single-step through the code.
- Move into and out of methods and functions, even stepping into classes written in other CLR-compliant languages.
- Perform any number of other debugging and analysis tasks.

Setting a breakpoint

You can set a breakpoint in any window editing a .NET compliant language, such as C# or VB2005, by single-clicking on the gray vertical bar along the left margin of the window. A red dot will appear in the left margin and the line of code will be high-lighted, as shown in Figure 7-6.

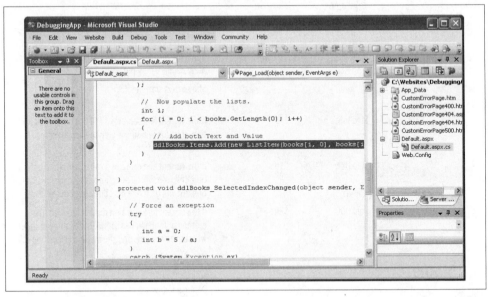

Figure 7-6. Setting a breakpoint

Breakpoint window

You can see all the breakpoints currently set by looking at the *Breakpoint window*. To display the Breakpoint window, perform any one of the following actions:

- Press Ctrl-Alt-B.
- Select Breakpoints from the Debug → Windows menu command.
- Click on the Windows icon of the Debug toolbar and select Breakpoints.

A Breakpoint window is shown in Figure 7-7.

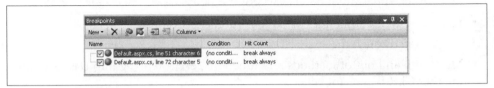

Figure 7-7. Breakpoint window

You can toggle a breakpoint between Enabled and Disabled by clicking on the corresponding checkbox in the Breakpoint window.

Breakpoint properties

Sometimes you don't want a breakpoint to stop execution every time the line is reached. VS2005 offers several properties that can be set to modify the behavior of a breakpoint. These properties can be set via the property menu, arrived at in either of two ways:

- Right-click on the breakpoint glyph in the left margin.
- Open the Breakpoint window and right-click on the desired breakpoint.

 The user interface for dealing with breakpoints is somewhat different, and extended, in VS2005 relative to previous versions.

In either case, you will see the dialog box shown in Figure 7-8.

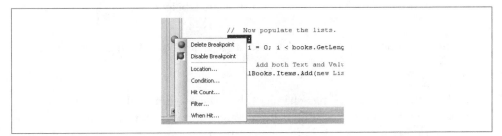

Figure 7-8. Breakpoint properties menu

The first two items in the breakpoint properties menu allow you to delete or disable the selected breakpoint. The Disable menu item will toggle each time you click it, and when the breakpoint is disabled, the icon will appear as an empty circle.

The following menu items are available:

Location. The Location menu item brings up the dialog box shown in Figure 7-9, which is fairly self-explanatory.

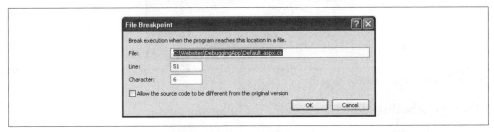

Figure 7-9. Breakpoint Location dialog box

Condition. The Condition button brings up the dialog shown in Figure 7-10.

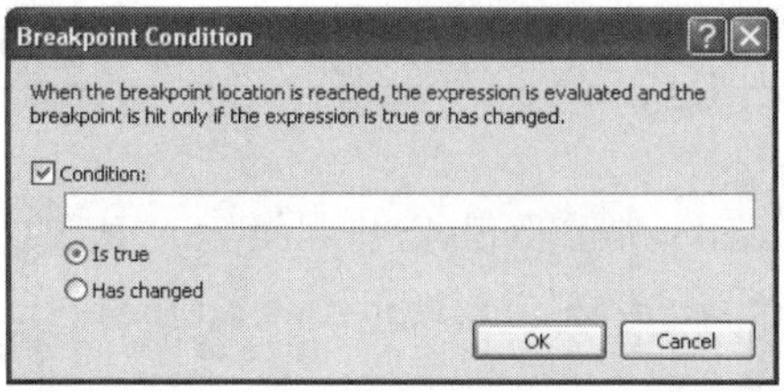

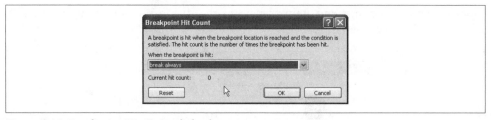

Figure 7-10. Breakpoint Condition dialog box

You can enter any valid expression in the edit field. This expression is evaluated when program execution reaches the breakpoint. Depending on which radio button is selected and how the Condition expression evaluates, the program execution will either pause or move on. The two radio buttons are labeled:

Is true

> If the Condition entered evaluates to a Boolean true, then the program will pause.

Has changed

> If the Condition entered has changed, then the program will pause. On the first pass through the piece of code being debugged, the breakpoint will never pause execution because there is nothing to compare against. On the second and subsequent passes, the expression will have been initialized and the comparison will take place.

Hit count. Hit count is the number of times that spot in the code has been executed since either the run began or the Reset Hit Count button was pressed. The Hit Count button brings up the dialog shown in Figure 7-11.

Figure 7-11. Breakpoint Hit Count dialog box

Clicking on the drop-down list presents the following options:

- Break always
- Break always when the hit count is equal to
- Break always when the hit count is a multiple of
- Break always when the hit count is greater than or equal to

If you click on any option other than "break always" (the default), the dialog box will add an edit field for you to enter a target hit count.

Suppose this is a breakpoint set in a loop of some sort. You select "break when the hit count is a multiple of" and enter 5 in the edit field. The program will pause execution every fifth time it runs.

When a hit count is set, the red breakpoint icon in the left margin of the window has a plus sign in the middle of it.

Filter. Setting a breakpoint filter allows you to specify machines, processes, or threads, or any combination thereof, for which a breakpoint will be in effect. The Filter menu item brings up the dialog box shown in Figure 7-12.

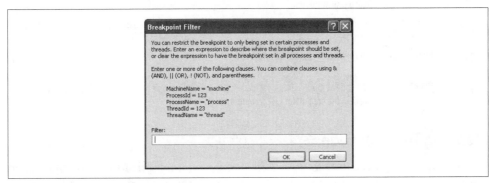

Figure 7-12. Breakpoint Filter dialog box

When Hit.... The When Hit menu item brings up the dialog box shown in Figure 7-13. By default, the Print a message checkbox is unchecked. When this box is checked, the red circular breakpoint icon in the left margin of the window changes to a diamond shape.

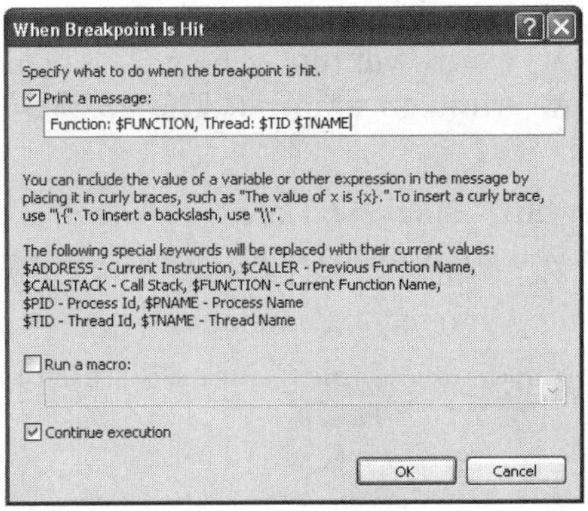

Figure 7-13. Breakpoint When Hit dialog box

You can also elect to run one of a large selection of pre-defined macros, such as Find-Case, SaveView and SaveBackup.

By default, the Continue execution checkbox is checked.

Breakpoint icons

Each breakpoint symbol, or glyph, conveys a different type of breakpoint. These glyphs appear in Table 7-4.

Table 7-4. Breakpoint icons

Icon	Type	Description
●	Enabled	A normal, active breakpoint. If breakpoint conditions or hit count settings are met, execution will pause at this line.
○	Disabled	Execution will not pause at this line until the breakpoint is re-enabled.
◐	Error	The location or condition is not valid.
❷	Warning	The code at this line is not yet loaded, so a breakpoint can't be set. If the code is subsequently loaded, the breakpoint will become enabled.

Stepping Through Code

One of the most powerful techniques for debugging an application is to single-step through the code, giving you the opportunity to see the execution flow and to examine the value of variables, properties, objects, and so on. To see this in action, go to the code-behind file in the example. Place a breakpoint on the call to the Add method of the DropDownList control's Items collection, the line in the Page_Load method where the items are added to the DropDownList. Set the Hit Count to be a multiple of five (break always when hit count is a multiple of five). Then run the program.

The breakpoint will be hit, and the program will stop execution at the line of code containing the breakpoint, which will turn yellow. The breakpoint glyph in the left margin will have a yellow arrow on top of it. The VS2005 screen should look like Figure 7-14.

You can now move forward a single statement or line at a time, stepping into any methods or functions as you go, by using one of the following techniques:

- Select the Debug → Step Into menu command.
- Click on the Step Into icon (see Table 7-3 for a picture of the icon).
- Press F11.

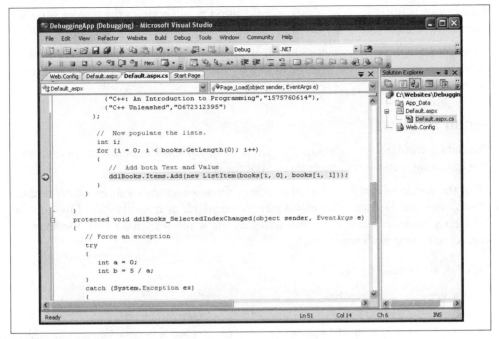

Figure 7-14. Breakpoint hit

You can step through the code without going through called functions or methods. That is, you can step over the calls rather than into the calls, using one of the following techniques:

- Select the Debug → Step Over menu item.
- Click on the Step Over icon (see Table 7-3 for a picture of the icon).
- Press F10.

Finally, if you are debugging in a called method or function, you can step out of that method or function call, using one of the following techniques:

- Select the Debug → Step Out menu command.
- Click on the Step Out icon (see Table 7-3 for a picture of the icon).
- Press Shift-F11.

Examining Variables and Objects

Once the program is stopped, it is incredibly intuitive and easy to examine the value of objects and variables currently in scope. Place the mouse cursor over the top of any variable or object in the code, wait a moment, and a little pop-up window will appear with its current value.

If the cursor is hovering over a variable, the pop-up will contain the type of variable, its value (if relevant), and any other properties it may have.

If the cursor is hovering over some other object, the pop-up window will contain information relevant to its type, including its full namespace, syntax and a descriptive line of help.

Debug Windows

The debug windows are optimized to show program information in a specific way. The following sections will describe each of the windows.

All of the windows can be accessed in one of three ways: with a shortcut key combination, from the Debug → Windows menu command, or from the Windows icon of the Debug toolbar. Table 7-5 summarizes all the windows, along with the shortcut keys for accessing each window.

Table 7-5. Accessing debug windows

Window name	Shortcut keys	Description
Immediate	Ctrl-Alt-I	View any variable or expression.
Autos	Ctrl-Alt-V followed by A	View all variables in the current and previous statement.
Locals	Ctrl-Alt-V followed by L	View all variables in the current context.
Watch	Ctrl-Alt-W, followed by either 1, 2, 3, or 4	View up to four different sets of variables of your choosing.
Call Stack	Ctrl-Alt-C	View all methods on the call stack.
Threads	Ctrl-Alt-H	View and control threads.
Modules	Ctrl-Alt-U	View all modules in use.
Disassembly	Ctrl-Alt-D	View current program in assembly code.
Registers	Ctrl-Alt-G	View microprocessor registers.
Memory	Ctrl-Alt-M followed by n, where n is either 1, 2, 3, or 4	View contents of up to four different memory addresses.

Immediate window

The *Immediate window* allows you to type almost any variable, property, or expression and immediately see its value.

You can enter expressions for immediate execution in the Immediate window. If you want to see the value of an expression, prepend it with a question mark. For instance, if the breakpoint is on the line shown in Figure 7-14, you will see the value of the integer i by entering either of the following lines (they are equivalent):

```
?i
i
```

in the Immediate window and press Enter. Figure 7-15 shows the result of that exercise; additionally, this figure shows the process of assigning a new value to the variable i and then viewing its value again. If you change the value of a variable in the Immediate window and then continue to run the program, the new value will now be in effect.

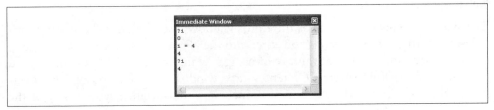

Figure 7-15. Immediate window

You can clear the contents of the Immediate window by right-clicking anywhere in the window and selecting Clear All. Close the window by clicking on the X in the upper-right corner. If you close the window and subsequently bring it back up in the same session, it will still have all the previous contents.

Autos window

The *Autos window* shows all the variables used in the current statement and the previous statement displayed in a hierarchical table.

A typical Autos window is shown in Figure 7-16.

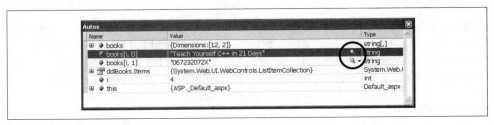

Figure 7-16. Autos window

There are columns for the name of the object, its value, and its type. A plus sign next to an object indicates that it has child objects that are not displayed while a minus sign indicates that its child objects are visible. Clicking on a plus symbol expands out the tree and shows any children, while clicking on a minus symbol contracts the tree and displays only the parent. Values that change in the current step display in red.

You can select and edit the value of any variable. The value will display as red in the Autos window. Any changes to values take effect immediately.

Locals window

The *Locals window* is the same as the Autos window, except that it shows variables local to the current context. The current context is the method or function containing the current execution location.

Watch window

The *Watch window* is the same as the Autos window, except that it shows only variables, properties, or expressions you enter into the Name field in the window or drag from another window. The advantage of using a Watch window is that it allows you to watch objects from several different source windows simultaneously. This overcomes the inability to add object types other than the specified type to any of the other debug windows.

In addition to typing in the name of the object you want to watch, you can also drag and drop variables, properties, or expressions from a code window. Select the object in the code you want to put in the Watch window and then drag it to the Name field in the open Watch window.

You can also drag and drop objects from any of the following windows into the Watch window:

- Locals
- Autos
- This
- Disassembly

To drag something from one of these windows to the Watch window, both the source window and the Watch window must be open. Highlight a line in the source window and drag it down over the Watch tab. The Watch window will come to the foreground. Continue dragging the object to an empty line in the Watch window.

Call Stack window

The *Call Stack window* displays the names of the methods on the call stack and their parameter types and values. You can control which information is displayed in the Call Stack window by right-clicking anywhere in the window and toggling field names that appear in the lower portion of the pop-up menu.

Threads window

The *Threads window* allows you to examine and control threads in the program you are debugging. Threads are sequences of executable instructions. Programs can be single-threaded or multithreaded. The whole topic of threading and multiprocess programming is beyond the scope of this book.

Modules window

The *Modules window* allows you to examine the *.exe* and *.dll* files being used by the program being debugged.

A Modules window is shown in Figure 7-17.

Figure 7-17. Modules window

By default, the modules are shown in the order in which they were loaded. You can re-sort the table by clicking on any of the column headers.

Disassembly window

The *Disassembly window* shows the current program in assembly code. If you are debugging managed code, such as that which comes from VB2005, C#, or Managed C++, this will correspond to Microsoft Intermediate Language (MSIL) code.

A Disassembly window is shown in Figure 7-18.

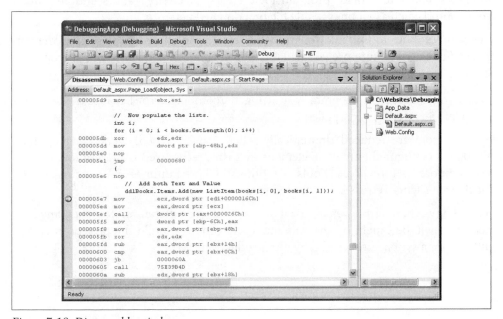

Figure 7-18. Disassembly window

Unlike the previous windows discussed in this chapter, the Disassembly window displays as a tabbed item as part of the main work surface. You can set breakpoints anywhere in the window, just as for any other Source code window.

Registers window

The *Registers window* allows you to examine the contents of the microprocessor's registers. Values that have changed recently are displayed in red.

You can select which pieces of information to view by right-clicking anywhere in the Registers window and clicking on the information you would like displayed.

Memory windows

There are four *Memory windows* available for viewing memory dumps of large buffers, strings, and other data that will not display well in any other window. These four memory windows are for watching four different memory addresses.

Error Handling

You can and should avoid bugs, but there are runtime errors that cannot be avoided and should be handled as gracefully as possible. You would like to avoid having the end user see ugly or cryptic error messages, or worse, having the application crash. Errors can arise from any number of causes: user action, such as entering invalidly formatted text into a field, program logic errors, or circumstances entirely out of your control, such as an unavailable file or a downed network.

The simplest bugs to find and fix are syntax errors: violations of the rules of the language. For example, suppose you had the following line of code in your C# program:

```
intt i;
```

When you compile the program, you will get a compiler error because the keyword to declare an integer is misspelled.

Syntax errors are reduced dramatically when using VS2005. Depending on how VS2005 is configured, any code element that isn't recognized is underlined. If Auto List Members is turned on (Tools → Options → Text Editor → All Languages), the incidence of syntax errors is further reduced.

Should any syntax errors remain or if you are using a different editor, then any syntax errors will be caught by the compiler every time you build the project. It is very difficult for a syntax error to slip by into production code.

When the compiler finds a syntax error, an error message containing the location of the error and a terse explanation will be displayed in the Output window of VS2005. If the error is caused by something such as an unbalanced parenthesis or bracket, or a missing semicolon in C#, then the actual error may not be on the exact reported line.

More problematic, and often more difficult to catch, are errors in *logic*. The program successfully compiles and may run perfectly well most of the time yet still contain errors in logic. The very hardest bugs to find are those that occur least often. If you can't reproduce the problem, it is terribly difficult to find it.

While you will try to eliminate all the bugs from your code, you do want your program to react gracefully when a subtle bug or unexpected problem rears its ugly head.

Unhandled Errors

To demonstrate what happens if there is no error handling in place, modify the sample project from this chapter to force some errors.

Go to the code-behind file. Find the for loop that populates the DropDownList in the Page_Load method. Change the test expression to cause an error intentionally at runtime. For example, change the line:

```
for (i = 0; i < books.GetLength(0); i++)
```

to:

```
for (i = 0; i < books.GetLength(0) + 2; i++)
```

When this code runs it will try to add more items than have been defined in the books array, thus causing a runtime error. This is not a subtle bug, but it serves to demonstrate how the system reacts to runtime errors.

Now run the program. As expected, an error is generated immediately, and the generic ASP.NET error page is displayed, as shown in Figure 7-19.

This error page is actually fairly useful to the developer or technical support person who will be trying to track down and fix any bugs. It tells you the error type, the line in the code that is the approximate error location, and a stack trace to help in tracking down how that line of code was reached.

You can replace this detailed error page with a custom error page and can control who gets to see what by setting the mode attribute of the CustomErrors element in the configuration file, as will be described next.

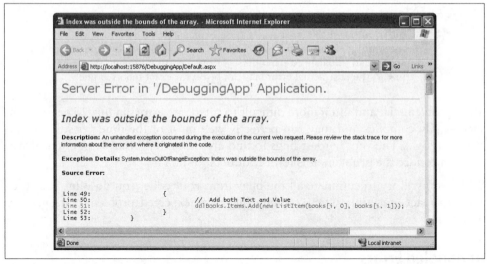

Figure 7-19. Generic error page

Application-Wide Error Pages

The previous section showed the default error pages presented for unhandled errors. This is fine for a developer, but if the application is in production, it would be much more aesthetically pleasing if the user were presented with an error page that looked less intimidating.

The goal is to intercept the error before it has a chance to send the generic error page to the client. This is done on an application-wide basis by modifying the configuration file, *web.config*, which is described more fully in Chapter 18.

The error-handling configuration information in *web.config* is contained within the <customErrors> section within the <system.web> section, which is contained within the <configuration> section. A typical <customErrors> section will look like Example 7-6.

Example 7-6. Custom error code snippet from web.config

```
<?xml version="1.0" encoding="utf-8" ?>
<configuration>

   <system.web>
.
.
.
   <customErrors
      defaultRedirect="CustomErrorPage.htm"
      mode="On"
   />
```

There are two possible attributes for the `<customErrors>` section: `defaultRedirect` and `mode`.

`defaultRedirect` is a text string that contains the URL of the page to display in the case of any error not otherwise handled. In Example 7-6, the `defaultRedirect` page is `CustomErrorPage.htm`. This example is a simple HTML page contained in the same application virtual root directory. The contents of this page are shown in Example 7-7.

Example 7-7. CustomErrorPage.htm

```html
<html>
   <body>
      <h1>Sorry - you've got an error.</h1>
   </body>
</html>
```

If the custom error page to be displayed is not in the application virtual root, then you need to include either a relative or a fully qualified URL in the `defaultRedirect` attribute.

`mode` is an attribute that enables or disables custom error pages for the application. It can have three possible values:

`On`

    Enables custom errors for the entire application.

`Off`

    Disables custom errors for the entire application.

`RemoteOnly`

    Enables custom errors only for remote clients. Local clients will see the generic error page. In this way, developers can see all the possible error information, but end users will see the custom error page.

If you edit your *web.config* file to look like Example 7-6, then put *CustomErrorPage. htm* in your application virtual root and run the program. Instead of Figure 7-19, you will see something like Figure 7-20.

Figure 7-20. Custom error page

Obviously, you'll want to put more information on your custom error page, such as instructions or contact information, but you get the idea. Showing dynamic information about the error on the custom error page is also possible.

You can even use a different custom error page for different errors. To do this, you need to include one or more <error> subtags in the <customErrors> section of *web.config*. You might, for example, modify *web.config* to look like the code snippet in Example 7-8.

Example 7-8. Custom error code snippet with <error> subtags from web.config

```
<?xml version="1.0" encoding="utf-8" ?>
<configuration>

    <system.web>
.
.
.
    <customErrors
        defaultRedirect="CustomErrorPage.htm"
        mode="On" >

        <error statusCode="400" redirect="CustomErrorPage400.htm"/>
        <error statusCode="404" redirect="CustomErrorPage404.htm"/>
        <error statusCode="500" redirect="CustomErrorPage500.htm"/>

    </customErrors>
```

Copy *CustomErrorPage.htm* three times and rename the copies to the filenames in the <error> subtags in Example 7-8. Edit the files so each displays a unique message.

Run the program again with the intentional error in the for loop still in place. You should see something like Figure 7-21.

Figure 7-21. Custom error page for Error 500

Fix the error in the for loop so the program will at least load correctly. Then run the program and click on the hyperlink you put on the test page. That control is configured to link to a nonexistent *.aspx* file. You should see something like Figure 7-22.

Figure 7-22. Custom error page for Error 404

Be aware that you can only display custom error pages for errors generated on *your* server. So, for example, if the hyperlink had been set to a nonexistent page, say, *http:// TestPage.comx* (note the intentional misspelling of the extension), you will not see your custom error page for error 404. Instead, you'll see whatever error page for which the remote server or your browser is configured. Also, you can only trap the 404 error if the page you are trying to link to has an extension of *.aspx*.

In addition to displaying a custom error page, you can add code to the `Application_OnError` event handler in the *global.asax* file to be executed every time an error occurs. Application and session events, as well as the *global.asax* file, are discussed in detail in Chapter 18. Here would be a good place to put functionality such as logging an error message, shutting down connections, cleaning up resources, and so on.

Page-Specific Error Pages

You can override the application-level error pages for any specific page by modifying the Page directive. (Chapter 6 fully discusses Page directives.)

Modify the Page directive in *Default.aspx* file of the DebuggingApp so it appears as follows (note the highlighted `ErrorPage` attribute, which has been added):

```
<%@ Page language="c#" Codebehind="WebForm1.aspx.cs" AutoEventWireup="false"
    Inherits="DebuggingApp.WebForm1" Trace="false"
    ErrorPage="PageSpecificErrorPage.aspx" %>
```

If there is an error on this page, the `PageSpecificErrorPage.aspx` page will be displayed. If there is an application-level custom error page defined in *web.config*, it will be overridden by the Page directive.

CHAPTER 8
Validation

As you have seen in the preceding chapters, many web applications involve user input. The sad fact is, however, that users make mistakes: they skip required fields, they put in six-digit phone numbers, and they return all manner of incorrectly formatted data to your application. Your database routines can choke on corrupted data, and orders can be lost, for example, if a credit card number is entered incorrectly or an address is omitted, so it is imperative to validate user input.

Traditionally, it takes a great deal of time and effort to write reliable validation code. Each field must be checked, and routines must be created for ensuring data integrity. If bad data is found, error messages must be displayed so the user knows there is a problem and how to correct it.

In a given application, you may choose to validate that certain fields have a value, that the values fall within a given range, or that the data is formatted correctly. For example, when processing an order, you may need to ensure that the user has input an address and phone number, that the phone number has the right number of digits (and no letters), and that the Social Security number entered is in the appropriate form of nine digits separated by hyphens.

Some applications require more complex validation, in which one field is validated to be within a range established by two other fields. For example, you might ask in one field what date the customer wishes to arrive at your hotel, and in a second field you might ask for the departure date. When the user books dinner, you'll want to ensure that the date is between the arrival and departure dates.

There is no limit to the complexity of the validation routines you may need to write. Credit cards have checksums built into their values, as do ISBN numbers. Zip and postal codes follow complex patterns, as do international phone numbers. You may need to validate passwords, membership numbers, dollar amounts, dates, runway choices, and launch codes.

In addition, you usually want all of this validation to happen client side so you can avoid the delay of repeated round trips to the server while the user is tinkering with his input. In the past, this was solved by writing client-side JavaScript to validate the input, and then writing server-side script to handle input from browsers that don't support client-side programming. In addition, as a security check, you may want to do server-side validation even though you have client-side validation, since users can circumvent validation code deliberately spoofing. Traditionally, this involved writing your validation code twice, once for the client and once for the server.

As you can see, in traditional Internet programming, validation requires extensive custom programming. The ASP.NET framework simplifies this process by providing rich controls for validating user input. The validation controls allow you to specify how and where the error messages will be displayed; either inline with the input controls, aggregated together in a summary report, or both. These controls can be used to validate input for both HTML and ASP.NET server controls.

You add validation controls to your ASP.NET document as you would add any other control. Within the declaration of the validation control, you specify which other control is being validated. You may freely combine the various validation controls, and you may even write your own custom validation controls as you'll see later in this chapter.

With uplevel browsers that support DHTML, such as Internet Explorer 4 or better, .NET validation is done client side, avoiding the necessity of a round trip to the server. With downlevel browsers, *your* code is unchanged, but the code sent to the client ensures validation at the server.

 Even when client-side validation is done, the values are ultimately validated server side as well as a security measure.

Because client-side validation will prevent your server-side code from ever running if the control is invalid, you may at times, want to force server-side validation. In that case, add a ClientTarget attribute to the @Page directive:

```
<%@ Page Language="C#"
    AutoEventWireup="true"
    CodeFile="Default.aspx.cs"
    Inherits="Default_aspx"
    ClientTarget="downlevel"
%>
```

This directive will cause the validation to happen on the server even if your browser would have supported DHTML and client-side validation.

Sometimes you don't want any validation to occur, such as when a Cancel button is clicked. To allow this, many postback controls, such as Button, ImageButton, LinkButton, ListControl, and TextBox, have a CausesValidation property, which dictates if validation is performed on the page when the control's default event is raised.

If CausesValiation is set to true, which is the default value, the postback will *not* occur if any control on the page fails validation. If CausesValiation is set to false, however, no validation will occur when that button is used to post the page.

ASP.NET supports the following validation controls:

RequiredFieldValidator

Ensures the user does not skip over your input control. A RequiredFieldValidator can be tied to a text box to force input into the text box. With selection controls, such as a drop-down or radio buttons, the RequiredFieldValidator ensures the user makes a selection other than the default value you specify. The RequiredFieldValidator does not examine the validity of the data but only ensures that some data is entered or chosen.

RangeValidator

Ensures that the value entered is within a specified lower and upper boundary. You can check the range within a pair of numbers (greater than 10 and less than 100), a pair of characters (greater than D and less than K), or a pair of dates (after 1/1/01 and before 2/28/01).

CompareValidator

Compares the user's entry against another value. It can compare against a constant you specify at design time or against a property value of another control. It can also compare against a database value.

RegularExpressionValidator

One of the most powerful validators, it compares the user's entry with a regular expression you provide. You can use this validator to check for valid Social Security numbers, phone numbers, passwords, and so forth.

CustomValidator

If none of these controls meets your needs, you can use the CustomValidator. This checks the user's entry against whatever algorithm you provide in a custom method.

In the remainder of this chapter, we'll examine how to use each of these controls to validate data in ASP.NET applications.

The RequiredFieldValidator

The RequiredFieldValidator, ensures the user provides a valid value for your control.

To get started, create a new web site called RequiredFieldValidator. You'll create the bug reporting web page shown in Design view in Figure 8-1.

When the user clicks the Submit Bug button, the page is validated to ensure each field has been modified. If not, the offending field is marked with an error message in red, as shown in Figure 8-2.

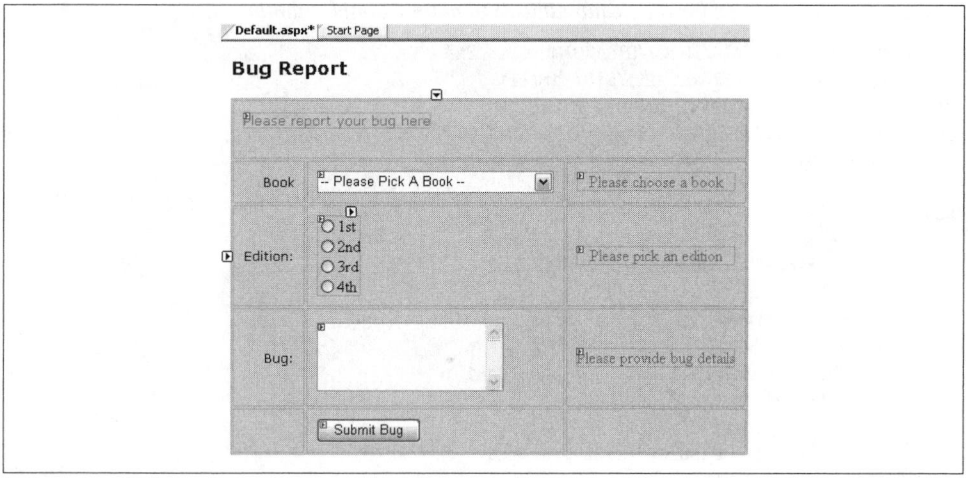

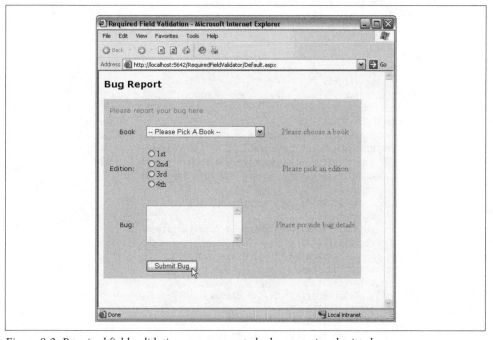

Figure 8-1. Validator bug report in the designer

Figure 8-2. Required field validation errors reported when page is submitted

The complete source code for the content file, *default.aspx*, for this example is shown in Example 8-1.

Example 8-1. default.aspx for the RequiredFieldValidator example

```
<%@ Page Language="C#" AutoEventWireup="true"  CodeFile="Default.aspx.cs"
      Inherits="Default_aspx" %>
```

```
<!DOCTYPE html PUBLIC "-//W3C//DTD XHTML 1.1//EN"
   "http://www.w3.org/TR/xhtml11/DTD/xhtml11.dtd">
<html xmlns="http://www.w3.org/1999/xhtml" >
<head runat="server">
    <title>Required Field Validation</title>
</head>
<body>
    <h3>
        <font face="Verdana">Bug Report</font>
    </h3>
    <form runat="server" ID="frmBugs">
        <div>
          <table bgcolor=gainsboro cellpadding=10>
            <tr valign="top">
                <td colspan=3>
                    <!-- Display error messages -->
                    <asp:Label ID="lblMsg"
                    Text="Please report your bug here"
                    ForeColor="red" Font-Names="Verdana"
                    Font-Size="10" runat=server />
                    <br>
                </td>
            </tr>
            <tr>
                <td align=right>
                    <font face=Verdana size=2>Book</font>
                </td>
                <td>
                <!-- Drop down list with the books (must pick one) -->
                    <ASP:DropDownList id=ddlBooks runat=server>
                        <asp:ListItem>-- Please Pick A Book --</asp:ListItem>
                        <asp:ListItem>Programming ASP.NET</asp:ListItem>
                        <asp:ListItem>
                            Programming .NET Windows Applications
                        </asp:ListItem>
                        <asp:ListItem>Programming C#</asp:ListItem>
                        <asp:ListItem>
                                Programming Visual Basic 2005
                        </asp:ListItem>
                        <asp:ListItem>
                            Teach Yourself C++ In 21 Days
                        </asp:ListItem>
                        <asp:ListItem>
                            Teach Yourself C++ In 24 Hours
                        </asp:ListItem>
                        <asp:ListItem>TY C++ In 10 Minutes</asp:ListItem>
                        <asp:ListItem>TY More C++ In 21 Days</asp:ListItem>
                        <asp:ListItem>C++ Unleashed</asp:ListItem>
                    </ASP:DropDownList>
                </td>
                <!-- Validator for the drop down -->
                <td align=center rowspan=1>
```

```
<asp:RequiredFieldValidator
id="reqFieldBooks"
ControlToValidate="ddlBooks"
Display="Static"
InitialValue="-- Please Pick A Book --"
Width="100%" runat=server>
    Please choose a book
</asp:RequiredFieldValidator>
        </td>
    </tr>
    <tr>
        <td align=right>
        <!-- Radio buttons for the edition -->
            <font face=Verdana size=2>Edition:</font>
        </td>
        <td>
            <ASP:RadioButtonList id=rblEdition
            RepeatLayout="Flow" runat=server>
                <asp:ListItem>1st</asp:ListItem>
                <asp:ListItem>2nd</asp:ListItem>
                <asp:ListItem>3rd</asp:ListItem>
                <asp:ListItem>4th</asp:ListItem>
            </ASP:RadioButtonList>
        </td>
        <!-- Validator for editions -->
        <td align=center rowspan=1>
            <asp:RequiredFieldValidator
            id="reqFieldEdition"
            ControlToValidate="rblEdition"
            Display="Static"
            InitialValue=""
            Width="100%" runat=server>
                Please pick an edition
            </asp:RequiredFieldValidator>
        </td>
    </tr>
    <tr>
        <td align=right style="HEIGHT: 97px">
            <font face=Verdana size=2>Bug:</font>
        </td>
        <!-- Multi-line text for the bug entry -->
        <td style="HEIGHT: 97px">
            <ASP:TextBox id=txtBug runat=server width="183px"
            textmode="MultiLine" height="68px"/>
        </td>
        <!-- Validator for the text box-->
        <td style="HEIGHT: 97px">
            <asp:RequiredFieldValidator
            id="reqFieldBug"
            ControlToValidate="txtBug"
            Display="Static"
            Width="100%" runat=server>
```

```
                      Please provide bug details
                   </asp:RequiredFieldValidator>
                </td>
            </tr>
            <tr>
                <td>
                </td>
                <td>
                   <ASP:Button id=btnSubmit
                   text="Submit Bug" runat=server />
                </td>
                <td>
                </td>
            </tr>
        </table>
    </div>
    </form>
</body>
</html>
```

To lay out this page, you'll put the controls inside an HTML table. For each field that you want validated, however, you'll add a RequiredFieldValidator control, (which is a control like any other).

The RequiredFieldValidator control has its own ID, and it also asks for the ID of the control you wish to validate. Thus, the first RequiredFieldValidator you'll add will have the ID of reqFieldBooks, but its ControlToValidate property will be set to ddlBooks (the drop-down list that you are validating):

```
<asp:RequiredFieldValidator runat=server
    id="reqFieldBooks"
    ControlToValidate="ddlBooks"
    Display="Static"
    InitialValue="-- Please Pick A Book --"
    Width="100%" >
    Please choose a book
</asp:RequiredFieldValidator>
```

The Display attribute is set to Static, which tells ASP.NET to allocate room on the page for the validator whether or not there is a message to display. If this is set to Dynamic, space will not be allocated until (and unless) an error message is displayed. Dynamic allocation is powerful, but it can cause your controls to bounce around on the page when the message is displayed.

In the example, if you set all the validation controls to dynamic, no space will be allocated for them, and the browser will decide that your table is only two columns wide rather than three. That is, the table will not allocate any space for the validation messages and will recognize only one column for the prompt and the other for the controls. When you validate the controls (by clicking the Submit button), the table will widen, which can be disconcerting or attractive depending on how you manage the display.

The RequiredFieldValidator has an additional attribute, InitialValue, which is set to the initial value of the drop-down box. If the user clicks Submit, this initial value will be compared with the value of the drop-down, and if they are the same, the error message will be displayed. This forces the user to change the initial value, picking a particular book to report.

The second RequiredFieldValidator ensures that one of the radio buttons in rblEdition is selected:

```
<!-- Validator for editions -->
<td align=middle rowspan=1>
   <asp:RequiredFieldValidator runat=server
      id="reqFieldEdition"
      ControlToValidate="rblEdition"
      Display="Static"
      Width="100%" >
      Please pick an edition
   </asp:RequiredFieldValidator>
</td>
```

You do not need to indicate an initial value this time. Since the control is a radio button list, the validator knows the user is required to pick one of the buttons; if any button is chosen, the validation will be satisfied.

Finally, to complete the example, add a text box and require the user to enter some text in it. The validator is straightforward; set the text box as the ControlToValidate and enter the error message to display if the box is left empty:

```
<!-- Validator for the text box-->
<td style="HEIGHT: 97px">
   <asp:RequiredFieldValidator runat=server
      id="reqFieldBug"
      ControlToValidate="txtBug"
      Display="Static"
      Width="100%" >
      Please provide bug details
   </asp:RequiredFieldValidator>
</td>
</tr>
```

The only code required in the code-behind file is the event handler for the Submit button:

```
protected void btnSubmit_Click(object sender, EventArgs e)
{
   if (Page.IsValid)
   {
      lblMsg.Text = "Page is Valid!";
   }
   else
```

```
        {
            lblMsg.Text = "Some of the required fields are empty";
        }
    }
```

When the Submit button is clicked, the page is posted to the server. The validation for each control is checked, and if every control is valid, the IsValid property of the page will return true.

You can make your pages a bit friendlier for your users by placing the focus on the first control that fails validation. To do so, add the SetFocusOnError property to each validation control and set it to true (the default is false):

```
<asp:RequiredFieldValidator runat=server
    id="reqFieldBug"
    ControlToValidate="txtBug"
    Display="Static"
    SetFocusOnError=true
    Width="100%" >
    Please provide bug details
</asp:RequiredFieldValidator>
```

When one or more controls uses SetFocusOnError and if the page is invalid, the focus will be set to the first control that fails validation and has this property set to true.

The Summary Control

You can decide how validation errors are reported. For example, rather than putting error messages alongside the control, you can summarize all the validation failures with a ValidationSummary control. This control can place a summary of the errors in a bulleted list, a simple list, or a paragraph that appears on the web page or in a pop-up message box.

Create a copy of RequiredFieldValidator called RequiredFieldValidatorSummary. Add a ValidationSummary control at the bottom of the page, which requires that you add the following code after the </table> tag:

```
<asp:ValidationSummary
    ID="ValSum" runat="server"
    DisplayMode="BulletList"
    HeaderText="The following errors were found: "
    ShowSummary="True" />
```

You've named the ValidationSummary control ValSum and set its DisplayMode property to BulletList. The HeaderText attribute holds the header that will be displayed only if there are errors to report. You can mix the ShowMessageBox and ShowSummary attributes to display the errors in the body of the HTML document (ShowSummary="true"), in a pop-up message box (ShowMessageBox="true"), or both.

To make this work, you'll need to add an `ErrorMessage` attribute to the other validation controls. For example, you might modify the first validation control as follows:

```
<asp:RequiredFieldValidator runat=server
    id="reqFieldBooks"
    ControlToValidate="ddlBooks"
    Display="Static"
    SetFocusOnError=true
    InitialValue="-- Please Pick A Book --"
    ErrorMessage = "You did not choose a book from the drop-down"
    Width="100%" > * </asp:RequiredFieldValidator>
```

The text in the `ErrorMessage` attribute will be displayed in the summary if this control reports a validation error. You've also modified the validator to display an asterisk rather than the more complete error message. Now that you have a summary, you need only flag the error. You can make similar changes for each of the other `RequiredFieldValidator` controls.

Rather than choose which of the three types of summary reports (bulleted list, list, or summary paragraph) to provide, you'll let the user choose from a drop-down. You do this by inserting the following code before the row that holds the Submit button:

```
<tr>
    <td align="right">
            <font face=Verdana size=2>Display Report</font>
    </td>
    <td>
        <asp:DropDownList id="lstFormat"
        AutoPostBack=true
        OnSelectedIndexChanged="lstFormat_SelectedIndexChanged"
        runat=server >
            <asp:ListItem >List</asp:ListItem>
            <asp:ListItem Selected="true">Bulleted List</asp:ListItem>
            <asp:ListItem>Single Paragraph</asp:ListItem>
        </asp:DropDownList>
    </td>
</tr>
```

This drop-down posts back the page so you can update the display. You have assigned an event handler, lstFormat_SelectedIndexChanged, to handle the event when the user changes the current selection. The event handler code is simple:

```
protected void lstFormat_SelectedIndexChanged(object sender, EventArgs e)
{
    ValSum.DisplayMode =
        (ValidationSummaryDisplayMode)
        lstFormat.SelectedIndex;
}
```

The validation summary object (ValSum) has its DisplayMode set to the index of the selected item. This is a bit of a cheat. The ValidationSummary DisplayMode is controlled by the ValidationSummaryDisplayMode enumeration, in which BulletList = 0,

`List` = 1, and `SingleParagraph` = 2. You take advantage of this and order your list so the index of the selected item will equal the choice you want.

Similarly, you'll add a drop-down to allow the user to control if the error report appears in the page or in a pop-up menu. To do this, insert the following row before the row that allows the user to choose the type of summary report:

```
<tr>
    <td align=right>
    <!-- Drop down for the error display -->
        <font face=Verdana size=2>Display Errors</font>
    </td>
    <td>
        <asp:DropDownList id="lstDisplay"
        AutoPostBack=true
        OnSelectedIndexChanged="lstDisplay_SelectedIndexChanged"
        runat=server >
                <asp:ListItem Selected ="true">Summary</asp:ListItem>
                <asp:ListItem>Msg. Box</asp:ListItem>
        </asp:DropDownList>
    </td>
    <td>
     
    </td>
</tr>
```

Once again, this control posts back the page, and the changed selection event is handled in an event handler:

```
protected void lstDisplay_SelectedIndexChanged(object sender, EventArgs e)
{
    ValSum.ShowSummary = lstDisplay.SelectedIndex == 0;
    ValSum.ShowMessageBox = lstDisplay.SelectedIndex == 1;
}
```

 To keep the example simple, we've allowed the order of the items in the drop-down to be tightly coupled with the event handling code. That is, we're assuming that Show Summary is the first item in the list. In a real application, these would be decoupled to make maintenance easier.

Figure 8-3 shows the page with the summary validator at the bottom using the bulleted list.

Changing the first drop-down to `Msg. Box` and the second to `List` causes the message box shown in Figure 8-4 to appear on the user's screen.

The Compare Validator

While the ability to ensure that the user has made some sort of entry is great, you will often want to validate that the entry content is within certain guidelines. One of

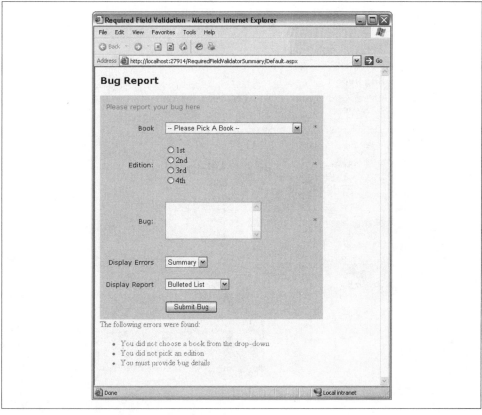

Figure 8-3. Summary validator: summary

the most common requirements for validation is to compare the user's input to (a value constant, the value of another control, or a database value).

To see this at work, make a new copy of the RequiredValidationSummary protect and name the new web site CompareValidator. Add a new control that asks the user how many copies of the book he has purchased.

To do so, you will insert a text box, a required field validator, and a compare validator into a new row before the row for the Display Errors drop-down:

```
<tr>
    <td>Number purchased:</td>
    <td><ASP:TextBox id="txtNumPurch" runat=server width="50px" /></td>
    <td>
        <asp:RequiredFieldValidator runat="server"
            id="RequiredFieldValidatorNumPurch"
            ControlToValidate="txtNumPurch"
            SetFocusOnError=true
            ErrorMessage ="You did not enter the number purchased"
            Width="100%" >*
        </asp:RequiredFieldValidator>
```

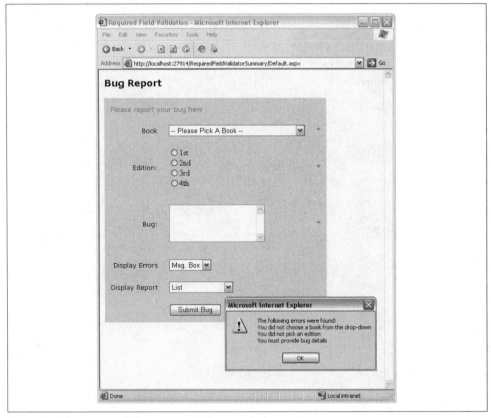

Figure 8-4. Summary validator: message box

```
        <asp:CompareValidator runat="server"
            id="CompareValidatorNumPurch"
            ControlToValidate="txtNumPurch"
            SetFocusOnError=true
            ErrorMessage ="Invalid number purchased"
            Type="Integer"
            Operator="GreaterThan"
            ValueToCompare=0>*</asp:CompareValidator>
    </td>
  </tr>
```

Both validators are placed into the same cell in the table, and both validators validate the same control: *txtNumPurch*. The required field validator is needed because the compare validator will always return true for null or empty values.

The Compare validator's ValueToCompare attribute takes a constant, in this case zero. The Operator attribute determines how the comparison will be made (that is, how the input value must be related to the ValueToCompare).

The possible values for the Operator attribute are Equal, NotEqual, GreaterThan, GreaterThanEqual, LessThan, LessThanEqual, and DataTypeCheck. In this example case, to be valid, the input value must be greater than the ValueToCompare constant. The user must order more than zero books (always my philosophy). You must use the Type attribute to tell the control what type of value it is using. The Type attribute takes one of the ValidationDataType enumerated values: Currency, Date, Double, Integer, or String. In the example, the values are compared as integers, and thus, entering (for example) a character will cause the validation to fail.

Run the application and satisfy yourself that the Compare validator does require a nonzero value to be entered.

Checking the Input Type

Rather than checking that the number of books purchased is greater than zero, you might want to check that it is a number (rather than a letter or date). To do this, you make a minor change to the CompareValidator.

To accomplish this change, remove the ValueToCompare attribute and change the Operator attribute from GreaterThan to DataTypeCheck. Since the Type attribute is Integer, the control will report any integer value as valid. The following code should replace the code for the CompareValidator you added in the last section:

```
<asp:CompareValidator runat="server"
    id="CompareValidatorNumPurch"
    SetFocusOnError=true
    ControlToValidate="txtNumPurch"
    ErrorMessage ="Invalid number purchased"
    Type="Integer"
    Operator="DataTypeCheck">*
</asp:CompareValidator>
```

Comparing to Another Control

You can compare a value in one control to the value in another control rather than to a constant. A classic use of this might be to ask the user to enter his password twice and then validate that both entries are identical.

The common scenario is that you've asked the user to pick a new password. For security, when the password is entered, the text is disguised with asterisks. Because this will be the password the user will need to log in, you must validate the user entered the password as intended. The usual solution is to ask the user to reenter the password, and then you validate the same password was entered each time. The CompareValidator is perfect for this.

Insert the following code, again before the rows for the Display Errors control.

```
<!-- Text fields for passwords -->
<tr>
```

```
    <td>Enter your password:</td>
    <td>
    <asp:TextBox id="txtPasswd1" runat=server
        TextMode="Password"
        Width="80"></asp:TextBox>
    </td>
    <td>
    <!-- required to enter the password -->
    <asp:RequiredFieldValidator runat=server
        id="ReqFieldTxtPassword1"
        ControlToValidate="txtPasswd1"
        ErrorMessage ="Please enter your password"
        Width="100%" >*</asp:RequiredFieldValidator>
    </td>
</tr>

<!-- Second password for comparison -->
<tr>
    <td>Re-enter your password:</td>
    <td>
    <asp:TextBox id="txtPasswd2" runat=server
        TextMode="Password"
        Width="80"></asp:TextBox>
    </td>

    <td>
    <!-- Second password is required -->
    <asp:RequiredFieldValidator runat=server
        id="ReqFieldTxtPassword2"
        ControlToValidate="txtPasswd2"
        SetFocusOnError=true
        ErrorMessage ="Please re-enter your password"
        Width="100%" >*</asp:RequiredFieldValidator>

    <!-- Second password must match the first -->
    <asp:CompareValidator runat=server
        id="CompValPasswords"
        ControlToValidate="txtPasswd2"
        ErrorMessage ="Passwords do not match"
        SetFocusOnError=true
        Type="String"
        Operator="Equal"
        ControlToCompare="txtPasswd1">*</asp:CompareValidator>
    </td>
</tr>
```

The first row contains the text box (with the attribute TextMode="Password" set) and a RequiredField validator to ensure the user doesn't leave it blank.

The second row contains a second password text box and a second RequiredField validator (again, it can't be blank), but it uses a compare validator to make sure the two controls have the same content. Notice the two properties set:

```
ControlToValidate="txtPasswd2"
ControlToCompare="txtPasswd1"
```

This says that the CompareValidator (whose ID is CompValPasswords) is validating the text box control whose ID is txtPasswd2 by comparing its value with the text box control whose ID is txtPasswd1. The Operator property is set to Equal and the Type property is set to String, so the two strings must match.

 Both text boxes need a RequiredField validator because the CompareValidator will validate as matching a string against a null or empty string value.

Range Checking

At times, you'll want to validate that a user's entry falls within a range. That range can be within a pair of numbers, characters, or dates. In addition, you can express the boundaries for the range by using constants or by comparing its value with values found in other controls.

In this example, you'll prompt the user for a number between 10 and 20 and then validate his answer to ensure it was entered properly. To do so, create a new web site named RangeValidator. Let's do this project entirely in Design mode. To begin, drag four controls onto your page: a label, a text box, a button, and of course, a RangeValidator control, as shown in Figure 8-5.

Figure 8-5. Dragging controls onto a range validator

Click on the label and set its text to "Enter a number between 10 and 20:." Click on the text box, set its ID to txtValue. Click the button and set its text to "Submit." Finally, click on the RangeValidator and in the Properties window click Type. Choose Integer from the drop-down. Set the MinimumValue property to 10 and the MaximumValue property to 20. Next, click on the ControlToValidate property, pick the text box, and set the Text property to "Between 10 and 20 please."

Run your program. Enter a value and click Submit. The text "Between 10 and 20 please" will be displayed if the value is not within the range of values specified by the MinimumValue and MaximumValue attributes. The Type attribute designates how the value should be evaluated and may be any of the following types: Currency, Date, Double, Integer, or String.

If there are no validation errors, the page can be submitted; otherwise, the range checking error message is displayed.

If you leave the text blank, the validation will pass and the page will be submitted. If you want to ensure *some* value is entered, you'll need to add a RequiredField validator.

Regular Expressions

Often, a simple value or range check is insufficient; you must check that the *form* of the data entered is correct. For example, you may need to ensure that a Zip Code is five digits, an email address is in the form *name@place.com*, a credit card matches the right format, and so forth.

A regular expression validator allows you to validate that a text field matches a *regular expression*. Regular expressions are a language for describing and manipulating text.

 For complete coverage of regular expressions, see *Mastering Regular Expressions*, Second Edition, by Jeffrey Friedl (O'Reilly).

A regular expression consists of two types of characters: literals and metacharacters. A *literal* is a character you wish to match in the target string. A *metacharacter* is a special symbol that acts as a command to the regular expression parser. (The parser is the engine responsible for understanding the regular expression.) Consider this regular expression:

```
^\d{5}$
```

This will match any string that has five numerals. The initial metacharacter, ^, indicates the beginning of the string. The second metacharacter, \d, indicates a digit. The third metacharacter, {5}, indicates five of the digits, and the final metacharacter, $, indicates the end of the string. Thus, this regular expression matches five digits between the beginning and end of the line and nothing else.

 When you use a `RegularExpressionValidator` control with client-side validation, the regular expressions are matched using JScript. This may differ in small details from the regular expression checking done on the server.

A more sophisticated algorithm might accept a five-digit Zip Code or a nine-digit Zip Code in the format of 12345-1234. Rather than using the \d metacharacter, you could designate the range of acceptable values:

```
[0-9]{5}|[0-9]{5}-[0-9]{4}
```

Make a copy of the `RangeValidator` example named `RegularExpressionValidator` and replace the `RangeValidator` control with a `RegularExpressionValidator` control. Use the Properties window to set the `ControlToValidate` to txtValue and set the text to "Please enter a valid U. S. zip code." Finally, click on the property for Validation Expression, and click on the ellipsis. A Regular Expression Editor pops up with a few common regular expressions, or you can enter your own. Scroll down and choose U.S. ZIP Code, as shown in Figure 8-6.

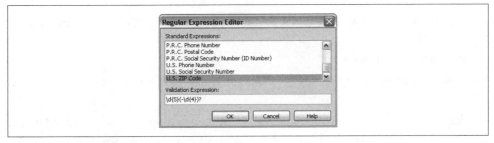

Figure 8-6. Regular Expression Editor

 If you choose "Custom," the validation expression will be left blank and you can enter any expression you choose. For help with *creating* custom regular expressions, we recommend the program RegEx Buddy (*http://www.RegExBuddy.com*).

Custom Validation

There are times when the validation of your data is so specific to your application that you will need to write your own validation method. The `CustomValidator` is designed to provide all the infrastructure support you need. You point to your validation method and have it return a Boolean value: `true` or `false`. The `CustomValidator` control takes care of all the rest of the work.

Because validation can be done on the client or on the server, depending on the browser, the `CustomValidator` has attributes for specifying a server-side and a client-side method for validation. The server-side method can be written in any .NET language, such as C# or VB.NET, but the client-side method must be written in a scripting language understood by the browser, such as VBScript or JavaScript.

Once again, create a new web site, named `CustomValidator`, and copy the `RegularExpressionValidator` web site to get you started. In this example, you want to ensure that the user enters an even number.

This time, you'll report an error if the number is not evenly divisible by 2. You can imagine, however, that you could use this technique perform a checksum on a credit card or ISBN or otherwise perform complex data checking.

 Most of these checks can be done more easily with a Regular Expression Validator; the custom validator should be used only as a last resort.

Replace the `RegularExpressionValidator` with a `CustomValidator`. Set the `ControlTo-Validate` field, and set `EnableClientScript` to true (the default). Set the text property to *Please enter an even number*.

`CustomValidators` have an additional property that can save you a lot of special coding: `ValidateEmptyText`.

```
ValidateEmptyText=false
```

The default is true, but by setting it to false, the text field will be considered invalid if it is empty.

The key to making your custom validator work is in setting the client-side validator, which you do in the `ClientValidationFunction` property (set this to `ClientValidator`). Also, click the Events lightning bolt button and set the `ServerValidate` event handler to `ServerValidator`. Each of these is the name of a method. The first is a JavaScript method that you'll add to the content file (*default.aspx* in this case):

```
<script language="javascript">
    function ClientValidator(source, args)
    {
        if (args.Value % 2 == 0)
            args.IsValid=true;
        else
            args.IsValid=false;
        return;
    }
</script>
```

This function examines the value passed to the script by the validator, and if it is an even number, it will return true; otherwise, it will return false.

You'll implement the server-side method in the code behind file, *default.aspx.cs*:

```
protected void ServerValidator (object source, ServerValidateEventArgs e)
{
    try
    {
        e.IsValid = false;
        int evenNumber = Int32.Parse(e.Value);
        if (evenNumber % 2 == 0)
            e.IsValid = true;
    }
    catch (Exception)
    {
        // error handler here
    }
}
```

This method does the same thing as the client-side validator, only in C# rather than in JavaScript. There are a few things to notice about these methods. First, the value that the `CustomValidator` is examining is passed to your routine as the Value property of the `ServerValidateEventArgs` event argument. You convert that string to an `int` using the Base Class Library Int32 object's static `Parse` method, as shown.

The declaration for the `CustomValidator` in the content file sets the client-side method and the server-side method you've designated.

```
<asp:CustomValidator runat="server"
    ID="CustomValidator1"
    ControlToValidate="txtValue"
    ValidateEmptyText=false
    ClientValidationFunction="ClientValidator"
    OnServerValidate="ServerValidator">
    Please enter an even number
</asp:CustomValidator>
```

If you run this program in an uplevel browser and enter an odd number, the page will never be posted back to the server; the JavaScript handles the validation. If you enter an even number, however, the client-side script *and* the server-side script will run (to protect against spoofing from the client).

Validation Groups

The examples shown in this chapter have been kept intentionally simple. In a real application, however, you might have a page with many controls on it. In addition, the page may be divided into sections, with more than one button that can submit the page, depending on what the user is doing.

At times, it is convenient to be able to say, "When I press the first button I want to validate only these first five controls, but when I press the second button I want to validate only the last four controls." This allows you to create forms in which you *expect* that some of the controls will be invalid. For example, you might have a page in which you ask the user to enter her username and password (if registered) or to enter other information if creating a new account. Clearly, one or the other will be left blank.

To accomplish this, you set the `ValidationGroup` property on all the controls (and the button that submits the page) to the same value for each group. In the example described above, the first five controls and the first button might all have `ValidationGroup` set to `GroupOne`, yet all the other controls would have `ValidationGroup` set to `GroupTwo`.

To try this out, create a new web site called `ValidationGroup` and copy the `CompareValidator` web site as a starting point.

Make two changes. First, move the two rows for password entry *after* the row that holds the Submit button. Then, add an additional row after the passwords to hold a new button with the ID of `btnPW` and the text `Login`. Your page should look like Figure 8-7.

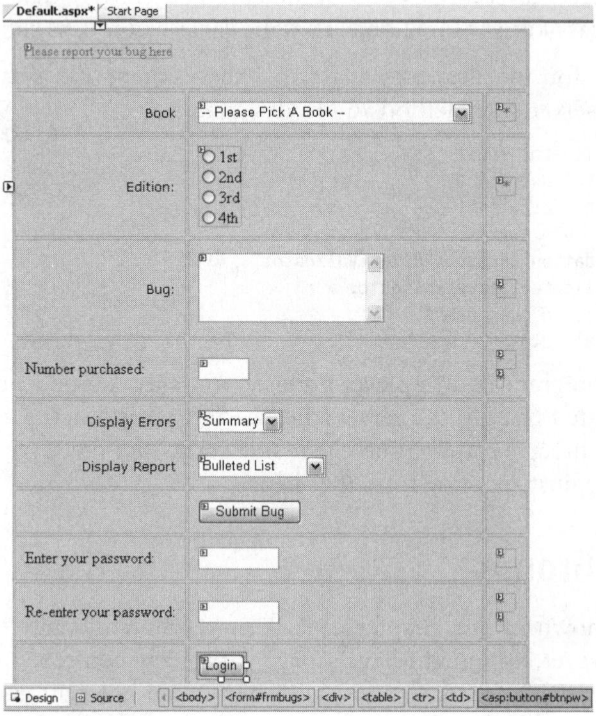

Figure 8-7. Rearranging the form for ValidationGroups

That done, you can add the ValidationGroup to each of your validation controls and to the buttons. For all the controls above the Submit Bug button, add the group name Bug, and for all the controls below the Submit Bug button, add the group name Login as in this example:

```
<asp:RequiredFieldValidator runat=server
    id="reqFieldBooks"
    ControlToValidate="ddlBooks"
    Display="Static"
    SetFocusOnError=true
    InitialValue="-- Please Pick A Book --"
    ErrorMessage = "You did not choose a book from the drop-down"
    ValidationGroup="Bug"
    Width="100%" > *
</asp:RequiredFieldValidator>
```

The drop-down lists have their AutoPostBack property set to true. This will cause a postback (and, thus, validation) when the drop-down value changes. Be sure to set the ValidationGroup to Bug for these controls as well.

When you click the Submit Bug button, only the controls in its group are validated, as shown in Figure 8-8.

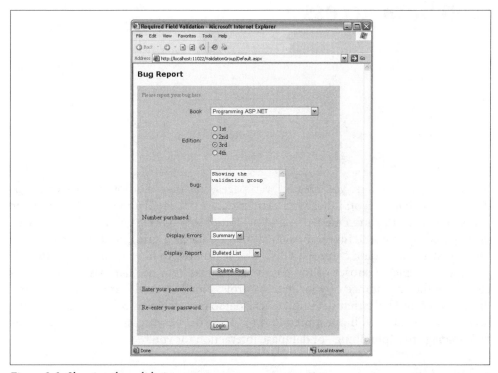

Figure 8-8. Showing the validation group

Look carefully at Figure 8-8. The password fields are not filled in, though they have a required field validator. Because the Submit Bug button was pressed, and the validators for the password controls were not in the Bug group, they were not validated at all. If you click Login, the password controls will be validated, but none of the other controls will be validated.

CHAPTER 9

Web Data Access

In the previous chapters, you created web pages, but they did not interact with real data. In this chapter, you'll begin to extract data from the database and fill in your pages. You'll do this incrementally, adding complexity as you go. You'll see how to display and update a GridView (which displays data in a grid), and how to handle events generated by data controls. You'll also learn how to filter your data on the client side to display a subset of the data you retrieve from the database and how to customize the appearance of your data controls. Finally, you'll learn how to edit the data in place and have that data update the database safely and efficiently in a multi-user environment. You'll put a premium on using data controls and letting the controls manage the "plumbing" of database interaction for you.

Getting Data from a Database

To see how to interact with a database, you'll begin by creating a web application that can be used to display information about the NorthWind database (that comes with SQLExpress and SQL Server).

Start by creating a new web site called *WebNorthWind*.

You'll be working with the Customers table in the NorthWind database, so rename your *.aspx* file from *default.aspx* to *Customers.aspx*.

Remember to change the class name in the code file and in the page directive.

You need a connection to the database. You can explicitly create one, or you can use a control that depends on having a connection and one will be created for you. Let's start by explicitly creating one.

Drag a `SqlDataSource` control onto the form (see Figure 9-1). You can drag and drop this control either into Design view or into Source view. Switch to Design view, and click on the smart tag to open its menu. Clicking on Configure Data Source... opens the Configure Data Source Wizard. Your first option is to choose an existing connection or to press the button to create a new connection.

Figure 9-1. SqlDataSource control on form

 If you do not see the `SqlDataSource` control, choose View → Non Visual Controls.

Click on New Connection. When you create a new connection, you'll be asked to fill in the Server name. Decide if you want to use a trusted connection (Windows Authentication) or use a specific username and password, and you'll be asked which database to connect to (as shown in Figure 9-2).

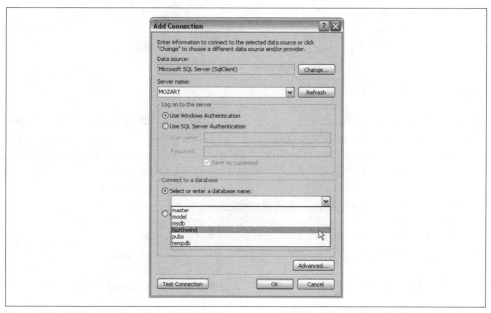

Figure 9-2. Adding connection to Northwind

To use a trusted connection, you will need to modify your SQL Server Database through SqlServer Enterprise Manager. First, go to the security section, and add machineName\ASPNET as a user. Second, go to the Northwind database and add the ASPNET user as a user and set its role to dbo_owner.

Click the Test Connection button to ensure that your connection is correct. Then click OK to save the connection.

You have the option to save the connection string in the application file (the alternative is to save the connection string in the page as a property of the control). Generally, you'll want to save the connection string in the application file where it is more secure and encrypted, as shown in Figure 9-3.

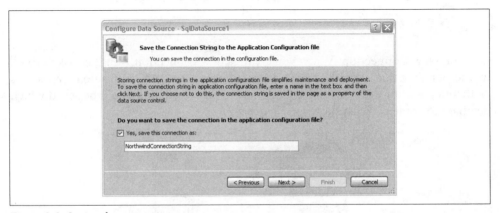

Figure 9-3. Saving the connection

The next step is to specify your query or to pick the columns you want from a specific table (see Appendix B for a crash course on relational databases and querying for data). For this example, you'll choose all the columns from the Customers table, as shown in Figure 9-4.

 While you are here, click the Advanced button to see that you can instruct the wizard to generate the update statements used to update the database, which you'll need later in this chapter. For now, however, you can leave this unchecked.

The next step in the wizard allows you to test your query, as shown in Figure 9-5.

Clicking Finish creates the connection.

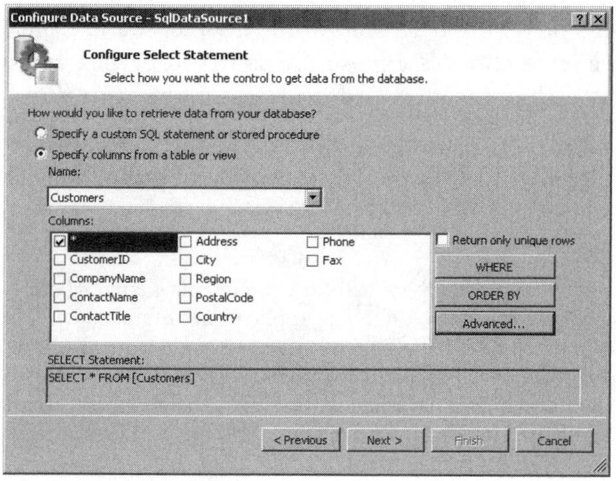

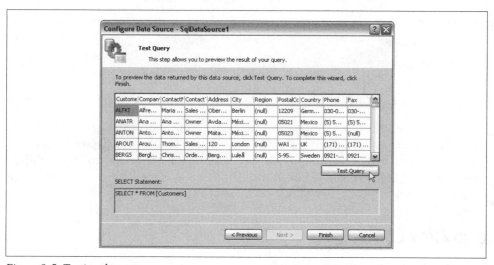

Figure 9-4. Choosing the Customers table

Figure 9-5. Testing the query

Data Source Controls

A data source control, which is derived from the System.Web.UI.DataSourceControl class, provides a single object that you can define declaratively (in your web page) or programmatically (in your code-behind). The data source control will own the connection information, the query information, the parameters and the behavior (such as paging and caching), so that you can then bind to various UI objects for display on your web page.

Many data source controls exist, including controls for accessing SQL from SQL Server, from ODBC or OLE DB servers, from XML files, and from business objects. All of these data source controls expose the same properties and methods, and all bind to UI objects (such as DataList and GridView) in the same way.

Thus, you have various UI controls all binding in the same way to underlying data sources, and the details (the plumbing) are handled by the data source controls for you, simplifying complex data manipulation tasks in web applications.

 ASP.NET 1.x developers will find significant changes (and simplifications) in how your ASP.NET application interacts with underlying data. The ADO.NET object model has been encapsulated in controls, and the details (data sources, tables, relations, and so on) have been pushed down into the framework layer. This frees you from worrying about the details and provides a more uniform API for interacting with various types of data sources.

The data source controls included with the ASP.NET include:

- ObjectDataSource
- SqlDataSource
- AccessDataSource, which is derived from SqlDataSource
- XMLDataSource
- SiteMapDataSource

You will see the SQLDataSource (and controls derived from it) used frequently in this book. The SiteMapDataSource is used in the navigation section of Chapter 12, and the ObjectDataSource is used in Chapter 10. The other data source control are not illustrated in this book explicitly, but work in much the same way as those that are demonstrated.

GridView Control

Now that you have a working data source control on your web page, let's hook it up to a control to display the data you've retrieved. You will use a GridView control, the workhorse data grid in ASP.NET.

The GridView is derived from the BaseDataBoundControl class, along with many other controls, such as the AdRotator, DetailsView, and FormView controls, the members of the ListControl class, such as CheckBoxList, RadioButtonList, and so on, and composite controls, such as the password controls, wizards, and so on. The DataGrid and DataList controls derive from BaseDataList, not BaseDataBoundControl. (Refer to Figure 3-3 in Chapter 3 for a schematic diagram of the class structure of System.Web.UI.Control.) Though they derive from different base classes, the GridView and the DataList (described later in this chapter) share many of the same properties.

Users of ASP.NET Version 1.x, will probably now use a GridView rather than a DataGrid control. GridView does all that the DataGrid does and much more, including providing easier paging and sorting. The DataGrid is fully compatible with Version 2.0, with no requirement to modify existing projects to run under the new version.

Many of the most commonly used properties of the GridView control not inherited from the control or WebControl classes are listed in Table 9-1. Many of these properties are described and used in subsequent sections of this chapter.

Table 9-1. GridView properties not inherited from WebControl

Property	Type	Get	Set	Values	Description
AllowPaging	Boolean	✗	✗	true, false	Specifies if paging is enabled. Default is false.
AllowSorting	Boolean	✗	✗	true, false	Specifies if sorting is enabled. Default is false.
AlternatingRowStyle	TableItemStyle	✗			Derived from the WebControls.Style class, the style properties for the alternate rows.
AutoGenerateColumns	Boolean	✗	✗	true, false	If true, the default, bound fields are automatically created for each field in the data source.
AutoGenerate-DeleteButton	Boolean	✗	✗	true, false	If true, a delete button will be automatically added to each data row. The default is false.
AutoGenerate-EditButton	Boolean	✗	✗	true, false	If true, an edit button will be automatically added to each data row. The default is false.
AutoGenerate-SelectButton	Boolean	✗	✗	true, false	If true, a select button will be automatically added to each data row. The default is false.
BottomPagerRow	GridViewRow	✗			Returns the bottom pager row as a GridViewRow object.
Caption	String	✗	✗		Text rendered to an HTML caption element.
CaptionAlign	TableCaptionAlign	✗	✗	Bottom, Left, NotSet, Right, Top	Specifies placement of the caption element. If the CaptionAlign property is set to NotSet, the browser's default will be used.

Table 9-1. GridView properties not inherited from WebControl (continued)

Property	Type	Get	Set	Values	Description
CellPadding	Integer	✗	✗		Number of pixels between a cell's contents and its border.
CellSpacing	Integer	✗	✗		Number of pixels between the cells of the grid.
Columns	DataControlField-Collection	✗			Returns a collection of `DataControlField` objects.
DataKeyNames	String	✗	✗		An array of the primary key fields of the items.
DataKeys	DataKeyCollection	✗			A collection of the key values of each record.
DataMember	String	✗	✗		Specifies the data member in a multimember data source
DataSource	Object	✗	✗		Specifies the data source for the control.
EditIndex	Integer	✗	✗		The zero-based index of the row to edit. A value of -1 (the default) indicates no row to edit.
EditRowStyle	TableItemStyle	✗			Derived from the `WebControls.Style` class, the style properties for the row currently selected for editing.
EmptyDataRowStyle	TableItemStyle	✗			Derived from the `WebControls.Style` class, the style properties for an empty data row.
EmptyDataTemplate	ITemplate	✗	✗		User-defined content to render a row with no data.
EmptyDataText	String	✗	✗		Text to display when control is bound to a data source with no records.
EnableSortingAnd-Paging-Callbacks	Boolean	✗	✗	`true, false`	If `true`, client-side callbacks will be used for sorting and paging. The default is `false`.
FooterRow	GridViewRow	✗			Returns the footer row as a `GridViewRow` object.
FooterStyle	TableItemStyle	✗			Derived from the `WebControls.Style` class, the style properties for the footer section.

Property	Type	Get	Set	Values	Description
GridLines	GridLines	✗	✗	Both, Horizontal, None, Vertical	Specifies which gridlines to display. The default is None.
HeaderRow	GridViewRow	✗			Returns the header row as a GridViewRow object.
HeaderStyle	TableItemStyle	✗			Derived from the WebControls.Style class, the style properties for the header section.
HorizontalAlign	HorizontalAlign	✗	✗	Center, Justify, Left, NotSet, Right	Specifies the horizontal alignment for items within containers, such as cells. Default is NotSet.
PageCount	Integer	✗			Number of pages required to display the data.
PageIndex	Integer	✗	✗		Zero-based index of the current page.
PagerSettings	PagerSettings	✗		See note below	Returns a PagerSettings object which allows the pager buttons to be configured.
PagerStyle	TableItemStyle	✗		See below	Derived from the WebControls.Style class, the style properties for the pager row. See paragraph after table for details on this property.
PagerTemplate	ITemplate	✗	✗		User-defined content to render a pager row.
PageSize	Integer	✗	✗		The number of records to display on one page.
RowHeaderColumn	String	✗	✗		Allows the optional setting of a column header.
Rows	GridViewRow-Collection	✗			Returns a collection of GridRowView objects comprising the data in the control.
RowStyle	TableItemStyle	✗			Derived from the WebControls.Style class, the default style properties for rows in the control.
SelectedDataKey	DataKey	✗			Returns the DataKey with the key value of the currently selected row.

Property	Type	Get	Set	Values	Description
SelectedIndex	Integer	✗	✗		The zero-based index of the currently selected item. If no items are selected, or to unselect an item, set the value to -1.
SelectedRow	GridViewRow	✗			Returns the row currently selected.
SelectedRowStyle	TableItemStyle	✗			Derived from the WebControls.Style class, the default style properties for the selected row in the control.
SelectedValue	Object	✗			Returns the DataKey value of the currently selected row.
ShowFooter	Boolean	✗	✗	true, false	Specifies if a footer is to be displayed. Default is true. Only relevant if FooterTemplate property is not null.
ShowHeader	Boolean	✗	✗	true, false	Specifies if a header is to be displayed. Default is true. Only relevant if HeaderTemplate property is not null.
SortDirection	SortDirection	✗		Ascending, Descending	Returns the direction currently used for sorting.
SortExpression	String	✗			Returns the name of the column being sorted.
TopPagerRow	GridViewRow	✗			Returns the top pager row as a GridViewRow object.

The PagerSettings property requires a bit more explanation. This property returns an instance of the PagerSettings class. The PagerSettings class's most important property is Mode, which allows you to specify one of four enumerated values: NextPrevious, NextPreviousFirstLast, Numeric, NumericFirstLast. Each of these sets the pagination controls. If you choose any but Numeric, you may specify the column text for the non-numeric buttons by setting other properties such as FirstPageText, NextPageText, and so on. Alternatively, you can specify images for the non-numeric buttons using the properties FirstPageImageURL, NextPageImageURL, and so on.

Drag a GridView onto the page. The GridView recognizes a SqlDataSource is on the page and does not create its own. Click on the GridView's smart tag and choose your Data Source, as shown in Figure 9-6.

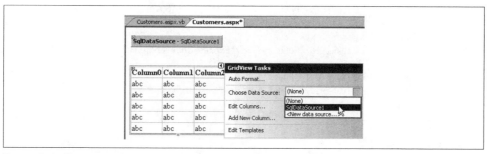

Figure 9-6. Choosing an existing Data Source

As soon as you set the data source, the data grid is redrawn, with a column for each field returned by the data source. The column headers have been filled in for you. Open the smart tag again and click on Paging (which will allow the grid to show a limited number of entries on each page and will make the display easier to view).

Switch to Source view, and examine the declaration of the GridView, as shown in Example 9-1.

Example 9-1. GridView control bound to data source

```
<asp:GridView ID="GridView1" runat="server"
          PageSize="4"
          DataSourceID="SqlDataSource1"
          AutoGenerateColumns="False"
          DataKeyNames="CustomerID">
    <Columns>
        <asp:BoundField ReadOnly="True" HeaderText="CustomerID"
                    DataField="CustomerID" SortExpression="CustomerID">
        </asp:BoundField>
        <asp:BoundField HeaderText="CompanyName"
                    DataField="CompanyName" SortExpression="CompanyName">
        </asp:BoundField>
        <asp:BoundField HeaderText="ContactName"
                    DataField="ContactName" SortExpression="ContactName">
        </asp:BoundField>
        <asp:BoundField HeaderText="ContactTitle"
                    DataField="ContactTitle" SortExpression="ContactTitle">
        </asp:BoundField>
        <asp:BoundField HeaderText="Address"
                    DataField="Address" SortExpression="Address">
        </asp:BoundField>
        <asp:BoundField HeaderText="City"
                    DataField="City" SortExpression="City">
        </asp:BoundField>
        <asp:BoundField HeaderText="Region"
```

Example 9-1. GridView control bound to data source (continued)

```
                         DataField="Region" SortExpression="Region">
        </asp:BoundField>
        <asp:BoundField HeaderText="PostalCode"
                         DataField="PostalCode" SortExpression="PostalCode">
        </asp:BoundField>
        <asp:BoundField HeaderText="Country"
                         DataField="Country" SortExpression="Country">
        </asp:BoundField>
        <asp:BoundField HeaderText="Phone"
                         DataField="Phone" SortExpression="Phone">
        </asp:BoundField>
        <asp:BoundField HeaderText="Fax"
                         DataField="Fax" SortExpression="Fax">
        </asp:BoundField>
    </Columns>
</asp:GridView>
```

VS2005 has done a lot of work for you. It has examined the data source and created a BoundField for each column in the data. Further, it has set the HeaderText to the name of the DataField. Finally, you'll notice on the declaration of the GridView that it has set AutoGenerateColumns to False (highlighted in Example 9-1).

If you were creating the GridView by hand, and if you were going to let the grid create all the columns right from the retrieved data, you could simplify the code by setting AutoGenerateColumns to True. To see this at work, create a second GridView in the Source view of the content file below the one you just created using drag and drop.

```
<asp:GridView ID="GridView2" runat="server"
            AllowPaging="true"PageSize="4"
            DataSourceID="SqlDataSource1"
            AutoGenerateColumns="True"
            DataKeyNames="CustomerID"/>
```

Run the application. You should see two data grids, one above the other, as shown in Figure 9-7.

They are indistinguishable. So why does VS2005 create the more complex version? By turning off AutoGenerate Column VS2005 gives you much greater control over the presentation of your data. You can, for example, set the headings on the columns (such as changing ContactTitle to Title). You can remove columns you don't need, and you can add new columns with controls for manipulating the rows.

You can make these changes by hand-coding the HTML in the Source view or by clicking on the smart tag for the GridView and choosing Edit Columns. Doing so brings up the Fields dialog box, as shown in Figure 9-8.

The dialog box is divided into three main areas: the list of available fields, the list of selected fields (with arrows to remove fields or reorder the list), and the Bound Field Properties window on the right. Click on a selected field (such as ContactTitle), and you can set the way that field will be displayed in the data grid (such as changing the header to Title).

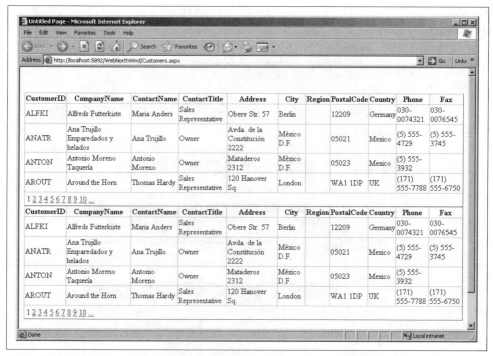

Figure 9-7. Creating two grids—one by hand

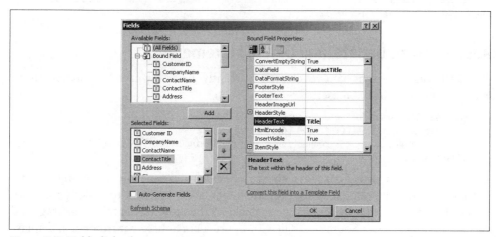

Figure 9-8. Fields dialog box

While you're examining what you can do with the `GridView`, let's make it look nicer. First, delete (or comment out) the second (simpler) grid. Second, open the smart tag on the first grid. Click on AutoFormat and choose one of the formatting options. (You can, of course format it by hand, but why work so hard?) I'll choose "Brown Sugar" because it shows up well in the printed book. While you're at it, click on

Enable Sorting (Presto! The columns can be sorted). Run the application. You'll see the output in Figure 9-9.

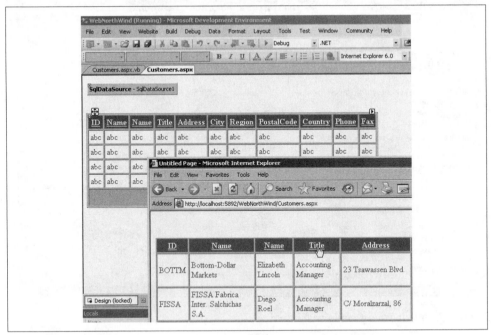

Figure 9-9. Running the formatted grid

Adding Insert, Update, and Delete Statements

The SqlDataSource that you've created currently has only a select statement to extract data from the database:

```
<asp:SqlDataSource ID="SqlDataSource1" runat="server"
    SelectCommand="SELECT * FROM [Customers]"
    ConnectionString="<%$ ConnectionStrings:NorthwindConnectionString %>">
</asp:SqlDataSource>
```

You can, however, ask your data source control to create the remaining Create, Retrieve, Update and Delete (CRUD) statements using a wizard to make your work easier. To do so, switch to Design view, click on the SqlDataSource's smart tag, and choose Configure Data Source.... The Configure Data Source wizard opens, displaying your current connection string. Click Next and the Configure Select Statement dialog box is displayed. Click the Advanced button.

This opens the Advanced SQL Generation Options dialog box. Click the Generate Insert, Update, and Delete statements checkbox, as shown in Figure 9-10.

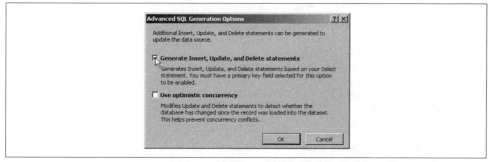

Figure 9-10. Add the CRUD methods

Clicking this checkbox instructs the wizard to create the remaining CRUD methods, and it enables the second checkbox: Use optimistic concurrency. Do not check this yet. Click OK, Next, and then Finish. You will be asked to update your grid, which unfortunately will wipe out all your customization, but the good news is that you are now bound to a data source control that provides all four CRUD methods.

Open the smart tag, add back the look and feel you want, and check Enable Editing and Enable Deleting.

Take a look at the HTML generated for the SqlDataSource control, as shown in Example 9-2.

Example 9-2. Source code for SQL with CRUD

```
<asp:SqlDataSource ID="SqlDataSource1" runat="server"
    SelectCommand="SELECT * FROM [Customers]"
    ConnectionString="<%$ ConnectionStrings:NorthwindConnectionString %>"
    DeleteCommand="DELETE FROM [Customers]
        WHERE [CustomerID] = @original_CustomerID"
    InsertCommand="INSERT INTO [Customers] ([CustomerID], [CompanyName],
                [ContactName], [ContactTitle], [Address], [City], [Region],
                [PostalCode], [Country], [Phone], [Fax])
        VALUES (@CustomerID, @CompanyName, @ContactName, @ContactTitle, @Address,
                @City, @Region, @PostalCode, @Country, @Phone, @Fax)"
    UpdateCommand="UPDATE [Customers] SET [CompanyName] = @CompanyName,
                [ContactName] = @ContactName, [ContactTitle] = @ContactTitle,
                [Address] = @Address, [City] = @City, [Region] = @Region,
                [PostalCode] = @PostalCode, [Country] = @Country,
                [Phone] = @Phone, [Fax] = @Fax
        WHERE [CustomerID] = @original_CustomerID">
    <DeleteParameters>
        <asp:Parameter Type="String" Name="original_CustomerID" />
    </DeleteParameters>
    <UpdateParameters>
        <asp:Parameter Type="String" Name="CompanyName" />
        <asp:Parameter Type="String" Name="ContactName" />
        <asp:Parameter Type="String" Name="ContactTitle" />
        <asp:Parameter Type="String" Name="Address" />
        <asp:Parameter Type="String" Name="City" />
```

Example 9-2. Source code for SQL with CRUD (continued)

```
        <asp:Parameter Type="String" Name="Region" />
        <asp:Parameter Type="String" Name="PostalCode" />
        <asp:Parameter Type="String" Name="Country" />
        <asp:Parameter Type="String" Name="Phone" />
        <asp:Parameter Type="String" Name="Fax" />
        <asp:Parameter Type="String" Name="original_CustomerID" />
    </UpdateParameters>
    <InsertParameters>
        <asp:Parameter Type="String" Name="CustomerID" />
        <asp:Parameter Type="String" Name="CompanyName" />
        <asp:Parameter Type="String" Name="ContactName" />
        <asp:Parameter Type="String" Name="ContactTitle" />
        <asp:Parameter Type="String" Name="Address" />
        <asp:Parameter Type="String" Name="City" />
        <asp:Parameter Type="String" Name="Region" />
        <asp:Parameter Type="String" Name="PostalCode" />
        <asp:Parameter Type="String" Name="Country" />
        <asp:Parameter Type="String" Name="Phone" />
        <asp:Parameter Type="String" Name="Fax" />
    </InsertParameters>
</asp:SqlDataSource>
```

Taking this apart, you see first the declaration for the SqlDataSource (and the closing tag at the bottom). After the ID and the obligatory runat="server", you see four attributes: the SelectCommand (which was there previously) and the new DeleteCommand, InsertCommand, and UpdateCommand.

```
SelectCommand="SELECT * FROM [Customers]"
DeleteCommand="DELETE FROM [Customers]
WHERE [CustomerID] = @original_CustomerID"
InsertCommand="INSERT INTO [Customers] ([CustomerID], [CompanyName], [ContactName],
[ContactTitle], [Address], [City], [Region], [PostalCode], [Country], [Phone], [Fax])
VALUES (@CustomerID, @CompanyName, @ContactName, @ContactTitle, @Address, @City,
@Region,
@PostalCode, @Country, @Phone, @Fax)"
UpdateCommand="UPDATE [Customers] SET [CompanyName] = @CompanyName,
[ContactName] = @ContactName, [ContactTitle] = @ContactTitle, [Address] = @Address,
[City] = @City, [Region] = @Region, [PostalCode] = @PostalCode, [Country] = @Country,
[Phone] = @Phone, [Fax] = @Fax
WHERE [CustomerID] = @original_CustomerID">
```

The DeleteCommand takes a single parameter (@original_CustomerID), specified in the DeleteParameters element.

```
<DeleteParameters>
    <asp:Parameter Type="String" Name="original_CustomerID" />
</DeleteParameters>
```

The UpdateCommand requires more parameters, one for each column you'll be updating, as well as a parameter for the original CustomerID (to make sure the correct record is updated). Similarly, the InsertCommand takes parameters for each column for the new record. All of these parameters are within the definition of the SqlDataSource.

Multiuser Updates

So far, you have not enabled support for optimistic concurrency. You are now going to go back and check the "use optimistic concurrency" checkbox, but before you do, let's take a moment to put this concept in context.

As things stand now, you read data from the database and move the data into your data grid through the `SqlDataSource`. You have now added the ability to update (or delete) that information. Of course, more than one person may be interacting with the database simultaneously (few web applications support only single-user access).

You can easily imagine that this could cause tremendous problems of data corruption. Imagine, for example, that two people download a record:

```
Liberty Associates, Inc. / Boston / Jesse Liberty
```

The first editor changes the City from Boston to New York. The second editor changes the Contact Name from Jesse Liberty to Milo Liberty. Now, things get interesting. The first editor writes back the data record, and the database has the following:

```
Liberty Associates, Inc. / New York / Jesse Liberty
```

A moment later, the second editor updates the database. The database then has the following record:

```
Liberty Associates, Inc. / Boston / Milo Liberty
```

These earlier updated values are overwritten and lost. The technical term for this is *bad*.

To prevent this problem, you might be tempted to use any of the following strategies:

- Lock the records. When one user is working with a record, other users can read the records but they cannot update them. This is called *pessimistic record locking*, and if you have many users, the database quickly becomes fully locked and unusable.

- Update only the columns you change. This is great in theory, but it exposes you to the risk of having a database that is internally consistent but that no longer reflects reality. Suppose two sales people each check the inventory for a given book. The `NumberOnHand` is 1. They each change only the `NumberOnHand` field to 0. The database is perfectly happy, but one customer is not going to get the book because you can only sell a given book once (much to my chagrin). To prevent this, you are back to locking records, and you read that we don't like that solution.

- You could decide that before you make an update, you'll check to see if the record has changed and only make the update to unchanged records. Unfortunately, this still does not solve the problem. If you look at the database before updating it, there is the (admittedly small) chance that someone else will update the database between the time you peek at it and the time you write your changes. Given enough transactions over enough time, collisions and corrupted data will occur.

This is also inefficient because it requires accessing the database twice for each update (to read and then to write). In a high-volume application, the performance hit will be costly.

- Attempt the change in a way guaranteed to generate an error if the record has changed and then handle these (rare) errors as they occur. This is called Optimistic Concurrency and is the method implemented for .NET.

Optimistic Concurrency

To implement optimistic concurrency, your WHERE clause will include the original values (stored for you automatically by the data set) so you can ensure the record will not be updated if it has been changed by another user. Thus, you do not need to "pre-read" the record; you can write (once) and if the record has changed, it will not be updated.

This approach has tremendous efficiency advantages. In the vast majority of cases, your update will succeed, and you will not have bothered with extra reads of the database. If your update succeeds, no lag exists between checking the data and the update, so there is no chance of someone sneaking in another write. Finally, if your update fails, you will know why and can take corrective action.

For this approach to work, your updates must fail if the data has changed in the database since the time you retrieved the data. Since the data source can tell you the original values it received from the database, you only need to pass those values back into the stored procedure as parameters and then add them to the Where clause in your Update statement. That is, you must extend your Where statement to say "where each field still has its original value."

When you update the record, the original values are checked against the values in the database. If they are different, you will not update any records until you fix the problem (which could only have been caused by someone else updating the records before you did).

To see how this is done, let's go back and turn on Optimistic Concurrency. Reopen the wizard (click on the smart tag on the data source and then click Next → Advanced…), but this time ensure both checkboxes are checked.

Click OK, click Next, and click Finish. Once more, examine the source code, as shown in Example 9-3.

Example 9-3. Data source control with Optimistic Concurrency

```
<asp:SqlDataSource ID="SqlDataSource1" runat="server"
    SelectCommand="SELECT * FROM [Customers]"
    ConnectionString="<%$ ConnectionStrings:NorthwindConnectionString %>"
    DeleteCommand="DELETE FROM [Customers]
        WHERE [CustomerID] = @original_CustomerID
            AND [CompanyName] = @original_CompanyName
            AND [ContactName] = @original_ContactName
            AND [ContactTitle] = @original_ContactTitle
            AND [Address] = @original_Address
            AND [City] = @original_City
            AND [Region] = @original_Region
            AND [PostalCode] = @original_PostalCode
            AND [Country] = @original_Country
            AND [Phone] = @original_Phone
            AND [Fax] = @original_Fax"
    InsertCommand="INSERT INTO [Customers] ([CustomerID],
        [CompanyName], [ContactName], ContactTitle], [Address], [City], [Region],
        [PostalCode], [Country], [Phone], [Fax])
        VALUES (@CustomerID, @CompanyName, @ContactName, @ContactTitle,
            @Address, @City, @Region, @PostalCode, @Country, @Phone, @Fax)"
    UpdateCommand="UPDATE [Customers] SET [CompanyName] = @CompanyName,
        [ContactName] = @ContactName, [ContactTitle] = @ContactTitle,
        [Address] = @Address, [City] = @City, [Region] = @Region,
        [PostalCode] = @PostalCode, [Country] = @Country, [Phone] = @Phone,
        [Fax] = @Fax
        WHERE [CustomerID] = @original_CustomerID
            AND [CompanyName] = @original_CompanyName
            AND [ContactName] = @original_ContactName
            AND [ContactTitle] = @original_ContactTitle
            AND [Address] = @original_Address
            AND [City] = @original_City
            AND [Region] = @original_Region
            AND [PostalCode] = @original_PostalCode
            AND [Country] = @original_Country
            AND [Phone] = @original_Phone
            AND [Fax] = @original_Fax"
    ConflictDetection="CompareAllValues">
    <DeleteParameters>
        <asp:Parameter Type="String" Name="original_CustomerID" />
        <asp:Parameter Type="String" Name="original_CompanyName" />
        <asp:Parameter Type="String" Name="original_ContactName" />
        <asp:Parameter Type="String" Name="original_ContactTitle" />
        <asp:Parameter Type="String" Name="original_Address" />
        <asp:Parameter Type="String" Name="original_City" />
        <asp:Parameter Type="String" Name="original_Region" />
        <asp:Parameter Type="String" Name="original_PostalCode" />
        <asp:Parameter Type="String" Name="original_Country" />
        <asp:Parameter Type="String" Name="original_Phone" />
        <asp:Parameter Type="String" Name="original_Fax" />
    </DeleteParameters>
    <UpdateParameters>
        <asp:Parameter Type="String" Name="CompanyName" />
```

Example 9-3. Data source control with Optimistic Concurrency (continued)

```
    <asp:Parameter Type="String" Name="ContactName" />
    <asp:Parameter Type="String" Name="ContactTitle" />
    <asp:Parameter Type="String" Name="Address" />
    <asp:Parameter Type="String" Name="City" />
    <asp:Parameter Type="String" Name="Region" />
    <asp:Parameter Type="String" Name="PostalCode" />
    <asp:Parameter Type="String" Name="Country" />
    <asp:Parameter Type="String" Name="Phone" />
    <asp:Parameter Type="String" Name="Fax" />
    <asp:Parameter Type="String" Name="original_CustomerID" />
    <asp:Parameter Type="String" Name="original_CompanyName" />
    <asp:Parameter Type="String" Name="original_ContactName" />
    <asp:Parameter Type="String" Name="original_ContactTitle" />
    <asp:Parameter Type="String" Name="original_Address" />
    <asp:Parameter Type="String" Name="original_City" />
    <asp:Parameter Type="String" Name="original_Region" />
    <asp:Parameter Type="String" Name="original_PostalCode" />
    <asp:Parameter Type="String" Name="original_Country" />
    <asp:Parameter Type="String" Name="original_Phone" />
    <asp:Parameter Type="String" Name="original_Fax" />
  </UpdateParameters>
  <InsertParameters>
    <asp:Parameter Type="String" Name="CustomerID" />
    <asp:Parameter Type="String" Name="CompanyName" />
    <asp:Parameter Type="String" Name="ContactName" />
    <asp:Parameter Type="String" Name="ContactTitle" />
    <asp:Parameter Type="String" Name="Address" />
    <asp:Parameter Type="String" Name="City" />
    <asp:Parameter Type="String" Name="Region" />
    <asp:Parameter Type="String" Name="PostalCode" />
    <asp:Parameter Type="String" Name="Country" />
    <asp:Parameter Type="String" Name="Phone" />
    <asp:Parameter Type="String" Name="Fax" />
  </InsertParameters>
</asp:SqlDataSource>
```

Don't panic. The only difference between Examples 9-2 and 9-3 is that in Example 9-3, the Where clause is extended to ensure the record has not been altered. The DeleteCommand illustrates this, and the UpdateCommand works the same way:

```
DeleteCommand="DELETE FROM [Customers]
WHERE [CustomerID] = @original_CustomerID
AND [CompanyName] = @original_CompanyName
AND [ContactName] = @original_ContactName
AND [ContactTitle] = @original_ContactTitle
AND [Address] = @original_Address
AND [City] = @original_City
AND [Region] = @original_Region
AND [PostalCode] = @original_PostalCode
AND [Country] = @original_Country
AND [Phone] = @original_Phone
AND [Fax] = @original_Fax"
```

You must, therefore, send in the parameter for the CustomerID and the original values of these fields:

```
<DeleteParameters>
    <asp:Parameter Type="String" Name="original_CustomerID" />
    <asp:Parameter Type="String" Name="original_CompanyName" />
    <asp:Parameter Type="String" Name="original_ContactName" />
    <asp:Parameter Type="String" Name="original_ContactTitle" />
    <asp:Parameter Type="String" Name="original_Address" />
    <asp:Parameter Type="String" Name="original_City" />
    <asp:Parameter Type="String" Name="original_Region" />
    <asp:Parameter Type="String" Name="original_PostalCode" />
    <asp:Parameter Type="String" Name="original_Country" />
    <asp:Parameter Type="String" Name="original_Phone" />
    <asp:Parameter Type="String" Name="original_Fax" />
</DeleteParameters>
```

All of that work is done for you by the wizard.

The wizard has added the following attribute:

```
ConflictDetection="CompareAllValues"
```

The two possible values for the `ConflictDetection` parameter are `CompareAllValues` (in which case no changes will be made to the database if the original values have changed) or `OverwriteChanges`, in which case the new values will overwrite the old.

> `OverwriteChanges` blasts away anything anyone else has entered and writes your updates to the database. As you can imagine, this is used rarely and only with great caution. Most of the time, you'll use `CompareAllValues`.

Displaying and Updating the Grid

Now that your `SqlDataSource` object is ready to go, you only have to set up your `GridView`. First, in Design view, click on the smart tag and choose Edit Columns, restore the titles to the way you want and click the checkboxes to enable editing and deleting, as shown in Figure 9-11.

If you prefer to have buttons for Edit and Delete, rather than links, click on the smart tag and click on Edit Columns.... When the Fields dialog box opens, click in Selected Fields on the Command Field entry. This brings up the Command Field Properties in the righthand window, where you can change the `ButtonType` from Link to Button by clicking on `ButtonType` in the Appearance section of the Fields editor.

The result is that the commands (Edit and Delete) are shown as buttons, as shown in Figure 9-12.

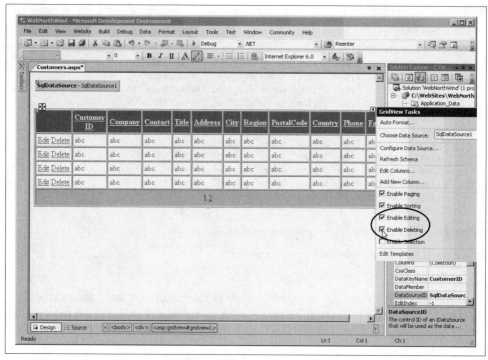

Figure 9-11. Enabling deleting and editing

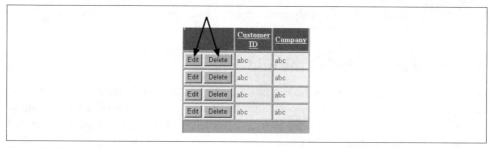

Figure 9-12. Button commands

Take It for a Spin

Start the application. The customer database information is loaded into your GridView. When you click the Edit button, the data grid automatically enters edit mode. You'll notice that the editable text fields change to text boxes, and the command buttons change from Edit and Delete to Save and Cancel. Make a small change to one field, as shown in Figure 9-13.

When you click Update, the grid and the database are updated, as you can confirm by opening the table in the database, as shown in Figure 9-14.

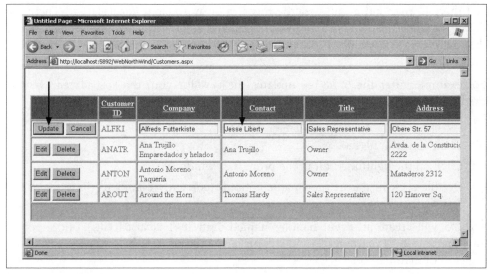

Figure 9-13. Editing

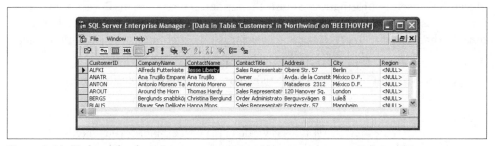

Figure 9-14. Updated database

 To create Figure 9-14, I opened SQL Server and drilled down to the NorthWindDatabase tables. I then right-clicked on the Customers table and chose Open Table → Return All Rows.

Tracking the Update with Events

Some programmers get nervous when a control does so much work invisibly. After all, when all goes well, it is great not to have to sweat the details, but if something does go wrong, how can you tell whether your connection failed, no records were updated, an exception was thrown, or exactly what happened? Related to that, what if you want to modify the behavior of the control in some way?

The ASP.NET controls, in general, and the data controls, in particular, overcome these concerns by providing numerous events that you can handle. For example, the GridView control has more than 20 events, such as RowCreated and RowDeleted. There is an event that fires when you press the Save button after editing a row (RowUpdating), and there is a second event after the row has been updated (RowUpdated). There are events for when the data is about to be bound and when it has been bound, and when the row is created, when it is about to be deleted and when it has been deleted, and more.

For example, after the GridView updates the row for you, the RowUpdated event is fired. To see this at work, create a handler:

1. Click on Design view.
2. Click on the GridView.
3. Click on the lightning bolt in the properties window.
4. Double-click in the method name column (currently blank) to the right of the RowUpdated event.

VS2005 will create an event handler named GridView1_RowUpdated( ) (more generally, controlName_EventName( )) and will place you in the code-behind page within the skeleton of that method.

The second argument to this method is of type GridViewUpdatedEventArgs. This object has useful information about the update, including a Boolean property, ExceptionHandled, that will be True if an exception was thrown when updating the data. In that case, the GridViewUpdatedEventArgs object contains the exception object.

Another property of GridViewUpdatedEventArgs tells you how many rows were affected by your update (AffectedRows). Three ordered collections tell you what changes have taken place: Keys, OldValues, and NewValues.

 To use DictionaryEntry (as we do in the next example), you'll need to add using System.Collections to the top of your file.

You can examine the collection in the debugger to see the values for each column in the row in turn, as shown in Example 9-4.

Example 9-4. Handling the Row Updated event

```
protected void GridView1_RowUpdated(
    object sender, GridViewUpdatedEventArgs e )
{
    if ( e.ExceptionHandled )
    {
        string exceptionMessage = e.Exception.Message;
    }
    else
    {
        int numRowsChanged = e.AffectedRows;
        foreach ( DictionaryEntry myDE in e.NewValues )
```

Example 9-4. Handling the Row Updated event (continued)

```
    {
        string key = myDE.Key.ToString( );
        string val = myDE.Value.ToString( );
    }         // end for each Dictionary Entry
  }           // end else no exception
}             // end method GridView1_RowUpdated
```

The `if` block tests to see if an exception was handled, and if so, sets a string (`exceptionMessage`) to the value of the `Message` in that exception. You would, presumably, display this message or log it, and then present the user with options on how to handle the exception.

If no exception has been thrown, you will get the number of rows that were affected, storing it in the local variable `numRowsChanged`. Again, you would presumably log this number or take action if it is zero. It might be zero because of a multiuser update conflict, as explained above.

Finally, in the example, you iterate through the `NewValues` collection to see that the values you updated on the grid are the values that were in the collection passed back to the database. In this example, you don't do anything with these values, but in a production program, you might log them or use them to provide progress reports.

Modifying the Grid Based on Events

Suppose you would like you to modify the grid so the contents of the Title column are red when the person listed is the owner of the company. You can do this by handling the `RowDataBound` event (which fires after each row's data is bound), as shown in Example 9-5.

Example 9-5. Handling the Row Data Bound event

```
protected void GridView1_RowDataBound(
    object sender, GridViewRowEventArgs e )
{
    if ( e.Row.RowType == DataControlRowType.DataRow )
    {
        TableCell cell = e.Row.Cells[4];
        if ( cell.Text.ToUpper( ) == "OWNER" )
        {
            cell.ForeColor = System.Drawing.Color.Red;
        }    // end if OWNER
    }        // end if DataRow
}            // end method GridView1_RowDataBound
```

The first `if` statement (highlighted in Example 9-5) tests if the type of `Row` passed in as a parameter is a `DataRow` (rather than a header, footer, or something else).

Once you know you are dealing with a `DataRow`, you can extract the cell you want to examine from that row (in this case, Title is the fifth cell, at offset 4).

You are ready to compare the cell's text field to the text string "OWNER." If they match, set the `ForeColor` property for the cell itself to Red, rendering the word Owner in red.

```
if ( cell.Text.ToUpper() == "OWNER" )
{
    cell.ForeColor = System.Drawing.Color.Red;
}
```

One question that might arise is how do you know that the cell a is `TableCell` type? This is another place where the development environment helps you. When you open the bracket on the `Cells` collection to place the index, a *tool tip* opens that tells you the index must be of type `integer` (that explains what that index does) and tells you the return type of the object obtained from the collection, as shown in Figure 9-15.

```
TableCell cell = e.Row.Cells[
```
TableCell TableCellCollection [int index]
index: An ordinal index value that specifies the System.Web.UI.WebControls.TableCell to return.

Figure 9-15. Indexing into the Cells collection—tool tip

It turns out that the Row's `Cells` collection holds objects of type `TableCell`, but the cell within the `DataGrid` is a `DataControlFieldCell` type (which derives from `TableCell`). If there are properties of `DataControlFieldCell` that are unavailable in `TableCell` (such as Containing Field, which gets the `DataControlField` that contains the current cell), you may safely cast to the "real" type:

```
DataControlFieldCell fieldCell =
    e.Row.Cells[4] as DataControlFieldCell;
```

Passing Parameters to the Select Query

Sometimes you do not want to display all the records in a table. For example, you might create a second grid on your current page that would display the Orders for the selected Company. To do this, you'll need a way to select a company and a way to pass the ID of the selected company to a second grid to display that company's orders.

To keep the downloadable source code clear, I've created a new Web Application named *WebNorthWindTwoGrids* and used Website → Copy Web Site to copy over the web site from the prior example as previously described in Chapter 4.

The first step is to add a Select button on the existing Grid. You can do this from Design view by clicking on the smart tag on the grid and checking the Enable Selection checkbox. The grid immediately adds a Select button to the first cell alongside the Edit and Delete buttons, as shown in Figure 9-16.

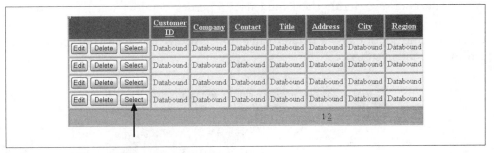

Figure 9-16. Adding the Select button

Next, create a second GridView, that will be used to display the orders. Drag the second grid onto the page and then open its smart tag. Create a new data source (name it NorthWindOrders), but use the existing connection string. Choose the Orders table and then click the Where button, as shown in Figure 9-17.

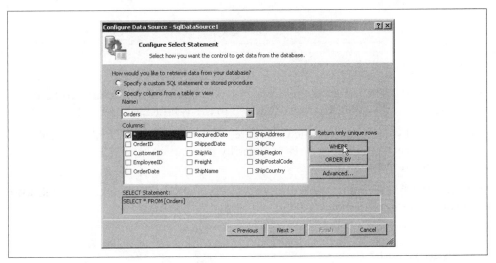

Figure 9-17. Configuring the Orders table

The Add WHERE Clause dialog opens. First, pick the column you want to match on, in this case CustomerID. Next, pick the operator, which can be equals, less than/greater than, like, contains, and so on. In this case, you'll use the default (=).

The third drop-down lets you pick the source for the CustomerID. You can pick None if you will be providing a source, or you can obtain the source from the form, a user's profile, a QueryString, or Session State. In this case, you'll obtain the source of the CustomerID from the first GridView, so choose Control.

When you choose Control, the Parameter Properties window wakes up. You are asked to provide the ID of the Control providing the parameter, in this case GridView1, and (optionally) a default value. Once you've made all your choices, the screen will look like Figure 9-18.

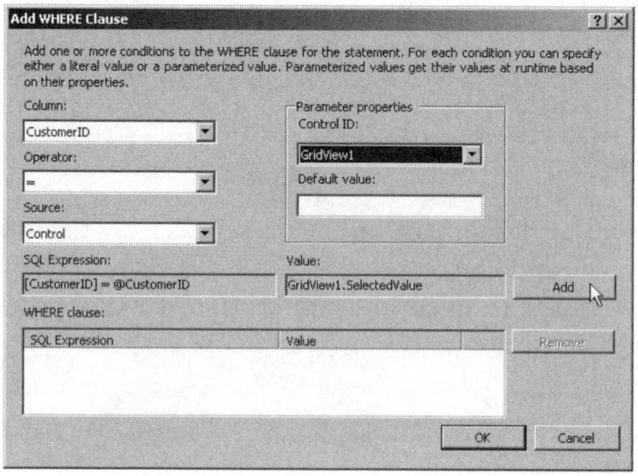

Figure 9-18. Adding a WHERE clause

Now click Add. When you do, the upper portion of the dialog returns to its initial (blank) state and the WHERE clause is added to the WHERE Clause window.

Click OK until you are back at the Configure Select Statement dialog box. While you are at it, sort the results in OrderDate order by clicking on the Order By button, as shown in Figure 9-19.

After you finish creating this SqlDataSource control, switch to Source view and look at the declaration created by VS2005:

```
<asp:SqlDataSource ID="NorthWindOrders" runat="server"
    ConnectionString="<%$ ConnectionStrings:NorthwindConnectionString %>"
    SelectCommand="SELECT * FROM [Orders]
        WHERE ([CustomerID] = @CustomerID)
        ORDER BY [OrderDate]">
    <SelectParameters>
        <asp:ControlParameter
```

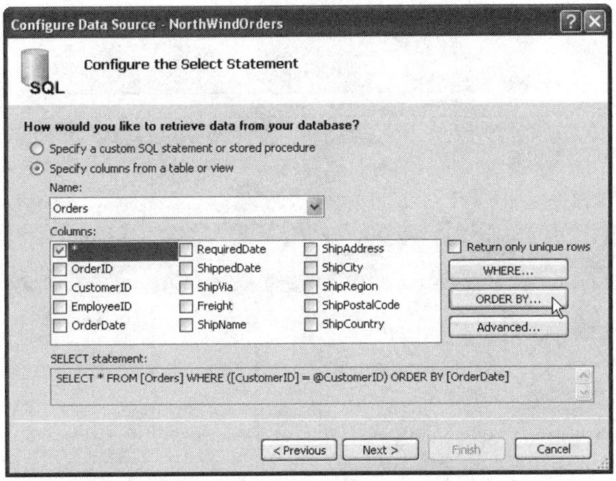

Figure 9-19. Select the Order By button

```
            Name="CustomerID"
            ControlID="GridView1"
            PropertyName="SelectedValue"
            Type="String" />
    </SelectParameters>
</asp:SqlDataSource>
```

The select statement now has a WHERE clause that includes a parameterized value (@CustomerID). In addition, within the definition of the SqlDataSource control is a definition of the SelectParameters, which includes one parameter of type asp: ControlParameter, and is a parameter that knows how to get its value from a control. The asp:ControlParameter has a property ControlID that tells it which control to check for its value, and a second property, PropertyName, that tells it which property in the GridView to check. A third property, Type, tells it that the type of the value it is getting is of type string, so it can properly pass that parameter to the Select statement.

You may now reformat your grid and edit the columns as you did for the first grid, and then try out your new page, which should look something like Figure 9-20.

As you click on each select button in the upper grid, the orders for that customer are displayed in the new grid.

The DataGrid allows you to create various fields, as shown in Table 9-2.

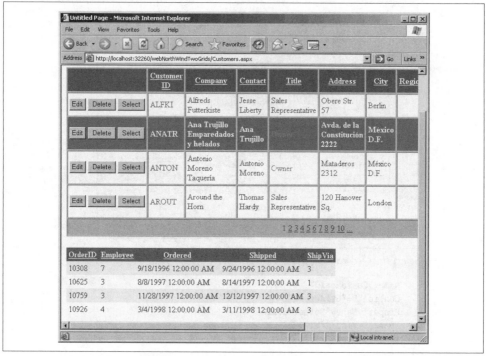

Figure 9-20. Order grid displayed

Table 9-2. Column fields in GridView

Field	Description
BoundField	The value of a field in a data source (default column type for `GridView`).
ButtonField	Command button (Add, Remove, Select).
CheckBoxField	Displays a checkbox for an item in the `GridView` (typically used for Boolean values).
HyperLinkField	Like `BoundField` but displayed as a link—you specify the destination URL.
ImageField	Display and image for an item in the `GridView`.
TemplateField	Allows the user to define the content for each item according to a specified template.

DataList Control

The toolbox provides a `DataList` control for creating *templated* lists of data. A templated list is one in which you control the HTML used to render the list by defining templates: HTML that describes how to display one item in the list.

DataList controls provide simple templates; if you need precise control of the layout, consider using the Repeater control, covered below.

There are seven different templates available for defining the appearance of a DataList control, listed in Table 9-3. Of those templates, all but the ItemTemplate are optional.

Table 9-3. DataList templates

Template name	Description
AlternatingItemTemplate	Provides content and layout for every other item. If not defined, then the ItemTemplate will be used for every item in the DataList.
EditItemTemplate	Provides content and layout for the item currently being edited. If not defined, then the ItemTemplate will be used for the currently edited item.
FooterTemplate	Provides content and layout for the footer. If not defined, then the DataList will not have a footer.
HeaderTemplate	Provides content and layout for the header. If not defined, then the DataList will not have a header.
ItemTemplate	Required. Default definition for every item's content and layout.
SelectedItemTemplate	Provides content and layout for the currently selected item. If not defined, then the ItemTemplate will be used.
SeparatorTemplate	Provides content and layout for the separator between items. If not defined, then item separators will not be used.

To get started with the DataList control, create a new application (*WebNorthWind-DataControls*) or add a page to your existing application named *DataControls*. Drag a DataList control onto the form. In Design view, the smart tag opens, offering you an opportunity to choose a Data Source. Choose New Data Source for this exercise, and choose SQL Database, naming the new data source *DataListCustomerData-Sources*. Use your existing connection to NorthWind, and specify that you want all the fields in the Customers table. When you finish, the DataList will be populated with labels that represent the field names and labels that are bound to the data control, as shown in Figure 9-21.

If you click on Source, you will see that the DataList has been defined with a number of attributes to identify its data source:

```
<asp:DataList runat="server"
    ID="DataList1"
    DataKeyField="CustomerID"
    DataSourceID="DataListCustomerDataSources">
```

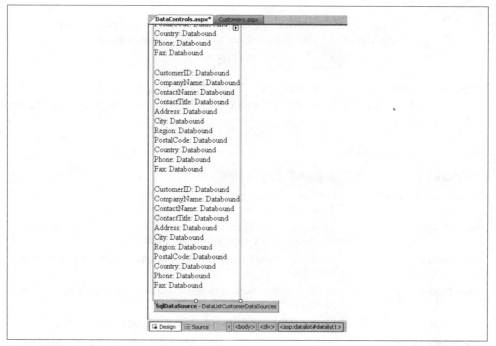

Figure 9-21. DataList bound to data control

Between the opening and closing tags of the DataList is an <ItemTemplate> tag that defines how each item will be displayed. In the default <ItemTemplate> tag, each column is represented by literal text, and the bound value is represented by a Label control whose Text property is created using the Eval method passing in the name of a column in the underlying data, as in the following:

```
<asp:Label ID="CustomerIDLabel" runat="server"
    Text='<%# Eval("CustomerID") %>' >
</asp:Label>
```

 Eval returns the value of the underlying data in the column whose name is passed in as a string.

There are a number of ways to improve the look and feel of this control. First, you can return to Design view, and click the Auto Format... link to choose a scheme (such as Classic). Doing so adds a number of styles to the DataList:

```
<asp:DataList runat="server"
    ID="DataList1"
```

```
            DataKeyField="CustomerID"
            DataSourceID="DataListCustomerDataSources"
            CellPadding="4"
            ForeColor="#333333">
            <ItemTemplate>
   ...
               <!  ItemTemplates here -->
   ...
            </ItemTemplate>
            <FooterStyle BackColor="#507CD1" Font-Bold="True" ForeColor="White" />
            <SelectedItemStyle BackColor="#D1DDF1" Font-Bold="True" ForeColor="#333333" />
            <AlternatingItemStyle BackColor="White" />
            <ItemStyle BackColor="#EFF3FB" />
            <HeaderStyle BackColor="#507CD1" Font-Bold="True" ForeColor="White" />
         </asp:DataList>
```

In addition, you may return to the smart tag, and this time choose Edit Templates. This changes the smart tag to Template Editing Mode (which continues until you click the link End Template Editing) and offers you a drop-down to choose which template you want to edit, as shown in Figure 9-22.

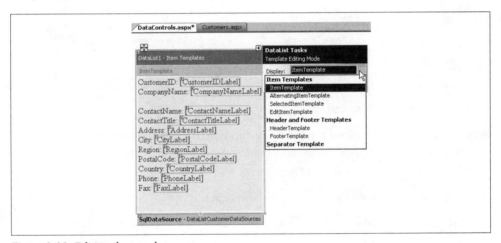

Figure 9-22. Editing the templates

You are now free to manipulate the template by expanding or moving the various elements within the templates, adding new controls, and so forth.

As an alternative, you may add or edit templates directly in the content file. The technique you choose is a matter of personal preference. Each template supports its own style object, which can be set at design time and modified at runtime.

By default, each item is displayed below the next, in a vertical column. You may modify this by setting the Repeat Direction property of the DataList from Vertical to Horizontal and by setting the number of columns by setting the RepeatColumns property, as shown in Figure 9-23.

Figure 9-23. Data list column layout

Some of the commonly used properties not inherited from the `Control` or `WebControl` classes to control the appearance and behavior of the `DataList` control are listed in Table 9-4.

Table 9-4. DataList properties not inherited from WebControl

Property	Type	Get	Set	Values	Description
Caption	String	✗	✗		Text rendered to an HTML caption element.
CaptionAlign	TableCaptionAlign	✗	✗	Bottom, Left, NotSet, Right, Top	Specifies placement of the caption element.
CellPadding	Integer	✗	✗		Number of pixels between a cell's contents and its border.
CellSpacing	Integer	✗	✗		Number of pixels between the cells of the grid.
DataKeyField	String	✗	✗		Specifies the key field in the data source.
DataKeys	DataKeyCollection	✗			A collection of the key values of each record.

Property	Type	Get	Set	Values	Description
DataMember	String	✗	✗		Specifies the data member in a multimember data source.
DataSource	Object	✗	✗		Specifies the data source for the control.
EditItemIndex	Integer	✗	✗		The zero-based index of the item currently selected for editing. If no items are selected for editing, or to unselect an item, set the value to -1.
EditItemStyle	TableItemStyle	✗			Derived from the WebControls.Style class, the style properties for the item currently selected for editing.
FooterStyle	TableItemStyle	✗			Derived from the WebControls.Style class, the style properties for the footer section.
GridLines	GridLines	✗	✗	Both, Horizontal, None, Vertical	Specifies which gridlines to display. The default is None.
HeaderStyle	TableItemStyle	✗			Derived from the WebControls.Style class, the style properties for the header section.
Items	DataListItem-Collection	✗			A collection of all the items in the control.
ItemStyle	TableItemStyle	✗			Derived from the WebControls.Style class, the default style properties for each item in the control.
RepeatColumns	Integer	✗	✗		Specifies the number of columns to display.
RepeatDirection	RepeatDirection	✗	✗	Horizontal, Vertical	If Horizontal, items will be displayed left to right, then top to bottom. If Vertical, items will be displayed top to bottom, then left to right. Default is Vertical.
RepeatLayout	RepeatLayout	✗	✗	Flow, Table	If Flow, items will be displayed without a table structure, otherwise with a table structure. Default is Table.

Property	Type	Get	Set	Values	Description
SelectedIndex	Integer	✗	✗		The zero-based index of the currently selected item. If no items are selected, or to unselect an item, set the value to -1.
SelectedItem	DataListItem	✗			Returns the item currently selected.
SelectedItemStyle	TableItemStyle	✗			Derived from the WebControls.Style class, the default style properties for the selected item in the control.
SelectedValue	Object	✗			Returns the currently selected item.
SeparatorStyle	TableItemStyle	✗			Derived from the WebControls.Style class, the default style properties for the separators between items.
ShowFooter	Boolean	✗	✗	true, false	Specifies if a footer is to be displayed. Default is true. Only relevant if FooterTemplate property is not null.
ShowHeader	Boolean	✗	✗	true, false	Specifies if a header is to be displayed. Default is true. Only relevant if HeaderTemplate property is not null.

In addition, the DataList has a number of events to which you will want to respond. Some of the most important are listed in Table 9-5.

Table 9-5. DataList events

Event	Event argument	Event argument properties	Description
DataBinding	EventArgs	None	Raised when the control binds to a data source (inherited from Control).
DeleteCommand	DataListcommandEventArgs	CommandArgument, CommandName	Raised when the Delete button is clicked.
EditCommand	DataListcommandEventArgs	CommandArgument, CommandName	Raised when the Edit button is clicked.
Init	EventArgs	None	Raised when the control is initialized (inherited from Control).

Table 9-5. DataList events (continued)

Event	Event argument	Event argument properties	Description
ItemCommand	DetailsViewCommandEventArgs Form-ViewCommandEventArgs	CommandArgument, CommandName, CommandSource	Raised when a button in the control is clicked.
ItemCreated	EventArgs	none	Raised after all the rows in the control are created.
ItemDataBound	DataListItemEventArgs	Item	Raised on binding to data.
PreRender	EventArgs	none	Raised just before the control is rendered to the Page (inherited from Control).
UpdateCommand	DataListcommandEventArgs	CommandArgument, CommandName	Raised when the Update button is clicked.

Editing Items in List Controls

The ListControl provides support for editing items in place. To accomplish this, you must add an EditItemTemplate to your DataList. You can do this by copying the ItemTemplate and pasting it as EditItemTemplate in the content file (unfortunately, you cannot use Drag and Drop to add an EditItemTemplate), and then using Search and Replace (within the selected EditItemTemplate) to replace *Label* with *Textbox* (replace the control and the ID):

```
<EditItemTemplate>
    CustomerID:
    <asp:TextBox runat="server"
        Text='<%# Eval("CustomerID") %>'
        ID="CustomerIDTextBox" />
```

Second, you must provide a way to enter Edit mode from your existing ItemTemplate. The easiest way is to add a button to the ItemTemplate. Set the button's CommandName attribute to "edit" to cause the list to fire the EditCommand event, for which you can then create a handler:

```
<ItemTemplate>
    <!-- the rest of the ItemTemplate in here -->

    <asp:Button runat="server"
        ID="ItemEditButton"
        Text="Edit"
        CommandName="edit"  />
</ItemTemplate>
```

CommandName attributes are case-sensitive.

The EditCommand event handler receives a DataListCommandEventArgs object as its second parameter. The DataListCommandEventArgs contains an Item property, representing the list item the user wants to edit. The DataListItem returned by the Item property has an ItemIndex property, which you'll assign to the EditItemIndex property of the DataList. You'll then rebind the DataList:

```
protected void DataList1_EditCommand(
    object source, DataListCommandEventArgs e )
{
    DataList1.EditItemIndex = e.Item.ItemIndex;
    DataBind( );
}
```

As you can see, it sounds harder than it is.

You'll want to add buttons to your EditItemTemplate to handle the Update (save changes) and Cancel commands, which will raise the UpdateCommand and CancelCommand events respectively:

```
<EditItemTemplate>

    <!-- the rest of the EditItemTemplate in here -->

    <asp:Button runat="server"
        ID="ItemSaveButton"
        Text="Save"
        CommandName="update" />
    <asp:Button runat="server"
        ID="ItemCancelButton"
        Text="Cancel"
        CommandName="cancel" />

</EditItemTemplate>
```

 The easiest way to create the EditCommand, UpdateCommand, and CancelCommand event handlers is to return to the Design view and click on the DataList control. In the Properties window, click on the lightning bolt to bring up the list of events, and you'll find EditCommand, UpdateCommand, and CancelCommand.

Run the application and click the Edit button. You'll see the selected item switch to your EditItemTemplate view, as shown in Figure 9-24.

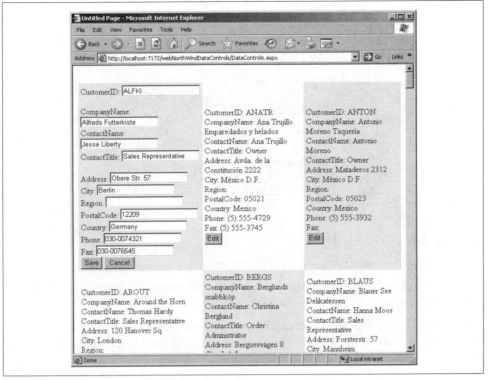

Figure 9-24. DataList control in Edit mode

You can use other kinds of controls besides textboxes. For example, for some data items, a set of radio buttons or a checkbox might be a more appropriate choice. If you wish to control the data entry, you might use a drop-down list that is bound to data (perhaps from another table in the database).

Deleting Items from a List Control

To allow your user to delete a record, add a Delete button to the ItemTemplate:

```
<  <asp:Button runat="server"
    ID="ItemDeleteButton"
    Text="Delete"
    CommandName="delete" />
```

You'll need to add another data source control to the page to handle the Delete command (name it *DataListCustomerDeleteDataSource*). Set the Delete command by clicking on the DeleteQuery property in the Properties window of the new data source, which brings up the Command and Parameter Editor, as shown in Figure 9-25.

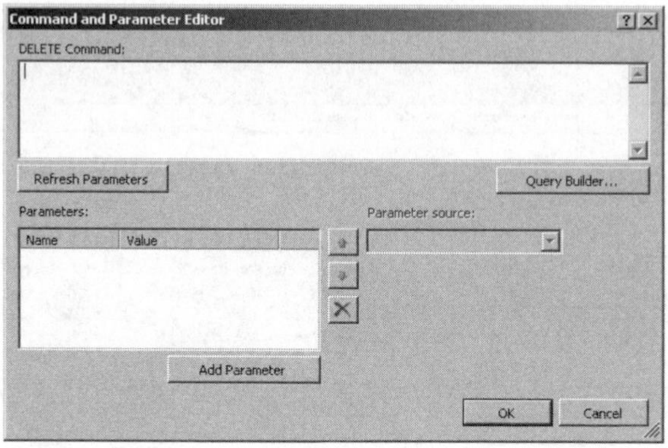

Figure 9-25. Command and Parameter Editor

Enter the delete command:

```
delete from Customers where CustomerID = @CustomerID
```

Click on the Add Parameter button and add the parameter CustomerID. (You do not
enter an @ character as part of the parameter.)

You need to create a Select command for your control to ensure it is properly connected when you call Delete. Thus, the complete source code for your new
SqlDataSource object should look like this:

```
<asp:SqlDataSource
ID="DataListCustomerDeleteDataSource"
runat="server"
ConnectionString="<%$ ConnectionStrings:NorthwindConnectionString %>"
SelectCommand="Select * from Customers"
DeleteCommand="Delete from Customers where CustomerID = @CustomerID">
    <DeleteParameters>
        <asp:Parameter Name="CustomerID" />
    </DeleteParameters>
</asp:SqlDataSource>
```

> Set the DataKeyField property of the DataList control to the primary
> key of the table you'll be deleting records from. It should be set to
> CustomerID.

Create an event handler for the DeleteCommand event, as you created a handler for the
Edit event. Here are the steps:

1. Get the record ID from the selected record (the one whose Delete button was
   pushed).

2. Get the parameter from the Parameters collection of the new data source object.

3. Set the parameter's DefaultValue to the record ID of the record to be deleted.

4. Call Delete on the data source.

5. Rebind the `DataList`.

These five steps are shown in Example 9-6.

Example 9-6. Deleting a record from a DataList

```
protected void DataList1_DeleteCommand(
    object source, DataListCommandEventArgs e )
{
    // (1) Get the recordID from the selected item
    string recordID = ( DataList1.DataKeys[e.Item.ItemIndex] ).ToString( );

    // (2) Get a reference to the customerID parameter
    System.Web.UI.WebControls.Parameter param =
        DataListCustomerDeleteDataSource.DeleteParameters["CustomerID"];

    // (3) Set the parameter's default value to the value for
    // the record to delete
    param.DefaultValue = recordID;

    // (4) Delete the record
    DataListCustomerDeleteDataSource.Delete( );

    // (5) Rebind the list
    DataBind( );
}
```

The first line is a bit tricky. Let's break this out into a number of substeps to make it easier to understand.

You are given a `DataListCommandEventArgs` object (e) as a parameter. That `DataList-CommandEventArgs` instance has an Item property of type `DataListItem`, which you can assign to a variable theItem.

```
// get the Item property from the parameter
DataListItem theItem = e.Item;
```

You can ask that `DataListItem` for its `ItemIndex` (the index into the list for the selected item):

```
// get the itemIndex from the Item
int itemIndex = theItem.ItemIndex;
```

Next, you can ask the `DataList` for its collection of `DataKeys`. Set the `DataKeyField` attribute of the list:

```
<asp:DataList
    DataKeyField="CustomerID"
```

This collection contains all the `CustomerID`s, one for each row:

```
// Get the DataKeys collection from the Data List
DataKeyCollection keyCollection = DataList1.DataKeys;
```

With a reference to that collection and the index, you can extract the contents of the key collection at that index. What you get back is of type Object.

```
// Get the object stored at the ItemIndex inside the collection
object theRecordAsObject = keyCollection[itemIndex];
```

You know what you have is a string, so you can cast that returned object to string:

```
// Cast the result from object to string
string recordID = theRecordAsObject.ToString( );
```

All of this work is done in the first line of the method:

```
string recordID = ( DataList1.DataKeys[e.Item.ItemIndex] ).ToString( );
```

The second line asks the DataListCustomerDeleteDataSource to index into its DeleteParameters property, which returns a collection of parameters, for the parameter whose name is "CustomerID," and return a reference to that parameter:

```
System.Web.UI.WebControls.Parameter param =
    DataListCustomerDeleteDataSource.DeleteParameters["CustomerID"];
```

You can search using an ordinal, so you could rewrite this line this way:

```
System.Web.UI.WebControls.Parameter param =
    DataListCustomerDeleteDataSource.DeleteParameters[0];
```

Using the name of the parameter is clearer.

The third line sets the DefaultValue property of this parameter to the recordID you extracted earlier. The fourth line calls the Delete method on the data source, and the final line rebinds the control, now missing the record you've deleted.

If you try this, it will almost certainly fail. The problem is that almost all the customer records have orders associated with them, and the NorthWind database is set up to prevent deleting any customer who has associated orders, to avoid data corruption.

You can work around this by creating a new customer using SQL Server Enterprise Manager, as shown in Figure 9-26.

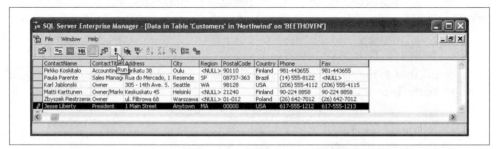

Figure 9-26. Creating a dummy record

Once this record is added, place a break point on the first line of your new event handler (DataList1_DeleteCommand) and run the application. Scroll down to the new record you've added and click the Delete button.

Once the button is clicked, your application will stop at the break point you've set. As you step through, you can see that the record ID retrieved matches the record that you've asked to delete, and once the method completes, you can scroll down and see that the record has been deleted (which you can verify directly in the database).

Repeater Control

There is one other major player in the game of displaying data: the Repeater Control. The most frequently asked question is which control to use at any given time. Table 9-6 summarizes the differences.

Table 9-6. Comparing Repeater DataList and GridView controls

Feature	Repeater	DataList	GridView
Table layout	No	No	Yes
Flow layout	Yes	Yes	No
Column layout	No	Yes	No
Style properties	No	Yes	Yes
Templates	Yes	Yes	Columns/optional
Select/ Edit/Delete	No	Yes	Yes
Sort	No	No	Yes
Paging	No	No	Yes

The Repeater provides a subset of the DataList and is typically used only when you do not want a column layout.

The Repeater control is "lookless"—that is, there is no predetermined look for the control; you determine how it will appear by adding templates. The potential templates are shown in Table 9-7.

Table 9-7. Repeater Control templates

Template	Description
AlternatingItemTemplate	Used as you would the item template; however, the alternating item is rendered for every other row in the control.
FooterTemplate	Elements to render after all items and other templates have been rendered.
HeaderTemplate	Elements to render before any other templates are rendered.
ItemTemplate	Elements rendered once for each row in the data source.
SeparatorTemplate	Elements to render between each row in the data source.

To get started, add a page to WebNorthWindDataControls named *RepeaterDemo.aspx*.
Drag a Repeater control onto the page from the Data tab in the toolbox. The smart tag
opens and asks you to choose (or create) a new data source. This process is identical to
the one you did for DataLists (name this datasource RepeaterCustomerDataSource).

The Repeater does not have a default appearance; you control it entirely with the
templates, which are, essentially, snippets of HTML and .NET Server Controls listed
within Template elements:

```
<asp:Repeater id="Repeater1" runat="server" DataSource="<%#
RepeaterCustomerDataSource %>">
   <ItemTemplate>
      <asp:Label id=Label1 runat="server"
         Customer='<%# DataBinder.Eval(Container, "DataItem.Name")%>'>
      </asp:Label>
   </ItemTemplate>
   <SeparatorTemplate>, </SeparatorTemplate>
</asp:Repeater>
```

DetailsView Control: Examining One Record at a Time

Another way to look at your data is one record at a time. ASP.NET offers a control
explicitly for this purpose: the DetailsView. This control allows you to edit, delete,
and insert records.

The DetailsView control is derived from the BaseDataBoundControl class as is the
GridView. As such it shares many of the same properties with GridView. Many of the
commonly used properties of the DetailsView control that are not inherited from
Control or WebControl are listed in Table 9-8.

Table 9-8. DetailsView properties not inherited from WebControl

Property	Type	Get	Set	Values	Description
AllowPaging	Boolean	x	x	true, false	Specifies if paging is enabled. Default is false.
Alternating-RowStyle	TableItemStyle	x			Derived from the WebControls. Style class, the style properties for the alternate rows.
AutoGenerate-DeleteButton	Boolean	x	x	true, false	If true, a Delete button will be automatically added to each data row. The default is false.

Property	Type	Get	Set	Values	Description
AutoGenerate-EditButton	Boolean	x	x	true, false	If true, an Edit button will be automatically added to each data row. The default is false.
AutoGenerate-InsertButton	Boolean	x	x	true, false	If true, an Insert button will be automatically added to each data row. The default is false.
AutoGenerateRows	Boolean	x	x	true, false	If true, the default, automatically generated data-bound fields will be displayed.
BottomPagerRow	GridViewRow	x			Returns the bottom pager row as a DetailsViewRow object.
Caption	String	x	x		Text rendered to an HTML caption element.
CaptionAlign	TableCaption-Align	x	x	Bottom, Left, NotSet, Right, Top	Specifies placement of the caption element.
CellPadding	Integer	x	x		Number of pixels between a cell's contents and its border.
CellSpacing	Integer	x	x		Number of pixels between the cells of the grid.
CommandRowStyle	TableItemStyle	x			Derived from the WebControls.Style class, the style properties for a command row.
CurrentMode	DetailsView-Mode	x		Edit, Insert, ReadOnly	Returns the current edit mode of the control. Unless set otherwise with the DefaultMode property, the default is ReadOnly.

Property	Type	Get	Set	Values	Description
DataItem	Object	x			Returns a reference to the current item displayed in the control.
DataItemCount	Integer	x			Returns the number of items in the data source.
DataItemIndex	Integer	x	x		Zero-based index of the current item in the data source.
DataKey	DataKey	x			Returns the primary key of the current item.
DataKeyNames	String	x	x		An array of the primary key fields of the items.
DataMember	String	x	x		Specifies the data member in a multi-member data source.
DataSource	Object	x	x		Specifies the data source for the control.
DefaultMode	DetailsView-Mode	x	x	Edit, Insert, ReadOnly	The default edit mode of the control. The default is ReadOnly.
EditRowStyle	TableItemStyle	x			Derived from the WebControls. Style class, the style properties for the row currently selected for editing.
EmptyDataRowStyle	TableItemStyle	x			Derived from the WebControls. Style class, the style properties for an empty data row.
EmptyDataTemplate	ITemplate	x	x		User-defined content to render a row with no data.
EmptyDataText	String	x	x		Text to display when control is bound to a data source with no records.

Property	Type	Get	Set	Values	Description
EnablePaging-Callbacks	Boolean	x	x	true, false	If true, client-side callbacks will be used for paging. The default is false.
FieldHeaderStyle	TableItemStyle	x			Derived from the WebControls. Style class, the style properties for the field header section.
Fields	DataControl-FieldCollection	x			Returns a collection of all the fields in the control.
FooterRow	GridViewRow	x			Returns the footer row as a DetailsViewRow object.
FooterStyle	TableItemStyle	x			Derived from the WebControls. Style class, the style properties for the footer section.
FooterTemplate	ITemplate	x	x		User-defined content to render a footer row.
FooterText	String	x	x		The text displayed in a footer row.
GridLines	GridLines	x	x	Both, Horizontal, None, Vertical	Specifies which gridlines to display. The default is None.
HeaderRow	GridViewRow	x			Returns the header row as a DetailsViewRow object.
HeaderStyle	TableItemStyle	x			Derived from the WebControls. Style class, the style properties for the header section.
HeaderTemplate	ITemplate	x	x		User-defined content to render a header row.
HeaderText	String	x	x		The text displayed in a header row.

Property	Type	Get	Set	Values	Description
HorizontalAlign	HorizontalAlign	x	x	Center, Justify, Left, NotSet, Right	Specifies the horizontal alignment for items within containers, such as cells. Default is NotSet.
InsertRowStyle	TableItemStyle	x			Derived from the WebControls.Style class, the style properties for an insert row.
PageCount	Integer	x			Number of pages required to display the data.
PageIndex	Integer	x	x		Zero-based index of the current page.
PagerSettings	PagerSettings	x		Mode, FirstPageText, PageButtonCount, Position, PreviousPageText, NextPageText, LastPageText, FirstPageImageUrl, PreviousPageImage-Url, NextPageImage-Url, LastPageImage-Url, Visible	Returns a PagerSettings object, which allows the pager buttons to be configured.
PagerStyle	TableItemStyle	x			Derived from the WebControls.Style class, the style properties for the pager row.
PagerTemplate	ITemplate	x	x		User-defined content to render a pager row.
Rows	GridViewRow-Collection	x			Returns a collection of DetailsView-Row objects comprising the data in the control.
RowStyle	TableItemStyle	x			Derived from the WebControls.Style class, the default style properties for rows in the control.

Property	Type	Get	Set	Values	Description
SelectedValue	Object	x			Returns the data key value of the currently selected row.
TopPagerRow	GridViewRow	x			Returns the top pager row as a DetailsViewRow object.

The DetailsView can raise a large number of events in response to user interactions.

To see a DetailsView in action, create a new page in your application (*DetailsView. aspx*) and drag a DetailsView control onto the page from the Toolbox.

The smart tag will open in Design view and will offer you the opportunity to create a new data source. Call this one CustomersDetailsViewDataSource and set it to get all the records in the Customers table. Use the Autoformat... smart tag menu choice to pick a nice color scheme, check the *Enable Paging* checkbox so you can page through the records, and run the application. Hey, presto! A quick and nice way to examine one record at a time.

Customizing the UI for this control is easy, using the style properties listed in Table 9-8 (HeaderRowStyle, RowStyle, and so on) as well as by using templates.

In addition, you can set the AutoGenerateEditButton property to true, and the control will automatically render an Edit button. When the user clicks the Edit button, the control enters Edit mode, and the CurrentMode property changes from ReadOnly to Edit, and each field of the control is rendered in its Edit user interface (which can be customized using styles and templates), as shown in Figure 9-27.

The Edit text boxes were created for you automatically, as were the links for Update and Cancel. If you set the data source to create the Update and Delete commands (using the Advanced button in the configuration dialogs), the Update link works with no additional code:

```
<asp:DetailsView runat="server"
    ID="DetailsView1"
    Height="50px"
    Width="125px"
    DataSourceID="CustomersDetailsViewDataSource"
    AutoGenerateRows="False"
    DataKeyNames="CustomerID"
    ForeColor="#333333" GridLines="None"
    CellPadding="4" AllowPaging="True"
    AutoGenerateEditButton="True"
    AutoGenerateDeleteButton="True"
    AutoGenerateInsertButton="True">
    <FooterStyle ForeColor="White" Font-Bold="True" BackColor="#990000" />
    <CommandRowStyle Font-Bold="True" BackColor="#FFFFC0" />
```

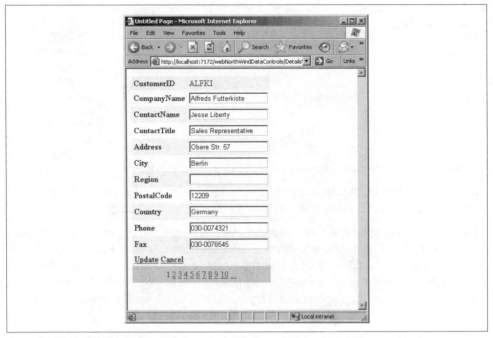

Figure 9-27. Detail View editing mode

```
<RowStyle ForeColor="#333333" BackColor="#FFFBD6" />
<PagerStyle ForeColor="#333333" HorizontalAlign="Center"
BackColor="#FFCC66" />
<Fields>
    <asp:BoundField ReadOnly="True" HeaderText="CustomerID"
       DataField="CustomerID" SortExpression="CustomerID"/>
    <asp:BoundField HeaderText="CompanyName"
       DataField="CompanyName" SortExpression="CompanyName"/>
    <asp:BoundField HeaderText="ContactName"
       DataField="ContactName" SortExpression="ContactName"/>
    <asp:BoundField HeaderText="ContactTitle"
       DataField="ContactTitle" SortExpression="ContactTitle"/>
    <asp:BoundField HeaderText="Address"
       DataField="Address" SortExpression="Address" />
    <asp:BoundField HeaderText="City"
       DataField="City" SortExpression="City" />
    <asp:BoundField HeaderText="Region"
       DataField="Region" SortExpression="Region" />
    <asp:BoundField HeaderText="PostalCode"
       DataField="PostalCode" SortExpression="PostalCode" />
    <asp:BoundField HeaderText="Country"
       DataField="Country" SortExpression="Country" />
    <asp:BoundField HeaderText="Phone"
       DataField="Phone" SortExpression="Phone" />
    <asp:BoundField HeaderText="Fax"
       DataField="Fax" SortExpression="Fax" />
</Fields>
```

```
        <FieldHeaderStyle Font-Bold="True" />
        <HeaderStyle ForeColor="White" Font-Bold="True" BackColor="#990000" />
        <AlternatingRowStyle BackColor="White" />
</asp:DetailsView>
```

FormView Control: Examining Single Records as Master/Detail

An alternative to the DetailsView control is the FormView control, which is built entirely with templates and, thus, gives you even greater control over the look and feel of the data.

DetailsView and FormView are derived from the CompositeDataBoundControl class. Therefore, they share almost all the same properties, as listed in Table 9-8. (The only significant exception is that the FormView does not have an AlternatingRowStyle property.)

To demonstrate the FormView, the next exercise will display details from the Products table, and will introduce the idea of navigating to a specific record based on the value chosen by a user from a drop down list of products.

Begin by adding a new page called *Products* to your web site.

Drag a DropDownList control from the Toolbox onto the page and give it an ID of ddlProducts. Go to Design view. You'll note that the smart tag opens. Choose New Data Source, and for this exercise, name the new data source NorthWindProductsDataSource. You may use your existing connection, and choose the Product Name (to display) and the product ID (to identify which product was selected), as shown in Figure 9-28.

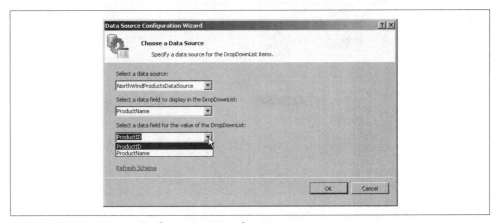

Figure 9-28. Data Source Configuration Wizard

Check Enable AutoPostBack in the smart tag or in the Properties window to ensure that when the user makes a selection in the drop down, the page is immediately posted back to the server for processing. You may want to run the application to test that the drop-down is properly filled as it has been in Figure 9-29. Select a product and watch to ensure the page is posted back and that the drop-down is filled with the name of the selected product when the page is redrawn.

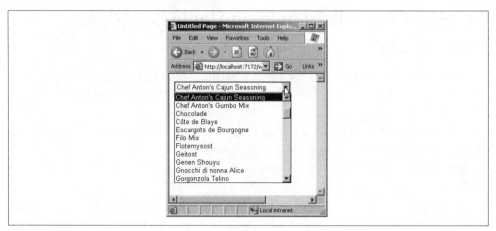

Figure 9-29. Testing the drop-down

With the `DropDownList` working, drag a `FormView` control onto the form. Using the smart tag, create a new data source, this time named `NorthWindProductsDetailsDataSource`. Select the product details you want to display, as shown in Figure 9-30.

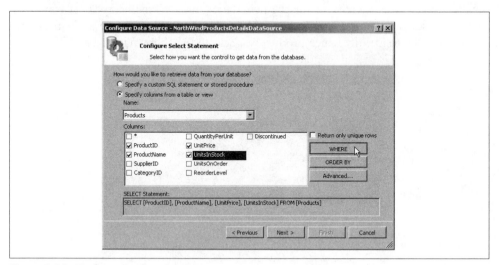

Figure 9-30. Configure product data source

You want to display product details only for the product chosen by the user. Click the WHERE button to set the parameters for the WHERE clause, which brings up the Add WHERE Clause dialog. Set the column to `ProductID` and the source to Control.

Set the ControlID to the name of the Control, and click Add to add the WHERE clause, as shown in Figure 9-31.

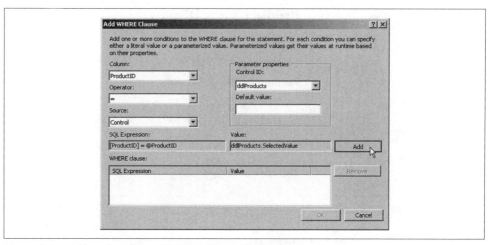

Figure 9-31. Adding drop-down WHERE clause

You'll want the control to support inserting and deleting records, as well as updating records. Click the Advanced button and check "Generate Insert, Update and Delete statements," then click OK.

Unlike the DetailsView, the FormControl's display is entirely controlled by templates that you can modify using standard ASP.NET and HTML controls. Before editing the templates, edit the page to type in the header: Form View Display, and set it to heading level 1.

```
<h1> Form View Display</h1>
```

Next, open the smart tag (or right-click on the control) and choose Edit Templates. The first template to edit is the ItemTemplate. You can click on the template box and grab the resizing handles to make it wider and taller.

Click in the top of the Item template, and hit enter a few times to make some room. Then type a heading such as Product Details. Select the title and set it to Heading 2 using the Toolbar, as shown in Figure 9-32.

Previously, you laid out the controls in a template by stacking them. Most web designers will use tables to control layout, and you can do so from within the template.

Click the menu choice Layout → Insert Table. In the Insert table dialog, set the Custom Layout to 5 rows (one for each of ProductID, ProductName, UnitPrice, Units in Stock, and the Edit/Delete/New buttons), and set two columns (one for display and one for the label). Set the cell width to 50 pixels and the cell height to 30 pixels, as shown in Figure 9-33.

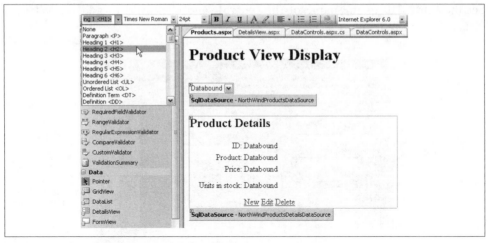

Figure 9-32. Setting the Item template heading

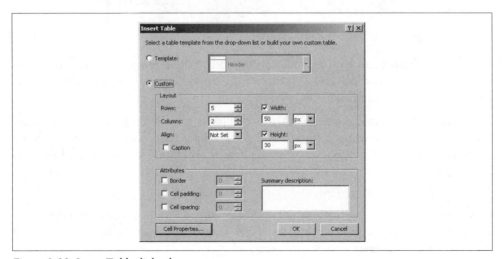

Figure 9-33. Insert Table dialog box

To set the prompt for the ProductID, type ID into the upper-left cell. Then click and drag the ProductIDLabel control into the upper-righthand cell. Your first row is now laid out with precision.

Similarly, drag the ProductNameLabel control into the second row's righthand cell, and put a prompt (Product:) in the cell to its left. Do the same with the two remaining label controls.

To right-align the prompts, click to highlight the left column, and set the Align property in the properties window. Expand the righthand column (highlight and then drag the column) to make room for large product names, as shown in Figure 9-34.

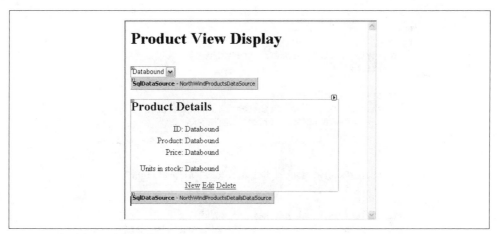

Figure 9-34. Editing the Product Item template

When the template is set the way you want, click on the smart tag and choose End Editing Templates.

Examine the source. Everything you've done with wizards is reflected here, and you can edit the source directly:

```
<asp:FormView runat="server"
    ID="FormView1"
    DataSourceID="NorthWindProductsDetailsDataSource"
    DataKeyNames="ProductID"
    Width="410px">
```

Within the FormView (between the opening tag shown above, and the closing tag much later in the file), you'll find a series of ItemTemplates. The first dictates how the item should look when you first see it (not editing):

```
<ItemTemplate>
    <h2>Product Details</h2>
    <table>
        <tr>
            <td style="width: 120px" align="right">
                ID:
            </td>
            <td style="width: 391px">
                <asp:Label ID="ProductIDLabel" runat="server"
                Text='<%# Eval("ProductID") %>' />
            </td>
        </tr>
        <tr>
            <td style="width: 120px" align="right">
                Product:
            </td>
            <td style="width: 391px">
                <asp:Label ID="ProductNameLabel" runat="server"
                Text='<%# Bind("ProductName") %>' />
```

```
                </td>
        </tr>
        <tr>
            <td style="width: 120px" align="right">
                Price:
            </td>
            <td style="width: 391px">
                <asp:Label ID="UnitPriceLabel" runat="server"
                Text='<%# Bind("UnitPrice") %>' />
            </td>
        </tr>
        <tr>
            <td style="width: 120px; height: 40px" align="right">
                Units in stock:
            </td>
            <td style="width: 391px; height: 40px">
                <asp:Label ID="UnitsInStockLabel" runat="server"
                Text='<%# Bind("UnitsInStock") %>' />
            </td>
        </tr>
        <tr>
            <td style="width: 120px; height: 21px" align="right">
            </td>
            <td style="width: 391px; height: 21px">
                <asp:LinkButton ID="NewButton"
                runat="server" Text="New"
                CommandName="New" />
                <asp:LinkButton ID="EditButton"
                runat="server" Text="Edit"
                CommandName="Edit" />
                <asp:LinkButton ID="DeleteButton"
                runat="server" Text="Delete"
                CommandName="Delete" />
            </td>
        </tr>
    </table>
</ItemTemplate>
```

Run the application to see how the items look. They should resemble Figure 9-35.

Editing with FormView

The FormView includes links to create new records, edit existing records, or delete records. When you click Edit, the FormView automatically enters edit mode (you do not have to write code to make this happen) and switches to its EditItem template. You want that EditItem template to present the data using, for example, text box controls.

The ProductIDLabel control is not editable, so drag this into the header so your page will inform the user which record is being edited.

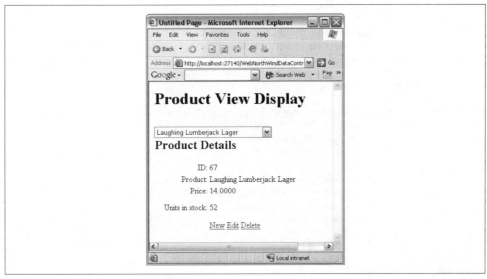

Figure 9-35. Testing the Form View display

Next, recreate the table from the previous template into the `EditItems` template, but use text boxes where you previously used labels:

```
<EditItemTemplate>
    <h2>
        Product Detail - Editing
        <asp:Label Text='<%# Eval("ProductID") %>'
        runat="server" ID="ProductIDLabel1" />
    </h2>
    <br />
    <table style="width: 273px">
        <tr>
            <td style="width: 100px" align="right">
                Name:</td>
            <td style="width: 543px">
                <asp:TextBox ID="ProductNameTextBox"
                runat="server" Text='<%# Bind("ProductName") %>'
                Width="271px" />
            </td>
        </tr>
        <tr>
            <td style="width: 100px" align="right">
                Price:</td>
            <td style="width: 543px">
                <asp:TextBox ID="UnitPriceTextBox"
                runat="server" Text='<%# Bind("UnitPrice") %>'
                Width="75px" />
            </td>
        </tr>
        <tr>
            <td style="width: 100px" align="right">
```

```
            Units in stock:</td>
        <td style="width: 543px">
            <asp:TextBox ID="UnitsInStockTextBox"
            runat="server" Text='<%# Bind("UnitsInStock") %>'
            Width="76px" />
        </td>
    </tr>
    <tr>
        <td style="width: 100px" align="right">
            <asp:LinkButton ID="UpdateButton"
            runat="server" Text="Update"
            CommandName="Update" />
        </td>
        <td style="width: 543px">
            <asp:LinkButton ID="UpdateCancelButton"
            runat="server" Text="Cancel"
            CommandName="Cancel"/>
        </td>
    </tr>
    </table>
</EditItemTemplate>
```

The result is shown in Figure 9-36.

Figure 9-36. Edit Item template

Run the program and use the drop-down to pick a product (e.g., Laughing Lumberjack Lager). Click Edit and the Edit window (based on the EditItem template) opens. You are free to enter new values, as shown in Figure 9-37.

Figure 9-37. Testing editing

The Header shows the product ID. Change the values and click Update. You are returned to the updated display page showing the new values. You can check that the database was updated, as shown in Figure 9-38.

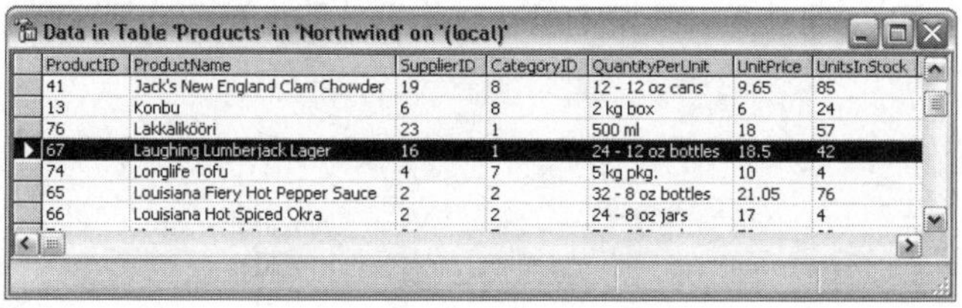

Figure 9-38. Updated product in DB

Inserting New Records

Just as clicking Edit in the FormView put you in edit mode and used the EditItem template, clicking New puts you in Insert mode and uses the InsertItem template. Rather than recreating the same work, copy and paste the EditItem template to the InsertItem template, being sure to fix the header and the names of the controls. The result is shown in Figure 9-39.

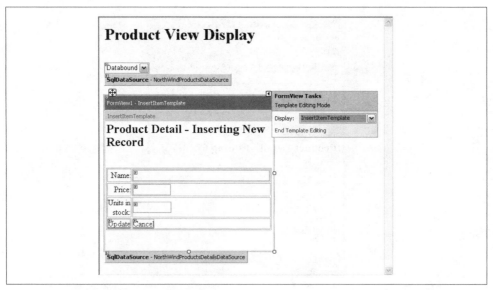

Figure 9-39. Insert Item template

DetailsView and FormView Events

Both the DetailsView and FormView controls can raise events in response to a large number of user interactions, such as inserting, updating, or deleting items. A list of the most commonly used events is contained in Table 9-9. A common scenario for using these events follows.

Table 9-9. DetailsView and FormView events

Event	Event argument	Event argument properties	Description
DataBinding	EventArgs	None	Raised when the control binds to a data source. (Inherited from Control.)
DataBound	EventArgs	None	Raised after the control binds to a data source. (Inherited from BaseDataBound Control.)
Init	EventArgs	None	Raised when the control is initialized. (Inherited from Control.)

Table 9-9. DetailsView and FormView events (continued)

Event	Event argument	Event argument properties	Description
ItemCommand	DetailsViewCommandEventArgs FormViewCommandEventArgs	CommandArgument, CommandName, CommandSource	Raised when a button in the control is clicked.
ItemCreated	EventArgs	none	Raised after all the rows in the control are created.
ItemDeleted	DetailsViewDeletedEventArgs FormViewDeletedEventArgs	AffectedRows, Exception, ExceptionHandled, Keys, Values	Raised after the delete operation when a Delete button is clicked.
ItemDeleting	DetailsViewDeletedEventArgs FormViewDeletedEventArgs	AffectedRows, Exception, ExceptionHandled, Keys, Values	Raised before the delete operation when a Delete button is clicked.
ItemInserted	DetailsViewInsertedEventArgs FormViewInsertedEventArgs	AffectedRows, Exception, ExceptionHandled, KeepInInsertMode, Values	Raised after the insert operation when an Insert button is clicked.
ItemInserting	DetailsViewInsertedEventArgs FormViewInsertedEventArgs	AffectedRows, Exception, ExceptionHandled, KeepInInsertMode, Values	Raised before the insert operation when an Insert button is clicked.
ItemUpdated	DetailsViewUpdatedEventArgs FormViewUpdatedEventArgs	AffectedRows, Exception, ExceptionHandled, KeepInEditMode, Keys, NewValues, OldValues	Raised after the update operation when an Update button is clicked.
ItemUpdating	DetailsViewUpdatedEventArgs FormViewUpdatedEventArgs	AffectedRows, Exception, ExceptionHandled, KeepInEditMode, Keys, NewValues, OldValues	Raised before the update operation when an Update button is clicked.
ModeChanged	EventArgs	None	Raised after the control switches between edit, insert, and read-only modes.

Table 9-9. DetailsView and FormView events (continued)

Event	Event argument	Event argument properties	Description
ModeChanging	DetailsViewModeEventArgs FormView-ModeEventArgs	`Cancel,` `CancelingEdit,` `NewMode`	Raised before the control switches between `edit,` `insert,` and read-only modes.
PageIndexChanged	EventArgs	None	Raised after the `PageIndex` property changes.
PageIndexChanging	DetailsViewPageEventArgs FormView-PageEventArgs	`Cancel,` `NewPageIndex`	Raised before the `PageIndex` property changes.
PreRender	EventArgs	None	Raised just before the control is rendered to the Page. (Inherited from `Control`.)

When you change the name of a product or add a new product, you want those changes reflected in the drop-down. To accomplish this, you'll want to update the `DropDownList` control after each edit. To do this, you'll handle the `ItemInserted` and the `ItemUpdated` events of the `FormView` to rebind the drop-down list with the new data:

```
protected void FormView1_ItemInserted(
    object sender, FormViewInsertedEventArgs e )
{
    ddlProducts.DataBind( );
}
protected void FormView1_ItemUpdated(
    object sender, FormViewUpdatedEventArgs e )
{
    ddlProducts.DataBind( );
}
```

To test this, navigate to Ipoh Coffee and click Edit. In the name field, enter the name of your favorite coffee (being from the Boston area, mine is Green Mountain). While you are at it, drop the price from $46 (only people in Seattle pay that much for coffee) down to a somewhat more reasonable $9.00. Click Update. Ipoh Coffee is no longer in the drop-down, but Green Mountain is as shown in Figure 9-40.

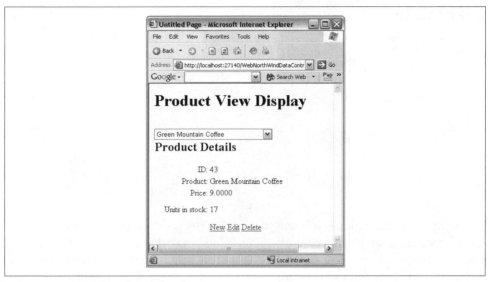

Figure 9-40. Drop-down list updated

CHAPTER 10

ADO.NET

For many web applications, you will use the DataSource controls, and you need not know anything at all about the underlying "plumbing" that interacts with the database. On the other hand, most *serious* commercial applications will have needs that go beyond what the DataSource control can do, and you will then need to dive into the ADO.NET object model to understand how the data source works and how to accomplish more advanced tasks.

To illustrate the utility of understanding the ADO.NET object model, you'll undertake two tasks in this chapter:

- Utilize connection-based transactions.
- Create a business tier object that mediates between the user-interface level and the database, binding the UI to an instance of ObjectDataSource.

Before you can accomplish either of these tasks, we must back up and examine the ADO.NET object model.

The ADO.NET Object Model

The goal of ADO.NET is to provide a bridge between your objects in ASP.NET and your back-end database. ADO.NET provides an object-oriented view into the database, encapsulating many of the database properties and relationships within ADO.NET objects. Further, and in many ways most important, the ADO.NET objects encapsulate and hide the details of database access; your objects can interact with ADO.NET objects without you knowing or worrying about the details of how the data is moved to and from the database.

An overview of the ADO.NET architecture is shown in Figure 10-1. We will return to the aspects of this figure throughout the chapter.

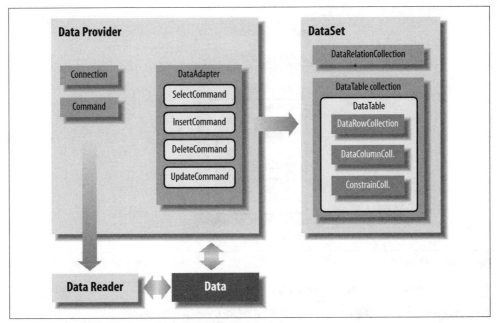

Figure 10-1. ADO.NET architecture diagram

The DataSet Class

The ADO.NET object model is rich, but at its heart, it is a fairly straightforward set of classes. The key class is the DataSet, which is located in the System.Data namespace (shown in the upper right-hand corner of Figure 10-1).

The dataset represents a rich subset of the entire database, cached in session state or in memory, without a continuous connection to the database. Periodically, you'll reconnect the dataset to its parent database, which is how you update the database with changes to the dataset you've made, and update the dataset with changes in the database made by other processes.

The dataset doesn't just capture a few rows from a single table but represents a set of tables with all the metadata necessary to represent the relationships and constraints among the tables recorded in the original database, as shown in Figure 10-2.

The dataset consists of DataTable objects as well as DataRelation objects. These are accessed as the Tables and Relations properties, respectively, of the DataSet object. The most important methods and properties of the DataSet class are shown in Tables 10-1 and 10-2.

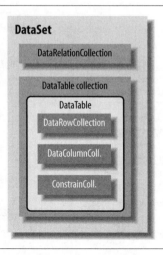

Figure 10-2. Dataset

Table 10-1. Important DataSet properties (all read-only)

Property name	Type	Get	Set	Description
DefaultViewManager	DataViewManager	✗		Returns a view of the data in the DataSet that allows filtering, searching, and navigation.
HasErrors	BooleanBoolen	✗		Returns true if there are any errors in any of the rows of any of the tables.
Relations	DataRelationCollection	✗		Returns a collection of DataRelation objects.
Tables	DataTableCollection	✗		Returns a collection of DataTable objects.

Table 10-2. Important DataSet methods

Method name	Return type	Description
AcceptChanges	void	Accepts all the changes made since loaded or since last time AcceptChanges was called (see GetChanges).
Clear	void	Clears the dataset of any data.
GetChanges	DataSet	Returns a copy of the dataset containing all the changes made since loaded or since AcceptChanges was called.
GetXML	string	Returns the XML representation of the data in the dataset.
GetXMLSchema	string	Returns the XSD schema for the XML representation of the data in the dataset.
Merge	void	Merges the data in this dataset with another dataset. Overloaded.
ReadXML	XmlReadMode	Reads an XML schema and data into the dataset. Overloaded.
ReadXMLSchema	void	Reads an XML schema into the dataset.

Table 10-2. *Important DataSet methods (continued)*

Method name	Return type	Description
RejectChanges	void	Rolls back to the state since last AcceptChanges (see AcceptChanges).
WriteXML	void	Writes out the XML schema and data from the dataset. Overloaded.
WriteXMLSchema	void	Writes the structure of the dataset as an XML schema. Overloaded.

The DataRelation class contains a DataRelationCollection object, which contains DataRelation objects. Each DataRelation object represents a relationship between two tables through DataColumn objects. For example, in the Northwind database, the Orders table is in a relationship with the Customers table through the CustomerID column. The nature of this relationship is parent/child: for any given Order, there will be exactly one customer, but any given customer may be represented in any number of Orders.

The DataTable class

The DataSet object's Tables property returns a DataTableCollection collection, which in turn contains all the DataTable objects in the dataset. For example, the following line of code creates a reference to the first DataTable in the Tables collection of a DataSet object named myDataSet.

```
DataTable dataTable = myDataSet.Tables[0];
```

The DataTable has a number of public properties, including the Columns property, which returns the ColumnsCollection object, which in turn consists of DataColumn objects. Each DataColumn object represents a column in a table.

The most important properties and methods of the DataTable class are shown in Tables 10-3 and 10-4.

Table 10-3. *Important DataTable properties*

Property name	Type	Get	Set	Description
ChildRelations	DataRelationCollection-DataRelationCollection	✗		Returns the collection of child relations (see Relations object).
Columns	DataColumnCollection	✗		Returns the columns collection.
Constraints	ConstraintCollection	✗		Returns the constraints collection.
DataSet	DataSet	✗		Returns the dataset this table belongs to.
DefaultView	DataView	✗		Returns a view of the table for filtering.
ParentRelations	DataRelationCollection	✗		Returns the parent relations collection.
PrimaryKey	DataColumn	✗	✗	An array of columns as primary key for this table.
Rows	DataRowCollection	✗		Returns the rows collection.

Table 10-4. Important DataTable methods

Method name	Return type	Description
AcceptChanges	void	Commits all the changes since last AcceptChanges.
Clear	void	Clears the table of all data.
GetChanges	DataTable	Returns a copy of the DataTable that contains all the changes since last AcceptChanges (see AcceptChanges).
GetErrors	DataRow[]	Returns an array of rows with errors.
ImportRow	void	Copies a row into a table, including all settings and values.
LoadDataRow	DataRow	Finds and updates a specific row. Creates a new row if no matching row is found. Overloaded.
Merge	void	Merges the specified DataTable with the current DataTable. Overloaded.
NewRow	DataRow	Creates a new DataRow with the same schema as the table.
RejectChanges	void	Rolls back changes since last AcceptChanges (see AcceptChanges).
Reset	void	Resets the table to its original state.
Select	DataRow[]	Returns an array of DataRow objects. Overloaded.

The DataTable DefaultView returns an object of type DataView, which can be used for data binding to controls such as the GridView.

The DataRow class

The Rows collection returns a set of rows for any given table. You use this collection to examine the results of queries against the database, iterating through the rows to examine each record in turn.

Programmers experienced with classic ADO may be confused by the absence of the RecordSet, with its moveNext and movePrevious commands. With ADO.NET, you do not iterate through the dataset; instead you access the table you need, and then you can iterate through the rows collection, typically with a foreach loop. You'll see this in the first example in this chapter.

The most important methods and properties of the DataRow class are shown in Tables 10-5 and 10-6.

Table 10-5. Important DataRow properties

Name	Type	Get	Set	Description
HasErrors	Boolean	✗		Returns true if the row has any errors.
Item	object	✗	✗	Gets or sets the data stored in a specific column (in C#, this is the indexer).

Table 10-5. Important DataRow properties (continued)

Name	Type	Get	Set	Description
ItemArray	object	✗	✗	Gets or sets all the values for the row using an array.
Table	DataTable	✗		Gets the table this row is owned by.

Table 10-6. Important DataRow methods

Name	Return type	Description
AcceptChanges	voidVoid	Accepts all the changes since the last time AcceptChanges was called.
BeginEdit	voidVoid	Begins an edit operation.
CancelEdit	voidVoid	Cancels the edit operation.
Delete	voidVoid	Deletes the DataRow from the DataTable.
EndEdit	voidVoid	Ends the edit operation.
GetChildRows	DataRows[]	Gets the child rows for this row. Overloaded.
GetParentRow	DataRow	Gets the parent row of this row. Overloaded.
GetParentRows	DataRow[]	Gets parent rows of a DataRow. Overloaded.
RejectChanges	voidVoid	Rejects all the changes since the last time AcceptChanges was called (see AcceptChanges).

DbCommand and DbConnection

The DbConnection object represents a connection to a data source. This connection may be shared among different command objects and is used in support of transactions (explained later in this chapter).

The DbCommand object allows you to send a command (typically a SQL statement or the name of a stored procedure) to the database. Often DbCommand objects are implicitly created when you create your dataset, but you can explicitly access these objects as you'll see in a subsequent example.

The DataAdapter Object

Rather than tie the DataSet object too closely to your database architecture, ADO. NET uses a DataAdapter object to mediate between the DataSet object and the database. This decouples the dataset from the database and allows a single dataset to represent more than one database or other data source.

ASP.NET provides different versions of the DataAdapter object. For example, there is one for use with SQL Server, and another for use with OLE DB providers such as Access. If you are connecting to a SQL Server database (or SQLExpress), you will increase the performance of your application by using SqlDataAdapter (from System. Data.SqlClient) along with SqlCommand and SqlConnection.

There are two ways programmers pronounce the letters "SQL." One is Ess-Queue-Ell, the other (preferred by many of the cognoscente) is "SEE-Quill." Thus, in this book we will write "*a SQL query*," which is to be read "a see-quill query".

The DataAdapter class provides several properties, such as AcceptChangesDuringFill, AcceptChangesDuringUpdate, and ContinueUpdateOnError, to control the behavior of the object. It has a number of useful methods; the three most important are listed in Table 10-7.

Table 10-7. Important DataAdapter methods

Name	Return type	Description
Fill	integer	Fills a DataTable by adding or updating rows in the dataset. The return value is the number of rows successfully added or updated. Overloaded.
FillSchema	DataTable[]	Adds a DataTable object to the specified dataset. Configures the schema (the logical design of the database) to the specified SchemaType. It returns a DataTable object containing the schema data.
Update	integer	Updates all the modified rows in the specified table of the DataSet. Returns the number of rows successfully updated.

The Data Reader Object

An alternative to the dataset is the DataReader object. The DataReader provides database-connected forward-only access to a record set records executing a SQL statement or a stored procedure. DataReaders are lightweight objects ideally suited for filling a web page with read-only data, such as populating lists, and then breaking the connection to the back-end database.

The base class for all DataReaders is DbDataReader in the System.Data.Common namespace.

The classes derived from DbDataReader are DataTableReader, OdbcDataReader, OleDbDataReader, OracleDataReader, SqlDataReader, and SqlCeDataReader.

The DbDataReader class has properties such as FieldCount and HasRows for obtaining information about the data. Of particular interest is the Item property, which returns an object representing the value of a specified column in the row. In C#, the item property is the indexer for the class.

The DbDataReader class has a large number of methods for extracting the data as you iterate through the reader, such as GetBytes, GetData, GetName, and GetString. Other important methods are listed in Table 10-8.

Table 10-8. Important DbDataReader methods

Name	Return type	Description
Close	void	Closes the data reader. Overridden.
NextResult	Boolean	When reading the results of a batch SQL statement, advances to the next result set (set of records). Will return true if there are more result sets. Overridden.
Read	Boolean	Advances to the next record. Will return true if there are more records.

The DataReader is a powerful object, but you don't often use many of its methods or properties. Most of the time, you use the DataReader to retrieve and iterate through the records that represent the result of your query.

Getting Started with ADO.NET

Create a new web site named *SimpleADONetGridView*. Drag a GridView onto the page and accept all its default values. Do *not* attach a data source. Switch to the code-behind file. In the code-behind page, you will create a DataSet and then assign one of the tables from that DataSet to the DataSource property of the GridView.

To get started, add a using statement for the SqlClient namespace to your source code:

```
using System.Data.SqlClient;
```

 You'll need to add this using statement in all the examples in this chapter.

That done, you will implement the Page_Load method to get the Customers table from the Northwind database and bind it to your GridView. You do this in a series of steps:

1. Create a connection string and a command string.
2. Pass the strings to the constructor of the SqlDataAdapter.
3. Create an instance of a DataSet.
4. Ask the DataAdapter to fill the DataSet.
5. Extract the table from the DataSet.
6. Bind the GridView to that table.

The complete source code for this example is shown in Example 10-1.

Example 10-1. SimpleADONetGridView Default.aspx.csSource

```
using System;
using System.Data;
```

Example 10-1. SimpleADONetGridView Default.aspx.csSource (continued)

```
using System.Data.SqlClient;
using System.Configuration;
using System.Web;
using System.Web.Security;
using System.Web.UI;
using System.Web.UI.WebControls;
using System.Web.UI.WebControls.WebParts;
using System.Web.UI.HtmlControls;

public partial class _Default : System.Web.UI.Page
{
    protected void Page_Load(object sender, EventArgs e)
    {
        // 1. Create the connection string and command string
        string connectionString =
            "Data Source=Mozart;Initial Catalog=Northwind;Integrated Security=True";

        string commandString =
        "Select * from Customers";

        // 2. Pass the strings to the SqlDataAdapter constructor
        SqlDataAdapter dataAdapter =
            new SqlDataAdapter(
                commandString, connectionString);

        // 3. Create a DataSet
        DataSet dataSet = new DataSet();

        // 4. fill the dataset object
        dataAdapter.Fill(dataSet,"Customers");

        // 5. Get the table from the dataset
        DataTable dataTable = dataSet.Tables["Customers"];

        // 6. Bind to the Gridview
        GridView1.DataSource=dataTable;
        GridView1.DataBind();
    }
}
```

Easy as pie. The result is indistinguishable from using a DataSource control, as shown in Figure 10-3.

Using a DataReader

In the previous example, the grid was filled from a table in a dataset. Though datasets are powerful, disconnected data sources, they may require more overhead than you want. If you want to retrieve a set of records and then immediately display them, an SqlDataReader object, introduced above, may be more efficient.

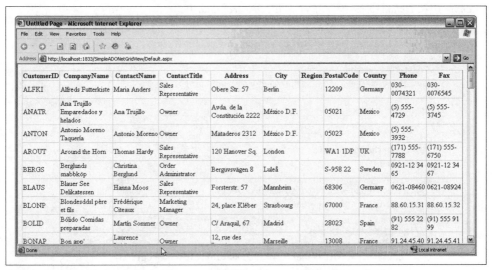

Figure 10-3. SimpleADONetGridView - a GridView from ADO.NET

DataReaders are limited compared to datasets (see below). They offer only a "fire-hose" cursor for forward-only iteration through a set of results.

To demonstrate a DataReader, create a new website named SimpleDataReader and use Copy Web Site to copy over SimpleADONetGridView. Copy all the old files over the new files created by VS2005 and open *Default.aspx.cs* and replace the existing code with the code shown in Example 10-2.

Example 10-2. Default.aspx.cs SimpleDataReader

```
using System;
using System.Data;
using System.Data.SqlClient;
using System.Configuration;
using System.Web;
using System.Web.Security;
using System.Web.UI;
using System.Web.UI.WebControls;
using System.Web.UI.WebControls.WebParts;
using System.Web.UI.HtmlControls;

public partial class _Default : System.Web.UI.Page
{
    protected void Page_Load(object sender, EventArgs e)
    {
        // Create the connection string
        string connectionString =
            "Data Source=Mozart;Initial Catalog=Northwind;Integrated
                Security=True";

        string commandString = "Select * from Customers";
```

Example 10-2. Default.aspx.cs SimpleDataReader (continued)

```
    // Create the connection object
    SqlConnection conn = new SqlConnection(connectionString);

    // Create a command object
    SqlCommand command = new SqlCommand(commandString);

    // open the connection
    try
    {
        // open the connection
        conn.Open( );

        // attach connection to command object
        command.Connection = conn;

        // get the data reader
        SqlDataReader reader =
            command.ExecuteReader(CommandBehavior.CloseConnection);

        // bind to the data reader
        GridView1.DataSource = reader;
        GridView1.DataBind( );

    }
    finally
    {
        conn.Close( );    // make sure the connection closes
    }

    }
}
```

The connection is opened in a try block and closed in the finally block. Database transactions are limited resources, and it is important to ensure they are closed. Normally, you would catch any exceptions and handle them, but you do want to make sure that whatever happens, the connection is explicitly closed before leaving this method.

You begin by setting the connection string and command string as you did previously. The last time you passed your Connection string and a Command string to the DataAdapter object, which implicitly created a Connection object and a Command object for you. This time you create those objects explicitly:

```
SqlConnection conn = new SqlConnection(connectionString);
SqlCommand command = new SqlCommand(commandString);
```

Once your `Command` object is established, create the `DataReader`. You cannot call the `DataReader`'s constructor directly; instead, you call `ExecuteReader` on the `SqlCommand` object. What you get back is an instance of `SqlDataReader`:

```
SqlDataReader reader =
    command.ExecuteReader(CommandBehavior.CloseConnection);
```

You can now bind the `GridView` to the `DataReader` you created:

```
GridView1.DataSource = reader;
GridView1.DataBind( );
```

Run the application, and the `DataReader` acts as the data source, populating your grid, as shown in Figure 10-4.

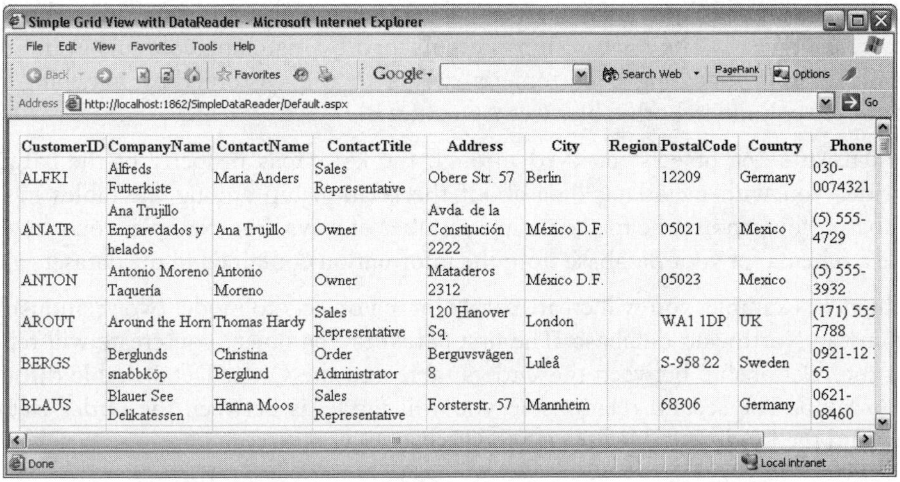

Figure 10-4. DataReader Grid View

`DataReaders` have less overhead that `DataSets` (covered next); when you use a `DataReader`, it can be more efficient to do so. That said, there are significant limitations to `DataReaders`. For one, `DataReaders` are *not* disconnected.

In any case, you will need a dataset to meet any of the following requirements:

- To pass a disconnected set of data to another tier in your application or to a client application.

- To persist your results either to a file or to a `Session` object.

- To provide access to more than one table and to relationships among the tables.

- To bind the same data to multiple controls. Remember, a `DataReader` object provides forward-only access to the data; you cannot reiterate through the data for a second control.

- To jump to a particular record or to go backwards through a set of data.

- To update a number of records in the back-end database using a batch operation.

Creating Data Relations Within DataSets

Because the DataSet acts as a disconnected model of the database, it must be able to represent the tables within the database and the relations among the tables as well.

The DataSet captures these relationships in a DataRelationCollection that you access through the read-only Relations property. The DataRelationCollection is a collection of DataRelation objects, each of which represents a relationship between two tables.

Each DataRelation object relates a pair of DataTable objects to each other through DataColumn objects. The relationship is established by matching columns in the two tables, such as matching a customer's orders to the customer by matching the CustomerID column in both tables (see Appendix B).

The DataRelation objects retrieved through the Relations property of the DataSet provides you with metadata: data about the relationship among the tables in the database. You can use the metadata in a number of ways. For example, you can generate a schema for your database from the information contained in the dataset.

In the next example, you will create DataRelation objects to model two relationships within the Northwind database. The first DataRelation object you create will represent the relationship between the Orders table and the Order Details table through the OrderID. The second relationship you will model is between the Order Details table and the Products table through the ProductID.

To begin, create a new web site name DataRelations. On the *default.aspx* page, add three grids, one of which is in a panel. The first grid represents the orders and displays five orders at a time, with a button to select a particular order:

```
<asp:GridView ID="GridView1" runat="server"
    CellPadding="4"
    ForeColor="#333333"
    GridLines="None"
    DataKeyNames="OrderID"
    AutoGenerateColumns="False"
    PagerSettings-Mode="Numeric"
    AllowPaging="true"
    PageSize="5"
    OnSelectedIndexChanged="OnSelectedIndexChangedHandler" >
    <FooterStyle BackColor="#5D7B9D" Font-Bold="True" ForeColor="White" />
    <RowStyle BackColor="#F7F6F3" ForeColor="#333333" />
    <PagerStyle BackColor="#284775" ForeColor="White" HorizontalAlign="Center" />
    <SelectedRowStyle BackColor="#E2DED6" Font-Bold="True" ForeColor="#333333" />
    <HeaderStyle BackColor="#5D7B9D" Font-Bold="True" ForeColor="White" />
    <EditRowStyle BackColor="#999999" />
    <AlternatingRowStyle BackColor="White" ForeColor="#284775" />
```

```
        <Columns>
            <asp:ButtonField ButtonType="Button" CommandName="Select" Text="Details" />
            <asp:BoundField DataField="OrderID" HeaderText="Order ID" />
            <asp:BoundField DataField="OrderDate" HeaderText="Order Date" />
            <asp:BoundField DataField="CompanyName" HeaderText="Company" />
            <asp:BoundField DataField="ContactTitle" HeaderText="Contact" />
            <asp:BoundField DataField="Phone" HeaderText="Phone" />
        </Columns>
    </asp:GridView>
```

A few things to notice about this grid. First, it is set up for paging so you see only five rows at a time:

```
PagerSettings-Mode="Numeric"
AllowPaging="true"
PageSize="5"
```

Second, the columns are not automatically created; they will be created at your discretion. This was done by using the *Edit Columns* choice from the smart tag which brings up the Fields editing dialog, as shown in Figure 10-5. Ensure the fields to be displayed are the fields in the table you bind to.

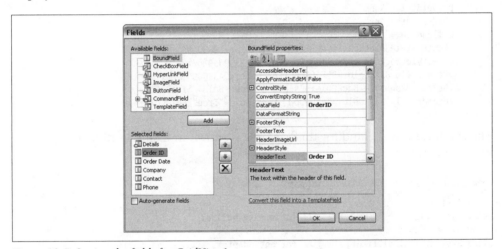

Figure 10-5. Setting the fields for GridView1

The second data grid is in a panel so you can show or hide it as necessary. This second data grid displays the details for a particular order:

```
<asp:Panel ID="OrderDetailsPanel" runat="server" Height="50px" Width="125px">
    <asp:GridView ID="DetailsGridView" runat="server"
        AutoGenerateColumns="False"
        BackColor="LightGoldenrodYellow"
        BorderColor="Tan"
        BorderWidth="1px"
        CellPadding="2"
        ForeColor="Black"
        GridLines="None">
```

```
          <FooterStyle BackColor="Tan" />
          <Columns>
             <asp:BoundField DataField="OrderDate" HeaderText="Order Date" />
             <asp:BoundField DataField="ProductName" HeaderText="Product" />
             <asp:BoundField DataField="UnitPrice" HeaderText="Price" />
             <asp:BoundField DataField="Quantity" HeaderText="Quantity" />
          </Columns>
       <PagerStyle BackColor="PaleGoldenrod"
          ForeColor="DarkSlateBlue" HorizontalAlign="Center" />
       <SelectedRowStyle BackColor="DarkSlateBlue" ForeColor="GhostWhite" />
       <HeaderStyle BackColor="Tan" Font-Bold="True" />
       <AlternatingRowStyle BackColor="PaleGoldenrod" />
    </asp:GridView>
  </asp:Panel>
```

This grid turns off AutoGenerateColumns and shows only the columns of interest.

Finally, create a third grid that will display the relations in the dataset:

```
<asp:GridView ID="OrderRelationsGridView" runat="server"
    BackColor="White"
    BorderColor="#CC9966"
    BorderStyle="None"
    BorderWidth="1px"
    CellPadding="4">
    <FooterStyle BackColor="#FFFFCC" ForeColor="#330099" />
    <RowStyle BackColor="White" ForeColor="#330099" />
    <PagerStyle BackColor="#FFFFCC" ForeColor="#330099" HorizontalAlign="Center" />
    <SelectedRowStyle BackColor="#FFCC66" Font-Bold="True" ForeColor="#663399" />
    <HeaderStyle BackColor="#990000" Font-Bold="True" ForeColor="#FFFFCC" />
</asp:GridView>
```

The complete code-behind for this example is shown in Example 10-3 and analyzed immediately after.

Example 10-3. Data Relations Default.aspx.cs

```
using System;
using System.Text;                // for string builder
using System.Data;
using System.Data.SqlClient;      // for dataadapter, etc.
using System.Configuration;
using System.Web;
using System.Web.Security;
using System.Web.UI;
using System.Web.UI.WebControls;
using System.Web.UI.WebControls.WebParts;
using System.Web.UI.HtmlControls;

public partial class _Default : System.Web.UI.Page
{
    protected void Page_Load(object sender, EventArgs e)
    {
```

Example 10-3. Data Relations Default.aspx.cs (continued)

```
        if (!IsPostBack)
        {
            UpdateDetailsGrid( );

            DataSet ds = CreateDataSet( );
            GridView1.DataSource = ds.Tables[0];
            GridView1.DataBind( );

            // create the dataview and bind to the details grid
            DataView detailsView = new DataView(ds.Tables[1]);
            DetailsGridView.DataSource = detailsView;
            Session["DetailsView"] = detailsView;
            DetailsGridView.DataBind( );

            // bind the relations grid to the relations collection
            OrderRelationsGridView.DataSource = ds.Relations;
            OrderRelationsGridView.DataBind( );

        }
    }

    // get order details
    public void OnSelectedIndexChangedHandler(
        Object sender, EventArgs e)
    {
        UpdateDetailsGrid( );
    }

    private void UpdateDetailsGrid( )
    {

        int index = GridView1.SelectedIndex;
        if (index != -1)
        {
            // get the order id from the data grid
            DataKey key = GridView1.DataKeys[index];
            int orderID = (int) key.Value;
            DataView detailsView = (DataView)Session["detailsView"];
            detailsView.RowFilter = "OrderID = " + orderID;
            DetailsGridView.DataSource = detailsView;
            DetailsGridView.DataBind( );
            OrderDetailsPanel.Visible = true;
        }
        else
        {
            OrderDetailsPanel.Visible = false;
        }
    }

    private DataSet CreateDataSet( )
    {
```

Example 10-3. Data Relations Default.aspx.cs (continued)

```csharp
// connection string to connect to the Orders Database
string connectionString =
"Data Source=Mozart;Initial Catalog=Northwind;Integrated Security=True";

// Create connection object, initialize with
// connection string and open the connection
System.Data.SqlClient.SqlConnection connection =
    new System.Data.SqlClient.SqlConnection(connectionString);

connection.Open( );


// Create a SqlCommand object and assign the connection
System.Data.SqlClient.SqlCommand command =
    new System.Data.SqlClient.SqlCommand( );
command.Connection = connection;


StringBuilder s = new StringBuilder(
    "select OrderID, c.CompanyName, c.ContactName, ");
s.Append(" c.ContactTitle, c.Phone, orderDate");
s.Append(" from orders o ");
s.Append("join customers c on c.CustomerID = o.CustomerID");

// set the command text to the select statement
command.CommandText = s.ToString( );

// create a data adapter and assign the command object
// and add the table mapping for bugs
SqlDataAdapter dataAdapter = new SqlDataAdapter( );
dataAdapter.SelectCommand = command;
dataAdapter.TableMappings.Add("Table", "Orders");

// Create the dataset and use the data adapter to fill it
DataSet dataSet = new DataSet( );
dataAdapter.Fill(dataSet);


// create a second command object for the order details
System.Data.SqlClient.SqlCommand command2 =
    new System.Data.SqlClient.SqlCommand( );
command2.Connection = connection;

// This time be sure to add a column for Severity so that you can
// create a relation to Products
StringBuilder s2 =
    new StringBuilder(
    "Select od.OrderID, OrderDate, p.ProductID, ");
s2.Append(" ProductName, od.UnitPrice, Quantity ");
s2.Append("from Orders o ");
s2.Append("join [Order Details] od on o.orderid = od.orderid ");
s2.Append("join products p on p.productID = od.productid ");
```

Example 10-3. Data Relations Default.aspx.cs (continued)

```csharp
command2.CommandText = s2.ToString( );

// create a second data adapter and
// add the command and map the table
// then fill the dataset  from this second adapter
SqlDataAdapter dataAdapter2 = new SqlDataAdapter( );
dataAdapter2.SelectCommand = command2;
dataAdapter2.TableMappings.Add("Table", "Order Details");
dataAdapter2.Fill(dataSet);


// create a third command object for the Products table
System.Data.SqlClient.SqlCommand command3 =
    new System.Data.SqlClient.SqlCommand( );
command3.Connection = connection;

string strCommand3 = "Select ProductID, ProductName from Products";
command3.CommandText = strCommand3;

// create a third data adapter
// and add the command and map the table
// then fill the dataset  from this second adapter
SqlDataAdapter dataAdapter3 = new SqlDataAdapter( );
dataAdapter3.SelectCommand = command3;
dataAdapter3.TableMappings.Add("Table", "Products");
dataAdapter3.Fill(dataSet);


// declare the DataRelation and DataColumn objects
System.Data.DataRelation dataRelation;
System.Data.DataColumn dataColumn1;
System.Data.DataColumn dataColumn2;

// set the dataColumns to create the relationship
// between Bug and Order Details on the OrderID key
dataColumn1 =
    dataSet.Tables["Orders"].Columns["OrderID"];
dataColumn2 =
    dataSet.Tables["Order Details"].Columns["OrderID"];

dataRelation =
    new System.Data.DataRelation(
    "OrdersToDetails",
    dataColumn1,
    dataColumn2);

// add the new DataRelation to the dataset
dataSet.Relations.Add(dataRelation);

// reuse the DataColumns and DataRelation objects
// to create the relation between Order Details and Products
dataColumn1 = dataSet.Tables["Products"].Columns["ProductID"];
dataColumn2 = dataSet.Tables["Order Details"].Columns["ProductID"];
```

Example 10-3. Data Relations Default.aspx.cs (continued)

```
            dataRelation =
                new System.Data.DataRelation(
                "ProductIDToName",
                dataColumn1,
                dataColumn2);

            // add the HistoryToSeverity relationship to the dataset
            dataSet.Relations.Add(dataRelation);

            return dataSet;
        }     // end createDataSet
}               // end class
```

The key to the code-behind page is in the `CreateDataSet` method, shown high-lighted. The job of this method is to create a dataset with three tables and two sets of relations. A connection to the Northwind database is created and opened as you've seen previously.

The first select statement is created to fill the Orders table in the DataSet:

```
StringBuilder s = new StringBuilder(
    "select OrderID, c.CompanyName, c.ContactName, ");
s.Append(" c.ContactTitle, c.Phone, orderDate");
s.Append(" from orders o ");
s.Append("join customers c on c.CustomerID = o.CustomerID");

command.CommandText = s.ToString();
SqlDataAdapter dataAdapter = new SqlDataAdapter();
dataAdapter.SelectCommand = command;
dataAdapter.TableMappings.Add("Table", "Orders");

// Create the dataset and use the data adapter to fill it
DataSet dataSet = new DataSet();
dataAdapter.Fill(dataSet);
```

A second command object is used to create the Order Details table, which will provide the order details for a given order, joining the Product table to turn a `ProductID` (stored in Order Details) into a product name:

```
System.Data.SqlClient.SqlCommand command2 =
    new System.Data.SqlClient.SqlCommand();
command2.Connection = connection;

StringBuilder s2 =
    new StringBuilder(
    "Select od.OrderID, OrderDate, p.ProductID, ");
s2.Append(" ProductName, od.UnitPrice, Quantity ");
s2.Append("from Orders o ");
s2.Append("join [Order Details] od on o.orderid = od.orderid ");
s2.Append("join products p on p.productID = od.productid ");

command2.CommandText = s2.ToString();
```

```
SqlDataAdapter dataAdapter2 = new SqlDataAdapter( );
dataAdapter2.SelectCommand = command2;
dataAdapter2.TableMappings.Add("Table", "Order Details");
dataAdapter2.Fill(dataSet);
```

The second command object shares the original connection. The second table is added to the original dataset using the second DataAdapter. Similarly, a third command object is used to fill a third table: Products.

With the three tables in place, two DataRelation objects will be created. To get started, you'll create an instance of a DataRelation and two instances of DataColumn objects:

```
System.Data.DataRelation dataRelation;
System.Data.DataColumn dataColumn1;
System.Data.DataColumn dataColumn2;
```

You assign each of the DataColumn objects to a column in a table that creates a relationship:

```
dataColumn1 = dataSet.Tables["Orders"].Columns["OrderID"];
dataColumn2 = dataSet.Tables["Order Details"].Columns["OrderID"];
```

This corresponds to the OrderID column in Order Details being a foreign key into the Orders table, where it is the primary key. With these two data columns in place, you can create the DataRelation object:

```
dataRelation =
    new System.Data.DataRelation(
        "OrdersToDetails",
        dataColumn1,
        dataColumn2);
```

The constructor for the DataRelation object takes an (arbitrary) name for the data relation, in this case, "OrdersToDetails." You can now add your new DataRelation object to the Relations collection in the dataset:

```
dataSet.Relations.Add(dataRelation);
```

Then reuse the DataColumns to establish the relationship between the ProductID column in Order Details and the ProductID column in Products, create a second DataRelation object, and add that to the DataSet as well.

That done, you return the DataSet to the calling method, in this case Page_Load. Once Page_Load has the newly created dataset, it can bind the first GridView to the first table in the dataset:

```
protected void Page_Load(object sender, EventArgs e)
{
    if (!IsPostBack)
    {
        UpdateDetailsGrid( );
        DataSet ds = CreateDataSet( );
        GridView1.DataSource = ds.Tables[0];
        GridView1.DataBind( );
```

It can get a DataView (a filtered view) of the second table and stash that in Session-State and bind the Details table to that view:

```
DataView detailsView = new DataView(ds.Tables[1]);
DetailsGridView.DataSource = detailsView;
Session["DetailsView"] = detailsView;
DetailsGridView.DataBind( );
```

Finally, Page_Load can bind the Relations collection to the third GridView to display all the relations in the dataset:

```
OrderRelationsGridView.DataSource = ds.Relations;
OrderRelationsGridView.DataBind( );
```

Because the details panel's Visible property is initially set false, when you first open the page, you see only the Orders grid and the relations grid, as shown in Figure 10-6.

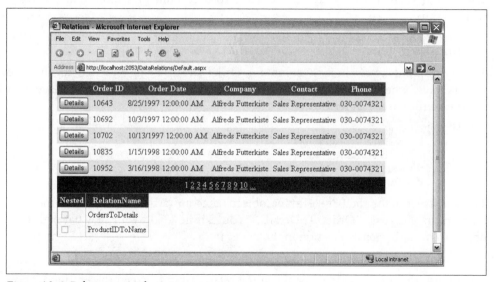

Figure 10-6. Relations page first view

If you click on a Details button, the OnSelectedIndexChanged method will fire (as set declaratively in the first GridView):

```
public void OnSelectedIndexChangedHandler(Object sender, EventArgs e)
{
    UpdateDetailsGrid( );
}
```

This method calls the UpdateDetailsGrid method, which asks the GridView for its DataKeys collection and then extracts the DataKey using the GridView's selected index and translates the key's value to an integer (ordered).

It then extracts the details view from session state, applies a row filter (to get only those rows with the appropriate OrderID) and binds the second gridView to the resulting view, which makes the panel visible.

```
private void UpdateDetailsGrid( )
{

    int index = GridView1.SelectedIndex;
    if (index != -1)
    {
        // get the order id from the data grid
        DataKey key = GridView1.DataKeys[index];
        int orderID = (int) key.Value;
        DataView detailsView = (DataView)Session["detailsView"];
        detailsView.RowFilter = "OrderID = " + orderID;
        DetailsGridView.DataSource = detailsView;
        DetailsGridView.DataBind( );
        OrderDetailsPanel.Visible = true;
    }
    else
    {
        OrderDetailsPanel.Visible = false;
    }
}
```

The result is that the details for the given order are displayed in the panel, as shown in Figure 10-7.

Creating Data Objects by Hand

In all of the examples so far, you have created the DataSet object and its DataTable and DataRow objects by selecting data from the database. There are, however, occasions when you will want to fill a dataset or a table by hand.

For example, you may want to gather data from a user, and push that data into the database. It can be convenient to add records to a table manually and update the database from that table.

The dataset is an excellent transport mechanism for data. You may even want to create a dataset by hand only to pass it to another tier in your application where it will be used as a data source.

In the next example, you will create a dataset and populate three tables by hand. Once the tables are created, you'll set constraints on a number of columns, set default values, establish identity columns, and create keys. In addition, you'll establish a foreign key relationship between two tables, and you'll create a data relation tying two tables together. It sounds like more work than it really is.

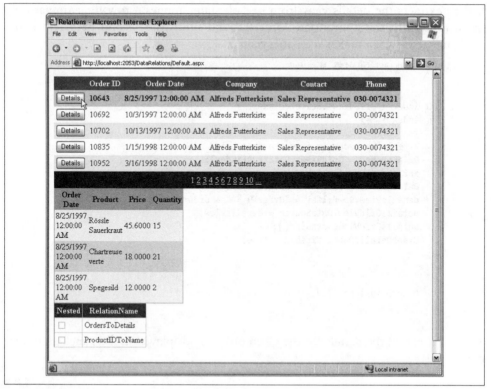

Figure 10-7. Details panel displayed

Bug Database Design

Rather than use the Northwind database for this exercise, you will create a database for tracking bugs in a software development project. Imagine that you have been asked to create a tool to manage bugs for a large development effort. You will be supporting three developers along with a user interface designer and a few quality control engineers. You would like your design to be reasonably flexible so you can reapply your bug tracking application to future projects.

Your first decision is to create a web application. This has the great advantage that all the participants will be able to access the application from their home computers. Since the developers work off-site, this is almost a necessity. You will, of course, develop your web application in ASP.NET.

There will be a web page for entering bugs, as well as a page for reviewing and editing bugs. To support this, you will need to design a relational database; we'll use SQL Server.

You begin by thinking about the kinds of information you want to capture in the database and how that information will be used. You will want to allow any user of the system to create a bug report. You'll also want certain users (such as developers and Quality Assurance, or QA) to update the bug reports. Developers will want to be able to record progress in fixing a bug or to mark a bug fixed. QA will want to check the fix and close the bug or reopen it for further investigation. The original reporter of the bug will want to find out who is working on the bug and track the progress.

One requirement imposed early in the design process is that the bug database ought to provide an audit trail. If the bug is modified, you'll want to be able to say who modified it and when they did so. In fact, you'll want to be able to track all the changes to the bug, so you can generate a report like the excerpt shown in Example 10-4.

Example 10-4. Excerpt from a bug report

```
Bug 101 - System crashes on login
101.1 - Reporter: Osborn
Date: 1/1/2002  Original bug filed
Description: When I login I crash.
Status: Open
Owner: QA

101.2 - Modified by: Smith
Date: 1/2/2002 Changed Status, Owner
Action: Confirmed bug.
Status: Assigned
Owner: Hurwitz

101.3 - Modified by Hurwitz
Date 1/2/2002 Changed Status
Action: I'll look into this but I don't think it is my code.
Status: Accepted
Owner: Hurwitz

101.4 - Modified by Hurwitz
Date 1/3/2002 Changed Status, Owner
Action: Fault lies in login code. Reassigned to Liberty
Status: Assigned
Owner: Liberty

101.5 - Modified by Liberty
Date: 1/3/2002 Changed Status
Action: Yup, this is mine.
Status: Accepted
Owner: Liberty

101.6 - Modified by Liberty
Date 1/4/2002 Changed Status, Owner
Action: Added test for null loginID in DoLogin( )
Status: Fixed
Owner: QA
```

Example 10-4. Excerpt from a bug report (continued)

```
101.7 - Modified by Smith
Date: 1/4/2002 Changed Status
Action: Tested and confirmed
Status: Closed
Owner: QA
```

To track this information, you'll need to know the date and time of each modification, who made the modification, and what they did. There will probably be other information you'll want to capture as well though this may become more obvious as you build the application and as you use it.

One way to meet these requirements is to create two tables to represent each bug. Each record in the Bugs table will represent a single bug, but you'll need an additional table to keep track of the revisions. Call this second table BugHistory.

A bug record will have a `BugID` and will include the information that is constant for the bug throughout its history. A `BugHistory` record will have the information specific to each revision.

The bug database design described in this chapter includes three significant tables: `Bugs`, `BugHistory`, and `People`. `Bugs` and `BugHistory` work together to track the progress of a bug. For any given bug, a single record is created in the `Bugs` table, and a record is created in `BugHistory` each time the bug is revised in any way. The `People` table tracks the developers, QA, and other personnel who might be referred to in a bug report. See the design diagram in Figure 10-8.

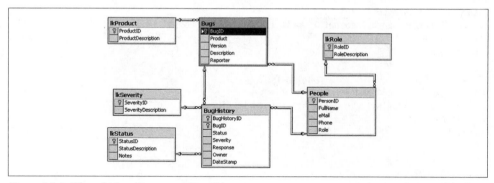

Figure 10-8. The relationship among the tables

 This is a simplified design that meets the detailed specifications, but which focuses on the key technologies; a robust professional design would necessarily be more complex.

When a bug is first entered, a record is created in each of the Bugs and BugHistory tables. Each time the bug is updated, a record is added to BugHistory. During the evolution of a bug, the status, severity, and owner of a bug may change, but the initial description and reporter will not. Those items that are consistent for the entire bug are in the Bugs table; those that are updated as the bug is corrected are in the BugHistory table.

Creating the DataTable by Hand

Create a new web application named *BugTrackerByHand*. Drag two GridView objects onto the form. Name the first Bugs and the second BugConstraints. Use Auto Format to make them look reasonably nice. The ASPX page is shown in Example 10-5.

Example 10-5. BugTrackerbyhand Default.aspx

```
<%@ Page Language="C#" AutoEventWireup="true"  CodeFile="Default.aspx.cs"
   Inherits="_Default" %>

<!DOCTYPE html PUBLIC "-//W3C//DTD XHTML 1.1//EN"
   "http://www.w3.org/TR/xhtml11/DTD/xhtml11.dtd">

<html xmlns="http://www.w3.org/1999/xhtml" >
<head runat="server">
    <title>Bug Tracker</title>
</head>
<body>
    <form id="form1" runat="server">
    <div>
        <asp:GridView ID="Bugs" runat="server"
          CellPadding="4" ForeColor="#333333" GridLines="None">
            <FooterStyle BackColor="#507CD1" Font-Bold="True" ForeColor="White" />
            <RowStyle BackColor="#EFF3FB" />
            <PagerStyle BackColor="#2461BF" ForeColor="White"
                HorizontalAlign="Center" />
            <SelectedRowStyle BackColor="#D1DDF1" Font-Bold="True"
                ForeColor="#333333" />
            <HeaderStyle BackColor="#507CD1" Font-Bold="True" ForeColor="White" />
            <EditRowStyle BackColor="#2461BF" />
            <AlternatingRowStyle BackColor="White" />
        </asp:GridView>

        <asp:GridView ID="BugConstraints" runat="server"
            BackColor="#DEBA84" BorderColor="#DEBA84"
            BorderStyle="None" BorderWidth="1px" CellPadding="3" CellSpacing="2">
            <FooterStyle BackColor="#F7DFB5" ForeColor="#8C4510" />
            <RowStyle BackColor="#FFF7E7" ForeColor="#8C4510" />
            <PagerStyle ForeColor="#8C4510" HorizontalAlign="Center" />
            <SelectedRowStyle BackColor="#738A9C" Font-Bold="True"
                ForeColor="White" />
            <HeaderStyle BackColor="#A55129" Font-Bold="True" ForeColor="White" />
        </asp:GridView>
    </div>
    </form>
</body>
</html>
```

The supporting code-behind is shown in Example 10-6 and analyzed immediately afterward.

Example 10-6. BugTrackerbyhand Default.aspx.cs

```
using System;
using System.Data;
using System.Configuration;
using System.Web;
using System.Web.Security;
using System.Web.UI;
using System.Web.UI.WebControls;
using System.Web.UI.WebControls.WebParts;
using System.Web.UI.HtmlControls;

public partial class _Default : System.Web.UI.Page
{
    protected void Page_Load(object sender, EventArgs e)
    {
        if (!IsPostBack)
        {
            // call the method whichthat creates the tables and the relations
            DataSet ds = CreateDataSet();

            // set the data source for the grid to the first table
            Bugs.DataSource = ds.Tables["Bugs"];
            Bugs.DataBind();

            BugConstraints.DataSource = ds.Tables["Bugs"].Constraints;
            BugConstraints.DataBind();
        }

    }
    //hand carved
    private DataSet CreateDataSet()
    {
        // instantiate a new DataSet object that
        // you will fill with tables and relations
        DataSet dataSet = new DataSet();

        // make the bug table and its columns
        // mimic the attributes from the SQL database
        DataTable tblBugs = new DataTable("Bugs");

        DataColumn newColumn; // hold the new columns as you create them

        newColumn =
          tblBugs.Columns.Add(
              "BugID", Type.GetType("System.Int32"));
```

Example 10-6. BugTrackerbyhand Default.aspx.cs (continued)

```
newColumn.AutoIncrement = true;      // autoincrementing
newColumn.AutoIncrementSeed=1;       // starts at 1
newColumn.AutoIncrementStep=1;       // increments by 1
newColumn.AllowDBNull=false;         // nulls not allowed

// or you can provide a named constraint
UniqueConstraint constraint =
    new UniqueConstraint("Unique_BugID",newColumn);
tblBugs.Constraints.Add(constraint);

// create an array of columns for the primary key
DataColumn[] columnArray = new DataColumn[1];
columnArray[0] = newColumn;

// add the array to the Primary key property
tblBugs.PrimaryKey=columnArray;

// The Product column
newColumn = tblBugs.Columns.Add(
    "Product", Type.GetType("System.Int32"));
newColumn.AllowDBNull=false;
newColumn.DefaultValue = 1;

// save for foreign key creation
DataColumn bugProductColumn = newColumn;

// The Version column
newColumn = tblBugs.Columns.Add(
  "Version", Type.GetType("System.String"));
newColumn.AllowDBNull=false;
newColumn.MaxLength=50;
newColumn.DefaultValue = "0.1";

// The Description column
newColumn = tblBugs.Columns.Add(
  "Description", Type.GetType("System.String"));
newColumn.AllowDBNull=false;
newColumn.MaxLength=8000;
newColumn.DefaultValue = "";

// The Reporter column
newColumn = tblBugs.Columns.Add(
  "Reporter", Type.GetType("System.Int32"));
newColumn.AllowDBNull=false;

// save for foreign key creation
DataColumn bugReporterColumn = newColumn;

// Add rows based on the db schema you just created
DataRow newRow;          // holds the new row
```

Example 10-6. BugTrackerbyhand Default.aspx.cs (continued)

```
newRow = tblBugs.NewRow( );
newRow["Product"] = 1;
newRow["Version"] = "0.1";
newRow["Description"] = "Crashes on load";
newRow["Reporter"] = 5;
tblBugs.Rows.Add(newRow);

newRow = tblBugs.NewRow( );
newRow["Product"] = 1;
newRow["Version"] = "0.1";
newRow["Description"] =
    "Does not report correct owner of bug";
newRow["Reporter"] = 5;
tblBugs.Rows.Add(newRow);

newRow = tblBugs.NewRow( );
newRow["Product"] = 1;
newRow["Version"] = "0.1";
newRow["Description"] =
    "Does not show history of previous action";
newRow["Reporter"] = 6;
tblBugs.Rows.Add(newRow);

newRow = tblBugs.NewRow( );
newRow["Product"] = 1;
newRow["Version"] = "0.1";
newRow["Description"] =
    "Fails to reload properly";
newRow["Reporter"] = 5;
tblBugs.Rows.Add(newRow);

newRow = tblBugs.NewRow( );
newRow["Product"] = 2;
newRow["Version"] = "0.1";
newRow["Description"] = "Loses data overnight";
newRow["Reporter"] = 5;
tblBugs.Rows.Add(newRow);

newRow = tblBugs.NewRow( );
newRow["Product"] = 2;
newRow["Version"] = "0.1";
newRow["Description"] = "HTML is not shown properly";
newRow["Reporter"] = 6;
tblBugs.Rows.Add(newRow);

// add the table to the dataset
dataSet.Tables.Add(tblBugs);


// Product Table
```

Example 10-6. BugTrackerbyhand Default.aspx.cs (continued)

```csharp
// make the Products table and add the columns
DataTable tblProduct = new DataTable("lkProduct");
newColumn = tblProduct.Columns.Add(
    "ProductID", Type.GetType("System.Int32"));
newColumn.AutoIncrement = true;       // autoincrementing
newColumn.AutoIncrementSeed=1;        // starts at 1
newColumn.AutoIncrementStep=1;        // increments by 1
newColumn.AllowDBNull=false;          // nulls not allowed
newColumn.Unique=true;                // each value must be unique

newColumn = tblProduct.Columns.Add(
    "ProductDescription", Type.GetType("System.String"));
newColumn.AllowDBNull=false;
newColumn.MaxLength=8000;
newColumn.DefaultValue = "";

newRow = tblProduct.NewRow( );
newRow["ProductDescription"] = "BugX Bug Tracking";
tblProduct.Rows.Add(newRow);

newRow = tblProduct.NewRow( );
newRow["ProductDescription"] =
    "PIM - My Personal Information Manager";
tblProduct.Rows.Add(newRow);

// add the products table to the dataset
dataSet.Tables.Add(tblProduct);


// People


// make the People table and add the columns
DataTable tblPeople = new DataTable("People");
newColumn = tblPeople.Columns.Add(
    "PersonID", Type.GetType("System.Int32"));
newColumn.AutoIncrement = true;       // autoincrementing
newColumn.AutoIncrementSeed=1;        // starts at 1
newColumn.AutoIncrementStep=1;        // increments by 1
newColumn.AllowDBNull=false;          // nulls not allowed

UniqueConstraint uniqueConstraint =
   new UniqueConstraint(
        "Unique_PersonID",newColumn);
tblPeople.Constraints.Add(uniqueConstraint);

// stash away the PersonID column for the foreign
// key constraint
DataColumn PersonIDColumn = newColumn;

columnArray = new DataColumn[1];
columnArray[0] = newColumn;
tblPeople.PrimaryKey=columnArray;
```

Example 10-6. BugTrackerbyhand Default.aspx.cs (continued)

```
newColumn = tblPeople.Columns.Add(
    "FullName", Type.GetType("System.String"));
newColumn.AllowDBNull=false;
newColumn.MaxLength=8000;
newColumn.DefaultValue = "";

newColumn = tblPeople.Columns.Add(
    "eMail", Type.GetType("System.String"));
newColumn.AllowDBNull=false;
newColumn.MaxLength=100;
newColumn.DefaultValue = "";

newColumn = tblPeople.Columns.Add(
    "Phone", Type.GetType("System.String"));
newColumn.AllowDBNull=false;
newColumn.MaxLength=20;
newColumn.DefaultValue = "";

newColumn = tblPeople.Columns.Add(
    "Role", Type.GetType("System.Int32"));
newColumn.DefaultValue = 0;
newColumn.AllowDBNull=false;

newRow = tblPeople.NewRow( );
newRow["FullName"] = "Jesse Liberty";
newRow["email"] = "jliberty@libertyassociates.com";
newRow["Phone"] = "617-555-7301";
newRow["Role"] = 1;
tblPeople.Rows.Add(newRow);

newRow = tblPeople.NewRow( );
newRow["FullName"] = "Dan Hurwitz";
newRow["email"] = "dhurwitz@stersol.com";
newRow["Phone"] = "781-555-3375";
newRow["Role"] = 1;
tblPeople.Rows.Add(newRow);

newRow = tblPeople.NewRow( );
newRow["FullName"] = "John Galt";
newRow["email"] = "jGalt@franconia.com";
newRow["Phone"] = "617-555-9876";
newRow["Role"] = 1;
tblPeople.Rows.Add(newRow);

newRow = tblPeople.NewRow( );
newRow["FullName"] = "John Osborn";
newRow["email"] = "jOsborn@oreilly.com";
newRow["Phone"] = "617-555-3232";
newRow["Role"] = 3;
tblPeople.Rows.Add(newRow);
```

Example 10-6. BugTrackerbyhand Default.aspx.cs (continued)

```
            newRow = tblPeople.NewRow( );
            newRow["FullName"] = "Ron Petrusha";
            newRow["email"] = "ron@oreilly.com";
            newRow["Phone"] = "707-555-0515";
            newRow["Role"] = 2;
            tblPeople.Rows.Add(newRow);

            newRow = tblPeople.NewRow( );
            newRow["FullName"] = "Tatiana Diaz";
            newRow["email"] = "tatiana@oreilly.com";
            newRow["Phone"] = "617-555-1234";
            newRow["Role"] = 2;
            tblPeople.Rows.Add(newRow);

            // add the People table to the dataset
            dataSet.Tables.Add(tblPeople);

            // create the Foreign Key constraint
            // pass in the parent column from people
            // and the child column from Bugs
            ForeignKeyConstraint fk =
                new ForeignKeyConstraint(
                    "FK_BugToPeople",PersonIDColumn,bugReporterColumn);
            fk.DeleteRule=Rule.Cascade;    // like father like son
            fk.UpdateRule=Rule.Cascade;
            tblBugs.Constraints.Add(fk);  // add the new constraint


            // declare the DataRelation and DataColumn objects
            System.Data.DataRelation dataRelation;
            System.Data.DataColumn dataColumn1;
            System.Data.DataColumn dataColumn2;

            // set the dataColumns to create the relationship
            // between Bug and BugHistory on the BugID key
            dataColumn1 =
                dataSet.Tables["People"].Columns["PersonID"];
            dataColumn2 =
                dataSet.Tables["Bugs"].Columns["Reporter"];

            dataRelation =
                new System.Data.DataRelation(
                "BugsToReporter",
                dataColumn1,
                dataColumn2);

            // add the new DataRelation to the dataset
            dataSet.Relations.Add(dataRelation);

            return dataSet;
        }
    }
```

The Page_Load method calls the CreateDataSet method and binds the first GridView to the Bugs table. Then it binds the second GridView to the constraints collection within the Bugs table (to demonstrate the creation of constraints in the dataset).

```
if (!IsPostBack)
{
    // call the method that creates the tables and the relations
    DataSet ds = CreateDataSet( );

    // set the data source for the grid to the first table
    Bugs.DataSource = ds.Tables["Bugs"];
    Bugs.DataBind( );

    BugConstraints.DataSource = ds.Tables["Bugs"].Constraints;
    BugConstraints.DataBind( );
}
```

The heart of this program is in CreateDataSet, where you have created the dataset.

You begin by instantiating a new (empty) dataset:

```
private DataSet CreateDataSet( )
{
    DataSet dataSet = new DataSet( );
```

Next, you declare a DataTable object, passing in the name of the table as a parameter to the constructor:

```
DataTable tblBugs = new DataTable("Bugs");
```

The table you are creating should mimic the data structure of the Bugs table in the SQL Server. Figure 10-9 shows that structure.

To add a column to this DataTable object, you do not call a constructor. Instead you call the Add method of the DataTable object's Columns collection. The Add method takes two parameters, which are the name of the column and its data type:

```
DataColumn newColumn;
newColumn =
    tblBugs.Columns.Add("BugID", Type.GetType("System.Int32"));
```

Setting column properties

The Add method creates the new column and returns a reference to it, which you may now manipulate. Since this is to be an identity column (see the highlighted field in Figure 10-9), you'll want to set its AutoIncrement property to true and you'll set the AutoIncrementSeed and AutoIncrementStep properties to set the seed and step values of the identity, respectively. The following code fragment does this:

```
newColumn.AutoIncrement = true;
newColumn.AutoIncrementSeed=1;
newColumn.AutoIncrementStep=1;
```

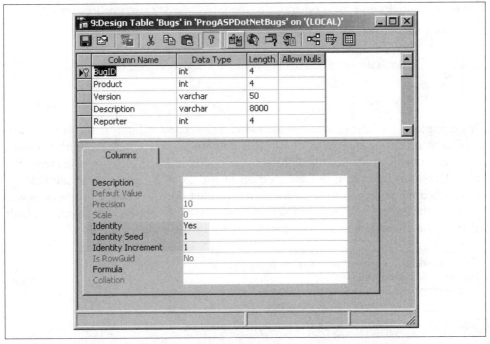

Figure 10-9. The structure of the Bugs table in SQL server

 The `AutoIncrementSeed` property sets the initial value for the identity column, and the `AutoIncrementStep` property sets the increment for each new record. Thus, if the seed were 5 and the step were 3, the first five records would have IDs of 5, 8, 11, 14, and 17. In the case shown, where the seed and step are 1, the first four records have IDs of 1,2,3,4.

Setting constraints

Identity columns must not be null, so you'll set the `AllowDBNull` property of the new column to false:

```
newColumn.AllowDBNull=false;
```

You can set the `Unique` property to `true` to ensure that each entry in this column must be unique:

```
newColumn.Unique=true;
```

Setting the `Unique` property to `true` creates an unnamed constraint in the Bugs table's `Constraints` collection. You can, if you prefer, add a named constraint. To do this, you create an instance of the `UniqueConstraint` class and pass a name for it into the constructor along with a reference to the column:

```
UniqueConstraint constraint =
    new UniqueConstraint("Unique_BugID",newColumn);
```

You then manually add that constraint to the table's Constraints collection:

```
tblBugs.Constraints.Add(constraint);
```

 If you do add a named constraint, be sure to comment out the Unique property.

This completes the first column in the table. The second column is the Product column, as you can see in Figure 10-10. This column is of type integer, with no nulls and a default value of 1 (see the highlighted property in Figure 10-10). You create the Product column by calling the Add method of the Columns collection of the tblBugs table, this time passing in the type for an integer. Set the AllowDBNull property as you did with the earlier column, and set the DefaultValue property to set the default value for the column. This is illustrated in the following code fragment:

```
newColumn = tblBugs.Columns.Add(
    "Product", Type.GetType("System.Int32"));
newColumn.AllowDBNull=false;
newColumn.DefaultValue = 1;
```

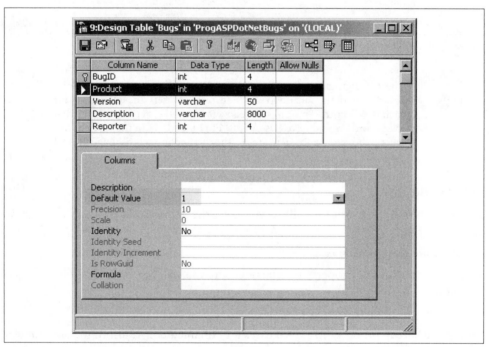

Figure 10-10. The Products column

Looking at Figure 10-10, you can see the third column is Version with a type of varChar.

A varChar is a variable length character string. A varChar can be declared to be any length between 1 and 8000 bytes. Typically you will limit the length of the string as a form of documentation indicating the largest string you expect in the field.

You declare the column type to be string for a varChar, and you can set the length of the string with the MaxLength property, as shown in the following code fragment:

```
newColumn = tblBugs.Columns.Add(
    "Version", Type.GetType("System.String"));
newColumn.AllowDBNull=false;
newColumn.MaxLength=50;
newColumn.DefaultValue = "0.1";
```

You declare the Description and Reporter columns in a like manner:

```
newColumn = tblBugs.Columns.Add("Description", Type.GetType("System.String"));
newColumn.AllowDBNull=false;
newColumn.MaxLength=8000;
newColumn.DefaultValue = "";

newColumn = tblBugs.Columns.Add(
    "Reporter", Type.GetType("System.Int32"));
newColumn.AllowDBNull=false;
```

Adding data to the table

With all the columns declared, you're ready to add rows of data to the table. You do this by calling the DataTable object's NewRow method, which returns an empty DataRow object with the right structure:

```
newRow = tblBugs.NewRow( );
```

You can use the column name as an index into the row's collection of DataColumns, assigning the appropriate value for each column, one by one:

```
newRow["Product"] = 1;
newRow["Version"] = "0.1";
newRow["Description"] = "Crashes on load";
newRow["Reporter"] = 5;
```

The authors of the DataRows class have implemented the indexer for their class to access the contained Columns collection invisibly. Thus, when you write newRow["Product"], you access the Product column within the Columns collection of the DataRow object.

When the columns are complete, you add the row to the table's Rows collection by calling the Add method, passing in the row you just created:

```
tblBugs.Rows.Add(newRow);
```

You are ready to create a new row:

```
newRow = tblBugs.NewRow( );
newRow["Product"] = 1;
newRow["Version"] = "0.1";
newRow["Description"] = "Does not report correct owner of bug";
newRow["Reporter"] = 5;
tblBugs.Rows.Add(newRow);
```

When all the rows have been created, you can create an instance of a DataSet object and add the table:

```
DataSet dataSet = new DataSet( );
dataSet.Tables.Add(tblBugs);
```

Adding additional tables to the DataSet

With the Bugs table added to the new dataset, you can create a new table for lkProduct as illustrated in the database diagram.

```
DataTable tblProduct = new DataTable("lkProduct")
```

You'll define the columns and add data. Then, you'll add a new table for People. In theory, you could add all the other tables from the previous example, but to keep things simpler, you'll stop with these three.

Adding rows with an array of objects

The DataRowCollection object's Add method is overloaded. In the code shown above, you created a new DataRow object, populated its columns, and added the row. You can create an array of Objects, fill the array, and pass the array to the Add method. For example, rather than writing:

```
newRow = tblPeople.NewRow( );
newRow["FullName"] = "Jesse Liberty";
newRow["email"] = "jliberty@libertyassociates.com";
newRow["Phone"] = "617-555-7301";
newRow["Role"] = 1;
tblPeople.Rows.Add(newRow);
```

you can create an array of five objects and fill that array with the values you would have added to the columns of the row:

```
Object[] PersonArray = new Object[5];
PersonArray[0] = 1;
PersonArray[1] = "Jesse Liberty";
PersonArray[2] = "jliberty@libertyassociates.com";
PersonArray[3] = "617-555-7301";
PersonArray[4] = 1;
tblPeople.Rows.Add(PersonArray);
```

In this case, you must manually add a value for the identity column, BugID. When you created the row object, the identity column value was automatically created for you with the right increment from the previous row. Since you are creating an array of objects, you must do this by hand.

 Though this technique works, it is generally not desirable. The overloaded version of the Add method that takes a DataRow object is *typesafe*. Each column must match the definition of the column you've created. With an array of objects, just about anything goes; in .NET, everything derives from Object, and thus, you can pass in any type of data to an array of objects.

Creating Primary Keys

The Bugs table uses the PersonID as a foreign key into the People table. To recreate this, you'll need to create a primary key (PersonID) in the People table.

You start by declaring the PersonID column as a unique non-null identity column as you did earlier for the BugID column in Bugs:

```
newColumn = tblPeople.Columns.Add("PersonID", Type.GetType("System.Int32"));
newColumn.AutoIncrement = true;       // autoincrementing
newColumn.AutoIncrementSeed=1;        // starts at 1
newColumn.AutoIncrementStep=1;        // increments by 1
newColumn.AllowDBNull=false;          // nulls not allowed

// add the unique constraint
UniqueConstraint uniqueConstraint =
  new UniqueConstraint("Unique_PersonID",newColumn);
tblPeople.Constraints.Add(uniqueConstraint);
```

To create the primary key, you must set the PrimaryKey property of the table. This property takes an array of DataColumn objects.

 In many tables, the primary key is not a single column but rather two or more columns. For example, you might keep track of orders for a customer. A given order might be order number 17. Your database may have many orders whose order number is 17. What uniquely identifies a given order is the order number combined with the customer number. Thus, that table would use a compound key of the order number and the customer number.

The primary key for the People table is a single column: PersonID. To set the primary key, you create an array (in this case, with one member) and assign to that member the column(s) you want to make the primary key:

```
columnArray = new DataColumn[1];
columnArray[0] = newColumn;
```

The newColumn object contains a reference to the PersonID column returned from calling Add. You assign the array to the PrimaryKey property of the table:

```
tblPeople.PrimaryKey=columnArray;
```

Creating Foreign Keys

The PersonID acts as a primary key in People and as a foreign key in Bugs. To create the foreign key relationship, you'll instantiate a new object of type ForeignKeyConstraint, passing in the name of the constraint (FK_BugToPeople) and a reference to the two columns.

To facilitate passing references from the key fields to the ForeignKeyConstraint constructor, you'll want to squirrel away a reference to the PersonID column in People and the Reporter column in Bugs. After you create the columns, save a reference:

```
newColumn =
    tblBugs.Columns.Add("Reporter", Type.GetType("System.Int32"));
newColumn.AllowDBNull=false;
DataColumn bugReporterColumn =
    newColumn; // save for foreign key creation
```

Assuming you've saved the Reporter column in bugReporterColumn and the PersonID column from People in PersonIDColumn, you can create the ForeignKeyConstraint object:

```
ForeignKeyConstraint fk =
  New ForeignKeyConstraint(
        "FK_BugToPeople",PersonIDColumn,bugReporterColumn);
```

This creates the Foreign Key Constraint named fk. Before you add it to the Bugs table, you must set two properties:

```
fk.DeleteRule=Rule.Cascade;
fk.UpdateRule=Rule.Cascade;
```

The DeleteRule determines the action that will occur when a row is deleted from the parent table. Similarly, the UpdateRule determines what will happen when a row is updated in the parent column. The potential values are enumerated by the Rule enumeration, as shown in Table 10-9.

Table 10-9. Rule enumeration

Member name	Description
Cascade	Delete or update related rows (this is the default).
None	Take no action on related rows.
SetDefault	Set the values in the related rows to the value contained in the DefaultValue property.
SetNull	Set the related rows to null.

In this case, the values are set to Rule.Cascade; if a record is deleted or updated from the parent table, all the child records will be deleted or updated as well. You can now add the foreign key constraint to the Bugs table:

```
tblBugs.Constraints.Add(fk);
```

Creating Data Relations

As you saw earlier in the chapter, you can encapsulate the relationship between tables in a DataRelation object. The code for building relationships among hand-crafted DataTables is like the code you saw earlier when you pulled the data structure from the database:

```
System.Data.DataRelation dataRelation;
System.Data.DataColumn dataColumn1;
System.Data.DataColumn dataColumn2;

// set the dataColumns to create the relationship
// between Bug and BugHistory on the BugID key
dataColumn1 =
    dataSet.Tables["People"].Columns["PersonID"];
dataColumn2 =
    dataSet.Tables["Bugs"].Columns["Reporter"];

dataRelation =
    new System.Data.DataRelation(
    "BugsToReporter",
    dataColumn1,
    dataColumn2);

// add the new DataRelation to the dat
dataSet.Relations.Add(dataRelation);
```

The output is shown in Figure 10-11.

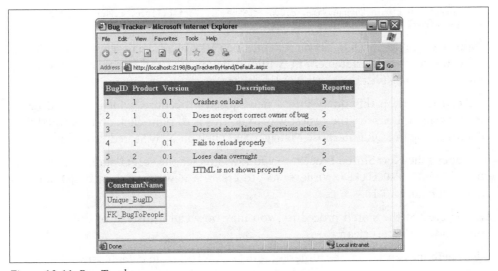

Figure 10-11. Bug Tracker

Stored Procedures

Until now, you've interacted with the database using nothing but SQL statements. Many real-world applications interacting with a SQL Server or other large databases use stored procedures. Stored procedures can be compiled by the database and, thus, offer better performance.

Creating a Simple Stored Procedure

The easiest way to create a stored procedure (often referred to as a *sproc*) is to begin with a working SQL statement. To see this at work, copy the web site you worked on previously in this chapter, *DataRelations*, to a new web site called *StoredProcedures*.

In the method `CreateDataSet`, you created a select statement for your first command object:

```
StringBuilder s = new StringBuilder(
    "select OrderID, c.CompanyName, c.ContactName, ");
s.Append(" c.ContactTitle, c.Phone, orderDate");
s.Append(" from orders o ");
s.Append("join customers c on c.CustomerID = o.CustomerID");
command.CommandText = s.ToString( );
```

Put a break point on the final line and run the program. Step one instruction, and in the Autos window, you should see `command.CommandText`. Double-click on the value to extract the complete select statement:

```
"select OrderID, c.CompanyName, c.ContactName,  c.ContactTitle, c.Phone, orderDate
from orders o join customers c on c.CustomerID = o.CustomerID"
```

If you have a copy of SQL Server Client, open its Query Analyzer and you should find you can drop this statement in (without the opening and closing double quotes) and have it run against the Northwind database, as shown in Figure 10-12.

You can now drop this query into a new stored procedure, which you will name `spOrders`. In SQL Server, the easiest way to do this is to right-click on the Stored Procedures listing in SQL Enterprise Manager and click on New Stored Procedure.

This opens the New Stored Procedure window. Preface the select statement with the string `"CREATE PROCEDURE spOrders AS"` to create a new sproc named `spOrders`, as shown in Figure 10-13.

Having created the stored procedure, you may now call it instead of using the SQL command. Let's start clean:

1. Delete the third `GridView` (`OrderRelationsGridView`) from *default.aspx*.

2. Replace `Page_Load` with the following code:

```
protected void Page_Load(object sender, EventArgs e)
{
    if (!IsPostBack)
```

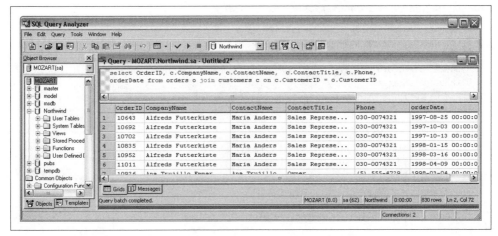

Figure 10-12. SQL QueryAnalyzer

Figure 10-13. Creating the new stored procedure

```
        {
            DataSet ds = CreateDataSet( );
            GridView1.DataSource = ds.Tables[0];
            GridView1.DataBind( );
        }
    }
```

3. Replace the CreateDataSet method with the code shown in Example 10-7.

Example 10-7. Invoking a stored procedure

```
private DataSet CreateDataSet( )
{

    // connection string to connect to the Orders Database
    string connectionString =
    "Data Source=Brahams;Initial Catalog=Northwind;Integrated Security=True";
```

Example 10-7. Invoking a stored procedure (continued)

```
    // Create connection object, initialize with
    // connection string and open the connection
    System.Data.SqlClient.SqlConnection connection =
        new System.Data.SqlClient.SqlConnection(connectionString);
    DataSet dataSet;
    try
    {
        connection.Open( );

        System.Data.SqlClient.SqlCommand command =
            new System.Data.SqlClient.SqlCommand( );
        command.Connection = connection;

        command.CommandText = "spOrders";
        command.CommandType = CommandType.StoredProcedure;

        SqlDataAdapter dataAdapter = new SqlDataAdapter( );
        dataAdapter.SelectCommand = command;
        dataAdapter.TableMappings.Add("Table", "Orders");

        // Create the dataset and use the data adapter to fill it
        dataSet = new DataSet( );
        dataAdapter.Fill(dataSet);

    }
    finally
    {
        connection.Close( );
    }
    return dataSet;
}       // end createDataSet
```

The significant change in this code (beyond simplification) is that you are calling the stored procedure spOrders rather than passing in the entire select statement. To do this, you remove the string builder, and you set the commandText to the name of the stored procedure and the command type to the enumerated constant CommandType. StoredProcedure:

```
    command.CommandText = "spOrders";
    command.CommandType = CommandType.StoredProcedure;
```

(The default CommandType is Text, and that is what you've been using until now.)

Running the application will demonstrate that the call to the stored procedure has the same effect as calling the query directly, with the advantage that, in larger applications, the stored procedure will be more efficient, because your database will optimize its execution.

Stored Procedures with Parameters

If the user clicks on a Details button, the current version of the program will throw an exception. Let's fix that. In the DataRelations program, you downloaded all the details and then selected which details to show in the grid in the panel by using a filtered view. This time, you'll create a parameterized stored procedure to retrieve the details for the specific orderID selected.

 Which approach is more efficient will depend on the volume of data, the frequency with which you want to go back to the database, how much data you can hold in memory, and so forth. Typically, you'll use the filtered view whenever possible to reduce the number of connections to the database.

Create a new stored procedure named spOrderDetails as follows:

```
CREATE PROCEDURE spOrderDetails
@OrderID int
AS
select od.orderid, orderDate, p.productid, productname, od.unitprice, quantity from
orders o
join [order details] od on o.orderid = od.orderid
join products p on p.productid = od.productid
where o.orderID = @OrderID
```

When you invoke the stored procedure, you must replace the parameter @OrderID with the OrderID you want to match, as shown in Example 10-8.

Example 10-8. Calling stored procedure with parameter

```
private void UpdateDetailsGrid( )
{
    int index = GridView1.SelectedIndex;
    if (index != -1)
    {
      DataKey key = GridView1.DataKeys[index];
      int orderID = (int) key.Value;
      string connectionString =
         "Data Source=Brahams;Initial Catalog=Northwind;Integrated Security=True";
       System.Data.SqlClient.SqlConnection connection =
          new System.Data.SqlClient.SqlConnection(connectionString);
       try
       {
           connection.Open( );
           System.Data.SqlClient.SqlCommand command =
              new System.Data.SqlClient.SqlCommand( );
           command.Connection = connection;
           command.CommandText = "spOrderDetails";
           command.CommandType = CommandType.StoredProcedure;

           SqlParameter param =
              command.Parameters.AddWithValue("@OrderID", orderID);
```

Example 10-8. Calling stored procedure with parameter (continued)

```
            param.Direction = ParameterDirection.Input;
            param.DbType = DbType.Int32;


            SqlDataAdapter dataAdapter = new SqlDataAdapter( );
            dataAdapter.SelectCommand = command;
            dataAdapter.TableMappings.Add("Table", "OrderDetails");
            DataSet dataSet = new DataSet( );
            dataAdapter.Fill(dataSet);

            DetailsGridView.DataSource = dataSet.Tables["OrderDetails"];
            DetailsGridView.DataBind( );
            OrderDetailsPanel.Visible = true;
        }
        finally
        {
            connection.Close( );
        }
    }
    else
    {
        OrderDetailsPanel.Visible = false;
    }
}
```

 In a production-quality program, the shared code for creating the connection to the database would be factored out of these methods. It is left intact so the examples stand on their own.

What's new in this code is that you have added an `SqlParameter` object to the command object's `Parameters` collection by invoking the method `AddWithValue` and passing in the name of the parameter and its value:

```
SqlParameter param =
    command.Parameters.AddWithValue("@OrderID", orderID);
param.Direction = ParameterDirection.Input;
param.DbType = DbType.Int32;
```

Setting the `Direction` to input and the type to `Int32` are optional as these are the default values, but it makes for good programming practice to set them explicitly. If you need to get a value out of a stored procedure, set the `Direction` property to `ParameterDirection.Output`. You can then pick up the value after calling the stored procedure:

```
string retVal = command.Parameters["@MyReturnValue"].Value.ToString( );
```

Updating with SQL and ADO.NET

There are two aspects to writing web applications that allow users to update data. The first aspect is providing the user with a form that facilitates data modification. The second is to provide the programmatic support for the update: how do you insert new records, or modify or delete existing records once you know what changes you want to make, if you use the ADO.NET object model directly?

Updating data in a database is simple if you update a single table, but once you update related tables, things get complicated. You can use *transactions* to ensure the integrity of your data, as shown below.

The simplest way to update the database using ADO.NET objects directly is to generate a SQL Insert, Update, or Delete statement, and execute it using the Command object's ExecuteNonQuery method. To see this at work, create a new web site called *UpdatingDBDirectly*. Drag a GridView to display the Shipper's table and add a Select button to the first column of the grid.

Below the grid, add three buttons and two text boxes. Name the buttons btnAdd, btnEdit and btnDelete, and name the text boxes txtName and txtPhone, as shown in Figure 10-14.

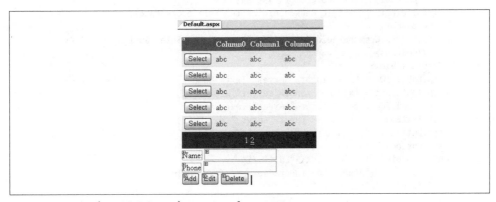

Figure 10-14. Updating DB Directly user interface

The content file to create this is shown in Example 10-9.

Example 10-9. default.aspx for UpdatingDBDirectly

```
<%@ Page Language="C#" AutoEventWireup="true"  CodeFile="Default.aspx.cs"
    Inherits="_Default" %>

<!DOCTYPE html PUBLIC "-//W3C//DTD XHTML 1.1//EN"
    "http://www.w3.org/TR/xhtml11/DTD/xhtml11.dtd">

<html xmlns="http://www.w3.org/1999/xhtml" >
<head runat="server">
```

Example 10-9. default.aspx for UpdatingDBDirectly (continued)

```
        <title>Updating Directly</title>
    </head>
    <body>       •
        <form id="form1" runat="server">
        <div>
            <asp:GridView
            ID="GridView1"
            runat="server"
            CellPadding="4"
            ForeColor="#333333"
            GridLines="None"
            PagerSettings-Mode="Numeric"
            AllowPaging="True"
            DataKeyNames="ShipperID"
            AutoGenerateColumns="true"
            PageSize="5" >
                <FooterStyle BackColor="#5D7B9D" Font-Bold="True" ForeColor="White" />
                <RowStyle BackColor="#F7F6F3" ForeColor="#333333" />
                <PagerStyle BackColor="#284775"
                ForeColor="White" HorizontalAlign="Center" />
                <HeaderStyle BackColor="#5D7B9D" Font-Bold="True" ForeColor="White" />
                <SelectedRowStyle BackColor="#E2DED6"
                 Font-Bold="True" ForeColor="#333333" />
                <AlternatingRowStyle BackColor="White" ForeColor="#284775" />
                <Columns>
                    <asp:CommandField ButtonType="Button" ShowSelectButton="True" />
                </Columns>
            </asp:GridView>
            <asp:Label ID="Label1" runat="server" Text="Name: "></asp:Label>
            <asp:TextBox ID="txtName" runat="server" Width="135px"/><br />
            <asp:Label ID="Label2" runat="server" Text="Phone" />
            <asp:TextBox ID="txtPhone" runat="server" Width="137px"/><br />
            <asp:Button ID="btnAdd" runat="server" Text="Add" OnClick="btnAdd_Click" />
            <asp:Button ID="btnEdit" runat="server"
            OnClick="btnEdit_Click" Text="Edit" />
            <asp:Button ID="btnDelete" runat="server" Text="Delete"
             OnClick="btnDelete_Click" />
        </div>
        </form>
    </body>
</html>
```

This time, you set AutoGenerateColumns to True, but you add an additional column for the CommandField. You can do this declaratively (in the *.aspx*) or through the properties in the Design window.

There are four tasks for this program:

1. Populate the data grid.

2. Add a new record to the table.

3. Edit the new record.

4. Delete the new record.

The code to populate the data grid is familiar and is shown in Example 10-10.

Example 10-10. Populating the DataGrid

```
private void PopulateGrid( )
{
    // connection string to connect to the Orders Database
    string connectionString =
    "Data Source=Brahams;Initial Catalog=Northwind;Integrated Security=True";

    // Create connection object, initialize with
    // connection string and open the connection
    System.Data.SqlClient.SqlConnection connection =
        new System.Data.SqlClient.SqlConnection(connectionString);
    DataSet dataSet;
    try
    {
        connection.Open( );

        // Create a SqlCommand object and assign the connection
        System.Data.SqlClient.SqlCommand command =
            new System.Data.SqlClient.SqlCommand( );
        command.Connection = connection;
        command.CommandText = "select * from Shippers";

        // create a data adapter and assign the command object
        // and add the table mapping for bugs
        SqlDataAdapter dataAdapter = new SqlDataAdapter( );
        dataAdapter.SelectCommand = command;
        dataAdapter.TableMappings.Add("Table", "Shippers");

        // Create the dataset and use the data adapter to fill it
        dataSet = new DataSet( );
        dataAdapter.Fill(dataSet);
        GridView1.DataSource = dataSet.Tables["Shippers"];
        GridView1.DataBind( );
    }
    finally
    {
        connection.Close( );
    }
}    // end createDataSet
```

Each of the buttons has an event handler. The Add button picks up the text from the name and phone textboxes and adds a new record to the database by passing a command string to UpdateDB. Once the database is updated, it calls PopulateGrid (again) to repopulate the grid:

```
    protected void btnAdd_Click(object sender, EventArgs e)
    {
```

```
    string cmd = @"Insert into Shippers values ('" +
        this.txtName.Text + "', '" + this.txtPhone.Text + "')";
    UpdateDB(cmd);
    PopulateGrid();
}
```

The interesting work is done in `UpdateDB`, which takes the command string to execute, as shown in Example 10-11.

Example 10-11. UpdateDB

```
private void UpdateDB(string cmd)
{
    // connection string to connect to the Orders Database
    string connectionString =
    "Data Source=Brahams;Initial Catalog=Northwind;Integrated Security=True";

    // Create connection object, initialize with
    // connection string and open the connection
    System.Data.SqlClient.SqlConnection connection =
        new System.Data.SqlClient.SqlConnection(connectionString);

    try
    {
        connection.Open();

        // Create a SqlCommand object and assign the connection
        System.Data.SqlClient.SqlCommand command =
            new System.Data.SqlClient.SqlCommand();
        command.Connection = connection;
        command.CommandText = cmd;
        command.ExecuteNonQuery();
    }
    finally
    {
        connection.Close();
    }
}
```

The `CommandText` property of the `Command` object is set to whatever is passed in, and then `ExecuteNonQuery` is called on the `Command` object. This `Command` returns the number of rows affected, and you could easily build error checking to ensure the expected number of rows were added.

The Edit button works the same way, but it must get the ID of the selected row. For that, you have a helper method:

```
protected int GetSelectedRecord()
{
    int shipperID = -1;
    int index = GridView1.SelectedIndex;
    if (index != -1)
    {
        DataKey key = GridView1.DataKeys[index];
```

```
        shipperID = (int)key.Value;
    }
    return shipperID;
}
```

 There is no error checking in this example to ensure that a row has been selected. That and other appropriate error checking is left as an exercise for the prudent reader.

The Edit button gets the shipperID and then formulates the update statement to send to UpdateDB:

```
protected void btnEdit_Click(object sender, EventArgs e)
{
    int shipperID = GetSelectedRecord( );
    string cmd = @"Update Shippers set CompanyName = '" +
        this.txtName.Text +
        "', Phone = '" + this.txtPhone.Text +
        @"' where ShipperID = " + shipperID;

    UpdateDB(cmd);
    PopulateGrid( );
}
```

Finally, the Delete button deletes the selected entry in the database:

```
protected void btnDelete_Click(object sender, EventArgs e)
{
    string cmd =
        @"delete from Shippers where ShipperID = " + GetSelectedRecord( );

    UpdateDB(cmd);
    PopulateGrid( );
}
```

Before running the program, check that your Page_Load method has been copied properly:

```
protected void Page_Load(object sender, EventArgs e)
{
    if (!IsPostBack)
    {
        DataSet ds = CreateDataSet( );
        GridView1.DataSource = ds.Tables[0];
        GridView1.DataBind( );
    }
}
```

The running program is shown in Figure 10-15.

Figure 10-15. Updating Directly

Updating Data with Transactions

An important feature of most industrial-strength databases is support for transactions. A *transaction* is a set of database operations that must all complete or fail together. That is, either all the operations must complete successfully (*commit* the transaction), or all must be undone (*roll back* the transaction) so the database is left in the state it was in before the transaction began.

The canonical transaction is transferring money at an ATM. If I transfer $50 from checking to savings, the bank will first reduce my checking account by $50 and then increase my savings account by $50. If it does the first step but not the second, I will be annoyed.

The bank system treats the entire set of reducing one account and increasing the other as a single transaction. The entire transaction occurs or none of it occurs; it is not valid for it to occur "partially."

The ACID Test

Database designers define the requirements of a transaction with the so-called "ACID" test. ACID is an acronym for *A*tomic, *C*onsistent, *I*solated, and *D*urable. Here's a brief summary of what each of these terms means:

Atomic

An atomic interaction is indivisible, i.e., it cannot be partially implemented. Every transaction must be atomic. For instance, in the previous banking example, it must be impossible to decrement my checking account but fail to increment my savings account. If the transaction fails, it must return the database to the state it would have been in without the transaction.

 All transactions, even failed ones, affect the database in trivial ways: resources are expended, performance is affected, and the log file is updated. The atomic requirement only implies that, if a transaction is rolled back, all of the tables and data (other than log tables) will be in the state they would have been in had the transaction not been attempted at all.

Consistent

The database is presumed to be in a consistent state before the transaction begins, and the transaction must leave it in a consistent state when it completes. While the transaction is being processed, the database need not be in a consistent state. To continue with our example of transferring money, the database need not be consistent during the transaction. (It is okay to decrement my checking account before incrementing my savings account.) It must end in a consistent state, i.e., when the transaction completes, the books must balance.

Isolated

Transactions are not processed one at a time. Typically, a database may be processing many transactions at once, switching its attention among various operations. This creates the possibility that a transaction can view and act upon data that reflects intermediate changes from another transaction that is still in progress and that, therefore, currently has its data in an inconsistent state. Transaction isolation is designed to prevent this problem. For a transaction to be isolated, the effects of the transaction must be exactly as if the transaction were acted on alone; there can be no effects on or dependencies on other database activities. For more information, see the sidebar "Data Isolation"

Durable

Once a transaction is committed, the effect on the database is permanent.

Implementing Transactions

You can implement transactions in ASP.NET in two ways. You can allow the database to manage the transaction by using transactions within your stored procedure, or you can use connection-based transactions. In the latter case, the transaction is created and enforced outside of the database. This allows you to add transaction support to databases that do not otherwise provide for it or to wrap several stored procedures and other database calls inside a single transaction.

In the following example, you will update the Order table and the Order Details table. To get started, create a new web site named *Transactions*.

The *Default.aspx* page has a GridView to display the orders (OrdersGridView) and a panel in which you will place a second GridView to display the order details (DetailsGridView).

Below the panel, you'll create a table in which you'll add a number of controls for updating the Orders and Order Details tables through a database transaction or through an ASP.NET connection-based transaction. The complete design view is shown in Figure 10-16.

The *default.aspx* file to create this is shown in Example 10-12.

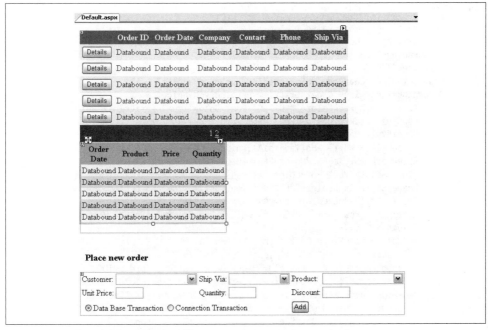

Figure 10-16. Transaction user interface

Example 10-12. Transactions default.aspx

```
<%@ Page Language="C#" AutoEventWireup="true"  CodeFile="Default.aspx.cs"
   Inherits="_Default" %>

<!DOCTYPE html PUBLIC "-//W3C//DTD XHTML 1.1//EN"
   "http://www.w3.org/TR/xhtml11/DTD/xhtml11.dtd">

<html xmlns="http://www.w3.org/1999/xhtml" >
<head runat="server">
    <title>Transactions</title>
</head>
<body>
    <form id="form1" runat="server">
    <div>
        <asp:GridView
        ID="OrdersGridView"
        runat="server"
        CellPadding="4"
        ForeColor="#333333"
        GridLines="None"
        DataKeyNames="OrderID"
```

Example 10-12. Transactions default.aspx (continued)

```
AutoGenerateColumns="False"
PagerSettings-Mode="Numeric"
AllowPaging="true"
PageSize="5"
OnSelectedIndexChanged="OnSelectedIndexChangedHandler"
OnPageIndexChanging="OrdersGridView_PageIndexChanging" >
    <FooterStyle BackColor="#5D7B9D" Font-Bold="True" ForeColor="White" />
    <RowStyle BackColor="#F7F6F3" ForeColor="#333333" />
    <PagerStyle BackColor="#284775"
      ForeColor="White" HorizontalAlign="Center" />
    <SelectedRowStyle BackColor="#E2DED6"
      Font-Bold="True" ForeColor="#333333" />
    <HeaderStyle BackColor="#5D7B9D" Font-Bold="True" ForeColor="White" />
    <EditRowStyle BackColor="#999999" />
    <AlternatingRowStyle BackColor="White" ForeColor="#284775" />
    <Columns>
        <asp:ButtonField ButtonType="Button"
          CommandName="Select" Text="Details" />
        <asp:BoundField DataField="OrderID" HeaderText="Order ID" />
        <asp:BoundField DataField="OrderDate" HeaderText="Order Date" />
        <asp:BoundField DataField="CompanyName" HeaderText="Company" />
        <asp:BoundField DataField="ContactTitle" HeaderText="Contact" />
        <asp:BoundField DataField="Phone" HeaderText="Phone" />
        <asp:BoundField DataField="ShipperName" HeaderText="Ship Via" />
    </Columns>
</asp:GridView>
<asp:Panel ID="OrderDetailsPanel" runat="server"
  Height="50px" Width="125px">
    <asp:GridView
    ID="DetailsGridView"
    runat="server"
    AutoGenerateColumns="False"
    BackColor="LightGoldenrodYellow"
    BorderColor="Tan"
    BorderWidth="1px"
    CellPadding="2"
    ForeColor="Black"
    GridLines="None">
        <FooterStyle BackColor="Tan" />
        <Columns>
            <asp:BoundField DataField="OrderDate"
                HeaderText="Order Date" />
            <asp:BoundField DataField="ProductName" HeaderText="Product" />
            <asp:BoundField DataField="UnitPrice" HeaderText="Price" />
            <asp:BoundField DataField="Quantity" HeaderText="Quantity" />
        </Columns>
        <PagerStyle BackColor="PaleGoldenrod"
            ForeColor="DarkSlateBlue" HorizontalAlign="Center" />
        <SelectedRowStyle BackColor="DarkSlateBlue"
            ForeColor="GhostWhite" />
        <HeaderStyle BackColor="Tan" Font-Bold="True" />
        <AlternatingRowStyle BackColor="PaleGoldenrod" />
```

Example 10-12. Transactions default.aspx (continued)

```
        </asp:GridView>
    </asp:Panel>
     <br />
    <h3>
          Place new order</h3>
    <asp:Table ID="tblAddOrder" runat="server">
        <asp:TableRow>
            <asp:TableCell>Customer:</asp:TableCell>
            <asp:TableCell>
                <asp:DropDownList
                ID="ddlCustomer"
                DataValueField="CustomerID"
                DataTextField="CompanyName"
                runat="server"
                Width="160" />
            </asp:TableCell>
            <asp:TableCell>Ship Via:</asp:TableCell>
            <asp:TableCell>
                <asp:DropDownList
                ID="ddlShipper"
                DataValueField="ShipperID"
                DataTextField="CompanyName"
                runat="server"
                Width="120" />
            </asp:TableCell>
            <asp:TableCell>Product:</asp:TableCell>
            <asp:TableCell>
                <asp:DropDownList
                ID="ddlProduct"
                DataValueField="ProductID"
                DataTextField="ProductName"
                runat="server"
                Width="160px" />
            </asp:TableCell>
        </asp:TableRow>

        <asp:TableRow>
            <asp:TableCell>Unit Price:</asp:TableCell>
            <asp:TableCell>
                <asp:TextBox ID="txtUnitPrice" runat="server" Width="48px" />
            </asp:TableCell>
            <asp:TableCell>Quantity:</asp:TableCell>
            <asp:TableCell>
                <asp:TextBox ID="txtQuantity" runat="server" Width="48px" />
            </asp:TableCell>
            <asp:TableCell>Discount:</asp:TableCell>
            <asp:TableCell>
                <asp:TextBox ID="txtDiscount" runat="server" Width="48px" />
            </asp:TableCell>
        </asp:TableRow>
        <asp:TableRow>
        <asp:TableCell ColumnSpan="4">
```

Example 10-12. Transactions default.aspx (continued)

```
                    <asp:RadioButtonList
                    ID="rbTransactionType"
                    runat="server"
                    RepeatDirection="Horizontal">
                        <asp:ListItem Value="DB" Selected="true">
                            Data Base Transaction</asp:ListItem>
                        <asp:ListItem Value="Connection">
                            Connection Transaction</asp:ListItem>
                    </asp:RadioButtonList>
                </asp:TableCell>
                <asp:TableCell>
                    <asp:Button
                    ID="btnAdd"
                    runat="server"
                    Text="Add"
                    OnClick="btnAdd_Click"/>
                </asp:TableCell>
                <asp:TableCell>
                    <asp:Label ID="lblNewOrderID" runat="server" Text="" />
                </asp:TableCell>
            </asp:TableRow>
          </asp:Table>

    </div>
    </form>
</body>
</html>
```

In a previous example, you made a single database call to get all the order details records, and when an order was selected, you filtered on that view to get the details you wanted. This time, to show another approach, when you select an order, you'll go to the database with a query that only extracts the order detail records for the appropriate order ID.

The complete code-behind is shown in Example 10-13 and analysis follows.

Example 10-13. Default.aspx.cs for Transactions

```
using System;
using System.Text;
using System.Data;
using System.Data.SqlClient;      //  necessary for data access
using System.Configuration;
using System.Web;
using System.Web.Security;
using System.Web.UI;
using System.Web.UI.WebControls;
using System.Web.UI.WebControls.WebParts;
using System.Web.UI.HtmlControls;

public partial class _Default : System.Web.UI.Page
{
```

Example 10-13. Default.aspx.cs for Transactions (continued)

```
protected void Page_Load(object sender, EventArgs e)
{
    if (!IsPostBack)
    {
        BindGrid( );
        ddlCustomer.DataSource = GetDataReader("Customers");
        ddlCustomer.DataBind( );
        ddlShipper.DataSource = GetDataReader("Shippers");
        ddlShipper.DataBind( );
        ddlProduct.DataSource = GetDataReader("Products");
        ddlProduct.DataBind( );
    }
}

private void BindGrid( )
{
    DataSet ds = CreateDataSet(WhichTable.Orders);
    OrdersGridView.DataSource = ds.Tables[0];
    OrdersGridView.DataBind( );
}

private SqlDataReader GetDataReader(string whichTable)
{
    // connection string to connect to the Bugs Database
    string connectionString =
    "Data Source=Brahams;Initial Catalog=Northwind;Integrated Security=True";

    // Create connection object, initialize with
    // connection string. Open it.
    System.Data.SqlClient.SqlConnection connection =
        new System.Data.SqlClient.SqlConnection(
        connectionString);

    connection.Open( );

    // Create a SqlCommand object and assign the connection
    System.Data.SqlClient.SqlCommand command =
        new System.Data.SqlClient.SqlCommand( );
    command.Connection = connection;

    // hard code the select statement
    command.CommandText = "select * from " + whichTable;

    // return the data reader
    return command.ExecuteReader(
        CommandBehavior.CloseConnection);
}

// get order details
public void OnSelectedIndexChangedHandler(
    Object sender, EventArgs e)
{
```

Example 10-13. Default.aspx.cs for Transactions (continued)

```
        UpdateDetailsGrid( );
    }

    private void UpdateDetailsGrid( )
    {
        BindGrid( );
        DataSet ds = CreateDataSet(WhichTable.OrderDetails);
        if (ds.Tables[0].Rows.Count > 0)
        {
            this.OrderDetailsPanel.Visible = true;
            this.DetailsGridView.DataSource = ds.Tables[0];
            this.DetailsGridView.DataBind( );
        }
        else
        {
            this.OrderDetailsPanel.Visible = false;
        }
    }

    private enum WhichTable
    {
        Orders,
        OrderDetails,
    };

    private DataSet CreateDataSet(WhichTable theTable)
    {
        // connection string to connect to the Orders Database
        string connectionString =
        "Data Source=Brahams;Initial Catalog=Northwind;Integrated Security=True";

        // Create connection object, initialize with
        // connection string and open the connection
        System.Data.SqlClient.SqlConnection connection =
            new System.Data.SqlClient.SqlConnection(connectionString);

        DataSet dataSet = new DataSet( );
        try
        {
            connection.Open( );

            // Create a SqlCommand object and assign the connection
            System.Data.SqlClient.SqlCommand command =
                new System.Data.SqlClient.SqlCommand( );
            command.Connection = connection;

            StringBuilder sb = new StringBuilder( );
            if (theTable == WhichTable.Orders)
            {
                sb.Append("select OrderID, c.CompanyName, c.ContactName, ");
                sb.Append(" c.ContactTitle, c.Phone, orderDate, ");
                sb.Append(" s.CompanyName as ShipperName");
```

Example 10-13. Default.aspx.cs for Transactions (continued)

```
                sb.Append(" from orders o ");
                sb.Append(" join customers c on c.CustomerID = o.CustomerID");
                sb.Append(" join shippers s on s.ShipperID = o.ShipVia");
                sb.Append(" ORDER BY OrderID DESC");
            }
            else
            {
                int index = OrdersGridView.SelectedIndex;
                int theOrderID = -1;
                if (index != -1)
                {
                    // get the order id from the data grid
                    DataKey key = OrdersGridView.DataKeys[index];
                    theOrderID = (int)key.Value;
                }

                sb.Append("Select od.OrderID, OrderDate, p.ProductID, ");
                sb.Append(" ProductName, od.UnitPrice, Quantity ");
                sb.Append("from Orders o ");
                sb.Append("join [Order Details] od on o.orderid = od.orderid ");
                sb.Append("join products p on p.productID = od.productid ");
                sb.Append("where od.OrderID = " + theOrderID);
            }

            command.CommandText = sb.ToString( );
            SqlDataAdapter dataAdapter = new SqlDataAdapter( );
            dataAdapter.SelectCommand = command;
            dataAdapter.TableMappings.Add("Table", theTable.ToString( ));
            dataAdapter.Fill(dataSet);
        }
        finally
        {
            connection.Close( );
        }
        return dataSet;
    }

    protected void btnAdd_Click(object sender, EventArgs e)
    {
        string whichTransaction = this.rbTransactionType.SelectedValue.ToString( );
        if (whichTransaction == "DB")
            UpdateDBTransaction( );
        else
            UpdateConnectionTransaction( );
    }

    private void UpdateConnectionTransaction( )
    {
        string connectionString =
        "Data Source=Brahams;Initial Catalog=Northwind;Integrated Security=True";
```

Example 10-13. Default.aspx.cs for Transactions (continued)

```
    // Create connection object, initialize with
    // connection string. Open it.
    System.Data.SqlClient.SqlConnection connection =
        new System.Data.SqlClient.SqlConnection(connectionString);

    // declare the command object for the sql statements
    System.Data.SqlClient.SqlCommand command =
        new System.Data.SqlClient.SqlCommand( );

    // declare an instance of SqlTransaction
    SqlTransaction transaction = null;
    int OrderID = -1;

    try
    {
        // connection string to connect to the Bugs Database
        connection.Open( );

        // begin the transaction
        transaction = connection.BeginTransaction( );

        // attach the transaction to the command
        command.Transaction = transaction;

        // attach connection to the command
        command.Connection = connection;

        command.CommandText = "spAddOrder";
        command.CommandType = CommandType.StoredProcedure;

        // declare the parameter object
        System.Data.SqlClient.SqlParameter param;

        // add each parameter and set its direciton and value
        param = command.Parameters.Add("@CustomerID", SqlDbType.NChar);
        param.Direction = ParameterDirection.Input;
        param.Value = this.ddlCustomer.SelectedItem.Value;

        param = command.Parameters.Add(
            "@ShipperID", SqlDbType.Int);
        param.Direction = ParameterDirection.Input;
        param.Value = this.ddlShipper.SelectedValue;

        param = command.Parameters.Add(
            "@OrderID", SqlDbType.Int);
        param.Direction = ParameterDirection.Output;

        command.ExecuteNonQuery( ); // execute the sproc

        // retrieve the identity column
        OrderID = Convert.ToInt32(command.Parameters["@OrderID"].Value);
```

Example 10-13. Default.aspx.cs for Transactions (continued)

```
            // formulate the string to update the orderDetails
            string strAddOrderDetails = "Insert into [Order Details] " +
                "(OrderID, ProductID, UnitPrice, Quantity, Discount) " +
                "values(" + OrderID + ", " + this.ddlProduct.SelectedValue + ", " +
                this.txtUnitPrice.Text + ", " + this.txtQuantity.Text + ", " +
                this.txtDiscount.Text + ")";

            // set up the command object to update the bug hsitory
            command.CommandType = CommandType.Text;
            command.CommandText = strAddOrderDetails;

            // execute the insert statement
            command.ExecuteNonQuery( );

            // commit the transaction
            transaction.Commit( );
        }
        catch (Exception e)
        {
            Trace.Write(e.Message);
            transaction.Rollback( );
        }
        finally
        {
            connection.Close( );
        }
        this.txtDiscount.Text = string.Empty;
        this.txtQuantity.Text = string.Empty;
        this.txtUnitPrice.Text = string.Empty;
        this.lblNewOrderID.Text = OrderID.ToString( );
    }

    private void UpdateDBTransaction( )
    {
        // connection string to connect to the Bugs Database
        string connectionString =
        "Data Source=Brahams;Initial Catalog=Northwind;Integrated Security=True";

        // Create connection object, initialize with
        // connection string. Open it.
        System.Data.SqlClient.SqlConnection connection =
            new System.Data.SqlClient.SqlConnection(connectionString);
        connection.Open( );

        // create a second command object for the bugs hisotry table
        System.Data.SqlClient.SqlCommand command =
            new System.Data.SqlClient.SqlCommand( );
        command.Connection = connection;

        command.CommandText = "spAddOrderTransactions";
        command.CommandType = CommandType.StoredProcedure;
```

Example 10-13. Default.aspx.cs for Transactions (continued)

```
        // declare the parameter object
        System.Data.SqlClient.SqlParameter param;

        // add each parameter and set its direciton and value
        string customerID = this.ddlCustomer.SelectedValue.ToString( );
        param = command.Parameters.AddWithValue("@CustomerID", customerID);
        param.DbType = DbType.StringFixedLength;
        param.Direction = ParameterDirection.Input;

        int shipperID = Convert.ToInt32(this.ddlShipper.SelectedValue);
        param = command.Parameters.AddWithValue("@ShipperID", shipperID);
        param.DbType = DbType.Int32;
        param.Direction = ParameterDirection.Input;

        int productID = Convert.ToInt32(this.ddlProduct.SelectedValue);
        param = command.Parameters.AddWithValue("@ProductID", productID);
        param.DbType = DbType.Int32;
        param.Direction = ParameterDirection.Input;

        decimal price = Convert.ToDecimal(this.txtUnitPrice.Text);
        param = command.Parameters.AddWithValue("@UnitPrice", price);
        param.DbType = DbType.Decimal;
        param.Direction = ParameterDirection.Input;

        Int16 quantity = Convert.ToInt16(this.txtQuantity.Text);
        param = command.Parameters.AddWithValue("@Quantity", quantity);
        param.DbType = DbType.Int16;
        param.Direction = ParameterDirection.Input;

        double discount = Convert.ToDouble(this.txtDiscount.Text);
        param = command.Parameters.AddWithValue("@Discount", discount);
        param.DbType = DbType.Double;
        param.Direction = ParameterDirection.Input;

        param = command.Parameters.AddWithValue("@orderID", 0);
        param.DbType = DbType.Int32;
        param.Direction = ParameterDirection.Output;

        command.ExecuteNonQuery( ); // execute the sproc

        param = command.Parameters["@OrderID"];
        int newOrderID = (int) param.Value;
        this.lblNewOrderID.Text = newOrderID.ToString( );
    }

    protected void OrdersGridView_PageIndexChanging(
        object sender, GridViewPageEventArgs e)
    {
        OrdersGridView.PageIndex = e.NewPageIndex;
        this.OrderDetailsPanel.Visible = false;
```

Example 10-13. Default.aspx.cs for Transactions (continued)

```
        BindGrid( );
    }
}               // end class
```

In Example 10-13, you factor out the common code for getting the Order and Order Details records into a single method, CreateDataSet, that takes an enumerated constant called WhichTable as an argument to indicate which table's records you are retrieving:

```
private enum WhichTable
{
    Orders,
    OrderDetails,
};
```

The CreateDataSet method tests the enumeration passed in to decide whether to query the Orders table or the Order Details table:

```
if (theTable == WhichTable.Orders)
{
    sb.Append("select OrderID, c.CompanyName, c.ContactName, ");
    sb.Append(" c.ContactTitle, c.Phone, orderDate, ");
    sb.Append(" s.CompanyName as ShipperName");
    sb.Append(" from orders o ");
    sb.Append(" join customers c on c.CustomerID = o.CustomerID");
    sb.Append(" join shippers s on s.ShipperID = o.ShipVia");
    sb.Append(" ORDER BY OrderID DESC");
}
else    // get order details
{
    int index = OrdersGridView.SelectedIndex;
    int theOrderID = -1;
    if (index != -1)
    {
        // get the order id from the data grid
        DataKey key = OrdersGridView.DataKeys[index];
        theOrderID = (int)key.Value;
    }

    sb.Append("Select od.OrderID, OrderDate, p.ProductID, ");
    sb.Append(" ProductName, od.UnitPrice, Quantity ");
    sb.Append("from Orders o ");
    sb.Append("join [Order Details] od on o.orderid = od.orderid ");
    sb.Append("join products p on p.productID = od.productid ");
    sb.Append("where od.OrderID = " + theOrderID);
}
```

When the page is first loaded the data grid is bound by calling BindGrid:

```
if (!IsPostBack)
{
```

```
    BindGrid();
    //...
}
```

BindGrid gets the dataset for Orders and binds the OrdersGridView to that dataset's first table:

```
private void BindGrid()
{
    DataSet ds = CreateDataSet(WhichTable.Orders);
    OrdersGridView.DataSource = ds.Tables[0];
    OrdersGridView.DataBind();
}
```

The full Page_Load method then goes on to fill the three drop-downs (Customers, Shippers, and Products):

```
if (!IsPostBack)
{
    BindGrid();
    ddlCustomer.DataSource = GetDataReader("Customers");
    ddlCustomer.DataBind();
    ddlShipper.DataSource = GetDataReader("Shippers");
    ddlShipper.DataBind();
    ddlProduct.DataSource = GetDataReader("Products");
    ddlProduct.DataBind();
}
```

The common work of getting the DataReader to bind to is factored out into the GetDataReader method, which takes the name of the table as a parameter:

```
private SqlDataReader GetDataReader(string whichTable)
{
    // connection string to connect to the Bugs Database
    string connectionString =
    "Data Source=Brahams;Initial Catalog=Northwind;Integrated Security=True";

    // Create connection object, initialize with
    // connection string. Open it.
    System.Data.SqlClient.SqlConnection connection =
        new System.Data.SqlClient.SqlConnection(
        connectionString);

    connection.Open();

    // Create a SqlCommand object and assign the connection
    System.Data.SqlClient.SqlCommand command =
        new System.Data.SqlClient.SqlCommand();
    command.Connection = connection;

    // set the stored procedure to get the bug records
    command.CommandText = "select * from " + whichTable;
```

```
    // return the data reader
    return command.ExecuteReader(
        CommandBehavior.CloseConnection);
}
```

The drop-down's job is to present the text to the user and to return the ID to the program. This is accomplished by declaring the DataValueField and the DataTextField for each drop-down, as shown in Example 10-12:

```
<asp:DropDownList ID="ddlShipper" runat="server"
    DataValueField="ShipperID"
    DataTextField="CompanyName"
    Width="120" />
```

To create a new order using transactions, the user chooses a customer, shipper, and product from the drop-downs and then fills in the Unit Price, Quantity, and Discount. To illustrate the different code for DB-based versus connection-based transactions, you'll ask the user to select which type of transaction support to use (via the radio buttons) and then to click the Add button, as shown in Figure 10-17.

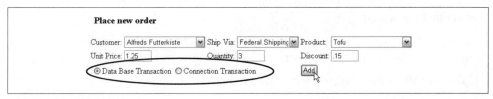

Figure 10-17. Placing a new order

Data Base transactions

If the user chooses Data Base Transaction, the code branches to the method UpdateDBTransaction. This invokes the stored procedure *spAddOrderTransactions* shown in Example 10-14.

Example 10-14. spAddOrderTransactions stored procedure

```
CREATE PROCEDURE spAddOrderTransactions
@CustomerID nchar (5),
@ShipperID int,
@ProductID int,
@UnitPrice money,
@Quantity smallint,
@Discount real,
@OrderID int output
 AS
Begin Transaction
-- declare @OrderID int
Insert into Orders (CustomerID, ShipVia)
values (@CustomerID, @ShipperID)
select @OrderID = @@identity
if @@Error <> 0 goto ErrorHandler
```

Example 10-14. spAddOrderTransactions stored procedure (continued)

```
Insert into [Order Details]
(OrderID, ProductID, UnitPrice, Quantity, Discount)
values
( @OrderID, @ProductID, @UnitPrice, @Quantity, @Discount)

if @@Error <> 0 goto ErrorHandler
commit transaction
return
ErrorHandler:
rollback transaction
return
GO
```

The responsibility for managing the transaction, committing it if both tables are updated, and rolling it back if anything goes wrong, is entirely within the stored procedure. The only job of UpdateDBTransactions is to invoke the stored procedure and pass in the appropriate parameters.

Connection transactions

If, on the other hand, the user chooses to use connection transactions, then your code will be more complex. The steps are as follows:

1. Create the connection string and the SqlConnection object.
2. Create the SqlCommand object and assign the connection to its Connection property:

   ```
   command.Connection = connection;
   ```

3. Open a try block in which you will try to update the two tables. If an exception is thrown, you will catch the exception and roll back the transaction; otherwise, you'll commit the transaction.
4. Open the connection.
5. Instantiate a SqlTransaction object by calling the BeginTransaction method of the SqlConnection object:

   ```
   transaction = connection.BeginTransaction();
   ```

6. Set the SqlCommand object's Transaction property to the SqlTransaction object you've instantiated:

   ```
   command.Transaction = transaction;
   ```

7. Set the SqlCommand object's Connection property to the SqlConnection object you've created.

Your transaction, in this case, will consist of a call to a stored procedure to add the record to the Orders table (spAddOrder) which will return the OrderID of the new order, as shown in Example 10-15.

Example 10-15. spAddOrder

```
CREATE PROCEDURE spAddOrder
@CustomerID nChar,
@ShipperID integer,
@OrderID integer out
as
Insert into Orders values ( @CustomerID, 1, GetDate( ), GetDate( ), GetDate( ),
@ShipperID, 0, null, null, null, null, null, null)
```

You'll then use direct SQL code to add to the OrdersDetail page. If both steps succeed, you will commit the transaction; otherwise, you'll roll back the entire transaction.

You accomplish this by putting all the work into a try/catch block. If an exception is caught, something went wrong, and you will roll back the transaction; otherwise, you commit it.

```
try
{
    // db work done here
    transaction.Commit( );
}
catch (Exception e)
{
    Trace.Write(e.Message);
    transaction.Rollback( );
}
finally
{
    connection.Close( );
}
```

The last line in the try block is the Commit statement. This will only be called if no exception has been thrown.

Binding to Business Objects

Most of the applications that we've looked at in this book have been two-tier, separating the User Interface from the back-end data. Many larger commercial applications, however, are n-tier, with at least a middle business-logic layer to separate retrieval of data from the database from manipulation (and validation) of that data before presentation.

An example of a middle-tier business object would be to create a stateless class to encapsulate business logic, and a "model" class that knows how to load and store data from the database.

 This follows the Model View Controller (MVC) design pattern popular with many object-oriented programmers (see, for example, the article "Model-View-Controller" on MSDN.com: *http://msdn.microsoft. com/library/default.asp?url=/library/en-us/dnpatterns/html/desmvc.asp*).

To illustrate implementing the n-tier MVC pattern, we'll create a stateless business class *CustomerBusinessLogic* and a "model" of the Customer class named North-Wind customer. We'll bind an ObjectDataSource to the stateless business-logic class which will use the Model class to get and retrieve data about customers in the North-Wind database.

To begin, create a new web application called *NTierDataSource*. Add a GridView and use the smart tag and the properties to set the columns from the Customer table you'd like to display, as shown in Example 10-16.

Example 10-16. GridView declaration in default.aspx from NTierDataSource

```
<asp:GridView ID="GridView1" runat="server"
    DataSourceID="ObjectDataSource1"
    AllowPaging="True"
    AutoGenerateColumns="False"
    CellPadding="4" ForeColor="#333333" GridLines="None" >
    <FooterStyle BackColor="#5D7B9D" Font-Bold="True" ForeColor="White" />
    <RowStyle BackColor="#F7F6F3" ForeColor="#333333" />
    <Columns>
        <asp:BoundField DataField="CompanyName" HeaderText="Company" />
        <asp:BoundField DataField="ContactName" HeaderText="Contact" />
        <asp:BoundField DataField="ContactTitle" HeaderText="Title" />
        <asp:BoundField DataField="Address" HeaderText="Address" />
        <asp:BoundField DataField="City" HeaderText="City" />
        <asp:BoundField DataField="Region" HeaderText="Region" />
        <asp:BoundField DataField="PostalCode" HeaderText="Postal Code" />
        <asp:BoundField DataField="Phone" HeaderText="Phone" />
        <asp:BoundField DataField="Fax" HeaderText="Fax" />
    </Columns>
    <PagerStyle BackColor="#284775" ForeColor="White" HorizontalAlign="Center" />
    <SelectedRowStyle BackColor="#E2DED6" Font-Bold="True" ForeColor="#333333" />
    <HeaderStyle BackColor="#5D7B9D" Font-Bold="True" ForeColor="White" />
    <EditRowStyle BackColor="#999999" />
    <AlternatingRowStyle BackColor="White" ForeColor="#284775" />
</asp:GridView>
```

The only thing surprising in this declaration is that we've set the DataSourceID to *ObjectDataSource1*. Declare that object below the DataGrid:

```
<asp:ObjectDataSource ID="ObjectDataSource1" runat="server"
    SelectMethod="GetAllCustomers"
    TypeName="CustomerBusinessLogic" />
```

Two key attributes of this ObjectDataSource are new in ASP 2.0: the SelectMethod attribute tells the ObjectDataSource which method to call on its business object to respond to the DataGrid's select request (to populate the grid), and the TypeName attribute tells the ObjectDataSource which class will have that method.

The SelectMethod is invoked on the TypeName class using reflection at runtime.

From this declaration, you can see your stateless business-logic class will be named CustomerBusinessLogic, and it will have a (static) method named GetAllCustomers.

To create this class, right-click on the project in the Solution Explorer and add a new Class named *CustomerBusinessLogic.cs*. VS2005 will offer to put the file in the *App_Code* directory, which is what you want.

The Business Logic class, which is listed in Example 10-17, is declared to be static because all its members will be static. The member methods represent the capabilities of the business logic class:

GetAllCustomers
 Responds to the select method.

UpdateCustomerInformation
 Responds to the Update method (stubbed out for this example).

GetCustomer
 Gets an individual customer instance given a CustomerID.

Example 10-17. CustomerBusinessLogic

```
using System;
using System.Data;
using System.Data.SqlClient;
using System.Collections;
using System.Collections.Specialized;
using System.Configuration;
using System.Text;
using System.Web;
using System.Web.Security;
using System.Web.UI;
using System.Web.UI.WebControls;
using System.Web.UI.WebControls.WebParts;
using System.Web.UI.HtmlControls;

/// <summary>
/// Stateless business logic that encapsulates what
/// can be done with a Customer object
/// All methods are static
/// </summary>
public static class CustomerBusinessLogic
{
    public static ICollection GetAllCustomers( )
    {
        ArrayList allCustomers = new ArrayList( );
```

Example 10-17. CustomerBusinessLogic (continued)

```csharp
        string connectionString =
        "Data Source=Brahams;Initial Catalog=Northwind;Integrated Security=True";

        string selectCommand = "Select CustomerID from Customers";

        SqlDataSource dataSource =
            new SqlDataSource(connectionString, selectCommand);

        try
        {
            // select with no arguments
            IEnumerable CustomerIDs =
              dataSource.Select(DataSourceSelectArguments.Empty);

            IEnumerator enumerator = CustomerIDs.GetEnumerator( );
            while (enumerator.MoveNext( ))
            {
                DataRowView drv = enumerator.Current as DataRowView;
                if (drv != null)
                {
                    string customerID = drv["CustomerID"].ToString( );
                    NorthWindCustomer cust = new NorthWindCustomer(customerID);
                    allCustomers.Add(cust);
                }   // end if not null
            }       // end while enumerating
        }           // end try block
        finally
        {
            dataSource.Dispose( );
        }
        return allCustomers;
    }

    public static void UpdateCustomerInformation(NorthWindCustomer customer)
    {
        bool returnValue = customer.Save( );
        if (returnValue == false)
        {
            throw new ApplicationException("Unable to update customer");
        }
    }

    public static NorthWindCustomer GetCustomer(string custID)
    {
        return new NorthWindCustomer(custID);
    }
}
```

The only interesting method is GetAllCustomers, whose job is to return an ICollection to which the grid may bind. You do this by creating an instance of SqlDataSource initialized with the connection string and a select statement that gets all the CustomerIDs from the Customers table. What you get back from calling dataSource.Select (passing in no arguments) is a collection of DataRowViews.

You enumerate the collection, extracting each DataRowView, and from that you extract the CustomerID. Using that CustomerID, you instantiate a NorthWindCustomer object (defined below in Example 10-18) which you add to your ArrayList. Once you have created an instance of the NorthWindCustomer for every ID in the database, that collection is used as the data source for the GridView.

This process allows you to manipulate the data object (the NorthWindCustomer) to add business logic to any or all of its properties. In this example, the NorthWindCustomer object does nothing more than store the data for a customer from the Customers table, but you can imagine it performing operations on that data or extending the definition of a customer beyond a single table (or even beyond the data in a single database). Example 10-18 shows the definition of the NorthWindCustomer implemented in *CustomerBusinessLogic.cs*.

Example 10-18. NorthWindCustomer

```
public class NorthWindCustomer
{
    private object customerID;

    private string companyName;
     public string CompanyName
    {
        get { return companyName; }
        set { companyName = value; }
    }

    private string contactName;
    public string ContactName
    {
        get { return contactName; }
        set { contactName = value; }
    }

    private string contactTitle;
    public string ContactTitle
    {
        get { return contactTitle; }
        set { contactTitle = value; }
    }
```

Example 10-18. NorthWindCustomer (continued)

```csharp
    private string address;
    public string Address
    {
        get { return address; }
        set { address = value; }
    }

    private string city;
    public string City
    {
        get { return city; }
        set { city = value; }
    }

    private string region;
    public string Region
    {
        get { return region; }
        set { region = value; }
    }

    private string postalCode;
    public string PostalCode
    {
        get { return postalCode; }
        set { postalCode = value; }
    }

    private string country;
    public string Country
    {
        get { return country; }
        set { country = value; }
    }

    private string phone;
    public string Phone
    {
        get { return phone; }
        set { phone = value; }
    }

    private string fax;
    public string Fax
    {
        get { return fax; }
        set { fax = value; }
    }
```

Example 10-18. NorthWindCustomer (continued)

```csharp
public bool Save( )
{
    return true;
}

// default constructor
public NorthWindCustomer( )
{
    this.customerID = DBNull.Value;
    this.companyName = string.Empty;
    this.contactName = string.Empty;
    this.contactTitle = string.Empty;
    this.address = string.Empty;
    this.city = string.Empty;
    this.region = string.Empty;
    this.postalCode = string.Empty;
    this.country = string.Empty;
    this.phone = string.Empty;
    this.fax = string.Empty;
}

// Business object representing a Customer from the Northwind database
public NorthWindCustomer(string customerID)
{
    string connectionString =
    "Data Source=Brahams;Initial Catalog=Northwind;Integrated Security=True";

    StringBuilder sb =
        new StringBuilder("Select CompanyName, ContactName, ContactTitle,");
    sb.Append(" Address, City, Region, PostalCode, Country, Phone, ");
    sb.Append(" Fax from Customers ");
    sb.Append(" where CustomerID = @customerID");

    // Create connection object, initialize with
    // connection string.
    System.Data.SqlClient.SqlConnection connection =
        new System.Data.SqlClient.SqlConnection(connectionString);

    // declare the command object for the sql statements
    System.Data.SqlClient.SqlCommand command =
        new System.Data.SqlClient.SqlCommand(sb.ToString( ), connection);

    SqlParameter param =
        command.Parameters.AddWithValue("@customerID", customerID);
    param.DbType = DbType.String;
    param.Direction = ParameterDirection.Input;
    SqlDataReader dataReader = null;
    try
    {
```

Example 10-18. NorthWindCustomer (continued)

```
            connection.Open( );
            dataReader = command.ExecuteReader( );
            if (dataReader != null && dataReader.Read( ))
            {
                this.companyName = dataReader["companyName"].ToString( );
                this.contactName = dataReader["contactName"].ToString( );
                this.contactTitle = dataReader["contactTitle"].ToString( );
                this.address = dataReader["address"].ToString( );
                this.city = dataReader["city"].ToString( );
                this.region = dataReader["region"].ToString( );
                this.postalCode = dataReader["postalCode"].ToString( );
                this.country = dataReader["country"].ToString( );
                this.phone = dataReader["phone"].ToString( );
                this.fax = dataReader["fax"].ToString( );
            }
            else
            {
                throw new ApplicationException(
                    "Data not found for customer ID" + customerID);
            }
        }
        finally
        {
            try
            {
                if (dataReader != null)
                {
                    dataReader.Close( );
                }
                connection.Close( );
            }
            catch (SqlException)
            {
                // handle the exception here
                throw;
            }
        }
    }           // end constructor
}               // end class
```

This code extracts information about a given customer (based on the CustomerID) from the database and creates instance data from that database-bound data. It starts by creating a parameterized select statement (the at-sign [@] in front of CustomerID indicates it is a parameter that is passed in) that extracts the fields needed to create the business object:

```
StringBuilder sb =
    new StringBuilder("Select CompanyName, ContactName, ContactTitle,");
sb.Append(" Address, City, Region, PostalCode, Country, Phone, ");
sb.Append(" Fax from Customers ");
sb.Append(" where CustomerID = @customerID");
```

The code creates a connection and command object in the normal way and then adds the parameter with customerID as the value:

```
SqlParameter param = command.Parameters.AddWithValue("@customerID", customerID);
param.DbType = DbType.String;
param.Direction = ParameterDirection.Input;
```

Within the try block, the connection is opened, and a DataReader is fetched based on the parameterized selection statement:

```
connection.Open( );
dataReader = command.ExecuteReader( );
```

Assuming you get back data (and it is an exception if you don't), you will populate the fields of the business object from the columns within dataReader:

```
if (dataReader != null && dataReader.Read( ))
{
    this.companyName = dataReader["companyName"].ToString( );
    this.contactName = dataReader["contactName"].ToString( );
    this.contactTitle = dataReader["contactTitle"].ToString( );
    this.address = dataReader["address"].ToString( );
    this.city = dataReader["city"].ToString( );
    this.region = dataReader["region"].ToString( );
    this.postalCode = dataReader["postalCode"].ToString( );
    this.country = dataReader["country"].ToString( );
    this.phone = dataReader["phone"].ToString( );
    this.fax = dataReader["fax"].ToString( );
}
```

After you close the DataReader and the connection, your object is fully instantiated and can be used to bind data in the GridView.

In the example shown, the data in the database is isomorphic with the fields in the business object, but in a real-world application, the customer business object might be larger, smaller, or more complex than the data stored in a single table in the database.

When the application is run, the GridView is bound to the ObjectDataSource as previous GridViews have been bound to SqlDataSources, and the data is displayed appropriately based on the bound columns you chose earlier, as shown in Figure 10-18.

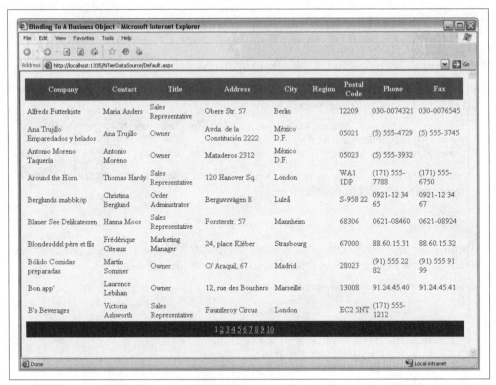

Figure 10-18. Binding to a business object

CHAPTER 11

Forms-Based Security

Back in the primitive days of personal computing, when each user's computer stood alone and isolated, security was not such a big deal. Until computers became networked and viruses were let loose as a scourge on the Internet, security for most PCs meant screen-saver passwords and a lock on the office door.

All that has changed. Today's computers are interconnected in myriad ways, on local networks and over the Internet. The pipes of data that connect your machine to the rest of the world are tremendously beneficial, but at the same time potentially harmful, opening your machine to outsiders. Some of those outsiders are malicious or just plain unwelcome. In any case, it is the job of security to let the good stuff in and keep the bad stuff out.

As part of the .NET Framework, ASP.NET 2.0 has a robust security infrastructure. ASP.NET is designed to work with Microsoft Internet Information Server (IIS), Windows 2000/XP/2003, and the NTFS filesystem. Consequently, there is tight integration with the security provided inherently in those environments. If you are on an intranet and are certain that all your clients will be using Windows and Internet Explorer, there are features you can use to make your job as software developer easier. Alternatively, you can implement your security system independent of Windows and NTFS using the new forms-based security controls.

The fundamental role of security in ASP.NET is to restrict access to portions of a web site. It does this through the following methods:

Authentication
  Verifying that a client is who he says he is.

Authorization
  Determining whether the client has permission to access the resource he is requesting.

Impersonation

ASP.NET assumes the role of the user gaining access, limiting system access to that which is allowed to the user.

Delegation

A more powerful form of impersonation that allows remote resources to be accessed by the web server while it is impersonating the client.

The decision to allow or deny access is based on Windows 2000/XP/2003 and NTFS security features in conjunction with IIS or by verifying credentials against a security database. ASP.NET 2.0 makes creating a security database simple, setting up all the tables you need for authentication and authorization and for personalization and role-based access.

Security in ASP.NET is a two-layered process, as shown in Figure 11-1. All web requests are first handled by IIS. This gives IIS security a chance to accept or reject the request. If the request is accepted by IIS, it will be passed to ASP.NET, where it will be again subjected to a security decision and accepted or rejected. The security systems of IIS and ASP.NET are independent of each other. They can be used independently or in coordination, as will be described later in this chapter.

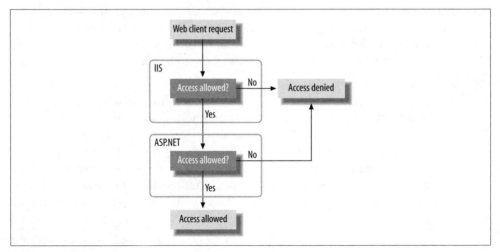

Figure 11-1. Security overview

Authentication

Authentication is the process of ensuring that clients are who they claim to be. Authentication is accomplished using *credentials*, or some form of identification. The requesting client presents the credentials to IIS and the ASP.NET application, usually in the form of a username and password.

The credentials are validated against some authority. Depending on how authentication is configured, that authority might be Windows 2000/XP/2003 security, or it might be a store of names, passwords, and rights maintained in a configuration file such as *web.config*, a relational database such as SQL Server, or an XML file.

Authentication is not required. If no authentication is performed, then the client will be an *anonymous* user. By default, all web sites allow anonymous access. However, if you need to restrict access to any part of the web site, authentication is a necessary step.

If the system cannot identify a user based on the credentials presented and if anonymous users are disallowed, then access will be denied. If the system can identify the user, then that user will be considered an authenticated identity and allowed to proceed on to authorization. Sometimes the identity is known as a *principal*.

Authentication is provided through code modules called *authentication providers*. Authentication providers are enabled using the ASP.NET configuration files, either *machine.config* or the copy of *web.config* in the application virtual root directory. (For a complete description of the configuration files, see Chapter 18.)

A typical entry in a configuration file to enable authentication would look like the following:

```
<configuration>
    <system.web>
        <authentication mode="Windows" />
    </system.web>
</configuration>
```

The mode attribute determines which authentication provider is used. There are four possible values for the mode attribute, as shown in Table 11-1. Each of these authentication modes will be described in the following sections.

Table 11-1. Values of the Authentication key's mode attribute

Mode value	Description
None	No authentication will be performed. Enables anonymous access.
Windows	Windows authentication will be used in conjunction with IIS. This is the default.
Passport	Centralized commercial authentication service offered by Microsoft to web site developers, providing single logon across web sites.
Forms	Unauthenticated requests are redirected to a web page that gathers credentials from the user and submits them to the application for authentication.

Anonymous Access

Anonymous access occurs when a web application does not need to know the identity of users. In this case, credentials are not requested by IIS, and authentication is not performed. Allowing anonymous access is the default configuration for web sites.

To configure IIS to disable anonymous authentication, use the Computer Management console or the Internet Services console. Click Start → Settings → Control Panel → Administrative Tools. Now you have a choice of two ways to get to the same place. Click on Internet Services Manager or Computer Management.

From either, you get the Microsoft Management Console (MMC), which is used throughout Windows for displaying and controlling many system functions. In the left pane is a hierarchical tree structure showing resources relevant to the aspect(s) of the computer being managed. The right pane contains the child nodes of the currently selected node on the left.

From Computer Management, select Services and Applications in the left-hand pane, then drill down to IIS, then Web Sites, then Default Web Site. From Internet Services Manager go directly to IIS, then Web Sites, then Default Web Site. At this point, you can right-click on Default Web Site to set the properties for the entire server (that is, all the web applications on the server), or you can drill down further to the application virtual directory to set the properties for a specific application. In either case, right-clicking will present a menu, from which you select Properties. Select the Directory Security tab. This tab is shown in Figure 11-2.

Figure 11-2. ASPNet Directory Security tab

The Directory Security tab has sections for enabling server certificates and imposing restrictions based on Internet Protocol (IP) address and domain name. (This latter section will be available only for Windows 2000 Server and Windows 2003 and will be grayed out for Windows 2000 Professional and Windows XP Professional.)

Click the Edit button in the "Anonymous access and authentication control" section. You will get the dialog box shown in Figure 11-3.

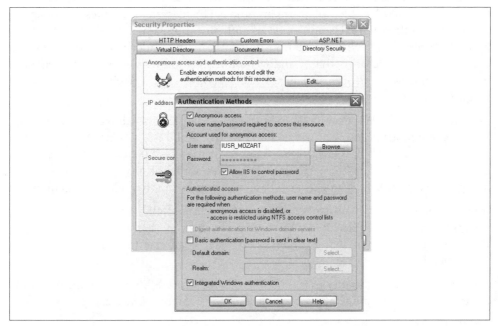

Figure 11-3. Authentication Methods dialog box

If the "Anonymous access" checkbox is checked, then any request will be accepted by IIS without credentials being requested by IIS and with no authentication performed. This is the default configuration for web sites.

Since all requests made to IIS must have credentials, anonymous requests are assigned to a standard user account. This account defaults to IUSR_MachineName, where MachineName is the name of the web server. You can change the account assigned to anonymous access by clicking on the Edit button in that section. The IUSR_MachineName account is a built-in account, created when IIS is installed on the machine. It has a limited set of permissions, just enough to allow access to the web site.

Anonymous access is appropriate if your application has no need to know the username or password of the person or application calling on the application, and if the information or service contained in the application is considered public. It is also possible to personalize a site without requiring login through the use of cookies. This would be useful where the content on the site is public, but you want to preserve user preferences or previous selections.

Of all the security configurations available to a web site, anonymous access provides the best performance but is the least secure.

Windows Authentication

Windows authentication offers the developer a way to leverage the security built into the Windows 2000/XP/2003 platform and the NTFS filesystem. It takes advantage of the security built into IIS. Using Windows authentication, a high level of security can be built into an ASP.NET application with little or no code being written by the developer. The trade-off is that Windows authentication only works if the client is using a Windows platform and has a user account on the web server or in the Windows domain to which the web server belongs.

To configure IIS for Windows authentication, follow the steps above for configuring IIS for anonymous access, shown in Figures 11-2 and 11-3. Uncheck the "Anonymous access" checkbox. Check one or more of the checkboxes under "Authenticated access". There are three types of Windows authentication: basic, digest, and integrated Windows authentication. These are described in the following sections.

If more than one type of authentication access is checked, IIS will first attempt to use Integrated Windows authentication if it is checked. If that fails, it will attempt Digest authentication if that is checked. Finally, if all else fails, it will use Basic authentication.

To use the Windows identity that IIS authenticates with ASP.NET, you must include the following section in the appropriate *web.config* configuration file:

```
<configuration>
  <system.web>
    <authentication mode="Windows" />
  </system.web>
</configuration>
```

Basic authentication

Basic authentication is the simplest and least secure type of Windows authentication. In this type of authentication, the browser presents a standard Windows-supplied dialog box for the user to enter his credentials, consisting of a username and password. These credentials are compared against valid user accounts on the domain server or on the local machine. If the credentials match, the user will be authenticated and access to the requested resource will be provided.

The reason that basic authentication is the least secure method of authentication is that the username and password are sent to the server encoded as a Base64 string. However, they are not encrypted. The username and password are available to your application code in clear text. A skilled person using a network sniffer can easily intercept and extract the username and password. Therefore, basic authentication is best suited for those applications where a high level of security is not a requirement, or no other authentication method will work.

You can use basic authentication in conjunction with Secure Sockets Layer (SSL) to achieve a high level of security. This encrypts the information passed over the network and prevents the password from being deciphered, though the performance hit from SSL is significant.

To set the authentication method to Basic, refer back to Figure 11-3. Uncheck "Anonymous access", "Digest authentication", and "Integrated Windows authentication" if any of them is checked. Then check "Basic authentication". That is all that is necessary to implement basic authentication in IIS. To configure ASP.NET, include the following section in the relevant *web.config* configuration file:

```
<configuration>
  <system.web>
    <authentication mode="Windows" />
  </system.web>
</configuration>
```

By default, the local domain of the web server is active and is used for basic authentication. If you wish to authenticate against a different domain, click the Edit button and select a different default domain.

Basic authentication works across proxy servers and through firewalls. It is supported by essentially all browsers. Basic authentication allows for delegation from one computer to another but only for a single hop, i.e., only to one other computer. If you need to access resources beyond the first hop, you will need to log on locally to each of the other computers in the call chain. This is possible since the username and password are available to your application in clear text.

Digest authentication

Digest authentication is similar to basic authentication, except that the credentials are encrypted and a hash is sent over the network to the server. It is a fairly secure method of authentication though not as secure as basic authentication used with SSL, Windows integrated authentication, or certificate authentication. Like basic authentication, digest works through firewalls and proxy servers. Digest authentication does not support delegation, i.e., impersonated requests to remote machines.

Digest authentication works only with Internet Explorer 5.x and higher and .NET web services. It requires that the web server is running on Windows 2000, XP, or Server 2003 and that all users have Windows accounts stored in an Active Directory. Because of these requirements, digest authentication is generally limited to intranet applications.

When the user requests a resource that requires digest authentication, the browser presents the same credentials dialog box as with basic authentication. The username and password are combined with a server-specified string value and encrypted to a hash value. This hash value is sent over the network. Since the server knows the string used to create the hash, it is able to decrypt the hash and extract the username and password. These are compared with the user accounts to determine if the user is authenticated, and if so, if the user has permission to access the requested resource.

To set the authentication method to Digest, refer back to Figure 11-3. Uncheck "Anonymous access", "Basic authentication", and "Integrated Windows authentication" if any of them are checked. Then check "Digest authentication". The Digest authentication checkbox will be unavailable if the machine is unconnected to a domain.

In addition, to configure ASP.NET you must include the following section in the relevant *web.config* configuration file:

```
<configuration>
  <system.web>
    <authentication mode="Windows" />
  </system.web>
</configuration>
```

For a user to be able to use digest authentication, the user account must be set to store the password using reversible encryption. To do this, go to the management console for Active Directory Users and Computers on the domain controller. Open the domain you want to administer and double-click on the username that you want to use digest authentication. On the Account Options tab, select "Store password using reversible encryption".

Integrated Windows authentication

Integrated Windows authentication uses the current users' credentials presented at the time they logged into Windows. A dialog box is never presented to the user to gather credentials unless the Windows logon credentials are inadequate for a requested resource.

Integrated Windows authentication comprises two different types of authentication: NT LAN Manager (NTLM) challenge/response, and Kerberos. NTLM is the protocol used in Windows NT, Windows 2000 work groups, and environments with mixed NT and 2000 domains. If the environment is a pure Windows 2000 or Windows XP Active Directory domain, then NTLM is automatically disabled and the authentication protocol switches to Kerberos.

 Kerberos is named after the three-headed, dragon-tailed dog (Cerberus) who guarded the entrance to Hades in Greek mythology.

Integrated Windows authentication works well in intranet environments, where all the users have Windows domain accounts and presumably all users are using IE 3.01 or later. It is secure since the encrypted password is not sent over the network. Integrated Windows authentication does not work through a proxy server. NTLM does not support delegation though Kerberos does.

Integrated Windows authentication does not require any login dialog boxes. This is more convenient for the user and is well suited to automated applications, such as those using web services.

To set the authentication method to Integrated Windows authentication, refer back to Figure 11-3. Uncheck "Anonymous access", "Basic authentication", and "Digest authentication" if any of them are checked. Then check "Integrated Windows authentication".

In addition, to configure ASP.NET, you must include the following section in the relevant *web.config* configuration file:

```
<configuration>
    <system.web>
        <authentication mode="Windows" />
    </system.web>
</configuration>
```

Kerberos is faster than NTLM though neither is as fast as basic authentication or well-designed custom authentication methods. If you are anticipating a large number of concurrent users or are delegating security to back-end servers (such as SQL Server), then scalability may become an issue with Integrated Windows Authentication.

Role-based security

Windows 2000/XP/2003 also provides *role-based security*. In this security scheme, *roles*, also known as *groups*, are defined. A role defines the range of actions and access that is permitted to users assigned to the role. Users are assigned to one or more roles, or groups. For example, if a user is a member of the Administrator role, then that person will have complete access to the computer and all its resources. If a user is a member only of the Guest group, then he will have very few permissions.

Groups and users are assigned by going to Control Panel, clicking on Administrative Tools, and then clicking on Computer Management. You will see the MMC console shown in Figure 11-4.

All the groups shown in Figure 11-4 were installed by default.

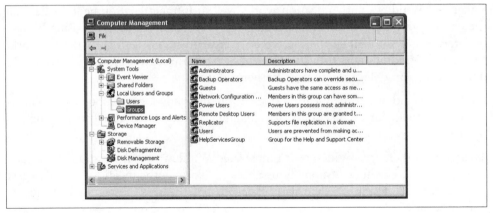

Figure 11-4. Groups in the Computer Management console

Windows users log in to the operating system, providing a username and password. These constitute their *credentials*. At login time, those credentials are authenticated by the operating system. Once their credentials are verified, they will have certain permissions assigned, depending on which role(s) they have been assigned. As you will see, these credentials and roles are used by ASP.NET if the web application makes use of Windows authentication.

When a client requests an ASP.NET page or web service, all the requests are handled by IIS. If Windows authentication is the currently configured authentication scheme, then IIS will hand off the authentication chores to the Windows NT, Windows 2000, or Windows XP operating system. The user is authenticated based on the credentials that were presented when they first logged into their Windows system. These credentials are verified against the Windows user accounts contained on the web server or on the domain controller that handles the web server.

Passport Authentication

Passport is a centralized authentication service provided by Microsoft. It offers a single logon for all web sites that have registered with the Passport service, accepted the license agreement, paid the requisite fee, and installed the Passport SDK.

When a client makes a request to a Passport protected site, the server detects that the request does not contain a valid Passport ticket as part of the query string. The client is redirected to the Passport Logon Service along with encrypted parameters about the original request. The Passport Logon Service presents the client with a logon form, which the user fills out and posts back to the logon server using the SSL protocol. If the logon server authenticates the user, the request is redirected back to the original site, this time with the authentication ticket encrypted in the query string. When the original site receives this new request, it detects the authentication ticket and authenticates the request.

Subsequent requests to the same site are authenticated using the same authentication ticket. Provisions exist for expiring the authentication ticket and for using the same ticket at other sites.

For sites that have implemented Passport and installed the Passport SDK, the Passport-AuthenticationModule provides a wrapper around the SDK for ASP.NET applications.

Passport uses Triple-DES encryption to encrypt and decrypt the authentication key when passed as part of the query string. When a site registers with the Passport service, it is given a site-specific key that is used for this encryption and decryption.

Using delegation is impossible if you are using Passport authentication.

To use Passport authentication, ASP.NET must be configured by including the following section in the relevant *web.config* configuration file:

```
<configuration>
    <system.web>
        <authentication mode="Passport" />
    </system.web>
</configuration>
```

Forms Authentication

Integrated Windows authentication offers many advantages to the developer who is deploying to an environment where all the clients are known to have user accounts in the requisite Windows domain or Active Directory and are known to be using a recent version of Internet Explorer. However, in many web applications, one or both of these conditions will not be true. In these cases, forms authentication allows the developer to collect credentials from the client and authenticate them.

In *forms authentication*, a login form is presented to the user to gather credentials. This form does not necessarily authenticate the user, but submits the credentials, via form post, to application code that performs the authentication. The application code generally authenticates by comparing the credentials submitted with usernames and passwords contained in a data store of some sort. ASP.NET 2.0 does most of the work of setting up the database to support Forms Authentication as described below.

The credentials submitted by the login form are sent unencrypted over the network and are vulnerable to interception by a skilled and malicious user of a network sniffer. A forms authentication scheme can be made fully secure by sending the credentials and all subsequent authenticated requests using the SSL protocol.

Once the client is authenticated, the server returns a small piece of data, called a *cookie*, back to the client. This authentication cookie is then passed from the client to the server on each subsequent request, which tells the server that this client has been authenticated. If a request is made without a valid authentication cookie, then the user will be automatically redirected to the login form, where credentials are again gathered and authenticated.

Forms-Based Authentication in Detail

ASP.NET 2.0 forms-based security is based on a set of tables that must be created in your database, typically SQL Server or SQL Server Express. Fortunately, ASP.NET provides a utility named *aspnet_regsql.exe*, located in the *<Drive:>\Windows\ Microsoft.NET\Framework\versionNumber* folder on your Web server, that sets up the tables for you. (The version number will be determined by which version of the 2.0 framework you have installed on your machine.) This utility program will create the required database and all its tables.

The easiest way to use this utility is to run aspnet_regsql.exe utility from the .NET command box with no arguments. A wizard will be started that will walk you through the process.

 You can set up the tables using the ASP.NET Web Site Administration Tool, as described later.

The database is *.\SQLEXPRESS*, the authentication type is Windows, and the name of the db is *aspnetdb*. For more details, see the MSDN article "Installing the SQL Server Provider Database".

Create the Application

To begin, create an empty directory called *Security*. In the IIS manager (accessed through the Control Panel), create a virtual directory to point to the *Security* folder, and after it is created, right-click the new virtual directory and select Properties.

In the Properties window, click the ASP.NET tab, and then click Edit Configuration. Within the ASP.NET Configuration Settings dialog, click the Authentication tab, and within that tab, set the Authentication mode to Forms, and the Membership provider class to AspNetSqlMembershipProvider, as shown in Figure 11-5.

Click OK to close all the dialogs. A *web.config* file is created (or updated) for you in the Security folder, as shown in Example 11-1.

Figure 11-5. Set Authentication to Forms

Example 11-1. web.config file generated

```
<?xml version="1.0" encoding="utf-8"?>
<configuration xmlns="http://schemas.microsoft.com/.NetConfiguration/v2.0"
    <system.web>
        <authentication mode="Forms" />
        <membership defaultProvider="AspNetSqlMembershipProvider" />
    </system.web>
</configuration>
```

In VS2005, create a new web site in the same location. A dialog box will open warning that you have a web site in that location; choose Open Existing Site, as shown in Figure 11-6.

Figure 11-6. Open Existing Site

This instructs Visual Studio to use the site you've created, complete with the *web.config* file available for that site.

Creating accounts

Your initial goal will be to have two pages: a default page that displays different information to users who are logged in than to users who are not yet logged in and a login page that allows the user to log in.

To have users log in, however, you must create a database of users. So, you'll want a page that lets your users create an account. Let's start there, by creating a new page called *CreateAccount.aspx*. Click the Website → Add New Item menu item or right-click the top level folder in the Solution Explorer and select Add New Item. From the Add New Item dialog, select Web Form and type in the form name. Be sure to select the correct language from the drop-down.

Click the Design tab for your page, and then click the Login tab in the toolbox. Drag an instance of CreateUserWizard onto your page, as shown in Figure 11-7.

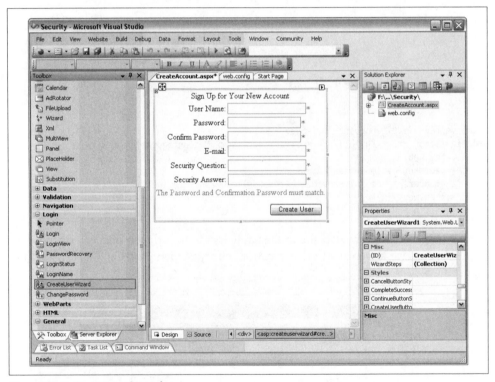

Figure 11-7. CreateUserWizard

The CreateUserWizard prompts the user for a username, a password (twice), an email address, and a security question and answer. All of this is configurable through the

declaration is created by this control in the content file or, more commonly, through the smart tag, as shown in Figure 11-8.

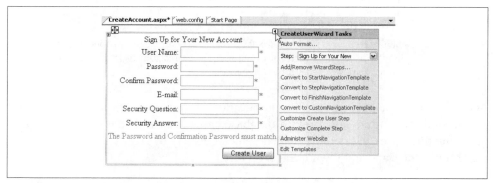

Figure 11-8. CreateUserWizard tasks

Click on the control and scroll through the Properties window to find the `ContinueDestinationPageURL`. Click the Browse button and choose the create account page (*CreateAccount.aspx*), so you'll be brought back to the same page after the new user is confirmed. Finally, set the *CreateAccount.aspx* page as your Start page and fire up the application. You will be prompted to add a new user, as shown in Figure 11-9.

Figure 11-9. Testing Create Account wizard

When you click Create User, the account is created, and you are brought to a confirmation screen. Click Continue, and you are brought back to the Create Account screen to create a second account.

By default, passwords must be "strong," which is defined as having at least six characters and at least one element of at least three of the four types of characters: English upper case, English lower case, Arabic numerals, and special characters (such as ! and @). This is documented in the MSDN article "Strong Password Enforcement."

The `CreateUserWizard` has a `PasswordRegularExpression` property that allows you to substitute your own regular expression to determine the characteristics of acceptable passwords.

Add a couple of accounts, stop the application, and examine your database. You should find that within `SqlExpress` a database named `aspnetdb` has extensive tables, including the `aspnet_Users` table, which you can display by right-clicking and choosing Show Table Data, as shown in Figure 11-10.

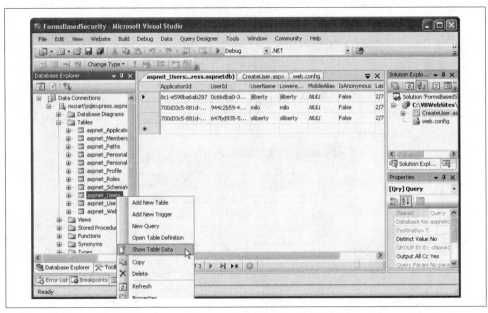

Figure 11-10. Personalization Database Updated

Creating the welcome page

With your user database in place, you are ready to create your welcome page that will welcome the logged in user.

Add a new page called *Welcome.aspx*. Drag a `LoginStatus` control from the Login section of the toolbox onto the new page.

A link marked Login is placed on the page. Click the smart tag and you'll see you are looking at the template for when no user is logged in, as shown in Figure 11-11.

Figure 11-11. Not Logged In

You can set the properties of the `LoginStatus` control, for example, to change the text of the link with the Login Text and Logout Text properties. You can also drop down the view window to see the link and text for Logged In status.

Drag a `LoginView` control from the toolbox, and drop it onto the page below the `LoginStatus` control. Here you may enter text and controls that will be displayed based on whether or not the user is logged in. This control has two views, visible from the smart tag: Anonymous Template and Logged In Template. Which template's contents will be displayed will be decided by whether or not the user has yet logged in.

Click on the smart tag and confirm that the view is set to Anonymous Template and type some text in the box, as shown in Figure 11-12.

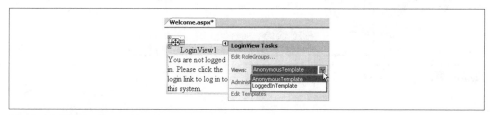

Figure 11-12. Not Logged In view

Now set the `LoggedInTemplate`. Since the user will be logged in when this template is displayed, you can use the `LoginName` control to welcome the user by name. After typing some text onto the `LoginView` template, drag the `LoginName` control right onto the `LoginView` template, as shown in Figure 11-13.

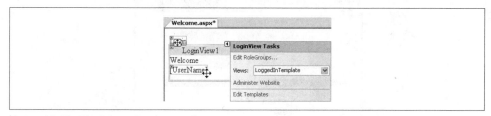

Figure 11-13. The Login Name control

Creating the Login page

You are ready to create the Login page for users to log in to the system (after having created an account). Add a new page named *Login.aspx*. Change to Design view, and drag a Login control onto the page. To make this look a bit more professional, click on the AutoFormat link from the smart tag, as shown in Figure 11-14, and pick one of the predefined formats for the control, as shown in Figure 11-15.

Figure 11-14. Creating the Login control

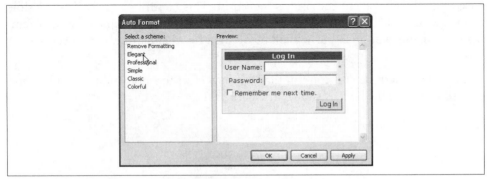

Figure 11-15. Pick Auto Format for Login control

Make sure that the Welcome page is the start page and run the application. The welcome page will display its "Not Logged In" message. Click the link to go to the log in page.

Enter a false name or an incorrect password. The Login control will show you your mistake, as shown in Figure 11-16.

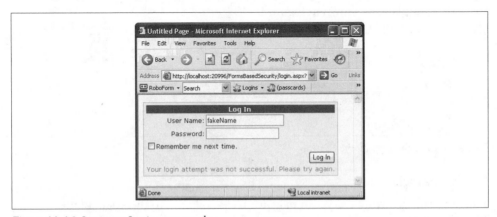

Figure 11-16. Incorrect Logins are caught

Enter the correct name and password, and you are brought back to the Welcome page. Your status as logged in is noted, you are greeted by name, and you are offered the opportunity to log out, as shown in Figure 11-17.

Figure 11-17. Logged In view

Adding a Password Reminder

To add a password reminder, you must change your existing login control to a template by clicking on the smart tag and choosing "Convert to Template," as shown in Figure 11-18.

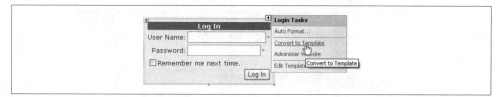

Figure 11-18. Convert to Template

The display will change to a template you can modify, adding a link titled (for example) Recover Password, as shown in Figure 11-19.

Set the NavigateURL to the name of the page that will hold your PasswordRecovery control, and then click the smart tag and choose End Editing.

Your next step is to create the new *.aspx* page to link to (*RecoverPW.aspx*). Drag a PasswordRecovery control onto this new page, and click the smart tag to choose the view you wish to edit, as shown in Figure 11-20.

In the Properties window for the PasswordRecovery control, set the SuccessPageUrl property to Login.aspx. You may want to confirm or change the Success text and other text fields (e.g., QuestionInstructionText, QuestionLabelText).

For password recovery to work, you must place the sender's email address in the smtpMail config section, in the PasswordRecovery.MailDefinition.From field, or in the Sending Mail event handler.

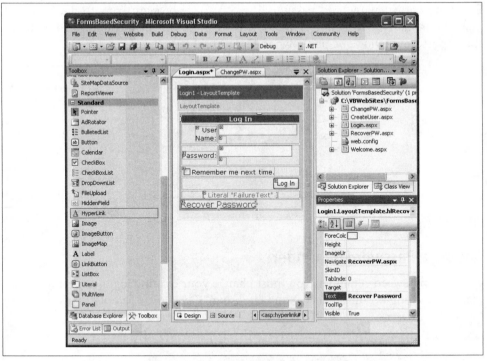

Figure 11-19. Adding Password hyperlink to Login Template

Figure 11-20. Password Recovery control

On the Welcome page, add a link to *ChangePW.aspx* (which you'll create shortly), and while you're at it, add a link for *CreateAccount.asxp* in case you want to add any additional users.

Create the *ChangePW.aspx* page and drag on a `ChangePassword` control (see Figure 11-21). Use the smart tag to format the control to match the others you've created.

Set the `ContinueDestinationPageURL` property to *Login.aspx*. On *Login.aspx*, make sure the `DestinationPageURL` property of the Login control is set to *Welcome.aspx*. You may want to confirm or change the Success text as well as the other text fields (e.g., `ChangePasswordTitleText`, `ChangePasswordFailure` text).

Figure 11-21. Change Password Control

Run the application. You should be able to log in and out, change your password, and so forth. You have added the essential aspects of form-based security without writing any code.

Add Roles to ASP.NET Accounts

You can assign a set of permissions to a group of people. You do so in two steps: first, you assign permissions to a *role*, and then you assign users to the roles you've created. Any given user may be in more than one role (for example, administrator and manager). The permissions you assign to each role may determine access to a page, or it may determine the content of a given page displayed to members of that role.

Creating a New Application with RolesTo demonstrates how to create roles and assign users to those roles; you'll need to create a new application, setting the appropriate IIS configuration. In the previous exercise, you created the directory for your application before you created the application itself. To see that there is more than one way to accomplish creating the relationship between physical and virtual directories, let's reverse the order.

Start by creating a new web site from within VS2005 and naming it *ASPSecurityRoles*.

Find the directory in which the *Default.aspx* page is held by clicking on the page in Solution Explorer and looking at the Properties window. Use the IIS administrator to create a virtual directory and call it *ASPSecurityRoles* that points to that physical directory. Right-click on the virtual directory and select properties.

Click the ASP.NET tab and then click the Edit Configuration button (as you did in the previous exercise). Again, click the Authentication tab and set Forms authentication, but this time check the Role management enabled checkbox, as shown in Figure 11-22.

When you click OK and close the configuration dialogs, you'll find that a *web.config* file has been added to the directory, with a system.web element that defines the authentication mode and the membership provider and enables roleManager.

```
<system.web>
    <authentication mode="Forms" />
    <membership defaultProvider="AspNetSqlMembershipProvider" />
    <roleManager enabled="True" defaultProvider="AspNetSqlRoleProvider" />
</system.web>
```

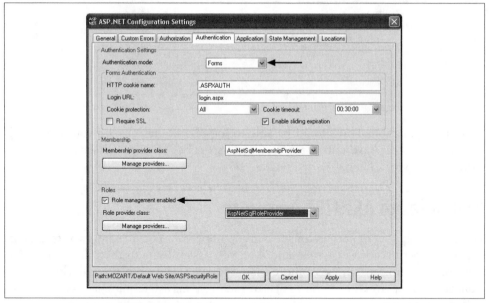

Figure 11-22. Role management enabled

This time, the roleManager element has been added and its enabled attribute has been set to True.

You need to add the pages you had in the previous exercise to this one. The preferred way is to choose the menu choice WebSite → CopyWebsite command.

When you click the Connect to button, as shown in Figure 11-23 (see the cursor), the Open Web Site dialog opens allowing you to navigate to the folder for the original exercise, which we called *Security*. After you pick the folder, the Remote web site is filled in, as shown in Figure 11-24.

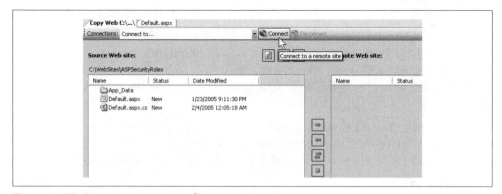

Figure 11-23. Connect to previous web site

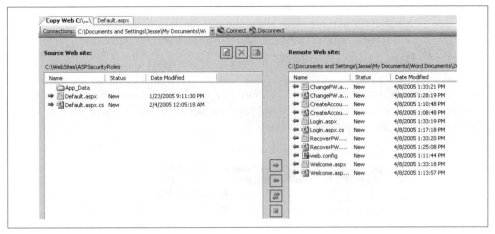

Figure 11-24. Copy Web Site

As you can see, the wizard has detected that you have a *Default.aspx* that is not in the original (i.e., remote) site, and it has found a conflict in that both sites have a *web.config*. You'll want to copy over all the non-conflicted files. To do that, high-light the files you want to copy, using standard Windows selection techniques and click the left-facing arrow, as shown in Figure 11-25.

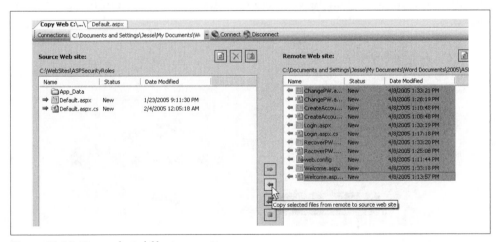

Figure 11-25. Copy selected files to new site

After copying the files, delete the *Default.aspx* and *Default.aspx.cs* files since you won't need them. You can do this right from the Copy Web page by highlighting the files in the Source Web Site list, right-clicking, and selecting Delete.

Check your *web.config* file and make sure that you have the line:

```
<membership defaultProvider="AspNetSqlMembershipPRovider" />
```

from the previous example.

Add a third hyperlink to the Logged In Template on the Welcome page, with the text "Manage Roles" that will link to a new *ManageRoles.aspx page*. (Click on End Template Editing, as shown in Figure 11-26.)

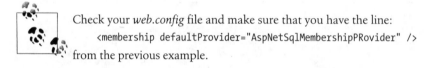

Figure 11-26. End Editing Logged In Template

The Manage Roles page, *ManageRoles.aspx*, has a somewhat complex layout since it must display the list of roles and the list of users supported by your site, as well as which users have been assigned which roles. The page is shown in Figure 11-27. The controls are listed in Table 11-2 and the complete *.aspx* listing is shown in Example 11-2 though it may be easier to download this code from the O'Reilly or Liberty Associates web sites.

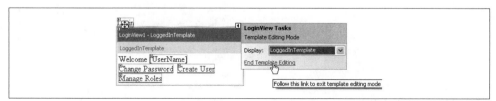

Figure 11-27. ManageRoles.aspx

Table 11-2. Controls in ManageRoles.aspx

Control name	Control type	Control text
linkHome	Hyperlink	Home Page
Msg	Label	
RolesListBox	ListBox	
btnAddUsersToRole	Button	Add User(s) to Role
btnCreateRole	Button	Create new Role
pnlCreateRole	Panel	
Label2	Label	New Role:
txtNewRole	TextBox	
btnAddRole	Button	Add
UsersInRoleGrid	GridView	

Example 11-2. Manage Roles page

```
<%@ Page Language="C#" AutoEventWireup="true" CodeFile="ManageRoles.aspx.cs"
Inherits="ManageRoles_aspx" %>

<!DOCTYPE html PUBLIC "-//W3C//DTD XHTML 1.1//EN" "http://www.w3.org/TR/xhtml11/DTD/
xhtml11.dtd">

<html xmlns="http://www.w3.org/1999/xhtml" >
<head id="Head1" runat="server">
   <title>Manage Roles</title>
</head>
<body>
   <form id="form1" runat="server">
   <h3>Role Membership
     <asp:HyperLink ID="linkHome" Runat="server" NavigateUrl="Welcome.aspx">Home page</asp:
HyperLink>
   </h3>
   <asp:Label id="Msg" ForeColor="maroon" runat="server" /><BR>
   <table CellPadding="3" border="0">
    <tr>
     <td valign="top">Roles:</td>
     <td valign="top" style="width: 186px"><asp:ListBox id="RolesListBox"
         runat="server" Rows="8" AutoPostBack="True">
     </asp:ListBox></td>
     <td valign="top">Users:</td>
     <td valign="top"><asp:ListBox id="UsersListBox" DataTextField="Username"
       Rows="8" SelectionMode="Multiple" runat="server" /></td>
     <td valign="top" visible="false">
         <table>
         <tr>
           <td>
              <asp:Button Text="Add User(s) to Role" id="btnAddUsersToRole"
              runat="server" OnClick="AddUsers_OnClick" />
           </td>
         </tr>
```

Example 11-2. Manage Roles page (continued)

```
    <tr>
        <td>
            <asp:Button Text="Create new Role" id="btnCreateRole"
            runat="server" OnClick="CreateRole_OnClick"
            Width="170px" Height="24px" />
        </td>
    </tr>
    <tr>
    <td>
    <asp:Panel ID="pnlCreateRole" Runat="server" Width="259px"
    Height="79px" Visible="False" BackColor="#E0E0E0">
        <br />
          
        <asp:Label ID="Label2" Runat="server" Text="New Role:"
         Width="72px" Height="19px"/>
        <asp:TextBox ID="txtNewRole" Runat="server"/> <br />
          <br />
                  
                  
        <asp:Button ID="btnAddRole" Runat="server"
          Text="Add" OnClick="btnAddRole_Click"
          Width="64px" Height="24px" /><br />
    </asp:Panel>

    </td>
    </tr>
    </table>
  </td>
 </tr>
 <tr>
  <td valign="top">Users In Role:</td>
  <td valign="top" style="width: 186px">
      <asp:GridView runat="server" CellPadding="4" id="UsersInRoleGrid"
                    AutoGenerateColumns="false" Gridlines="None"
                    CellSpacing="0"
    OnRowCommand="UsersInRoleGrid_RemoveFromRole">
              <HeaderStyle BackColor="navy" ForeColor="white" />
              <Columns>
               <asp:TemplateField HeaderText="User Name">
                 <ItemTemplate>
                  <%# Container.DataItem.ToString( ) %>
                 </ItemTemplate>
               </asp:TemplateField>
               <asp:ButtonField Text="Remove From Role" ButtonType="Link" />
              </Columns>
      </asp:GridView>
    </td>
  </tr>
 </table>
 </form>
</body>
</html>
```

This page is not designed to be pretty, just useful. It is based on a demonstration *.aspx* page provided by Microsoft with Beta software.

The code-behind page must implement five event handlers:

- `Page_Load`
- `AddUsers_OnClick` (adding users to roles)
- `UsersInRoleGrid_RemoveFromRole` (removing users from roles)
- `CreateRole_OnClick` (opening panel to create a new role)
- `btnAddRole_Click` (adding new role)

To accomplish this, your class will declare three *member variables*:

- A string array named `rolesArray`
- A string array named `usersInRole`
- An instance of `MembershipUserCollection` named `users`

The `MembershipUserCollection` is defined by the framework to hold `MembershipUser` objects (surprise!). A `MembershipUser` object, in turn, is defined by the framework to represent a single user in the membership data store (in this case, the tables created in `SqlServerExpress`). This class exposes information about the user such as the user's email address, and methods such as those needed to change or reset the user's password.

The complete code behind is shown in Example 11-3 and analyzed in detail immediately afterward.

Example 11-3. ManageRoles.aspx Code Behind

```
using System;
using System.Data;
using System.Configuration;
using System.Collections;
using System.Web;
using System.Web.Security;
using System.Web.UI;
using System.Web.UI.WebControls;
using System.Web.UI.WebControls.WebParts;
using System.Web.UI.HtmlControls;

public partial class ManageRoles_aspx : System.Web.UI.Page
{
    // Page events are wired up automatically to methods
    // with the following names:
```

Example 11-3. ManageRoles.aspx Code Behind (continued)

```csharp
    // Page_Load, Page_AbortTransaction, Page_CommitTransaction,
    // Page_DataBinding, Page_Disposed, Page_Error, Page_Init,
    // Page_Init Complete, Page_Load, Page_LoadComplete, Page_PreInit
    // Page_PreLoad, Page_PreRender, Page_PreRenderComplete,
    // Page_SaveStateComplete, Page_Unload

    private string[] rolesArray;
    private string[] usersInRole;
    MembershipUserCollection users;


    protected void Page_Load(object sender, EventArgs e)
    {

        //if ( User.IsInRole("Manager") == false )
        //{
        //     Response.Redirect("NoPrivs.aspx");
        //}
        Msg.Text = string.Empty;
        if ( ! IsPostBack )
        {
            rolesArray = Roles.GetAllRoles( );
            RolesListBox.DataSource = rolesArray;
            RolesListBox.DataBind( );
            users = Membership.GetAllUsers( );
            this.UsersListBox.DataSource = users;
            this.UsersListBox.DataBind( );
        }
        if ( RolesListBox.SelectedItem != null )
        {
            usersInRole = Roles.GetUsersInRole
                    (this.RolesListBox.SelectedItem.Value);
            UsersInRoleGrid.DataSource = usersInRole;
            UsersInRoleGrid.DataBind( );
        }
    }

    protected void AddUsers_OnClick(object sender, EventArgs e)
    {

        if (RolesListBox.SelectedItem == null)
        {
            this.Msg.Text = "Please select a role.";
            return;
        }
        if (UsersListBox.SelectedItem == null)
        {
            Msg.Text = "Please select one or more users";
            return;
        }
```

Example 11-3. ManageRoles.aspx Code Behind (continued)

```
        int sizeOfArray = UsersListBox.GetSelectedIndices( ).Length;
        string[] newUsers = new string[sizeOfArray];

        //for (int i = 0; i < newUsers.Length; i++)
        //{
        //     newUsers[i] =
        //          UsersListBox.Items[UsersListBox.GetSelectedIndices( )[i]].Value;
        //}


        // get the array of selected indices from the (multiselect) list box
        int[] selectedIndices = UsersListBox.GetSelectedIndices( );

        for ( int i = 0; i < newUsers.Length; i++)
        {
            // get the selectedIndex that corresponds to the counter[i]
            int selectedIndex = selectedIndices[i];
            //get the ListItem in the UserListBox Items collection at that offset
            ListItem myListItem = UsersListBox.Items[selectedIndex];
            //get the string that is that ListItem's value property
            string newUser = myListItem.Value;
            //add that string to the newUsers collection of string
            newUsers[i] = newUser;
        }

        // Add users to the selected role
        Roles.AddUsersToRole(newUsers, RolesListBox.SelectedItem.Value);
        usersInRole = Roles.GetUsersInRole(RolesListBox.SelectedItem.Value);
        UsersInRoleGrid.DataSource = usersInRole;
        UsersInRoleGrid.DataBind( );


    }
    protected void CreateRole_OnClick(object sender, EventArgs e)
    {
        this.pnlCreateRole.Visible = true;
    }
    protected void btnAddRole_Click(object sender, EventArgs e)
    {
        if (txtNewRole.Text.Length > 0 )
        {
            string newRole = txtNewRole.Text;
            if ( Roles.RoleExists(newRole) == false )
            {
                Roles.CreateRole(newRole);
                rolesArray = Roles.GetAllRoles( );
                this.RolesListBox.DataSource = rolesArray;
                this.RolesListBox.DataBind( );
            }
        }
        txtNewRole.Text = string.Empty;
        pnlCreateRole.Visible = false;
    }
```

Example 11-3. ManageRoles.aspx Code Behind (continued)

```
    protected void UsersInRoleGrid_RemoveFromRole(
        object sender, GridViewCommandEventArgs e)
    {
        int index = Convert.ToInt32(e.CommandArgument);
        DataBoundLiteralControl theControl = (DataBoundLiteralControl)
                (UsersInRoleGrid.Rows[index].Cells[0].Controls[0]);
        string userName = theControl.Text;
        Roles.RemoveUserFromRole(userName, RolesListBox.SelectedItem.Value);
         usersInRole = Roles.GetUsersInRole(RolesListBox.SelectedItem.Value);
         UsersInRoleGrid.DataSource = usersInRole;
         UsersInRoleGrid.DataBind( );
    }
}
```

Here's how the code works. The logic begins with the CreateRole button's onClick event handler, which makes the CreateRole panel visible:

```
    protected void CreateRole_OnClick(object sender, EventArgs e)
    {
        this.pnlCreateRole.Visible = true;
    }
```

The purpose of this is to make the panel visible, which contains a text box for the user to enter a new role, and an Add button, as shown in Figure 11-28.

Figure 11-28. Create new Role

When you click the Add button in the panel, the btnAddRole_Click event handler is called:

```
    protected void btnAddRole_Click(object sender, EventArgs e)
    {
        if (txtNewRole.Text.Length > 0 )
        {
            string newRole = txtNewRole.Text;
            if ( Roles.RoleExists(newRole) == false )
            {
                Roles.CreateRole(newRole);
                rolesArray = Roles.GetAllRoles( );
                this.RolesListBox.DataSource = rolesArray;
                this.RolesListBox.DataBind( );
            }
        }
        txtNewRole.Text = string.Empty;
        pnlCreateRole.Visible = false;
    }
```

You check to ensure text is in the New Role text box, and then you check to ensure the role does not exist. If it does not, you will create the new role using the static CreateRole method of the Roles class, provided by the framework.

 You do not need an instance of Roles to call CreateRole because CreateRole is static.

You get all the roles by calling the static method GetAllRoles and store the roles in the member array rolesArray, to which you bind the list box. When the role is added, the text box is cleared and the panel is made invisible.

Run the application. If you are starting with a new database, add some users. Next, click Add Roles and add a couple of roles. Click on a role (to highlight it) and one or more users (to highlight the users), and then click Add User(s) to Role. This invokes the AddUsers_OnClick event handler.

You first check to ensure that a role has been selected:

```
protected void AddUsers_OnClick(object sender, EventArgs e)
{

    if (RolesListBox.SelectedItem == null)
    {
        this.Msg.Text = "Please select a role.";
        return;
    }
```

and that at least one user has been selected:

```
if (UsersListBox.SelectedItem == null)
{
    Msg.Text = "Please select one or more users";
    return;
}
```

Create an array to hold the users to be added:

```
int sizeOfArray = UsersListBox.GetSelectedIndices().Length;
string[] newUsers = new string[sizeOfArray];
```

and iterate through the users, retrieving each selected user's name:

```
for (int i = 0; i < newUsers.Length; i++)
{
    newUsers[i] =
        UsersListBox.Items[UsersListBox.GetSelectedIndices()[i]].Value;
}
```

The statement in the for loop is somewhat complicated. The best way to understand it is to rewrite the for loop using interim variables, like this:

```
for ( int i = 0; i < newUsers.Length; i++)
{
```

```
        // get the array of selected indices from the (multiselect) list box
        int[] selectedIndices = UsersListBox.GetSelectedIndices();

        // get the particular selected selectedIndex that corresponds
        // to the counter[i]
        int selectedIndex = selectedIndices[i];

        //get the ListItem in the UserListBox Items collection at that offset
        ListItem myListItem = UsersListBox.Items[selectedIndex];

        //get the string that is that ListItem's value property
        string newUser = myListItem.Value;

        //add that string to the newUsers collection of string
        newUsers[i] = newUser;
    }
```

The advantage of the interim variables is that you can set break points on them and see what their value is, and you can more easily document the code. The disadvantage is minimal, but many programmers (especially those from the "C" culture) prefer the terser version aesthetically.

Call the static AddUsersToRole on the Roles class, passing in the array of user names and the role you want these users added to. You then rebind the users who are in that role to the UsersInRoleGrid.

```
Roles.AddUsersToRole(newUsers, RolesListBox.SelectedItem.Value);
usersInRole = Roles.GetUsersInRole(RolesListBox.SelectedItem.Value);
UsersInRoleGrid.DataSource = usersInRole;
UsersInRoleGrid.DataBind();
```

The results are shown in Figure 11-29.

Add each user to one or more roles, and when you are done, you'll be ready to test if these roles have any effect. To do so, stop the application and edit the Welcome page. Click the smart tag for the LoginView and click Edit RoleGroups, as shown in Figure 11-30.

Add a couple of the roles you created earlier, as shown in Figure 11-31.

Switch to Source view on your *Welcome.aspx* page. You'll see that a new section has been added to the LoginView:

```
<RoleGroups>
    <asp:RoleGroup Roles="Supervisor">
    </asp:RoleGroup>
    <asp:RoleGroup Roles="Manager">
    </asp:RoleGroup>
</RoleGroups>
```

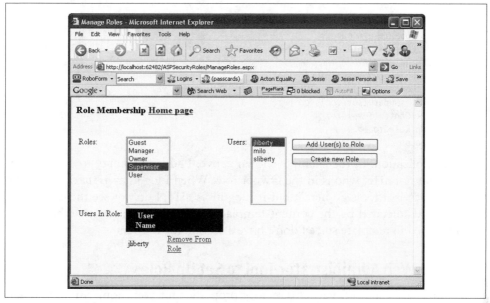

Figure 11-29. Adding users to roles

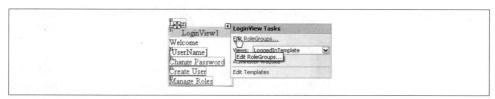

Figure 11-30. Edit RoleGroups

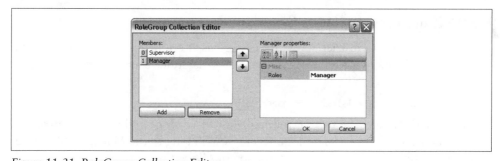

Figure 11-31. RoleGroup Collection Editor

You can now control what content is seen by members of each role by using contentTemplate elements. You add these between the opening and closing tag of each role, like this:

```
<RoleGroups>
    <asp:RoleGroup Roles="Manager">
        <ContentTemplate>
```

```
    Welcome
    <asp:LoginName ID="LoginNameManager" Runat="server" />
    You are a manager
  </ContentTemplate>
</asp:RoleGroup>
<asp:RoleGroup Roles="Supervisor">
    <ContentTemplate>
        Supervisor tools go here
    </ContentTemplate>
</asp:RoleGroup>
</RoleGroups>
```

Run the application. In the example shown above, I added jliberty to the Supervisor role, but not milo, who is in the Owner role. When I log in as jliberty, I see the words "Supervisor tools go here", but if I log in as milo, I do not see those words. I see the words dictated by the content template associated with owners (that is, the default logged in template since I don't have a section for Owners).

Using the Web Administrator Tool to Set Up Roles

Rather than using the IIS virtual directory properties for your application, you can open the *Web Site Administration Tool* and click on the security tab.

Stop the application. On the Visual Studio menu bar, click Website → Asp.NET Configuration, and then choose the Security tab. Click Enable roles, as shown in Figure 11-32.

After you click on Enable roles, the only change will be that the string that currently says "Roles are not enabled" will change to "Existing Roles: 0" and the link will change to "Disable roles".

Restricting Access to Pages Based on Roles

There are two ways to restrict access to a page based on membership in a role. The first is to test if the logged-in user is in a particular role, using the User.IsInRole method:

```
Bool isManager = User.IsInRole("Manager");
```

You might redirect the user to an error page if the user is not in the role. As an example, let's add code that blocks non-managers from linking to the Manage Roles page. To do this, add a test in the Page_Load method of *ManageRoles.aspx.cs:*

```
if (User.IsInRole("Manager") == false)
{
    Response.Redirect("NoPrivs.aspx");
}
```

If the user is not in the role of "Manager", the user is redirected to the page *NoPrivs. aspx*. That page can display an error message and then allow the user to take other actions. A very simple example is shown in Figure 11-33.

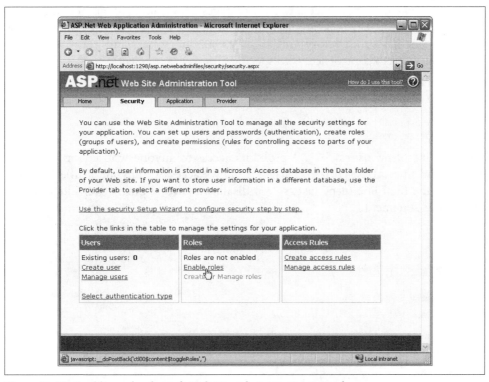

Figure 11-32. Enabling roles through Web Site Administration wizard

Figure 11-33. NoPrivs.aspx

The code for the button on the *NoPrivs.aspx.cs* page is simple:

```
protected void btnHome_Click(object sender, EventArgs e)
{
    Response.Redirect("Welcome.aspx");
}
```

The second way to restrict access to a set of pages is by adding an authorization section to a *web.config* file. You can place this section in a subdirectory to control access to all files in that subdirectory and all of its subdirectories, and you can use the `location` element to control access to specific files.

```
<authorization>
  <deny users='?' />
  <allow roles='Manager' />
  <deny users='*' />
</authorization>
```

The first line (`deny users = '?'`) prohibits access to anyone who is not logged in. The second line (`allow roles='Manager'`) allows access to anyone in the Manager role, and the final line (`deny users='*'`) disallows anyone but is overridden by the `allow` roles statement.

CHAPTER 12

Master Pages and Navigation

Web sites look better and are less confusing to users when they have a consistent "look and feel" as you move from page to page. ASP.NET 2.0 facilitates the creation of consistency with *master pages*, which allow you to create a consistent frame in which each page will place its content.

Navigation adds to the user's ease of use of your site by providing a site map and/or by providing "bread crumbs" that tell the user how he got to the current page.

By placing your navigation aides in master pages, you can provide consistent navigational cues to your users, making for an enhanced user experience.

Master Pages

A master page provides shared HTML, controls, and code that can be used as a template for all of the pages of a site. Everything on your master page is shown on every page that uses that master page. For example, you might have a master page with a logo and a menu; these will show on every "child" of the master page. Each master page has a content area where you put the content that varies on each child page.

 Unlike CSS, which helps ensure that similar controls have similar appearances (see the section "Themes and Skins" in Chapter 13) master pages ensure that all the pages have common elements such as logos, headings, footers, or navigation aides.

The O'Reilly web site (*http://www.oreilly.com*) is a good example of a site that could be implemented using a master page. With a master page the logo (the O'Reilly tarsier) and an image (the O'Reilly header) can be shared across multiple pages, as shown in Figure 12-1.

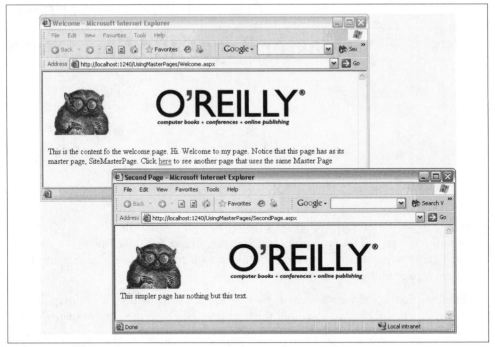

Figure 12-1. The O'Reilly site with master pages

 The O'Reilly site shown in these examples is a mockup and not taken from the O'Reilly site, which can be reached at *http://www.oreilly.com*.

To use master pages, you'll take the following steps:

1. Create a new web site.
2. Add a master page to the site.
3. Add content pages based on the master page.

To begin, create a new web site and call it *UsingMasterPages*. Once the new site opens, right-click the project and choose Add New Item. In the dialog box that opens, choose Master Page and name your master page *SiteMasterPage.master*, as shown in Figure 12-2.

 All master pages *must* have the extension *.master*.

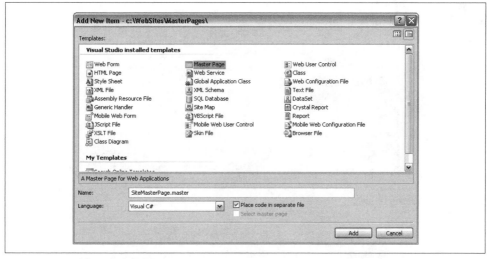

Figure 12-2. Adding the master page

Your new master page has been created with an `<asp:contentplaceholder>` control declaration already in place:

```
<asp:contentplaceholder id="ContentPlaceHolder1" runat="server">
</asp:contentplaceholder>
```

It is this placeholder that will be filled by the page content that uses this master page (the child pages). Within the master page, you may add anything you like surrounding the `<asp:contentplaceholder>`. For example, you might add the logos at the top of the page using a pair of image controls.

To set this up, download the images that come with the source code or save your own images. Create a folder by right-clicking the application and choosing Add Folder → Regular Folder. Name the folder *Images*. Put your images in that folder.

 As usual, the images used in this book can be downloaded with the source code from *http://www.LibertyAssociates.com*. Click Books, scroll down to this book and click Source Code.

Then, right-click the *Images* folder and choose Add Existing Item. You can highlight all your images and add them to the project, as shown in Figure 12-3.

Add two image controls to the master page. You can drag these onto the page in either design or source mode. Set the ID for the first to `Animal` and set its `ImageURL` by clicking the ellipsis in the Properties window and navigating to the appropriate image, as shown in Figure 12-4.

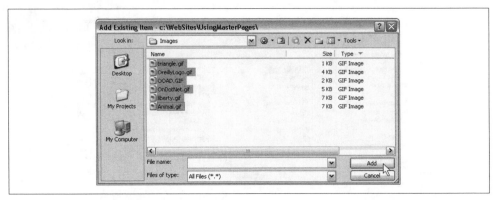

Figure 12-3. Adding images

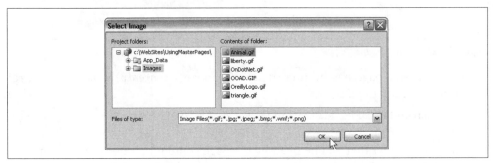

Figure 12-4. Adding the animal image

Drag a second image onto the form, name it `Oreilly`, and add the *OreillyLogo.gif* file. Your form now has three objects, as shown in Figure 12-5.

For convenience, I've numbered the three areas in Figure 12-5: the first image (*1*), the second image (*2*), and the `ContentPlaceHolder` object (*3*). You may add text to the master page's `ContentPlaceHolder` by typing directly on it, which will act as default text (typically replaced in the pages that use this master page).

The *.master* page file that resulted in Figure 12-5 is listed in Example 12-1. The `ID` property of the `ContentPlaceHolder` control has been changed from its default value to `TopPageContent` in preparation for use in the example.

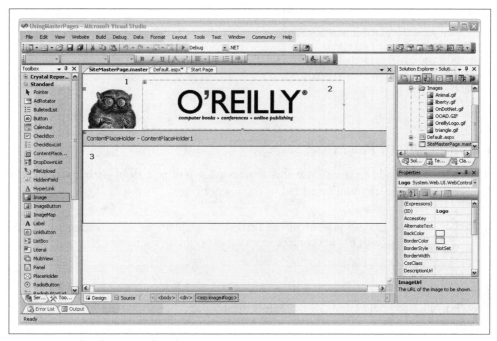

Figure 12-5. Three areas on the master page

Example 12-1. SiteMasterPage.master

```
<%@ Master Language="C#" AutoEventWireup="true"
   CodeFile="SiteMasterPage.master.cs"
   Inherits="SiteMasterPage" %>

<!DOCTYPE html PUBLIC "-//W3C//DTD XHTML 1.1//EN"
   "http://www.w3.org/TR/xhtml11/DTD/xhtml11.dtd">

<html xmlns="http://www.w3.org/1999/xhtml" >
<head runat="server">
    <title>Untitled Page</title>
</head>
<body>
    <form id="form1" runat="server">
    <div>
       <asp:Image ID="Animal" runat="server"
           ImageUrl="Images/animal.gif" />
       <asp:Image ID="Oreilly" runat="server"
            ImageUrl="Images/OreillyLogo.gif" />
```

Example 12-1. SiteMasterPage.master (continued)

```
        <asp:contentplaceholder id="TopPageContent" runat="server">
        This is some default text.
         </asp:contentplaceholder>
     </div>
     </form>
</body>
</html>
```

Adding Content Pages

The pages you'll add that will use this master page will put all of *their* content into the ContentPlaceHolder you've added to the master page.

 You can put more than one ContentPlaceHolder control on a master page (each has its own ID), so this does not limit your flexibility.

Create two new *.aspx* pages, *Welcome.aspx* and *PageTwo.aspx*. Make these "normal" Web Form (*.aspx*) pages and check "Select master page," as shown in Figure 12-6.

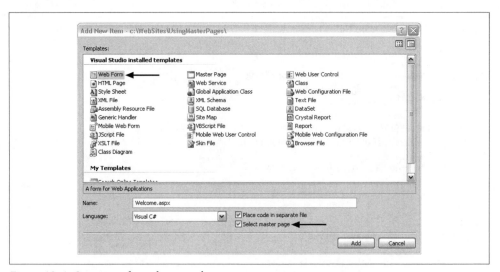

Figure 12-6. Creating a form that uses the master page

When you click the Add button, the Select a Master Page dialog will open. Choose SiteMasterPage.master and click OK.

Your new *Welcome.aspx* page will be shown (in Design Mode) within the master page. The Content box will allow you to add any content you like, including controls, text, and so forth, but the contents of the master page will be disabled, as shown in Figure 12-7.

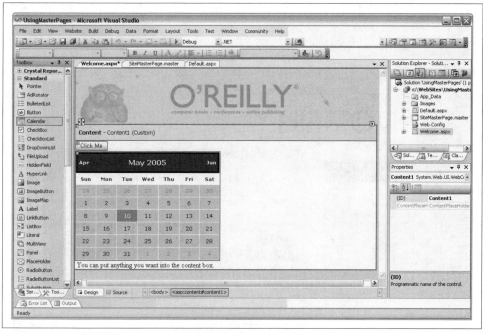

Figure 12-7. Editing content in the Content control

 The terminology can get a bit confusing, so let's clarify. A master page has an empty `ContentPlaceHolder` control. This control is populated within child pages. A child page is a normal *.aspx* file, with a `Page` directive but minus the `<html>`, `<form>`, `<head>`, and `<body>` tags. All of the content of the child control is contained within the area designated in its master page's `ContentPlaceHolder` control.

This allows you to see how your new page will look when it is combined with the master page at runtime. When you create *SecondPage.aspx*, you'll use the same master page, thus ensuring that the look and feel of the two pages is identical. Take a quick look at the asp that is generated:

```
<%@ Page Language="C#" MasterPageFile="~/SiteMasterPage.master"
AutoEventWireup="true" CodeFile="SecondPage.aspx.cs"
Inherits="SecondPage" Title="Second Page" %>

<asp:Content ID="Content1"
ContentPlaceHolderID="ContentPlaceHolder1" Runat="Server">

</asp:Content>
```

The @Page directive contains a reference to this page's *MasterPage* file and that a content ASP.NET web control was added for you.

You can put in some simple text and bring up the two pages, as shown in Figure 12-8.

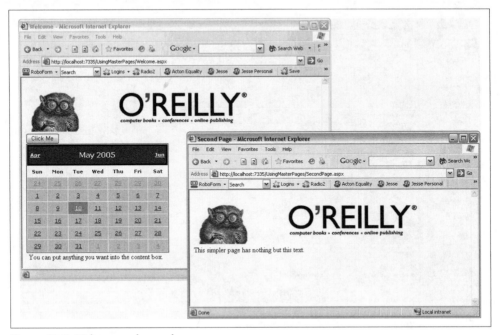

Figure 12-8. Welcome and second page

Using Nested Master Pages

It is not unusual for you to want to have certain stable elements throughout the entire application, but other elements are shared only within one part of your application. For example, you might have a company-wide header but have division-wide elements as well. ASP.NET 2.0 lets you create nested pages. Any given web page can be combined with a nested page or with the original master, whichever makes more sense for that individual page.

To illustrate this, we'll create a nested master page called *ASPNet.master*. Create a new master page, and then edit the page, as shown in the highlighted lines of code in Example 12-2.

When creating a nested page, VS2005 will automatically insert the normal boilerplate for a page, including the following:

```
<!DOCTYPE html PUBLIC "-//W3C//DTD XHTML 1.1//EN"
    "http://www.w3.org/TR/xhtml11/DTD/xhtml11.dtd">
```

```
<html xmlns="http://www.w3.org/1999/xhtml" >
<head runat="server">
    <title>Untitled Page</title>
</head>
<body>
    <form id="form1" runat="server">
    <div>
    </div>
    </form>
</body>
</html>
```

This default HTML must be deleted and replaced, as shown in Example 12-2.

Example 12-2. ASPNET.master nested page

```
<%@ Master Language="C#"
    MasterPageFile="~/SiteMasterPage.master"
    AutoEventWireup="true"
    CodeFile="ASP.NET.master.cs"
    Inherits="ASP.NET" %>

<asp:Content runat="server" ID="OnDotNetMasterContent"
    ContentPlaceHolderID="TopPageContent" >
    <table>
        <tr>
            <td>
                <asp:Image ID="Image1" runat="server"
                    ImageUrl="~/Images/OnDotNet.gif" />
            </td>
        </tr>
        <tr>
            <td>
                <div>
                    <asp:contentplaceholder id="OnDotNetContent"
                        runat="server">
                    This is default content for OnDotNet
                    </asp:contentplaceholder>
                </div>
            </td>
        </tr>
    </table>
</asp:Content>
```

This nested page will have as *its* master page the *SiteMasterPage* you created earlier, but it will add, within its Content control, an image and its own Content placeholder (with its own default text). Unfortunately, you cannot use the designer to examine nested pages, as shown in Figure 12-9, but you can see the effect once you create a web page that uses this nested master page.

Figure 12-9. You cannot use Design view to create nested master pages

Like the topmost master page, the new nested page has a `Master` directive but this nested page adds one attribute: `MasterPageFile` (shown highlighted in Example 12-2). This indicates that the current master page (*ASP.Net.master*) is a nested page to *SiteMasterPage.master*.

To use the nested page, create two additional web pages (*OnDotNetPage1.aspx* and *OnDotNetPage2.aspx*). Set *ASP.Net.Master* as the master page for both by adding a `MasterPageFile` attribute to the `Page` directive. The results are shown in Figure 12-10.

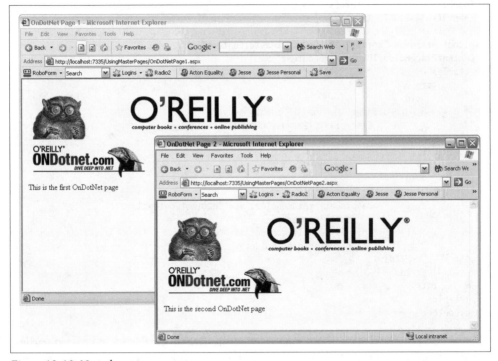

Figure 12-10. Nested master pages

Each of these pages is divided into three areas. The topmost area has the O'Reilly logos from *SiteMasterPage.master*. The middle area has the OnDotNet.com logo from the nested page *OnDotNet.master*. Finally, each of the *.aspx* pages has content.

You can have multiple nested pages that all share a common master page. For example, you might create a second nested page named *LibertyMaster.master*, as shown in Example 12-3. Delete the extraneous code from the boilerplate inserted by VS2005.

Example 12-3. LibertyMaster.master

```
<%@ Master Language="C#"
    MasterPageFile="~/SiteMasterPage.master"
    AutoEventWireup="true"
    CodeFile="LibertyMaster.cs"
    Inherits="Liberty" %>

<asp:Content ID="LibertyMasterContent" runat="server"
        ContentPlaceHolderID="ContentPlaceHolder1" >
    <table>
        <tr>
            <td>
                <asp:Image ID="libertyImage" runat="server"
                        ImageUrl="~/Images/liberty.gif" />
            </td>
            <td>
                <h2>Liberty Sub-Master</h2>
            </td>
        </tr>
        <tr>
            <td colspan="2">
                <div>
                    <asp:contentplaceholder id="LibertyContent" runat="server">
                        This is default content for Liberty
                    </asp:contentplaceholder>
                </div>
            </td>
        </tr>
    </table>
</asp:Content>
```

This new nested page uses a different image and adds text to a second column. You could make significant differences in each of your nested pages (e.g., one might add a layer of menus, another might add a site map).

To see your new nested page at work, create two new pages: *LibertyPage1.aspx* and *LibertyPage2.aspx*. These new pages will share the top master page with the OnDot-Net pages, but these new pages will have their own middle section created by the *Liberty.master* sub-page, as shown in Figure 12-11.

Dynamically Editing the Master

You may decide that in response to certain events, you'd like to reach up into the master page (from a child page) and change its presentation. To do this, you will create a public property in your master page that sub-pages can reach up and change.

Figure 12-11. Four nested pages

To see this in action, add the following property to *SiteMasterPage.master.cs*:

```
public Image AnimalImage
{
    get { return this.Animal; }
    set { this.Animal = value; }
}
```

The value this.Animal is defined in *SiteMasterPage.master*:

```
<asp:Image ID="Animal" runat="server" ImageUrl="~/Images/Animal.gif" />
```

To access this property, add two new pages to the web site, *Welcome1.aspx* and *Welcome2.aspx*. Check the Select Master Page checkbox in the Add New Item dialog. Both will use *SiteMasterPage.master* as their master page.

Add the following directive at the top of *Welcome2.aspx*:

```
<%@ MasterType TypeName="SiteMasterPage" %>
```

You can now write code in *Welcome2.aspx.cs* that reaches up to the `SiteMasterPage` and sets its property as highlighted in the following code snippet:

```
protected void Page_Load(object sender, EventArgs e)
{
    this.Master.AnimalImage.ImageUrl = "~//images//procCS.gif";
}
```

 You may need to build the web site before Intellisense will make the `AnimalImage` property available.

Put some content into each. For example, here is the content for *Welcome1.aspx*, which you will find startlingly original:

```
<asp:Content ID="Content1"
ContentPlaceHolderID="TopPageContent"
Runat="Server">
    <h2>This is Welcome 1</h2>
</asp:Content>
```

When you run the two pages, you can see that *Welcome2.aspx* has had its master page modified at runtime, as shown in Figure 12-12.

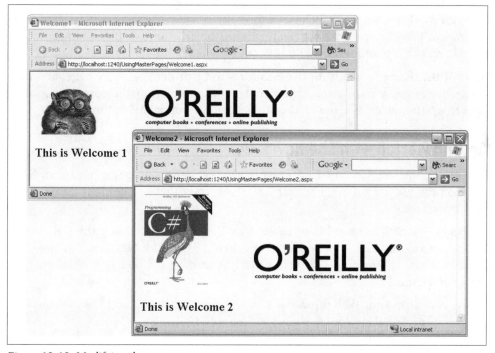

Figure 12-12. Modifying the master page

The alternative to using properties is to use late binding. If you replace the Page_Load method in *Welcome2.aspx* with the following, the results will be identical (if a bit slower):

```
protected void Page_Load(object sender, EventArgs e)
{
    Control ctrl = Master.FindControl( "Animal" );
    Image img = ctrl as Image;
    if ( img != null )
    {
        img.ImageUrl = "~//images//procCS.gif";
    }
}
```

In this case, rather than using a property, you are finding the Image control at runtime and then setting its property. Both approaches work, but the use of properties is preferred because late binding is less efficient and harder to maintain.

Navigation

Web sites are becoming larger and more complex. Consequently, developers are called upon to provide navigational hints and menus to keep visitors from "getting lost," and to enable them to find all the features of the site.

The ASP.NET toolset now includes a number of new controls that facilitate this assistance. There are controls for creating both "bread crumbs" (how did I get to this page?) and site maps (how do I find that other page?).

Most of the time you will want these features to be present on every page, and thus master pages are a great asset. If you change the site map or the control, you only have to update the master and all the other pages are "updated" automatically.

Getting Started with Site Navigation

The most common way to create a site navigation data source is to create an XML file. You can use a database, multiple XML files, and other sources, but for now let's keep things simple.

To begin, create a new web site called *SiteNavigation*. Right-click the web site in Solution Explorer and choose Add New Item. The Add New Item dialog box appears. Choose Site map and verify that the name provided is *Web.sitemap*, as shown in Figure 12-13.

When you click Add, *Web.sitemap* is added to your web site, and the skeleton of a site map is provided for you, as shown in Example 12-4.

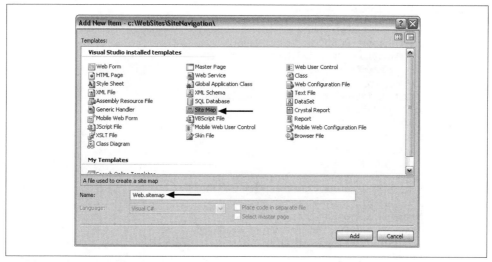

Figure 12-13. Creating the site map

Example 12-4. Web.sitemap skeleton

```xml
<?xml version="1.0" encoding="utf-8" ?>
<siteMap xmlns="http://schemas.microsoft.com/AspNet/SiteMap-File-1.0" >
    <siteMapNode url="" title=""  description="">
        <siteMapNode url="" title=""  description="" />
        <siteMapNode url="" title=""  description="" />
    </siteMapNode>
</siteMap>
```

The title attribute defines the text that is (usually) used as the link, and the description attribute is used in the tool tip.

> VS2005 provides no drag-and-drop support for creating your site map file. You can implement your own SiteMap provider to automate this process or to get the site map from another source (such as a database) but this is a very advanced topic, beyond the scope of this book.

Replace the contents of *Web.sitemap* with the site map XML shown in Example 12-5.

Example 12-5. Web.sitemap

```xml
<?xml version="1.0" encoding="utf-8" ?>
<siteMap xmlns="http://schemas.microsoft.com/AspNet/SiteMap-File-1.0" >
    <siteMapNode title="Welcome" description="Welcome" url="~/welcome.aspx">
        <siteMapNode title="Writing" description="Writing"
            url="~/Writing.aspx">
            <siteMapNode title="Books" description="Books"
                url="~/Books.aspx">
                <siteMapNode title="In Print Books"
                    description="Books in Print"
```

Example 12-5. Web.sitemap (continued)

```
            url="~/BooksInPrint.aspx" />
            <siteMapNode title="Out Of Print Books"
                description="Books no longer in Print"
            url="~/OutOfPrintBooks.aspx" />
        </siteMapNode>
        <siteMapNode title="Articles" description="Articles"
            url="~/Articles.aspx" />
    </siteMapNode>
    <siteMapNode title="Programming"
        description="Contract Programming"
        url="~/Programming.aspx">
        <siteMapNode title="On-Site Programming"
            description="On-site contract programming"
            url="~/OnSiteProgramming.aspx" />
        <siteMapNode title="Off-Site Programming"
            description="Off-site contract programming"
            url="~/OffSiteProgramming.aspx" />
    </siteMapNode>
    <siteMapNode title="Training"
        description="On-Site Training"
        url="~/OnSiteTraining.aspx">
        <siteMapNode title="C# Training"
            description="C# Training"
            url="~/TrainCSharp.aspx" />
        <siteMapNode title="ASP.NET Training"
            description="ASP.NET Training"
            url="~/TrainASPNET.aspx" />
        <siteMapNode title="Windows Forms Training"
            description="Windows Forms Training"
            url="~/TrainWinForms.aspx" />
    </siteMapNode>
    <siteMapNode title="Consulting"
        description="Consulting"
        url="~/Consulting.aspx">
        <siteMapNode title="Application Analysis"
            description="Analysis"
            url="~/ApplicationAnalysis.aspx" />
        <siteMapNode title="Application Design"
            description="Design"
            url="~/ApplicationDesign.aspx" />
        <siteMapNode title="Mentoring"
            description="Team Mentoring"
            url="~/Mentoring.aspx" />
    </siteMapNode>
    </siteMapNode>
</siteMap>
```

The site map file has a single <sitemap> element that defines the namespace:

```
<siteMap xmlns="http://schemas.microsoft.com/AspNet/SiteMap-File-1.0" >
```

Within the siteMap element is nested exactly one <SiteMapNode> (in this case, Welcome). Nested within that first <SiteMapNode>, however, is any number of children <SiteMapNode> elements.

In Example 12-5, there are four such children: Writing, Programming, Training and Consulting. Nested within each of these <SiteMapNode> elements can be more nodes. For example, Writing has Books and Articles. You may nest the nodes arbitrarily deep. The Books node has nested within it nodes for Books in print and books no longer in print.

ASP.NET is configured to protect files with the extension .*sitemap* so that they cannot be downloaded to a client (web browser). If you change providers and need to use a different extension, be sure to place your file in the protected *App_Data* folder.

Setting Up the Pages

To experiment with the site map, create a master page called *MasterPage.master* (the default name offered by VS2005).

All the controls you will now add to the master page must be placed *outside* the ContentPlaceHolder tags but inside the <\form> tag.

From the toolbox, drag a SiteMapDataSource control from the Data tab onto the master page. By default, the SiteMapDataSource control will look for and use the file named *Web.sitemap*.

To create a robust example of navigation, you'll want to create a site map as well as bread crumbs. (Bread crumbs are links, often at the top of a page, that show how the user got to the current page—for example, "MainPage → Books → Programming ASP.NET").

To get started, switch to Design view and drag a TreeView control from the Navigation tab of the Toolbox onto the form, outside of the Content area. In Design view, click its smart tag and set the data source to the SiteMapDataSource control you just created, as shown in Figure 12-14.

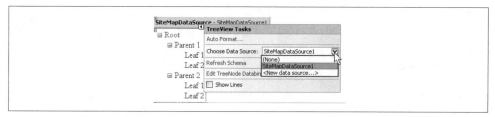

Figure 12-14. Creating the Tree view

To take control of the layout of the various elements on the master page, drag a table control into Source view and set its width to 100%. Drag the TreeView you just created into the first cell; it will act as the site map navigation control, as shown in Figure 12-15.

```
⊟ Welcome
    ⊟ Writing
        ⊟ Books
            In Print Books
                Out Of Print Books
        Articles
        ⊟ Programming
            On-Site Programming
            Off-Site Programming
        ⊟ Training
            VB Training
            ASP.NET Training
            Windows Forms Training
        ⊟ Consulting
            Application Analysis
            Application Design
            Mentoring
```

Figure 12-15. Site Map Tree view

Drag a SiteMapPath control into a second cell, which will act as your bread crumbs, as shown in Figure 12-16.

<u>Welcome</u> > <u>Writing</u> > <u>Books</u> > Out Of Print Books

Figure 12-16. Site Map Path control

 If you switch to Design view, you'll notice the page doesn't show any of this because your TreeView does not have contents yet.

Add two <br/> elements after the SiteMapPath and then drag the ContentPlaceHolder control on the master page into the same cell, as shown in Example 12-6.

Example 12-6. MasterPage.master

```
<%@ Master Language="C#" AutoEventWireup="true"
    CodeFile="MasterPage.master.cs" Inherits="MasterPage" %>

<!DOCTYPE html PUBLIC "-//W3C//DTD XHTML 1.1//EN"
    "http://www.w3.org/TR/xhtml11/DTD/xhtml11.dtd">

<html xmlns="http://www.w3.org/1999/xhtml" >
<head runat="server">
    <title>Liberty Associates, Inc.</title>
</head>
<body>
    <form id="form1" runat="server">
```

Example 12-6. MasterPage.master (continued)

```
    <div>
        <asp:SiteMapDataSource ID="SiteMapDataSource1" runat="server" />
        <asp:Table ID="Table1" runat="server" Width="100%" >
            <asp:TableRow>
                <asp:TableCell>
                    <asp:TreeView ID="TreeView1" runat="server"
                        DataSourceID="SiteMapDataSource1" />
                </asp:TableCell>
                <asp:TableCell VerticalAlign="Top">
                    <asp:SiteMapPath ID="SiteMapPath1" runat="server" />
                    <br /><br />
                    <asp:contentplaceholder id="ContentPlaceHolder1"
                        runat="server">
                    </asp:contentplaceholder>
                </asp:TableCell>
            </asp:TableRow>
        </asp:Table>
    </div>
    </form>
</body>
</html>
```

To test this master page, you'll need to create at least a few of the pages defined in the site map. Delete the Default page from the web site and create a new page named *Welcome.aspx*. Check the Select master page checkbox and set the master page to *MasterPage.master*. Within the content control, add the line of code shown in bold below:

```
<asp:Content ID="Content1" ContentPlaceHolderID="ContentPlaceHolder1"
    Runat="Server">
    <h1>Welcome</h1>
</asp:Content>
```

Create each of the other pages, providing whatever stubbed out data you want as long as you can tell what page you are on. When you are done, your solution explorer should look more or less like Figure 12-17. Set *Welcome.aspx* as the start page.

Start the application and navigate from the Welcome page to another page, such as Programming, as shown in Figure 12-18.

There are a few things to notice about this page. The tree view was built for you by reading the XML file through the SiteMapDataSource control. You can see that each node can be collapsed (see Training) or expanded (see Writing). When you click on a node (in this case Off-Site Programming), you are brought directly to that page. The bread crumbs, put in place by the SiteMapPath, show you how you got here and how to get back to home.

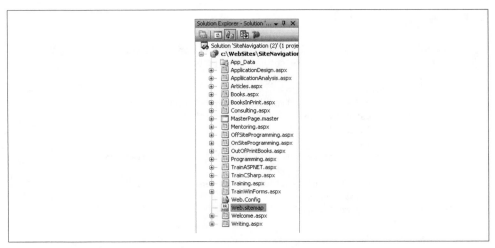

Figure 12-17. Solution Explorer with site navigation pages

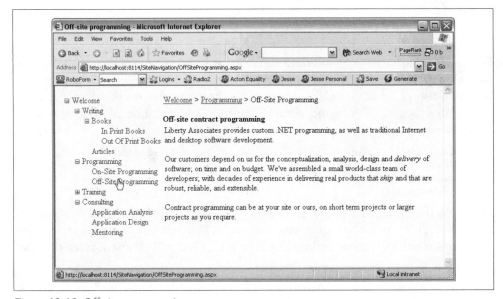

Figure 12-18. Off-site programming

 It is uncommon in production applications to provide both a map and bread crumbs on the same page.

Customizing the Look and Feel

You can set a number of properties for the TreeView. To begin with, you may click the Smart Tag and choose Auto Format... to bring up the Auto Format dialog, which offers a series of preset formats for the tree, as shown in Figure 12-19.

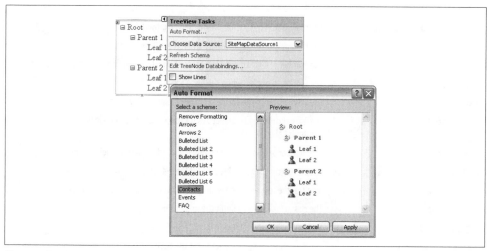

Figure 12-19. Treeview Auto Format

In addition, you can click the TreeView control and then set its properties through the Properties window. Most of the TreeView's properties have to do with the styles used for the various nodes. Some of the most important properties are shown in Figure 12-20.

Figure 12-20. Tree view node styles

There are a large number of other properties, many of which are listed in Table 12-1.

Table 12-1. Tree View properties

Property	Description
AutoGenerateDataBindings	If set to `true`, the default lets you manually set the bindings between data and tree nodes.
CheckedNodes	Returns a collection of `TreeNode` objects that contains only those nodes whose checkbox was selected.
CollapseImageToolTip	The tool tip to display when the node is collapsed.
CollapseImageUrl	The URL for the image to display when the node is collapsed.
ExpandDepth	The number of levels to which the tree should be expanded when it is first displayed.
ExpandImageToolTip	The tool tip to display when the node is expanded.
ExpandImageUrl	The URL for the image to display when the node is expanded.
HoverNodeStyle	The `TreeNodeStyle` object to set the appearance of a node when the mouse pointer is hovering over it.
NodeIndent	The number of pixels that child nodes are indented from their parent.
NodeStyle	The `TreeNodeStyle` object to set the default appearance of a node.
NodeWrap	If `true`, the text of a node wraps if it runs out of space. The default is `false`.
PathSeparator	The character used to delimit the node values.
SelectedNode	Returns the selected `TreeNode` object.
SelectedNodeStyle	The `TreeNodeStyle` object to set the appearance of the selected node.
ShowCheckBoxes	A bitwise combination of `TreeNodeTypes` to indicate which types of nodes will display with checkboxes.
	In this example, none of the nodes has checkboxes; in other applications, you might open a `TreeView` control to display, for example, directories, and allow the user to check which directories are to be acted on (e.g., deleted).
ShowExpandCollapse	If `true`, the default, the expand/collapse indicators will be displayed .
ShowLines	If `true`, lines connecting the nodes will be displayed. The default is `false`.

The `TreeView` has a number of public methods that allow you to poke into the control and pick out specific nodes or to programmatically change, expand, and contract nodes. The most important methods are shown in Table 12-2.

Table 12-2. Tree view methods

Method	Description
CollapseAll	Collapses the entire tree
ExpandAll	Expands the entire tree
FindNode	Retrieves the designated `TreeNode`

Finally, there are a number of events that the `TreeView` control raises that allow you to hook into the user's interaction with the `TreeView` and modify the results. The most important events are shown in Table 12-3.

Table 12-3. Tree view events

Event	Description
SelectedNodeChanged	Raised when a node is selected in the TreeView
TreeNodeCheckChanged	Raised when the checkbox status of a node is changed
TreeNodeCollapsed	Raised when a node is collapsed
TreeNodeExpanded	Raised when a node is expanded
TreeNodePopulate	Raised when a node whose PopulateOnDemand property is set to true is expanded in the TreeView (gives you an opportunity to fill in the subnodes for that node)

Similarly, the SiteMapPath control can be modified by using the smart tag to set AutoFormatting or by setting properties on the control. Some common tasks include customizing the link *style* properties (such as RootNodeStyle-Font-Names and RootNodeStyle-BorderWidth). These can be set declaratively in the declaration of the control itself. Intellisense will help; when you press the spacebar while within the declaration of the control, a list of its properties, methods, and events will pop up, as shown in Figure 12-21.

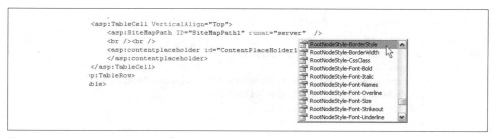

Figure 12-21. Setting SiteMapPath properties

> In addition to setting styles for the RootNode, you can set separate styles for the ParentNode, the CurrentNode, and the PathSeparator. You can use the NodeTemplate to customize the style of all the links at once.

In the previous example, the bread crumbs separated the various pages with the greater-than symbol (>). Adding the PathSeparator property is easy to change that to, for example, an arrow:

```
<asp:SiteMapPath ID="SiteMapPath1" runat="server"  PathSeparator="->"  />
```

The result is shown in Figure 12-22.

Welcome->Programming->Off-Site Programming

Figure 12-22. Arrow Path separator

For "deep" web sites, the bread crumbs may become unwieldy. You have the option to limit the number of levels shown by setting the ParentLevelDisplayed property:

```
<asp:SiteMapPath ID="SiteMapPath1" runat="server" ParentLevelDisplayed="3" />
```

Populating on Demand

You may decide you would like your tree view to populate on demand. That is, rather than loading all the contents of each node when the tree is first shown and displaying the full tree, you can display (for example) the first node, and as each node is clicked on, it will populate the next level.

To do this, you'll make some simple changes to the master page. First, modify the TreeView not to be a self-closing element; you'll be adding content between the opening and closing tags. Add an ExpandDepth attribute to the TreeView, which you will set to 0 (or whatever level, zero-based, you want the tree to expand to when loaded).

Within the Treeview, you'll add a DataBindings element, and within *that,* you'll add a TreeNodeBinding control, as shown in Example 12-7.

Example 12-7. Adding Tree node bindings for Populate On Demand

```
<asp:TreeView ID="TreeView1" runat="server"
 DataSourceID="SiteMapDataSource1" ExpandDepth="0">
    <DataBindings>
        <asp:TreeNodeBinding DataMember="SiteMapNode" NavigateUrlField="URL"
        PopulateOnDemand="true" TextField="Title" />
    </DataBindings>
</asp:TreeView>
```

Run the application with *Welcome.aspx* as the start page. The tree is fully closed. Expand the TreeView to choose Off-Site Programming. When you get to the page, again the tree is fully closed, as shown in Figure 12-23.

The nodes will be loaded as you click on each level of the menu.

Using a Menu for Navigation

Open *MasterPage.master* in source mode and locate the TreeView control. Comment it out and replace it with a menu:

```
<!-- <asp:TreeView ID="TreeView1" runat="server" DataSourceID="SiteMapDataSource1"
/> -->
 <asp:Menu ID="Menu1" runat="server" DataSourceID="SiteMapDataSource1" />
```

Run the application. Presto! A menu control for navigation, as shown in Figure 12-24.

In this case, I hovered over welcome (opening the next level) and then hovered over Programming (opening the third level).

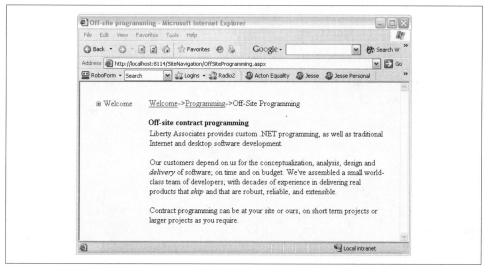

Figure 12-23. Menu fully closed

Figure 12-24. Using a menu for navigation

If the menus start to eat into your content, you can set their Orientation property to Horizontal (the default is Vertical) and rearrange your table to make room for them.

Enumerate Site Map Nodes Programatically

There are times when you may want access to the current node and its subnodes so you can manipulate them programmatically. You can add code to a page to get that information. In the next example, you will display the name of the current node in the *Programming.aspx* page, and you will also display its subnodes. Add the code in Example 12-8 inside the Content tags in *programming.aspx*.

Example 12-8. Programming.aspx with Site Map controls

```
<hr />
<table>
    <tr>
        <td>
            <b>Current Node:</b>
        </td>
        <td>
            <asp:Label ID="lblCurrentNode" runat="server" />
```

Example 12-8. Programming.aspx with Site Map controls (continued)

```
            </td>
        </tr>
        <tr>
            <td>
                <b>Child Nodes:</b>
            </td>
            <td>
                <asp:Label ID="lblChildNodes" runat="server" />
            </td>
        </tr>
</table>
```

You have added two labels: lblCurrentNode and lblChildNodes

Open the code-behind for this page and modify the Page_Load method, as shown in Example 12-9.

Example 12-9. Modifed Page_Load method

```
protected void Page_Load(object sender, EventArgs e)
{
   try
   {
      this.lblCurrentNode.Text = SiteMap.CurrentNode.Title;

      if ( SiteMap.CurrentNode.HasChildNodes )
      {
         foreach ( SiteMapNode childNode in SiteMap.CurrentNode.ChildNodes )
         {
            lblChildNodes.Text += childNode.Title + "<br/>";
         }
      }
   }
   catch ( System.NullReferenceException )
   {
      lblCurrentNode.Text = "The xml file is not in the site map!";
   }
   catch ( Exception ex )
   {
      lblCurrentNode.Text = "Exception! " + ex.Message;
   }
}
```

In this code, you are setting the text of lblCurrentNode to reflect the SiteMap's CurrentNode. The SiteMap is an in-memory representation of a site's navigational structure. The SiteMap object itself is created by the site map provider (in this case, by the SiteMapDataSource).

The CurrentNode property returns an object of type SiteMapNode, and the Text property of that SiteMapNode returns that SiteMapNode's title.

The `SiteMapNode`'s property `HasChildNodes` returns a Boolean, true if there are sub-nodes to the `SiteMapNode`. If this is the case, you can iterate through the `SiteMapNodeCollection` returned by the `ChildNodes` property.

When you view this page, the labels display the name of the current node and all its child nodes, as shown in Figure 12-25.

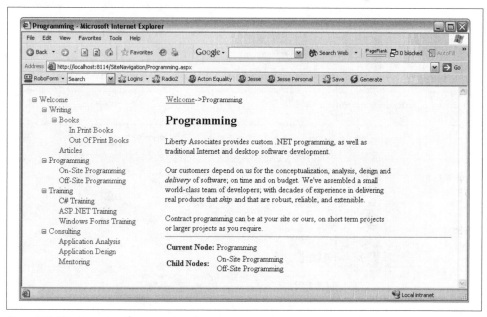

Figure 12-25. Accessing the current node

Filtering Based on Security

In Chapter 11, we covered the creation of login accounts and roles. In the next example, we'll use that information combined with the navigation tools covered to make aspects of the navigation aids visible and accessible to users in specific roles.

To get started, you will create a new web site called *SecureNavigation* with an IIS virtual directory. When the New Web Site dialog box appears, click Browse next to the location. The Choose Location dialog box appears. On the left are four buttons; click Local IIS and select the default web site. Then click the New Web Application icon in the upper-right corner of the dialog box, as shown in Figure 12-26.

A new web site will appear under Default Web Site; name it *SecureNavigation*, as shown in Figure 12-27.

Clicking Open will return you to the New Web Site dialog box with the location set to HTTP and the site name *http://localhost/SecureNavigation*. Click OK.

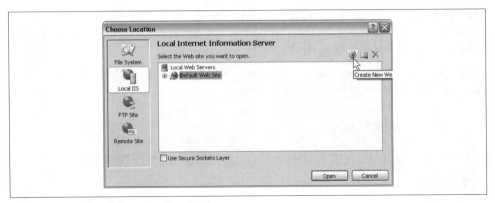

Figure 12-26. Choose Location: Local IIS

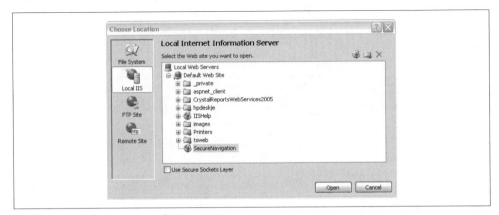

Figure 12-27. Creating new web site

Enable Membership

Select the menu choice Website → ASP.NET Configuration. This opens the Web Site Administration Tool. Click the Security tab. Under Users, click the link "Select authentication type," choose From the Internet and then click Done. This will set the authentication type to Forms.

In the same Users section, click Create User Fill in the form to create three user accounts. By default, you must use a *strong password*, one that includes all of the following:

- Uppercase letters
- Lowercase letters
- Punctuation
- A minimum of eight characters

To make things easy to remember, use the following password: Liberty! (that's an exclamation point at the end):

The Create user dialog box is shown in Figure 12-28.

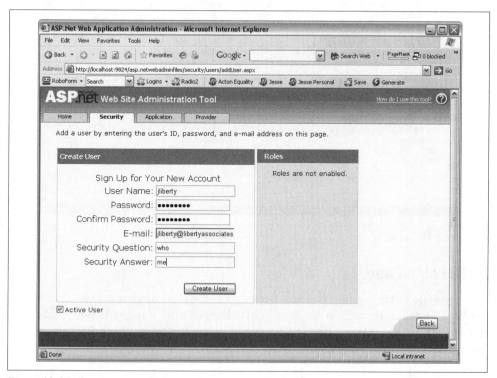

Figure 12-28. Create user

The three users I'll create for this application are jliberty, milo, and allegra. Make sure you check the Active User checkbox in the lower left and click Create User to create each in turn. After you've created all three, click the Back button in the lower right to return to the Security tab.

Adding Roles

Under the Roles box, click Enable roles, as shown in Figure 12-29.

Create two roles, Authors and Customers, by clicking Create or Manage Roles. Once the two roles are created, click Manage for Authors. This brings you to a search page. Click on the first letter of the first user's name (e.g., jliberty) and that user will appear with a checkbox (not yet checked). Check the box to add that user to the role.

Click Back, click Manage next to Customers, and add your second user to that role. You now have one user in each role and one user who is not in any roles.

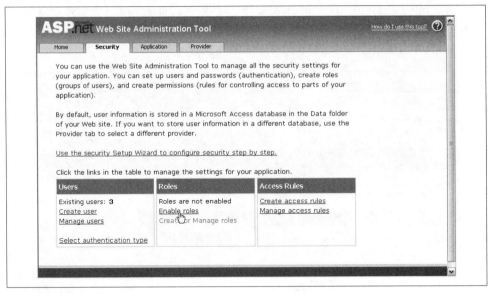

Figure 12-29. Enable roles

Add a Login Page

Before you go much further, you will need a page for your three users to log in. Close the Web Site Administration Tool and open *Default.aspx*. Drag a Login Status control onto the page, as described in Chapter 11. Type the word "Hello" followed by a space and drag a LoginName control onto the page.

You now need a page for users to log in to. Create a new page named *Login.aspx* and switch to Design view and drag a Login control onto the new page. Click your new Login control and set its DestinationPageURL to ~/default.aspx.

Your goal is to create pages that are accessible to users who are in the Authors role and other pages accessible only to users in the Customers role. To do this, you must create a pair of folders. Right-click on the solution and create two new regular folders by selecting Add Folder → Regular Folder. Name them Authors and Customers.

In the Authors folder, create a page named *AuthorInfo.aspx*. Similarly, in the Customers folder, create a page named *CustomerInfo.aspx*.

Add two more *aspx* pages to the root of your site: Books and Articles. To keep life simple, open each of the four pages you've just created and add an <h1> header with the name of the file (so when you view it in the browser you'll know immediately which page you are on), like this:

```
<form id="form1" runat="server">
<div>
  <h1>Books</h1>
</div>
</form>
```

Rules are covered in depth in Chapter 11.

Create Access Rules

Once again, open the Web Site Administration Tool (by clicking Website → ASP. NET Configuration). Click the Security tab, and under Access Rules click Create access rules. Click first on the Authors folder. In the second column, set the rule to apply to a specific role and choose Authors from the drop-down. In the third column, click the Allow radio button, as shown in Figure 12-30.

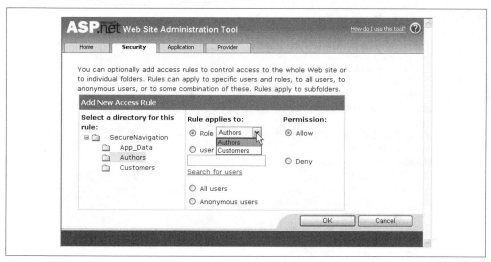

Figure 12-30. Create access rule for authors

Click OK and you are returned to the Web Site Administration Tool home page. Repeat the same steps to create an access rule for the Customers folder, granting permission only to the Customers role.

Return to the Web Site Administration Tool home page and click Manage Access Rules. Click the Authors Folder and click Add new access rule. This time, with the Authors folder highlighted, click the radio button All Users and set the permission to Deny, then click OK. Do the same for Customers.

You've now created four rules. The Author rules say that users in the role of Authors are allowed access and all others are denied. The same is true for the Customers page: only Customers have access.

By highlighting a rule and clicking the Move Up or Move Down button, you can move the rule up or down. This is important because rules are checked in the order of their appearance. If the Deny All rule is at the top and an author tries to access that page she will be denied. On the other hand, if you set the order Allow Authors, then Deny All, you'll have the results you expect: Authors will be granted access, and all other roles (including users who are not identified or not in a role) will be denied access to the page.

Close the Web Site Administration Tool.

Creating a Permission-Driven Site Map

The goal is to limit which parts of the SiteMap are displayed to the user based on which groups (or roles) the user is a member of. To get started, create a site map as described above. Right-click the web site root in the Solution Explorer and select Add New Item, and choose SiteMap. Accept the default name, *Web.sitemap*, and copy the SiteMap shown in Example 12-10.

Example 12-10. web.sitemap

```
<?xml version="1.0" encoding="utf-8" ?>
<siteMap xmlns="http://schemas.microsoft.com/AspNet/SiteMap-File-1.0" >
   <siteMapNode url="~/Default.aspx" title="Home"  description="Home" >
      <siteMapNode url="~/Books.aspx" title="Books"
      description="Books" />
      <siteMapNode url="~/Articles.aspx" title="Articles"
      description="Articles" />
      <siteMapNode url="~/Authors/AuthorInfo.aspx"
         title="Author Info"
         description="Author Information" />
      <siteMapNode url="Customers/CustomerInfo.aspx"
      title="customer information"
      description ="customer information" />
      <siteMapNode url="~/Login.aspx" title="login"
      description="login" />
   </siteMapNode>
</siteMap>
```

At this point, you have three users, two roles, a default page, a login page, and a SiteMap. You are all set to add security trimming to your SiteMap navigation so that which parts of the SiteMap are displayed will be controlled by which role the user is in.

Security trimming is the technique of displaying only those parts of your navigation for which the user is authorized, based on the user's role.

To do this, you'll need to make an entry in your *web.config* file, as shown in Example 12-11.

Example 12-11. Web.config for Security Trimming

```
<?xml version="1.0"?>
<configuration xmlns="http://schemas.microsoft.com/.NetConfiguration/v2.0">
    <system.web>
        <roleManager enabled="true"/>
        <authentication mode="Forms"/>
        <compilation debug="true"/>
        <siteMap defaultProvider="XmlSiteMapProvider" enabled="true">
            <providers>
                <add name="XmlSiteMapProvider"
                    type="System.Web.XmlSiteMapProvider "
                    description="Default SiteMap provider."
                    siteMapFile="Web.sitemap"
                    securityTrimmingEnabled="true" />
            </providers>
        </siteMap>
    </system.web>
</configuration>
```

You've put some pages into secured folders and established which roles should have access to those folders. When you turn security trimming on, ASP.NET checks if the page is available to the current user and, if not, the page *will not be* displayed in any representation of the site map.

You can see this by logging in as jliberty. This user is in the group Authors and should have access to the AuthorInfo page along with the unsecured pages: Articles, Books, Default and Login, which is exactly what we see in Figure 12-31.

Figure 12-31. Security Trimming at work

In Figure 12-31, we see that user jliberty has logged in and *does* have access to Author Info but *does not* have access to Customer Info.

CHAPTER 13

Personalization

Most modern web sites are designed for users to visit repeatedly and, therefore, support some level of personalization. Personalization enables the site to remember the user's preferences and, if appropriate, previous user choices, such as "You have 3 items in your shopping cart."

Creating Personalized Web Sites

To get started, you'll want a new web site that duplicates the work you accomplished in the security chapter. Create a new web site called *SitePersonalization* and copy the *ASPSecurityRoles* web site from Chapter 11 (Website → Copy Web Site). Copy over all the files, including the data files. Set *Welcome.aspx* as the start page and run the program to make sure you have a working duplicate.

Recording Personalization Information

The simplest form of personalization is to record information about the user and then to make that information available whenever the user logs on. This requires a kind of persistence that goes beyond session state. To create true personalization, you'll want to store the user's choices and information in a database that associates the saved information with a particular user and persists indefinitely. Fortunately, ASP.NET 2.0 provides all of the plumbing required. You do not have to design, edit, or manage the database tables; all of that is done for you.

To get started, you'll need to modify your project to handle user Profiles.

Setting Up Profile Handling

ASP.NET 2.0 has decoupled the Profile API (how you programmatically interact with profile data) from the underlying data provider (how you store the data). This allows you to use the default provider (SqlServerExpress), or one of the other providers supplied (SQL server) or even write your own provider (for example, if you have an existing customer relationship management system) without changing the way you interact with the profile in the rest of your code.

To add data to the user's profile, you must first alert the system about the data you wish to store. You do this in *web.config* by adding a profile section to the system.web element:

```
<?xml version="1.0"?>
<configuration>
  <connectionStrings>
    <remove name="LocalSqlServer"/>
    <add name="LocalSqlServer" connectionString="data source=.\sqlExpress;Integrated
Security=SSPI;&#xA;          Initial Catalog=aspnetdb"/>
  </connectionStrings>
  <system.web>
    <authentication mode="Forms"/>
    <membership defaultProvider="AspNetSqlMembershipProvider"/>
    <roleManager enabled="True" defaultProvider="AspNetSqlRoleProvider"/>
    <compilation debug="true"/>
    <profile enabled="True" defaultProvider="AspNetSqlProfileProvider">
      <properties>
        <add name="lastName" />
        <add name="firstName" />
        <add name="phoneNumber" />
        <add name="birthDate" type="System.DateTime"/>
      </properties>
    </profile>
  </system.web>
</configuration>
```

This causes the Profile API to create storage for four pieces of information: lastName, firstName, phoneNumber, and birthDate. The default storage type is string. Notice, however, that you are storing the birthdate as a DateTime object.

You can gather this personalization information any way you like. To keep the example simple, we'll remove the role groups section from *Welcome.aspx* and add a new hyperlink to the LoggedInTemplate:

```
<asp:LoginView ID="LoginView1" runat="server">
    <LoggedInTemplate>
        Welcome
        <asp:LoginName ID="LoginName1" runat="server" />
        <br />
        <asp:HyperLink
            ID="hlChangePW"
            NavigateUrl="ChangePW.aspx"
            runat="server">Change Password
        </asp:HyperLink>
         
        <asp:HyperLink
            ID="hlCreateUser"
```

```
                    NavigateUrl="CreateUser.aspx"
                    runat="server">Create User
              </asp:HyperLink>
              <br />
              <asp:HyperLink
                    ID="hlManageRoles"
                    NavigateUrl="ManageRoles.aspx"
                    runat="server">Manage Roles
              </asp:HyperLink> <br />
              <asp:HyperLink
                    ID="hlProfile"
                    NavigateUrl="ProfileInfo.aspx"
                    runat="server">Add Profile Information
              </asp:HyperLink>
        </LoggedInTemplate>
```

As you can see, the link brings you to *ProfileInfo.aspx*, a page you'll now create. Add a table, and within the table, add labels, checkboxes, and a Save button, as shown in Figure 13-1.

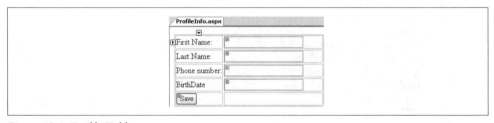

Figure 13-1. Profile Table

The content file for the Profile Table is shown in Example 13-1.

Example 13-1. Content file for Profile Table

```
<%@ Page Language="VB" AutoEventWireup="false" CodeFile="ProfileInfo.aspx.cs"
    Inherits="ProfileInfo_aspx" %>

<!DOCTYPE html PUBLIC "-//W3C//DTD XHTML 1.1//EN"
    "http://www.w3.org/TR/xhtml11/DTD/xhtml11.dtd">

<html xmlns="http://www.w3.org/1999/xhtml" >
<head runat="server">
    <title>Untitled Page</title>
</head>
<body>
    <form id="form1" runat="server">
    <div>
            <table>
            <tr>
                <td>First Name: </td>
                <td style="width: 193px">
                    <asp:TextBox ID="firstName" Runat="server" />
                </td>
```

Example 13-1. Content file for Profile Table (continued)

```
              </tr>
              <tr>
                  <td>Last Name: </td>
                  <td style="width: 193px">
                   <asp:TextBox ID="lastName" Runat="server" /></td>
              </tr>
              <tr>
                  <td>Phone number: </td>
                  <td style="width: 193px">
                     <asp:TextBox ID="phone" Runat="server" />
                  </td>
              </tr>
              <tr>
                  <td>BirthDate</td>
                  <td style="width: 193px">
                     <asp:TextBox ID="birthDate" Runat="server" />
                  </td>
              </tr>
               <tr>
                  <td>
                     <asp:Button ID="save" Text="Save" Runat="server"
                        OnClick="save_Click" />
                   </td>
                  <td style="width: 193px"></td>
              </tr>
          </table>

    </div>
    </form>
</body>
</html>
```

All that remains to be done is for you to add an event handler for the Save button:

```
protected void save_Click(object sender, EventArgs e)
{
    if (Profile.IsAnonymous == false)
    {
        Profile.lastName = this.lastName.Text;
        Profile.firstName = this.firstName.Text;
        Profile.phoneNumber = this.phone.Text;
        DateTime birthDate = Convert.ToDateTime(this.birthDate.Text);
        Profile.birthDate = birthDate;        }
    Response.Redirect("Welcome.aspx");
}
```

 If Intellisense does not recognize the Profile.lastName field, leave the
if statement empty, build the application, and try again, which will
force VS2005 to reread the configuration file.

When you start the application, you are asked to log in. Once you're logged in, a new hyperlink appears: Add Profile Info. This was created by the hyperlink you added to the LoggedInTemplate (above). Clicking on that link brings you to your new profile page.

The Profile object has properties that correspond to the properties you added in *web.config*. To test that the Profile object has stored this date, you want to add a panel to the bottom of the Welcome page just before the closing </div> tag:

```
<asp:Panel ID="pnlInfo" Runat="server" Visible="False" Width="422px" Height="63px">
  <br />
  <table width="100%">
    <tr>
      <td>
        <asp:Label ID="lblFullName" Runat="server"
         Text="Full name unknown">
        </asp:Label></td>
      </tr>
    <tr>
      <td>
        <asp:Label ID="lblPhone" Runat="server"
          Text="Phone number unknown">
        </asp:Label>
      </td>
    </tr>
    <tr>
      <td>
        <asp:Label ID="lblBirthDate" Runat="server"
            Text="Birthdate unknown">
        </asp:Label>
      </td>
    </tr>
  </table>
</asp:Panel>
```

The panel has a table with three rows, and each row has a label initialized to say the value is unknown (this is not normally needed, but is included here to ensure the data you see was in fact retrieved from the Profile object.) When the page is loaded, you check to see if you have Profile data for this user and, if so, you assign that data to the appropriate controls.

To do so, implement Page_Load in *Welcome.aspx.cs*:

```
protected void Page_Load(object sender, EventArgs e)
{
    if (Profile.UserName != null && Profile.IsAnonymous == false)
    {
        this.pnlInfo.Visible = true;
        this.lblFullName.Text = Profile.firstName + " " + Profile.lastName;
        this.lblPhone.Text = Profile.phoneNumber;
        this.lblBirthDate.Text = Profile.birthDate.ToShortDateString();
    }
    else
```

```
    {
        this.pnlInfo.Visible = false;
    }
}
```

Run the application, log in, and click Add Profile Info. You will be brought to the Profile Information form, as shown in Figure 13-2.

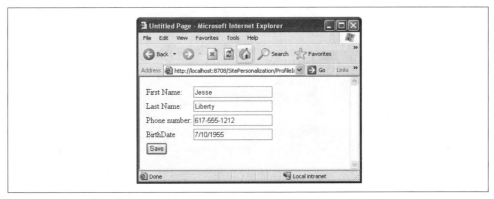

Figure 13-2. Profile information page

When you click Save and return to the Welcome page, the Page_Load event fires, both parts of the if statement return true, that is the UserName value is in the profile (and is not null), and the user is logged in and not anonymous.

```
if (Profile.UserName != null && Profile.IsAnonymous == false)
```

Your profile information is displayed, as shown in Figure 13-3.

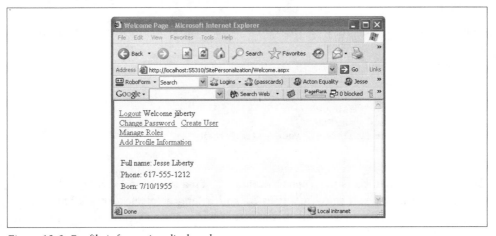

Figure 13-3. Profile information displayed

Exploring the Profile Tables

Open the Database Explorer window, and look at the Tables in the aspnetdb database. Open two tables: aspnet_Users (which lists all the users your security system knows about) and aspnet_Profile (which lists the profile information for those users). To see these next to each other, click and drag the tab for one of the views, as shown in Figure 13-4.

Figure 13-4. Drag tab

When you let go a menu will open, offering to create a new tab group, as shown in Figure 13-5.

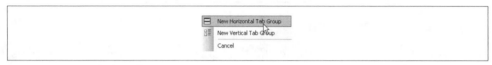

Figure 13-5. Create new tab group

This done, you can see the Profile tab and the Users tab in a single window. The Users tab shows you that each user has a unique UserID. The profile table has a foreign key into that table (UserID) and lists the PropertyNames and PropertyValues, as shown in Figure 13-6.

PropertyNames matches up with the entries you created in the <profile> section of *web.config*:

```
<profile>
    <properties>
        <add name="lastName" />
        <add name="firstName" />
        <add name="phoneNumber" />
        <add name="birthDate" type="System.DateTime"/>
    </properties>
</profile>
```

Each property is named (such as phoneNumber), given a type (S for string), and a starting offset (phoneNumber begins at offset 5) and a length (phoneNumber's value has a length of 12). This offset and value are used to find the value within the PropertyValueString field.

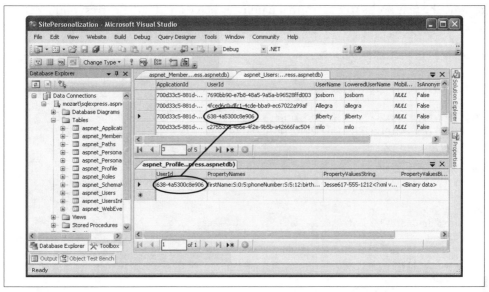

Figure 13-6. Profile Tables

birthDate is listed as a string that begins at offset 17 and is 95 characters long, but if you look at the propertyValuesString column, you'll find that the birthdate is encoded as XML.

Personalizing with Complex Types

While personalizing a site for your users is terrific, to make a useful commercial site, you often have to store complex user-defined types (classes) or collections.

In the next exercise, you'll edit the *web.config* file to add a collection of strings called CHOSENBOOKS. Doing so will allow the user to choose one or more books and have those choices stored in the user's profile.

Add a line to *web.config* for your new property:

```
<profile>
  <properties>
    <add name="lastName" />
    <add name="firstName" />
    <add name="phoneNumber" />
    <add name="birthDate" type="System.DateTime"/>
    <add name="CHOSENBOOKS"
        type="System.Collections.Specialized.StringCollection" />
  </properties>
</profile>
```

To see this collection at work, edit the page *ProfileInfo.aspx*, inserting a row with a checkbox list just above the row with the Save button. While you are there, let's rename the text boxes to our normal naming scheme and fix the corresponding code. The complete content file is shown in Example 13-2.

Example 13-2. Revised ProfileInfo.aspx

```
<%@ Page Language="VB" AutoEventWireup="false" CodeFile="ProfileInfo.aspx.cs"
   Inherits="ProfileInfo_aspx" %>

<!DOCTYPE html PUBLIC "-//W3C//DTD XHTML 1.1//EN"
   "http://www.w3.org/TR/xhtml11/DTD/xhtml11.dtd">

<html xmlns="http://www.w3.org/1999/xhtml" >
<head runat="server">
    <title>Untitled Page</title>
</head>
<body>
    <form id="form1" runat="server">
    <div>
        <table>
        <tr>
            <td>First Name: </td>
            <td style="width: 193px">
              <asp:TextBox ID="txtFirstName" Runat="server" />
            </td>
        </tr>
        <tr>
            <td>Last Name: </td>
            <td style="width: 193px">
             <asp:TextBox ID="txtLastName" Runat="server" /></td>
        </tr>
        <tr>
            <td>Phone number: </td>
            <td style="width: 193px">
                <asp:TextBox ID="txtPhone" Runat="server" />
            </td>
        </tr>
        <tr>
            <td>BirthDate</td>
            <td style="width: 193px">
                <asp:TextBox ID="txtBirthDate" Runat="server" />
            </td>
        </tr>
         <tr>
            <td>
                <asp:CheckBoxList ID="cblChosenBooks" runat="server">
                    <asp:ListItem>Programming C#</asp:ListItem>
                    <asp:ListItem>Programming ASP.NET</asp:ListItem>
                    <asp:ListItem>Programming .NET Apps</asp:ListItem>
                    <asp:ListItem>Agile Software Development</asp:ListItem>
                    <asp:ListItem>UML2 For Dummies</asp:ListItem>
                    <asp:ListItem>
                        Object Oriented Design Heuristics
                    </asp:ListItem>
```

Example 13-2. Revised ProfileInfo.aspx (continued)

```
                        <asp:ListItem>Design Patterns</asp:ListItem>
                    </asp:CheckBoxList>
                </td>
            </tr>
            <tr>
                <td>
                    <asp:Button ID="save" Text="Save" Runat="server"
                        OnClick="save_Click" />
                </td>
                <td style="width: 193px"></td>
            </tr>
        </table>

    </div>
    </form>
</body>
</html>
```

Modify the Save button handler to add the selected books to the profile:

```
protected void save_Click(object sender, EventArgs e)
{
    if (Profile.IsAnonymous == false)
    {
        Profile.lastName = this.lastName.Text;
        Profile.firstName = this.firstName.Text;
        Profile.phoneNumber = this.phone.Text;
        DateTime birthDate = Convert.ToDateTime(this.birthDate.Text);
        Profile.birthDate = birthDate;
        Profile.CHOSENBOOKS =
                new System.Collections.Specialized.StringCollection( );
        foreach (ListItem li in this.cblChosenBooks.Items)
        {
            if (li.Selected)
            {
                Profile.CHOSENBOOKS.Add(li.Value.ToString( ));
            }
        }

    }
    Response.Redirect("Welcome.aspx");
}
```

To make your code a bit easier to maintain, you want to have the selected values (e.g., name, phone, selected books) pre-filled when you return to the profile editing page, so you'll implement a bit of code on Page_Load to get the initial values from the Profile object:

```
protected void Page_Load(object sender, EventArgs e)
{
    if (Profile.IsAnonymous == false)
    {
        this.lastName.Text = Profile.lastName;
```

```
            this.firstName.Text = Profile.firstName;
            this.phone.Text = Profile.phoneNumber;
            this.birthDate.Text = Profile.birthDate.ToShortDateString( );

            if (Profile.CHOSENBOOKS != null)
            {
               foreach (ListItem li in this.cblChosenBooks.Items)
               {
                  foreach (string profileString in Profile.CHOSENBOOKS)
                  {
                     if (li.Text == profileString)
                     {
                        li.Selected = true;
                     }          // end if text matches
                  }             // end for each profile string
               }                // end for each item in list
            }                   // end if chosen books not null
         }                      // end if not anonymous
      }                         // end page load
```

 Each time you save the books, you create an instance of the string collection and then iterate through the checked list boxes, looking for the selected items. Each selected item is added to the string collection within the profile (the CHOSENBOOKS property).

To confirm that this data has been stored, add a list box (lbBooks) to the *Welcome.aspx* file:

```
<tr>
   <td>
      <asp:ListBox  ID="lbBooks" runat="server" />
   </td>
</tr>
```

Update Welcome.aspx.cs.Page_Load to reflect the contents of the chosen books:

```
protected void Page_Load(object sender, EventArgs e)
{
   if (Profile.UserName != null && Profile.IsAnonymous == false)
   {
      this.pnlInfo.Visible = true;
      this.lblFullName.Text = Profile.firstName + " " + Profile.lastName;
      this.lblPhone.Text = Profile.phoneNumber;
      this.lblBirthDate.Text = Profile.birthDate.ToShortDateString( );

      this.lbBooks.Items.Clear( );
      if (Profile.CHOSENBOOKS != null)
      {
         foreach (string bookName in Profile.CHOSENBOOKS)
         {
            this.lbBooks.Items.Add(bookName);
         }
      }
```

```
   }
   else
   {
      this.pnlInfo.Visible = false;
   }
```

When you click on the profile, you will have the option to add (or change) the books associated with your profile, as shown in Figure 13-7.

Figure 13-7. Adding books to the profile

When you click Save and return to the welcome page, your saved profile information will be reflected, as shown in Figure 13-8.

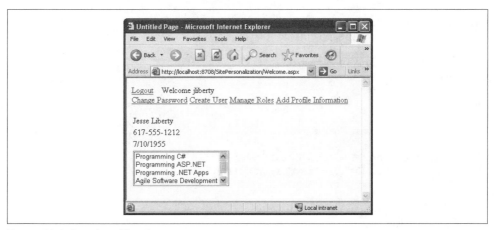

Figure 13-8. Saved profile information

Anonymous Personalization

It is common to allow your users to personalize your site before identifying them-selves. A classic example of this is *Amazon.com,* which lets you add books to your shopping cart *before* you log in (you only need to log in when you are ready to pur-chase what is in your cart).

ASP.NET 2.0 supports the ability to link anonymous personalized data with a spe-cific user's personalized data, once that user logs in (you don't want to lose what's in your cart when you do log in).

Begin by creating a new web site named *AnonymousPersonalization.* Delete *Default.aspx* and copy the *SitePersonalization* web site to your new site, and test that it is working as expected.

Next, to enable anonymous personalization, you must update your *web.config* file, adding the following in the `<system.web>` section:

```
<anonymousIdentification enabled="true" />
```

Also, add the attribute-value pair `allowAnonymous="true"` to the `CHOSENBOOKS` element of *web.config.*

Redesign your *Welcome.aspx* page so the hyperlink that links to the profile informa-tion page, and the `lbBooks` list box, are both outside of the `LoginView` control (so you can see the hyperlink and the list, even if you are not logged in). While you are at it, rename Add Profile Info to Profile Info, since you will be using this link to add, and edit, the profile info, as shown in Example 13-3.

Example 13-3. Modified Welcome.aspx

```
<%@ Page Language="VB" AutoEventWireup="false" CodeFile="Welcome.aspx.cs"
   Inherits="Welcome_aspx" %>

<!DOCTYPE html PUBLIC "-//W3C//DTD XHTML 1.1//EN"
   "http://www.w3.org/TR/xhtml11/DTD/xhtml11.dtd">

<html xmlns="http://www.w3.org/1999/xhtml" >
<head runat="server">
    <title>Welcome</title>
</head>
<body>
    <form id="form1" runat="server">
    <div>
        <asp:LoginStatus ID="LoginStatus1" runat="server" />
        <asp:LoginView ID="LoginView1" runat="server">
            <LoggedInTemplate>
                Welcome
                <asp:LoginName ID="LoginName1" runat="server" />
                <br />
                <asp:HyperLink
                    ID="hlChangePW"
```

Example 13-3. Modified Welcome.aspx (continued)

```
                    NavigateUrl="ChangePW.aspx"
                    runat="server">Change Password
                </asp:HyperLink>
                 
                <asp:HyperLink
                    ID="hlCreateUser"
                    NavigateUrl="CreateUser.aspx"
                    runat="server">Create User
                </asp:HyperLink>
                <br />
                <asp:HyperLink
                    ID="hlManageRoles"
                    NavigateUrl="ManageRoles.aspx"
                    runat="server">Manage Roles
                </asp:HyperLink> <br />
        </LoggedInTemplate>
        <AnonymousTemplate>
            You are not logged in.
            Please click the login link to log in to this system.
        </AnonymousTemplate>
    </asp:LoginView>
<asp:HyperLink
    ID="hlProfile"
    NavigateUrl="ProfileInfo.aspx"
    runat="server">Profile Information
</asp:HyperLink>

<asp:ListBox  ID="lbBooks" runat="server" />

    <asp:Panel ID="pnlInfo" Runat="server" Visible="False"
      Width="422px" Height="63px">
        <br />
        <table width="100%">
            <tr>
            <td style="height: 21px">
                <asp:Label ID="lblFullName" Runat="server"
                Text="Full name unknown">
                </asp:Label></td>
            </tr>
            <tr>
            <td>
                <asp:Label ID="lblPhone" Runat="server"
                Text="Phone number unknown">
                </asp:Label>
            </td>
            </tr>
            <tr>
            <td>
                <asp:Label ID="lblBirthDate" Runat="server"
                    Text="Birthdate  unknown">
                </asp:Label>
            </td>
```

Example 13-3. Modified Welcome.aspx (continued)

```
              </tr>
           </table>
        </asp:Panel>
    </div>
 </form>
</body>
</html>
```

When an anonymous user chooses books, that user will automatically be assigned a Globally Unique Identifier (GUID), and an entry will be made in the database. However, only those properties marked with allowAnonymous will be stored, so you must modify your save_Click event handler in *ProfileInfo.aspx.cs*. Bracket the entries for all the profile elements *except* CHOSENBOOKS in an if statement that tests whether the user is currently Anonymous, as shown in the following snippet:

```
protected void Page_Load(object sender, EventArgs e)
{
   if ( !IsPostBack )
   {
      if (Profile.IsAnonymous == true)
      {
         this.pnlNonAnonymousInfo.Visible = false;
      }
      else
      {
         this.lastName.Text = Profile.lastName;
         this.firstName.Text = Profile.firstName;
         this.phone.Text = Profile.phoneNumber;
         this.birthDate.Text = Profile.birthDate.ToShortDateString( );
      }                     // end if not anonymous
      if (Profile.CHOSENBOOKS != null)
      {
         foreach (ListItem li in this.cblChosenBooks.Items)
         {
            foreach (string profileString in Profile.CHOSENBOOKS)
            {
               if (li.Text == profileString)
               {
                  li.Selected = true;
               }            // end if text matches
            }               // end for each profile string
         }                  // end for each item in list
      }                     // end if chosen books not null
   }                        // end if not postback /user name not null
}                           // end page load
```

When saving your Profile data, you check if the IsAnonymous property is false. If it is false, you will know you are dealing with a logged-in user, and you may get all of the properties; otherwise, you may get only those that are allowed for anonymous users.

Modify the *ProfileInfo* page so the non-anonymous data is in a panel that will be invisible for users who are not logged in, as shown in Example 13-4.

Example 13-4. Modified ProfileInfo.aspx

```
<%@ Page Language="VB" AutoEventWireup="false" CodeFile="ProfileInfo.aspx.cs"
   Inherits="ProfileInfo_aspx" %>

<!DOCTYPE html PUBLIC "-//W3C//DTD XHTML 1.1//EN"
   "http://www.w3.org/TR/xhtml11/DTD/xhtml11.dtd">

<html xmlns="http://www.w3.org/1999/xhtml" >
<head runat="server">
    <title>Profile Information</title>
</head>
<body>
    <form id="form1" runat="server">
    <div>
        <asp:Panel ID="pnlNonAnonymousInfo" runat="server">
            <table>
            <tr>
                <td>First Name: </td>
                <td style="width: 193px">
                  <asp:TextBox ID="txtFirstName" Runat="server" />
                </td>
            </tr>
            <tr>
                <td>Last Name: </td>
                <td style="width: 193px">
                  <asp:TextBox ID="txtLastName" Runat="server" /></td>
            </tr>
            <tr>
                <td>Phone number: </td>
                <td style="width: 193px">
                   <asp:TextBox ID="txtPhone" Runat="server" />
                </td>
            </tr>
            <tr>
                <td>BirthDate</td>
                <td style="width: 193px">
                   <asp:TextBox ID="txtBirthDate" Runat="server" />
                </td>
            </tr>
            </table>
        </asp:Panel>
        <table>
            <tr>
                <td>
                    <asp:CheckBoxList ID="cblChosenBooks" runat="server">
                        <asp:ListItem>Programming C#</asp:ListItem>
                        <asp:ListItem>Programming ASP.NET</asp:ListItem>
                        <asp:ListItem>Programming .NET Apps</asp:ListItem>
                        <asp:ListItem>Agile Software Development</asp:ListItem>
```

Example 13-4. Modified ProfileInfo.aspx (continued)

```
                        <asp:ListItem>UML2 For Dummies</asp:ListItem>
                        <asp:ListItem>
                            Object Oriented Design Heuristics
                        </asp:ListItem>
                        <asp:ListItem>Design Patterns</asp:ListItem>
                    </asp:CheckBoxList>
                </td>
            </tr>
            <tr>
                <td>
                    <asp:Button ID="save" Text="Save" Runat="server"
                        OnClick="save_Click" />
                </td>
                <td style="width: 193px"></td>
            </tr>
        </table>
    </div>
    </form>
</body>
</html>
```

Remove the test for whether IsAnonymous is false in *Profile.info.aspx.cs* save_Click so the assignment to the profile happens whether or not the user is anonymous:

```
protected void save_Click(object sender, EventArgs e)
{
    if (Profile.IsAnonymous == false)
    {
        Profile.lastName = this.lastName.Text;
        Profile.firstName = this.firstName.Text;
        Profile.phoneNumber = this.phone.Text;
        DateTime birthDate = Convert.ToDateTime(this.birthDate.Text);
        Profile.birthDate = birthDate;
    }
    Profile.CHOSENBOOKS = new System.Collections.Specialized.StringCollection( );
    foreach (ListItem li in this.cblChosenBooks.Items)
    {
        if (li.Selected)
        {
            Profile.CHOSENBOOKS.Add(li.Value.ToString( ));
        }
    }

    Response.Redirect("Welcome.aspx");
}
```

Fix Page_Load in *Welcome.aspx.cs* as well to display the anonymous list of books:

```
protected void Page_Load(object sender, EventArgs e)
{
    if ( ! Profile.IsAnonymous )
    {
        this.pnlInfo.Visible = true;
```

```
            this.lblFullName.Text = Profile.firstName + " " + Profile.lastName;
            this.lblPhone.Text = Profile.phoneNumber;
            this.lblBirthDate.Text = Profile.birthDate.ToShortDateString( );

            this.lbBooks.Items.Clear( );
        }
        else
        {
            this.pnlInfo.Visible = false;
        }

        if (Profile.CHOSENBOOKS != null)
        {
            foreach (string bookName in Profile.CHOSENBOOKS)
            {
                this.lbBooks.Items.Add(bookName);
            }
        }
    }
}
```

Run the application. Do *not* log in; click the Profile Info link. Select a few books and click Save. When you return to the Welcome page, you will still not be logged in, but your selected books are displayed, as shown in Figure 13-9.

Figure 13-9. Anonymous user information

Stop the application and reopen the database. Open the apsnet_Users table and the aspnet_Profile tables. You'll see that an ID has been created for the anonymous user (and the UserName has been set to the GUID generated). In addition, the chosen books list has been stored in the corresponding record, as shown in Figure 13-10.

When the user *does* log in, you must migrate the Profile data you've accumulated for the anonymous user to the appropriate authenticated user's record (so, for example, shopping cart items are not lost). You do this by writing a handler for the global MigrateAnonymous event that is fired when a user logs in. This handler must be named

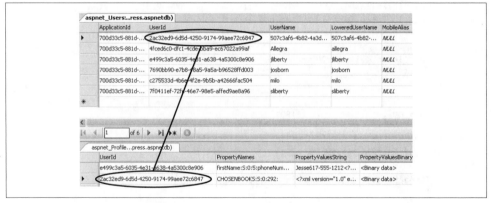

Figure 13-10. Anonymous user record in database

Profile_MigrateAnonymous (case sensitive) and is created within the script tags in *global.asax*:

```
void Profile_MigrateAnonymous(object sender,
    ProfileMigrateEventArgs e)
{
    ASP.ProfileCommon anonymousProfile =
        Profile.GetProfile(e.AnonymousId);

    if (anonymousProfile != null &&
        anonymousProfile.CHOSENBOOKS != null)
    {
        foreach (string s in anonymousProfile.CHOSENBOOKS)
        {
            Profile.CHOSENBOOKS.Remove(s); // remove dupes
            Profile.CHOSENBOOKS.Add(s);
        }
    }
}
```

 If your project does not have a *global.asax* file, right-click on the project and choose Add New Item. One of your choices will be Global Application Class, and it will default to the name *global.asax*. Click Add.

The first step in the event handler is to get a reference to the profile that matches the AnonymousID passed in as a property of the ProfileMigrateEventArgs structure (shown in bold).

If the reference is not null, then you will know there is a matching anonymous profile, and that you may pick up whatever data you need from that profile. In this case, you copy over the CHOSENBOOKS collection.

The user's profile is updated, and the books chosen as an anonymous user are now part of that user's profile, as shown in Figure 13-11.

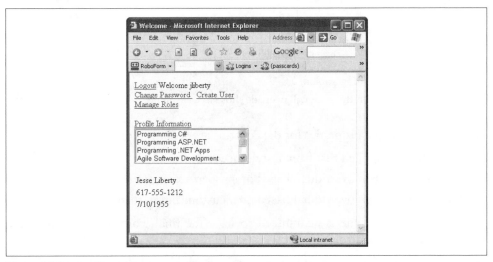

Figure 13-11. Profiles merged

Themes and Skins

Many users like to personalize their favorite web sites by setting the look and feel of the site's controls to meet their own personal aesthetic preferences. ASP.NET 2.0 provides support for *themes* that enable you to offer that level of personalization to your users.

A *theme* is a collection of skins. A *skin* describes how a *control* should look. A skin can define stylesheet attributes, images, colors, and so forth.

Having multiple themes allows your users to choose how they want your site to look by switching from one set of skins to another at the touch of a button. Combined with personalization, your site can remember the look and feel your user prefers.

There are two types of themes. The first, called *stylesheet themes,* define styles that may be overridden by the page or control. These are, essentially, equivalent to CSS style sheets. The second type, called *customization themes*, can*not* be overridden. You set a stylesheet theme by adding the StyleSheetTheme attribute to the Page directive, and, similarly, you set a Customization theme by setting the Theme attribute in the Page directive.

You can set the default theme for the entire web site in *web.config* by adding the pages element to the system.web element within the configuration element, as follows:

```
<configuration>
<system.web>
        <pages theme="Psychedelic" />
    </system.web>
</configuration>
```

Settings in the page will override those in *web.config*.

In any given page, the properties for the controls are set in this order:

1. Properties are applied first from a stylesheet theme.
2. Properties are then overridden based on properties set in the control.
3. Properties are then overridden based on a customization theme.

The customization theme is guaranteed to have the final word in determining the look and feel of the control.

Skins come in two flavors: default skins and explicitly named skins. Thus, you might create a Labels skin file with this declaration:

```
<asp:Label runat="server"
ForeColor="Blue" Font-Size="Large"
Font-Bold="True" Font-Italic="True" />
```

This is a default skin for all Label controls. It looks like the definition of an asp:Label server control, but it is housed in a skin file and is used to define the look and feel of all Label objects.

In addition, however, you might decide that some labels must be red. To accomplish this, you create a second skin, but you assign this skin a SkinID property:

```
<asp:Label runat="server" SkinID="RedLabel"
ForeColor="Red" Font-Size="Large"
Font-Bold="True" Font-Italic="True" />
```

Any Label that does not have a SkinID attribute will get the default skin; any Label that sets SkinID="RedLabel" will get your named skin.

The steps to providing a personalized web site are the following:

1. Create the test site.
2. Organize your themes and skins.
3. Enable themes and skins for your site.
4. Specify themes declaratively if you wish.

Create the Test Site

To demonstrate the use of themes and skins, you'll create a new web site (*Themes*) but you will use Copy Web Site to bring over all the personalization code from the previous example and set the start page to *Welcome.aspx*.

To begin your new application, you'll need some controls whose look and feel you can set. Open *Welcome.aspx* and add the following controls to the page, using the code shown in Example 13-5 (add this new code after the panel but before the closing <div>).

Example 13-5. Controls for demonstrating skins

```
<table width ="100%">
    <tr>
        <td >
            <asp:Label ID="lblListBox" Runat="server" Text="ListBox"/>
        </td>
        <td >
            <asp:ListBox ID="lbItems" Runat="server">
                <asp:ListItem>First Item</asp:ListItem>
                <asp:ListItem>Second Item</asp:ListItem>
                <asp:ListItem>Third Item</asp:ListItem>
                <asp:ListItem>Fourth Item</asp:ListItem>
                </asp:ListBox>
        </td>
        <td >
            <asp:Label ID="lblRadioButtonList" Runat="server"
                Text="Radio Button List"/>
        </td>
        <td >
            <asp:RadioButtonList ID="RadioButtonList1" Runat="server">
                <asp:ListItem>Radio Button 1</asp:ListItem>
                <asp:ListItem>Radio Button 2</asp:ListItem>
                <asp:ListItem>Radio Button 3</asp:ListItem>
                <asp:ListItem>Radio Button 4</asp:ListItem>
                <asp:ListItem>Radio Button 5</asp:ListItem>
                <asp:ListItem>Radio Button 6</asp:ListItem>
                </asp:RadioButtonList><br />
        </td>
    </tr>
    <tr>
        <td>
            <asp:Label ID="lblCalendar" Runat="server"
            Text="Calendar"></asp:Label>
        </td>
        <td>
            <asp:Calendar ID="Calendar1" Runat="server" />
        </td>
        <td>
            <asp:Label ID="lblTextBox" Runat="server"
            Text="TextBox"/>
        </td>
```

Example 13-5. Controls for demonstrating skins (continued)

```
        <td>
            <asp:TextBox ID="TextBox1" Runat="server"/>
        </td>
    </tr>
</table>
```

You will use skins to change the look and feel of these controls, and you will organize sets of skins into themes.

Organize Site Themes and Skins

Themes are stored in your project in a folder named App_Themes. To create this folder, go to Solution Explorer, right-click on the project folder and choose Add Folder → Theme Folder. Name the new folder Dark Blue –, the folder *App_Themes* will be created automatically, with a Theme folder named *Dark Blue* under it. Create a second theme folder, named *Psychedelic*.

Right-click on the *Dark Blue* theme folder and choose Add New Item. From the template lists, choose Skin File and name it *Button.skin* (to hold all the button skins for your Dark Blue theme), as shown in Figure 13-12.

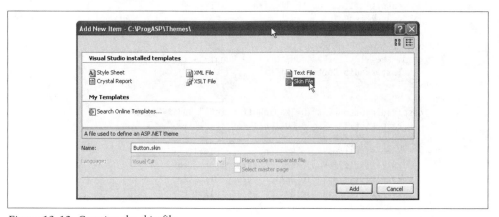

Figure 13-12. Creating the skin file

Each skin file is a text file that contains a definition for the control type but with no ID. For example, your Label.skin file might look like this (for the Dark Blue theme):

```
<asp:Label Runat="server"
    ForeColor="Blue" Font-Size="Large"
    Font-Bold="True" Font-Italic="True" />
```

Create skin files for each of the following types in both themes:

- *Button.skin*
- *Calendar.skin*

- *Label.skin*
- *ListBox.skin*
- *RadioButton.skin*
- *Text.skin*

At this point, your solution should look more or less like Figure 13-13.

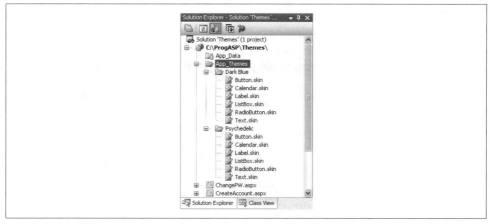

Figure 13-13. Themes and skins in your project

Enable Themes and Skins

To let your users choose the theme they like and have it stored in their profile, you need to add a single line to the <properties> element in the <profile> element of *web.config*:

```
<add name="Theme" />
```

Save and rebuild your application to make sure the profile is set properly.

Specify Themes for Your Page

You can set the themes on your page declaratively or programmatically. To set a theme declaratively, add the Theme attribute to the Page directive:

```
<%@ Page Language="C#" AutoEventWireup="true"
CodeFile="Welcome.aspx.cs" Inherits="Welcome_aspx" Theme="Dark Blue"%>
```

This will set the page's theme to the Dark Blue theme you've created

You can set the theme programmatically by hard coding it or (even better) by setting it from the user's profile.

Setting Stylesheet Themes

Stylesheet themes are set by overriding the StyleSheetTheme property for the page. Intellisense will help you with this. Open *Welcome.aspx.cs*, and scroll to the bottom of the class. Type the words *public override* and all the overridable members are shown. Start typing *sty* and Intellisense will scroll to the property you want, StyleSheetTheme, as shown in Figure 13-14.

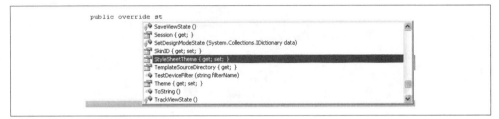

Figure 13-14. Overriding Stylesheet theme

Once Intellisense finds the method you want, press TAB to accept that property. Fill in the accessors as follows:

```
public override string StyleSheetTheme
{
    get
    {
        if ((!Profile.IsAnonymous) && Profile.Theme != null)
        {
            return Profile.Theme;
        }
        else
        {
            return "Dark Blue";
        }
    }
    set
    {
        Profile.Theme = value;
    }
}
```

Setting Customization Themes

If you are going to set a *customization* theme programmatically, however, you must do so from the PreInit event handler for the page because the theme must be set before the controls are created.

```
protected void Page_PreInit(object sender, EventArgs e)
{
    if (!Profile.IsAnonymous)
```

```
    {
        Page.Theme = Profile.Theme;
    }
}
```

 The PreInit event handler is new in ASP.NET 2.0.

Setting the theme in PreInit creates a bit of a difficulty when you want to allow the user to change the theme at runtime. If you create a control that posts the page back with a new theme, the PreInit code runs *before* the event handler for the button that changes the theme, and so by the time the theme is changed the buttons have already been drawn.

To overcome this you must, unfortunately, refresh the page. An alternative is to post to another page, for example, adding two buttons to the *ProfileInfo.aspx* page at the bottom of the table at the bottom of the page:

```
<tr>
    <td>
        <asp:Button ID="ThemeBlue" Text="Dark Blue"
          Runat="server" OnClick="Set_Theme" />
    </td>
    <td>
        <asp:Button ID="ThemePsych" Text="Psychedelic"
          Runat="server" OnClick="Set_Theme" />
    </td>
</tr>
```

The two buttons share a single click event handler. An easy way to have VS2005 set up that event handler for you is to switch to design view and click on one of the buttons. Click on the lightning bolt in the properties window to go to the events, and double-click on the Set_Theme event. You are ready to implement the event handler. You'll cast the sender to the button and check its text, setting the theme appropriately:

```
protected void Set_Theme(object sender, EventArgs e)
{
    Button btn = (Button)sender;
    if (btn.Text == "Psychedelic")
    {
        Profile.Theme = "Psychedelic";
    }
    else
    {
        Profile.Theme = "Dark Blue";
    }
}
```

When the user is not logged on, the page's default theme will be used. Once the user sets a theme in the profile, that theme will be used. Create skins for your two themes and run the application to see the effect of applying the themes.

Using Named Skins

You can override the theme for particular controls by using named skins. For example, you can set the lblRadioButtonList label in *Welcome.aspx* to be red even in the DeepBlue theme, by using a named skin. To accomplish this, create two Label skins in the *Label.skin* file within the *Deep Blue* folder:

```
<asp:Label Runat="server"
ForeColor="Blue" Font-Size="Large"
Font-Bold="True" Font-Italic="True" />

<asp:Label Runat="server" SkinID="Red"
ForeColor="Red" Font-Size="Large"
Font-Bold="True" Font-Italic="True" />
```

The first skin is the default, and the second is a named skin because it has a *SkinID* property set to "Red." Open the source for *Welcome.aspx* and find the label you want to make red, and add the attribute SkinID="Red", as shown in the following code snippet:

```
<asp:Label ID="lblRadioButtonList" Runat="server"
    Text="Radio Button List"
    SkinID="Red"/>
```

When you log in and set your theme to Dark Blue, you'll find that the label for the Radio Button List is Red (honest!), as shown in Figure 13-15.

Web Parts

Web Parts allow your users to reconfigure sections of your site to meet their own needs and preferences. Many information providers allow the user to pick which content they want displayed and in which column to display it. Web Parts allow you to provide that functionality with drag and drop "parts" of your page.

To learn about Web Parts, create a new web site (call it *WebParts*) and copy the SitePersonalization web site from the beginning of this chapter. Set the Welcome page as the start page and ensure you can log in with an account you created previously (or, alternatively, set *CreateAccount* as the start page and create a new account to use).

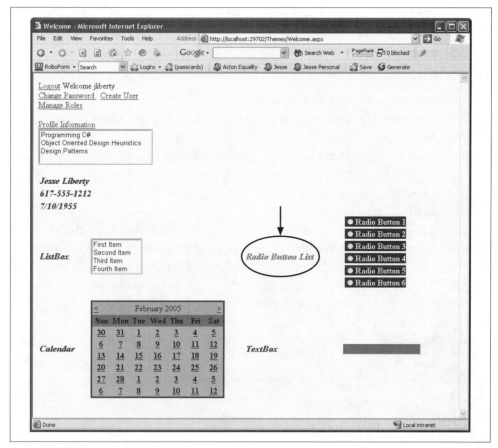

Figure 13-15. Radio button list label is red

Web Parts Architecture

Web Parts are created and managed on top of personalization using a structural component, called the WebPartManager control, to manage the interaction of Web Parts and UI Controls to create user-managed interface.

Every Web Parts page has a WebPartManager control. This invisible control tracks all the individual web part controls and manages the Web Parts Zones (described below). It also tracks the different display modes of the page and if personalization of your Web Parts page applies to a particular user or all users.

Creating Zones

A page that uses Web Parts is divided into *zones*: areas of the page that can contain content and controls that derive from the Part class (Part controls). They can contain consistent UI elements (header and footer styles, border styles, and so on) known as the *chrome* of the control.

It is typical (though certainly not required) to organize these zones using tables.

To see a simple example of Web Parts at work, follow these steps:

1. Create a new page called *WebPartsDemo.aspx*.

2. Open the WebParts section of your Toolbox and drag a WebPartsManager onto your page.

3. The job of the WebPartsManager is to track and coordinate all the web part controls on the page. It will not be visible when the page is running.

4. Add a new table, with two rows and three columns. Rearrange the columns so they are not of even size.

5. Drag a WebPartZone into each of the six table cells. Each WebPartZone will have a default name (such as WebPartZone6) and a default heading. You can modify either or both of these properties in the properties window, as shown in Figure 13-16.

6. Set the HeaderText property on the first web part control to News.

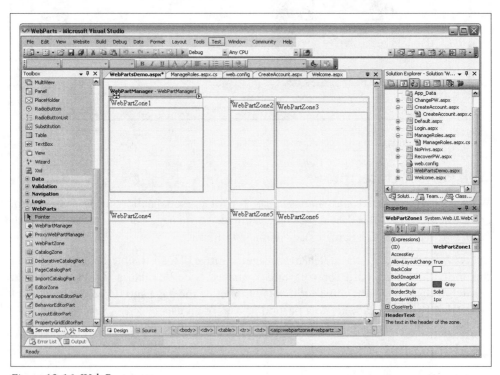

Figure 13-16. Web Parts zones

Adding Controls to Zones

Drag a Label control into the zone. The label is wrapped in a Web Part control, and its title is set to Untitled, as shown in Figure 13-17.

Figure 13-17. Label Web Part

Switch to source view and change the Title property of the label to *Today's News* and the text to the following:

```
<br/>Penguin Classics releases new translation of "In Search of Lost Time".
```

 Title is not normally a property of the Label control and will not show up in the Properties window or Intellisense. However, when you add it to a WebPartZone, it is wrapped, at runtime, in a GenericWebPart control that does recognize this property.

Switch back to Design view and drag a ListBox control into WebPartZone3. Set the header text for the WebPartZone to Sponsors. Click on the list box and then its smart tag and Edit Items to open the ListItems Collection Editor. Add a few items to the list box. Back in Source view, set the Title property to "Our Sponsors." (This control, like the Label control, does not inherently have a Title property, so Intellisense will complain; as the note above explains, all will be well.)

You'll need to log in using one of the accounts you set up previously, and you'll need to add a link to your new page from the Welcome page. Now run the application.

Click on the link to the Web Parts page which you added to *Welcome.aspx*. You should see two Web Parts, complete with Minimize and Close commands, as shown in Figure 13-18.

Minimizing and Restoring

Click on the Minimize tag and a menu appears allowing you to minimize or close the web part, as shown in Figure 13-19.

If you choose Minimize, the web part will be minimized to its title, and the minimize tag will offer the choices of Restore or Close, as shown in Figure 13-20.

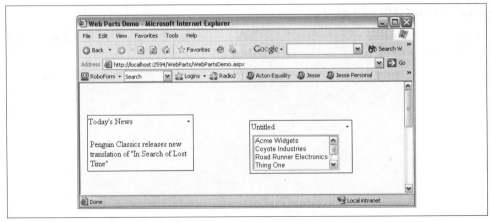

Figure 13-18. Two Web Parts visible

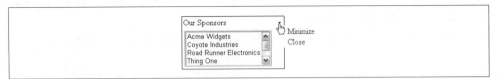

Figure 13-19. Minimize or Close

Figure 13-20. Restore or Close

Exit the application. Restart, sign back in, and navigate to these pages. Aha! The minimized zone remains minimized. The individual's personalized Web Parts are automatically persisted through the personalization database.

Web part controls derive from the Part class and are the essential UI of a Web Parts page. You can create custom Web Part controls, or you can use existing ASP.NET server controls, user controls, and custom controls.

Enabling Editing and Layout Changes

Web Parts provide users with the ability to change the layout of the web part controls by dragging them from zone to zone. You may also allow your users to modify the appearance of the controls, their layout, and their behavior.

The built-in Web Parts control set provides basic editing of any Web Part control on the page. You can create custom editor controls that allow users to do more extensive editing.

Creating a User Control to Enable Changing Page Layout

To edit the contents of zones or move controls from one zone to another, you need to be able to enter Edit and Design mode. To do this, you will create a new user control called *DisplayModeMenu.ascx* (see Chapter 14 for information on creating user controls), which will allow the user to change modes among Browse, Edit, and Design, as shown in Figure 13-21.

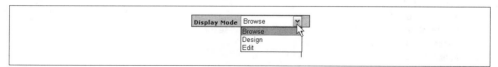

Figure 13-21. Display Mode user control

Right-click on the web project in the Solution Explorer and choose Add New Item. Select Web User Control and name the new user control `DisplayModeMenu`, as shown in Figure 13-22.

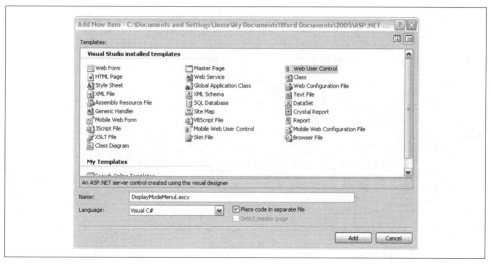

Figure 13-22. Adding a user control

Add the highlighted code listed in Example 13-6 to the content file of your new user control.

Example 13-6. DisplayModeMenu .ascx file

```
<%@ Control Language="C#" AutoEventWireup="true"
   CodeFile="DisplayModeMenu.ascx.cs"
   Inherits="DisplayModeMenu" %>

<div>
  <asp:Panel ID="Panel1" runat="server"
```

Example 13-6. DisplayModeMenu .ascx file (continued)

```
      Borderwidth="1"
      Width="230"
      BackColor="lightgray"
      Font-Names="Verdana, Arial, Sans Serif" >
      <asp:Label ID="Label1" runat="server"
        Text=" Display Mode"
        Font-Bold="true"
        Font-Size="8"
        Width="120" />
      <asp:DropDownList ID="ddlDisplayMode" runat="server"
        AutoPostBack="true"
        EnableViewState="false"
        Width="120"
        OnSelectedIndexChanged="ddlDisplayMode_SelectedIndexChanged" />
  </asp:Panel>
</div>
```

This code creates a panel, and within that panel, it adds a single drop-down list (ddlDisplayMode). It sets the event handler for when the Selected item changes in the drop-down list. To support this page, open the code-behind file (*DisplayModeMenu. ascx.cs*) and add the highlighted code shown in Example 13-7.

Example 13-7. DisplayModeMenu.ascx.cs

```
using System;
using System.Data;
using System.Configuration;
using System.Collections;
using System.Web;
using System.Web.Security;
using System.Web.UI;
using System.Web.UI.WebControls;
using System.Web.UI.WebControls.WebParts;
using System.Web.UI.HtmlControls;

public partial class DisplayModeMenu : System.Web.UI.UserControl
{
    // will reference the current WebPartManager control.
    WebPartManager webPartManager;

    public void Page_Init( object sender, EventArgs e )
    {
        Page.InitComplete += new EventHandler( InitComplete );
    }

    // when the page is fully initialized
    public void InitComplete( object sender, System.EventArgs e )
    {
        webPartManager = WebPartManager.GetCurrentWebPartManager( Page );

        String browseModeName = WebPartManager.BrowseDisplayMode.Name;
```

Example 13-7. DisplayModeMenu.ascx.cs (continued)

```
    foreach ( WebPartDisplayMode mode in
      webPartManager.SupportedDisplayModes )
    {
      String modeName = mode.Name;
      if ( mode.IsEnabled( webPartManager ) )
      {
        ListItem listItem = new ListItem( modeName, modeName );
        ddlDisplayMode.Items.Add( listItem );
      }
    }
  }

  // Change the page to the selected display mode.
  public void ddlDisplayMode_SelectedIndexChanged( object sender,
    EventArgs e )
  {
    String selectedMode = ddlDisplayMode.SelectedValue;

    WebPartDisplayMode mode =
     webPartManager.SupportedDisplayModes[selectedMode];
    if ( mode != null )
    {
      webPartManager.DisplayMode = mode;
    }
  }

  // Set the selected item equal to the current display mode.
  public void Page_PreRender( object sender, EventArgs e )
  {
    ListItemCollection items = ddlDisplayMode.Items;
    int selectedIndex =
      items.IndexOf( items.FindByText( webPartManager.DisplayMode.Name ) );
    ddlDisplayMode.SelectedIndex = selectedIndex;
  }
}
```

Open the *WebPartsDemo* page in Design mode and make a space between the WebPartManager and the table of zones. Drag the *DisplayModeMenu.ascx* file from the solution explorer into that space. Change to Source view; VS2005 has done two things for you: it has registered the new control:

```
<%@ Register Src="DisplayModeMenu.ascx" TagName="DisplayModeMenul"
TagPrefix="uc1" %>
```

Second, it has placed the control into the form:

```
<div>
    <asp:WebPartManager ID="WebPartManager1" runat="server" />
    <uc1:DisplayModeMenul ID="DisplayModeMenul1" runat="server" />
```

Before testing this, drag an Editor Zone into the lower righthand cell in the table (currently unoccupied) and drag an AppearanceEditorPart and a LayoutEditorPart onto the Editor Zone. To make the Editor Zone stand out, click on its smart tab and choose AutoFormat and then Professional. Your design page should look more or less like Figure 13-23.

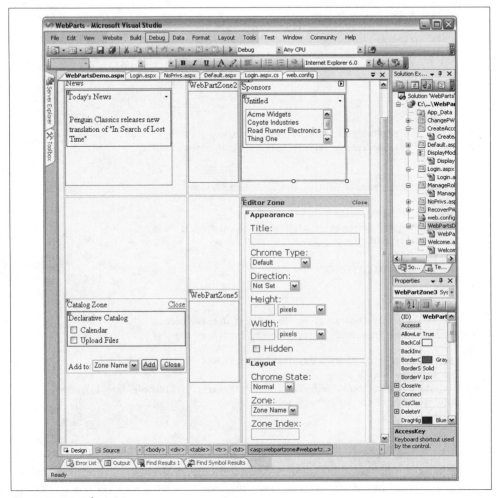

Figure 13-23. Editor zone

Moving a Part

Run the application. When you log in and go to the Web Parts page, you are in Browse mode. Use the Display mode drop-down to switch to Design mode and all the zones (except the editing zone) appear. You can click on any Web Part (e.g., *Today's News*) and drag it to any zone, as shown in Figure 13-24.

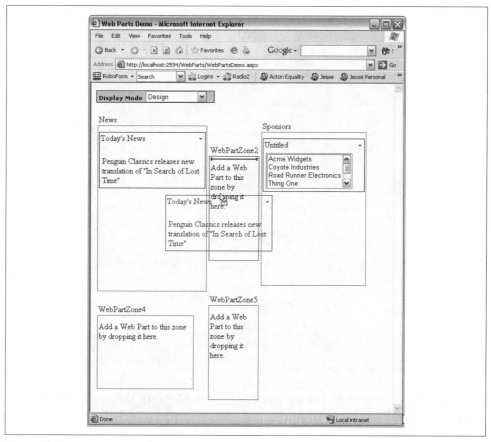

Figure 13-24. Dragging a Web Part

Editing a Part

Next, change the drop-down to Edit mode. Nothing much happens, but click on the drop-down tag on one of the web part controls. A menu appears that now includes Edit, as shown in Figure 13-25.

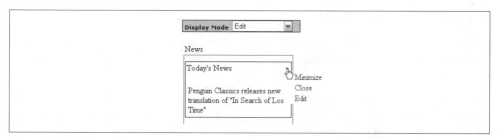

Figure 13-25. Edit mode

Click Edit and the Edit zone appears, allowing you to edit the current web part, as shown in Figure 13-26.

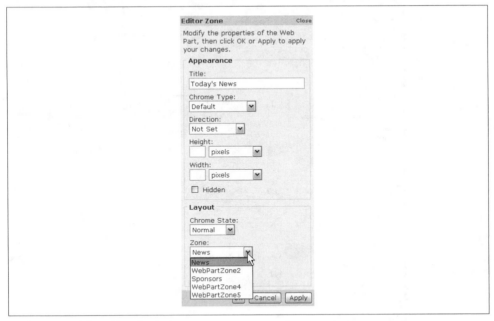

Figure 13-26. Editor Zone In Action

The Appearance editor lets you change the title and look of the Web Part, and the Layout lets you change, among other things, which zone the Web Part will appear in.

Adding Parts from a Catalog

You may want to provide a catalog of Web Parts that your users can add to the various zones. To do so, open *WebPartsDemo.aspx* in Source view and find Zone 4. Remove it from the cell so the cell is empty. Switch to Design view and drag a `CatalogZone` control into the newly empty cell. Click on the zone, and in the properties window, set the `HeaderText` property to Catalog Zone. Drag a `DeclarativeCatalogPart` control into the zone, as shown in Figure 13-27.

Click the smart tag on the `DeclarativeCatalogPart` and select Edit Templates. From the standard tab of the toolbox, drag on a `Calendar` and a `File Upload` control, as shown in Figure 13-28.

Before you run your program, switch to Source view and find the catalog zone you've added. Within the `<WebPartsTemplate>` element, add a Title attribute to both the calendar and the `File Upload` controls, as shown in Example 13-8. (Again, Intellisense will not like this attribute, but be strong and do it anyways.)

Figure 13-27. Adding a Declarative Catalog Part control

Figure 13-28. Dragging controls into the Declarative Template

Example 13-8. Catalog Zone

```
<asp:CatalogZone ID="CatalogZone1" runat="server">
   <ZoneTemplate>
      <asp:DeclarativeCatalogPart ID="DeclarativeCatalogPart1" runat="server">
         <WebPartsTemplate>
            <asp:Calendar ID="Calendar1" runat="server"
               title="Calendar" />
            <asp:FileUpload ID="FileUpload1" runat="server" title="Upload Files" />
         </WebPartsTemplate>
      </asp:DeclarativeCatalogPart>
   </ZoneTemplate>
</asp:CatalogZone>
```

Run the application. Drop down the Display Mode; the Catalog mode has been added, as shown in Figure 13-29.

When you select Catalog, the catalog zone will be exposed. You may select one of the controls and decide which zone to place it in, as shown in Figure 13-30.

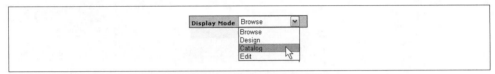

Figure 13-29. Catalog added to Display Mode

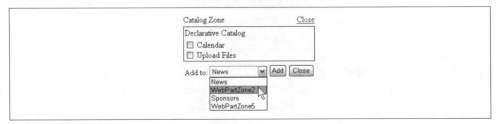

Figure 13-30. Adding a control from the catalog

Once you've picked your control and the zone to add it to, click Add and the control instantly appears in the designated zone.

Web Parts are the building blocks (along with personalization, themes, and skins) for the next generation of web applications, in which the user (rather than the designer) decides how the site appears and which information is given prominence.

CHAPTER 14

Custom and User Controls

This chapter discusses controls created by the developer. These are called custom controls, and a subset of them is called user controls.

Custom controls are compiled controls that act, from the client's perspective, much like ASP.NET controls. Custom controls can be created in one of three ways:

- By deriving a new custom control from an existing control (for example, deriving your own specialized text box from asp:textbox). This is known as a *derived custom control*.

- By composing a new custom control out of two or more existing controls. This is known as a *composite custom control*.

- By deriving from the base control class, thus creating a new custom control from scratch. This is known as a *full custom control*.

All three of these methods, and the three control types that correspond to them, are variations on the same theme. We'll consider these custom controls later in this chapter. The simplest category of custom controls is a subset called *user controls*. Microsoft distinguishes user controls as a special case because they differ from other types of custom controls. In short, *user controls* are segments of ASP.NET pages that can be reused from within other pages. This is similar to "include files" familiar to ASP developers. However, user controls are far more powerful. User controls support properties and events and, thus, provide reusable functionality as well as reusable HTML.

User Controls

User controls allow you to save a part of an existing ASP.NET page and reuse it in many other ASP.NET pages. A user control is almost identical to a normal *.aspx* page, with the following differences:

- User controls have an *.ascx* extension rather than an *.aspx* extension.

- User controls may not have `<html>`, `<body>`, or `<form>` tags.
- User controls have a `Control` directive rather than a `Page` directive.

The simplest user control is one that displays only HTML. A classic example of a simple user control is an HTML page that displays a copyright notice.

 User controls were originally called *pagelets*, which we think is more descriptive; alas, Microsoft has elected to call them User Controls and so shall we. When you see the term *user control*, think this: *a bit of a content page that can be reused in other content pages.*

VS2005 provides support for creating user controls. To see this at work, you'll create a new web site named *UserControls*. Right-click on the web site folder in the Solution Explorer and choose Add New Item to bring up the Add New Item dialog box. One of the choices is Web User Control. Select this and give it the name *Copyright.ascx*.

This choice opens the new file in Source view. Initially, the file contains only a `Control` directive:

```
<%@ Control Language="C#" AutoEventWireup="true"
    CodeFile="Copyright.ascx.cs" Inherits="Copyright" %>
```

This directive, similar to the `Page` directive described in Chapter 6, sets the language, the name of the code-behind file, and the class, and so on.

Copy the following code into the new *.ascx* file below the `Control` directive:

```
<table>
   <tr>
      <td align="center">Copyright 2005 Liberty Associates, Inc.</td>
   </tr>
   <tr>
      <td align="center">Support at http://www.LibertyAssociates.com</td>
   </tr>
</table>
```

You can now add this user control to any number of pages. You'll begin by returning to *Default.aspx* and adding a couple web controls to the page. Drag a `Label` control onto the page and set its Text property to `Hello`. Drag a `Button` control onto the page and set its Text property to `Change`. Double-click on the button in Design view to go to its default event handler and enter the following line of code:

```
Label1.Text = "Changed!";
```

Default.aspx now has a label and a button, but we want to add the copyright. You can reuse the copyright user control by adding two lines to *default.aspx*: the register directive for the user control and an instance of the user control itself.

Switch to source view and, at the top of *default.aspx* file, add the following Register directive immediately after the Page directive:

```
<%@Register tagprefix="OReilly" Tagname="copyright" src="copyright.ascx" %>
```

The tagprefix for the Label control is asp and its Tagname is Label. Your registration statement establishes *your* tagprefix (OReilly) and the Tagname of your user control (copyright).

 The tilde character (~) is interpreted by ASP.NET as indicating the path to the root of you web application as in:

```
~/myUserControls/mypage.ascx
```

You can add an instance of your user control like any other control. The complete source for the content file for UserControls is shown in Example 14-1.

Example 14-1. Default.aspx for UserControls

```
<%@ Page Language="C#" AutoEventWireup="true" CodeFile="Default.aspx.cs"
    Inherits="_Default" %>

<%@Register tagprefix="OReilly" Tagname="copyright"
   src="copyright.ascx" %>

<!DOCTYPE html PUBLIC "-//W3C//DTD XHTML 1.1//EN"
   "http://www.w3.org/TR/xhtml11/DTD/xhtml11.dtd">

<html xmlns="http://www.w3.org/1999/xhtml" >
<head runat="server">
    <title>User Controls</title>
</head>
<body>
    <form id="form1" runat="server">
    <div>
        <asp:Label ID="Label1" runat="server" Text="Hello"></asp:Label>
        <asp:Button ID="Button1" runat="server"
          OnClick="Button1_Click" Text="Change" />
    </div>
    </form>
    <OReilly:copyright ID="Copyright1" runat="server" />
</body>
</html>
```

Run the program and the copyright user control is displayed as if you had put its HTML into the content file, as shown in Figure 14-1.

The user control can be reused in any *.aspx* page. If you update the copyright, you will make that update only in the one *.ascx* file, and it will be displayed appropriately in all the pages that use that control.

Figure 14-1. Copyright user control

User Controls with Code

User controls can have events and other code associated with them to make for more sophisticated reusable code. Suppose, for example, that you'd like to reuse the customer data list that you developed in Chapter 9 in the application WebNorth-WindDataControls.

To convert this *.aspx* page and its code behind into a re-usable user control you will need to:

1. Create a user control skeleton in your new project.
2. Excise the reusable code from the *.aspx* and paste it into your new control.
3. Bring over the support code from the code-behind to the user control.
4. Bring over the appropriate connection string from *web.config*.

Begin by adding a new user control called *CustomerDataList.ascx* to the ongoing example. Open WebNorthWindDataControls in a separate instance of Visual Studio and pick out the entire *default.aspx* code from the opening to the closing <div> tags. Drop what you've copied into the new user control, CustomerDataList.

To make the control appear more natural in your page, change the first line of HTML from this:

```
<h1>DataList Demo</h1>
```

to this:

```
<h2>Customers</h2>
```

Open the code-behind for your new user control and copy over the implemented methods from *Default.aspx.cs*.

In the content file of the user control, you have a pair of SqlDataSource controls, each of which has the following connection string element:

```
ConnectionString="<%$ ConnectionStrings:NorthwindConnectionString %>"
```

To support that, copy the following lines from the WebNorthWindDataControl project's *web.config* file:

```
<connectionStrings>
    <add name="NorthwindConnectionString"
        connectionString="Data Source=Mozart;
        Initial Catalog=Northwind;
        Persist Security Info=True;
        User ID=<your user>;
        Password=<your password>"
        providerName="System.Data.SqlClient"/>
</connectionStrings>
```

Paste that connection string element over the empty connection string element in the *web.config* of the UserControls project and rebuild the web site.

Your control is now ready to use. Add it to *default.aspx* in the UserControls web site in two steps. First, register it by adding a Register directive:

```
<%@Register
    tagprefix="OReilly"
    Tagname="customerDL"
    src="CustomerDataList.ascx" %>
```

Second, place an instance of the control under the button as in the highlighted line in the following code snippet:

```
<asp:Button ID="Button1" runat="server"
   OnClick="Button1_Click" Text="Change" />
<OReilly:customerDL ID="custDL1" runat="server" />
```

The complete content file for UserControls after adding the customer DataList user control is listed in Example 14-2 with the additions highlighted.

Example 14-2. UserControls after adding Customer DataList user control

```
<%@ Page Language="C#" AutoEventWireup="true"  CodeFile="Default.aspx.cs
   " Inherits="_Default" %>
<%@Register tagprefix="OReilly" Tagname="copyright" src="copyright.ascx" %>
<%@Register tagprefix="OReilly"
    Tagname="customerDL"
    src="CustomerDataList.ascx" %>

<!DOCTYPE html PUBLIC "-//W3C//DTD XHTML 1.1//EN"
    "http://www.w3.org/TR/xhtml11/DTD/xhtml11.dtd">

<html xmlns="http://www.w3.org/1999/xhtml" >
<head runat="server">
    <title>User Controls</title>
</head>
<body>
    <form id="form1" runat="server">
    <div>
      <h1>User Controls</h1>
        <asp:Label ID="Label1" runat="server" Text="Hello"></asp:Label>
```

Example 14-2. UserControls after adding Customer DataList user control (continued)

```
        <asp:Button ID="Button1" runat="server" Text="Change"
                  OnClick="Button1_Click" />
        <OReilly:customerDL ID="custDL1" runat=server />
    </div>
    </form>
    <OReilly:copyright ID="Copyright1" runat="server" />
</body>
</html>
```

When you run the UserControls web site, *default.aspx* comes up with the complete and populated DataList in place as you would expect, as shown in Figure 14-2.

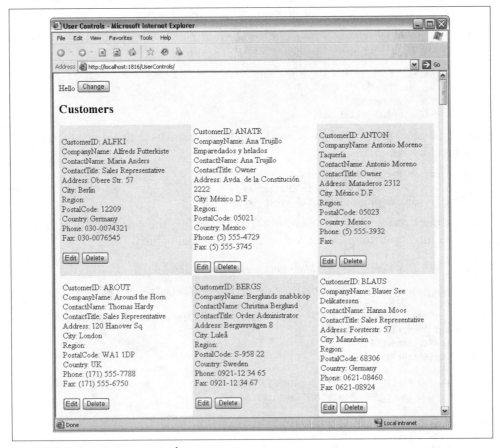

Figure 14-2. DataList user control

Clicking on the Edit button puts the record into Edit Mode as it did before you turned your page into a reusable data control, as shown in Figure 14-3.

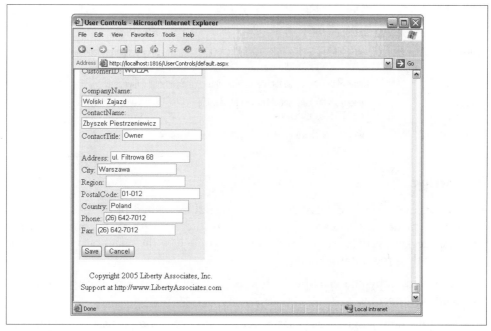

Figure 14-3. DataList user control in Edit Mode

@Control Directive

There can be only one @Control directive for each user control. This directive is used by the ASP.NET page parser and compiler to set attributes for your user control. Possible values are shown in Table 14-1.

Table 14-1. Values for @Control properties

Attribute	Description	Possible values
AutoEventWireup	true (the default) indicates the page automatically posts back to the server. If false, the developer must fire the server event manually.	true or false; default is true.
ClassName	The class name for the page.	Any valid class name.
CompilerOptions	Passed to compiler.	Any valid compiler string indicating options.
Debug	Whether to compile with debug symbols.	true or false; default is false.
Description	Text description of the page.	Any valid text.
EnableViewState	Indicates if view state is maintained for the user control.	true or false; default is true.
Explicit	Indicates whether the page should be compiled with VB.NET option explicit.	true or false; default is false.
Inherits	Defines a code-behind class.	Any class derived from UserControl.

Table 14-1. Values for @Control properties (continued)

Attribute	Description	Possible values
Language	The language used for inline rendering and server-side script blocks.	Any .NET-supported language.
Src	Name of the source file for the code-behind.	Any valid filename.
Strict	Indicates if the page should be compiled using VB.NET Strict option.	true or false; default is false.
WarningLevel	Compiler warning level at which compilation will abort.	0–4

Properties

You can make your user control far more powerful by adding properties. Properties allow your client (in this case *Default.aspx*) to interact with your control, setting attributes declaratively (when the user control is added to the page) or programmatically (while the program is running).

To get started, copy the example web site *UserControls* to a new web site called *UserControlsProperties*.

You can, for example, give your CustomerDataList control properties for the number of columns to render and if to lay them out vertically or horizontally. You do this in four steps:

1. Create properties in the control. You must decide if you will provide a read-write, read-only, or write-only property. For this example, you'll provide read-write properties.

2. Provide an underlying value for the property. You can do this by computing the property, retrieving it from a database, or, as you'll do here, storing the underlying value in a private member variable. You must decide if you'll provide a default value for your properties.

3. Integrate the underlying values into the body of the code; you'll do that, in this case, by setting these values in the PreRender event of the control.

4. Set the property from the client declaratively (as an attribute) or programmatically. In this case, you'll set them programmatically in response to user input.

Creating a property

There is nothing special about the property for the user control; you create it as you would any property for a class. To do this, add the following code to the CustomerDataList class in *CustomerDataList.ascx.cs*:

```
public int HowManyColumns
{
    get { return howManyColumns; }
    set { howManyColumns = value; }
}
```

```
public RepeatDirection WhichDirection
{
    get { return whichDirection; }
    set { whichDirection = value; }
}
```

Providing an underlying value for the property

You can compute the value of a property or look up the value in a database. In this example, you'll create member variables to hold the underlying value. Add these two lines of code to *CustomerDataList.ascx.cs*:

```
private int howManyColumns = 3;
private RepeatDirection whichDirection = RepeatDirection.Horizontal;
```

RepeatDirection is an enumerated constant provided by the framework. Intellisense will offer the valid choices when you type the dot following RepeatDirection.

Integrating the property into your code

Having declared the properties, you must modify the code so these values are used when creating the control. You can't do this in the Page_Load of the user control code-behind file because the event handler for setting the properties runs *after* Page_Load. You want to use the new property values before you render the control, so put the following code in the code-behind file to handle the PreRender event:

```
protected void Page_PreRender(object sender, EventArgs e)
{
    this.DataList1.RepeatColumns = this.howManyColumns;
    this.DataList1.RepeatDirection = this.whichDirection;
}
```

Setting the property from the client

You'll modify the client to lay out the controls within a table as a convenience. While you are at it, you'll add a text box for the number of columns and a drop-down to allow the user to decide vertical versus horizontal. Finally, you'll add a button which will repost the page so the new values are put into place. The complete content file for UserControlsProperties, *default.aspx*, is shown in Example 14-3. A Table control has been used to control the layout. The relevant changes (other than that Table control) are highlighted.

Example 14-3. Default.aspx for UserControlsProperties

```
<%@ Page Language="C#"
    AutoEventWireup="true"
    CodeFile="Default.aspx.cs"
    Inherits="_Default" %>

<%@Register
    tagprefix="OReilly"
```

Example 14-3. Default.aspx for UserControlsProperties (continued)

```
      Tagname="copyright"
      src="copyright.ascx" %>

<%@Register
    tagprefix="OReilly"
    Tagname="customerDL"
    src="CustomerDataList.ascx" %>

<!DOCTYPE html PUBLIC "-//W3C//DTD XHTML 1.1//EN"

"http://www.w3.org/TR/xhtml11/DTD/xhtml11.dtd">

<html xmlns="http://www.w3.org/1999/xhtml" >
<head runat="server">
    <title>User Controls</title>
</head>
<body>
    <form id="form1" runat="server">
    <div>
      <asp:Table ID="table1" runat="server">
        <asp:TableRow>
          <asp:TableCell ColumnSpan="3">
             <asp:Label ID="Label1" runat="server" Text="Hello" />  
             <asp:Button ID="Button1" runat="server"
             OnClick="Button1_Click" Text="Change" />
          </asp:TableCell>
        </asp:TableRow>
        <asp:TableRow>
          <asp:TableCell>
             <asp:Label ID="Label2" runat="server" Text="Columns" />
              
             <asp:TextBox ID="txtNumberColumns" runat="server"
                          width="25"/>
          </asp:TableCell>
           <asp:TableCell>
             <asp:Label ID="Label3" runat="server" Text="Direction" />
               
               <asp:DropDownList ID="ddlDirection" runat="server" >
                  <asp:ListItem Value="H">Horizontal</asp:ListItem>
                  <asp:ListItem Value="V">Vertical</asp:ListItem>
               </asp:DropDownList>
          </asp:TableCell>
          <asp:TableCell>
             <asp:Button ID="btnSetProperties" runat="server"
                         Text="Set Properties"
                         OnClick="btnSetProperties_OnClick" />
          </asp:TableCell>
        </asp:TableRow>
        <asp:TableRow>
          <asp:TableCell ColumnSpan="3">
             <OReilly:customerDL ID="custDL1" runat="server" />
          </asp:TableCell>
```

Example 14-3. Default.aspx for UserControlsProperties (continued)

```
        </asp:TableRow>
      </asp:Table>
    </div>
    </form>
    <OReilly:copyright ID="Copyright1" runat="server" />

</body>
</html>
```

The Click event handler for the Set Properties button will examine the drop-down and set the DataList control's RepeatDirection property accordingly. It will examine txtNumberColumns and set the HowManyColumns property of the user control from that value. Once these are set, the control will know how to render itself. The Click event handler for btnSetProperties has been declared in Example 14-3 to be btnSetProperties_OnClick, so add the code from Example 14-4 to the code-behind file for the page, *default.aspx.cs*:

Example 14-4. btnSetProperties Click event handler for UserControlsProperties

```
protected void btnSetProperties_OnClick(object sender, EventArgs e)
{
    if (ddlDirection.SelectedValue == "H")
    {
        this.custDL1.WhichDirection = RepeatDirection.Horizontal;
    }
    else
    {
        this.custDL1.WhichDirection = RepeatDirection.Vertical;
    }

    if (this.txtNumberColumns.Text.Length > 0)
    {
        this.custDL1.HowManyColumns =
            Convert.ToInt32(this.txtNumberColumns.Text);
    }

}
```

When you run the application, the page is displayed using the default values.

To simplify the code we are not using validators to ensure, for example, that the text in txtNumberColumns is actually a numeric value. For more on validators, please see Chapter 8.

If you set new values and then click Set Properties, the new values will be placed into the control's properties and used when the control is rendered, as shown in Figure 14-4.

Figure 14-4. Setting the data control properties

Handling Events

Event handling with user controls can be a bit confusing. Within a user control (e.g., CustomerDataList), you may have other controls (e.g., buttons). If those internal controls fire events, you'll need to handle them within the user control. The page the user control is placed in will never see those events.

That said, a user control can raise its own events. You may raise an event in response to events raised by internal controls, in response to user actions or system activity, or for any reason you choose.

Your user control can publish any event it chooses, and your consuming application (in this case *default.aspx*) may respond to those events if it chooses. Here are the steps:

1. The user control defines a delegate for the event.
2. The user control defines the event.

---

3. The user control defines a method that raises the event if anyone has registered to receive the event.

4. The user control calls that method from the place in the code where the event should be raised.

5. If the user control needs to pass along additional information for an event, the user control will define a class that derives from EventArgs, adds a parameter of that class to the delegate definition, and create an instance of that EventArgs-derived class when raising the event.

6. The consuming class registers for the event, indicating which method should be called if the event is raised.

7. The consuming class's event handler handles the event in whatever way is appropriate.

To demonstrate how this is all accomplished, copy the current example to a new web site, called *UserControlsEvents*. In this example, the CustomerDataList control will declare two events. The first, EditRecord, will be raised when a record is being edited, and will pass along, in ChangedRecordEventArgs (derived from EventArgs), the name of the company. The second event, FinishedEditRecord, will be raised when the user either saves the update or cancels the update.

You declare new events for the user control as you would for any class. In this case, you'll declare two delegates and two events for the CustomerDataList in the code-behind of the user control:

```
public delegate void EditRecordHandler(
    object sender, ChangedRecordEventArgs e);
public event EditRecordHandler EditRecord;

public delegate void FinishedEditRecordHandler(
    object sender, EventArgs e);
public event FinishedEditRecordHandler FinishedEditRecord;
```

The first delegate has, as its second argument, a ChangedRecordEventArgs object. This is a class defined within the definition of the CustomerDataList class, specifically to pass along the company name that is being edited:

```
public class ChangedRecordEventArgs : EventArgs
{
    private string companyName;

    public string CompanyName
    {
        get { return companyName; }
    }

    public ChangedRecordEventArgs(string companyName)
    {
        this.companyName = companyName;
    }
}
```

The company name is set in the constructor, and there is a read-only property for the event handler to read the name of the company that is being edited.

In addition to declaring the two events, you must declare methods in the CustomerDataList class that fire the events if anyone has registered to receive them:

```
protected virtual void OnEditRecord(ChangedRecordEventArgs e)
{
    if (EditRecord != null)
    {
        EditRecord(this, e);
    }
}

protected virtual void OnFinishedEditRecord(EventArgs e)
{
    if (FinishedEditRecord != null)
    {
        FinishedEditRecord(this, e);
    }
}
```

Finally, you must add calls to these methods to the places in your code where you want the events to be raised. The first place is when the user clicks the Edit button. An event handler exists for the EditCommand event of the DataList control. Add the highlighted lines from the following snippet to add these calls:

```
protected void DataList1_EditCommand(object source,
                                    DataListCommandEventArgs e)
{
    DataList1.EditItemIndex = e.Item.ItemIndex;
    DataBind( );
    Label lbl = (Label) e.Item.FindControl("CompanyNameLabel");
    string companyName = lbl.Text;
    ChangedRecordEventArgs cre = new ChangedRecordEventArgs(companyName);
    OnEditRecord(cre);
}
```

The first two lines are unchanged. The next two lines extract the company name from the Company Name Label within the selected DataList item. The next line creates an instance of your new ChangedRecordEventArgs class, and the final line calls the method that will raise the event.

You'll want to modify the pre-existing UpdateCommand and CancelCommand event handlers to raise the OnFinishedEditRecord. Add the highlighted line from the following snippet to both of those event handlers:

```
protected void DataList1_CancelCommand(object source,
                                      DataListCommandEventArgs e)
{
    DataList1.EditItemIndex = -1;
    DataBind( );
    OnFinishedEditRecord(new EventArgs( ));
}
```

There is no data to pass in, so instead pass in a new instance of the placeholder class EventArgs to follow the convention that every event has an EventArgs argument.

The client of your control (*default.aspx*) must register to receive these events. It will do so in its Page_Load method:

```
protected void Page_Load(object sender, EventArgs e)
{
    this.custDL1.EditRecord +=
        new CustomerDataList.EditRecordHandler(custDL1_EditRecord);
    this.custDL1.FinishedEditRecord +=
        new CustomerDataList.FinishedEditRecordHandler(
          custDL1_FinishedEditRecord);
}
```

The first line registers that you want to receive the EditRecord event and indicates that the method to call is custDL1_EditRecord. The second line registers that you want to receive the FinishedEditRecord event and indicates that the method to call is custDL1_FinishedEditRecord.

These two methods add or remove text to a new label added to the user interface of *default.aspx*. Add the highlighted code from this snippet inside the Table control:

```
<asp:Table ID="table1" runat="server">
  <asp:TableRow>
    <asp:TableCell >
      <asp:Label ID="Label1" runat="server" Text="Hello" />  
      <asp:Button ID="Button1" runat="server"
      OnClick="Button1_Click" Text="Change" />
    </asp:TableCell>
    <asp:TableCell ColumnSpan="2">
        <asp:Label ID="lblDisplayCompany" runat="server" Text="" />
    </asp:TableCell>
  </asp:TableRow>
```

Add the next two code snippets to the code-behind of the page, *default.aspx.cs*. The first method sets the text of this new label to the name of the company:

```
protected void custDL1_EditRecord(
    object sender,
    CustomerDataList.ChangedRecordEventArgs e)
{
    lblDisplayCompany.Text = "Editing " + e.CompanyName;
}
```

The second event handler sets the label back to an empty string (making it invisible):

```
protected void custDL1_FinishedEditRecord(object sender, EventArgs e)
{
    lblDisplayCompany.Text = string.Empty;
}
```

The result is that when you are editing a record, the name of the record you are editing is displayed by *default.aspx*, as shown in Figure 14-5. The complete listings for the two code-behind files in this example, with changes highlighted, are shown in Examples

14-5 and 14-6. There are no changes to the content file for the user control since the previous example and the single addition to the content file for the consuming page, so neither of those files are listed here.

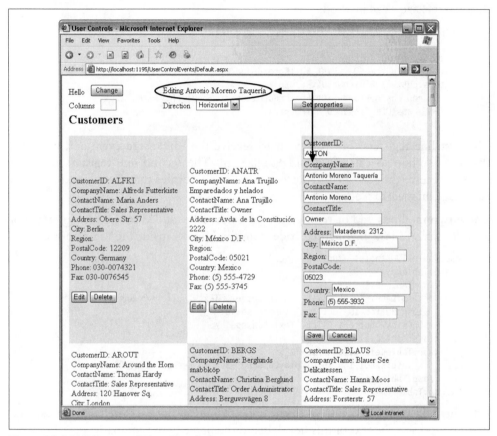

Figure 14-5. Editing record EventHandled

Example 14-5. CustomDataList.ascx.cs for UserControlsEvents

```
using System;
using System.Data;
using System.Configuration;
using System.Collections;
using System.Web;
using System.Web.Security;
using System.Web.UI;
using System.Web.UI.WebControls;
using System.Web.UI.WebControls.WebParts;
using System.Web.UI.HtmlControls;

public partial class CustomerDataList : System.Web.UI.UserControl
{
```

Example 14-5. CustomDataList.ascx.cs for UserControlsEvents (continued)

```csharp
public delegate void EditRecordHandler(object sender, ChangedRecordEventArgs e);
public event EditRecordHandler EditRecord;

public delegate void FinishedEditRecordHandler(object sender, EventArgs e);
public event FinishedEditRecordHandler FinishedEditRecord;


private int howManyColumns = 3;
private RepeatDirection whichDirection = RepeatDirection.Horizontal;

public int HowManyColumns
{
   get { return howManyColumns; }
   set { howManyColumns = value; }
}

public RepeatDirection WhichDirection
{
   get { return whichDirection; }
   set { whichDirection = value; }
}

protected void Page_Load(object sender, EventArgs e)
 {
 }

 protected void Page_PreRender(object sender, EventArgs e)
 {
    this.DataList1.RepeatColumns = this.howManyColumns;
    this.DataList1.RepeatDirection = this.whichDirection;
 }

protected void DataList1_EditCommand(object source,
                                    DataListCommandEventArgs e)
 {
    DataList1.EditItemIndex = e.Item.ItemIndex;
    DataBind( );

    Label lbl = (Label)e.Item.FindControl("CompanyNameLabel");
    string companyName = lbl.Text;
    ChangedRecordEventArgs cre =
       new ChangedRecordEventArgs(companyName);
    OnEditRecord(cre);
 }

protected void DataList1_CancelCommand(object source,
                                      DataListCommandEventArgs e)
 {
    DataList1.EditItemIndex = -1;
    DataBind( );
    OnFinishedEditRecord(new EventArgs( ));
 }
```

Example 14-5. CustomDataList.ascx.cs for UserControlsEvents (continued)

```
   protected void DataList1_UpdateCommand(object source,
                                          DataListCommandEventArgs e)
   {
      OnFinishedEditRecord(new EventArgs( ));
   }

   protected void DataList1_DeleteCommand(object source,
                                          DataListCommandEventArgs e)
   {
      // (1) Get the recordID from the selected item (a string)
      string recordID =
          (DataList1.DataKeys[e.Item.ItemIndex]).ToString( );

      // (2) Get a reference to the customerID parameter
      System.Web.UI.WebControls.Parameter param =
         DataListCustomerDeleteDataSource.DeleteParameters["CustomerID"];

      // (3) Set the parameter's default value to the value for
      // the record to delete
      param.DefaultValue = recordID;

      // (4) Delete the record
      DataListCustomerDeleteDataSource.Delete( );

      // (5) Rebind the list
      DataBind( );
   }

   public class ChangedRecordEventArgs : EventArgs
   {
      private string companyName;

      public string CompanyName
      {
         get { return companyName; }
      }

      public ChangedRecordEventArgs(string companyName)
      {
         this.companyName = companyName;
      }
   }

   protected virtual void OnEditRecord(ChangedRecordEventArgs e)
   {
      if (EditRecord != null)
      {
         EditRecord(this, e);
      }
   }
```

Example 14-5. CustomDataList.ascx.cs for UserControlsEvents (continued)

```
    protected virtual void OnFinishedEditRecord(EventArgs e)
    {
        if (FinishedEditRecord != null)
        {
            FinishedEditRecord(this, e);
        }
    }
}
```

Example 14-6. default.aspx.cs for UserControlsEvents

```
using System;
using System.Data;
using System.Configuration;
using System.Web;
using System.Web.Security;
using System.Web.UI;
using System.Web.UI.WebControls;
using System.Web.UI.WebControls.WebParts;
using System.Web.UI.HtmlControls;

public partial class _Default : System.Web.UI.Page
{
    protected void Page_Load(object sender, EventArgs e)
    {
        this.custDL1.EditRecord +=
            new CustomerDataList.EditRecordHandler(custDL1_EditRecord);
        this.custDL1.FinishedEditRecord +=
            new CustomerDataList.FinishedEditRecordHandler(
                custDL1_FinishedEditRecord);

    }

    protected void Button1_Click(object sender, EventArgs e)
    {
        Label1.Text = "Changed!";
    }

    protected void btnSetProperties_OnClick(object sender, EventArgs e)
    {
        if (ddlDirection.SelectedValue == "H")
        {
            this.custDL1.WhichDirection = RepeatDirection.Horizontal;
        }
        else
        {
            this.custDL1.WhichDirection = RepeatDirection.Vertical;
        }

        if (this.txtNumberColumns.Text.Length > 0)
        {
            this.custDL1.HowManyColumns =
```

Example 14-6. default.aspx.cs for UserControlsEvents (continued)

```
            Convert.ToInt32(this.txtNumberColumns.Text);
    }
}

protected void custDL1_EditRecord(object sender,
                       CustomerDataList.ChangedRecordEventArgs e)
{
    lblDisplayCompany.Text = "Editing " + e.CompanyName;
}

protected void custDL1_FinishedEditRecord(object sender, EventArgs e)
{
    lblDisplayCompany.Text = string.Empty;
}
}
```

Custom Controls

In addition to creating user controls, which are essentially reusable portions of web pages, you can create your own compiled custom controls. As noted earlier, there are three ways to create custom controls: derive from an existing control, create a control that combines existing controls, or create a new control from scratch.

Composite controls are most similar to user controls. The key difference is that composite controls are compiled into a *dll* and used as you would any server control.

To get started, you'll create a Web Control Library in which you'll create the various custom controls for this chapter. Open VS2005 and choose New Project. In the New Project dialog box, select Visual C# Projects, then Windows, and create a Web Control Library called *CustomControls*, as shown in Figure 14-6.

For inexplicable reasons, the Web Control Library is listed under Windows and not directly under Visual C#, nor under New Web Site.

Visual Studio has created a complete custom control named WebCustomControl1. Build the application.

If you try to run this application, you will get a message telling you that a project with an output type of Class Library cannot be started directly.

Before examining this control in detail, open a second instance of VS2005 and create a web site named *CustomControlWebPages*. This will act as your *consuming* application or your *client*. Both of these phrases mean the same thing: *CustomControlWebPages* will *use* the custom controls you'll put in your controls library. Right-click on the

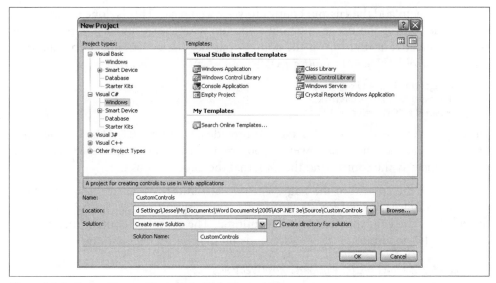

Figure 14-6. Create CustomControls in Web Control Library

solution and add a reference to the *CustomControls.dll* you built, as shown in Figure 14-7.

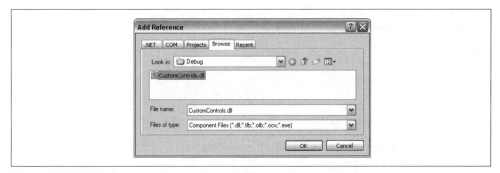

Figure 14-7. Add Reference to CustomControls.dll

The solution explorer will reflect the new reference, as shown in Figure 14-8.

Figure 14-8. Custom Controls DLL in Solution Explorer

You are ready to add the custom control to your web page. This is done in two steps: register the control and use it (much like you did with User Controls). First, add the Register directive to the top of the content page of the consuming web page (i.e., *CustomControlWebPages\Default.aspx*).

```
<%@ Register TagPrefix="OReilly"
    Namespace="CustomControls"
    Assembly="CustomControls" %>
```

Once again you use the @Register tag and provide a tag prefix (OReilly). Rather than providing a Tagname and src, however, you provide a Namespace and Assembly, which uniquely identify the control and the DLL that the page must use.

You can add the control to the page. The two attributes you must set are the Runat attribute, which is needed for all server-side controls, and the Text attribute, which dictates how the control is displayed at runtime. The complete content file, listed in Example 14-7, incorporates the registration and the control declaration:

Example 14-7. default.aspx for CustomControlWebPages

```
<%@ Page Language="C#" AutoEventWireup="true"  CodeFile="Default.aspx.cs"
    Inherits="_Default" %>
<%@ Register TagPrefix="OReilly" Namespace="CustomControls"
    Assembly="CustomControls" %>

<!DOCTYPE html PUBLIC "-//W3C//DTD XHTML 1.1//EN"
    "http://www.w3.org/TR/xhtml11/DTD/xhtml11.dtd">

<html xmlns="http://www.w3.org/1999/xhtml" >
<head runat="server">
    <title>Untitled Page</title>
</head>
<body>
    <form id="form1" runat="server">
    <div>
        <OReilly:WebCustomControl1 ID="wcc1" runat="server"
                                   Text="Hello Custom Control!" />
    </div>
    </form>
</body>
</html>
```

When you view this page, the text you passed in is displayed, as shown Figure 14-9.

For your convenience, Example 14-8 shows the complete custom control source code provided by VS2005.

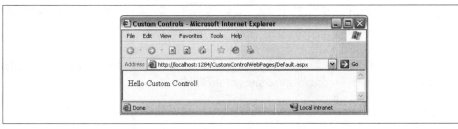

Figure 14-9. Custom Control running

Example 14-8. Custom Control provided by Visual Studio 2005

```csharp
using System;
using System.Collections.Generic;
using System.ComponentModel;
using System.Text;
using System.Web.UI;
using System.Web.UI.WebControls;

namespace CustomControls
{
    [DefaultProperty("Text")]
    [ToolboxData("<{0}:WebCustomControl1 runat=server></{0}:WebCustomControl1>")]
    public class WebCustomControl1 : WebControl
    {
        private string text;

        [Bindable(true)]
        [Category("Appearance")]
        [DefaultValue("")]
        public string Text
        {
            get
            {
                return text;
            }
            set
            {
                text = value;
            }
        }

        protected override void Render(HtmlTextWriter output)
        {
            output.Write(Text);
        }
    }
}
```

This control contains a single property, Text, backed by a private string variable, text.

Attributes are provided for the property and the class. These attributes are used by VS2005 and are not required when creating custom controls. The most commonly used attributes for custom controls are shown in Table 14-2.

Table 14-2. Common attributes for custom controls

Attribute	Description
Bindable	Boolean. true indicates that VS.NET will display this control in the data bindings dialog box.
Browsable	Boolean. Determines if the property is displayed in the designer.
Category	Determines in which category this control will be displayed when the Properties dialog is sorted by category.
DefaultProperty	The default property of the class.
DefaultValue	The default value.
Description	The text you provide is displayed in the description box in the Properties panel.
ToolboxData	Used by VS2005 to provide the tag when the object is dragged from the toolbox.

Properties

Custom controls can expose properties as any other class can. You access these properties programmatically (in code-behind) or declaratively by setting attributes of the custom control as you did in *CustomControlWebPages* and as shown here:

```
<OReilly:WebCustomControl1 ID="wcc1" runat="server"
                        Text="Hello Custom Control!" />
```

The Text property of the control is accessed through the Text attribute in the custom control declaration on the web page.

In the case of the Text property and the Text attribute, the mapping between the attribute and the underlying property is straightforward because both are strings. ASP. NET will provide intelligent conversion of other types, however. For example, if the underlying type is an integer or a long, the attribute will be converted to the appropriate value type. If the value is an enumeration, ASP.NET will match the string value against the evaluation name and set the correct enumeration value. If the value is a Boolean, ASP.NET will match the string value against the Boolean value, i.e., it will match the string "True" to the Boolean value true.

The Render Method

The key method of the custom control is Render. This method is declared in the base class and must be overridden in your derived class if you wish to take control of rendering to the page. The Render method uses the HtmlTextWriter object passed in as a parameter. In the case of the boilerplate custom control code provided by VS2005, this is used to write the string held in the Text property.

The HtmlTextWriter class derives from TextWriter and provides rich formatting capabilities. HtmlTextWriter will ensure the elements produced are well-formed, and it will manage the attributes, including style attributes, such as the following:

```
output.AddStyleAttribute("color", "fuchsia");
```

This style attribute needs to be attached to a tag. To do this, replace the contents of the Render method in *WebCustomControl1.cs* with the following code snippet:

```
output.AddStyleAttribute("color", "fuchsia");
output.RenderBeginTag("p");
output.Write(Text);
output.RenderEndTag( );
```

The style attribute is attached to an opening <p> tag, the text is written, and the RenderEndTag renders the end tag for the most recent begin tag.

The result is that when the text is output, the correct tags are created, as shown in Figure 14-10. (The source output that illustrates the HTML rendered by the HtmlTextWriter is circled.)

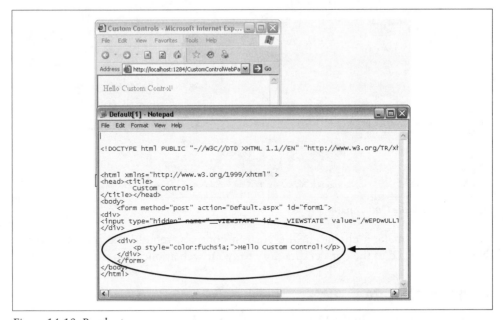

Figure 14-10. Render tag

Updating the Control

Each time you modify the control in the custom control library, you must get the rebuilt DLL into the *bin* directory of your web site. You can do that by deleting and recreating the reference or by copying the *.dll file* by hand.

An alternative is to teach the Custom Controls library to build its DLL right into the *bin* directory of the test web site. To do this, open the Custom Controls library in VS2005 and click on Project → Custom Controls Properties. Open the Build tab and set the Output path to the path for your web site, as shown in Figure 14-11.

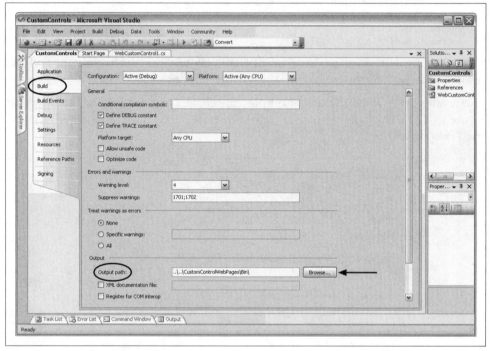

Figure 14-11. Set the Output path

Each time you make a change in the custom controls, rebuild the project and the DLL will be placed in the correct directory for your web application.

Maintaining State

In the next example, you'll add a button to the custom control to increase the size of the text. To accomplish this, right-click on the *CustomControls* project and choose Add → New Item. In the New Item dialog choose Web Custom Control and use the default name *WebCustomControl2*, as shown in Figure 14-12.

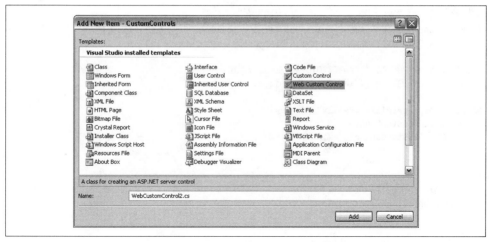

Figure 14-12. Add a second custom control

Once again, VS2005 creates a default custom control. This time you'll render the text while setting the font size based on a Size property you'll add to the class.

Replace the existing line in the Render method with the highlighted line from the following code snippet:

```
protected override void Render(HtmlTextWriter output)
{
    output.Write("<font size = " + Size + ">" + Text + "</font>");
}
```

This new line wraps the output text with an HTML <font> element and incorporates a property called Size, which you will define shortly.

First, open the consuming web application, *CustomControlWebPages*, and right-click on the web site folder in the Solution Explorer. Choose Add → New Item. Add a new Web Form, accepting the default name *Default2.aspx*.

Drag a Button onto the new form and set its ID to btnSize and its Text to Increase Size. In Design view, double-click on the button to create the skeleton of an event handler for the Click event in the code-behind file. The Button declaration in the content file will look something like the following:

```
<asp:Button ID="btnSize" runat="server"
    OnClick="btnSize_Click"
    Text="Increase Size" />
```

Add the Register directive for this custom control to the page file, and create an instance of the custom control within your page. The complete content file for the second web page, *default2.aspx*, is shown in Example 14-9.

Example 14-9. default2.aspx to test CustomControl2

```
<%@ Page Language="C#" AutoEventWireup="true" CodeFile="Default2.aspx.cs"
   Inherits="Default2" %>

<!DOCTYPE html PUBLIC "-//W3C//DTD XHTML 1.1//EN"
   "http://www.w3.org/TR/xhtml11/DTD/xhtml11.dtd">

<%@ Register TagPrefix="OReilly"
   Namespace="CustomControls"
   Assembly="CustomControls" %>


<html xmlns="http://www.w3.org/1999/xhtml" >
<head runat="server">
    <title>Untitled Page</title>
</head>
<body>
    <form id="form1" runat="server">
    <div>
        <asp:Button ID="btnSize" runat="server"
            OnClick="btnSize_Click"
            Text="Increase Size" />

        <OReilly:WebCustomControl2 ID="wc2" runat="server"
            Text="Hello Custom Control!" />

    </div>
    </form>
</body>
</html>
```

The registration statement is identical to that used in *Default.aspx* even though you are using a second control. Since they are both in the same control library, you only have to register the library and not each individual control.

Switch back to your new Custom control and add a Size property to WebCustomControl2 that stores its value in ViewState:

```
public int Size
{
    get { return Convert.ToInt32(ViewState["Size"]); }
    set { ViewState["Size"] = value; }
}
```

The property get method retrieves the value from ViewState and converts the value to an integer. The property set method stashes a string representing the size into ViewState.

To ensure a valid value is in ViewState to start with, you'll add a constructor to initialize the value:

```
public WebCustomControl2( )
{
```

```
        ViewState["Size"] = 1;
    }
```

The constructor initializes the value held in ViewState to 1. Each press of the button will update the Size property. To make that work, return to the web site and implement the btnSize_Click method in *Default2.aspx.cs*. Update the size in the btnSize_Click method:

```
    protected void btnSize_Click(object sender, EventArgs e)
    {
        wc2.Size += 1;
    }
```

To illustrate the effect of clicking the button, we created two instances of the program in Figure 14-13, and in the second instance we pressed the button three times. Before running the application, remember to rebuild the custom control project.

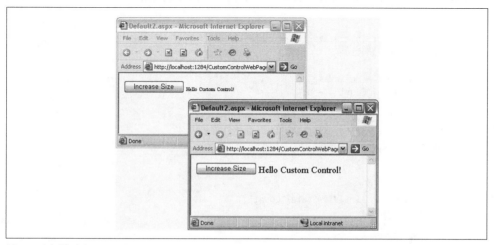

Figure 14-13. Maintaining state

Each time the button is clicked, the state variable Size is incremented. When the page is drawn, the state variable is retrieved and used to set the size of the text.

Creating Derived Controls

There are times when it is not necessary to create your own control from scratch. You may want to extend the behavior of an existing control type. You can derive from an existing control as you might derive from any class.

Imagine, for example, that you would like a button to maintain a count of the number of times it has been clicked. Such a button might be useful in any number of applications; unfortunately, the ASP.NET Button control does not provide this functionality.

To overcome this limitation of the Button class, you'll derive a new custom control from System.Web.UI.WebControls.Button, as shown in Example 14-10.

Example 14-10. CountedButton.cs

```csharp
using System;
using System.Collections.Generic;
using System.ComponentModel;
using System.Text;
using System.Web.UI;
using System.Web.UI.WebControls;

namespace CustomControls
{
    [DefaultProperty("Text")]
    [ToolboxData("<{0}:CountedButton runat=server></{0}:CountedButton>")]
    public class CountedButton : System.Web.UI.WebControls.Button
    {

        // constructor initializes view state value
        public CountedButton( )
        {
            this.Text = "Click me";
            ViewState["Count"] = 0;
        }

        // count as property maintained in view state
        public int Count
        {
            get
            {
                return (int)ViewState["Count"];
            }

            set
            {
                ViewState["Count"] = value;
            }
        }

        // override the OnClick to increment the count,
        // update the button text and then invoke the base method
        protected override void OnClick(EventArgs e)
        {
            ViewState["Count"] = ((int)ViewState["Count"]) + 1;
            this.Text = ViewState["Count"] + " clicks";
            base.OnClick(e);
        }

    }
}
```

Right-click on the *CustomControls* project and add a new Web Custom Control item named *CountedButton.cs*. Delete everything in the file and replace it with the code shown in Example 14-10.

You begin by deriving your new class from the existing Button type:

```
public class CountedButton : System.Web.UI.WebControls.Button
```

The work of this class is to maintain its state: how many times the button has been clicked. You provide a public property, Count, which is backed not by a private member variable but rather by a value stored in ViewState. This is necessary because the Button will post the page; otherwise, the state would be lost.

```
public int Count
{
   get
   {
      return (int) ViewState["Count"];
   }

   set
   {
      ViewState["Count"] = value;
   }
}
```

To retrieve the value "Count" from ViewState, you use the string Count as an offset into the ViewState collection. What is returned is an object that you cast to an int.

To ensure the property will return a valid value, you initialize the Count property in the constructor, where you set the initial text for the button.

```
public CountedButton( )
{
   this.Text = "Click me";
   ViewState["Count"] = 0;
}
```

Because CountedButton derives from Button, it is easy to override the behavior of a Click event. In this case, when the user clicks the button, you will increment the Count value held in ViewState and update the text on the button to reflect the new count. You will then call the base class's OnClick method to carry on with the normal processing of the Click event.

```
protected override void OnClick(EventArgs e)
{
   ViewState["Count"] = ((int)ViewState["Count"]) + 1;
   this.Text = ViewState["Count"] + " clicks";
   base.OnClick(e);
}
```

Remember to build the *CustomControls* project.

Create a new page (*Default3.aspx*) in *CustomControlWebPages*, the consuming web application, and add the Register directive and the highlighted control declaration:

```
<%@ Page Language="C#" AutoEventWireup="true" CodeFile="Default3.aspx.cs"
    Inherits="Default3" %>

<%@ Register TagPrefix="OReilly"
    Namespace="CustomControls"
    Assembly="CustomControls" %>

<!DOCTYPE html PUBLIC "-//W3C//DTD XHTML 1.1//EN"
    "http://www.w3.org/TR/xhtml11/DTD/xhtml11.dtd">

<html xmlns="http://www.w3.org/1999/xhtml" >
<head runat="server">
    <title>Counted Button</title>
</head>
<body>
    <form id="form1" runat="server">
    <div>
        <OReilly:CountedButton runat="server" ID="cb1" />
    </div>
    </form>
</body>
</html>
```

When you click the button four times, the button reflects the current count of clicks, as shown in Figure 14-14.

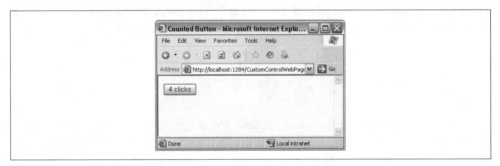

Figure 14-14. Counted Button

Creating Composite Controls

The third way to create a custom control is to combine two or more existing controls. In the next example, you will act as a contract programmer, and we will act as the client. We'd like you to build a more complex control that we might use to keep track of the number of inquiries we receive about our books.

As your potential client, we might ask you to write a control that lets us put in one or more books; each time we click on a book, the control will keep track of the number of clicks for that book, as shown in Figure 14-15.

Figure 14-15. Book counter

To begin, create a new web page in the *CustomControlsWebPages* web site named *BookCounter.aspx*. The complete listing for the content file is shown in Example 14-11.

Example 14-11. BookCounter.aspx

```
<%@ Page Language="C#" AutoEventWireup="true" CodeFile="BookCounter.aspx.cs"
Inherits="BookCounter" %>
<%@ Register TagPrefix="OReilly"
   Namespace="CustomControls"
   Assembly="CustomControls" %>

<!DOCTYPE html PUBLIC "-//W3C//DTD XHTML 1.1//EN" "http://www.w3.org/TR/xhtml11/DTD/
xhtml11.dtd">

<html xmlns="http://www.w3.org/1999/xhtml" >
<head runat="server">
   <title>Book Counter</title>
</head>
<body>
   <form id="form1" runat="server">
   <div>
      <OReilly:BookInquiryList ID="bookInquiry1" Runat="Server">
         <OReilly:BookCounter ID="Bookcounter1" Runat="server"
                           BookName="Programming ASP.NET" />
            <OReilly:BookCounter ID="Bookcounter2" Runat="server"
                           BookName="Programming C#" />
            <OReilly:BookCounter ID="Bookcounter3" Runat="server"
```

Example 14-11. BookCounter.aspx (continued)

```
                                BookName="Programming Visual Basic 2005" />
            <OReilly:BookCounter ID="Bookcounter4" Runat="server"
                                BookName="Visual C#: A Developers Notebook" />
            <OReilly:BookCounter ID="BookCounter5" Runat="server"
                                BookName="Teach Yourself C++ 21 Days" />
            <OReilly:BookCounter ID="Bookcounter6"  Runat="server"
                                BookName="Teach Yourself C++ 24 Hours" />
            <OReilly:BookCounter ID="Bookcounter7" Runat="server"
                                BookName="Clouds To Code" />
        </OReilly:BookInquiryList>
    </div>
    </form>
</body>
</html>
```

The key thing to note in this code is that the BookInquiryList component contains a number of BookCounter elements. There is one BookCounter element for each book we want to track in the control. The control is quite flexible. We can track one, seven (as shown here), or any arbitrary number of books. Each BookCounter element has a BookName attribute used to display the name of the book being tracked.

You can see in Figure 14-15 that each book is tracked using a CountedButton custom control, but you do not see a declaration of the CountedButton in the *.aspx* file. The CountedButton control is entirely encapsulated within the BookCounter custom control.

The entire architecture, therefore, is as follows:

1. The BookInquiryList composite control derives from WebControl and implements INamingContainer (described shortly).

2. The BookInquiryList control has a Controls property it inherits from the Control class (through WebControl) and that returns a collection of child controls.

3. Within this Controls collection is an arbitrary number of BookCounter controls.

4. BookCounter is a composite control that derives from WebControl and that implements INamingContainer.

5. Each instance of BookContainer has two properties, BookName and Count:

    Name
        Backed by ViewState and is initialized through the BookName in the *.aspx* file

    Count
        Delegates to a private CountedButton object, which is instantiated in BookContainer.CreateChildControls( )

The BookInquiryList object has two purposes: it acts as a container for the BookCounter objects, and it is responsible for rendering itself and ensuring that its contained BookCounter objects render themselves on demand.

The best way to see how all this works is to work your way through the code from the inside out. The most contained object is the CountedButton.

Modifying the CountedButton derived control

CountedButton needs minor modification. To keep the code clear, create a new user control named CountedButton2 and have it derive from Button, as shown in Example 14-12.

Example 14-12. CountedButton2.cs

```
using System;
using System.Collections.Generic;
using System.ComponentModel;
using System.Text;
using System.Web.UI;
using System.Web.UI.WebControls;

namespace CustomControls
{
    [DefaultProperty("Text")]
    [ToolboxData("<{0}:CountedButton2
     runat=server></{0}:CountedButton2>")]
    public class CountedButton2 : System.Web.UI.WebControls.Button
    {
        private string displayString;

        // default constructor
        public CountedButton2( )
        {
            displayString = "clicks";
            InitValues( );
        }

        // overloaded, takes string to display (e.g., 5 books)
        public CountedButton2(string displayString)
        {
            this.displayString = displayString;
            InitValues( );
        }

        // called by constructors
        private void InitValues( )
        {
            if (ViewState["Count"] == null)
                ViewState["Count"] = 0;
            this.Text = "Click me";
        }

        // count as property maintained in view state
        public int Count
        {
            get
```

Example 14-12. CountedButton2.cs (continued)

```
        {
            return (int) ViewState["Count"];
        }

        set
        {
            ViewState["Count"] = value;
        }
    }

    // override the OnClick to increment the count,
    // update the button text and then invoke the base method
    protected override void OnClick(EventArgs e)
    {
        ViewState["Count"] =  ((int)ViewState["Count"]) + 1;
        this.Text = ViewState["Count"] + " " + displayString;
        base.OnClick(e);
    }
  }
}
```

Because you want the button to be able to display the string 5 Inquiries rather than five clicks, you must change the line within the OnClick method that sets the button's text:

```
    this.Text = ViewState["Count"] + " " + displayString;
```

Rather than hard-wiring the string, you'll use a private member variable, displayString, to store a value passed in to the constructor:

```
    private string displayString;
```

You must set this string in the constructor. To protect client code that uses the default constructor (with no parameters), you'll overload the constructor, adding a version that takes a string:

```
    public CountedButton2(string displayString)
    {
        this.displayString = displayString;
        InitValues();
    }
```

You can now modify the default constructor to set the displayString member variable to a reasonable default value:

```
    public CountedButton2( )
    {
        displayString = "clicks";
        InitValues();
    }
```

The code common to both constructors has been factored out to the private helper method InitValues, which ensures that the Count property is initialized to zero and sets the initial text for the button:

```
private void InitValues()
{
    if (ViewState["Count"] == null)
        ViewState["Count"] = 0;
    this.Text = "Click me";
}
```

With these changes, the CountedButton is ready to be used in the first composite control, BookCounter.

Creating the BookCounter composite control

The BookCounter composite control is responsible for keeping track of and displaying the number of inquiries about an individual book. Create a new control in CustomControls named BookCounter and modify it, as shown in Example 14-13.

Example 14-13. BookCounter.cs composite control

```
using System;
using System.Collections.Generic;
using System.ComponentModel;
using System.Text;
using System.Web.UI;
using System.Web.UI.WebControls;

namespace CustomControls
{
    [ToolboxData("<{0}:BookCounter runat=server></{0}:BookCounter>")]
    public class BookCounter : WebControl, INamingContainer
    {
        // intialize the counted button member
        CountedButton2 btn = new CountedButton2("inquiries");

        public string BookName
        {
            get
            {
                return (string)ViewState["BookName"];
            }

            set
            {
                ViewState["BookName"] = value;
            }
        }

        public int Count
        {
            get
```

Example 14-13. BookCounter.cs composite control (continued)

```
                {
                    return btn.Count;
                }
                set
                {
                    btn.Count = value;
                }
            }

            public void Reset( )
            {
                btn.Count = 0;
            }

            protected override void CreateChildControls( )
            {
                Controls.Add(btn);
            }
        }
    }
```

INamingContainer. The BookCounter class implements the INamingContainer interface. This is a "marker" interface that has no methods. This interface identifies a container control that creates a new ID namespace, guaranteeing that all child controls have IDs that are unique to the page.

Containing CountedButton2. The BookCounter class contains an instance of CountedButton2:

```
            CountedButton2 btn = new CountedButton2("inquiries");
```

The btn member is instantiated in the CreateChildControls method inherited from System.Control:

```
            protected override void CreateChildControls( )
            {
                Controls.Add(btn);
            }
```

CreateChildControls is called in preparation for rendering and offers the BookCounter class the opportunity to add the btn object as a contained control.

 The complete control life cycle is presented in Chapter 6. That same life cycle applies to custom controls as to ASP.NET Web controls.

There is no need for BookCounter to override the Render method; the only thing it must render is the CountedButton, which can render itself. The default behavior of

Render is to render all the child controls, so you need not do anything special to make this work.

BookCounter has two properties: BookName and Count. BookName is a string to be displayed in the control and is managed through ViewState:

```csharp
public string BookName
{
    get
    {
        return (string) ViewState["BookName"];
    }

    set
    {
        ViewState["BookName"] = value;
    }
}
```

Count is the count of inquires about this particular book; responsibility for keeping track of this value is delegated to the CountedButton2:

```csharp
public int Count
{
    get
    {
        return btn.Count;
    }
    set
    {
        btn.Count = value;
    }
}
```

There is no need to place the value in ViewState since the button is responsible for its own data.

Creating the BookInquiryList composite control

Each of the BookCounter objects is contained within the Controls collection of the BookInquiryList. Create another control in the CustomControls project named BookInquiryList and modify it, as shown in Example 14-14. BookInquiryList has no properties or state. Its only method is Render.

Example 14-14. BookInquiryList.cs

```csharp
using System;
using System.Collections.Generic;
using System.ComponentModel;
using System.Text;
using System.Web.UI;
using System.Web.UI.WebControls;
```

Example 14-14. BookInquiryList.cs (continued)

```
namespace CustomControls
{
    [ControlBuilderAttribute(typeof(BookCounterBuilder)),
    ParseChildren(false)]
    public class BookInquiryList : WebControl, INamingContainer
    {
        protected override void Render(HtmlTextWriter output)
        {
            int totalInquiries = 0;
            BookCounter current;

            // Write the header
            output.Write("<Table border='1' width='90%' cellpadding='1'" +
                "cellspacing='1' align = 'center' >");
            output.Write("<TR><TD colspan = '2' align='center'>");
            output.Write("<B> Inquiries </B></TD></TR>");

            // if you have no contained controls, write the default msg.
            if (Controls.Count == 0)
            {
                output.Write("<TR><TD colspan='2' align='center'>");
                output.Write("<B> No books listed </B></TD></TR>");
            }
            // otherwise render each of the contained controls
            else
            {
                // iterate over the controls colelction and
                // display the book name for each
                // then tell each contained control to render itself
                for (int i = 0; i < Controls.Count; i++)
                {
                    current = (BookCounter)Controls[i];
                    totalInquiries += current.Count;
                    output.Write("<TR><TD align='left'>" +
                        current.BookName + "</TD>");
                    output.RenderBeginTag("TD");
                    current.RenderControl(output);
                    output.RenderEndTag();  // end td
                    output.Write("</tr>");
                }
                output.Write("<TR><TD colspan='2' align='center'> " +
                    " Total Inquiries: " +
                    totalInquiries + "</TD></TR>");
            }
            output.Write("</TABLE>");
        }
    }
}
```

ControlBuilder and ParseChildren attributes. The BookCounter class must be associated with the BookInquiryClass so ASP.NET can translate the elements in the *.aspx* page into the appropriate code. This is accomplished by adding the `ControlBuilderAttribute` attribute to the BookInquiryList class declaration:

```
[DefaultProperty("Text")]
[ToolboxData("<{0}:BookInquiryList
     runat=server></{0}:BookInquiryList>")]
[ControlBuilderAttribute(typeof(BookCounterBuilder)),
     ParseChildren(false)]
public class BookInquiryList : WebControl, INamingContainer
{
```

The first argument to the `ControlBuilderAttribute` attribute is a `Type` object that you obtain by passing in BookCounterBuilder, a class you will define to return the type of the BookCounter class given a tag named BookCounter. BookCounterBuilder is defined in the following code, added to *BookInquiryList.cs* inside the CustomControls namespace:

```
internal class BookCounterBuilder : ControlBuilder
{
    public override Type GetChildControlType(
        string tagName, System.Collections.IDictionary attributes)
    {
        if (tagName == "BookCounter")
            return typeof(BookCounter);
        else
            return null;
    }

    public override void AppendLiteralString(string s)
    {
    }
}
```

ASP.NET will use this BookCounterBuilder class, which derives from ControlBuilder, to determine the type of the object indicated by the BookCounter tag. Through this association, each of the BookCounter objects will be instantiated and added to the Controls collection of the BookInquiryClass.

 The BookCounterBuilder's method GetChildControlType uses the classic (non-generic) IDictionary interface.

The second argument of the ControlBuilderAttribute attribute, ParseChildren, must be set to false to tell ASP.NET you have handled the children attributes and no further parsing is required. A value of false indicates the nested child attributes are not properties of the outer object, but rather are child controls.

Render. The only method of the BookInquiryList class is the override of Render. The purpose of Render is to draw the table shown earlier in Figure 14-15, using the data managed by each of the BookCounter child controls.

The BookInquiryList class provides a count of the total number of inquiries, as shown in Figure 14-16.

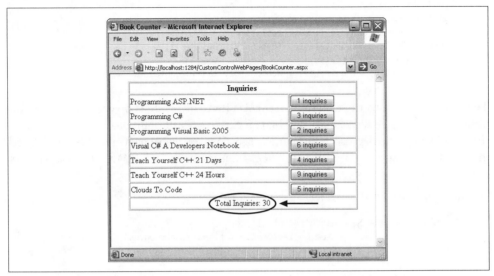

Figure 14-16. Total inquiries displayed

The code tallies inquiries by initializing an integer variable, totalInquiries, to 0 and then iterating over each control in turn, asking the control for its Count property:

```
totalInquiries += current.Count;
```

The Count property of the control delegates to the CountedButton's Count property.

Rendering the output. That same loop in the overridden Render method of the BookInquiryList class renders each of the child controls by iterating over each of the controls, building up the output HTML:

```
for (int i = 0; i < Controls.Count; i++)
{
    current = (BookCounter) Controls[i];
    totalInquiries += current.Count;
    output.Write("<TR><TD align='left'>" +
        current.BookName + "</TD>");
    output.RenderBeginTag("TD");
    current.RenderControl(output);
    output.RenderEndTag( );  // end td
    output.Write("</tr>");
}
```

The local BookCounter object, current, is assigned to each object in the Controls collection in succession:

```
for (int i = 0; i < Controls.Count; i++)
{
    current = (BookCounter) Controls[i];
```

With that object, you are able to get the Count, as described previously:

```
totalInquiries += current.Count;
```

Then you proceed to render the object. The HTMLTextWriter is used first to create a row and to display the name of the book, using the BookName property of the current BookCounter object:

```
output.Write("<TR><TD align='left'>" +
    current.BookName + "</TD>");
```

You then render a TD tag, and within that tag, you tell the BookCounter object to render itself. Finally, you render an ending TD tag using RenderEndTag and an ending row tag using the Write method of the HTMLTextWriter:

```
output.RenderBeginTag("TD");
 current.RenderControl(output);
 output.RenderEndTag();  // end td
 output.Write("</tr>");
```

You tell the contained control to render itself:

```
current.RenderControl(output);
```

When you do this, the ; method of BookCounter is called. Since you have not overridden this method, the Render method of the base class is called, which tells each contained object to render itself. The only contained object is CountedButton. Since you have not overridden Render in CountedButton, the base Render method in Button is called, and the button is rendered.

Assignment of Responsibilities

This example of a composite control is interesting because the various responsibilities are spread among the participating objects. The BookInquiryList object assumes all responsibility for laying out the control, creating the table, and deciding what will be rendered where. However, it delegates responsibility for rendering the Button object to the individual contained controls.

Similarly, the BookInquiryList is responsible for the total number of inquiries—because that information transcends what any individual BookCounter object might know. However, the responsibility for the count held by each BookCounter is delegated to the BookCounter itself. As far as the BookInquiryList is concerned, it gets that information directly from the BookCounter's Count property. It turns out, however, that BookCounter delegates that responsibility to the CountedButton.

Rendering the summary. Once all of the child controls have been rendered, the BookInquiryList creates a new row to display the total inquiries:

```
output.Write("<TR><TD colspan='2' align='center'> " +
    " Total Inquiries: " +
    totalInquiries + "</TD></TR>");
```

CHAPTER 15

Creating Web Services

The World Wide Web has opened up distributed computing on a large scale. However, normal web pages allow for interaction only between a client browser and the web server hosting the web page.

The goal of web services is to create web-based applications that interact with other applications with no user interface. If you're a web page developer, having such web services available can greatly increase your productivity. Imagine, for instance, you are creating a web site for a stock brokerage firm. Rather than integrating your back-end database with all the databases of the different stock exchanges, your application can communicate with their web services, exchanging data in XML format.

Web services are *loosely coupled* and are entirely independent of the operating system or programming language used on either the server or the client side. Unlike previous technologies for distributed computing (such as DCOM or CORBA), web services do not require that both ends of the connection be programmed in the same language or even be running on the same operating system. For example, the server code might be written in Visual Basic 2005 on Windows XP while the client is written in C++ running on a Unix machine.

If you own both ends of the wire (you are building both the client and the server), web services may not be the best solution. You will get better performance by using .NET remoting, a tightly coupled, proprietary format that sends binary data rather than XML files over the wire. For an introduction to .NET remoting, see *Programming C#*, Fourth Edition, by Jesse Liberty (O'Reilly). For comprehensive coverage, see *Advanced .NET Remoting*, Second Edition, by Ingo Rammer (Apress).

All that is necessary to create a web service is that both the server and the client support the industry standard protocols HTTP, SOAP, and XML. HTTP is the transport protocol used by the Web. Simple Object Access Protocol (SOAP) is a lightweight, object-oriented protocol based on XML, which in turn is a cross-platform standard for formatting and organizing information.

There are two broad aspects to web service development: creating the web service and consuming the web service. This chapter provides a high-level view of what web services are and how they work. It describes, briefly, the standard protocols that make web services possible and it introduces how web services are created and consumed. It then covers in detail what is involved in creating web services. We do this two different ways: letting VS2005 do all the work, and performing many of the steps manually. Through the development of a simple stock ticker, we will demonstrate how to create a web service that can be consumed by any number of different types of clients. We also show you how to create a discovery file and how to deploy the web service.

The next chapter looks at web services from the consumer's point of view. We will use the two different techniques of letting VS2005 do most of the work and performing all the steps manually. The first approach is shown with an extremely simple web service, and the latter builds on the stock ticker web service created in this chapter to create a client web application that consumes, or uses, the stock ticker web service.

How Web Services Work

Web services allow two programs to exchange XML documents. Microsoft has implemented a Remote Procedure Call (RPC) model on top of this architecture, and for the purposes of this book, we will treat web services as a way for a server to expose methods to a client.

There is a competing description of web services in which it is described in terms of messaging. From this perspective, a contract defines the content and type of the messages, and the web service is developed to implement that contract. Many developers believe that this approach yields a web service with fewer interoperability problems since all parties know in advance what types they can pass back and forth.

Though the tools in VS2005 are moving toward making this design approach more feasible, Microsoft's core tools still encourage and facilitate the RPC model.

The web services infrastructure has several defining characteristics:

- Both the web service server and the client application are connected to the Internet.
- The data format with which the two ends of the connection communicate conforms to the same open standard. This standard is almost always SOAP, though it is technically possible to communicate via HTTP-GET or HTTP-POST requests. SOAP messages consist of self-describing, text-based XML documents.
- The systems at the two ends of the connection are loosely coupled. In other words, web services do not care what operating system, object model, or programming

language is used on either end of the connection as long as both the web service and the consuming application are able to send and receive messages that conform to the proper protocol standard.

The logic behind the web services process is shown schematically in Figure 15-1.

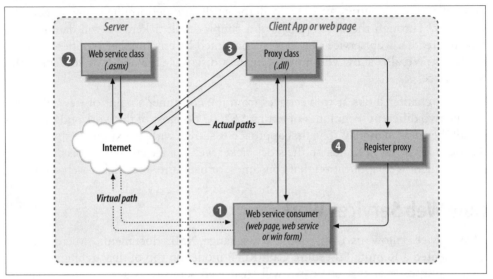

Figure 15-1. What goes on behind a web service

In Figure 15-1, at position 1, a web service consumer (a program that uses a particular web service, sometimes called the *consuming program*) makes a call to the web service (position 2). The consumer thinks it is talking directly to the web service over the Internet. This is an illusion.

The actual call is being made to a proxy class (position 3), which is local to the consumer. The proxy handles all the complex infrastructure of sending the request over the Internet to the server machine, as well as getting results back and presenting them to the consumer.

All of this is made possible because the proxy was previously registered with the consuming application (position 4). This is done by the developer of the consuming application.

This chapter and the next will explain and demonstrate all of the concepts outlined in Figure 15-1.

In addition to creating and consuming the web service, there are other aspects to consider:

Protocol
> The web service must communicate with the client, and vice versa, in a manner that both sides will understand.

Directories

Web services will be developed by thousands, or tens of thousands, of companies. Directories will be created to list these services and make them available to developers. For directories to be useful, however, there must be conventions for discovery and description.

Discovery

Potential clients will need to locate, or *discover*, documents that describe the web service. Thus, the service will often provide discovery documents, i.e., XML files that contain information allowing potential clients to find other files that describe the web service.

Description

Once a web service has been identified, through discovery or other means, it must make a document available that describes the protocols it supports (typically SOAP) and the programmatic interface to its usage. The Web Services Description Language (WSDL) describes all of the exposed methods and properties, including each method's parameters and return type.

Security

Most servers connected to the Internet are set up to be conscious of security, with firewalls and other means of blocking all traffic except that which is deemed safe. Web services must live within these security constraints. Web services must not be portals for malicious people or software to enter your network.

It is often necessary to restrict access to specific clients. For example, suppose you are developing a stock ticker for a brokerage firm. You might want to restrict access to the web service to paying clients, excluding anyone who has not paid a usage fee.

Chapter 12 discusses security for both web pages and web services.

State

Like web pages, web services use HTTP, which is a stateless protocol. And as with web pages, the .NET Framework will provide tools to preserve state if the application requires this.

Developing a Web Service

The process of developing a web service is nearly identical to developing a web page:

- All the source files that make up both web pages and services are text files. They can be created and edited in any text editor, and class files can be compiled using a command-line tool from a command prompt.

- Both web pages and services can be created in VS2005.

- Both web pages and web services can use either the *code-behind* or in-line coding model. Code-behind is generally considered a technique intended to separate visual content from programmatic content in web pages. As such, its use in web services is less imperative since a web service does not have any visual content. (For a full discussion of code-behind, see Chapter 6.)

- Both web pages and web services make full use of the CLR and the .NET Framework.

While a web page is defined by its *.aspx* file, a web service is defined by its *.asmx* file.

Think of a web service as a class in which some (but not necessarily all) of the methods are exposed to clients over the Internet.

You can easily test an *.asmx* file by entering its URL into any browser, as in this example:

```
http://localhost/websites/StockTickerInLine.asmx
```

The result is shown in Figure 15-2. This test shows a list of usable links to each of the web methods exposed by the web service. It also displays useful information and links pertaining to its deployment, including code samples in C#, VB2005, and C++.

Figure 15-2. Testing the .asmx file in a browser

The Proxy

Before a client application can use a web service, a *proxy* must be created. A proxy is a stand-in for the actual code you want to call. It is responsible for *marshalling* the call across the machine boundaries. Requests to the web service on the server must conform to the proper protocol and format, usually SOAP and/or HTTP. You could write all the code to serialize and send the proper data to the web service yourself, but that would be a lot of work. The proxy does it all for you.

The proxy is registered with the client application. Then the client application makes method calls *as though it were calling a local object*. The proxy does all the work of taking your calls, wrapping them in the proper format, and sending them as a SOAP request to the server. When the server returns the SOAP package to the client, the proxy decodes everything and presents it to the client application as though it were returning from a method on a local object. This process is shown schematically in Figure 15-3.

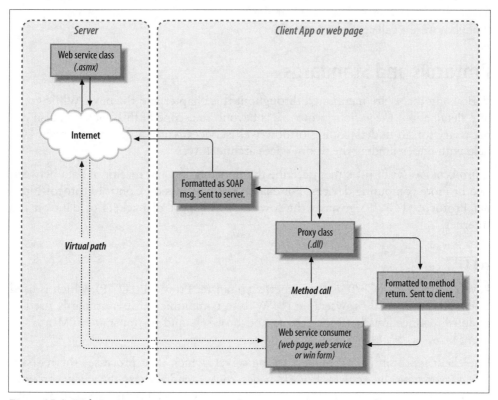

Figure 15-3. Web service proxy operation

To make this work, a developer must create the proxy and register it with the client application under development. This registration consists of a list of the exposed web methods and their signatures. The owner of the web service can add new web methods or update existing ones without changing their signature, and the existing proxy will not break.

Creating the Consumer

The consumer of a web service can be a desktop application, a web page, or another web service. All that is required is that the consumer be able to send and receive SOAP or HTTP packages.

The proxy class is compiled into an assembly, which must be registered with the consuming application. In the next chapter, you will see several ways to do this, ranging from a fully automated technique using VS2005 to a series of manual steps, either using VS2005 or not.

The consuming application is called the *client*, and the proxy is located on the client's machine. Once the proxy is created and registered with the client, all the client has to do to use your web service is make a method call against that proxy object as though it were a call against a local object.

Protocols and Standards

Various protocols are mentioned throughout this chapter and the next. While going into detail about the various protocols is beyond the scope of this book and also not necessary for an understanding of how web services work, a general overview will help with understanding the web services architecture.

A *protocol* is a set of rules that describe the transmission and receipt of data between two or more computing devices. For example, Transmission Control Protocol/Internet Protocol (TCP/IP) governs the low-level transport of packets of data on the Internet.

HTTP

Layered on top of TCP/IP is the Hypertext Transfer Protocol (HTTP), which is used to enable servers and browsers on the Web to communicate. It is primarily used to establish connections between servers and browsers and to transmit HTML to the client browser.

The client sends an HTTP request to the server, which then processes the request. The server typically returns HTML pages to be rendered by the client browser although, in the case of web services, the server may instead return a SOAP message containing the returned data of the web service method call.

HTTP requests pass name/value pairs from the requesting browser to a server. The request can be of two types: HTTP-GET, or HTTP-POST.

HTTP-GET

In GET requests, the name/value pairs are appended directly to the URL. The data is uuencoded (which guarantees that only legal ASCII characters are passed over the wire) and then appended to the URL, separated from the URL by a question mark.

For example, consider the following URL:

```
http://localhost/StockTicker/Service.asmx/GetName?StockSymbol=msft
```

The question mark indicates that this is an HTTP-GET request, the name of the variable passed to the GetName method is StockSymbol, and the value is msft.

GET requests are suitable when all the data that needs to be passed can be handled by name/value pairs, there are few fields to pass, and the length of the fields is relatively short. GET requests are also suitable when security is not an issue. This last point arises because the URL is sent over the wire and is included in server logs as plain text. As such, they can be easily captured by a network sniffer or an unscrupulous person.

The .NET Framework provides a class, HttpGetClientProtocol (shown in Figure 15-4), for using the HTTP-GET protocol in your clients.

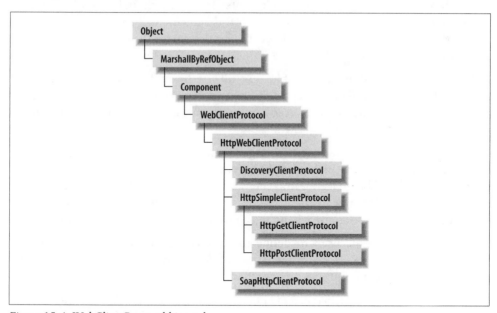

Figure 15-4. WebClientProtocol hierarchy

HTTP-POST

In POST requests, the name/value pairs are also uuencoded, but instead of being appended to the URL, they are sent as part of the request message.

POST requests are suitable for large numbers of fields or when lengthy parameters need to be passed. If security is an issue, a POST request is safer than a GET request since the HTTP request can be encrypted.

As with GET requests, with POST requests only name/value pairs can be passed. This precludes passing complex data types (such as classes, structs, or datasets).

The .NET Framework provides a class, `HttpPostClientProtocol` (see Figure 15-4), for using the HTTP-POST protocol in your clients.

XML

eXtensible Markup Language (XML) is an open standard promulgated by the World Wide Web Consortium (W3C) as a means of describing data. (For more information visit *www.w3c.org*.) The latest version of the XML protocol is Version 1.1, recommended by the W3C in February 2004. However, the version of XML currently in widespread use, including in VS2005, is Version 1.0.

XML is similar to HTML. In fact, both XML and HTML are derived from Standard Generalized Markup Language (SGML). Like HTML documents, XML documents are plain-text documents containing elements. However, though HTML uses predefined elements that specify how the HTML document will display in a browser, only XML allows elements to be defined by the document developer, so that virtually any data can be conveyed.

XML documents are human-readable text files. However, they typically are not meant to be read by humans, except developers doing programming and debugging. Most often XML documents are "read" by programs, and .NET provides extensive support for creating and reading XML.

XML documents are generally much larger than binary files containing the same data, but binary files must use proprietary encoding; the point of XML is to be a platform-neutral and language-neutral standard. In any case, file size, per se, is rarely an issue since the difference in transmission time over the Internet is usually negligible at today's speeds, especially when data compression is taken into account.

An XML *schema* is a file used to define the elements and how they relate to one another within a given XML document or set of documents. In the schema, both the element names and content types are specified.

One significant difference between HTML and XML: Most HTML readers (web browsers) are tolerant of coding errors; XML readers are not. XML must be *well-formed*. (For a complete discussion of well-formed XML markup, see the XHTML sidebar in Chapter 3.) For example, though browsers generally do not care if elements are uppercase or lowercase, in XML they must be lowercase or an error will be generated.

SOAP

Simple Object Access Protocol (SOAP) is an XML grammar that's tailored for exchanging web service data. In a .NET web service, you'll usually send SOAP messages over HTTP. SOAP is a simple, lightweight protocol for the exchange of information over the Internet. Like XML, the SOAP standard is promulgated by the W3C.

A SOAP message consists of the message content, plus one or more header blocks, all wrapped within the so-called SOAP envelope. The SoapEnvelope class derives from the System.Xml.XmlDocument class, so all the functionality provided by the .NET Framework for dealing with XML applies to SOAP.

SOAP uses XML syntax to format its content. It is, by design, as simple as possible and provides a minimum of functionality. Therefore, it is modular and flexible. Since SOAP messages consist of XML, which is plain text, they can easily pass through firewalls, unlike many proprietary, binary formats. At the time of this writing, the latest SOAP version is 1.2 (recommended by the W3C in June 2003). The SOAP protocol was originally developed by Compaq, HP, IBM, Lotus, Microsoft, and others.

SOAP is not limited to name/value pairs as HTTP-GET and HTTP-POST are. Instead, SOAP can be used to send more complex objects, including datasets, classes, and other objects.

One drawback to using SOAP to pass requests back and forth to web services is that SOAP messages tend to be verbose because of the nature of XML. Therefore, if bandwidth or transmission performance is an issue, you may be better off using HTTP-GET or HTTP-POST.

The .NET Framework provides a class, SoapHttpClientProtocol (see Figure 15-4) for using the SOAP protocol in your clients.

Web Services Enhancements (WSE)

Several firms, such as Microsoft, IBM, Intel, Oracle, Hewlett Packard, and others, have been collaborating and formulating platform-independent specifications aimed toward a more flexible, interoperable, and secure web service infrastructure. These specifications are collectively referred to as *WS-*.

For example, WS-I, the Web Services Interoperability Organization (*www.ws-i.org*) promotes interoperability. It promulgates a Basic Profile (of which 1.1 is the current version as of the initial release of VS2005), which provides guidance on interoperability issues related to SOAP, WSDL, messaging, and serialization.

A partial list of other frameworks recommended for use with web services includes the following:

- WS-Policy (*http://schemas.xmlsoap.org/ws/2004/09/policy/*)
- WS-ReliableMessaging (*http://schemas.xmlsoap.org/ws/2004/09/policy/*)

- WS-Addressing (*http://xml.coverpages.org/ni2004-08-10-a.html*)
- WS-Security (*http://www-106.ibm.com/developerworks/webservices/library/ws-secure/*)

As industry-wide initiatives, the timing of WS-* specifications may not correspond to Microsoft's product release schedule. Though Microsoft's stated intent is to conform to these industry-wide specifications, it could not tie the release of products or versions of products, such as VS2005, to WS-* release schedules. Therefore, it created *Web Services Enhancements*. WSE is a framework of classes and functionality that can be layered on top of Visual Studio to provide compliance with WS-*.

Prior to the release of VS2005, WSE was a separate download that could be installed alongside Visual Studio. Initially there was WSE 1.0, which was superseded by WSE 2.0. ASP.NET Version 2.0 and VS2005 incorporate WSE 3.0 directly.

You will see evidence of WSE 3.0, for example, in the new properties `ConformsTo` and `EmitConformanceClaims` of the `WebServiceBinding` attribute (described in this chapter). This attribute, along with these two properties, is inserted by default when VS2005 is used to create a new web service.

Creating a Simple Web Service

Though a web service has no user interface and no visual component, the architecture and files used to create a web service are similar to those used to create a web page, which are described in detail in previous chapters. Some of these similarities include the following:

- Full implementation of the .NET Framework and Common Language Runtime (CLR), including the object-oriented architecture, all the base class libraries, and features such as caching, state, and data access
- Nearly identical file and code structures
- All source code files in plain text, which can be created in any text editor
- Full support by VS2005, with all its productivity features, including IntelliSense, code completion, and integrated debugging
- Configurable on a global or application-wide basis using plain-text configuration files and the Web Site Administration Tool in VS2005

That said, web pages and web services are conceptually very different. A web page entails an interface designed for interaction with a person sitting at a web browser. A web service, on the other hand, consists only of methods, some of which are available for remote calls by client applications.

A web service can be coded in-line, in a single file with an extension of *.asmx*. Alternatively, the application logic of the web service can be segregated into a code-behind file, which is the default behavior of VS2005. One in-line example will be shown here, to aid in your understanding of how web services work, but all the other examples will be done using code-behind from within VS2005.

Code-Behind in Web Services

The rationale for code-behind is that it provides a clean separation between the presentation and programmatic portions of an application. Though this is extremely useful in the development of web pages, it is irrelevant to web services. However, since code-behind is the default coding technique for VS2005 (which offers so many productivity enhancements), code-behind becomes the *de facto* preferred technique.

In addition, code-behind will confer a performance advantage over in-line code the first time the web service app is run, *if* the web service class is manually compiled and placed in the *bin* directory under the virtual root, because the *.asmx* file is compiled into a class every time it is run. You won't see this advantage, by default, when using ASP.NET Version 2.0, which places the class source code in the *App_Code* directory and compiles on first use under all circumstances.

You can manually compile the class file and place it in the *bin* directory. Manual compilation and deployment issues will be covered in Chapter 19.

Whether using an inline or code-behind architecture, the *.asmx* file is the target entered into the browser for testing, or referenced by the utilities that create the proxy *dll*. (Recall from a previous section, "How Web Services Work," that the client application actually makes calls to a proxy *dll*. Creation of this proxy *dll* will be described in detail in the next chapter.)

As a first step in understanding how web services work, you will create a simple web service twice, the first called *StockTickerInLine*, using any favorite text editor. As the name implies, this example will use the in-line coding model. This is the only web service example in this book using that coding model and the only example made outside of VS2005. Then you will create essentially the same example, called *StockTickerSimple*, in VS2005.

This example web service will expose two web methods:

GetName
> Expects a stock symbol as an argument and returns a string containing the name of the stock

GetPrice
> Expects a stock symbol as an argument and returns a number containing the current price of the stock

If this web service were an actual production program, the data returned would be fetched from a live database. To keep web service issues and data access issues separate, for this example, the data will be stored in a two-dimensional array of strings. For a complete discussion of accessing a database, see Chapters 9 and 10.

In-Line with a Text Editor

In any text editor (Notepad works fine), open a new file called *StockTickerInLine.asmx*. Locate the file in a virtual directory somewhere on your machine. (To create an IIS virtual directory, go to Computer Management by right-clicking My Computer and selecting Manage, then drill down to Default Web Site under Internet Information Services, and right-click to create a new virtual directory.)

Enter the code shown in Example 15-1.

Example 15-1. StockTickerInLine.asmx

```
<%@ WebService Language="C#" Class="ProgAspNet.StockTickerInLine" %>

using System;
using System.Web.Services;

namespace ProgAspNet
{
    public class StockTickerInLine : System.Web.Services.WebService
    {
        //  Construct and fill an array of stock symbols and prices.
        //  Note: the stock prices are as of 5/1/05.
        string[,] stocks =
        {
            {"MSFT","Microsoft","25.30"},
            {"DELL","Dell Computers","34.83"},
            {"HPQ","Hewlett Packard","20.47"},
            {"YHOO","Yahoo!","34.50"},
            {"GE","General Electric","36.20"},
            {"IBM","International Business Machine","76.38"},
            {"GM","General Motors","26.68"},
            {"F","Ford Motor Company","9.11"}
        };

        [WebMethod]
        public double GetPrice(string StockSymbol)
        //  Given a stock symbol, return the price.
        {
            //  Iterate through the array, looking for the symbol.
            for (int i = 0; i < stocks.GetLength(0); i++)
            {
                //  Do a case-insensitive string compare.
                if (String.Compare(StockSymbol, stocks[i,0], true) == 0)
                    return Convert.ToDouble(stocks[i,2]);
            }
            return 0;
        }
```

Example 15-1. StockTickerInLine.asmx (continued)

```
    [WebMethod]
    public string GetName(string StockSymbol)
    //  Given a stock symbol, return the name.
    {
       //  Iterate through the array, looking for the symbol.
       for (int i = 0; i < stocks.GetLength(0); i++)
       {
          //  Do a case-insensitive string compare.
          if (String.Compare(StockSymbol, stocks[i,0], true) == 0)
             return stocks[i,1];
       }
       return "Symbol not found.";
    }
  }
}
```

This *.asmx* file contains the entire web service in-line. It defines a namespace called
ProgAspNet and creates a class called StockTickerInLine. The class instantiates and
fills an array to contain the stock data and then creates the two WebMethods that comprise the public aspects of the web service.

If you're familiar with web page code, you may notice in Example 15-1 that the code
for a web service is almost identical to the code in a code-behind page for an equivalent web page. There are some differences, however, which are highlighted in the
code example.

The first difference is in the use of a WebService directive at the top of the file rather
than a Page directive. As with Page directives (covered in detail in Chapter 6), the
WebService directive provides the compiler with necessary information. In this example, it specifies the language in use and the name of the web service class.

The next difference is that the web service class inherits from System.Web.Services.
WebService, rather than the Page class. Though this is not a strict requirement, it generally makes your life as the developer much easier. This issue will be covered in
detail later in this chapter.

The final difference is that any method that is to be made available as part of the web
service, called web methods, is decorated with the WebMethod attribute.

If you locate the file in a virtual directory, say one called *websites* (which is physically located at *c:\WebSites*), you can enter the following URL in a browser to see the
web service test page shown in Figure 15-2.

```
http://localhost/websites/StockTickerInLine.asmx
```

Code-Behind with Visual Studio 2005

VS2005 offers the programmer several advantages over a plain-text editor in addition to automating the creation of code-behind. Among them are color-coding of the

source code, integrated debugging, IntelliSense, integrated compiling, and full integration with the development environment. Chapter 2 covers VS2005 in detail.

To create a web service equivalent to the previous example in VS2005, open a new web site. From the list of Visual Studio Installed Templates in the New Web Site dialog, select ASP.NET Web Service. The Location selection will default to File System. Your choice here has the same ramifications as for web pages, described in Chapter 2. Name the web site StockTickerSimple.

As with a normal web site, several files and directories will be created, though the specifics are different for web services. The web service file, called *Service.asmx* by default (though it is probably a good idea to change it to something more meaningful) is created in the application root directory. It consists of a single line of code, shown in Example 15-2, containing the WebService directive, described in the next section.

Example 15-2. Service.asmx

```
<%@ WebService Language="C#" CodeBehind="~/App_Code/Service.cs"
    Class="Service" %>
```

The code-behind file is created in a subdirectory called *App_Code*.

 Version 1.x ASP.NET required that the web service class be compiled and placed in a *bin* directory under the virtual root if the code-behind model was used, as was default for Visual Studio. This is still supported in Version 2.0, to provide for backward compatibility and maximum performance.

However, the new deployment model in Version 2.0, which will be covered in detail in Chapter 19, requires only that any code files requiring compilation be placed in the *\App_Code* directory under the virtual root, and those files will be compiled automatically by the .NET Framework at runtime. This is all handled automatically by Visual Studio 2005.

The default code-behind file created by VS2005, listed in Example 15-3 (with one of the long lines wrapped for readability), is your basic Hello World type of program.

Example 15-3. Default web service code-behind file—App_Code\Service.cs

```
using System.Web;
using System.Web.Services;
using System.Web.Services.Protocols;

[WebService(Namespace = "http://tempuri.org/")]
[WebServiceBinding(ConformsTo = WsiProfiles.BasicProfile1_1,
    EmitConformanceClaims = true)]
public class Service : System.Web.Services.WebService
{
```

Example 15-3. Default web service code-behind file—App_Code\Service.cs (continued)

```
[WebMethod]
public string HelloWorld( ) {
    return "Hello World";
}

}
```

The code-behind file contains a class, named after the web service file, which derives from the System.Web.Services.WebService class. This class has two attributes, WebService and WebServiceBinding, both of which will be described shortly.

 You can rename a web service file in the Solution Explorer in VS2005 (just as you can rename a web page file) using the same techniques as in Windows Explorer: right-click on the file and select Rename, or highlight the file and press F2. Unlike web pages, renaming the .*asmx* will not automatically rename the code-behind file, nor will it rename the WebService class or change the Class attribute of the WebService directive.

Within the class Service, there is a boilerplate method called HelloWorld, which returns a string. This method is decorated with the WebMethod attribute, which identifies this method as available to consuming applications. The WebMethod attribute will be covered in detail shortly.

This boilerplate code comprises a fully functional, if limited, web service. You can see this by pressing F5 to run the web service app, which will produce a standard test page, similar to one shown in Figure 15-2.

To complete the simple web service example, replace the code within the class definition in Example 15-3 with the code highlighted in Example 15-4. This is exactly the same as the code within the class definition in the in-line example from Example 15-1.

Example 15-4. StockTickerSimple web service code-behind file—App_Code\Service.cs

```
using System.Web;
using System.Web.Services;
using System.Web.Services.Protocols;
using System;        //  necessary for String class

[WebService(Namespace = "http://tempuri.org/")]
[WebServiceBinding(ConformsTo = WsiProfiles.BasicProfile1_1,
    EmitConformanceClaims = true)]
public class Service : System.Web.Services.WebService
{
    //  Construct and fill an array of stock symbols and prices.
    //  Note: the stock prices are as of 5/1/05.
    string[,] stocks =
        {
```

```
            {"MSFT","Microsoft","25.30"},
            {"DELL","Dell Computers","34.83"},
            {"HPQ","Hewlett Packard","20.47"},
            {"YHOO","Yahoo!","34.50"},
            {"GE","General Electric","36.20"},
            {"IBM","International Business Machine","76.38"},
            {"GM","General Motors","26.68"},
            {"F","Ford Motor Company","9.11"}
        };

    [WebMethod]
    public double GetPrice(string StockSymbol)
    //  Given a stock symbol, return the price.
    {
        //  Iterate through the array, looking for the symbol.
        for (int i = 0; i < stocks.GetLength(0); i++)
        {
            //  Do a case-insensitive string compare.
            if (String.Compare(StockSymbol, stocks[i, 0], true) == 0)
                return Convert.ToDouble(stocks[i, 2]);
        }
        return 0;
    }

    [WebMethod]
    public string GetName(string StockSymbol)
    //  Given a stock symbol, return the name.
    {
        //  Iterate through the array, looking for the symbol.
        for (int i = 0; i < stocks.GetLength(0); i++)
        {
            //  Do a case-insensitive string compare.
            if (String.Compare(StockSymbol, stocks[i, 0], true) == 0)
                return stocks[i, 1];
        }
        return "Symbol not found.";
    }
}
```

Running the web service app will again produce a standard web service test page, as shown in Figure 15-2.

In the following sections, you will learn about the WebService directive and various attributes used in Examples 15-3 and 15-4, as well as all the other attributes available.

> Before proceeding, copy the previous example, *StockTickerSimple*, to a new web service called *StockTickerComplete*. In each of the next sections, you will add more features to the code listed in Example 15-4, eventually ending up with *StockTickerComplete*. At the end of this series of sections, the complete source code for *StockTickerComplete* is listed in Example 15-18.

WebService Directive

You can see the first difference between a web service and a web page in the web service file listed in Example 15-2. A normal *.aspx* file will have a `Page` directive as its first line, but a web service has a `WebService` directive as reproduced here:

```
<%@ WebService Language="C#" CodeBehind="~/App_Code/Service.cs"
    Class="Service" %>
```

The `WebService` directive is required of all web services. Like all directives, it has the following syntax:

```
<%@ DirectiveName attribute="value" [attribute="value"...]%>
```

You can have multiple attribute/value pairs. The order of the attribute/value pairs does not matter.

Language

> The `WebService` directive's `Language` attribute specifies the language used in the web service. Legal values include `C#`, `VB`, and `JS` for C#, VB2005, and Jscript.NET, respectively. The value is not case-sensitive. The `Language` attribute is not required. If it is missing, the compiler will deduce the language in use from the extension of the class file.

Class

> The `WebService` directive's `Class` attribute specifies the name of the class implementing the web service. The `Class` attribute is required. The class specified can reside either in a separate code-behind file, or in-line in a script block in the *.asmx* file.
>
> If the web service is developed in VS2005, the code-behind file containing the class will be located in a subdirectory under the application root (where the *.asmx* file resides) called *App_Code*. Any code files in a subdirectory with this name will automatically be compiled by the .NET Framework when the application is run.
>
> If the web service is developed outside of VS2005, or with a previous version of Visual Studio, then the class file must be compiled and the resulting *dll* placed in the *bin* subdirectory under the application root directory. Manual compilation is covered later in this chapter and in Chapter 19.

CodeBehind

> The `WebService` directive's `CodeBehind` attribute will specify the name of the source code file that implements the `WebService` class, if the class is not contained in-line with the web service file (*.asmx*) and if the class has not been manually compiled and placed in the *bin* subdirectory under the application root directory.

Debug

If true, the WebService directive's Debug attribute specifies that the web service will be compiled with debugging enabled. The default is false.

When you develop within VS2005, this attribute is typically omitted and the debug status is controlled by an entry in the web.config configuration file.

Deriving from the WebService Class

In the *StockTickerSimple* web service, with the class file listed in Example 15-4, the Service class inherits from the WebService class.

Deriving from the WebService class is optional, but it offers several advantages. The principal one is that you gain access to several common ASP.NET objects:

Application and Session

These objects allow the application to take advantage of state management. For a complete discussion of state management, see Chapter 6. State as it pertains specifically to web services will be covered in more detail later in this chapter.

User

This object is useful for authenticating the caller of a web service. For a complete discussion of security, see Chapter 12.

Context

This object provides access to all HTTP-specific information about the caller's request contained in the HttpContext class.

The main reason you might not want to inherit from WebService is to overcome the limitation imposed by the .NET Framework that a class can only inherit from one other class. Multiple inheritance is not supported. It would be very inconvenient to have to inherit from WebService if you needed to inherit from another class.

Application State via HttpContext

Web services have access to the Application object (as do all ASP.NET resources) via the HttpContext object.

So, for example, you could modify Example 15-4 to add the two web methods shown in Example 15-5, SetStockExchange and GetStockExchange, to set and retrieve a value in application state.

Example 15-5. Adding application state to StockTickerComplete

```
[WebMethod]
public void SetStockExchange(string Exchange)
{
   Application["exchange"] = Exchange;
}
```

Example 15-5. Adding application state to StockTickerComplete (continued)

```
[WebMethod]
public string GetStockExchange( )
{
   return Application["exchange"].ToString( );
}
```

You could accomplish the same thing without inheriting from System.Web.Services. WebService by using the HttpContext object, as shown in Example 15-6.

Example 15-6. Adding application state without inheriting WebService

```
using System.Web;
using System.Web.Services;
using System.Web.Services.Protocols;
using System;        //  necesary for String class
{
   public class Service
.
.
.
      [WebMethod]
      public void SetStockExchange(string Exchange)
      {
         HttpApplicationState app;
         app = HttpContext.Current.Application;
         app["exchange"] = Exchange;
      }

      [WebMethod]
      public string GetStockExchange( )
      {
         HttpApplicationState app;
         app = HttpContext.Current.Application;
         return app["exchange"].ToString( );
      }
}
```

In Example 15-6, you must add a reference to System.Web at the top of the listing (VS2005 does this by default.). The web service class, Service, no longer inherits from the class WebService. Finally, an HttpApplicationState object is declared to access the application state.

WebServiceBinding Attribute

A binding, as defined by Web Services Description Language (WSDL), is to a web service as an interface is to a .NET class. That is, it defines a specific set of operations. A WebService class has a default binding, which includes all the web methods in the class not specifically associated with a non-default binding. The WebServiceBinding attribute is used to identify non-default bindings, and also to set properties of the default and non-default bindings. (The WebServiceBinding attribute comes from the `WebServiceBindingAttribute` class, which is contained in the `System.Web.Services` namespace.)

A `WebService` class can have multiple `WebServiceBinding` attributes, each specifying a different binding. If the `Name` property is omitted, then that attribute will apply to the default binding. This is the case for the boilerplate `WebServiceBinding` attribute inserted by VS2005.

There are several properties of the `WebServiceBinding` attribute, listed in Table 15-1. The first two, `ConformsTo` and `EmitConformanceClaims`, are inserted into the `WebService` class by default by VS2005. These two properties implement the interoperability standards specified by Web Service Interoperability Basic Profiles (WS-I BP) Version 1.1. The two valid values of the `WsiProfiles` enumeration are `BasicProfile1_1` (seen in Example 15-4), indicating conformance with WS-I BP v1.1, and `None`, indicating no conformance claims.

Table 15-1. WebServiceBinding attribute properties

Property	Type	Get	Set	Description
ConformsTo	WsiProfiles	✗	✗	The WS-I specification to which the binding claims to conform.
EmitConformanceClaims	Boolean	✗	✗	If `true`, the binding will emit conformance claims when the WSDL description is published.
Location	String	✗	✗	The location where the binding is defined. The default is the URL of the current web service.
Name	String	✗	✗	The name of the binding.
Namespace	String	✗	✗	The namespace associated with the binding.

As you will see in the section on the `MessageName` property of the `WebMethod` attribute, there are circumstances under which creating a new binding, with a different name, location, or namespace is helpful.

WebMethod Attribute

As explained previously, a web service is defined by a `WebService` class. It is not necessary for the `WebService` class to expose all of its methods to consumers of the web service. Each method you do want to expose must do the following:

- Be declared as `public`.
- Have the `WebMethod` attribute placed before the method declaration. (The `WebMethod` attribute comes from the `WebMethodAttribute` class, which is contained in the `System.Web.Services` namespace.)

As you saw in the previous examples in this chapter, the basic `WebMethod` attribute looks something like the highlighted code in the following snippet:

```
[WebMethod]
public string GetName(string StockSymbol)
```

The WebMethod attribute has properties that are used to configure the behavior of the specific web method. Here is the syntax:

```
[WebMethod(PropertyName=value)]
```

PropertyName is a valid property accepted by the WebMethod attribute (these are described below), and value is the value to be assigned to that property. If there are multiple WebMethod properties, separate each property/value pair with a comma within a single set of parentheses as in this example:

```
[WebMethod(BufferResponse=false, Description="Sample description")]
```

The following sections describe the WebMethod properties.

The BufferResponse Property

By default, ASP.NET buffers the entire response to a request before sending it from the server to the client. Under most circumstances, this is the optimal behavior. However, if the response is very lengthy, you might want to disable this buffering by setting the WebMethod attribute's BufferResponse property to false. If it is set to false, the response will be returned to the client in 16KB chunks. The default value is true.

Here is the syntax for BufferResponse:

```
[WebMethod(BufferResponse=false)]
```

CacheDuration Property

Web services, like web pages, can cache the results returned to clients as is described fully in Chapter 17. If a client makes a request identical to a request made recently by another client, the server will return the response stored in the cache. This can result in a huge performance gain, especially if servicing the request is an expensive operation (such as querying a database or performing a lengthy computation).

For the cached results to be used, the new request must be identical to the previous request. If the web method has parameters, the parameter values must be identical. So, for example, if the GetPrice web method of the StockTicker web service is called with a value of msft passed in as the stock symbol, that result will be cached separately from a request with a value of dell passed in. If the web method has multiple parameters, all the parameter values must be the same as the previous request for the cached results from that request to be returned.

The CacheDuration property defines how many seconds after the initial request the cached page is sent in response to subsequent requests. Once this period has expired, a new page is sent. CacheDuration is set to 30 seconds as follows:

```
[WebMethod(CacheDuration=30)]
```

The default value for `CacheDuration` is zero, which disables caching of results.

If the web method is returning data that do not change much (say, a query against a database that is updated once hourly), then the cache duration can be set to a suitably long value, say 1800 (30 minutes). You could set the cache duration in this case to 3600 (60 minutes) if the process of updating the database forces the cache to refresh by making a call to the `WebMethod` after the database is updated.

On the other hand, if the data returned is very dynamic, then you will want to set the cache duration to a short time or to disable it altogether. Also, if the web method does not have a relatively finite range of possible parameters, then caching may not be appropriate.

Description Property

The `WebMethod` attribute's `Description` property allows you to attach a descriptive string to a web method. This description will appear on the web service help page when you test the web service in a browser.

Also, the `WebMethod` description will be made available to the consumer of the web service as you will see in the next chapter. When a representation of the web service is encoded into the SOAP message that is sent out to potential consumers, the `WebMethod` `Description` property is included.

The syntax for `Description` is as follows:

```
[WebMethod(Description="Returns the stock price for the input stock symbol.")]
```

EnableSession Property

The `WebMethod` attribute's `EnableSession` property, if set to `true`, will enable session state for the web method. The default value is `false`. (For a general discussion of session state, see Chapter 6.)

If the `EnableSession` property is set to `true` and the web service inherits from the `WebService` class (see earlier sections for a description of inheriting from the `WebService` class), the session state collection can be accessed with the `WebService.Session` property. If the web service does not inherit from the `WebService` class, the session state collection can be accessed directly from `HttpContext.Current.Session`.

As an example, the code in Example 15-7 adds a per-session hit counter to the ongoing *StockTickerComplete* web service example.

Example 15-7. HitCounter WebMethod with session state enabled

```
[WebMethod(Description="Number of hits per session.", EnableSession=true)]
public int HitCounter()
{
    if (Session["HitCounter"] == null)
```

Example 15-7. HitCounter WebMethod with session state enabled (continued)

```
    {
        Session["HitCounter"] = 1;
    }
    else
    {
        Session["HitCounter"] = ((int) Session["HitCounter"]) + 1;
    }

    return ((int) Session["HitCounter"]);
}
```

Enabling session state adds additional overhead to the application. Leaving session state disabled may improve performance.

In Example 15-7, it would probably be more efficient to use a member variable to maintain the hit counter, rather than session state, since the example as written entails two reads of the session state and one write, while a member variable would entail only one read and one write. However, session state is often useful as a global variable that can exceed the scope of a member variable.

Session state is implemented via HTTP cookies in ASP.NET web services, so if the transport mechanism is something other than HTTP (say, SMTP), then the session state functionality will be unavailable.

MessageName Property

You can have more than one method in your C# class with the same name. They are differentiated by their *signature* (the quantity, data type, and order of their parameters). Each unique signature can be called independently. This is called method *overloading*.

Web services forbid overloaded methods. The WebMethod attribute's MessageName property eliminates the ambiguity caused by having more than one method with the same name. It allows you to assign a unique alias to each version of the overloaded method. When the overloaded method is referred to in SOAP messages, the MessageName, and not the method name, will be used.

Consider Example 15-8. Two methods are added to the *StockTickerComplete* web service, both named GetValue. They differ in that one accepts a single string parameter, and the other takes a string and an integer.

Example 15-8. GetValue WebMethods which generate an error

```
// WebMethod generates an error
[WebMethod(Description="Returns the value of the users holdings " +
                      " in a specified stock symbol.")]
public double GetValue(string StockSymbol)
{
    /* Put code here to get the username of the current user, fetch both
       the current price of the specified StockSymbol and number of shares
```

Example 15-8. GetValue WebMethods which generate an error (continued)

```
        held by the current user, multiply the two together, and return the
        result.
    */
    return 0;
}

// WebMethod generates an error
[WebMethod(Description="This method returns the value of a " +
           "specified number of shares in a specified stock symbol.")]
public double GetValue(string StockSymbol, int NumShares)
{
    /*  Put code here to get the current price of the specified
        StockSymbol, multiply it times NumShares, and return the result.
    */
    return 0;
}
```

If you attempt to test either of these in a browser, it will return an error similar to that shown in Figure 15-5.

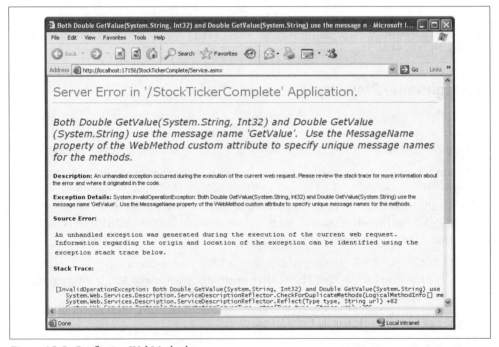

Figure 15-5. Conflicting WebMethod names

If you modify the code in Example 15-8 by adding the MessageName property, high-lighted in Example 15-9, then everything should compile nicely. Except you get another error page with a lengthy error message to the effect that your web service does not conform to WS-I Basic Profile v.1.1 since "operation name overloading…is disallowed."

Example 15-9. GetValue WebMethods with MessageName property

```
[WebMethod(Description="Returns the value of the users holdings " +
            "in a specified stock symbol.",
        MessageName="GetValuePortfolio")]
public double GetValue(string StockSymbol)
{
    /*  Put code here to get the username of the current user, fetch
        both the current price of the specified StockSymbol and number
        of shares held by the current user, multiply the two together,
        and return the result.
    */   return 0;
}

[WebMethod(Description="Returns the value of a specified " +
            "number of shares in a specified stock symbol.",
        MessageName="GetValueStock")]
public double GetValue(string StockSymbol, int NumShares)
{
    /*  Put code here to get the current price of the specified
        StockSymbol, multiply it times NumShares, and return the
        result.
    */
    return 0;
}
```

Recall that the default `WebServiceBinding` attribute inserted by VS2005 specifies conformance with WS-I BP v1.1. That specification will disallow method overloading (even using the `MessageName` property) *if the two methods are in the same binding.* Your choices are the following:

- Rename the methods so the method is no longer overloaded.
- Turn off enforced conformance with WS-I BP v1.1. Do this by setting the value of the `ConformsTo` property of the `WebServiceBinding` attribute to `WsiProfiles.None`.

  This is a bad idea because it will cause interoperability problems. If you own both sides of the wire and don't have to conform to open standards, then you should not be using a web service at all; you should be using remoting, which is much more efficient.
- Create a new binding to hold the overloaded method.

The first choice is simplest. The third choice may be preferred if no client needs to connect to your web service and have access to more than one form of the overloaded method. To add a new binding, add another `WebServiceBinding` attribute to the class, adjacent to the original attribute. It will be identical to the original except for the addition of the `Name` property, highlighted in Example 15-10.

Example 15-10. WebServiceBinding attribute with Name

```
[WebServiceBinding(Name = "OverloadedGetValue",
    ConformsTo = WsiProfiles.BasicProfile1_1,
    EmitConformanceClaims = true)]
```

For a web method to use this binding, rather than the default binding, it must be decorated with the SoapDocumentMethod attribute shown highlighted in Example 15-11. The Binding property of this attribute specifies which non-default binding to use.

Example 15-11. SoapDocumentMethod attribute

```
[SoapDocumentMethod(Binding = "OverloadedGetValue")]
[WebMethod(Description = "Returns the value of a specified " +
                    "number of shares in a specified stock symbol.",
            MessageName = "GetValueStock")]
public double GetValue(string StockSymbol, int NumShares)
{
    /*  Put code here to get the current price of the specified
        StockSymbol, multiply it times NumShares, and return the result.
    */
    return 0;
}
```

Now consumers of the web service can call GetValuePortfolio or GetValueStock rather than GetValue.

To see the impact of this change, examine the WSDL, which is the description of the web service used by clients of the web service. You can look at the WSDL by clicking the Service Description link in the test page you get when you run the web service. Alternatively, you can enter in a browser directly (assuming you have created a virtual directory for the web service) the URL for the *.asmx*, followed by ?WSDL.

If you examine the WSDL for *StockTickerComplete* so far, then search for the first occurrence of GetValue (as a whole word), you will see something like Figure 15-6.

You can see that the tag for GetValue:

```
<wsdl:operation name="GetValue">
```

is defined within a <wsdl:portType> section where the name is OverloadedGetValue. The portType element name corresponds to the additional web service binding added in Example 15-10. This has the <wsdl:input> name of GetValueStock, as you would expect from Example 15-11.

Searching further, you will find the XML listed in the following code snippet:

```
<wsdl:portType name="ServiceSoap">
    <wsdl:operation name="GetPrice">
        <wsdl:documentation xmlns:wsdl="http://schemas.xmlsoap.org/wsdl/">
            Returns the stock price for the input stock symbol.
        </wsdl:documentation>
```

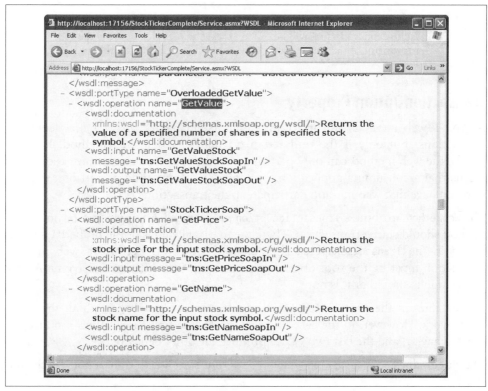

Figure 15-6. MessageName WSDL

```
        <wsdl:input message="tns:GetPriceSoapIn" />
        <wsdl:output message="tns:GetPriceSoapOut" />
    </wsdl:operation>
    .
    .
    .

    <wsdl:operation name="GetValue">
        <wsdl:documentation xmlns:wsdl="http://schemas.xmlsoap.org/wsdl/">
          Returns the value of the users holdings in a specified
          stock symbol.
        </wsdl:documentation>
        <wsdl:input name="GetValuePortfolio"
                    message="tns:GetValuePortfolioSoapIn" />
        <wsdl:output name="GetValuePortfolio"
                    message="tns:GetValuePortfolioSoapOut" />
    </wsdl:operation>
</wsdl:portType>
```

In this snippet, the web method GetValue is associated with the <wsdl:input> name
GetValuePortfolio, which corresponds to the MessageName property with that value,
all within a portType named ServiceSoap, which is the default binding.

If you run the WebServiceComplete example at the end of this chapter, the default binding will be called StockTickerService because the Name property of the WebService attribute, described shortly, will have been set.

TransactionOption Property

ASP.NET web methods can use transactions (see Chapter 10 for more details on transactions) but only if the transaction originates in that web method. In other words, the web method can only participate as the *root object* in a transaction. This means that a consuming application cannot call a web method as part of a transaction and have that web method participate in the transaction.

The WebMethod attribute's TransactionOption property specifies whether or not a web method should start a transaction. There are five legal values of the property, all contained in the TransactionOption enumeration. However, because a web method transaction must be the root object, there are only two different behaviors: A new transaction is started or it is not.

These values in the TransactionOption enumeration are used throughout the .NET Framework. However, in the case of web services, the first three values produce the same behavior, and the last two values produce the other behavior.

The three values of TransactionOption that do not start a new transaction are the following:

- Disabled (the default)
- NotSupported
- Supported

The two values that do start a new transaction are the following:

- Required
- RequiresNew

To use transactions in a web service, you must take three additional steps:

1. Add a reference to *System.EnterpriseServices.dll*.

   In VS2005, this is done through the Solution Explorer or the Website → Add Reference... menu item. To use the Solution Explorer, right-click the web site folder and select Add References.... In either case, you get the dialog box shown in Figure 15-7. Click on the desired component in the list and then click OK.

   This will have the effect of adding an <assemblies> section to *web.config*, which adds the System.EnterpriseServices assembly.

When you're coding outside of VS2005, you must add an Assembly directive pointing to System.EnterpriseServices:

```
<%@ assembly name="System.EnterpriseServices" %>
```

2. Add the System.EnterpriseServices namespace to the web service. This is done with the following code:

```
using System.EnterpriseServices;
```

3. Add a TransactionOption property with a value of RequiresNew to the WebMethod attribute. (The value of Required will have the same effect.)

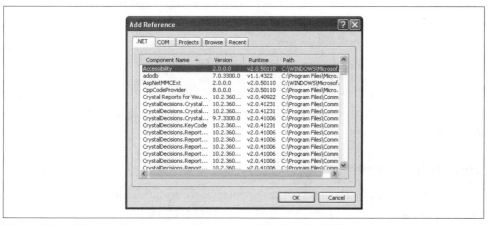

Figure 15-7. Adding a reference to a web service in Visual Studio 2005

Example 15-12 lists another web method added to *StockTickerComplete*, which has the TransactionOption property highlighted set to start a new transaction.

Example 15-12. TransactionOption property of WebMethod attribute

```
[WebMethod(Description = "Sets the value of the users holdings " +
        "in a specified stock symbol.",
        TransactionOption=TransactionOption.RequiresNew)]
public double SetValue(string StockSymbol)
{
    /*  Put code here to set the value of the specified
        StockSymbol.
        This method is starts a transaction.
    */
    return 0;
}
```

If there are no exceptions thrown by the web method, then the transaction will automatically commit unless the SetAbort method is explicitly called. If an unhandled exception is thrown, the transaction will automatically abort.

WebService Attribute

The `WebService` attribute (not to be confused with the `WebMethod` attribute or the `WebService` directive) allows you to add additional information to a web service. The `WebService` attribute is optional, though VS2005 inserts a default `WebService` attribute.

Here is the syntax for a `WebService` attribute:

```
[WebService(PropertyName=value)]
```

`PropertyName` is a valid property accepted by the `WebService` attribute (these are described shortly), and `value` is the value to be assigned to that property.

If there are multiple `WebService` properties, separate each property/value pair with a comma within a single set of parentheses as in this example:

```
[WebService (Description="A stock ticker using C#.",
        Name="StockTicker",
        Namespace="www.LibertyAssociates.com")]
```

There are three possible properties for a `WebService` attribute, described in the next three sections.

Description Property

The `WebService` attribute's `Description` property assigns a descriptive message to the web service. As with the `WebMethod` attribute's `Description` property, the `WebService` description will be displayed in the web service help page when the page is tested in a browser and will be made available in the SOAP message to any potential consumers of the web service.

Name Property

The name of a web service is displayed at the top of a web service help page when the page is tested in a browser and is made available to any potential consumers.

By default, the name of a web service is the name of the class implementing the web service. The `WebService` attribute's `Name` property allows you to change the name. If you glance back at the code listed in Example 15-4, you'll notice the class name is `Service`.

Prior to adding the `WebService` attribute, `Service` was displayed at the top of the test page when the service was run in a browser. After adding the above `WebService` attribute with the `Name` property set to `StockTicker`, that is the name displayed on the test page.

Namespace Property

Each web service has an XML namespace associated with it. An XML namespace allows you to create names in an XML document that are uniquely identified by a Uniform Resource Identifier (URI). The web service is described using a WSDL document, which is defined in XML. Each `WebService` attribute must have a unique XML namespace associated with it to ensure it can be uniquely identified by an application.

The default URI of a web service created in VS2005 is *http://tempuri.org/*. Typically, you will define a new namespace using a unique name, such as a firm's web site. Though the XML namespace often looks like a web site, it does not need to be a valid URL.

In the syntax given above for the `WebService` attribute, the `Namespace` property is set to *www.LibertyAssociates.com*, which happens to be a valid web site URL, though that is not required.

Data Types

ASP.NET web services can use any CLR-supported primitive data type as a parameter or a return value. Table 15-2 summarizes the valid types.

Table 15-2. CLR-supported primitive data types

Type	Description
byte	1-byte unsigned integer
short	2-byte signed integer
int	4-byte signed integer
long	8-byte signed integer
float	4-byte floating point
double	8-byte floating point
decimal	16-byte floating point
bool	True/false
char	Single Unicode character
string	Sequence of Unicode characters
DateTime	Represents dates and times
object	Any type

In addition to the primitive data types, you can use arrays and `ArrayLists` of the primitive types. Since data is passed between a web service and its clients using XML, whatever is used as either a parameter or return value must be represented in an XML schema or XSD.

Arrays

The examples shown so far in this chapter have used simple primitive types, such as strings and numbers, as parameters and return values. You can also use an array of primitive types as in the code shown here:

```
[WebMethod]
public string[] GetArray( )
{
    string[] TestArray = {"a","b","c"};
    return TestArray;
}
```

The main limitation of using arrays, of course, is that you must know the number of elements at design time. If the number of elements is dynamic, then an ArrayList will be called for. If an ArrayList is used in the web service, it will be converted to an object array when the web service description is created. The client proxy will return an array of objects, which will then have to be converted to an array of the proper type (string in this case).

The ArrayList is contained within the System.Collections namespace. To use an ArrayList, you must include the proper reference with the using keyword:

```
using System.Collections;
```

The code in Example 15-13 contains a web method called GetList. It takes a string as a parameter. This match string is then compared with all the firm names in the data store (the array defined at the top of the web service class shown in Example 15-4), and the web service returns all the firm names that contain the match string anywhere within the firm name.

Example 15-13. GetList web method

```
[WebMethod(Description="Returns all the stock symbols whose firm " +
                "matches the input string as *str*.")]
public ArrayList GetList(string MatchString)
{
    ArrayList a = new ArrayList( );

    //  Iterate through the array, looking for matching firm names.
    for (int i = 0; i < stocks.GetLength(0); i++)
    {
        //  Search is case sensitive.
        if ( stocks[i,1].ToUpper( ).IndexOf(MatchString.ToUpper( )) >= 0)
            a.Add(stocks[i,1]);
    }
    a.Sort( );
    return a;
}
```

The GetList web method first instantiates a new ArrayList and then iterates through the store of firms. The IndexOf method of the String class is used to do a case-sensitive search in a string, looking for the match string. If it finds a match, it will return the index of the first occurrence. If IndexOf does not find a match, it will return -1. To implement a case-insensitive search, the code in Example 15-13 first converts both the MatchString and the firm name to uppercase.

If the IndexOf method finds a match, the web method adds the firm name to the ArrayList. The firm name is contained in the second field of the array record, the field with index 1 (remember that array indices are zero-based). After completing the search, the web method sorts the ArrayList before returning it to the client. (As an alternative, you could convert the ArrayList to a strongly typed array using ArrayList.ToArray( ), before returning it.)

To test this, run the web service. From the test page, click on the GetList link. You will get a page similar to Figure 15-8.

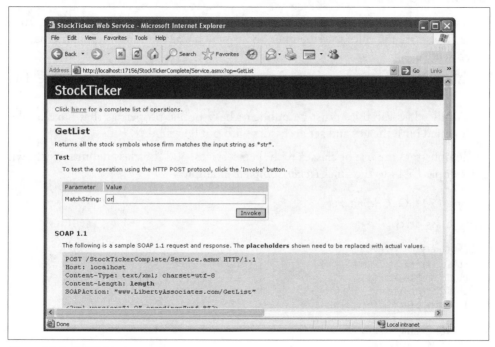

Figure 15-8. GetList test page

If you enter "or" (as shown in Figure 15-8), you will see the results that would be returned to a client, as shown in Figure 15-9. Notice that in the test output, Ford comes before General Motors even though their order has been reversed in the input data. That is a result of sorting the ArrayList prior to return.

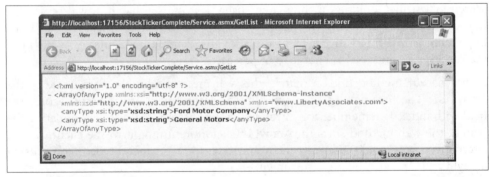

Figure 15-9. GetList test results

Classes and Structs

Web services can use user-defined classes and structs as either parameters or return types. These are the rules to remember about which class variables can participate in a web service:

- All the class variables must be primitive data types or arrays of primitive data types.
- All the class variables must be public or have public properties that have implemented both the get and set accessors with public visibility.

To demonstrate the use of classes with web services, add the class definitions shown in Example 15-14 to the *StockTickerComplete* example.

Example 15-14. Class definition

```
public class Stock
{
   public string StockSymbol;
   public string StockName;
   public double Price;
   public StockHistory[] History =
        new StockHistory[2];

   private string strBroker;
   public string Broker
   {
      get
      {
         return strBroker;
      }
      set
      {
         strBroker = value;
      }
   }
}
```

Example 15-14. Class definition (continued)

```csharp
public class StockHistory
{
    public DateTime TradeDate;
    public double Price;
}
```

The first class definition, Stock, consists of two strings, a double, an array of type StockHistory, and a public property with an underlying private string. The StockHistory class consists of a date, called the TradeDate, and the stock price on that date.

In a real-world application, you would never design a stock ticker like this. Instead of the Stock class having an array with a fixed number of stock history records, you would probably want to use a collection. You would also store the data in a database, rather than filling an array. That way, the number of history records returned by the web method would be dependent upon the number of records returned from the database query. In the example here, the data is hard-coded in an array to focus on the topic of using classes with web services.

The web method shown in Example 15-15, GetHistory, uses the Stock class to return stock history data for the stock symbol passed in to it.

Example 15-15. GetHistory web method

```csharp
[WebMethod(Description="Returns stock history for " +
           "the stock symbol specified.")]
public Stock GetHistory(string StockSymbol)
{
    Stock stock = new Stock( );

    //  Iterate through the array, looking for the symbol.
    for (int i = 0; i < stocks.GetLength(0); i++)
    {
        //  Do a case-insensitive string compare.
        if (String.Compare(StockSymbol, stocks[i,0], true) == 0)
        {
            stock.StockSymbol = StockSymbol;
            stock.StockName = stocks[i,1];
            stock.Price = Convert.ToDouble(stocks[i,2]);
            stock.Broker = "Dewy, Cheatum, & Howe";

            //  Populate the StockHistory data.
            stock.History[0] = new StockHistory( );
            stock.History[0].TradeDate = Convert.ToDateTime("5/1/2005");
            stock.History[0].Price = Convert.ToDouble(23.25);

            stock.History[1] = new StockHistory( );
            stock.History[1].TradeDate = Convert.ToDateTime("6/1/2005");
            stock.History[1].Price = Convert.ToDouble(28.75);
```

Example 15-15. GetHistory web method (continued)

```
        return stock;
    }
  }
  stock.StockSymbol = StockSymbol;
  stock.StockName = "Stock not found.";
  return stock;
}
```

In the GetHistory method listed in Example 15-15, each class is instantiated before it can be used. Iterating over the array of stocks finds the data to return. The class variables are populated from the array, and then the class itself is returned. If the stock symbol is not found, a message will be placed in a convenient field of the stock class and that is returned.

In the Stock object returned by the web service, the private string strBroker is not visible. Furthermore, the public property must have both a get and a set to be visible. Suppose you modified the Stock class by initializing the value of the private string and removing the set accessor from the property, as in the following code snippet:

```
private string strBroker = "Dewy,Cheatum, & Howe";
public string Broker
{
   get
   {
      return strBroker;
   }
}
```

Of course, you would then have to also remove the line of code in the GetHistory method that assigns a value to the Broker property, since the public property would now be read-only.

If you run the web service and put a breakpoint in the GetHistory method to examine the Stock object about to be returned, the debugger will show the Broker property was set. However, the Broker property will not be returned by the web service because it is not read/write.

DataSets

Since a web service can return any data that can be encoded in an XML file, it can return a DataSet since that is represented internally as XML by ADO.NET. A DataSet is the only type of ADO.NET data store that can be returned by a web service.

As an exercise, we will modify an example shown in Chapter 10 to return a DataSet from the Northwind database.

Though this sample web method does not conform to the ongoing Stock Ticker example, we will use it for convenience.

Add the namespaces shown in Example 15-16 to the *StockTickerComplete* example.

Example 15-16. Namespace references for using a DataSet

```
using System.Data;
using System.Data.SqlClient;
```

Now add the web method shown in Example 15-17. This web method, called GetDataSet, takes no parameters and returns a DataSet object consisting of data about customers from the Northwind database.

Example 15-17. GetDataSet web method

```
[WebMethod(Description="Returns a data set from the Northwind database.")]
public DataSet GetDataset( )
{
    // connect to the Northwind database
    string connectionString =
        "server=MyServer; uid=sa;pwd=secret;database= Northwind";

    // get records from the Customers table
    string commandString =
        "Select CompanyName,ContactName, City, Country from Customers";

    // create the data set command object and the DataSet
    SqlDataAdapter dataAdapter = new SqlDataAdapter(commandString,
                                                    connectionString);

    DataSet dataSet = new DataSet( );

    // fill the data set object
    dataAdapter.Fill(dataSet,"Customers");

    return dataSet;
}
```

The code is copied nearly verbatim from the Page_Load method in the code in Example 10-1 (described fully in that chapter). The important thing to note here is that a DataSet object is created from a query and then returned by the web method to the consuming client.

StockTickerComplete

Running the *StockTickerComplete* example produces the test page shown in Figure 15-10.

Figure 15-10. StockTickerComplete

The complete source code for the code-behind file, *App_Code/Service.cs*, is listed in Example 15-18. The code is included here to show how all the snippets of code presented fit together.

Example 15-18. Service.cs—StockTickerComplete code-behind file

```
using System.Web;
using System.Web.Services;
using System.Web.Services.Protocols;
using System;                       // necesary for String class
using System.EnterpriseServices;    // necessary for transactions
using System.Collections;           // necssary for ArrayLists
using System.Data;                  // necessary for DataSet
using System.Data.SqlClient;        // necessary for DataSet

[WebService(Description = "A stock ticker using C#.",
            Name = "StockTicker",
            Namespace = "www.LibertyAssociates.com")]
[WebServiceBinding(ConformsTo = WsiProfiles.BasicProfile1_1,
                   EmitConformanceClaims = true)]
[WebServiceBinding(Name = "OverloadedGetValue",
                   ConformsTo = WsiProfiles.BasicProfile1_1,
                   EmitConformanceClaims = true)]
public class Service : System.Web.Services.WebService
{
    //  Construct and fill an array of stock symbols and prices.
    //  Note: the stock prices are as of 5/1/05.
```

```csharp
string[,] stocks =
    {
        {"MSFT","Microsoft","25.30"},
        {"DELL","Dell Computers","34.83"},
        {"HPQ","Hewlett Packard","20.47"},
        {"YHOO","Yahoo!","34.50"},
        {"GE","General Electric","36.20"},
        {"IBM","International Business Machine","76.38"},
        {"GM","General Motors","26.68"},
        {"F","Ford Motor Company","9.11"}
    };

[WebMethod(Description =
            "Returns the stock price for the input stock symbol.")]
public double GetPrice(string StockSymbol)
//  Given a stock symbol, return the price.
{
    //  Iterate through the array, looking for the symbol.
    for (int i = 0; i < stocks.GetLength(0); i++)
    {
        //  Do a case-insensitive string compare.
        if (String.Compare(StockSymbol, stocks[i, 0], true) == 0)
            return Convert.ToDouble(stocks[i, 2]);
    }
    return 0;
}

[WebMethod(Description =
            "Returns the stock name for the input stock symbol.")]
public string GetName(string StockSymbol)
//  Given a stock symbol, return the name.
{
    //  Iterate through the array, looking for the symbol.
    for (int i = 0; i < stocks.GetLength(0); i++)
    {
        //  Do a case-insensitive string compare.
        if (String.Compare(StockSymbol, stocks[i, 0], true) == 0)
            return stocks[i, 1];
    }
    return "Symbol not found.";
}

[WebMethod]
public void SetStockExchange(string Exchange)
{
    Application["exchange"] = Exchange;
}

[WebMethod]
public string GetStockExchange()
{
    return Application["exchange"].ToString();
}
```

```csharp
[WebMethod(Description = "Number of hits per session.",
            EnableSession = true)]
public int HitCounter()
{
    if (Session["HitCounter"] == null)
    {
        Session["HitCounter"] = 1;
    }
    else
    {
        Session["HitCounter"] = ((int)Session["HitCounter"]) + 1;
    }
    return ((int)Session["HitCounter"]);
}

[WebMethod(Description = "Returns the value of the users holdings " +
                "in a specified stock symbol.",
            MessageName = "GetValuePortfolio")]
public double GetValue(string StockSymbol)
{
    /* Put code here to get the username of the current user, fetch both
       the current price of the specified StockSymbol and number of
       shares held by the current user, multiply the two together, and
       return the result.
    */
    return 0;
}

[SoapDocumentMethod(Binding = "OverloadedGetValue")]
[WebMethod(Description = "Returns the value of a specified " +
                "number of shares in a specified stock symbol.",
            MessageName = "GetValueStock")]
public double GetValue(string StockSymbol, int NumShares)
{
    /*  Put code here to get the current price of the specified
        StockSymbol, multiply it times NumShares, and return the result.
    */
    return 0;
}

[WebMethod(Description = "Sets the value of the users holdings " +
            "in a specified stock symbol.",
            TransactionOption=TransactionOption.RequiresNew)]
public double SetValue(string StockSymbol)
{
    /*  Put code here to set the value of the specified
        StockSymbol.
        This method is starts a transaction.
    */
    return 0;
}
```

```
[WebMethod(Description = "Returns all the stock symbols whose firm " +
               "matches the input string as *str*.")]
public ArrayList GetList(string MatchString)
{
    ArrayList a = new ArrayList();

    //  Iterate through the array, looking for matching firm names.
    for (int i = 0; i < stocks.GetLength(0); i++)
    {
        //  Search is case sensitive.
        if (stocks[i, 1].ToUpper().IndexOf(MatchString.ToUpper()) >= 0)
            a.Add(stocks[i, 1]);
    }
    a.Sort();
    return a;
}

[WebMethod(Description="Returns a data set from the Northwind db.")]
public DataSet GetDataset()
{
    // connect to the Northwind database
    string connectionString =
        "server=MyServer; uid=sa;pwd=secret;database= Northwind";

    // get records from the Customers table
    string commandString =
        "Select CompanyName,ContactName, City, Country from Customers";

    // create the data set command object and the DataSet
    SqlDataAdapter dataAdapter = new SqlDataAdapter(commandString,
                                              connectionString);

    DataSet dataSet = new DataSet();

    // fill the data set object
    dataAdapter.Fill(dataSet,"Customers");

    return dataSet;
}

[WebMethod(Description="Returns stock history for " +
           "the stock symbol specified.")]
public Stock GetHistory(string StockSymbol)
{
    Stock stock = new Stock();

    //  Iterate through the array, looking for the symbol.
    for (int i = 0; i < stocks.GetLength(0); i++)
    {
        //  Do a case-insensitive string compare.
        if (String.Compare(StockSymbol, stocks[i,0], true) == 0)
        {
```

```csharp
                stock.StockSymbol = StockSymbol;
                stock.StockName = stocks[i,1];
                stock.Price = Convert.ToDouble(stocks[i,2]);
                stock.Broker = "Dewy, Cheatum, & Howe";

                // Populate the StockHistory data.
                stock.History[0] = new StockHistory( );
                stock.History[0].TradeDate = Convert.ToDateTime("5/1/2005");
                stock.History[0].Price = Convert.ToDouble(23.25);

                stock.History[1] = new StockHistory( );
                stock.History[1].TradeDate = Convert.ToDateTime("6/1/2005");
                stock.History[1].Price = Convert.ToDouble(28.75);

                return stock;
            }
        }
        stock.StockSymbol = StockSymbol;
        stock.StockName = "Stock not found.";
        return stock;
    }
}   // close for class Service

public class Stock
{
    public string StockSymbol;
    public string StockName;
    public double Price;
    public StockHistory[] History =
            new StockHistory[2];

    private string strBroker;
    public string Broker
    {
        get
        {
            return strBroker;
        }
        set
        {
            strBroker = value;
        }
    }
}

public class StockHistory
{
    public DateTime TradeDate;
    public double Price;
}
```

Creating Discovery Documents

Once you have created a web service, the developers who develop the consuming applications will want a way to find out what web services are available on a server, the methods exposed by those web services, what parameters those methods and properties expect to receive, and what data type the web method returns. This process is called *discovery*, which is an optional process. If the developer of the consuming application knows the URL of the web service file (*.asmx*), then there will be no need to do discovery.

This discovery information is contained in discovery documents. These are XML files created with a command line utility called *disco.exe*, described next.

There are several ways for a web service consumer to access a discovery document, including viewing a discovery document with a query string and making use of a static discovery file.

These two methods are described in the following sections.

Discovery via Query String

A developer may be able to create a client application by obtaining the disco file created on the server. To see this file, append *?disco* to the URL of the *service.asmx* file:

```
http://localhost/StockTicker/service.asmx?disco
```

This will display the following disco file:

```
<?xml version="1.0" encoding="utf-8" ?>
- <discovery xmlns:xsi="http://www.w3.org/2001/XMLSchema-instance"
    xmlns:xsd="http://www.w3.org/2001/XMLSchema"
    xmlns="http://schemas.xmlsoap.org/disco/">
  <contractRef ref="http://localhost/StockTicker/service.asmx?wsdl"
    docRef="http://localhost/StockTicker/service.asmx"
    xmlns="http://schemas.xmlsoap.org/disco/scl/" />
  <soap address="http://localhost/StockTicker/service.asmx"
    xmlns:q1="www.LibertyAssociates.com" binding="q1:OverloadedGetValue"
    xmlns="http://schemas.xmlsoap.org/disco/soap/" />
  <soap address=http://localhost/StockTicker/service.asmx
    xmlns:q2="www.LibertyAssociates.com" binding="q2:StockTickerSoap"
    xmlns="http://schemas.xmlsoap.org/disco/soap/" />
  <soap address="http://localhost/StockTicker/service.asmx"
    xmlns:q3="www.LibertyAssociates.com" binding="q3:OverloadedGetValue1"
    xmlns="http://schemas.xmlsoap.org/disco/soap/" />
  <soap address="http://localhost/StockTicker/service.asmx"
    xmlns:q4="www.LibertyAssociates.com" binding="q4:StockTickerSoap12"
    xmlns="http://schemas.xmlsoap.org/disco/soap/" />
  </discovery>
```

Static Discovery Files

For the consumer of a web service to use a static discovery file, the developer of the web service must create it. (The client's use of discovery is covered in the next chapter.)

Though you can create the *.disco* file manually, it is far easier to use the *disco.exe* command-line utility. To do this, open a command prompt window (remember to use the Visual Studio 2005 Command Prompt from the Start Menu to get the correct path). Then enter a command similar to the following (all on one line):

```
disco /out:<output directory name>
    http://localhost/StockTicker/service.asmx
```

As an alternative to using the out switch to specify the *output* directory, change the current directory to where you want the output to be located in before executing the command and run the disco utility from that directory. The output will go to the current directory.

The disco utility executed in the previous command line will put three files (summarized in Table 15-3) in the output directory.

Table 15-3. Files output by the disco utility

Filename	Description
service.disco	Discovery document that contains references to descriptions of the resources available in the web service
service.wsdl	This is the exact same WSDL for the web service generated by entering the *.asmx* file in a browser with `?wsdl` appended to the URL
results.discomap	Contains a reference to both the *.disco* and *.wsdl* files

At this stage of the process, the *.disco* file is the main output that interests you. The other two files may be used by a developer creating a consuming application, as will be described in the next chapter.

For a complete listing of all the parameters available to the disco utility, enter the following command line:

```
disco /?
```

Deployment

Deploying web services is similar to deploying web pages, which will be covered in detail in Chapter 19. The *.asmx* file must be located in a virtual directory exposed by IIS so it is accessible to a browser on the Internet. If you have a *.disco* file for the web service (described in the previous section), then this file should also be in the application virtual directory. This allows the web service to be discovered and allows proxies to be created by consuming applications. Both of these concepts will be described in the next chapter.

If the application requires a *web.config* file (described fully in Chapter 18), then this file too should be copied to the application virtual directory.

As with web pages, you can make the compiled class (or classes) and other resources available with either pre-compiled assemblies or with dynamically compiled assemblies.

Pre-Compiled Assemblies

The technique from prior versions of Visual Studio, which is still fully supported, is to compile the source code manually into an assembly file (i.e., the *dll*) and locate that in the *bin* directory immediately beneath the virtual directory containing the *.asmx* file. Manual compilation of assemblies is described in the next chapter and in Chapter 19.

Figure 15-11 shows a typical directory structure on a production web server for a web service called StockTicker.

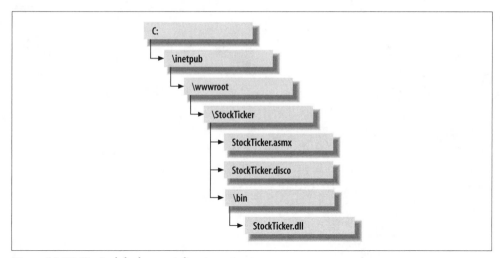

Figure 15-11. Typical deployment directory structure

Referring to Figure 15-11, if a virtual directory was defined on the web server called StockTicker, which was mapped to the directory called *StockTicker* (the name of the virtual directory and the physical directory do *not* have to be the same), then the URL for referring to the *.asmx* file would be the following:

```
http://YourDomain.com/StockTicker/StockTicker.asmx
```

Dynamically Compiled Assemblies

The .NET Framework automatically compiles any source code found in the \App_Code directory under the web application virtual root. VS2005 cooperates in this by automatically creating the \App_Code folder when it creates a new web service, and placing the code-behind file there. Every time the web app is started, any code found in the \App_Code folder is compiled into an assembly and cached.

The virtual directory and the URL used to access the web service would be the same, as shown in the previous section.

CHAPTER 16

Consuming Web Services

The previous chapter gave an overview of web services and described how to create a web service. This chapter explains how to create a web service client application, also called a web service *consumer*. The consuming application can be a web page, another web service, or a desktop application.

Once a web service is created and made available to consumers on the Internet, it is up to the developer creating the client application to find the web service, discover what methods are available, create the client proxy, and incorporate the proxy into the client. The client can then make method calls against the remote web service as though it were making local calls. In fact, the client application is making local method calls against the proxy—it just behaves as if it is making calls directly to the web service over the Internet.

Depending on the requirements of the consuming application, you can let VS2005 do all the work of creating and referencing the proxy, you can do it all manually, or somewhere in between. This chapter will demonstrate the range of possibilities.

Once the proxy is created, compiled, and referenced, the consuming application can make method calls against the remote web service. As long as the signatures and return types of the exposed web service methods do not change, the proxy will continue to work.

 The *signature* of a web method consists of the name of the method and its parameter list.

The web service can have additional web methods added without breaking the proxy, though the new web methods will be invisible to the consuming application until the proxy source code is regenerated and recompiled. Likewise, existing web methods can have their underlying code modified, but as long as their signature does not change, neither the proxy nor the client must be recompiled.

Discovery

As mentioned in the previous chapter, *discovery* is the process of finding out what web services are available, what methods and properties are exposed by a specific web service, what parameters those methods and properties expect to receive, and what data type the web method or property returns. All of this information is contained in the WSDL (Web Services Description Language) document, introduced in the previous chapter and described in more detail below.

As noted in the previous chapter, discovery is an optional process. If the consuming developer knows the URL of the web service file (*.asmx*) itself, there will be no need for discovery.

However, the consuming developer often will not know the location of the web service file or the WSDL document on a given server. In these instances, ASP.NET provides a discovery command-line utility called *disco.exe* that takes the URL of the web service as an argument, and creates discovery documents on the client machine from which the client-application developer can create the consuming application.

To do this, execute the disco utility from a command line, giving it the URL of the web service as an argument. For example:

```
disco http://WebSrvcDomain.com/StockTicker
```

This command will search the specified URL for any discovery documents and save them to the current directory of the local machine. A *.wsdl* file will be generated and saved there as well.

To force the output directory to be somewhere other than the current directory, use the /out: parameter, or /o: for short:

```
disco /out:<output directory name>
     http://WebSrvcDomain.com/StockTicker
```

The disco utility executed in the previous command line will put two files in the output directory:

service.wsdl

> This is the same WSDL for the web service generated by entering the *.asmx* file in a browser with *?wsdl* appended to the URL or created using the WSDL command line utility described below.

results.discomap

> Alternative discovery document. This can be used as input to the WSDL utility, described later in this chapter.

For a complete listing of all the parameters available to the disco utility, enter the following command line:

```
disco /?
```

Creating the Client with VS2005

The easiest way to create a web service client is to let VS2005 do all the work. This includes creating the proxy for the web service and adding a reference to that proxy to the client application. You will see how to do some or all of the steps outside VS2005 later in this chapter.

Why wouldn't you let VS2005 do all the work, you might ask? By taking control of the process and performing certain steps manually, you gain flexibility and features that may be helpful under certain (admittedly unusual) scenarios. In addition, you gain a more thorough understanding of how web services work and what is happening behind the scenes, so doing it yourself has great geek appeal and impresses your friends at parties.

To start, first create an ultra-simple web service in VS2005. Call it *WebServiceSimple*. This will bring up the default start-up boilerplate code in the code-behind file with a web method called HelloWorld. Modify this web method a bit to return the current time stamp, as shown highlighted in Example 16-1.

Example 16-1. App_Code\Service.cs for WebServiceSimple

```
using System;
using System.Web;
using System.Web.Services;
using System.Web.Services.Protocols;
```

Example 16-1. App_Code\Service.cs for WebServiceSimple (continued)

```
[WebService(Namespace = "http://tempuri.org/")]
[WebServiceBinding(ConformsTo = WsiProfiles.BasicProfile1_1)]
public class Service : System.Web.Services.WebService
{
    public Service () {

    }

    [WebMethod]
    public string HelloWorld( ) {
        return "Hello World. The time is " +
            DateTime.Now.ToLongTimeString( );
    }

}
```

After saving this web service, create the consuming web site. Be sure to select the correct template, ASP.NET Web Site, from the New Web Site dialog box. (If the previous web service was the last new web application created, the default template will remain ASP.NET Web Service.) Call this new web site *WebServiceSimpleConsumer*. When this page runs it will look something like Figure 16-1, with a label displaying a message and two buttons.

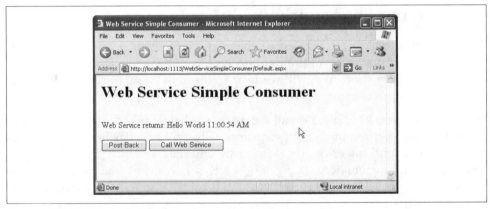

Figure 16-1. WebServiceSimpleConsumer

The content file for *WebServiceSimpleConsumer* is listed in Example 16-2, with the important controls highlighted. A click event handler exists for the Call Web Service button but not the Post Back button. The latter simply posts the form, and the only code that runs is that in Page_Load. You will see the code-behind file in a moment.

Example 16-2. Default.aspx for WebServiceSimpleConsumer

```
<%@ Page Language="C#" AutoEventWireup="true" CodeFile="Default.aspx.cs"
    Inherits="_Default" %>

<!DOCTYPE html PUBLIC "-//W3C//DTD XHTML 1.1//EN"
    "http://www.w3.org/TR/xhtml11/DTD/xhtml11.dtd">

<html xmlns="http://www.w3.org/1999/xhtml" >
<head runat="server">
    <title>Web Service Simple Consumer</title>
</head>
<body>
    <form id="form1" runat="server">
    <div>
      <h1>Web Service Simple Consumer</h1>
        <br />
        <asp:Label ID="lblMessage" runat="server" />
        <br />
        <br />
        <asp:Button ID="btnPost" runat="server"
                    Text="Post Back" />
        <asp:Button ID="btnWebService" runat="server"
                    Text="Call Web Service"
                    OnClick="btnWebService_Click" />
    </div>
    </form>
</body>
</html>
```

First, you must provide a reference to the web service. To be more precise, you must provide a reference to a proxy to the web service as was described in the previous chapter and illustrated in Figures 15-1 and 15-3.

This is where VS2005 does its magic, adding a web reference to your client. VS2005 can add a web reference to a web service only if that service is being served from a virtual directory. For web services accessed over the Internet, this is inherently the case. However, to consume the web service you just created on your local machine, you must have IIS installed on the machine and you must create a virtual directory pointing to that web service.

Create the virtual directory in the Computer Management window by right-clicking on My Computer and selecting Manage, or from the Start → Control Panel → Administrative Tools → Computer Management. Drill down to Services and Applications → Internet Information Services → Web Sites → Default Web Site, right-click Default Web Site, and choose New → Virtual Directory. Follow the wizard, entering WebServiceSimple as the alias (i.e., the name of the virtual directory) and browsing to the location of the web service file. You can verify that the virtual directory is made correctly by entering the following URL into a browser:

```
http://localhost/WebServiceSimple/service.asmx
```

You should get the web service test page, as shown in Figure 16-2.

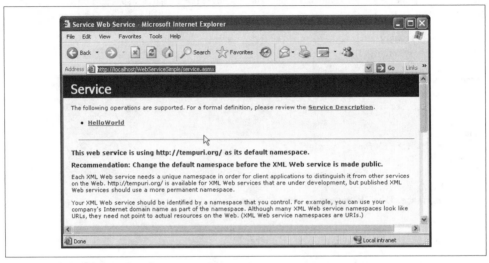

Figure 16-2. WebServiceSimple test page

Once the virtual directory for the web service is created, you can add that web service as a web reference to a consuming web site. To add a reference to a web service to your site, click on the Website → Add Web Reference… menu item, or right-click on the project file in the Solution Explorer and select Add Web Reference…. In either case, you will get the Add Web Reference dialog box shown in Figure 16-3.

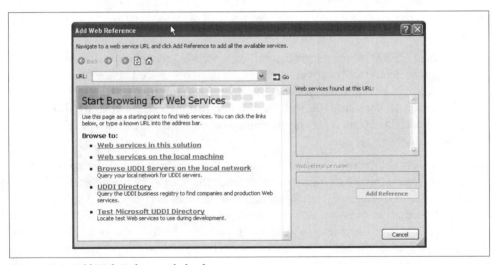

Figure 16-3. Add Web Reference dialog box

If the web service you wished to reference were on a different machine, you would enter the URL of either the web service file (*.asmx*), the *.wsdl* file, or a discovery file

(*.disco*). Then click the Go button. In this example, click on Web services on the local machine. Alternatively, you could search one of several UDDI directories.

In any case, VS2005 will search the specified location and present any available web services in a list of hyperlinks. Click on the web service you want to reference (Service, in this case). It will then display the test page for that web service, similar to what you saw in Figure 16-2. If this is the web service you want to reference, click on the Add Reference button. That is all there is to it.

VS2005 will add a folder to the project called *App_WebReferences*, which will display in the Solution Explorer. Under that folder will be another folder named after the web server, *localhost* in this case. Under that will be three files, all named after the web service file: *.disco*, *.discomap*, and *.wsdl*. These file types have all been described previously.

What you will not see anywhere is either the source code for the proxy class (which you will see when you perform the steps manually later in this chapter) or a compiled proxy assembly. This compiled assembly is there somewhere behind the scenes, but VS2005 manages it.

The reference is made available to the web page at runtime via an entry made automatically in the *web.config* file. This is an appSetting (appSettings will be described in Chapter 18) with a key comprised of the server name concatenated with the web service name, as in:

```
<appSettings>
   <add key="localhost.Service"
        value="http://localhost/WebServiceSimple/Service.asmx"/>
</appSettings>
```

Once the web reference has been added, your code-behind in the consuming web page can refer to the web service as though it were a class on the local machine.

The complete code-behind file for the consuming web site, *WebServiceSimpleConsumer*, is listed in Example 16-3.

Example 16-3. Default.aspx.cs for WebServiceSimpleConsumer

```
using System;
using System.Data;
using System.Configuration;
using System.Web;
using System.Web.Security;
using System.Web.UI;
using System.Web.UI.WebControls;
using System.Web.UI.WebControls.WebParts;
using System.Web.UI.HtmlControls;

public partial class _Default : System.Web.UI.Page
{
    protected void Page_Load(object sender, EventArgs e)
```

Example 16-3. Default.aspx.cs for WebServiceSimpleConsumer (continued)

```
   {
      if (!IsPostBack)
      {
         lblMessage.Text = "First loaded at " +
            DateTime.Now.ToLongTimeString( );
      }
      else
      {
         lblMessage.Text = "Postback at " +
            DateTime.Now.ToLongTimeString( );
      }
   }

   protected void btnWebService_Click(object sender, EventArgs e)
   {
      localhost.Service proxy = new localhost.Service( );
      lblMessage.Text = "Web Service returns: " + proxy.HelloWorld( );
   }
}
```

Looking at the Page_Load method, the Label control is populated with a relevant message and the timestamp every time the page posts, either from initial load or clicking the Post Back button.

The line of code in Example 16-3 that instantiates a reference to the web service is highlighted, as well the usage of a web method in the following line. This code is contained in the Click event handler for the Call Web Service button. As you type the server name (localhost) in the code window, you will see that Intellisense knows about the class and method names in the web service.

Creating the Client Manually

Occasionally, using web references in VS2005, does not meet your requirements. This could be due to specific deployment issues, such as language requirements for the proxy class, specification of the proxy class namespace, use of a non-default protocol, login or other security concerns, or any number of special circumstances. Using the command line tools, with their many optional switches and arguments, will often let you fine tune your application's deployment and usability.

This section will review the different ways you can take control of the process of creating and using the proxy, allowing your consuming app to talk to the web service as though they were on the same machine.

Creating the Consumer Web Page Content

Before proceeding with the steps of creating the proxy, it would be helpful to have a consumer application, in this case a web page, to use.

To demonstrate this and to provide a proxy class with a little more meat for analysis, we will work with the StockTickerComplete web service developed in the previous chapter, listed in its entirety in Example 15-18.

If you don't have a virtual directory for that web service on your machine, create one now called StockTicker. You can then see the test page for this web service by entering the following URL in a browser:

```
http://localhost/StockTicker/service.asmx
```

In VS2005, create a new web site called *StockTickerConsumer*. This web site will have several text boxes for entering the stock symbol of the firm. It will then return either the firm name, stock price, or stock history. It also has a text box for setting the name of the stock exchange. The web page in Design view will look something like Figure 16-4.

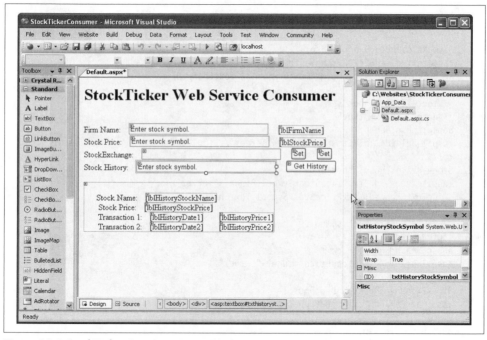

Figure 16-4. StockTickerConsumer Design view

The complete source code for the content file is listed in Example 16-4. This content provides only the minimum user input necessary to allow demonstration of the principles. There are four textboxes, with the following names: txtFirmNameStockSymbol, txtPriceStockSymbol, txtStockExchange, and txtHistoryStockSymbol. The first two have their AutoPostBack property set to true. Therefore, as soon as the value in those text boxes changes, it will fire the TextChanged event, which will cause the designated event handler to execute. Each event handler makes a call to the relevant proxy method and displays the returned value in a label next to the text box.

Example 16-4. default.aspx for StockTickerConsumer

```
<%@ Page Language="C#" AutoEventWireup="true"  CodeFile="Default.aspx.cs"
    Inherits="_Default" %>

<!DOCTYPE html PUBLIC "-//W3C//DTD XHTML 1.1//EN"
    "http://www.w3.org/TR/xhtml11/DTD/xhtml11.dtd">

<html xmlns="http://www.w3.org/1999/xhtml" >
<head runat="server">
    <title>StockTickerConsumer</title>
</head>
<body>
    <form id="form1" runat="server">
    <div>
        <h1>StockTicker Web Service Consumer</h1>
        <br/>
        Firm Name:   
        <asp:textBox id="txtFirmNameStockSymbol" runat="server"
            OnTextChanged="txtFirmNameStockSymbol_TextChanged"
            width="120"
            text="Enter stock symbol."
            AutoPostBack="true" />
           
        <asp:label id="lblFirmName" runat="server"/>
        <br/>
        Stock Price:   
        <asp:textBox id="txtPriceStockSymbol" runat="server"
            OnTextChanged="txtPriceStockSymbol_TextChanged"
            width="120"
            text="Enter stock symbol."
         AutoPostBack="true"/>
           
        <asp:label id="lblStockPrice" runat="server"/>
        <br/>
        StockExchange:   
        <asp:textBox id="txtStockExchange" runat="server"
            width="120" />
           
        <asp:button id="btnStockExchangeSet" runat="server"
            text="Set"
            onClick="btnStockExchangeSet_Click" />
           
        <asp:button id="btnStockExchangeGet" runat="server"
            text="Get"
            onClick="btnStockExchangeGet_Click" />
        <br/>
        Stock History:   
        <asp:textBox id="txtHistoryStockSymbol" runat="server"
            width="120"
```

Example 16-4. default.aspx for StockTickerConsumer (continued)

```
            text="Enter stock symbol." />
           
        <asp:button id="btnGetHistory" runat="server"
            text="Get History"
            onClick="btnGetHistory_Click" />
        <br/>
        <asp:Panel id="pnlHistory" runat="Server" visible="false">
            <br/>
                  
            Stock Name:   
            <asp:label id="lblHistoryStockName" runat="server"/>
            <br/>
                  
            Stock Price:   
            <asp:label id="lblHistoryStockPrice" runat="server"/>
            <br/>
                  
            Transaction 1:   
            <asp:label id="lblHistoryDate1" runat="server"/>
                  
            <asp:label id="lblHistoryPrice1" runat="server"/>
            <br/>
                  
            Transaction 2:   
            <asp:label id="lblHistoryDate2" runat="server"/>
                  
            <asp:label id="lblHistoryPrice2" runat="server"/>
        </asp:Panel>
    </div>
    </form>
</body>
</html>
```

The `txtStockExchange` text box does nothing when the value in the text box changes. However, it has two buttons associated with it. The Set button sets an application variable with the contents of the `txtStockExchange` text box, and the Get button fills the `txtStockExchange` text box with the contents of the application variable.

The `txtHistoryStockSymbol` text box also does nothing when the value in the text box changes. It has the `btnGetHistory` button associated with it. When that button is clicked, the `btnGetHistory_Click` event handler is called. This method demonstrates how to retrieve class member variables from within the web service class.

The code-behind file with the event handlers and other code will be developed shortly.

Creating the Proxy

As described in the previous chapter, and shown schematically in Figures 15-1 and 15-3, a web service is consumed by a client application by use of a *proxy*. A proxy is a substitute, or local stand-in, for the web service. Once the proxy is created and registered with the consuming application, method calls can be made against the web service. In actuality, those method calls will be made against the local proxy. It will seem to the consuming application that the web service is local to the application.

There are two ways to generate the proxy. The first way, demonstrated previously, is to allow VS2005 to create the proxy and register it with the consuming application with the single step of adding a web reference to the consuming app. The advantage to this method is that it requires little work.

The second way (described next) is to generate the source code manually for the proxy class and compile that into the proxy DLL. The advantages to this method are the following:

- You do not need to use VS2005.
- The command-line approach offers more flexibility and features over VS2005.

Manually generating the proxy class source code

To create the source code for the proxy class, you use a command-line utility called *wsdl.exe*. This utility takes a *.wsdl* file as input. The *.wsdl* file can be stored locally, having been previously created using the command-line utility, or it can be generated on the fly from the web service file itself. The following two command lines will yield the same result, assuming that the local *.wsdl* file came from the remote *.asmx* file:

```
wsdl MyWebService.WSDL
wsdl http://www.SomeVirtualDirectory/SomeWebService.asmx?wsdl
```

 For this, and any other ASP.NET command-line utilities, it is easiest to use the command prompt provided as part of the .NET installation, since this command prompt has the PATH environment variable set to include the location of all the command line utilities. To open this command prompt, go to Start → All Programs → Microsoft Visual Studio 2005 → Visual Studio Tools → Visual Studio 2005 Command Prompt.

Alternatively, the WSDL utility can take a *.discomap* file (described earlier in the "Discovery" section) created by the *disco* utility as input.

This source code will later be compiled into the proxy class, which a consuming application can get a reference to.

To generate the proxy class source code for this web service, enter the following command at a VS2005 command prompt after navigating to the *c:\websites\ StockTickerConsumer* folder (created in the previous section where the consumer web page was developed):

```
wsdl http://localhost/StockTicker/service.asmx?wsdl
```

The output from the WSDL utility is a source code file containing the proxy class, which can be compiled into a library, or *dll,* file. The default language for this output source is C#. To change the language of the output file, use the /language: parameter, or /l: for short. Valid values for the language parameter are CS, VB, or JS, for C#, VB2005, and JScript.NET, respectively. So, to force the output to be VB2005, you would use a command line similar to this:

```
wsdl /l:VB http://localhost/StockTicker/service.asmx?wsdl
```

By default, the first component of the output filename is based on the input file as follows. If the WebService attribute in the web service class has a Name property, the output file will have that name. If not, the output name will have the name of the web service class. Every output filename has an extension corresponding to the language.

For example, the code-behind file which contains the WebService class for the web service used here, *c:\websites\StockTickerComplete\service.cs,* has the following WebService attribute and class definition:

```
[WebService(Description = "A stock ticker using C#.",
            Name = "StockTicker",
            Namespace = "www.LibertyAssociates.com")]
.
.
.
public class Service : System.Web.Services.WebService
{
```

Running the WSDL utility against this WebService class, the output filename would be *StockTicker.cs.* However, if the Name property is removed from the WebService attribute, then the output name will be *Service.cs.* By default the output file will be in the current directory of the command prompt.

You can specify both the output filename and location by using the /out: parameter, or /o: for short. For example, the following command line will force the output file to use VB2005, have the name *test.vb,* and be located in the *bin* directory below the current directory:

```
wsdl /l:VB /o:bin\test.vb
    http://localhost/StockTicker/service.asmx?wsdl
```

Table 16-1 shows some of the other switches available to the WSDL utility.

Table 16-1. WSDL utility switches

Parameter	Description
/language	The language for the output proxy class source file. Valid values are CS, VB, JS, VJS, or CPP. The default is CS.
/nologo	Suppress the Microsoft banner.
/namespace:<namespace>	Specify the namespace for the generated proxy. The default is the global namespace.

Table 16-1. WSDL utility switches (continued)

Parameter	Description
/protocol:<protocol>	Specify the protocol to implement. Valid values are HttpGet, HttpPost, SOAP, or SOAP12 (corresponding to SOAP Version 1.2). The default is SOAP.
/username:<username>/ password:<password>/domain: <domain>	Credentials to use when connecting to a server that requires authentication.

For a complete list of parameters for *wsdl.exe*, enter the following from the command line:

```
wsdl /?
```

Proxy class details

Compare selected sections of the original web service class source file, *StockTicker-Complete\App_Code\service.cs*, reproduced here in Example 16-5, with the selected sections of the "manually" generated source code for the proxy class, *StockTicker.cs*, shown in Example 16-6. (Though you do not actually write any of the code in Example 16-6, it is manually generated in the sense that you run the WSDL utility manually rather than letting VS2005 to it for you.)

Example 16-5. Selected sections of the web service StockTickerComplete\App_Code\ service.cs

```
using System.Web;
using System.Web.Services;
using System.Web.Services.Protocols;
using System;                        //  necesary for String class
using System.EnterpriseServices;     // necessary for transactions
using System.Collections;            //  necssary for ArrayLists
using System.Data;                   //  necessary for DataSet
using System.Data.SqlClient;         //  necessary for DataSet

[WebService(Description = "A stock ticker using C#.",
          Name = "StockTicker",
          Namespace = "www.LibertyAssociates.com")]
[WebServiceBinding(ConformsTo = WsiProfiles.BasicProfile1_1,
               EmitConformanceClaims = true)]
[WebServiceBinding(Name = "OverloadedGetValue",
               ConformsTo = WsiProfiles.BasicProfile1_1,
               EmitConformanceClaims = true)]
public class Service : System.Web.Services.WebService
{
   // Construct and fill an array of stock symbols and prices.
   // Note: the stock prices are as of 5/1/05.
   string[,] stocks =
      {
         {"MSFT","Microsoft","25.30"},
         {"DELL","Dell Computers","34.83"},
```

```
            {"HPQ","Hewlett Packard","20.47"},
            {"YHOO","Yahoo!","34.50"},
            {"GE","General Electric","36.20"},
            {"IBM","International Business Machine","76.38"},
            {"GM","General Motors","26.68"},
            {"F","Ford Motor Company","9.11"}
    };

    [WebMethod(Description =
                "Returns the stock price for the input stock symbol.")]
    public double GetPrice(string StockSymbol)
    //  Given a stock symbol, return the price.
    {
        //  Iterate through the array, looking for the symbol.
        for (int i = 0; i < stocks.GetLength(0); i++)
        {
            //  Do a case-insensitive string compare.
            if (String.Compare(StockSymbol, stocks[i, 0], true) == 0)
                return Convert.ToDouble(stocks[i, 2]);
        }
        return 0;
    }

    [WebMethod(Description="Returns stock history for " +
                "the stock symbol specified.")]
    public Stock GetHistory(string StockSymbol)
    {
        Stock stock = new Stock( );

        //  Iterate through the array, looking for the symbol.
        for (int i = 0; i < stocks.GetLength(0); i++)
        {
            //  Do a case-insensitive string compare.
            if (String.Compare(StockSymbol, stocks[i,0], true) == 0)
            {
                stock.StockSymbol = StockSymbol;
                stock.StockName = stocks[i,1];
                stock.Price = Convert.ToDouble(stocks[i,2]);

                //  Populate the StockHistory data.
                stock.History[0] = new StockHistory( );
                stock.History[0].TradeDate = Convert.ToDateTime("5/1/2005");
                stock.History[0].Price = Convert.ToDouble(23.25);

                stock.History[1] = new StockHistory( );
                stock.History[1].TradeDate = Convert.ToDateTime("6/1/2005");
                stock.History[1].Price = Convert.ToDouble(28.75);

                return stock;
            }
        }
    }
```

```
      stock.StockSymbol = StockSymbol;
      stock.StockName = "Stock not found.";
      return stock;
   }
}   //  close for class Service

public class Stock
{
   public string StockSymbol;
   public string StockName;
   public double Price;
   public StockHistory[] History =
         new StockHistory[2];
}

public class StockHistory
{
   public DateTime TradeDate;
   public double Price;
}
```

Example 16-6. Selected sections of Proxy class source code file StockTicker.cs

```
//------------------------------------------------------------------------
// <auto-generated>
//    This code was generated by a tool.
//    Runtime Version:2.0.50215.44
//
//    Changes to this file may cause incorrect behavior and will be lost if
//    the code is regenerated.
// </auto-generated>
//------------------------------------------------------------------------

using System;
using System.ComponentModel;
using System.Data;
using System.Diagnostics;
using System.Web.Services;
using System.Web.Services.Protocols;
using System.Xml.Serialization;

//
// This source code was auto-generated by wsdl, Version=2.0.50215.44.
//
.
.
.
/// <remarks/>
[System.Diagnostics.DebuggerStepThroughAttribute( )]
[System.ComponentModel.DesignerCategoryAttribute("code")]
[System.Web.Services.WebServiceBindingAttribute(Name="StockTickerSoap",
```

Example 16-6. Selected sections of Proxy class source code file StockTicker.cs (continued)

```
        Namespace="www.LibertyAssociates.com")]
[System.Xml.Serialization.XmlIncludeAttribute(typeof(object[]))]
public partial class StockTickerSoap :
    System.Web.Services.Protocols.SoapHttpClientProtocol {

    private System.Threading.SendOrPostCallback
        GetHistoryOperationCompleted;

    /// <remarks/>
    public StockTickerSoap( ) {
        this.Url = "http://localhost/stockticker/service.asmx";
    }

    /// <remarks/>
    public event GetHistoryCompletedEventHandler GetHistoryCompleted;
.
.
.

    [System.Web.Services.Protocols.SoapDocumentMethodAttribute(
            "www.LibertyAssociates.com/GetHistory",
            RequestNamespace="www.LibertyAssociates.com",
            ResponseNamespace="www.LibertyAssociates.com",
            Use=System.Web.Services.Description.SoapBindingUse.Literal,
            ParameterStyle=
                System.Web.Services.Protocols.SoapParameterStyle.Wrapped)]
    public Stock GetHistory(string StockSymbol) {
        object[] results = this.Invoke("GetHistory", new object[] {
                    StockSymbol});
        return ((Stock)(results[0]));
    }

    /// <remarks/>
    public System.IAsyncResult BeginGetHistory(string StockSymbol,
        System.AsyncCallback callback, object asyncState) {
        return this.BeginInvoke("GetHistory", new object[] {
                    StockSymbol}, callback, asyncState);
    }

    /// <remarks/>
    public Stock EndGetHistory(System.IAsyncResult asyncResult) {
        object[] results = this.EndInvoke(asyncResult);
        return ((Stock)(results[0]));
    }

    /// <remarks/>
    public void GetHistoryAsync(string StockSymbol) {
        this.GetHistoryAsync(StockSymbol, null);
    }

    /// <remarks/>
    public void GetHistoryAsync(string StockSymbol, object userState) {
        if ((this.GetHistoryOperationCompleted == null)) {
```

```csharp
            this.GetHistoryOperationCompleted =
                new System.Threading.SendOrPostCallback(
                    this.OnGetHistoryOperationCompleted);
        }
        this.InvokeAsync("GetHistory", new object[] {
                    StockSymbol}, this.GetHistoryOperationCompleted,
                        userState);
    }

    private void OnGetHistoryOperationCompleted(object arg) {
        if ((this.GetHistoryCompleted != null)) {
            System.Web.Services.Protocols.InvokeCompletedEventArgs
                invokeArgs =
                  ((System.Web.Services.Protocols.InvokeCompletedEventArgs)
                    (arg));
            this.GetHistoryCompleted(this,
                new GetHistoryCompletedEventArgs(
                invokeArgs.Results, invokeArgs.Error,
                invokeArgs.Cancelled, invokeArgs.UserState));
        }
    }

    /// <remarks/>
    public new void CancelAsync(object userState) {
        base.CancelAsync(userState);
    }
}

/// <remarks/>
public delegate void GetHistoryCompletedEventHandler(object sender,
        GetHistoryCompletedEventArgs e);

/// <remarks/>
[System.SerializableAttribute()]
[System.Xml.Serialization.XmlTypeAttribute(Namespace=
    "www.LibertyAssociates.com")]
public partial class StockHistory {

    private System.DateTime tradeDateField;

    private double priceField;

    /// <remarks/>
    public System.DateTime TradeDate {
        get {
            return this.tradeDateField;
        }
        set {
            this.tradeDateField = value;
        }
    }
```

```
    /// <remarks/>
    public double Price {
        get {
            return this.priceField;
        }
        set {
            this.priceField = value;
        }
    }
}


/// <remarks/>
[System.SerializableAttribute( )]
[System.Xml.Serialization.XmlTypeAttribute(
        Namespace="www.LibertyAssociates.com")]
public partial class Stock {

    private string stockSymbolField;

    private string stockNameField;

    private double priceField;

    private StockHistory[] historyField;

    /// <remarks/>
    public string StockSymbol {
        get {
            return this.stockSymbolField;
        }
        set {
            this.stockSymbolField = value;
        }
    }

    /// <remarks/>
    public string StockName {
        get {
            return this.stockNameField;
        }
        set {
            this.stockNameField = value;
        }
    }

    /// <remarks/>
    public double Price {
        get {
            return this.priceField;
        }
        set {
            this.priceField = value;
```

```
        }
    }

    /// <remarks/>
    public StockHistory[] History {
        get {
            return this.historyField;
        }
        set {
            this.historyField = value;
        }
    }
}
```

There is no need to understand fully all the nuances of the proxy class source code file. Several points are worth noting:

- The namespaces referenced with the using statements at the beginning of the web service class in Example 16-5 and the proxy class in Example 16-6 differ. This is because the proxy class is not actually using System.Data. It is merely taking the call to the method that will ultimately use System.Data, wrapping it in the proper protocol (SOAP in this case), and passing it over the Internet to the web service. Therefore, the only namespaces actually needed by the proxy class are those necessary for interacting with a web service, serializing the data into an XML data stream, and sending and receiving those XML packages.

- The StockTickerSoap class in the proxy, which corresponds to the Service class in the web service, inherits from SoapHttpClientProtocol rather than from WebService. This inherited class provides the methods for the proxy to talk to the web service using the SOAP protocol. Notice how the class in the proxy is named based on the Name property of the WebService attribute (StockTicker) in the web service class, rather than the actual class name (Service).

- Immediately following the StockTickerSoap class declaration in the generated proxy is a *constructor*, which is a public method with the same name as the class. In the constructor, the URL of the web service is specified.

 A *constructor* is the method in a class that is invoked when the class is first instantiated. The constructor is used to initialize the class and put it into a valid state. If a class does not have a constructor, the CLR will create one by default.

- All the classes created in the web service class, including Stock and StockHistory, have equivalents in the proxy class.

- Though the original web service class file has the public method GetHistory, the proxy class has that method plus several additional, related, public methods:

BeginGetHistory and EndGetHistory, GetHistoryAsync (two overloaded forms), and OnGetHistoryOperationCompleted. In fact, every web method in the original web service class has the same method in the proxy class, plus these others, one for Begin..., one for End..., one or more for ...Async, and one for On...Completed. These additional methods are used to implement *asynchronous* processing.

Normal method calls are *synchronous*. In other words, the calling application halts all further processing until the called method returns. If this takes a long time, either because of a slow or intermittent Internet connection (not that that ever happens, of course) or because the method is inherently time-consuming (such as a lengthy database query), then the application will appear to hang and wait.

On the other hand, if the method call is made asynchronously, then the Begin method call is sent out, and processing can continue. When the results come back, the corresponding End method call receives the results. Asynchronous method calls will be demonstrated later in this chapter.

Compiling the Proxy Class

The output of the WSDL utility is a class source code file for the proxy. This source code then must be compiled into a class which can be instantiated in your code. There are two ways to do this: you can let the .NET Framework do it for you, or you can do it manually from the command line. You will see how both ways work in this section.

Automatic compilation in the App_Code folder

To let the .NET Framework compile the class for you, create a folder under the application root called *App_Code*. This is a special folder name in ASP.NET. Any source code in that folder will automatically be compiled and made available to the application at design time and at runtime.

To see this in action, create an *App_Code* folder under the *StockTickerConsumer* directory and copy the previously created *StockTicker.cs* proxy source file to that folder. Now you can instantiate a new StockTicker object in your code.

However, as you saw in the proxy class source code excerpted in Example 16-6, the StockTicker class has been renamed in the proxy class to StockTickerSoap. So, to instantiate a StockTicker object in the consuming application, add the following line of code inside the Page class:

```
StockTickerSoap proxy = new StockTickerSoap( );
```

Now you can call any of the public methods from the `StockTickerSoap` (previously called `StockTicker`) class, as in the following highlighted line of code:

```
protected void txtFirmNameStockSymbol_TextChanged(object sender,
                                                   EventArgs e)
{
    lblFirmName.Text = proxy.GetName(txtFirmNameStockSymbol.Text);
}
```

Manual compilation

You can take full manual control over the compilation process by compiling the proxy class with the appropriate command-line compiler (do not put in line breaks):

```
csc /out:bin\StockTickerProxy.dll /t:library
    /r:system.dll,system.web.dll,system.web.services.dll
    StockTicker.cs
```

Be certain no extraneous spaces are in the comma-separated list of DLLs.

 The C# compiler does not require explicit references to all the assemblies used in the proxy class, such as System.Data.dll., since a configuration file is located in the .NET Framework program directory, called *csc.rsp*, which contains the list of default references for the C# compiler.

The result of this command will be a compiled assembly called *StockTickerProxy.dll* in a folder called *bin* immediately under the application root. Any assembly files located in this folder will automatically be made available to the application at design time and at runtime.

With the compiled assembly in the *bin* folder, you can instantiate and use the proxy class the same way as if the proxy source was placed in the *App_Code* folder, described above.

Putting the compiled output in the *bin* folder is not required. It can go anywhere you want. However, if it is in the *bin* folder, then there is no need to create a reference to the assembly in the application. Adding such a reference will be described in the next section.

Creating and compiling the proxy file manually requires several steps, all performed at a command prompt. Further, several of those steps involve a fair amount of typing of parameters, with lots of places to make mistakes. Finally, when all is done, you probably need to move or copy the resulting *.dll* file to a different directory.

This entire process can be automated somewhat by creating a *batch file,* which are text files that contain one or more command-line operations. The batch file, which has an extension of *.bat*, can be executed from the command line, and all the operations within the file are executed one after the other as though they were manually entered at the command line.

Back in the days of DOS, batch files were used extensively. It is possible to make them fairly sophisticated, with replaceable parameters, conditional processing, and other programmatic niceties. For our purposes, a simple batch file will do.

Example 16-7 shows the contents of a batch file that changes to the correct current directory, runs the WSDL utility, compiles the resulting source code, and copies the resulting DLL from one *bin* directory to another.

Example 16-7. StockTickerProxy.bat

```
e:
cd \websites\StockTickerConsumer

rem   Generate the proxy class source file
wsdl http://localhost/StockTicker/service.asmx?wsdl

rem  Compile the proxy class source file
csc /out:bin\StockTickerProxy.dll /t:library
    /r:system.dll,system.web.dll,system.web.services.dll
    StockTicker.cs

rem  Copy the dll
copy bin\StockTickerProxy.dll
     c:\inetpub\wwwroot\WebServiceConsumer\bin
```

The first line in the batch file makes drive E the current drive. The next line changes the current directory. Blank lines are ignored. Lines beginning with rem are comments and are also ignored, though the contents are displayed on the screen as the file is processed. After the WSDL utility is run and the resulting file is compiled, it is copied. This last command is equivalent to the following:

```
copy e:\websites\StockTickerConsumer\bin\StockTickerProxy.dll
     c:\inetpub\wwwroot\WebServiceConsumer\bin
```

Be careful of inadvertent line breaks. A line break in a batch file is the equivalent of hitting the Enter key on the keyboard.

Finishing the Consumer App

There are three ways to make the proxy class available to the consuming application:

- Place the source code for the proxy class in the *App_Code* folder.
- Place the compiled assembly in the *bin* folder.
- Place the compiled assembly in an arbitrary location and add a reference to that assembly.

The first two techniques have been covered. To implement the third technique, adding a reference to an arbitrary assembly, click on the Website → Add Reference… menu item or right-click on the project file in the Solution Explorer and select Add Reference…. You will get the Add Reference dialog box. The assemblies listed on the .NET tab are those which have been installed to the Global Assembly Cache, or GAC. (Assemblies and the GAC will be covered in Chapter 19.) Click on the Browse tab to get the dialog box shown in Figure 16-5, where you can browse for the *.dll* file to reference.

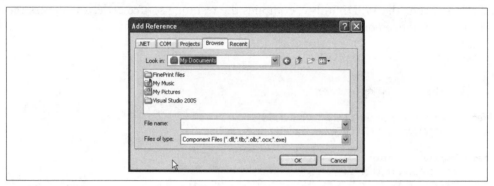

Figure 16-5. Add Reference dialog box

With the proxy class either compiled in the *bin* folder, the source in the *App_Code* folder, or a reference added, you can code the code-behind file to complete the *StockTickerConsumer* web page. The complete source code for the code-behind file is listed in Example 16-8 to go along with the content file listed previously in Example 16-4. All the references to the proxy are highlighted.

Example 16-8. default.aspx.cs for StockTickerConsumer

```
using System;
using System.Data;
using System.Configuration;
using System.Web;
using System.Web.Security;
using System.Web.UI;
using System.Web.UI.WebControls;
using System.Web.UI.WebControls.WebParts;
using System.Web.UI.HtmlControls;

public partial class _Default : System.Web.UI.Page
{
   StockTickerSoap proxy = new StockTickerSoap( );

   protected void Page_Load(object sender, EventArgs e)
   {

   }

   protected void txtFirmNameStockSymbol_TextChanged(object sender,
                                            EventArgs e)
   {
      lblFirmName.Text = proxy.GetName(txtFirmNameStockSymbol.Text);
   }
```

Example 16-8. default.aspx.cs for StockTickerConsumer (continued)

```
protected void txtPriceStockSymbol_TextChanged(object sender,
                                               EventArgs e)
{
    lblStockPrice.Text = "$ " +
        Convert.ToString(proxy.GetPrice(txtPriceStockSymbol.Text));
}

protected void btnStockExchangeSet_Click(object sender, EventArgs e)
{
    proxy.SetStockExchange(txtStockExchange.Text);
}

protected void btnStockExchangeGet_Click(object sender, EventArgs e)
{
    txtStockExchange.Text = proxy.GetStockExchange( );
}

protected void btnGetHistory_Click(object sender, EventArgs e)
{
    Stock theStock = proxy.GetHistory(txtHistoryStockSymbol.Text);
    string StockName = theStock.StockName;
    double StockPrice = theStock.Price;

    DateTime TradeDate1 = theStock.History[0].TradeDate;
    double Price1 = theStock.History[0].Price;

    DateTime TradeDate2 = theStock.History[1].TradeDate;
    double Price2 = theStock.History[1].Price;

    // Display the results.
    pnlHistory.Visible = true;
    lblHistoryStockName.Text = StockName;
    lblHistoryStockPrice.Text = "$ " + Convert.ToString(StockPrice);
    lblHistoryDate1.Text = TradeDate1.ToString("d");
    lblHistoryPrice1.Text = "$ " + Convert.ToString(Price1);
    lblHistoryDate2.Text = TradeDate2.ToString("d");
    lblHistoryPrice2.Text = "$ " + Convert.ToString(Price2);
}
}
```

The first line of code inside the class instantiates the web service class that was recently compiled (or placed in the *App_Code* directory). By instantiating the proxy here, the proxy variable can be used in any of the code that consumes the web service.

If you try to code against the proxy before you have provided the proxy class to VS2005, either as a web reference, a reference, compiled in the *bin* folder, or the source code in the *App_Code* folder, then any references to the proxy will be underlined by the editor as syntax errors.

To retrieve the Stock member variables, you must first instantiate the Stock class. Looking back at Example 15-15 in the previous chapter, you will recall that the

GetHistory web method returns an object of type Stock. The Stock object is instantiated here in the event handler with the following line of code:

```
Stock theStock = proxy.GetHistory(txtHistoryStockSymbol.Text);
```

Once the class is instantiated, it is a simple matter to assign its member variables to local variables in the event handler using dot notation:

```
string StockName = theStock.StockName;
```

Accessing the array variables contained in the StockHistory class contained within the Stock class is similar:

```
DateTime TradeDate1 = theStock.History[0].TradeDate;
```

Recall that array indices are zero-based.

 To repeat a point made in the previous chapter, when the web service example was first created, a real-world application would not store this type of history data in an array, nor would it display the history data in fixed variables as shown here. More likely, you would have the data in a collection or a dataset and display the data in some sort of data-bound control, as described in Chapter 9.

To display the history, several labels contained within an ASP.NET Panel control are used. The panel is used to control the labels' visibility. When the page is originally designed, the panel has its Visibility property set to false. When it is time to display the results in the Button event handler, the panel then has its Visibility property set to true, which makes all the labels contained within the panel visible.

The important point to understand here is that calls to the web service are made instead to the proxy as though the web service were a local DLL or component. When your code makes a method call to the proxy DLL, it has no idea that the call is being satisfied over the Internet by a web service. The proxy hides all the complex *stuff* required to package the method call up as a SOAP message, send it out over the wire using the proper protocol (typically HTTP), receive the SOAP message response, and return that back to your calling program as though the Internet was never involved.

When the *StockTickerConsumer* web page is run and some values inserted into the text boxes, you will see something like that shown in Figure 16-6.

Using Asynchronous Method Calls

As mentioned previously in this chapter, in the section on "Proxy Class Details," web services allow the developer to call any of the exposed web methods either synchronously or asynchronously.

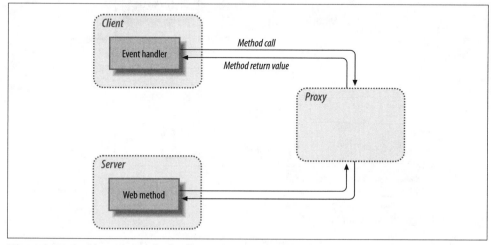

Figure 16-6. StockTickerConsumer in action

When a method is called synchronously, which is the "normal" way of doing method calls, the program execution waits for the method to return. As long as the method does not take too long to process and there is not too much network delay, this pause will not be a problem.

Figure 16-7 shows synchronous processing. Methods are called on the server via the proxy. The calling program is unaware a proxy is intervening in the process. A call goes out and when the results come back, the calling program continues processing.

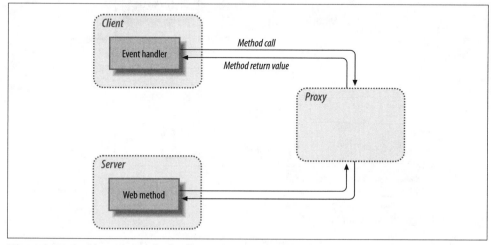

Figure 16-7. Synchronous method calls

However, in situations where the method is time-consuming to process (for example, a lengthy database operation or extensive computation) or where the network delay is significant, then this delay can be an unacceptable performance hit. In the case of web services, where all the method calls entail a round trip over the Internet, long network delays are common. Broadband Internet connections can help, but performance will still suffer.

One solution is to use asynchronous processing. In this model, a web service method is called, with instructions to notify the client when the result is ready. The client can go about its business, not waiting for the method to return. When the asynchronous method completes, a callback method is called. The client then retrieves the data from the server. Asynchronous processing is shown schematically in Figure 16-8.

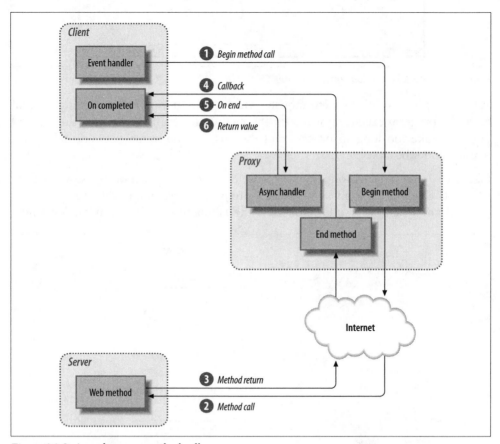

Figure 16-8. Asynchronous method calls

As with the synchronous method call, the client is unaware the proxy is intercepting the method call and passing it along to the server. The client event handler calls the Begin... method on the web service (actually on the proxy) passing in a delegate for the callback method (step 1 in Figure 16-8). The client then goes on to do other work.

The proxy calls the web method on behalf of the client (step 2). When the server has completed the method, it returns the result to the proxy (step 3). The proxy calls the client's callback method and passes in an object implementing IAsyncResult (step 4).

The client passes that IAsyncResult back to the proxy's End... method (step 5). The End... method then returns the data to the client (step 6).

The client does not have to poll the server; it is notified by the callback when the method completes.

The callback method is a *delegate,* which is a reference type that encapsulates a method with a specific signature and return type. The async Begin... and End... methods define a delegate for the callback mechanism you implement in your client.

To illustrate the use of delegates and asynchronous proxy calls, create a new web site named *StockTickerConsumerAsync* in VS2005. The page layout should look like Figure 16-9. It is nearly identical to the layout used in the *StockTickerConsumer* example, shown in Figure 16-4 and listed in Example 16-4, including the panel used to control the visibility of the labels it contains.

Figure 16-9. Asynchronous web page layout

The only difference between this example and the previous one is that there are now no field or buttons for Stock Exchange, the Get History button from Figure 16-4 is labeled Get Data, and the button ID is now btnGetData. In addition, the AutoPostBack property of the txtFirmNameStockSymbol and txtPriceStockSymbol text boxes should be set to false.

This web page will accept stock symbols in each of the text fields. When the Get Data button is clicked, all the processing for each field will be done asynchronously. If this were a real-world application where each field would typically be hitting a different web service on different servers, this asynchronous processing would prevent one slow connection from holding up the works. All three web service calls will essentially be occurring simultaneously.

Before entering the asynchronous code, you will make the page work synchronously to see how it works. To the end user, the synchronous and asynchronous implementations will look identical, except the latter should be somewhat faster (though that will not be noticeable in this example, where all of the web method calls are going to localhost).

Add the single event handler to the Get Data button by double-clicking on the button in Design view. This will bring you to the btnGetData_Click event handler in the code-behind page. Enter the code in Example 16-9 to the event handler.

Example 16-9. Synchronous event handler for btnGetData

```
lblFirmName.Text = proxy.GetName(txtFirmNameStockSymbol.Text);
lblStockPrice.Text = "$ " +
    Convert.ToString(proxy.GetPrice(txtPriceStockSymbol.Text));

Stock theStock = proxy.GetHistory(txtHistoryStockSymbol.Text);
string StockName = theStock.StockName;
double StockPrice = theStock.Price;

DateTime TradeDate1 = theStock.History[0].TradeDate;
double Price1 = theStock.History[0].Price;

DateTime TradeDate2 = theStock.History[1].TradeDate;
double Price2 = theStock.History[1].Price;

// Display the results.
pnlHistory.Visible = true;
lblHistoryStockName.Text = StockName;
lblHistoryStockPrice.Text = "$ " + Convert.ToString(StockPrice);
lblHistoryDate1.Text =TradeDate1.ToString("d");
lblHistoryPrice1.Text = "$ " + Convert.ToString(Price1);
lblHistoryDate2.Text = TradeDate2.ToString("d");
lblHistoryPrice2.Text = "$ " + Convert.ToString(Price2);
```

This code is identical to that in Example 16-8, except it is condensed into a single event handler rather than spread over three different event handlers.

Run the web application, fill in the stock symbols, and press the Get Data button; the resulting web page will look something like Figure 16-10.

Before adding the code to convert this web page from synchronous processing to asynchronous processing, examine the proxy class source code shown in Example 16-6. That segment of the source code shows the proxy method calls available for the GetHistory method. There are five (one of which has two overloaded forms), but we are particularly interested in three of them:

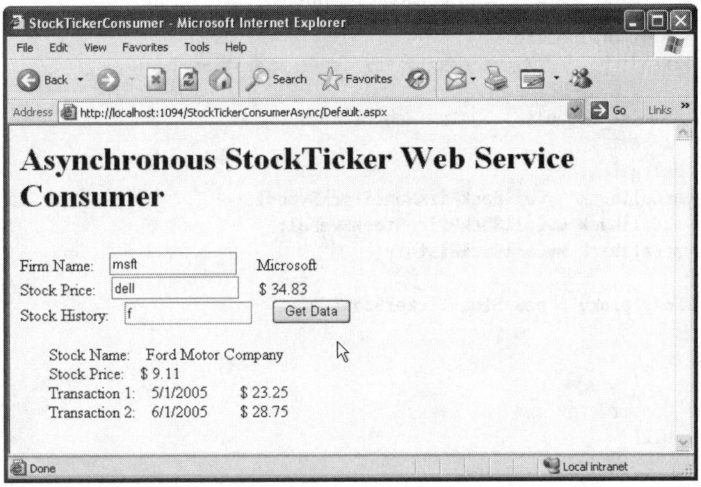

Figure 16-10. Synchronous test result

GetHistory

This is the synchronous method. It takes a single parameter, the StockSymbol string.

BeginGetHistory

This method starts the asynchronous processing. It takes three parameters: the StockSymbol string, the delegate callback method of type AsyncCallback, and an object called asyncState.

EndGetHistory

This method takes a single parameter, asyncResult, which is of type IAsyncResult.

Each of the methods exposed in the web service has equivalent Begin... and End... methods to enable asynchronous processing.

The code in Example 16-10 shows the complete code listing for the code-behind page demonstrating asynchronous event handling for a web service consumer. The lines of code relevant to converting the event handling from synchronous to asynchronous are highlighted.

Example 16-10. default.aspx.cs forStockTickerConsumerAsync

```
using System;
using System.Data;
using System.Configuration;
using System.Web;
using System.Web.Security;
using System.Web.UI;
using System.Web.UI.WebControls;
using System.Web.UI.WebControls.WebParts;
```

Example 16-10. default.aspx.cs forStockTickerConsumerAsync (continued)

```
using System.Web.UI.HtmlControls;
using System.Threading;      // necessary for async operation

public partial class _Default : System.Web.UI.Page
{
   // Create delegates.
   private AsyncCallback myCallBackFirmNameStockSymbol;
   private AsyncCallback myCallBackPriceStockSymbol;
   private AsyncCallback myCallBackHistory;

   StockTickerSoap proxy = new StockTickerSoap( );

   int flags;

   // default constructor for the class
   public _Default( )
   {
      // assign the call back
      myCallBackFirmNameStockSymbol = new
                  AsyncCallback(this.onCompletedGetName);
      myCallBackPriceStockSymbol = new
                  AsyncCallback(this.onCompletedGetPrice);
      myCallBackHistory = new
                  AsyncCallback(this.onCompletedGetHistory);
   }


   protected void Page_Load(object sender, EventArgs e)
   {
   }

   protected void txtFirmNameStockSymbol_TextChanged(object sender,
                                                      EventArgs e)
   {
      lblFirmName.Text = proxy.GetName(txtFirmNameStockSymbol.Text);
   }

   protected void txtPriceStockSymbol_TextChanged(object sender,
                                                   EventArgs e)
   {
      lblStockPrice.Text = "$ " +
         Convert.ToString(proxy.GetPrice(txtPriceStockSymbol.Text));
   }

   protected void btnGetData_Click(object sender, EventArgs e)
   {
      flags = 0;
      // lblFirmName.Text = proxy.GetName(txtFirmNameStockSymbol.Text);
      proxy.BeginGetName(txtFirmNameStockSymbol.Text,
                         myCallBackFirmNameStockSymbol,
                         0);
```

Example 16-10. default.aspx.cs forStockTickerConsumerAsync (continued)

```
    // lblStockPrice.Text = "$ " +
    Convert.ToString(proxy.GetPrice(txtPriceStockSymbol.Text));
    proxy.BeginGetPrice(txtPriceStockSymbol.Text,
                        myCallBackPriceStockSymbol,
                        0);

    // Stock theStock = proxy.GetHistory(txtHistoryStockSymbol.Text);
    proxy.BeginGetHistory(txtHistoryStockSymbol.Text,
                          myCallBackHistory,
                          0);

    while (flags < 3)
    {
        Thread.Sleep(100);
    }
}

private void onCompletedGetName(IAsyncResult asyncResult)
{
    string s = proxy.EndGetName(asyncResult);
    lblFirmName.Text = s;
    flags++;
}

private void onCompletedGetPrice(IAsyncResult asyncResult)
{
    lblStockPrice.Text = "$ " +
                Convert.ToString(proxy.EndGetPrice(asyncResult));
    flags++;
}

private void onCompletedGetHistory(IAsyncResult asyncResult)
{
    Stock theStock = proxy.EndGetHistory(asyncResult);
    string StockName = theStock.StockName;
    double StockPrice = theStock.Price;

    DateTime TradeDate1 = theStock.History[0].TradeDate;
    double Price1 = theStock.History[0].Price;

    DateTime TradeDate2 = theStock.History[1].TradeDate;
    double Price2 = theStock.History[1].Price;

    // Display the results.
    pnlHistory.Visible = true;
    lblHistoryStockName.Text = StockName;
    lblHistoryStockPrice.Text = "$ " + Convert.ToString(StockPrice);
    lblHistoryDate1.Text =TradeDate1.ToString("d");
    lblHistoryPrice1.Text = "$ " + Convert.ToString(Price1);
    lblHistoryDate2.Text = TradeDate2.ToString("d");
```

Example 16-10. default.aspx.cs forStockTickerConsumerAsync (continued)

```
    lblHistoryPrice2.Text = "$ " + Convert.ToString(Price2);
    flags++;
  }
}
```

The first step is to declare the delegates with the following lines of code inside the
_Default class:

```
private AsyncCallback myCallBackFirmNameStockSymbol;
private AsyncCallback myCallBackPriceStockSymbol;
private AsyncCallback myCallBackHistory;
```

These lines declare the delegates as private members of the class. The delegates are of
type AsyncCallback. This is the same type as the second parameter required by the
Begin... methods.

An AsyncCallback delegate is declared in the System namespace as follows:

```
public delegate void AsyncCallback (IAsyncResult ar);
```

Thus, this delegate can be associated with any method that returns void and takes
the IAsyncResult interface as a parameter.

You will create three methods in your client to act as callback methods:
onCompletedGetName, onCompletedGetPrice, and onCompletedGetHistory. You encapsulate these methods within their delegates in the constructor as follows:

```
myCallBackFirmNameStockSymbol = new
                AsyncCallback(this.onCompletedGetName);
myCallBackPriceStockSymbol = new AsyncCallback(this.onCompletedGetPrice);
myCallBackHistory = new AsyncCallback(this.onCompletedGetHistory);
```

You will see how to implement the three callback methods shortly.

The next step is to call all the Begin... methods to start the asynchronous processing. Replace each of the lines of code in btnGetData_Click that calls one of the proxy
methods with its equivalent Begin... method. (For now, comment out the original
lines of code and keep them for reference.) The first parameter for each Begin...
method is the same as the parameter for the original synchronous method. The second parameter is the delegate created previously. The third parameter is an object for
maintaining state, if necessary. For this example, use zero. The btnGetData_Click
event procedure should appear as follows:

```
private void btnGetData_Click(object sender, System.EventArgs e)
{
    flags = 0;
    // lblFirmName.Text = proxy.GetName(txtFirmNameStockSymbol.Text);
    proxy.BeginGetName(txtFirmNameStockSymbol.Text,
                    myCallBackFirmNameStockSymbol,
                    0);
    // lblStockPrice.Text = "$ " +
        Convert.ToString(proxy.GetPrice(txtPriceStockSymbol.Text));
```

```
proxy.BeginGetPrice(txtPriceStockSymbol.Text,
                    myCallBackPriceStockSymbol,
                    0);
// Stock theStock = proxy.GetHistory(txtHistoryStockSymbol.Text);
proxy.BeginGetHistory(txtHistoryStockSymbol.Text,
                      myCallBackHistory,
                      0);
while (flags < 3)
{
    Thread.Sleep(100);
}
}
```

The flags variable and the while loop will be explained shortly.

Create the three callback methods, and move the code from the synchronous btnGetData_Click to the appropriate method. Call the new methods onCompletedGet-Name, onCompletedGetPrice, and onCompletedGetHistory. The contents of these methods is shown in Example 16-9.

In each of the callback methods, the End... method associated with the appropriate web method in the proxy is called to construct the label Text properties to be set for display in the web page. In onCompletedGetName, a string is set to the return value from the proxy.EndGetName method. This string is then assigned to the label Text property. onCompletedGetPrice uses a similar technique, using a single line of code to replace the two lines in onCompletedGetName. onCompletedGetHistory is similar, except that it instantiates a Stock object with the return value from proxy.EndGetHistory. As you will recall from Example 16-5, a Stock object contains a stock symbol, stock name, price, and an array of StockHistory objects.

The last thing to explain is the flags variable, which is a counter. This variable is declared as a member variable:

```
int flags;
```

Each one of the callback methods increments the flags counter:

```
flags++;
```

Within the button click event handler, btnGetData_Click, the flags counter is reset to zero. Then every callback method increments the counter. The while loop prevents the button click event from completing until all three callback method methods have completed:

```
while (flags < 3)
{
    Thread.Sleep(100);
}
```

When the web page is run, the three Begin... methods are called. As each returns results, the onCompleted... methods call the appropriate End method and increment the counter.

When the counter reaches 3, the web page redraws. The end result looks indistinguishable from that shown in Figure 16-10.

Asynchronous consumption of web services can be very useful under the correct circumstances but may not scale well because each asynchronous method call spawns a new thread. So, *StockTickerConsumerAsync* would spawn three additional threads in addition to the main thread. This would be fine for a low-volume web site, but the performance penalty could overwhelm a large, busy web site.

CHAPTER 17

Caching and Performance

There are several ways to achieve higher performance and better scalability in ASP.NET. One way is through the use of caching. *Caching* is a technique whereby frequently requested data is stored in an accessible location, so the next time the same information is requested, it can be fetched quickly rather than regenerated by the application.

This can result in a significant performance boost, especially for dynamically generated content (such as ASP.NET web pages and components) and in cases where the data underlying the response is expensive to gather (such as database queries).

Most web browsers cache pages they receive, so if the same page is requested again, it does not have to be sent over the Internet, but rather is retrieved directly from the local hard drive. Most operating systems also employ caching of some sort to store frequently requested data in memory, rather than require additional hard drive reads. The only caching this chapter will be concerned with is server-side caching performed by the .NET Framework.

In some respects, caching is similar to the storage of state objects. (See Chapter 6 for a complete discussion of state in ASP.NET.) In both cases, data is saved for use across multiple requests, and, in the case of application state, across multiple sessions. However, don't be misled by this apparent similarity. With state objects, the developer explicitly saves a particular piece of data in a particular place, intending to retrieve that piece of data at a later time in the session or in other sessions. The data stored in state objects will last as long as the session or application and will not be lost until the developer specifies it is to be removed or replaced. In short, the developer can count on the data in a state object being available.

In contrast, cached data is non-deterministic. You cannot assume that any piece of data you are looking for will be in the cache. As will be shown later in this chapter, whenever your program attempts to retrieve data from the cache, it must test to see if the data is there and make provisions to retrieve the data elsewhere if it is not in the cache. The data may be missing because its lifetime expired, because the application freed memory for other purposes, or because the cache was never populated.

Types of Caching

There are several different types of caching in ASP.NET. Some are automatic and require no intervention on the part of the developer, while others require explicit coding.

In all types of caching, data or objects are placed in the *cache,* an area of memory managed by the server. Subsequent requests for that information are retrieved from the cache rather than the underlying source. If the cached item has *expired,* either because the underlying data has changed, the time limit has run out, or some dependency has changed, then the cache will be invalidated and the next request will retrieve fresh content from the underlying source rather than the cache. Your code can then refresh the cache. There are many ways to add items to the cache and expire items already in the cache, depending on the type of cache. The types of cache are covered in the next few sections, and the many ways of populating and expiring the cache will be covered in subsequent sections.

Class Caching

A web page or web service (*.aspx* or *.asmx* file, respectively) is compiled into a page class in an assembly the first time the page or service is run. This causes some delay, but that compiled assembly is then cached on the server and is called directly every subsequent time the page (or service) is referenced. This is done automatically; there is no user or developer interaction required for this to happen.

The CLR watches for source code changes. If the source code changes, the CLR will know to recompile the assembly the next time the page or service is called.

Configuration Caching

Application-wide configuration information is contained in the configuration files. Chapter 18 discusses the specifics of configuration in detail. For now, the relevant point is that when the application is started (the first time a page or service is called from the application virtual root directory), all the configuration information must be loaded. This can take some time, especially if the configuration files are extensive. Configuration caching, which occurs automatically, allows the application to store the configuration information in memory, thus saving time when the information is subsequently needed.

Data Caching

Caching data from a database is one of the most effective ways to improve performance and scalability of a web application, since database hits are a relatively expensive operation, especially when compared with retrieving the data from server

---

memory. The `DataSource` controls, new to ASP.NET Version 2.0 and covered in detail in Chapter 9, are specifically designed to enable easy and effective caching of data. Data caching will be covered in the next section of this chapter.

Output Caching

Output caching is the caching of pages or portions of pages that are sent to the client. This is one of the most significant performance-enhancing techniques available to the web-site developer. Since the page does not have to be recreated from scratch each time a request for it is made, the web site throughput, for example, measured in requests fulfilled per second, can be significantly increased.

Output caching is discussed later in this chapter.

Object Caching

Object caching is the caching of objects on the page, such as data bound controls. Object caching stores the cached data in server memory. Object caching will be covered in detail later in the chapter.

Data Caching

Data caching is (surprise!) the caching of data from a data source. As long as the cache is not expired, a request for data will be fulfilled from the cache rather than the original data source. If the cache is expired, for whatever reason, then fresh data will be obtained by the data source and the cache will be refreshed. There are many reasons the cache can expire, as you will see. These can include time outs, changed data, or changes to other objects.

There are two kinds of data caching: `DataSourceControl` caching and SQL cache dependency. Both are very useful.

DataSourceControl Caching

Data source controls, covered in Chapter 9, represent data in a data source, such as a database or an XML file. The abstract `DataSourceControl` class has two controls derived from it: `ObjectDataSource` and `SqlDataSource`, from which `AccessDataSource` is derived. Each of these derived classes (though not the base class) has a number of properties for implementing caching, listed in Table 17-1.

Table 17-1. Data source control properties for caching

Property	Type	Get	Set	Description
CacheDuration	Integer	✗	✗	Length of time, in seconds, that data is cached before the cache is invalidated. The default value is `Infinite`.
CacheExpirationPolicy	DataSourceCacheExpiry	✗	✗	Default is `Absolute`. Other possible value is `Sliding`, in which case the countdown to cache expiration is reset every time the cache is accessed.
CacheKeyDependency	string	✗	✗	Creates a dependency between cache entries and a key. When the key expires, so does the cache.
EnableCaching	Boolean	✗	✗	If `true`, caching will be enabled for the control. The default is `false`.

To show this in action, copy the web site called *WebNorthwind*, created back in Chapter 9 where data controls are first covered, to a new web site called *WebNorthwindCache*.

To simplify the demonstration, remove the UpdateCommand, DeleteCommand, and InsertCommand attributes from the SqlDataSource declaration, the associated Delete, Update, and Insert parameters, the bound columns from Region on, and the command field at the beginning of the Columns collection in the GridView declaration. Also, since you will not be updating data in this example, you can remove the OnRowUpdated attribute from the GridView declaration and the GridView1_RowUpdated method from the code-behind file, as well. Finally, to simplify the example more, remove the OnRowDataBound attribute from the GridView control in the content file and the associated event handler from the code-behind file.

To differentiate between when the page has been rendered from the server and when it has been retrieved from cache, add a Label control to the page and some code to the Page_Load in the code-behind file to populate the label with the current time.

The complete content file, with the Label control and associated caption highlighted, is listed in Example 17-1.

Example 17-1. Default.aspx for WebNorthwindCache

```
<%@ Page Language="C#" AutoEventWireup="true"
   CodeFile="Customers.aspx.cs" Inherits="Customers_aspx" %>

<!DOCTYPE html PUBLIC "-//W3C//DTD XHTML 1.1//EN"
   "http://www.w3.org/TR/xhtml11/DTD/xhtml11.dtd">
```

Example 17-1. Default.aspx for WebNorthwindCache (continued)

```
<html xmlns="http://www.w3.org/1999/xhtml" >
<head runat="server">
    <title>Data Caching</title>
</head>
<body>
    <form id="form1" runat="server">
    <div>
      <h1>Data Caching</h1>
      Page Posted: <asp:Label ID="lblPostTime" runat="server" />
      <br />
      <br />
      <asp:SqlDataSource ID="SqlDataSource1" runat="server"
        ConnectionString=
          "<%$ ConnectionStrings:NorthwindConnectionString %>"
        SelectCommand="SELECT * FROM [Customers]" >
      </asp:SqlDataSource>
      <asp:GridView ID="GridView1" runat="server"
        AutoGenerateColumns="False"
        DataKeyNames="CustomerID"
        DataSourceID="SqlDataSource1"
        AllowSorting="True"
        CellPadding="4"
        AllowPaging="True"
        ForeColor="#333333"
        GridLines="None">
        <Columns>
            <asp:BoundField DataField="CustomerID"
                HeaderText="CustomerID" ReadOnly="True"
                SortExpression="CustomerID" />
            <asp:BoundField DataField="CompanyName"
                HeaderText="CompanyName" SortExpression="CompanyName" />
            <asp:BoundField DataField="ContactName"
                HeaderText="ContactName" SortExpression="ContactName" />
            <asp:BoundField DataField="ContactTitle"
                HeaderText="ContactTitle"
                SortExpression="ContactTitle" />
            <asp:BoundField DataField="Address" HeaderText="Address"
                SortExpression="Address" />
            <asp:BoundField DataField="City" HeaderText="City"
                SortExpression="City" />
        </Columns>
        <FooterStyle BackColor="#5D7B9D" ForeColor="White"
                Font-Bold="True" />
        <RowStyle BackColor="#F7F6F3" ForeColor="#333333" />
        <PagerStyle ForeColor="White" HorizontalAlign="Center"
                BackColor="#284775" />
        <SelectedRowStyle BackColor="#E2DED6" Font-Bold="True"
                ForeColor="#333333" />
```

Example 17-1. Default.aspx for WebNorthwindCache (continued)

```
        <HeaderStyle BackColor="#5D7B9D" Font-Bold="True"
                ForeColor="White" />
        <EditRowStyle Font-Bold="False" Font-Italic="False"
                BackColor="#999999" />
        <AlternatingRowStyle BackColor="White" ForeColor="#284775" />
    </asp:GridView>
  </div>
  </form>
</body>
</html>
```

The complete code-behind file is listed in Example 17-2, with the highlighted line of code added to the Page_Load method.

Example 17-2. default.aspx.cs for WebNorthwindCache

```
using System;
using System.Data;
using System.Configuration;
using System.Web;
using System.Web.Security;
using System.Web.UI;
using System.Web.UI.WebControls;
using System.Web.UI.WebControls.WebParts;
using System.Web.UI.HtmlControls;

public partial class Customers_aspx : System.Web.UI.Page
{
    protected void Page_Load(object sender, EventArgs e)
    {
        lblPostTime.Text = DateTime.Now.ToLongTimeString( );
    }
}
```

When you run this web site, you will get something like that shown in Figure 17-1.

At this point, this web site has no caching enabled. You can see this by refreshing the browser window and seeing the displayed timestamp update. You can change the data in the underlying database (use SQL Server Enterprise Manager, Query Analyzer, or the Server Explorer in VS2005) and see the new values appear as soon as you refresh the page.

Now implement data caching in the SqlDataSource by adding the EnableCaching and CacheDuration attributes to the declaration from Example 17-1, as shown highlighted in Example 17-3.

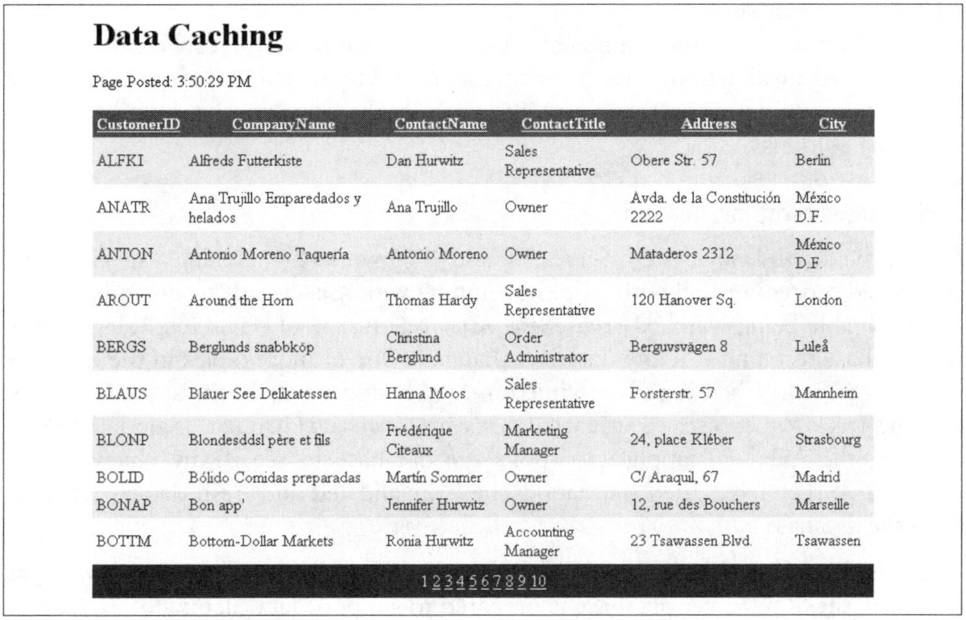

Data Caching

Page Posted: 3:50:29 PM

CustomerID	CompanyName	ContactName	ContactTitle	Address	City
ALFKI	Alfreds Futterkiste	Dan Hurwitz	Sales Representative	Obere Str. 57	Berlin
ANATR	Ana Trujillo Emparedados y helados	Ana Trujillo	Owner	Avda. de la Constitución 2222	México D.F.
ANTON	Antonio Moreno Taquería	Antonio Moreno	Owner	Mataderos 2312	México D.F.
AROUT	Around the Horn	Thomas Hardy	Sales Representative	120 Hanover Sq.	London
BERGS	Berglunds snabbköp	Christina Berglund	Order Administrator	Berguvsvägen 8	Luleå
BLAUS	Blauer See Delikatessen	Hanna Moos	Sales Representative	Forsterstr. 57	Mannheim
BLONP	Blondesddsl père et fils	Frédérique Citeaux	Marketing Manager	24, place Kléber	Strasbourg
BOLID	Bólido Comidas preparadas	Martín Sommer	Owner	C/ Araquil, 67	Madrid
BONAP	Bon app'	Jennifer Hurwitz	Owner	12, rue des Bouchers	Marseille
BOTTM	Bottom-Dollar Markets	Ronia Hurwitz	Accounting Manager	23 Tsawassen Blvd.	Tsawassen

1 2 3 4 5 6 7 8 9 10

Figure 17-1. WebNorthwindCache

Example 17-3. SqlDataSource with caching implemented

```
<asp:SqlDataSource ID="SqlDataSource1" runat="server"
  ConnectionString="<%$ ConnectionStrings:NorthwindConnectionString %>"
  SelectCommand="SELECT * FROM [Customers]"
  EnableCaching=true
  CacheDuration=60>
</asp:SqlDataSource>
```

Setting EnableCaching to true implements caching, and setting the CacheDuration to 60 means the cache will expire every minute. You can verify this by changing some data in the Customers table and refreshing the web page in the browser. Though the timestamp displayed on the page will update every time, the data will not refresh until the 60 seconds have passed.

The CacheDuration is subject to the value of the CacheExpirationPolicy property, which is covered in detail in the section below on Time Dependency under Object Caching. In short, the default value for CacheExpirationPolicy is Absolute, which causes the cache to expire at the end of the CacheDuration setting whether or not data access has occurred during that time.

SQL Cache Dependency

SQL cache dependency is the caching of data from a SQL Server database, specifically, SQL Server 7.0 or later, and expiring the cache whenever data in the database changes. It is not supported for other databases, including Access and Oracle (surprise!). There are two different mechanisms used to support SQL cache dependency. Polling-based invalidation is used for SQL Server 7.0 and 2000. Notification-based invalidation is used for SQL Server 2005. Both mechanisms will be described in the following sections.

Polling-based cache invalidation

SQL cache dependency in SQL Server 7.0 and 2000 works by inserting a special table, five stored procedures (all with names beginning with AspNet_SqlCache), and a trigger for each table being watched (***tableName*_AspNet_SqlCacheNotification_Trigger**) into the database to monitor if any data has changed. One or more tables in the database can be watched. When data is modified in a table under watch, the special table for keeping track, called AspNet_SqlCacheTablesForChangeNotification, is updated. Periodically, the ASP.NET application polls the database to see if any changes have occurred. If they have, then the data cache is invalidated and fresh data is retrieved from the database.

The actual implementation of SQL cache dependency is a three-part process. In the first part, the SQL Server database is prepared to support data caching or *SQL cache dependency*. In the second step, the cache is set up in the *web.config* file for the application. (Configuration is covered in Chapter 18.) Both of those steps will be covered in this section. Finally, the data cache is actually used, typically in the context of an output cache. Output caching will be covered in the next section.

Preparing the database. To prepare SQL Server to support SQL cache dependency, you must first run the SQL Server administrative command line tool, *aspnet_regsql*.

 To open a command line with the environment properly set to execute all the command line tools directly, go to Start → Programs → Microsoft Visual Studio 2005 → Visual Studio Tools → Visual Studio Command Prompt.

You can see all the options available to this tool by running the following command:

```
aspnet_regsql -?
```

There is a wizard mode to this utility, entered by running the command from the command line without any options, but the wizard mode does not handle setting up the database for SQL cache dependency, so you must do it all from the command line. This is easy if you either have a working connection string to the database or are using Windows integrated security on the database.

The command-line switches relevant to SQL cache dependency are listed in Table 17-2. Note that this utility serves many functions, including configuration of SQL Server Express, session state options, and other ASP.NET application services.

Table 17-2. aspnet_regsql command line switches relevant to SQL cache dependency

Switch	Description
-?	Display help.
-S *servername*	SQL Server instance to work with.
-U *loginID*	Username to authenticate with. Requires -P option.
-P *password*	Password to authenticate with. Requires -U option.
-E	Authenticate with current Windows credentials.
-C *connection string*	Connection string to use instead of username, password, and server name.
-d *database*	Database name for SQL Server 7.0 & 2000. The database can optionally be specified as part of the connection string.
-ed	Enable a database for SQL cache dependency.
-dd	Disable a database for SQL cache dependency.
-et	Enable a table for SQL cache dependency. Requires -t option.
-dt	Disables a table for SQL cache dependency. Requires -t option.
-t *tablename*	Name of the table to enable or disable.
-lt	List all tables enabled for SQL cache dependency.

First, you must prepare the database by creating the table `AspNet_SqlCacheTablesFor-ChangeNotification` for keeping track of changes and by creating the stored procedures. If you are using Windows integrated security, enter the following command:

```
aspnet_regsql -E -d Northwind -ed
```

The first argument, `-E`, says to use Windows authentication. `-d` specifies the database, and `-ed` says enable data caching.

If you are using a connection string, you do not specify the database since that is in the connection string, as in the following example:

```
aspnet_regsql -C "Data Source=MyServer;Initial Catalog=Northwind;Persist Security
Info=True;User ID=sa;Password=secret" -ed
```

Alternatively, you could use the `-S`, `-U`, and `-P` options to provide the credentials individually.

Adding a table for SQL cache dependency depends on your security method. If you are using Windows integrated security, use the following line:

```
aspnet_regsql -E -d Northwind -t Customers -et
```

or, with a connection string:

```
aspnet_regsql -C "Data Source=MyServer;Initial Catalog=Northwind;Persist Security
Info=True;User ID=sa;Password=secret" -t Customers -et
```

This adds a trigger called `Customers_AspNet_SqlCacheNotification_Trigger` to the Customers table, which calls the stored procedure `AspNet_SqlCacheUpdateChangeId-StoredProcedure` every time there is a change to the data in the Customers table.

To list all the tables enabled, use the following command:

```
aspnet_regsql -C "Data Source=MyServer;Initial Catalog=Northwind;Persist Security
Info=True;User ID=sa;Password=secret" -lt
```

An alternative to using the above command to list all the tables being monitored is to query the table AspNet_SqlCacheTablesForChangeNotification directly.

The database is now ready to support SQL cache dependency.

All of the above functionality can also be accomplished in code, using the SqlCacheDependencyAdmin class. This class has five methods for setting up and administering a SQL Server database for SQL cache dependency:

- DisableNotifications

- DisableTableForNotifications

- EnableNotifications

- EnableTableForNotifications

- GetTablesEnabledForNotifications

Usage of these SqlCacheDependencyAdmin classes is beyond the scope of this book.

Edit web.config. The second step in implementing SQL cache dependency is to edit the *web.config* file of the application. Continue working with the web site called *WebNorthwindCache* copied from *WebNorthwind* in the section "DataSourceControl Caching."

Open *web.config* in VS2005. It should have a <connectionStrings> section under <configuration> shown in the partial *web.config* listed in Example 17-4. Add the highlighted <caching> section under <system.web> from Example 17-4.

Example 17-4. Partial web.config for WebNorthwindCache

```
<configuration
    xmlns="http://schemas.microsoft.com/.NetConfiguration/v2.0">
    <appSettings/>
    <connectionStrings>
        <add name="NorthwindConnectionString"
            connectionString="Data Source=myServer;
                Initial Catalog=Northwind;Persist Security Info=True;
                User ID=sa;Password=secret"
            providerName="System.Data.SqlClient"/>
    </connectionStrings>
    <system.web>
        <caching>
            <sqlCacheDependency enabled="true"  >
                <databases>
                    <add name="Northwind"
                    connectionStringName="NorthwindConnectionString"
                    pollTime="1000" />
                </databases>
```

Example 17-4. Partial web.config for WebNorthwindCache (continued)

```
      </sqlCacheDependency>
    </caching>
.
.
.
  </system.web>
```

The `<sqlCacheDependency>` element has two possible attributes. `enabled` can be `true` or `false`. `pollTime` is the number of milliseconds between polls that SQL Server does to determine if the data has changed. If the latter is omitted from this element, the value in the `<add>` sections for individual databases will apply.

Within the `<sqlCacheDependency>` element are one or more `<databases>` sections. This contains `<add>`, `<clear>`, or `<remove>` sections. To add a database, as in Example 17-4, you provide the `name`, `connectionString`, and `pollTime` properties as attributes. To remove a database, you need only provide the `name` attribute. `<clear>` takes no attributes.

With the SQL cache dependency configured in *web.config*, you are ready to cache the data and have the cache expire when the data changes.

Notification-based cache invalidation

SQL cache dependency in SQL Server 2005 works by using the query change notification mechanism built into the database. It requires much less setup than polling-based cache invalidation used in earlier versions of SQL Server. There is no need to configure the database with *aspnet_regsql.exe*, and there is no need to add any `<sqlCacheDependency>` element to *web.config*.

To enable notification-based cache invalidation for a page, add a `SqlDependency` attribute to the `OutputCache` directive, described below, with a value of `CommandNotification`:

```
<%@ OutputCache Duration="999999" SqlDependency="CommandNotification"
    VaryByParam="none" %>
```

To enable notification-based cache invalidation for a `DataSource` control, add a `SqlCacheDependency` attribute to the control declaration, again with a value of `CommandNotification`:

```
<asp:SqlDataSource ID="SqlDataSource1" runat="server"
.
.
.
  SqlCacheDependency="CommandNotification"
  EnableCaching="true"
  CacheDuration="Infinite">
</asp:SqlDataSource>
```

In either case, ASP.NET and ADO.NET will work together to create a cache dependency that detects change notifications sent from SQL Server and invalidates the cache when the data is changed.

Output Caching

Output caching is the caching of pages or portions of pages that are output to the client. This does not happen automatically. The developer must enable output caching using either the OutputCache directive or the HttpCachePolicy class. Both methods will be described.

Output caching can be applied to an entire page or a portion of the page. To cache only a portion of a page, the caching is applied to a user control contained within the page. This will be described later in this section.

The OutputCache Directive

The OutputCache directive, like all page directives, goes at the top of the page file. (For a complete description of page directives, see Chapter 6.) A typical example of an OutputCache directive looks something like the following:

```
<%@ OutputCache Duration="60" VaryByParam="*" %>
```

The full syntax is:

```
<%@ OutputCache
    Duration="number of seconds"
    VaryByParam="parameter list"
    CacheProfile=""
    DiskCacheable=""
    Locaton="Any | Client | Downstream | Server | None"
    NoStore=""
    SqlDependency="database:table"
    VaryByControl="control list"
    VaryByCustom="custom output"
    VaryByHeader="header list" %>
```

Only the first two parameters, Duration and VaryByParam, are required, though the VaryByParam attribute will not be required for user controls if there is a VaryByControl attribute.

The VaryBy... parameters allow different versions of the cached page to be stored with each version satisfying the combination of conditions being varied.

The various parameters are described in the following sections.

Duration

The Duration parameter specifies the number of seconds that the page or user control is cached. Items placed in the output cache are only valid for this specified time period. When the time limit is reached, then the cache is said to be *expired*. The next request for the cached page or user control after the cache is expired causes the page or user control to be regenerated, and the cache is refilled with the fresh copy.

An example will clarify this. Create a new web site called *OutputCaching*, which contains only a Label control on the content page and a Page_Load that populates that Label control with the current time similar to the way you displayed the current time in the previous example. Add the OutputCache directive highlighted near the top of the content file in Example 17-5. The complete content file is listed in Example 17-5 and the complete code-behind file is listed in Example 17-6.

Example 17-5. Default.aspx for OutputCaching

```
<%@ Page Language="C#" AutoEventWireup="true"  CodeFile="Default.aspx.cs"
   Inherits="_Default" %>
<%@ OutputCache Duration="10" VaryByParam="*" %>

<!DOCTYPE html PUBLIC "-//W3C//DTD XHTML 1.1//EN"
"http://www.w3.org/TR/xhtml11/DTD/xhtml11.dtd">

<html xmlns="http://www.w3.org/1999/xhtml" >
<head runat="server">
    <<%@ Page Language="C#" AutoEventWireup="true"
CodeFile="Default.aspx.cs" Inherits="_Default" %>
<%@ OutputCache Duration="10" VaryByParam="*" %>

<!DOCTYPE html PUBLIC "-//W3C//DTD XHTML 1.1//EN"
"http://www.w3.org/TR/xhtml11/DTD/xhtml11.dtd">

<html xmlns="http://www.w3.org/1999/xhtml" >
<head runat="server">
    <title>Output Caching</title>
</head>
<body>
    <form id="form1" runat="server">
    <div>
      <h1>Output Caching</h1>
        <asp:Label ID="lblTime" runat="server" />
    </div>
    </form>
</body>
</html>
```

Example 17-6. Default.aspx.cs for OutputCaching

```
using System;
using System.Data;
using System.Configuration;
using System.Web;
using System.Web.Security;
using System.Web.UI;
using System.Web.UI.WebControls;
```

Example 17-6. Default.aspx.cs for OutputCaching (continued)

```
using System.Web.UI.WebControls.WebParts;
using System.Web.UI.HtmlControls;

public partial class _Default : System.Web.UI.Page
{
    protected void Page_Load(object sender, EventArgs e)
    {
        lblTime.Text = "This page was loaded at " +
            DateTime.Now.ToLongTimeString( );
    }
}
```

This OutputCache directive is all that is necessary to implement output caching. It specifies a Duration of 10 seconds. (The other parameter, VaryByParam, will be explained in the next section.) This means that if the same page is requested from the server within 10 seconds of the original request, the subsequent request will be served out of the cache rather than be regenerated by ASP.NET.

This is easy to verify. Run the page and note the time. Quickly refresh the page in the browser. If you refresh within 10 seconds of originally running the page, the displayed time will not have changed. You can refresh the page as many times as you wish, but the displayed time will not change until 10 seconds have passed.

VaryByParam

The VaryByParam parameter allows you to cache different versions of the page depending on which parameters are submitted to the server when the page is requested. These parameters are contained in a semicolon-separated list of strings.

In the case of a GET request, the strings in the parameter list represent query string values contained in the URL. In the case of a POST request, the strings represent variables sent as part of the form.

There are two special values for the VaryByParam parameter:

Value	Description
none	Don't vary by parameter, i.e., save only a single version of the page in the cache and return that version no matter what query string values or form variables are passed in as part of the request.
*	Save a separate version of the page in cache for each unique combination of query string values or form variables. The order of the query string values or form variables have no effect on the caching. However, the parameter values are case sensitive: state=ma differs from state=MA.

To see the effects of the VaryByParam parameter, modify the previous example, *OutputCaching*. Add two Labels for displaying parameters passed in as a query string as part of the URL in a GET request. Also, change the Duration parameter to 60 seconds to give you more time to explore the effects. The complete content file, with the changed code highlighted, is listed in Example 17-7.

Example 17-7. Default.aspx for OutputCaching demonstrating VaryByParam

```
<%@ Page Language="C#" AutoEventWireup="true"  CodeFile="Default.aspx.cs"
   Inherits="_Default" %>
<%@ OutputCache Duration="60" VaryByParam="*" %>

<!DOCTYPE html PUBLIC "-//W3C//DTD XHTML 1.1//EN" "http://www.w3.org/TR/xhtml11/DTD/
xhtml11.dtd">

<html xmlns="http://www.w3.org/1999/xhtml" >
<head runat="server">
    <title>Output Caching</title>
</head>
<body>
    <form id="form1" runat="server">
    <div>
      <h1>Output Caching</h1>
      <asp:Label ID="lblTime" runat="server" />
      <br/>
      <br/>
      UserName:   
      <asp:Label ID="lblUserName" runat="server" />
      <br/>
      State:   
      <asp:Label ID="lblState" runat="server" />
    </div>
    </form>
</body>
</html>
```

In the code-behind file, add two lines to the Page_Load method to populate the additional Labels. The complete code-behind file is listed in Example 17-8 with the additional lines highlighted.

Example 17-8. Default.aspx.cs for OutputCaching demonstrating VaryByParam

```
using System;
using System.Data;
using System.Configuration;
using System.Web;
using System.Web.Security;
using System.Web.UI;
using System.Web.UI.WebControls;
using System.Web.UI.WebControls.WebParts;
using System.Web.UI.HtmlControls;

public partial class _Default : System.Web.UI.Page
{
    protected void Page_Load(object sender, EventArgs e)
    {
        lblTime.Text = "This page was loaded at " +
          DateTime.Now.ToLongTimeString( );
```

```
        lblUserName.Text = Request.Params["username"];
        lblState.Text = Request.Params["state"];
    }
}
```

To test the version of *OutputCaching* listed in Examples 17-7 and 17-8, you will have to run the page from a browser outside of VS2005 so you can include query strings as part of the URL. Go to Computer Management and create a virtual directory pointing to the folder where this web site is located. Call the virtual directory *OutputCaching*, open a browser, and enter the following URL:

```
http://localhost/OutputCaching/default.aspx?username=Dan&state=MA
```

This will give the result shown in Figure 17-2.

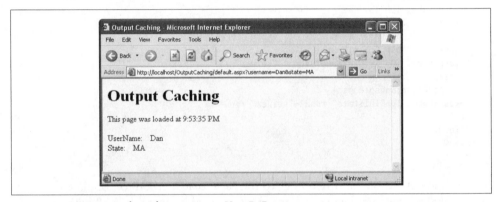

Figure 17-2. OutputCaching demonstrating VaryByParam

Now enter the same URL but with different parameters, say username=Jesse and state=NY, as in:

```
http://localhost/OutputCaching/default.aspx?username=Jesse&state=NY
```

This will give a different time in the resulting page. Now go back and enter the original URL with username=Dan and state=MA. You will see the original time shown in Figure 17-2, assuming 60 seconds have not passed since you first entered the URL.

Suppose the previous example was part of an application where the username was needed for login purposes and the state was used to query a database to return information about publicly-traded firms in that state. In that case, it would make no sense to cache based on the username, but it would make a lot of sense to cache based on the state parameter.

To accomplish this, set VaryByParam equal to the parameter(s) you wish to cache by. So, for example, to cache only by state, use the following OutputCache directive:

```
<%@ OutputCache Duration="60" VaryByParam="state" %>
```

If you need to cache by the unique combination of two parameters, say state and city, use a directive similar to this:

```
<%@ OutputCache Duration="60" VaryByParam="state;city" %>
```

CacheProfile

If you find yourself using the same OutputCache directives on many pages, you can use CacheProfiles to reuse the same attributes. To do this, add an <outputCacheProfiles> section to a configuration file. The <add> element specifies the name of the profile, as well as all the directive attributes, as in the following code snippet:

```
<outputCacheProfiles>
    <add name="StateCityCacheProfile"
        enabled="true"
        duration="60"
        varyByParam=" state;city " />
</outputCacheProfiles>
```

To make this CacheProfile available to all the pages on the server, add it either to *machine.config* or the globally scoped *web.config* file. To make it available only to a specific web site, add it to the *web.config* file in the application root. (Configuration files are covered in detail in Chapter 18.)

To use this profile, use the CacheProfile attribute of the OutputCache directive as in the following:

```
<%@ OutputCache CacheProfile="StateCityCacheProfile" %>
```

DiskCacheable

ASP.NET will remove items from cache if the amount of memory available falls below a certain threshold, in a practice known as *scavenging*. This is described later in this chapter. By default, ASP.NET (in a feature new to Version 2.0) also saves the output cache to disk. That way, the data can be retrieved from disk rather than regenerated from scratch even if memory is short. In addition, this enables cached data to survive an application restart.

To disable disk caching, set the DiskCacheable attribute to false, as in the following:

```
<%@ OutputCache Duration="60" VaryByParam="*" DiskCacheable="false" %>
```

Location

The Location parameter specifies the machine where the cached data is stored. The permissible values for this parameter are contained in the OutputCacheLocation enumeration (see Table 17-3).

Table 17-3. Location parameter values

Parameter value	Description
Client	The cache is located on the same machine as the client browser. Useful if the page requires authentication.
Downstream	The cache is located on a server downstream from the web server. This might be a proxy server.
Server	The cache is located on the web server processing the request.
None	Output caching is disabled.
Any	The output cache can be located either on the client, on a downstream server, or on the web server. This is the default value.

The Location parameter is not supported when output caching user controls.

SqlDependency

The SqlDependency attribute of the OutputCache directive allows you to expire the output cache when the underlying data changes. To implement this requires setting up the database and editing *web.config*, as described in the previous section, "SQL cache dependency."

To see how this works, copy the example used in that section, *WebNorthwindCache*, to a new web site, called *WebNorthwindSqlDependency*.

Remove the EnableCaching and CacheDuration attributes from the SqlDataSource declaration. Add the following OutputCache directive to the top of the content file:

```
<%@ OutputCache SqlDependency="Northwind:Customers"
    Duration="600" VaryByParam="none" %>
```

The value supplied to the SqlDependency attribute is a concatenation of the database name that was previously set up for SQL cache dependency, specified in the *web. config* file listed in Example 17-4, and the table that was also previously set up for SQL cache dependency, in this case the Customers table. The database name and table name are separated by a semicolon.

In this example, the OutputCache duration is set for 10 minutes and VaryByParam is disabled (none).

When you run the page, you can refresh the page all you want and the displayed timestamp will not be updated for 10 minutes. However, go into the database, change a value in the Customers table, and refresh the page, and the timestamp will be updated immediately.

You can see that the page will expire whenever the specified duration is exceeded or the data changes, whichever occurs first.

VaryByControl

The VaryByControl parameter is used when caching user controls, which will be described in the next section, "Fragment Caching: Caching Part of a Page." This parameter is not supported in OutputCache directives in web pages (*.aspx* files).

The values for this parameter consist of a semicolon-separated list of strings. Each string represents a fully qualified property name on a user control.

VaryByCustom

The VaryByCustom parameter allows the cache to be varied by browser if the value of the parameter is set to browser. In this case, the cache is varied by browser name and major version. In other words, there will be separate cached versions of the page for IE 4, IE 5, IE 6, Netscape 6, or any other browser type or version used to access the page.

VaryByHeader

The VaryByHeader parameter allows the cache to by varied by HTTP header. The value of the parameter consists of a semicolon-separated list of HTTP headers. This parameter is not supported in OutputCache directives in user controls.

Fragment Caching: Caching Part of a Page

All the examples shown so far have cached the entire page. Sometimes all you want to cache is part of the page. To do this, wrap that portion of the page you want to cache in a user control and cache the user control. This is known as *fragment caching*. (For a complete discussion of user controls, see Chapter 14.)

For example, suppose you develop a stock portfolio analysis page, where the top portion of the page displays the contents of the user's stock portfolio, and the bottom portion contains a data grid showing historical data about one specific stock. There would be little benefit in caching the top portion of the page since it will differ for every user. However, it is likely that in a heavily used web site, many people will be requesting historical information about the same stock, so there would be a benefit to caching the bottom portion of the page. This is especially true since generating the historical data requires a relatively expensive database query. In this case, you can wrap the data grid in a user control and cache just that.

To demonstrate fragment caching, create a new web site called *FragmentCaching*. Before adding any content to *default.aspx*, add a new Web User Control to the project and call it *SimpleUserControl.ascx*. The content file for *SimpleUserControl* is listed in Example 17-9 and the associated code-behind file is listed in Example 17-10.

Example 17-9. SimpleUserControl.ascx for FragmentCaching

```
<%@ Control Language="C#" AutoEventWireup="true"
     CodeFile="SimpleUserControl.ascx.cs"
     Inherits="SimpleUserControl_ascx" %>
<%@ OutputCache Duration="10" VaryByParam="*" %>

<hr />
<h3>User Control</h3>
<asp:Label ID="lblTime" runat="server" />
<hr />
```

Example 17-10. SimpleUserControl.ascx.cs for FragmentCaching

```
using System;
using System.Data;
using System.Configuration;
using System.Collections;
using System.Web;
using System.Web.Security;
using System.Web.UI;
using System.Web.UI.WebControls;
using System.Web.UI.WebControls.WebParts;
using System.Web.UI.HtmlControls;

public partial class SimpleUserControl_ascx : System.Web.UI.UserControl
{
    protected void Page_Load(object sender, EventArgs e)
    {
      lblTime.Text = "This user control was loaded at " +
         DateTime.Now.ToLongTimeString( );
    }
}
```

This user control does nothing more than display the time it was loaded. The visible portion of the control is surrounded by horizontal rules (<hr/>) to distinguish it when it is used in a web page. The OutputCache directive, highlighted in the content file in Example 17-9, specifies a Duration of 10 seconds.

Once the user control is ready, you can add some content to *Default.aspx*, including placing the user control. The complete listing of *Default.aspx* is shown in Example 17-11. The lines of code related to implementing the user control are highlighted.

Example 17-11. Default.aspx for FragmentCaching

```
<%@ Page Language="C#" AutoEventWireup="true"  CodeFile="Default.aspx.cs"
   Inherits="_Default" %>
<%@ Register TagPrefix="MyUserControl" TagName="LoadTime"
   Src="~/SimpleUserControl.ascx"%>

<!DOCTYPE html PUBLIC "-//W3C//DTD XHTML 1.1//EN"
"http://www.w3.org/TR/xhtml11/DTD/xhtml11.dtd">
```

Example 17-11. Default.aspx for FragmentCaching (continued)

```
<html xmlns="http://www.w3.org/1999/xhtml" >
<head runat="server">
    <title>Fragment Caching</title>
</head>
<body>
    <form id="form1" runat="server">
    <div>
      <h1>Fragment Caching</h1>
        <asp:Label ID="lblTime" runat="server" />
        <br />
        <MyUserControl:LoadTime runat="server" />
    </div>
    </form>
</body>
</html>
```

The associated code-behind file is listed in Example 17-12.

Example 17-12. Default.aspx.cs for FragmentCaching

```
using System;
using System.Data;
using System.Configuration;
using System.Web;
using System.Web.Security;
using System.Web.UI;
using System.Web.UI.WebControls;
using System.Web.UI.WebControls.WebParts;
using System.Web.UI.HtmlControls;

public partial class _Default : System.Web.UI.Page
{
    protected void Page_Load(object sender, EventArgs e)
    {
        lblTime.Text = "This page was loaded at " +
            DateTime.Now.ToLongTimeString( );
    }
}
```

Notice that the web page that uses the user control does not have any caching implemented; there is no OutputCache directive.

When you run the *FragmentCaching* example, you will initially see something like Figure 17-3.

The time displayed for both the user control and the containing page are identical. However, if you refresh the view, you will notice that the time the page was loaded will be the current time and the time the user control was loaded is static until the 10-second cache duration has expired.

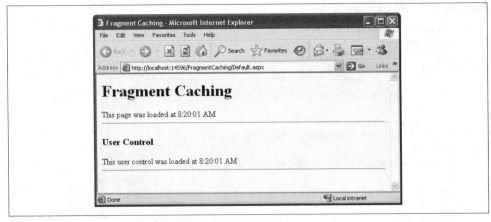

Figure 17-3. FragmentCaching initial screen

One caveat to keep in mind when caching user controls is that it is not possible to programmatically manipulate the user control being cached. This is because a user control in cache is only generated dynamically the first time it is requested. After that, the object is unavailable for the code to interact with. If you need to manipulate the contents of the user control programmatically, the code to do so must be contained within the user control.

To demonstrate this, copy the *FragmentCaching* web site to a new web site called *FragmentCachingWithProperty*. Add a Label control to the user control to display a user's name. For now, this label is hard-coded to Dan. Also add a public property, called Username, with a Get and a Set method to the code-behind file of the user control. The modified content and code-behind files are listed in Examples 17-13 and 17-14, respectively, with the code additions highlighted.

Example 17-13. SimpleUserControl.ascx for FragmentCachingWithProperty

```
<%@ Control Language="C#" AutoEventWireup="true"
   CodeFile="SimpleUserControl.ascx.cs"
   Inherits="SimpleUserControl_ascx" %>
<%@ OutputCache Duration="10" VaryByParam="*" %>

<hr />
<h3>User Control</h3>
<asp:Label ID="lblTime" runat="server" />
<br />
<asp:Label ID="lblUserName" runat="server" Text="Dan" />
<hr />
```

Example 17-14. SimpleUserControl.ascx.cs for FragmentCachingWithProperty

```
using System;
using System.Data;
using System.Configuration;
```

Example 17-14. SimpleUserControl.ascx.cs for FragmentCachingWithProperty (continued)

```
using System.Collections;
using System.Web;
using System.Web.Security;
using System.Web.UI;
using System.Web.UI.WebControls;
using System.Web.UI.WebControls.WebParts;
using System.Web.UI.HtmlControls;

public partial class SimpleUserControl_ascx : System.Web.UI.UserControl
{
    public string UserName
    {
        get
        {
            return lblUserName.Text;
        }
        set
        {
            lblUserName.Text = value;
        }
    }

    protected void Page_Load(object sender, EventArgs e)
    {
        lblTime.Text = "This user control was loaded at " +
            DateTime.Now.ToLongTimeString( );
    }
}
```

Now modify the default page, as shown in the highlighted code in Example 17-15 and its associated code-behind file in Example 17-16. In this content file, you will add an ID attribute to the user control, so you can refer to it elsewhere in the code, plus a Label to display the value of the user control property, UserName, and a button to change the value of the property. The code-behind file adds a line in the Page_Load method to populate that label, as well as a Click event handler for the button.

 This example demonstrates the error that occurs when attempting to manipulate a cached user control programmatically.

Example 17-15. Default.aspx for FragmentCachingWithProperty

```
<%@ Page Language="C#" AutoEventWireup="true" CodeFile="Default.aspx.cs"
    Inherits="_Default" %>
<%@ Register TagPrefix="MyUserControl" TagName="LoadTime"
    Src="~/SimpleUserControl.ascx"%>

<!DOCTYPE html PUBLIC "-//W3C//DTD XHTML 1.1//EN"
    "http://www.w3.org/TR/xhtml11/DTD/xhtml11.dtd">
```

Example 17-15. Default.aspx for FragmentCachingWithProperty (continued)

```
<html xmlns="http://www.w3.org/1999/xhtml" >
<head runat="server">
    <title>Fragment Caching</title>
</head>
<body>
    <form id="form1" runat="server">
    <div>
      <h1>Fragment Caching</h1>
        <asp:Label ID="lblTime" runat="server" />
        <br />
        <MyUserControl:LoadTime runat="server"
            ID="MyUserControl"/>
        <br />
        <asp:Label ID="lblUserControlText" runat="server" />
        <br />
        <asp:Button ID="btn" runat="server"
                    Text="Change Name to Jesse"
                    OnClick="btn_Click" />
    </div>
    </form>
</body>
</html>
```

Example 17-16. Default.aspx.cs for FragmentCachingWithProperty

```
using System;
using System.Data;
using System.Configuration;
using System.Web;
using System.Web.Security;
using System.Web.UI;
using System.Web.UI.WebControls;
using System.Web.UI.WebControls.WebParts;
using System.Web.UI.HtmlControls;

public partial class _Default : System.Web.UI.Page
{
    protected void Page_Load(object sender, EventArgs e)
    {
        lblTime.Text = "This page was loaded at " +
            DateTime.Now.ToLongTimeString( );
        lblUserControlText.Text = MyUserControl.UserName;
    }

    protected void btn_Click(object sender, EventArgs e)
    {
        MyUserControl.UserName = "Jesse";
    }
}
```

The *FragmentCachingWithProperty* example works fine when the page is first called, giving the result shown in Figure 17-4.

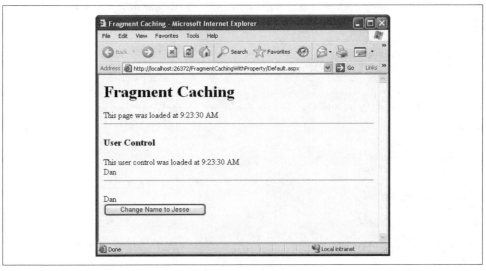

Figure 17-4. Results of FragmentCachingWithProperty

It will even work as expected if you click the button to change the name to Jesse. This is because the button causes the form to be posted to the server, so everything is regenerated and the request for the user control is not being satisfied from the cache. However, as soon as you refresh the page in the browser, either by clicking the browser Refresh icon or clicking the Change Name button a third time, and ASP.NET attempts to satisfy the request for the user control from the cache, a server error occurs.

The only way around this is to move all the code that accesses the user control property into the user control itself. To see this, copy the *FragmentCachingWithProperty* example to a new web site, called *FragmentCachingWithPropertyCorrect*.

The calling page reverts back to the exact same page originally shown in Examples 17-11 and 17-12.

The user control picks up the Button control and the Click event handler for the button. The content and code-behind files for the user control are shown in Examples 17-17 and 17-18, respectively, with the changed code highlighted.

Example 17-17. SimpleUserControl.ascx for FragmentCachingWithPropertyCorrect

```
<%@ Control Language="C#" AutoEventWireup="true"
   CodeFile="SimpleUserControl.ascx.cs"
   Inherits="SimpleUserControl_ascx" %>
<%@ OutputCache Duration="10" VaryByParam="*" %>

<hr />
<h3>User Control</h3>
<asp:Label ID="lblTime" runat="server" />
<br />
<asp:Label ID="lblUserName" runat="server" Text="Dan" />
```

```
<br />
<asp:Button ID="btn" runat="server"
    Text="Change Name to Jesse"
    OnClick="btn_Click" />
<hr />
```

Example 17-18. SimpleUserControl.ascx.cs for FragmentCachingWithPropertyCorrect

```
using System;
using System.Data;
using System.Configuration;
using System.Collections;
using System.Web;
using System.Web.Security;
using System.Web.UI;
using System.Web.UI.WebControls;
using System.Web.UI.WebControls.WebParts;
using System.Web.UI.HtmlControls;

public partial class SimpleUserControl_ascx : System.Web.UI.UserControl
{
    public string UserName
    {
        get
        {
            return lblUserName.Text;
        }
        set
        {
            lblUserName.Text = value;
        }
    }

    protected void Page_Load(object sender, EventArgs e)
    {
        lblTime.Text = "This user control was loaded at " +
            DateTime.Now.ToLongTimeString( );
    }

    protected void btn_Click(object sender, EventArgs e)
    {
        lblUserName.Text = "Jesse";
    }
}
```

Though this restriction on programmatically modifying user controls that are in the cache might seem significant, as a practical matter it should not be. The entire point of putting user controls in the cache is that they will not change while cached. If that is not the case, then they will probably not be a good candidate for caching.

Object Caching

All the examples in the previous section have cached pages, or parts of pages wrapped in user controls. But ASP.NET allows you much more caching flexibility. You can use *object caching* to place any object in the cache. The object can be of any type: a data type, a web control, a class, a DataSet, and so on.

The object cache is stored in server memory, a limited resource, and the careful developer will conserve that resource. That said, it is an easy way to buy significant performance benefits when used wisely, especially since ASP.NET will evict older items if memory becomes scarce.

Suppose you are developing a retail shopping catalogue web application. Many of the page requests contain queries against the same database to return a relatively static price list and description data. Instead of your control querying the database each time the data is requested, the data set is cached, so subsequent requests for the data will be satisfied from the high-speed cache rather than forcing a relatively slow and expensive regeneration of the data. You might want to set the cache to expire every minute, hourly, or daily, depending on the needs of the application and the frequency with which the data is likely to change.

Object caching is implemented by the Cache class. One instance of this class is created automatically per application when the application starts. The class remains valid for the life of the application. The Cache class uses syntax very similar to that of session and application state. Objects are stored in Cache as key/value pairs in a dictionary object. The object being stored is the value, and the key is a descriptive string.

The next example, ObjectCaching, will clarify object caching. A web page will display a GridView containing data from the Northwind database. It will initially query data from the Northwind database into a DataSet and then store the DataSet in cache for subsequent requests.

Create a new web site and call it *ObjectCaching*. Drag a Label, called lblMessage, a GridView, called gv, and two Buttons onto the form. The complete listing of the content file is shown in Example 17-19, with the controls highlighted.

Example 17-19. Default.aspx for ObjectCaching

```
<%@ Page Language="C#" AutoEventWireup="true"  CodeFile="Default.aspx.cs"
    Inherits="_Default" %>

<!DOCTYPE html PUBLIC "-//W3C//DTD XHTML 1.1//EN"
    "http://www.w3.org/TR/xhtml11/DTD/xhtml11.dtd">

<html xmlns="http://www.w3.org/1999/xhtml" >
<head runat="server">
    <title>Object Caching</title>
</head>
```

Example 17-19. Default.aspx for ObjectCaching (continued)

```
<body>
    <form id="form1" runat="server">
    <div>
      <h1>Object Caching</h1>
        <asp:Label ID="lblMessage" runat="server" />
        <br />
        <br />
        <asp:GridView ID="gv" runat="server" />
        <br />
        <asp:Button ID="btnClear" runat="server"
            Text="Clear Cache"
            OnClick="btnClear_Click" />
        <asp:Button ID="btnPost" runat="server" Text="Post" />
    </div>
    </form>
</body>
</html>
```

It would simplify matters greatly if you could just use a SqlDataSource control, set the EnableCache property of that control, and then set the DataSource property of the GridView to point to the SqlDataSource. However, there are certain circumstances in which you must "manually" create the data source and bind the source to the control. This is covered in detail in Chapter 10, but two of these circumstances are when you need to implement connection-based transactions or you are building an n-tier data architecture and your data is being retrieved from a business object. Example 17-19 demonstrates the principles involved in caching an arbitrary object.

Looking at the directive at the top of the content file, no OutputCache directive exists since this example does not use output caching.

The associated code-behind file is listed in Example 17-20, with an analysis to follow.

Example 17-20. Default.aspx.cs for ObjectCaching

```
using System;
using System.Data;
using System.Configuration;
using System.Web;
using System.Web.Security;
using System.Web.UI;
using System.Web.UI.WebControls;
using System.Web.UI.WebControls.WebParts;
using System.Web.UI.HtmlControls;
using System.Data.SqlClient;      // necessary for SqlDataAdapter

public partial class _Default : System.Web.UI.Page
{
    protected void Page_Load(object sender, EventArgs e)
    {
        CreateGridView();
    }
```

Example 17-20. Default.aspx.cs for ObjectCaching (continued)

```
    private void CreateGridView( )
    {
        DataSet dsGrid;
        dsGrid = (DataSet)Cache["GridViewDataSet"];
        if (dsGrid == null)
        {
            dsGrid = GetDataSet( );
            Cache["GridViewDataSet"] = dsGrid;
            lblMessage.Text = "Data from database.";
        }
        else
        {
            lblMessage.Text = "Data from cache.";
        }

        gv.DataSource = dsGrid.Tables[0];
        gv.DataBind( );
    }

    private DataSet GetDataSet( )
    {
        // connect to the Northwind database
        string connectionString = "Data Source=MyServer;
            Initial Catalog=Northwind;Persist Security Info=True;
            User ID=sa;Password=secret";

        // get records from the Customers table
        string commandString = "Select top 10 CustomerID, CompanyName,
                    ContactName, City from Customers";

        // create the data set command object and the DataSet
        SqlDataAdapter dataAdapter = new SqlDataAdapter(commandString,
                        connectionString);

        DataSet dsData = new DataSet( );

        // fill the data set object
        dataAdapter.Fill(dsData, "Customers");

        return dsData;
    }

  protected void btnClear_Click(object sender, EventArgs e)
  {
    Cache.Remove("GridViewDataSet");
    CreateGridView( );
  }
}
```

The heart of the *ObjectCaching* example involves data access. For a complete discussion of data access using ADO.NET in ASP.NET, see Chapter 10. For now, notice the using System.Data.SqlClient statement added at the top of the code-behind file to allow working with the `SqlDataAdapter` class without typing fully qualified namespaces.

A method named `CreateGridView` is called every time the grid needs to be created. It is called in the `Page_Load` every time the page is loaded, as well as when the Clear Cache button is clicked.

Looking at the `CreateGridView` method, a `DataSet` object is instantiated to contain the data that will be bound and displayed by the grid:

```
DataSet dsGrid;
```

The `Cache` object with the key `GridViewDataSet` is then retrieved and assigned to the `dsGrid` `DataSet` object:

```
dsGrid = (DataSet)Cache["DataGridDataSet"];
```

As with the `Session` and `Application` objects seen in Chapter 6, whatever is retrieved from the `Cache` object must be explicitly *cast*, or converted, to the correct data type, in this case `DataSet`. For this purpose, C# uses an explicit cast.

 You can use the Cache, Session, and View syntax even from within *global.asax* files. (See Chapter 18 for a complete discussion on the *global.asax* file.) However, in that case, you must qualify the keyword with the current context:

```
dsGrid = (DataSet)HttpContext.Current.Cache[
            "GridViewDataSet"];
```

The `dsGrid` data set is then tested to see if it actually exists. Though the `DataSet` object has been instantiated, it is only a placeholder until it actually contains data. If the `Cache` object with the key `GridViewDataSet` has not been created or has expired, then `dsGrid` still has no data in it.

```
if (dsGrid == null)
```

If the `DataSet` object already contains data, meaning the `Cache` had been previously filled and had not expired, the `Label` control's `Text` property will be set accordingly to convey this to you on the web page. Otherwise, the `GetDataSet` method is called, the cache is filled with the data set returned by `GetDataSet`, and the `Label` control's `Text` property is set accordingly:

```
dsGrid = GetDataSet();
Cache["GridViewDataSet"] = dsGrid;
lbl.Text = "Data from database.";
```

In either case, once the Data Set is filled, the `DataSource` property of the `GridView` control on the web page is set to be the first `DataTable` in the `DataSet` and the `GridView` control is data bound:

```
dg.DataSource=dsGrid.Tables[0];
dg.DataBind();
```

The result of running `ObjectCaching` is shown in Figure 17-5.

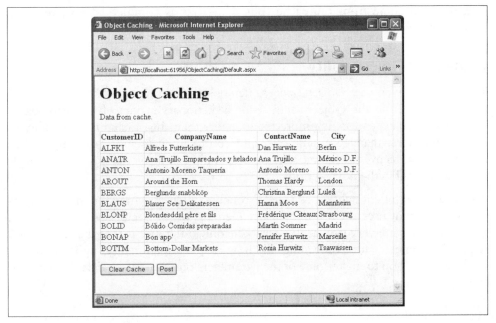

Figure 17-5. ObjectCaching

The first time the web page is run, the label just above the `GridView` control will indicate that the data is coming directly from the database. Every subsequent time the form is requested, the label will change to "Data from cache."

There is no way for the cache, in this example, to expire unless memory becomes scarce on the server and ASP.NET removes it automatically. As you will see shortly, there are several ways to force a cache to expire. In this example, however, even opening a new browser instance on a different machine will cause the data to come from the cache unless the application on the server is restarted. That is because the cache is available to the entire application just as the `Application` object is.

In this example, a button, called `btnClear`, is added to the form to empty the cache and refill it. The event handler for this button calls the `Cache.Remove` method. This method removes the cache record specified by the key named as the parameter to the method.

```
Cache.Remove("GridViewDataSet");
```

In Example 17-20, the button event handler refills the cache by calling the `CreateGridView` method. As an exercise in observing different behavior, comment out the line that calls `CreateGridView` in the `btnClear_OnClick` event procedure and observe the different behavior when you repost the page after clicking the Clear Cache button. When the line calling the `CreateGridView` method is *not* commented out, the next time a browser is opened after the Clear Cache button is clicked, the data will still come from the cache. But if the line *is* commented out, the next browser instance will get the data directly from the database.

Cache Class Functionality

The previous example, *ObjectCaching*, demonstrates how to add values to and retrieve values from the Object cache using a dictionary syntax of key/value pairs. The Cache class exposes much more functionality than this, including the ability to set dependencies, manage expirations, and control how memory used by cached objects can be recovered for more critical operations. All of these features will be covered in detail in the next sections.

This additional functionality is exposed through a different syntax for adding objects to the cache that uses the Add and Insert methods of the Cache class. The Add and Insert methods are very similar in effect. The only difference is that the Add method requires parameters for controlling all the exposed functionality, and the Insert method allows you to make some of the parameters optional, using default values for those parameters.

The syntax for the Add method is:

```
Cache.Add(
    KeyName,
    KeyValue,
    Dependencies,
    AbsoluteExpiration,
    SlidingExpiration,
    Priority,
    CacheItemRemovedCallback);
```

In this syntax, KeyName is a string with the name of the key in the Cache dictionary, and KeyValue is the object, of any type, to be inserted into the cache. All the other parameters will be described below.

The syntax examples for the overloaded Insert methods are:

- To insert a key/value pair with default values for all the other parameters:

  ```
  Cache.Insert(KeyName, KeyValue);
  ```

- To insert a key/value pair with dependencies and with default values for the other parameters:

  ```
  Cache.Insert(KeyName, KeyValue, Dependencies);
  ```

- To insert a key/value pair with dependencies and expiration policies and with default values for the other parameters:

  ```
  Cache.Insert(KeyName, KeyValue, Dependencies, AbsoluteExpiration,
      SlidingExpiration);
  ```

- To insert a key/value pair with dependencies, expiration policies, and priority policy, and a delegate to notify the application when the inserted item is removed from the cache:

```
Cache.Insert(KeyName, KeyValue, Dependencies, AbsoluteExpiration,
SlidingExpiration, Priority, CacheItemRemovedCallback);
```

To see this syntax in action, replace a single line from Example 17-20. Find the line in the CreateGridView method that looks like this:

```
Cache["GridViewDataSet "] = dsGrid;
```

Replace it with the following:

```
Cache.Insert("GridViewDataSet ", dsGrid);
```

On running the modified page in a browser, you will see no difference from the prior version.

By using the Insert method rather than the Add method, you are only required to provide the key and value, just as with the dictionary syntax.

Dependencies

One useful feature exposed by the Cache class is dependencies. A *dependency* is a relationship between a cached item and a point in time or an external object. If the designated point in time is reached or if the external object changes, the cached item will expire and be removed from the cache.

The external object controlling the dependency can be a file, a directory, an array of files or directories, another item stored in the cache (represented by its key), or an array of items stored in the cache. The designated point in time can be either an absolute time or a relative time. In the following sections, we'll examine each of these dependencies and how they can be used to control the contents of the cache programmatically.

 One of the more useful dependencies is data dependency, new to Version 2.0 of ASP.NET, where the cache is expired if the data in the underlying SQL Server database change. This feature is not part of object caching but is available to DataSourceControls and output caching. Data dependencies were covered earlier in this chapter.

File change dependency

With a file change dependency, a cached item will expire and be removed from the cache if a specified file changes. This feature is typically used when a cached data set is derived from an XML file. You do not want the application to get the data set from the cache if the underlying XML file has changed.

To generate an XML file containing the first five records from the `Customers` table of the Northwind database, an excerpt of which is listed in Example 17-21, perform the following steps:

1. Use Start → Programs → Microsoft SQL Server → Configure SQL XML Support in IIS.

2. Set a virtual directory called *Northwind*. Be sure to check the checkbox on the Settings tab which enables sql=URL queries.

3. Use the following URL in a browser:

   ```
   http://localhost/
   Northwind?sql=select+top+5*+from+Customers+for+xml+auto&root=ROOT
   ```

4. Copy the contents of the browser window into a text file called *Northwind.xml*.

5. Add the first line in the XML file, shown in Example 17-21, specifying the UTF-16 character set. This 16-bit character set allows the higher-order characters common to many non-English languages.

Example 17-21. Excerpt from Northwind.xml (with line breaks added for readability)

```
<?xml version="1.0" encoding="UTF-16" ?>
<ROOT>
  <Customers CustomerID="ALFKI" CompanyName="Alfreds Futterkiste"
    ContactName="Dan Hurwitz" ContactTitle="Sales Representative"
    Address="Obere Str. 57" City="Berlin" PostalCode="12209"
    Country="Germany" Phone="030-0074321" Fax="030-0076545" />
  .
  .
  .
</ROOT>
```

The next example, *ObjectCachingFileDependency*, will use this XML file as a data source. You can then edit the XML file to demonstrate a file change dependency. To create this next example, copy the previous example, *ObjectCaching*, to a new web site, called *ObjectCachingFileDependency*.

The content file, *default.aspx*, is unchanged (unless you want to add a descriptive heading). Copy the XML file you have created into the root directory of the application. (Though this is not strictly necessary, it simplifies the code.)

In the code-behind file, you will modify the `GetDataSet` method to populate the dataset from the XML file rather than from the Northwind database, and you will modify the `CreateGridView` method to implement a `Cache` object with a file change dependency. The complete code-behind file is listed in Example 17-22, with the modified code highlighted.

Example 17-22. Default.aspx.cs for ObjectCachingFileDependency

```
using System;
using System.Data;
```

```csharp
using System.Configuration;
using System.Web;
using System.Web.Security;
using System.Web.UI;
using System.Web.UI.WebControls;
using System.Web.UI.WebControls.WebParts;
using System.Web.UI.HtmlControls;
using System.Web.Caching;          // necessary for CacheDependency
using System.Xml;                  // necessary for Xml stuff

public partial class _Default : System.Web.UI.Page
{
    protected void Page_Load(object sender, EventArgs e)
    {
        CreateGridView( );
    }

    private void CreateGridView( )
    {
        DataSet dsGrid;
        dsGrid = (DataSet)Cache["GridViewDataSet"];
        if (dsGrid == null)
        {
            dsGrid = GetDataSet( );
            CacheDependency fileDepends =
                    new CacheDependency(Server.MapPath("Northwind.xml"));
            Cache.Insert("GridViewDataSet", dsGrid, fileDepends);
            lblMessage.Text = "Data from XML file.";
        }
        else
        {
            lblMessage.Text = "Data from cache.";
        }

        gv.DataSource = dsGrid.Tables[0];
        gv.DataBind( );
    }

    private DataSet GetDataSet( )
    {
        DataSet dsData = new DataSet( );
        XmlDataDocument doc = new XmlDataDocument( );
        doc.DataSet.ReadXml(Server.MapPath("Northwind.xml"));
        dsData = doc.DataSet;
        return dsData;
    }

    protected void btnClear_Click(object sender, EventArgs e)
    {
```

```
    Cache.Remove("GridViewDataSet");
    CreateGridView( );
  }
}
```

In the using statements at the beginning of the file, you can delete the reference to `System.Data.SqlClient` since the code is no longer using any members of that namespace. Instead, add the two highlighted using statements from Example 17-22: one for caching and one for XML.

The goal of the `GetDataSet` method is still to return a dataset. However, the source of the data for the dataset is now the XML file called *Northwind.xml*. Since ASP.NET stores datasets internally as XML, moving back and forth between XML and datasets is easy. The XML object equivalent to a dataset is the `XmlDataDocument`. An `XmlDataDocument` object named `doc` is instantiated. This `XmlDataDocument` object is filled using the `ReadXml` method. The `MapPath` method maps a virtual path of a file on the server to a physical path.

The `DataSet` object is obtained from the `DataSet` property of the `XmlDataDocument` object, then returned to the calling method.

In the `CreateGridView` method, only three lines have changed from the original *ObjectCaching* example. A `CacheDependency` object is defined against the source XML file. Again, `MapPath` is used to map the virtual path to a physical path.

The dictionary syntax used in the original *ObjectCaching* example to add the item to the cache is changed to use the `Insert` method of the `Cache` class. Using the `Insert` method allows you to specify a dependency in addition to the key name and value.

The text string assigned to the label has been updated to reflect that the data is now coming from an XML file rather than a database.

When you run this page, you will get something similar to Figure 17-6.

If you repost the page by highlighting the URL and pressing Enter, the label at the top of the page will indicate the data is coming from the cache.

Now open the *Northwind.xml* file in a text editor and make a change to one of the values in one of the records. Remember to save the XML file. When you repost the page in the browser, instead of the data still coming from the cache, it will once again be coming from the XML file.

As soon as the XML source file was changed, the cached data set was expired and removed from the cache. The next time the page requested the data set from the server, it had to retrieve it fresh from the XML file.

If you want the cache dependency to monitor an array of files or directories, the syntax for the `CacheDependency` constructor in Example 17-22 can take an array of file paths or directories rather than a single filename. So, for example, the single line of

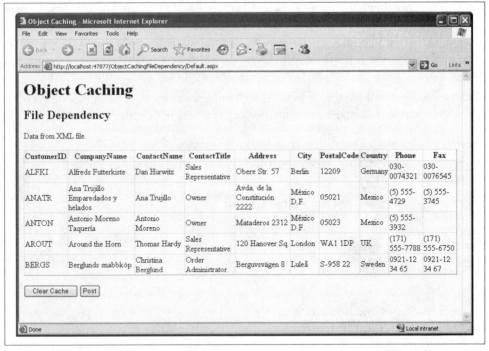

Figure 17-6. ObjectCachingFileDependency

code in Example 17-22 that defines the CacheDependency object would be preceded by code defining a string array with one or more files or paths, and the CacheDependency constructor itself would take the array as a parameter. It would look like this:

```
string[] fileDependsArray = {Server.MapPath("Customers.xml"),
                             Server.MapPath("Employees.xml")};
CacheDependency fileDepends = new CacheDependency(fileDependsArray);
```

Cached item dependency

A cached item can be dependent on other items in the cache. If a cached item is dependent on one or more other cached items, it will be expired and removed from the cache if any of those cached items upon which it depends change. These changes include either removal from the cache or a change in value.

To make a cached item dependent on other cached items, the keys of all of the controlling items are put into an array of strings. This array is passed in to the CacheDependency constructor, along with an array of file paths. (If you do not want to define a dependency on any files or paths, then the array of file paths can be null.)

This is demonstrated in the next example, *ObjectCachingItemDependency*. To create this example, copy the previous example, *ObjectCachingFileDependency*, to a new web site with the new example name.

In *ObjectCachingItemDependency*, two buttons are added to the UI. The first button initializes several other cached items. The second button changes the value of the cached text string in one of the controlling cached items. As with the previous examples, a label near the top of the page indicates if the data was retrieved directly from an XML file or from cache. The Clear Cache and Post buttons are unchanged.

The complete content file for *ObjectCachingItemDependency* is listed in Example 17-23, with the code that is changed from the previous example highlighted.

Example 17-23. Default.aspx for ObjectCachingItemDependency

```
<%@ Page Language="C#" AutoEventWireup="true"  CodeFile="Default.aspx.cs"
   Inherits="_Default" %>

<!DOCTYPE html PUBLIC "-//W3C//DTD XHTML 1.1//EN"
   "http://www.w3.org/TR/xhtml11/DTD/xhtml11.dtd">

<html xmlns="http://www.w3.org/1999/xhtml" >
<head runat="server">
    <title>Object Caching</title>
</head>
<body>
    <form id="form1" runat="server">
    <div>
      <h1>Object Caching</h1>
      <h2>Item Dependency</h2>
       <asp:Label ID="lblMessage" runat="server" />
       <br />
       <br />
       <asp:GridView ID="gv" runat="server" />
       <br />
       <asp:Button ID="btnClear" runat="server" Text="Clear Cache"
                   OnClick="btnClear_Click" />
       <asp:Button ID="btnPost" runat="server" Text="Post" />
       <br />
       <br />
       <asp:Button ID="btnInit" runat="server" Text="Initialize Keys"
                   OnClick="btnInit_Click" />
       <asp:Button ID="btnKey0" runat="server" Text="Change Key 0"
                   OnClick="btnKey0_Click" />
    </div>
    </form>
</body>
</html>
```

The code-behind file, listed in Example 17-24, modifies only the `CreateGridView` method from the previous example and adds `Click` event handlers for the two new buttons. The changes in Example 17-24 are highlighted.

Example 17-24. Default.aspx.cs for ObjectCachingItemDependency

```
using System;
using System.Data;
using System.Configuration;
using System.Web;
using System.Web.Security;
using System.Web.UI;
using System.Web.UI.WebControls;
using System.Web.UI.WebControls.WebParts;
using System.Web.UI.HtmlControls;
using System.Web.Caching;          // necessary for CacheDependency
using System.Xml;                  // necessary for Xml stuff

public partial class _Default : System.Web.UI.Page
{
    protected void Page_Load(object sender, EventArgs e)
    {
        CreateGridView( );
    }

    private void CreateGridView( )
    {
        DataSet dsGrid;
        dsGrid = (DataSet)Cache["GridViewDataSet"];
        if (dsGrid == null)
        {
            dsGrid = GetDataSet( );
            string[] fileDependsArray = {Server.MapPath("Northwind.xml")};
            string[] cacheDependsArray = {"Depend0", "Depend1", "Depend2"};
            CacheDependency cacheDepends = new CacheDependency
                             (fileDependsArray, cacheDependsArray);
            Cache.Insert("GridViewDataSet", dsGrid, cacheDepends);
            lblMessage.Text = "Data from XML file.";
        }
        else
        {
            lblMessage.Text = "Data from cache.";
        }

        gv.DataSource = dsGrid.Tables[0];
        gv.DataBind( );
    }

    private DataSet GetDataSet( )
    {
        DataSet dsData = new DataSet( );
        XmlDataDocument doc = new XmlDataDocument( );
        doc.DataSet.ReadXml(Server.MapPath("Northwind.xml"));
        dsData = doc.DataSet;
        return dsData;
    }
```

```
  protected void btnClear_Click(object sender, EventArgs e)
  {
    Cache.Remove("GridViewDataSet");
    CreateGridView( );
  }

  protected void btnInit_Click(object sender, EventArgs e)
  {
    //  Initialize caches to depend on.
    Cache["Depend0"] = "This is the first dependency.";
    Cache["Depend1"] = "This is the 2nd dependency.";
    Cache["Depend2"] = "This is the 3rd dependency.";
  }

  protected void btnKey0_Click(object sender, EventArgs e)
  {
    Cache["Depend0"] = "This is a changed first dependency.";
  }
}
```

In the `btnInit_Click` event handler, the controlling cache items are created. The values of the cached items are unimportant for this example, except as something to change when the `Change Key 0` button is clicked, which is done in the event handler for that button, `btnKey0_OnClick`.

The real action here occurs in the `CreateGridView` method. Two string arrays are defined, one to hold the file to depend upon, and one to hold the keys of the other cached items to depend upon.

The file dependency is exactly as described in the preceding section. If you do not wish to implement any file or directory dependency here, then use `null`:

```
  CacheDependency cacheDepends = new CacheDependency(null,
                                          cacheDependsArray);
```

Running the *ObjectCachingItemDependency* example brings up the page shown in Figure 17-7. Initially, the label above the data grid will show that the data is from the XML file. After you click the Initialize Keys button, clicking the Post button or re-entering the URL will cause the data to come from the cache. Clicking any of the other buttons or changing the contents of *Northwind.xml* will cause the cached data set to expire and the data to be retrieved fresh from the XML file the next time the page is posted. Though this example does not explicitly demonstrate what would happen if one of the controlling cached items was removed from the cache, that, too, would cause the dependent cached item to expire.

Time dependency

Items in the cache can be given a dependency based on time. This is done with two parameters in either the `Add` or `Insert` methods of the `Cache` object.

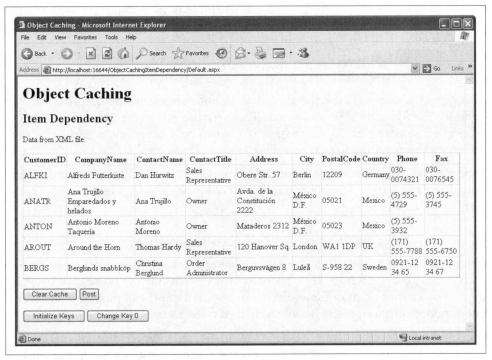

Figure 17-7. ObjectCachingItemDependency

The two parameters that control time dependency are `AbsoluteExpiration` and `SlidingExpiration`. Both parameters are required in the `Add` method and are optional in the `Insert` method through method overloading.

To insert a key/value pair into the cache with file or cached item dependencies and time-based dependencies, use the following syntax:

```
Cache.Insert(KeyName,
             KeyValue,
             Dependencies,
             AbsoluteExpiration,
             SlidingExpiration);
```

If you don't want any file or cached item dependencies, then the `Dependencies` parameter should be `null`. If this syntax is used, default values will be used for the scavenging and callback parameters (described in the next sections).

The `AbsoluteExpiration` parameter is of type `DateTime`. It defines a lifetime for the cached item. The time provided can be an absolute time, such as August 21, 2006, at 1:23:45 P.M. The code to implement that type of absolute expiration would look something like the following:

```
DateTime expDate = new DateTime(2006,8,21,13,23,45);
Cache.Insert("GridViewDataSet", dsGrid, null, expDate,
             Cache.NoSlidingExpiration);
```

Obviously, this is not very flexible. Of greater utility is an absolute expiration based on the current time, say 30 minutes from now. The syntax for that expiration would be the following:

```
Cache.Insert("GridViewDataSet ", dsGrid, null,
        DateTime.Now.AddMinutes(30), Cache.NoSlidingExpiration);
```

This line of code inserts the specified data set into the cache and then expires that item 30 minutes after it was inserted. This scenario would be useful when you're accessing a slowly changing database where it was only necessary to ensure the data presented was no more than 30 minutes old.

Suppose that the data was volatile or needed to be very current. Perhaps the data presented must never be more than 10 seconds old. The following line of code implements that scenario:

```
Cache.Insert("DataGridDataSet", dsGrid, null,
        DateTime.Now.AddSeconds(10), Cache.NoSlidingExpiration);
```

If your web page is receiving hundreds of hits per minute, implementing a 10-second cache would provide a huge performance boost by reducing the number of database queries by a factor of 20 or more. Even a one-second cache can provide a significant performance enhancement to heavily trafficked web servers.

The other time-based parameter is SlidingExpiration, of type TimeSpan. This parameter specifies a time interval between when an item is last accessed and when it expires. If the sliding expiration is set for 30 seconds, for example, then the cached item will expire if the cache is not accessed within 30 seconds. If it is accessed within that time period, the clock will be reset, so to speak, and the cached item will persist for at least another 30 seconds. If the cache were accessed every 29 seconds, for example, it would never expire. You might use this for data which does not change often but is not used often either. To implement this scenario, use the following line of code:

```
Cache.Insert("DataGridDataSet", dsGrid, null,
        Cache.NoAbsoluteExpiration, TimeSpan.FromSeconds(30));
```

Cache.NoAbsoluteExpiration is used for the AbsoluteExpiration parameter. Alternatively, you could use DateTime.MaxValue. This constant is the largest possible value of DateTime, corresponding to 11:59:59 P.M., 12/31/9999. (That's a millennium problem we can live with.) This indicates to ASP.NET that absolute expiration should not be used. If you attempt to use both types of expiration policies at once (absolute and sliding), an error will occur.

Scavenging

ASP.NET can scavenge memory by removing seldom-used or low-priority items from the cache if server memory falls below a given threshold. Doing so frees up memory to handle a higher volume of page requests.

Scavenging is influenced by the `Priority` parameter of the `Add` and `Insert` methods of the `Cache` class. This parameter is required of the `Add` method and optional for the `Insert` method

The `Priority` parameter indicates the value of the cached item relative to the other items stored in the cache. This parameter is used by the cache when it evicts objects to free up system memory when the web server runs low on memory. Cached items with a lower priority are evicted before items with a higher priority.

The legal values of the `Priority` parameter are contained in the `CacheItemPriority` enumeration, as shown in Table 17-4 in descending order of priority.

Table 17-4. Members of the CacheItemPriority enumeration

Priority value	Description
NotRemovable	Items with this priority will not be evicted.
High	Items with this priority level are the least likely to be evicted.
AboveNormal	Items with this priority level are less likely to be evicted than items assigned Normal priority.
Default	This is equivalent to Normal.
Normal	The default value.
BelowNormal	Items with this priority level are more likely to be evicted than items assigned Normal priority.
Low	Items with this priority level are the most likely to be evicted.

To implement scavenging, use the following line of code:

```
Cache.Insert("DataGridDataSet", dsGrid, null,
        Cache.NoAbsoluteExpiration,
        Cache.NoSlidingExpiration,
        CacheItemPriority.High,
        null);
```

The final parameter in the above lines of code pertains to callback support, which will be covered in the next section.

Since the `Insert` method calls use all seven parameters, you could use the `Add` method with the same parameters.

Callback Support

A `CacheItemRemovedCallback` event is raised when an item is removed from the cache for any reason. You may want to implement an event handler for this event, perhaps to reinsert the item into the cache or to log the event to evaluate whether your server needs more memory. The `Add` and `Insert` methods take a parameter that specifies the event handler (callback) method.

The next example demonstrates using the `CacheItemRemovedCallback` event. This example will behave identically to the previous example, shown in Figure 17-7, except that it will make an entry in a log file, hardcoded to be in *c:\test.txt*, every time the cache is expired.

Create a new web site called *ObjectCachingCallback* by copying the previous example, *ObjectCachingItemDependency*. The content file is functionally unchanged from the previous example. The code-behind file, listed in Example 17-25, has a number of changes, all of which are highlighted and then described in the analysis following the example.

Example 17-25. ObjectCachingCallback

```
using System;
using System.Data;
using System.Configuration;
using System.Web;
using System.Web.Security;
using System.Web.UI;
using System.Web.UI.WebControls;
using System.Web.UI.WebControls.WebParts;
using System.Web.UI.HtmlControls;
using System.Web.Caching;          //  necessary for CacheDependency
using System.Xml;                  //  necessary for Xml stuff

public partial class _Default : System.Web.UI.Page
{
   public static CacheItemRemovedCallback onRemove = null;

   protected void Page_Load(object sender, EventArgs e)
   {
      CreateGridView();
   }

   private void CreateGridView()
   {
      DataSet dsGrid;
      dsGrid = (DataSet)Cache["GridViewDataSet"];

      onRemove = new CacheItemRemovedCallback(this.RemovedCallback);

      if (dsGrid == null)
      {
         dsGrid = GetDataSet();
         string[] fileDependsArray = {Server.MapPath("Northwind.xml")};
         string[] cacheDependsArray = {"Depend0", "Depend1", "Depend2"};
         CacheDependency cacheDepends = new CacheDependency
                           (fileDependsArray, cacheDependsArray);
         Cache.Insert("GridViewDataSet", dsGrid, cacheDepends,
                     DateTime.Now.AddSeconds(10),
                     Cache.NoSlidingExpiration,
                     CacheItemPriority.Default,
                     onRemove);
         lblMessage.Text = "Data from XML file.";
      }
```

Example 17-25. ObjectCachingCallback (continued)

```
      else
      {
         lblMessage.Text = "Data from cache.";
      }

      gv.DataSource = dsGrid.Tables[0];
      gv.DataBind( );
   }

   private DataSet GetDataSet( )
   {
      DataSet dsData = new DataSet( );
      XmlDataDocument doc = new XmlDataDocument( );
      doc.DataSet.ReadXml(Server.MapPath("Northwind.xml"));
      dsData = doc.DataSet;
      return dsData;
   }

   public void RemovedCallback(string cacheKey,
                               Object cacheObject,
                               CacheItemRemovedReason reasonToRemove)
   {
      WriteFile("Cache removed for following reason: " +
         reasonToRemove.ToString( ));
   }

   private void WriteFile(string strText)
   {
      System.IO.StreamWriter writer = new System.IO.StreamWriter(
                                           @"C:\test.txt", true);
      string str;
      str = DateTime.Now.ToString( ) + "   " + strText;
      writer.WriteLine(str);
      writer.Close( );
   }

   protected void btnClear_Click(object sender, EventArgs e)
   {
      Cache.Remove("GridViewDataSet");
      CreateGridView( );
   }

   protected void btnInit_Click(object sender, EventArgs e)
   {
      // Initialize caches to depend on.
      Cache["Depend0"] = "This is the first dependency.";
      Cache["Depend1"] = "This is the 2nd dependency.";
      Cache["Depend2"] = "This is the 3rd dependency.";
   }

   protected void btnKey0_Click(object sender, EventArgs e)
   {
```

Example 17-25. ObjectCachingCallback (continued)

```
        Cache["Depend0"] = "This is a changed first dependency.";
    }
}
```

Looking at the lines of code that call the Insert method, you can see that one more parameter has been added: onRemove (in addition to the three parameters for time and priority dependencies). This is the callback.

```
Cache.Insert("GridViewDataSet", dsGrid, cacheDepends,
            DateTime.Now.AddSeconds(10),
            Cache.NoSlidingExpiration,
            CacheItemPriority.Default,
            onRemove);
```

The callback method is encapsulated within a *delegate*, which is a reference type that encapsulates a method with a specific signature and return type. The callback method is of the same type and must have the same signature as the CacheItemRemovedCallback delegate. The callback method is declared as a private member of the Page class with the following line of code:

```
private static CacheItemRemovedCallback onRemove = null;
```

Further down, in the CreateGridView method, the callback delegate is instantiated, passing in a reference to the appropriate method:

```
onRemove = new CacheItemRemovedCallback(this.RemovedCallback);
```

This instantiation associates the onRemove delegate with the RemovedCallback method, which is implemented further down.

```
public void RemovedCallback(String cacheKey,
                            Object cacheObject,
                            CacheItemRemovedReason reasonToRemove)
{
    WriteFile("Cache removed for following reason: " +
        reasonToRemove.ToString( ));
}
```

This code has the required signature, which consists of three parameters:

- A string containing the key of the cached item
- An object that is the cached item
- A member of the CacheItemRemovedReason enumeration

This last parameter, CacheItemRemovedReason, provides the reason that the cached item was removed from the cache. It can have one of the values shown in Table 17-5.

Table 17-5. Members of the CacheItemRemovedReason enumeration

Reason	Description
DependencyChanged	A file or item key dependency has changed.
Expired	The cached item has expired.
Removed	The cached item has been explicitly removed by the Remove method or replaced by another item with the same key.
Underused	The cached item was removed to free up system memory.

In this example, the only thing the RemovedCallback method does is call WriteFile to make a log entry. It does this by instantiating a StreamWriter on the log file:

```
System.IO.StreamWriter writer = new System.IO.StreamWriter(
                                      @"C:\test.txt",true);
```

The second parameter for the StreamWriter class, the Boolean, specifies to append to the file if it exists and to create the file if it doesn't exist. If false, it would have over-written the file if it existed. For this to work as written, the account used by the ASP. NET process must have sufficient rights to create files in the root directory.

The WriteLine method is then used to write the string to be logged to the log file.

The HttpCachePolicy Class

Just as the OutputCache directive provides a high-level API for implementing caching, a low-level API is available through the HttpCachePolicy class. This class is contained within the System.Web namespace. It uses HTTP headers to control the caching. The HttpCachePolicy class mirrors the functionality provided by the page directive. It also provides additional low-level control, comparable to the type of control provided for object caching.

To use the HttpCachePolicy class to control output caching, do not include an OutputCache directive in the page file. Instead, use the Response.Cache syntax, as shown in the next example, *OutputCacheLowLevel*. Create this example by copying the *OutputCaching* example from early in this chapter, as shown in Figure 17-2.

The content file of *OutputCacheLowLevel* is functionally unchanged from the previous example, except for removing the OutputCache directive from the top of the file. If you leave the OutputCache directive in, it will override the calls using Response.Cache.

The code-behind file has two additional lines added to the Page_Load method, highlighted in Example 17-26.

Example 17-26. default.aspx.cs for OutputCacheLowLevel

```
using System;
using System.Data;
using System.Configuration;
using System.Web;
using System.Web.Security;
using System.Web.UI;
using System.Web.UI.WebControls;
using System.Web.UI.WebControls.WebParts;
using System.Web.UI.HtmlControls;

public partial class _Default : System.Web.UI.Page
{
    protected void Page_Load(object sender, EventArgs e)
    {
        Response.Cache.SetExpires(DateTime.Now.AddSeconds(10));
        Response.Cache.SetCacheability(HttpCacheability.Public);

        lblTime.Text = "This page was loaded at " +
            DateTime.Now.ToLongTimeString();
        lblUserName.Text = Request.Params["username"];
        lblState.Text = Request.Params["state"];
    }
}
```

The first highlighted line in Example 17-26 sets the cache duration to 10 seconds. It is equivalent to a Duration parameter in an OutputCache directive.

The second line corresponds to the Location parameter in the OutputCache directive. Table 17-6 compares the SetCacheability values, which are members of the HttpCacheability enumeration, with the Location values.

Table 17-6. SetCacheability versus Location

Location value	SetCacheability values	SetCacheability description
Client	Private	Default value. Response is cacheable on the client. Useful if page requires authentication.
Downstream	Public	Uses SetNoServerCaching method to disallow caching on the web server.
Server	Server	Response is cached on the web server.
None	NoCache	Disables caching.
Any	Public	Response is cacheable by clients and shared (proxy) caches.

There are many other HttpCachePolicy methods and properties available. Some of the more common ones include the following:

SetMaxAge

Another method, in addition to SetExpires, to set an expiration. Accepts a TimeSpan value. The following line of code would set the expiration time to 45 seconds:

```
Response.Cache.SetMaxAge(new TimeSpan(0,0,45))
```

SetNoServerCaching

Disables all further server caching. For example:

```
Response.Cache.SetNoServerCaching( )
```

SetSlidingExpiration

A method to enable sliding expiration. Takes a Boolean parameter. If true, it will enable sliding expiration. Sliding expiration forces the clock to restart, so to speak, every time the cache is accessed. So, if SetMaxAge (described above) is set to 30 seconds, every time the cache is accessed, the 30-second clock will be reset to zero. As long as the cache is accessed at least every 30 seconds, it will never expire. The following statement, for example, enables sliding expiration of the cache:

```
Response.Cache.SetSlidingExpiration(true)
```

VaryByParams

This property is the equivalent of the VaryByParam parameter in the OutputCache directive (note the slight difference in spelling). It forces a separate cache for each unique combination of parameters passed to the server in the page request.

To duplicate the VaryByParam parameter in the following OutputCache directive:

```
<%@ OutputCache Duration="60" VaryByParam="state;city" %>
```

you would use the following lines of code:

```
Response.Cache.VaryByParams.Item("state")=true
Response.Cache.VaryByParams.Item("city")=true
```

Performance

Performance is often an important issue in computer applications, especially in web applications receiving a large number of requests. One obvious way to improve performance is to buy faster hardware with more memory. But you can also tune your code to enhance performance in many ways, some of them significant. We'll begin by examining some of the areas specific to ASP.NET that offer the greatest performance improvements and then examine some of the general .NET topics related to improving performance.

 Several Microsofties involved with writing the .NET Framework used the word *performant* to mean that something is delivering higher performance. We can't find it in any dictionary, but it seems like a good word.

ASP.NET-Specific Issues

Correctly using the following features of ASP.NET offers the greatest performance improvements when an ASP.NET application is running.

Session state

Session state is a wonderful thing, but not all applications or pages require it. For any that do not, disable it. You can disable session state for a page by setting the EnableSessionState attribute in the Page directive to false, as in this example:

```
<%@ Page Language="C#" EnableSessionState="false"%>
```

If a page will not be creating or modifying session variables but still needs to access them, set the session state to read-only:

```
<%@ Page Language="C#" EnableSessionState="ReadOnly"%>
```

By default, web services do not have session state enabled. They only have access to session state if the EnableSession property of the WebMethod attribute is set to true:

```
[WebMethod(EnableSession=true)]
```

Session state can be disabled for an entire application by editing the sessionState section of the application's *web.config* file:

```
<sessionState mode="off" />
```

Session state can be stored in one of three ways:

- In-process
- Out-of-process, as a Windows service
- Out-of-process, in a SQL Server database

Each has advantages and disadvantages. Storing session state in-process is by far the most performant. The out-of-process stores are necessary in web farm or web garden scenarios (see the section "Web gardening and web farming" later in this chapter) or if the data must not be lost if a server or process is stopped and restarted.

For a complete discussion of session state, see Chapter 6.

View state

Automatic view state management is another great feature of ASP.NET server controls that enables the controls to show property values correctly after a round trip with no work on the part of the developer. However, there is a performance penalty. This information is passed back and forth via a hidden field, which consumes bandwidth and takes time to process. To see the amount of data used in view state, enable tracing and look at the ViewState column of the Control Tree table displayed as part of the trace ouput.

By default, view state is enabled for all server controls. To disable view state for a server control, set the `EnableViewState` attribute to `false`, as in the following example:

```
<asp:TextBox
    id="txtBookName"
    text="Enter book name."
    toolTip="Enter book name here."
    EnableViewState="false"
    runat="server" />
```

You can disable view state for an entire page by setting the `EnableViewState` attribute of the `Page` directive to `false`, as in this example:

```
<%@ Page Language="C#" EnableViewState="false" %>
```

Caching

Use output and data caching whenever possible. This is especially valuable for database queries that return relatively static data or have a limited range of query parameters. Effective use of caching can have a profound effect on the performance of a web site.

Server controls

Server controls are convenient and offer many advantages. In VS2005, they are practically the default type of control. However, they have a certain amount of overhead and are sometimes not the optimal type of control to use.

In general, if you do not need to manipulate a control programmatically, do not use a server control. Use a classic HTML control instead. For example, if placing a simple label on a page, there will be no need to use a server control unless you need to read or change the value of the label's Text property.

If you need to substitute values into HTML sent to the client browser, you can achieve the desired result (without using a server control) by using data binding or a simple rendering. For example, the following example shows three ways of displaying a hyperlink in a browser:

```
<script language="C#" runat="server">

    string strLink = "www.anysite.com";

    void Page_Load(Object sender, EventArgs e)
    {
        //..retrieve data for strLink here
        //  Call the DataBind method for the page.
        DataBind( );
    }

</script>
```

```
<%--the server control is not necessary...--%>
<a href='<%# strLink %>' runat="server">The Name of the Link</a>

<br><br>

<%-- use DataBinding to substitute literals instead...--%>
<a href='<%# strLink %>' > The Name of the Link</a>

<br><br>

<%-- or a simple rendering expression...--%>
<a href='<%= strLink %>' > The Name of the Link</a>
```

Web gardening and web farming

Adding multiple processors to a computer is called *web gardening*. The .NET Framework takes advantage of this by distributing work to several processes, one process per CPU.

For truly high-traffic sites, multiple web server machines can work together to serve the same application. This is referred to as a *web farm*.

At the least, locating the web server on one machine and the database server on another will buy a large degree of stability and scalability.

Round trips

Round trips to the server are expensive. In low bandwidth situations, they are slow for the client, and in high-volume applications, they bog down the server and inhibit scaling. You should design your applications to minimize round trips.

The only truly essential round trips to the server are those that read or write data. Most validation and data manipulations can occur on the client browser. ASP.NET server controls do this automatically for validation with uplevel browsers (IE 4, 5, and 6, or any browser that supports ECMAScript).

When developing custom server controls, having the controls render client-side code for uplevel browsers will reduce the number of round trips.

Another way to minimize round trips is to use the `IsPostBack` property in the `Page_Load` method. Often, you will want the page to perform some process the first time the page loads, but not on subsequent postbacks. For example, the following code shows how to make code execution conditional on the `IsPostBack` property:

```
void Page_Load(Object sender, EventArgs e)
{
    if (! IsPostBack)
    {
        // Do the expensive operations only the
        // first time the page is loaded.
    }
}
```

For a complete discussion of the IsPostBack property, see Chapter 3.

General .NET Issues

Many of the performance enhancements that affect an ASP.NET application are general ones that apply to any .NET application. This section lists some of the major .NET-related areas to consider when developing your ASP.NET applications.

String concatenation

Strings are immutable in the .NET Framework. This means that methods and operators that appear to change the string are actually returning a modified copy of the string. This has huge performance implications. If you're doing a lot of string manipulation, using the StringBuilder class is much faster.

Consider the code shown in Example 17-27. It measures the time to create a string from 10,000 substrings in two different ways. The first time, a simple string concatenation is used, and the second time the StringBuilder class is used. If you want to see the resulting string, uncomment the two commented lines in the code.

Example 17-27. String concatenation benchmark in C#, StringConcat-cs.aspx

```
<%@ Page Language="C#" %>

<script runat="server">
    void Page_Load(Object Source, EventArgs E)
    {
        int intLimit = 10000;
        DateTime startTime;
        DateTime endTime;
        TimeSpan elapsedTime;
        string strSub;
        string strWhole = "";

        // Do string concat first
        startTime = DateTime.Now;
        for (int i=0; i < intLimit; i++)
        {
            strSub = i.ToString();
            strWhole = strWhole + " " + strSub;
        }
        endTime = DateTime.Now;
        elapsedTime = endTime - startTime;
        lblConcat.Text = elapsedTime.ToString();
//      lblConcatString.Text = strWhole;

        // Do stringBuilder next
        startTime = DateTime.Now;
        StringBuilder sb = new StringBuilder();
        for (int i=0; i < intLimit; i++)
        {
```

```
            strSub = i.ToString( );
            sb.Append(" ");
            sb.Append(strSub);
        }
        endTime = DateTime.Now;
        elapsedTime = endTime - startTime;
        lblBuild.Text = elapsedTime.ToString( );
//      lblBuildString.Text = sb.ToString( );
    }

</script>
<html>
    <body>
    <form runat="server">

        <h1>String Concatenation Benchmark</h1>

        Concatenation:  
        <asp:Label
            id="lblConcat"
            runat="server"/>

        <br/>

        <asp:Label
            id="lblConcatString"
            runat="server"/>

        <br/>
        <br/>

        StringBuilder:  
        <asp:Label
            id="lblBuild"
            runat="server"/>

        <br/>

        <asp:Label
            id="lblBuildString"
            runat="server"/>

    </form>
    </body>
</html>
```

When this page is run, you should see something like Figure 17-8. The difference between the two techniques is dramatic: the StringBuilder's Append method is more than 300 times faster than string concatenation.

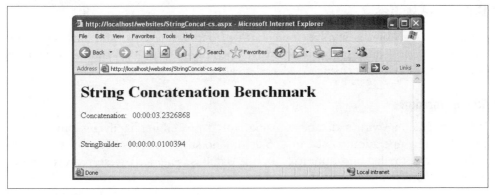

Figure 17-8. String concatenation

Minimize exceptions

You can use `try...catch` blocks to control program flow. However, this coding technique is a serious impediment to performance. You will do much better if you first test whether some condition will cause a failure; if so, code around it.

For example, rather than dividing two integers inside a `try...catch` block and catching any Divide By Zero exceptions thrown, first test if the divisor is zero; if it is, do not do the operation. Similarly, it is as expensive to throw exceptions of your own creation though there are times when it cannot be avoided.

Use early binding

.NET languages allow both early and late binding. Early binding occurs when all objects are declared and the object type known at compile time. Late binding occurs when the object type is not determined until runtime, at which point the CLR determines the type of object it is working with.

Early binding is much faster than late binding, though the latter can be very convenient. Late binding is implemented with reflection, the details of which are beyond the scope of this book.

Use managed code

Managed code is more performant than unmanaged code. It may be worthwhile to port heavily used COM components to managed code.

Disable debug mode

When you deploy your application, remember to disable Debug mode. For a complete discussion of deployment issues, refer to Chapter 19.

Database Issues

Almost all applications involve some form of database access, and accessing data from a database is necessarily an expensive operation. Data access can be made more efficient, however, by focusing on several areas.

Stored procedures

When interacting with a database, using stored procedures is always much faster than the same operation passed in as a command string. This is because stored procedures are compiled and optimized by the database engine. Use stored procedures whenever possible.

Use DataReader class

There are two main ways to get data from a database: from a `DataReader` object or a `DataSet` object. The `DataReader` classes (`SqlDataReader`, `OleDbDataReader`, or `OracleDataReader`) are a much faster way of accessing data if all you need is a forward-only data stream.

Use SQL or Oracle classes rather than OleDB classes

Some database engines have managed classes specifically designed for interacting with that database. It is much better to use the database-specific classes rather than the generic `OleDB` classes. So, for example, it is faster to use a `SqlDataReader` rather than an `OleDbDataReader`.

Benchmarking and Profiling

Benchmarking is the process of conducting reproducible performance tests to see how fast an application is running. It may involve coding the same task two different ways and seeing which one runs faster. The web page shown previously in Example 17-27, which tested the relative speed of string concatenation techniques, is an example of a simple benchmarking program. Obviously, benchmarking programs will often be more complex than that example. They should be designed to emulate your environment as closely as possible.

Profiling is the gathering of performance information about an application. There are several ways to profile an application. Two that are part of the .NET Framework are the following:

- Windows NT, Windows 2000, and Windows XP System Performance Monitor
- The .NET performance counters API

The Performance Monitor can be used to watch a huge variety of system parameters, both .NET-specific and otherwise, in real time. You can open the Performance Monitor by going to Start → Settings → ControlPanel → Administrative Tools → Performance, or you can do this by opening a Command Prompt and entering `perfmon`. When the Performance Monitor opens, click on the Add icon on the toolbar to select and add any number of performance counters. The available counters cover the processor, memory, hard disk, SQL Server, .NET, and ASP.NET.

The performance counter's API includes several classes. The `PerformanceCounter` component in the `System.Diagnostics` namespace can be used for reading existing performance counters and for creating and writing to custom counters.

 Benchmarking is a vast subject and this section only scratches the surface. Many articles and books have been written on the subject. To see what support is available within the .NET Framework, search for `Monitoring Performance` in the documentation index.

CHAPTER 18

Application Logic and Configuration

The original versions of ASP.NET offered many improvements over classic ASP in the areas of controlling, configuring, and deploying web applications. ASP.NET 2.0 builds on this infrastructure. This chapter and the next will cover all of these issues.

ASP.NET provides easy access to application-wide program logic through the *global.asax* file. This text file allows you to create event handlers for many events exposed by the application as a whole and by individual sessions. You can also include variables and methods that will apply globally to the entire application.

Configuration of web applications is handled using the XML configuration files *machine.config* and *web.config*, which provide a flexible and hierarchical configuration scheme. Configuration settings can apply to every application on the web server, to specific applications, or to specific subdirectories within an application. Two tools new to ASP.NET 2.0, the ASP.NET Configuration Settings dialog box and the Web Site Administration Tool, are provided as a welcome alternative to hand-editing application-specific configuration files.

Since all of the configuration and control for ASP.NET applications is done with text files, either XML or some other variant of plain text, you can maintain and update a web application remotely. You don't need to be physically present at a web server to reconfigure the application through IIS (though access to these files is tightly controlled so your users cannot modify them).

Internet Information Server (IIS)

IIS is Microsoft's web server that works in conjunction with ASP.NET. We will cover the topics relevant to developing and deploying ASP.NET web applications.

IIS Versions

This chapter assumes that you are using IIS 5 or 5.1, the versions that are included with the Windows 2000 and Windows XP operating systems, respectively. IIS 6 (included with Windows Server 2003) features a similar interface but adds enhanced options and a revamped request processing architecture. You can use all the instructions in this chapter to configure virtual directories in IIS 6.

You can determine which version of IIS is serving a page by enabling tracing on that page (add trace="true" to the Page directive) and looking for the value of SERVER_SOFTWARE under Server Variables. Alternatively, add a Label control to the form and set its Text property as follows:

```
lblVersion.Text = Request.ServerVariables["Server_Software"];
```

If the page is being served from VS2005 rather than IIS, the value of SERVER_SOFT-WARE will be blank.

Virtual Directories

When you work with web applications, you will frequently need to create, configure, or examine the properties of a virtual directory. Virtual directories in IIS are central to web applications. A *virtual directory* is any directory on the server, or accessible to the server, that has been made available by IIS to requests from the Web. Virtual directories are isomorphic with applications, i.e., each virtual directory is a separate application, and each IIS-served application must have a single virtual root directory.

Virtual directories are accessible to requests from browsers coming in over the Internet. The URL is the domain name, followed by the virtual directory and the web page (or service) file. For example, if an application with a starting web page called MyPage.aspx was using a virtual directory called MyVirtualDirectory, and the domain name of the hosting web server was SomeDomainName.com, the URL to access that application would be the following:

```
http://www.SomeDomainName.com/MyVirtualDirectory/MyPage.aspx
```

When a new web application is created in VS2005 and the Location is set to HTTP, an IIS virtual directory for the app is created automatically. If the Location is set to either File System (the default) or FTP, IIS does not come into play and no virtual directory is created. In these latter two cases, VS2005 provides its own built-in, lightweight web server to serve the pages during development only.

If you wish to deploy the app or look at the app in a browser by navigating using a URL, you will have to create the virtual directory manually using IIS.

 For a discussion of the Location setting, see Chapter 2.

There are several ways to create a virtual directory in IIS:

- Click Start → Run. In the Run dialog box, enter inetmgr, and click on OK.
- Click Start → Control Panel → Administrative Tools. Click on either Internet Information Services or Computer Management.
- Right-click on My Computer and select Manage.

All of these techniques bring up the Microsoft Management Console (MMC), which is used throughout Windows for displaying and controlling system functions. In the left pane is a hierarchical tree structure showing resources for the computer being managed. The right pane displays the child nodes of the currently selected node.

Depending on how you opened the MMC, you will have the Computer Management window or the IIS Window. The latter is one of the nodes within the former; both are fully equivalent except that the Computer Management window allows you to see nodes in addition to IIS.

Looking at Computer Management, the tree on the left has top-level nodes for System Tools, Storage, and Services and Applications. Drilling down through Services and Applications, then Internet Information Services, then Web Sites, to the Default Web Site, the MMC window should look something like that shown in Figure 18-1. If you opened the IIS window directly, you would see the same thing except the top level node would already be Internet Information Services.

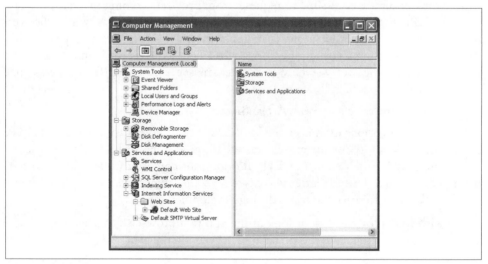

Figure 18-1. Computer Management console

Click on Default Web Site. The contents of the default web site will be visible, as shown in Figure 18-2.

The Default Web Site corresponds to the physical directory *c:\inetpub\wwwroot* unless you've changed it. When IIS is installed on a machine, it creates this directory, along

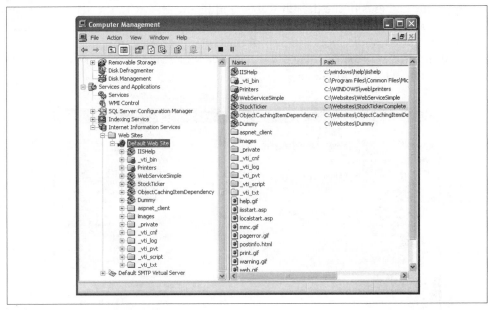

Figure 18-2. *Virtual directories*

with several subdirectories (beginning with the underscore character). If you open a browser window and enter the following URL, you will see the default page for the default web site:

```
http://localhost
```

If your web server is accessible over the Internet through a domain name, a remote user at a browser who entered that domain name as a URL (say for example, as the following), would see the same thing:

```
http://www.SomeDomainName.com
```

You will not see anything in the browser (other than help pages put up by IIS) unless one of the following conditions is true:

- A suitably named file (*default.htm*, *default.asp*, *default.aspx*, or *iisstart.asp*) containing a valid web page exists in the physical directory.
- Directory Browsing is enabled by right-clicking on Default Web Site, going to the Home Directory tab in the Default Web Site Properties dialog box, and checking the Directory browsing checkbox.

 Be aware that enabling Directory Browsing can be a serious gap in security. It is generally not something to do on a production site unless you have a very good reason and suitable security precautions are in place, such as stringent permissions.

Compare the contents of the default web site in Figure 18-2 with the actual contents of *c:\inetpub\wwwroot* shown in Figure 18-3. You can see that all the files and directories in the physical directory are also in the default web site in Figure 18-2. These physical directories, such as *images* and *_private*, are normal directories with standard Explorer-style directory icons.

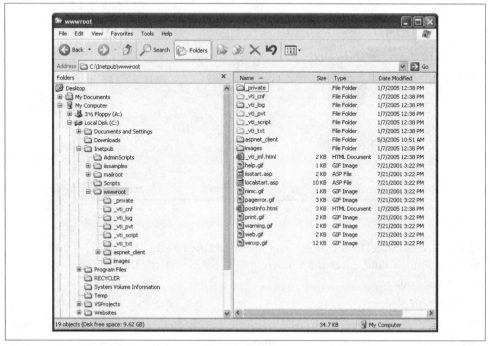

Figure 18-3. c:\inetpub\wwwroot

Other directories in the Default Web Site shown in Figure 18-2, such as *_vti_bin* and *Printers*, have a directory icon with a small globe on the lower-right corner. These are *virtual directories*, created either by IIS or by a developer.

Finally, some of the directories in the default web site shown in Figure 18-2 have an icon that looks like a cardboard box with a green thing inside (it's a package, get it?). These are *web application directories*. They can be either physical directories or virtual directories. The virtual directories created by developers are also application directories by default. This can be changed by right-clicking on the directory in question in the left pane, selecting Properties, then clicking the Create Application Settings button to make it an application directory or the Remove Application Settings button to convert the directory to a plain virtual directory.

When a new web application or web service is created in VS2005 and the Location is set to HTTP, the virtual directory is created. To access the web site in a browser, you must provide the web site name appended to a valid URL, such as one of the following:

```
http://localhost/MyNewWebSite
http://MyDomain.com/MyNewWebSite
```

In this case, VS2005 automatically creates a physical directory called *MyNewWebSite*. In the case of localhost, it will be located (by default) under *c:\inetpub\wwwroot*. In the case of a remote domain, the physical directory will be located under the virtual root of the domain. This new physical directory is both a virtual directory and an application directory.

You can make a new virtual directory outside VS2005 using the Computer Management window shown in Figure 18-2 (or the equivalent Internet Services Manager window) by right-clicking on Default Web Site in the left pane, selecting New… → Virtual Directory, and following the wizard. Once the new virtual directory is created, you can right-click on it and select Properties to modify its properties.

Back in Chapter 6, you created a virtual directory called *Websites*. This was mapped to the physical directory *c:\Websites*. To access this virtual directory, enter one of the following URLs from a browser, depending on whether you are on a local machine or accessing the application over a local intranet or the Internet:

```
http://localhost/Websites                [local]
http://SomeComputerName/Websites         [intranet]
http://www.SomeDomainName.com/Websites   [Internet]
```

 Internet Explorer can determine if a URL is pointing to an intranet or an Internet address by the presence of periods in the first node. If there are any periods, then it is an Internet address. For example, both of the following URLs are Internet addresses:

```
http://www.SomeDomainName.com/Websites
123.456.789.123/Websites
```

This determination is important for imposing the proper security settings.

Understanding Web Applications

The term *application* has been used throughout this book. You probably know intuitively what a web application is. Here is a working definition for a web application: "A web application consists of all of the web pages, files, code, objects, executables, images, and other resources located in an IIS virtual directory or a subdirectory of that virtual directory." In other words, a web application is either a web site or a web service.

The web application will start the first time any of its pages are requested from the web server. It will run until any of a number of events cause it to shut down. These events include the following:

- Editing *global.asax* or a configuration file
- Restarting IIS
- Restarting the machine

If a page is requested and the application is not running, the application will automatically restart.

Unlike traditional EXE applications, web applications do not have a fixed starting point. A user can drop in through any number of paths or entry points. Web application flow and security should be designed accordingly.

For example, a virtual directory may contain three web pages: *default.aspx*, *login.aspx*, and *bugs.aspx*. If you enter the following URL in a browser, you will go to *default.aspx*, which may send you to *login.aspx*:

```
http://localhost
```

On the other hand, users may enter the following URL to go directly to the login page:

```
http://localhost/login.aspx
```

Once logged in, they can go to *bugs.aspx*. If a user tries to go directly to *bugs.aspx* without logging in, your code should redirect them to *login.aspx* to log in first.

Classic ASP and ASP.NET applications can coexist side-by-side on the same server and can coexist in the same application directory. However, configuration, application, and session objects cannot be shared between them. They are totally distinct and independent.

Each application runs in its own *application domain*, which is created by the runtime server. Each application domain is isolated from every other application domain. If one application crashes or otherwise compromises its own stability, it cannot affect any other domains. This greatly enhances security and stability.

Since each application is independent from any other application, this means that each application has its own independent configuration and control structures.

Application-Wide Logic

All code contained in the page class is scoped to the page. In other words, it is only visible to other code within that page class. This is true for variables and members such as methods, properties, and events. For most code, this is the appropriate behavior. However, there are often situations where it is either convenient or necessary to have code scoped more globally. For example, you may have a common method used in several pages. Though you can replicate the code on all the pages, it is far better to have a single source. Another example would be an application where a variable—a TrackingID, for example—is needed by every page as the user moves from page to page.

It is possible to scope your code application-wide (rather than per page). There are two ways of doing this: using the HttpApplication object and using the *global.asax* file.

HttpApplication Object

Just as a web page instantiates the Page class, when an application runs, it instantiates an object from the HttpApplication class. This object has methods, properties, and events available to all the objects within the application. It provides several objects that allow you to interact with the HTTP request:

- The Application object for using application state
- The Request object for getting access to the incoming request
- The Response object for sending an HttpResponse back to the client
- The Session object for access to session state

ASP.NET maintains a pool of HttpApplication instances during the lifetime of each application. Every time a page is requested from the server, an HttpApplication instance is assigned to it. This instance manages the request from start to end. Once the request is completed, that instance is freed up for reuse.

You can also program against the HttpApplication object by using a file called *global.asax*, described next.

global.asax

global.asax is a text file that provides globally available code. Such code can include event handlers for application and session events, methods, and static variables. This file is sometimes called an application file.

Any code contained in the *global.asax* file becomes part of the application in which it is located. There can be only a single *global.asax* file per application, located in the root directory of the application. However, this file is optional. If there is no *global.asax* file, then the application will run using default behavior for all the events exposed by the HttpApplication class.

Classic ASP had a file with similar format and structure, called *global.
asa*. In fact, if you copy all the code from a working copy of *global.asa*
into *global.asax*, the application should run fine.

When the application runs, the contents of *global.asax* are compiled into a class that
derives from the `HttpApplication` class. Thus, all the methods, classes, and objects of
the `HttpApplication` class are available to your application.

The CLR monitors *global.asax* for changes. If it detects a change in the file, a new
copy of the application will be automatically started, creating a new application
domain. Any requests that are currently being handled by the old application domain
are allowed to complete, but any new requests are handled by the new application
domain. When the last request on the old application domain is finished, that application domain is removed. This effectively *reboots* the web application without any
users being aware of the fact.

To prevent application users from seeing the code underlying the application, ASP.NET
is configured by default to prevent users from seeing the contents of *global.asax*. If
someone enters the following URL in a browser:

```
http://localhost/progaspnet/Global.asax
```

she will receive a 403 (forbidden) error message or an error message similar to the
following:

```
This type of page is not served.
```

web.config files, described shortly, have behaviors similar to *global.
asax*. If the file is changed, the application will automatically "restart".
It is also not possible to view *web.config* files in a browser.

The *global.asax* file looks and is structured similarly to a page file (*.aspx*). It can have
one or more sections, which will be described in detail shortly:

- Directives
- Script blocks
- Object declarations

Just as web pages and web services can use code-behind, the *global.asax* file can use
code-behind. However, unlike the situation with web pages and web services, the
default behavior of VS2005 is *not* to use the code-behind technique with *global.asax*.

Versions of Visual Studio prior to 2005 by default did use the code-behind model with *global.asax*. Code-behind is still supported though not used by default.

To use code-behind with *global.asax*, the Application directive at the top of the file (which is analogous to the Page directive in a Page file, and will be described fully in the next section) has an Inherits property that points to the code-behind class created in *global.asax.cs*.

There is also a CodeBehind attribute which can be used to point to a code-behind file. However, if this points to a file located anywhere other than the *App_Code* folder, then the class file will have to be manually compiled.

You can add a *global.asax* file to a web application by right-clicking on the website in the Solution Explorer or clicking on the Website menu, and selecting Add New Item…, then selecting a Global Application Class. Leave the default name of *global.asax*.

VS2005 will create the file listed in Example 18-1. This boilerplate has empty declarations for five events: Application_Start and _End, Session_Start and _End, and Application_Error.

Example 18-1. Boilerplate global.asax

```
<%@ Application Language="C#" %>

<script runat="server">

    void Application_Start(Object sender, EventArgs e) {
        // Code that runs on application startup

    }

    void Application_End(Object sender, EventArgs e) {
        //  Code that runs on application shutdown

    }

    void Application_Error(Object sender, EventArgs e) {
        // Code that runs when an unhandled error occurs

    }

    void Session_Start(Object sender, EventArgs e) {
        // Code that runs when a new session is started

    }

    void Session_End(Object sender, EventArgs e) {
      // Code that runs when a session ends.
      // Note: The Session_End event is raised only when the sessionstate
      //       mode
```

Example 18-1. Boilerplate global.asax (continued)

```
    // is set to InProc in the Web.config file. If session mode is set
    //       to StateServer
    // or SQLServer, the event is not raised.


    }

</script>
```

The sample *global.asax* file listed in Example 18-2 sets some values in Application state and writes an entry to a log file every time the application starts. To use this example, the ASP.NET account must have permission to write to the root directory *c:* (which is not recommended in a production system).

Example 18-2. Sample global.asax

```
<%@ Application  Language="C#"%>
<script runat="server">

    protected void Application_Start(Object sender, EventArgs e)
    {
        Application["strConnectionString"] =
                    "SERVER=MyServer;DATABASE=Pubs;UID=myID;PWD=secret;";

        string[] Books = {"SciFi","Novels", "Computers",
                    "History", "Religion"};
        Application["arBooks"] = Books;

        WriteFile("Application Starting");
    }

    protected void Application_End(Object sender, EventArgs e)
    {
        WriteFile("Application Ending");
    }

    void WriteFile(string strText)
    {
        System.IO.StreamWriter writer =
                    new System.IO.StreamWriter(@"C:\test.txt",true);
        string str;
        str = DateTime.Now.ToString() + "   " + strText;
        writer.WriteLine(str);
        writer.Close();
    }
</script>
```

Directives

As with web page and web service files, the *global.asax* file may begin with any number of directives. These are used to specify settings to be used by the application compilers when they process the ASP.NET files. As with Page directives, Application directives use a dictionary structure that accepts one or more attribute/value pairs. There are three supported directives: `Application`, `Import`, and `Assembly`.

Application. The `Application` directive specifies application-specific attributes used by the compiler. A sample `Application` directive might look something like this:

```
<%@ Application  Language="C#" Inherits="WebServiceConsumer.Global"
          Description="A sample application" %>
```

The `Language` attribute can have any of the standard language values: `VB`, `C#`, `JS`, or `VJ#` for VB2005, C#, JScript .NET, or J#, respectively. (Any third-party language that supports the .NET platform can also be used.) The default is `C#`. The language specified here applies only to the language used in the *global.asax* file and not to any of the other code files in the application. It is perfectly legal to use C# in the *global.asax* file and VB2005 in the *.aspx* file, or vice versa, for example.

The `Inherits` attribute specifies the name of a class to inherit from, typically a class in a code-behind file.

The `Description` attribute accepts a text description of the application, which is then ignored by the parser and compiler.

The `CodeBehind` attribute was used by Visual Studio .NET (not VS2005) to keep track of the file that contains the code-behind.

Import. The `Import` directive takes a single attribute, a `namespace`. The specified namespace is explicitly imported into the application, making all its classes and interfaces available. The imported `namespace` can be part of the .NET Framework or a custom namespace.

A typical `Import` directive might look like this:

```
<%@ Import Namespace="System.Data" %>
```

There can only be one `Namespace` attribute. If you need to import multiple namespaces, use multiple `Import` directives.

The following namespaces are automatically imported into all web applications and so do not need an `Import` directive:

- `System`
- `System.Collections`
- `System.Collections.Specialized`
- `System.Configuration`
- `System.IO`
- `System.Text`
- `System.Text.RegularExpressions`
- `System.Web`

- `System.Web.Caching`
- `System.Web.Security`
- `System.Web.SessionState`
- `System.Web.UI`
- `System.Web.UI.HtmlControls`
- `System.Web.UI.WebControls`

Assembly. The `Assembly` directive links an assembly to the current application during compilation. This makes all the assembly's classes and interfaces available to the application.

 Assemblies are, typically, *.dll* or *.exe* files and are described in detail in the next chapter.

Using the `Assembly` directive enables both early and late binding since the assembly can be referenced at compile time, then loaded into the application domain at runtime.

Assemblies that are physically located in the application assembly cache (that is, the *bin* directory and code files located in the *App_Code* directory) are automatically linked to the application. Therefore, any assemblies located in the *bin* directory, or any assemblies compiled from code contained in the *App_Code* directory, need not be linked with an `Assembly` directive.

There are two possible attributes for the `Assembly` directive: `Name` and `Src`. `Name` is a string with the name of the assembly to link to the application. It should not include a path. `Src` is the path (relative only) to a source file that will be dynamically compiled and linked.

Each `Assembly` directive can only have one attribute. If you need to link to multiple assemblies, use multiple `Assembly` directives.

Assembly directives will look something like this:

```
<%@ Assembly Name="SomeAssembly" %>
<%@ Assembly Src="sources/SomeSourceFile.cs" %>
```

Script blocks

The typical *global.asax* file contains the bulk of its code in a script block contained between script tags:

```
<script runat="server">
  .
  .
  .
</script>
```

If you are using code-behind, the code contained within the code-behind class in the code-behind file is equivalent to putting the code in a script block, although code in the code-behind file itself is not enclosed by script tags.

The code contained within the script block can consist of event handlers or methods, as will be demonstrated in the following section.

Events

Just as web pages and the controls they contain expose events, the application and sessions running under the application also expose events. These events can be handled by event handlers contained in the *global.asax* file, as well as in page-specific files. For example, the `Application_Start` event is fired when the application starts, and the `Application_End` event is fired when the application ends. Some of the application events fire every time a page is requested, while others, such as `Application_Error`, only fire under certain conditions.

The sample *global.asax* file shown in Example 18-2 demonstrates event handlers for the `Application_Start` and `Application_End` events. The `Application_Start` event in Example 18-2 sets two Application properties: a string called `strConnectionString` and an array of strings called `arBooks`. The event handler then calls a helper method, `WriteFile`, that is also contained within the *global.asax* file. This helper method writes a line containing the string argument to a log file. `WriteFile` is reproduced here from Example 18-2:

```
void WriteFile(string strText)
{
    System.IO.StreamWriter writer =
                new System.IO.StreamWriter(@"C:\test.txt",true);
    string str;
    str = DateTime.Now.ToString() + "   " + strText;
    writer.WriteLine(str);
    writer.Close();
}
```

The `WriteFile` method is a simple logging method. It opens a `StreamWriter` object on a text file, hard-coded to be *c:\test.txt*. It adds a line to the file containing a timestamp and whatever text string is passed in to the method. The Boolean parameter `true` in the `StreamWriter` method call specifies that if the file already exists, the line will be appended to the file. If the file does not exist, it will be created.

The `Application_End` event handler makes another call to `WriteFile` to make a log entry that the application has ended.

To see the results of these two event handlers, make some meaningless edit to *global.asax* and save the file. This will force the application to end. Then request any URL in the virtual directory. For this example, use one of the web pages from a previous chapter—it doesn't really matter which one—or a web page of your own creation. Example 18-3 shows an excerpt from the resulting log file.

Example 18-3. Excerpt from Test.txt

```
8/26/2006 5:46:23 PM   Application Starting
8/26/2006 6:13:35 PM   Application Ending
8/27/2006 10:17:39 PM  Application Starting
8/27/2006 10:18:23 PM  Application Ending
8/27/2006 10:18:36 PM  Application Starting
```

Just as there are Start and End events for the Application, there are Start and End events for each session Session_Start and Session_End. This allows you to have code that will run every time each session within the application starts and ends.

By putting an event handler in *global.asax* for every possible application event, as shown in Example 18-4 with all the method names highlighted for readability, it is easy to see the cycle of application events as the page request is received, processed, and rendered.

Example 18-4. global.asax event demonstration

```
<%@ Application  Language="C#" %>

<script runat="server">

    protected void Application_Start(Object sender, EventArgs e)
    {
       WriteFile("Application Starting");
    }

    protected void Application_End(Object sender, EventArgs e)
    {
       WriteFile("Application Ending");
    }

    protected void Session_Start(Object sender, EventArgs e)
    {
       Response.Write("Session_Start" + "<br/>");
    }

    protected void Session_End(Object sender, EventArgs e)
    {
       Response.Write("Session_End" + "<br/>");
    }

    protected void Application_Disposed(Object sender, EventArgs e)
    {
       Response.Write("Application_Disposed" + "<br/>");
    }

    protected void Application_Error(Object sender, EventArgs e)
    {
       string strError;
       strError = Server.GetLastError( ).ToString( );
```

Example 18-4. global.asax event demonstration (continued)

```
    if (Context!= null)
       Context.ClearError( );

    Response.Write("Application_Error" + "<br/>");
    Response.Write("<b>Error Msg: </b>" + strError + "<br/>" +
                   "<b>End Error Msg</b><br/>");
}

protected void Application_BeginRequest(Object sender, EventArgs e)
{
    Response.Write("Application_BeginRequest" + "<br/>");
}

protected void Application_EndRequest(Object sender, EventArgs e)
{
    Response.Write("Application_EndRequest" + "<br/>");
}

protected void Application_AcquireRequestState(Object sender, EventArgs
                                               e)
{
    Response.Write("Application_AcquireRequestState" + "<br/>");
}

protected void Application_AuthenticateRequest(Object sender, EventArgs
                                               e)
{
    Response.Write("Application_AuthenticateRequest" + "<br/>");
}

protected void Application_AuthorizeRequest(Object sender, EventArgs e)
{
    Response.Write("Application_AuthorizeRequest" + "<br/>");
}

protected void Application_PostRequestHandlerExecute(Object sender,
                                                     EventArgs e)
{
    Response.Write("Application_PostRequestHandlerExecute" + "<br/>");
}

protected void Application_PreRequestHandlerExecute(Object sender,
                                                    EventArgs e)
{
    Response.Write("Application_PreRequestHandlerExecute" + "<br/>");
}

protected void Application_PreSendRequestContent(Object sender,
                                                 EventArgs e)
{
    Response.Write("Application_PreSendRequestContent" + "<br/>");
}
```

Example 18-4. global.asax event demonstration (continued)

```
    protected void Application_PreSendRequestHeaders(Object sender,
                                                    EventArgs e)
    {
        Response.Write("Application_PreSendRequestHeaders" + "<br/>");
    }

    protected void Application_ReleaseRequestState(Object sender, EventArgs
                                                    e)
    {
        Response.Write("Application_ReleaseRequestState" + "<br/>");
    }

    protected void Application_ResolveRequestCache(Object sender, EventArgs
                                                    e)
    {
        Response.Write("Application_ResolveRequestCache" + "<br/>");
    }

    protected void Application_UpdateRequestCache(Object sender, EventArgs
                                                    e)
    {
        Response.Write("Application_UpdateRequestCache" + "<br/>");
    }

    void WriteFile(string strText)
    {
        System.IO.StreamWriter writer =
            new System.IO.StreamWriter(@"C:\test.txt",true);
        string str;
        str = DateTime.Now.ToString() + "   " + strText;
        writer.WriteLine(str);
        writer.Close();
    }
</script>
```

The following are all the events fired with every page request, in the order in which they are fired:

Application_BeginRequest
> Raised for every request handled by ASP.NET. Code in this event handler is executed before the web page or service processes the request.

Application_AuthenticateRequest
> Raised prior to authentication of the request. (As was covered in Chapter 12, authentication is the process whereby a user is verified as being who they say they are.) Code in this event handler allows custom security routines to be implemented.

Application_AuthorizeRequest
> Raised prior to authorization of the request. (Authorization is the process of determining if the requesting user has permission to access a resource as discussed in

Chapter 12.) Code in this event handler allows custom security routines to be implemented.

Application_ResolveRequestCache

Raised before ASP.NET determines whether the output should be generated fresh or filled from cache. Code in this event handler is executed in either case.

Application_AcquireRequestState

Raised prior to acquiring the session state.

Application_PreRequestHandlerExecute

Raised just prior to the request being passed to the handler that is servicing the request. After the event is raised, the page is processed by the HTTP handler processing the request.

Application_PostRequestHandlerExecute

Raised when the HTTP handler is finished with the page request. At this point, the Response object now has the data to send back to the client.

Application_ReleaseRequestState

Raised when the session state is released and updated.

Application_UpdateRequestCache

Raised when the output cache is updated, if the output is to be cached.

Application_EndRequest

Raised when the request is finished.

Application_PreSendRequestHeaders

Raised prior to sending the HTTP headers to the client. If response buffering is enabled, meaning that none of the data will be sent until all the data is ready (the default condition), this event will always follow Application_EndRequest. If response buffering is disabled, then this event will be raised whenever the data is sent back to the client. Response buffering is controlled by an attribute to a Page directive or, in the case of web services, a WebMethod attribute.

Application_PreSendRequestContent

Raised prior to sending the HTTP content to the client. As with Application_PreSendRequestHeaders, the order in which the event is raised depends on if response buffering is enabled.

The following are the application events that fire only under certain conditions:

Application_Start

Raised whenever the application is started. An application is started the first time any page is requested from an application virtual directory and the application is not already running.

Application_End

Raised whenever an application ends. An application ends whenever one of the configuration files (*global.asax*, *global.asax.cs*, *global.asax.vb*, or *web.config*) is modified, or the server is crashed or restarted. Cleanup code, such as closing database connections, is normally executed in this event handler.

Session_Start

Raised for every session that starts. This is a good place to place code that is session-specific.

Session_End

Raised for every session that ends. This provides an opportunity to save any data stored in session state.

Application_Disposed

Raised when the CLR removes the application from memory.

Application_Error

Raised whenever an unhandled error occurs anywhere in the application. This provides an excellent opportunity to implement generic application-wide error handling.

You can handle specific error conditions where necessary in your code, using try...catch blocks. You can also trap for errors at the page level using the ErrorPage attribute of the Page directive. Any errors handled in these ways will not trigger the Application_Error event.

To test this new version of *global.asax*, create the web page shown in Example 18-5. Call the website *GlobalEvents*. When this web page is run, you will get the screen shown in Figure 18-4.

Example 18-5. default.aspx for GlobalEvents

```
<%@ Page Language="C#" AutoEventWireup="true"  CodeFile="Default.aspx.cs"
   Inherits="_Default" %>

<!DOCTYPE html PUBLIC "-//W3C//DTD XHTML 1.1//EN"
   "http://www.w3.org/TR/xhtml11/DTD/xhtml11.dtd">

<html xmlns="http://www.w3.org/1999/xhtml" >
<head runat="server">
    <title>Global Events</title>
</head>
<body>
    <form id="form1" runat="server">
    <div>
      <h1>Global Events</h1>
      <asp:Button ID="btnPost" runat="server" Text="Post" />
      <asp:Button ID="btnEndSession" runat="server"
                  Text="End Session"
                  OnClick="btnEndSession_Click" />
      <asp:Button ID="btnError" runat="server"
                  Text="Generate Error"
                  OnClick="btnError_Click" />
    </div>
    </form>
```

Example 18-5. default.aspx for GlobalEvents (continued)

```
</body>
</html>
```

Figure 18-4. GlobalEvents

In Figure 18-4, you see that a series of application events have fired. About midway through the sequence of events, the *.aspx* file itself is finally rendered, followed by another series of application events.

 The *GlobalEvents* example must be run from an actual IIS virtual directory to behave properly.

The first time the page is displayed, the Session_Start event is fired, but on subsequent displays, the Session_Start event may not be fired. This is because the request is part of the same session. Clicking on the End Session button causes the Session.Abandon method to be called, which ends the current session. The next time the page is submitted to the server, the Session_Start event will fire.

The Post button simply provides a way to repost the page.

Most of the Application event handlers in Example 18-4 use the Response.Write method to indicate the event has been called. However, the Application_Start and Application_End methods call the WriteFile method instead. If you try using Response.Write in these event handlers, they will not display on the web page because the session in which the page is to be rendered is not running. However, by examining the log file, *c:\test.txt*, you will see entries that indicate when the application starts and ends.

The sample *global.asax* file shown in Example 18-4 demonstrates one way of using the `Application_Error` event. That code is reproduced here for reference:

```
protected void Application_Error(Object sender, EventArgs e)
{
    string strError;
    strError = Server.GetLastError( ).ToString( );

    if (Context!= null)
        Context.ClearError( );

    Response.Write("Application_Error" + "<br/>");
    Response.Write("<b>Error Msg: </b>" + strError + "<br/>" +
                "<b>End Error Msg</b><br/>");
}
```

This event handler uses the `HttpServerUtility` object's `GetLastError` method to report the last error that occurred. That error is converted to a string and assigned to a string variable:

```
strError = Server.GetLastError( ).ToString( )
```

Next the `HttpContext` object's `ClearError` method is called to clear all the errors for the current HTTP request:

```
Context.ClearError( )
```

If the errors are not cleared, the error will still display on the client browser and the subsequent `Response.Write` statements will remain invisible.

Finally, the `Response.Write` statements display a message and the current error to the client browser.

An alternative technique for reporting an error to the user would display a custom error handling page. To do this, replace the `Response.Write` lines in the `Application_Error` event handler with the following line of code:

```
Response.Redirect("CustomErrorPage.aspx?Msg=" +
                Server.UrlEncode(strError));
```

This line of code uses the `HttpServerUtility` object's `UrlEncode` method to pass the error message as a query string parameter to the custom error page coded in *CustomErrorPage.aspx*. *CustomErrorPage.aspx* would have a `Label` control, called `lblMessage`, and the following code in its `Page_Load` method:

```
void Page_Load(Object Source, EventArgs E)
{
    lblMessage.Text = Request.QueryString["Msg"];
}
```

The Generate Error button on *Default.aspx* intentionally causes an error to see error handling in action. The Click event handler for that button contains the following code, which will raise a Divide By Zero exception:

```
protected void btnError_Click(object sender, EventArgs e)
{
    int a = 5;
    int b = 0;
    int c;
    c = a / b;
}
```

Server-side includes

External source code files can be included in the application using *server-side includes*. The code contained within an include file is added to *global.asax* before it is compiled. The language used in the include file must match the language used in the *global.asax* file though that may be different from the language(s) used within the application.

The following syntax is used for a server-side:

```
<!--#Include PathType="fileName" -->
```

In this syntax, PathType can have one of two values, as shown in Table 18-1.

Table 18-1. PathType attributes

Type of path	Description
File	*fileName* is a string containing a relative path from the directory containing the *global.asax* file.
Virtual	*fileName* is a string containing a full virtual path from a virtual directory in your web site.

Looking at the sample *global.asax* listed in Example 18-4, add the following line as the second line in the file:

```
<!--#Include File="IncludeFile.cs" -->
```

Create a new text file, called *IncludeFile.cs* and store it in the same directory that contains *global.asax*. This file requires a pair of script tags as with the *global.asax* file.

Move a copy of the WriteFile method from *global.asax* to the include file. Finally, comment out (or delete) the WriteFile method from *global.asax*. The include file should look like Example 18-6.

Example 18-6. Include file for global.asax

```
<script runat="server">

    public void WriteFile(string strText)
    {
        System.IO.StreamWriter writer =
                new System.IO.StreamWriter(@"C:\test.txt",true);
```

Example 18-6. Include file for global.asax (continued)

```
    string str;
    str = DateTime.Now.ToString( ) + "  " + strText;
    writer.WriteLine(str);
    writer.Close( );
  }
```

```
</script>
```

If you run any of your web pages, there should be no difference in behavior because all you did was move the code for a method from one file to another.

Just as the CLR watches for changes in *global.asax* and restarts the application if any occur, it also watches for changes in any include files. If an include file changes, then the application will restart for that as well.

Include files are useful for including the same standard code into multiple applications. This common code could include such things as methods for database access, writing log entries, error handling routines, logins, or any number of infrastructure-type pieces that are part of every application.

Object declarations

An additional way to include code in the *global.asax* file is as declarative object tags. These static objects are declared as either `Application` or `Session` objects. They are then available for the duration of the application or each session.

Here is a code snippet showing how an object might be declared in the *global.asax* file. This snippet would be located *outside* the script block in the file:

```
<object id="strDSN"
    class="System.String"
    scope="Application"
    runat="server"/>
```

The object in this snippet can be referred to in the application by the value of the `id` attribute, which in this example is `strDSN`.

The `class` attribute specifies the type of this object. In this case, it is a string object. The `class` attribute implies that the object is derived from a .NET assembly. Alternatively, you can use a `progid` or `classid` instead of the `class` attribute to instantiate a COM object rather than a .NET object. Each object declaration can have only one `class`, `progid`, or `classid`.

In this snippet, the `scope` attribute specifies this will be an `Application` object. The other legal value for this attribute is `Session`.

Objects declared in this way are not created upon declaration. They are created the first time they are referenced in the application. To reference the static object shown in the code snippet above in your code, refer to the following:

```
Application["strDSN"];
```

Storing application or session information elsewhere is also possible, such as in the *web.config* file, which will be described shortly.

Global Members

It was noted previously that the code contained in the *global.asax* file is compiled into a class derived from `HttpApplication` and becomes part of the application. You can also create a separate class file that will contain globally available code, such as public member variables and methods. These global members can be either static or instance.

Static methods and member variables are those that do not require that the class containing the method or variable to be instantiated. Static member variables are defined using the `static` keyword in *C#*. *Instance* members require an instance of the class in order to be invoked. Any member not declared as static is an instance member. Both static and instance members will be demonstrated.

New to C# 2.0 is the `static` class, which contains only static members.

The trick to getting access to this global class is to place the class file in the *App_Code* directory under the application root. Placed there, it will automatically be compiled every time the application is run. (Alternatively, the class can be manually compiled and the resulting assembly located in the *bin* directory.) The class can then be referred to throughout the application, making available global static and instance members.

Version 1.x of ASP.NET provided a `ClassName` attribute of the `Application` directive, which allowed you to directly specify the name of the global class. That attribute is no longer supported in Version 2.0. Though it will not cause a compiler error, it will be ignored.

To see this in action, create a new web site in VS2005 called *GlobalMembers*. Right-click on the web site root folder in the Solution Explorer, or click on the Website menu item, and select Add Folder → App_Code Folder. Then right-click on the new *App_Code* folder in the Solution Explorer and select Add New Item. From the Add New Item dialog, click on Class. Change the name to *GlobalMembers.cs*.

The name used for this file and for the name of the class within the file is not important as long as it is consistent throughout the application.

This class file will open in the editor with the class declared and an empty default constructor. Add the highlighted lines of code listed in Example 18-7.

Example 18-7. GlobalMembers.cs

```csharp
using System;
using System.Data;
using System.Configuration;
using System.Web;
using System.Web.Security;
using System.Web.UI;
using System.Web.UI.WebControls;
using System.Web.UI.WebControls.WebParts;
using System.Web.UI.HtmlControls;

public class GlobalMembers
{
    public static int successRate = 50;

    public Global( )
    {
    }

    protected void Application_Start(Object sender, EventArgs e)
    {
        WriteFile("Application Starting");
    }

    protected void Application_End(Object sender, EventArgs e)
    {
        WriteFile("Application Ending");
    }

    public void WriteFile(string strText)
    {
        System.IO.StreamWriter writer =
            new System.IO.StreamWriter(@"C:\test.txt", true);
        string str;
        str = DateTime.Now.ToString( ) + "   " + strText;
        writer.WriteLine(str);
        writer.Close( );
    }

    public static void StaticWriteFile(string strText)
    {
        System.IO.StreamWriter writer =
            new System.IO.StreamWriter(@"C:\test.txt", true);
        string str;
        str = DateTime.Now.ToString( ) + "   " + strText;
        writer.WriteLine(str);
        writer.Close( );
    }
}
```

The first highlighted line of code in Example 18-7 implements a global static variable, called successRate. You can access this variable from anywhere in the application simply by pre-pending the class name. So, for example, if your web page has a

Label control named lblGlobalStatic, you could set its Text property with the following line of code:

```
lblGlobalStatic.Text = GlobalMembers.successRate.ToString( );
```

The ToString method must be called to convert the variable to a string so it can be assigned to the Text property of the label.

The next two highlighted methods are event handlers for the Application_Start and Application_End events, exactly the same as seen in the previous example, *GlobalEvents*. These event handlers call the method WriteFile, listed further down in the class file. The public accessibility modifier has been added to the WriteFile method declaration, changing it from the default accessibility of private. This makes the method available to the entire application.

WriteFile is not static. That is, it requires an instance of the class to be invoked. The following two lines of code in a web page code-behind file get a reference to an instance of the class, then invoke WriteFile:

```
GlobalMembers g = new GlobalMembers( );
g.WriteFile("Instance method - Now in Page_Load of web page.");
```

Example 18-7 also demonstrates a static version of WriteFile, called StaticWriteFile. It is made static by the use of the static keyword. It can be invoked directly without first instantiating the class, similar to the static variable:

```
GlobalMembers.StaticWriteFile("Static method - Now in Page_Load of web page.");
```

In this example, there is no real reason to use the static instead of the instance methods, since the method content itself is identical. In the general case, however, instance methods are required when the method needs to refer to the specific instance of the class. Suppose the global method is working with a DataSet or some other object specific to this invocation of the page; then an instance global method would be called for. Otherwise, a static global method can be used.

Configuring the Application

ASP.NET is configured with XML files. The base server-wide configuration file is called *machine.config*, described in the next section, "Hierarchical Configuration." This is supplemented by an optional server-wide *web.configuration* file located in the same directory as *machine.config*, and a number of application-specific configuration files, all called *web.config*, located in the application root directory and subdirectories.

The XML files that control the configuration can be edited with any standard text editor. It is not necessary to use the IIS control panel, as was the case with classic ASP. Although the configuration files can be edited in any text editor, VS2005 and IIS provide UIs for editing the most common configurations.

Since the configuration is accomplished with XML files and since these files are text, it is easy to administer your configuration remotely. Files can be created or edited from a development machine and then copied into place via FTP or remote network access by anyone with suitable security clearance. There is no need for the developer to be physically present at the server machine hosting the application in order to perform configuration chores, as was the case with classic ASP.

The configuration system is hierarchical. Each application inherits a baseline configuration from *machine.config*, located on the server. An optional *web.config* file, located in the same folder as *machine.config*, layers on top of that baseline configuration. The application-specific *web.config* files then apply successive configuration attributes and parameters as the application directory tree structure is traversed. This will be explained in detail in the next section, "Hierarchical Configuration." A corollary of the hierarchical nature of the system is that each application can have its own independent configuration. All applications do not need to share a server-wide configuration.

The configuration system is *extensible*. The baseline system provides configurability to a large number of standard program areas. In addition, you can add custom parameters, attributes, and section handlers as required by your application. This will be explained in detail later in this chapter.

You can modify the configuration of a running application without stopping and restarting either the application or the server. The changes automatically and immediately apply themselves to any *new* client requests. Any clients online at the time the changes are made will be unaware changes are being made, other than perhaps a slight delay for the first request made after the change is put in place.

The configuration settings for each unique URL are computed at application runtime, using all the hierarchical configuration files. These configuration settings are then cached so requests to each URL can retrieve the configuration settings in a performant manner. ASP.NET automatically detects if any configuration files anywhere in the hierarchy are modified and recomputes and recaches the configuration settings accordingly.

Configuration files are hidden from browser access. If a browser directly requests a configuration file in a URL, an HTTP access error 403 (forbidden) will be returned. This is the same behavior you would see if you tried to request the *global.asax* file directly from a browser.

Hierarchical Configuration

The configuration system is hierarchical. The file at the top of the hierarchy is called *machine.config*. This file is located in the subdirectory:

```
c:\Windows\Microsoft.NET\Framework\version number\CONFIG
```

where version number will be replaced with the version of the .NET runtime installed on your machine, such as v2.5.12215.

All the other configuration files are called *web.config*, of which there might be several. A machine-scoped *web.config* can be located in the same directory as *machine.config*, plus locally scoped versions can be found in virtual directories or subdirectories. These files are optional: if none are anywhere in an application virtual directory or its subdirectories, the configuration settings contained in *machine.config* or the machine-scoped *web.config* will apply to your application without any modifications.

Each directory and subdirectory contained in the application can have at most a single *web.config* file. The configuration settings contained in a specific instance of *web.config* apply to the directory in which it is contained and to all its child directories. If a specific instance of *web.config* contains a setting that is in conflict with a setting higher up in the configuration hierarchy (i.e., in a parent directory or *machine.config*), then the lower-level setting will override and apply to its own directory and all child subdirectories below it (unless, of course, any of those child subdirectories have their own copies of *web.config*, which will further override the settings).

For example, consider the directory structure shown in Figure 18-5. The virtual root of the web site is called *MyWebSite*, corresponding to the physical directory *c:\inetpub\wwwroot\MyWebSite*. Underneath the virtual root are two subdirectories, each of which has additional subdirectories. The URL for this web site would be *www.MyWebSite.com* (assuming that the domain name *MyWebSite.com* was registered to the IP address assigned to the server and the startup page was named *Default.aspx* or one of the other default document names specified in IIS, as will be described shortly).

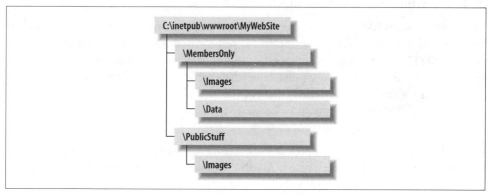

Figure 18-5. Hierarchical configuration

If there were no *web.config* files in any of these directories, then all the configuration would come directly from the globally scoped *web.config*. If that file was not present, it would come from *machine.config*. If there is a *web.config* in the directory *MyWebSite*, then any settings it contains will apply to the entire application (but only to that application), including all the subdirectories beneath it. If there were another version of *web.config* in the *MembersOnly* directory, then its configuration settings would apply to the *MembersOnly* directory and its subdirectories, but not to *PublicStuff*. If any of the settings in the *web.config* in *MembersOnly* conflicted with those in *machine.config* or the *web.config* in *MyWebSite*, the settings in *MembersOnly* would be in effect.

It is important to note that the hierarchical nature of the configuration files is based on application virtual directories. Refer again to Figure 18-5. The only virtual directory defined so far for that application is *MyWebSite*. However, suppose another virtual directory, *MyPublicWebSite*, were defined, corresponding to *c:\inetpub\wwwroot\ MyWebSite\PublicStuff*. The URL for this application might be *www.MyPublicWebSite. com*. This application would inherit the configuration settings from *machine.config* but not from *c:\inetpub\wwwroot\MyWebSite\web.config*. Though *c:\inetpub\wwwroot\ MyWebSite* is the physical parent directory of *c:\inetpub\wwwroot\MyWebSite\ PublicStuff*, it is not the virtual parent. In fact, *c:\inetpub\wwwroot\MyWebSite\ PublicStuff* is a virtual root and does not have a virtual parent. Configuration settings inherit from virtual parents and not physical parents.

Format

Most of the content of the application-specific configuration files, *web.config*, can be handled by the configuration tools, covered in the next two sections. However, it is often useful to be able to look at and edit a *web.config* file directly, and the tools provided by VB2005 do not modify *machine.config* at all (although the IIS Configuration page will edit the machine-scoped *web.config*). Therefore, it is worth examining the format requirements of these files.

The configuration files, *machine.config* and *web.config*, are XML files. As such they must be well-formed. (For a description of well-formed XML, see the sidebar "Well-Formed XHTML" in Chapter 3.) Specifically, these files consist of a nested hierarchy of XML tags. All opening tags must have the corresponding closing tag or be self-closing (with a trailing / character just inside the closing angle bracket). The tags must not overlap though tags may be nested. All tags may have attributes. All of these elements are case-sensitive.

Typically, tag and attribute names consist of one or more words run together. Tag and attribute names are camel-cased. Attribute values are *usually* Pascal-cased.

Camel-casing means that all the characters are lowercase, including the first character, except the first character of each run-on word after the first. Examples of camel-casing are `appSettings`, `configSections`, `section`, and `sessionState`.

Pascal-casing is the same as camel-casing except that the first character of the name is also uppercase. Examples of Pascal-casing are Sort-ByTime, InProc, and StateServer.

There are a couple of exceptions to these naming conventions:

- true and `false` are always lowercase.
- Literal strings do not adhere to either camel- or Pascal-casing. A database connection string may be specified as:

      SERVER=MyServer;DATABASE=Pubs;UID=sa;PWD=secret;

- If the value is the name of another tag in a configuration file, then it will be camel-cased.

The first line in the configuration file declares the file to be an XML file, with attributes specifying the version of the XML specification to which the file adheres and the character encoding used. Here is a typical XML declaration line:

    <?xml version="1.0" encoding="UTF-8" ?>

The character encoding specified here is UTF-8, which is a superset of ASCII. The character encoding parameter may be omitted if, and only if, the XML document is written in either UTF-8 or UTF-32. Therefore, if the XML file is written in pure ASCII, the encoding parameter may be omitted, though self-documentation is enhanced if the attribute is included.

The next line in the configuration files is the opening `<configuration>` tag:

    <configuration>

The entire contents of the configuration file, except the initial XML declaration, is contained between the opening `<configuration>` tag and the closing `</configuration>` tag, which comprise the `<configuration>` element.

Comments can be contained within the file using the standard XML (and HTML) format:

    <!-- Your comments here -->

Within the `<configuration>` element are two broad categories of entries. They are, in the order in which they appear in the configuration files:

- Configuration section handler declarations
- Configuration sections

Configuration section handler declarations

The handler declarations are contained between an opening <configSections> tag and a closing </configSections> tag. Each handler declaration specifies the name of a configuration section, contained elsewhere in the file, that provides specific configuration data. Each declaration also contains the name of the .NET class that will process the configuration data in that section.

 This terminology can be confusing. The first part of the file is enclosed in <configSections> tags but contains only a list of the configuration sections and their handlers and not the configuration sections themselves. And, as you will see shortly, the configuration sections are contained within tags, but there is no grouping tag to contain all the separate configuration sections, analogous to <configSections>.

The *machine.config* file contains, in the default installation, many configuration section handler declarations that cover the areas subject to configuration by default. Since this is an extensible system, you can also create your own. A typical entry containing a handler declaration is shown in Example 18-8.

Example 18-8. Typical configuration section handler declaration

```
<section name="compilation"
        type="System.Web.Configuration.CompilationSection,
            System.Web,
            Version=2.0.0.0,
            Culture=neutral,
            PublicKeyToken=b03f5f7f11d50a3a" />
```

 In the actual *machine.config* file, the contents of Example 18-8 were all contained in a single line. It is wrapped here for readability, as are many of the examples in this book.

Despite appearances to the contrary, the <section> tag has only two attributes: name and type. In Example 18-8, the name is compilation. This implies that somewhere else in the configuration file is a configuration section called compilation that will contain the actual configuration settings. These settings are name/value pairs to be used by the application(s). It will be described in detail shortly.

The type attribute has a lengthy parameter enclosed in quotation marks. This parameter contains the following:

- The class that will handle the named configuration section
- The assembly file (*dll*) that contains that class
- Version and culture information to coordinate with the assembly file
- A public-key token used to verify that the *dll* being called is secure

Each handler need only be declared once: in the base level *machine.config* file or in a *web.config* file further down the configuration hierarchy. The configuration section it refers to can then be specified as often as desired in other configuration files.

Example 18-9 shows a truncated version of the default *machine.config*.

Example 18-9. Truncated machine.config file

```
<?xml version="1.0" encoding="UTF-8"?>
<configuration>
  <configSections>
    <section name="appSettings"
             type="System.Configuration.AppSettingsSection,.../>
    <section name="connectionStrings"
             type="System.Configuration.ConnectionStringsSection,.../>
    <section name="mscorlib"
             type="System.Configuration.IgnoreSection,.../>

    <sectionGroup name="system.net"
                  type="System.Net.Configuration.NetSectionGroup,...>
      <section name="authenticationModules"
         type="System.Net.Configuration.AuthenticationModulesSection,.../>
      <section name="connectionManagement"
         type="System.Net.Configuration.ConnectionManagementSection,.../>
      <section name="defaultProxy"
         type="System.Net.Configuration.DefaultProxySection,.../>
      <sectionGroup name="mailSettings"
         type="System.Net.Configuration.MailSettingsSectionGroup,...>
        <section name="smtp"
                 type="System.Net.Configuration.SmtpSection,.../>
      </sectionGroup>
      <section name="requestCaching"
               type="System.Net.Configuration.RequestCachingSection,.../>
      <section name="settings"
               type="System.Net.Configuration.SettingsSection,.../>
      <section name="webRequestModules"
             type="System.Net.Configuration.WebRequestModulesSection,.../>
    </sectionGroup>

    <sectionGroup name="system.web"
            type="System.Web.Configuration.SystemWebSectionGroup,...>
      <section name="compilation"
               type="System.Web.Configuration.CompilationSection,.../>
      <section name="customErrors"
               type="System.Web.Configuration.CustomErrorsSection,.../>
      <sectionGroup name="caching"
           type="System.Web.Configuration.SystemWebCachingSectionGroup,...>
        <section name="cache"
                 type="System.Web.Configuration.CacheSection,.../>
        <section name="outputCache"
                 type="System.Web.Configuration.OutputCacheSection,.../>
      </sectionGroup>
    </sectionGroup>
  </configSections>
```

Example 18-9. Truncated machine.config file (continued)

```xml
  <runtime />

  <connectionStrings>
    <add name="LocalSqlServer"
      connectionString="data source=.\SQLEXPRESS;Integrated Security=SSPI;
                        AttachDBFilename=|DataDirectory|aspnetdb.mdf;
                        User Instance=true"
      providerName="System.Data.SqlClient" />
  </connectionStrings>

  <system.web>
    <processModel autoConfig="true" />
    <httpHandlers />
    <membership>
      <providers>
        <add name="AspNetSqlMembershipProvider"
             type="System.Web.Security.SqlMembershipProvider,.../>
      </providers>
    </membership>
    <profile>
      <providers>
        <add name="AspNetSqlProfileProvider"
             connectionStringName="LocalSqlServer"
             applicationName="/"
             type="System.Web.Profile.SqlProfileProvider,.../>
      </providers>
    </profile>
    <roleManager>
      <providers>
        <add name="AspNetSqlRoleProvider"
             connectionStringName="LocalSqlServer"
             applicationName="/"
             type="System.Web.Security.SqlRoleProvider,.../>
      </providers>
    </roleManager>
  </system.web>
</configuration>
```

Only a small subset of the entries in *machine.config* are included in Example 18-9. The type attribute of each entry has been edited to remove all but the class, and lines have been broken to enhance the readability.

In Example 18-9, you can see that many of the handler declarations are contained within <sectionGroup> tags. The name attribute of these tags corresponds to the namespace that contains the handlers. This groups together all the configuration sections that are handled out of the same namespace.

Configuration sections

The configuration sections contain the actual configuration data. Each are contained within tags corresponding to the name of the section specified in the configuration section handler declaration. Alternatively, a single self-closing tag can be used. For example, the following two configuration sections are equivalent:

```
<globalization requestEncoding="utf-8" responseEncoding="utf-8" />
```

and:

```
<globalization>
    requestEncoding="utf-8"
    responseEncoding="utf-8"
</globalization>
```

Configuration sections contain name/value pairs that hold the configuration data. They may also contain subsections.

machine.config contains one configuration section for each handler declaration. If the handler declaration was contained within a `<sectionGroup>` tag, then its corresponding configuration section will be contained within a tag containing the name of the `<sectionGroup>`. This can be seen in Example 18-9 for `system.web`.

The two configuration tools described in the next several sections provide an easy-to-use UI for editing and maintaining the configuration files. You can also edit any of them using any text editor, including Notepad.

The sections that follow provide a description of each of the configuration sections contained in the default *machine.config*. There are other configuration sections that are beyond the scope of this book, including `system.diagnostics`, `system.runtime.remoting`, and `system.windows.forms`.

Configuration Settings UI

Two configuration tools are provided: the ASP.NET Configuration Settings dialog box (described here), and the Web Site Administration Tool (described later in this chapter). The ASP.NET Configuration Settings dialog box is used to set configuration settings of web sites from within the IIS management window. You can get at this window as described in the section above on IIS Virtual Directories. Drill down to the Default Web Site.

Right-click on Default Web Site and select Properties to bring up the Default Web Site Properties dialog box, as shown in Figure 18-6 after selecting the ASP.NET tab.

Similarly, you can right-click on any virtual directory under Default Web Site and select Properties to get a dialog box nearly identical to that shown in Figure 18-6, this time pertaining only to that specific virtual directory.

There are two buttons in the Properties dialog shown in Figure 18-6: Edit Global Configuration and Edit Configuration. If the Properties dialog is for a specific virtual

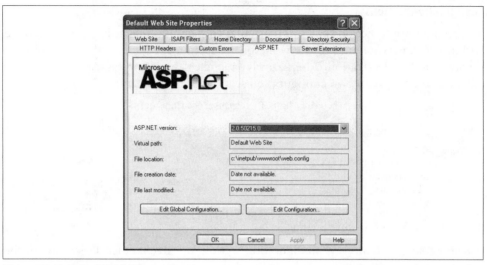

Figure 18-6. Default Web Site properties

directory, only the Edit Configuration button will be present. In any case, clicking one of the configuration buttons will bring up the Settings window shown in Figure 18-7.

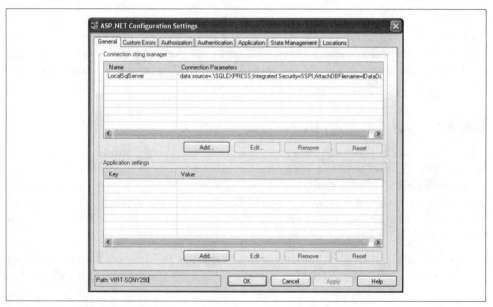

Figure 18-7. ASP.NET configuration settings

The box in the lower left of Figure 18-7 indicates the Path, or scope, to which this configuration applies. In Figure 18-7, it is the global configuration, because VIRT-

SONY290 is the name of the server. If you arrived at this window by editing the properties of the Default Web Site, the Path would be VIRT-SONY290/Default Web Site. If you were editing a specific virtual directory, the Path would be VIRT-SONY290/Default Web Site/VirtualDirectoryName.

The Path of the configuration will dictate where the settings are saved. In all cases, the settings will be saved to a *web.config* file. As mentioned above, configuration is hierarchical. The root of the hierarchy is *machine.config*, located in:

```
c:\Windows\Microsoft.NET\Framework\version number\CONFIG
```

However, this tool cannot be used to edit *machine.config*. That file can be edited manually in a text editor.

Configuration settings applied to the global configuration will be saved in the globally scoped *web.config* file located in the same directory as *machine.config*. Configuration settings applied to the Default Web Site will be saved in *c:\inetpub\wwwroot\web.config*. These settings will override equivalent settings in *machine.config* or a machine scoped *web.config*.

Configuration settings applied to a specific virtual directory will be saved to a *web.config* file located in the virtual directory. If that *web.config* does not exist, it will be created. If it exists, it will be modified. Any settings in this *web.config* will supersede settings higher in the hierarchy.

If a web app is created in VS2005 with the Location set to File System (the default), there will be no virtual directory automatically created. In this situation, you cannot edit the configuration using this tool unless you first manually create a virtual directory as described previously in this chapter.

Many of the configuration settings, including those on the General tab shown in Figure 18-7, consist of key/value pairs displayed in a grid. Clicking on the Add button below one of these grids brings up a dialog for entering a new key and associated value. The Edit button brings up the same dialog, filled in with the currently highlighted key/value pair, and the Remove button deletes a key/value pair.

The Apply button at the bottom of the dialog box will be disabled until any change is made. Clicking on the Apply button will apply the settings and allow you to continue working. Clicking on the OK button will apply the changes and dismiss the dialog box.

The sections that follow cover all of the settings accessible through this tool.

General

This tab, shown in Figure 18-7, allows editing of connection strings and application settings, discussed in the following two sections.

Connection strings. Connection strings are stored in the configuration file within a connectionStrings configuration section. The default setting, located in *machine.config*, looks like the following (wrapped for readability):

```
<connectionStrings>
    <add name="LocalSqlServer"
         connectionString=
            "data source=.\SQLEXPRESS;Integrated Security=SSPI;
             AttachDBFilename=|DataDirectory|aspnetdb.mdf;User Instance=true"
         providerName="System.Data.SqlClient" />
</connectionStrings>
```

Application Settings. The Application Settings grid allows you to store application-wide name/value pairs for read-only access. It is similar in function to application objects in the *global.asax* file.

This setting is saved within *web.config* files in an appSettings element.

 In versions of ASP.NET prior to 2.0, the appSettings section was handled by the NameValueSectionHandler class, which hinted at the underlying architecture. In Version 2.0, appSettings has a dedicated class, AppSettingsSection.

Example 18-10 shows a *web.config* file with an appSettings section added to provide two application-wide values. The appSettings section is not contained within any higher-level tag other than <configuration>.

Example 18-10. appSettings configuration section

```
<?xml version="1.0" encoding="utf-8"?>
<configuration
  xmlns="http://schemas.microsoft.com/.NetConfiguration/v2.0">
    <appSettings>
        <add key="appISBN" value="0-596-00487-7" />
        <add key="appTitle" value="Programming ASP.NET" />
    </appSettings>
</configuration>
```

These values can be accessed anywhere in the application to which this configuration is applicable (that is, its current directory and any child directories in which the value is not overridden by another *web.config* file). The code in Example 18-11 demonstrates retrieving the appSettings assigned in Example 18-10.

Example 18-11. Using appSettings

```
string strTitle = ConfigurationManager.AppSettings["appTitle"];
lblISBN.Text = ConfigurationManager.AppSettings["appISBN"];
```

ASP.NET 1.x retrieved appSettings with the AppSettings property of the ConfigurationSettings class. Though this class is still supported, it is deprecated and will cause a warning to be displayed by the compiler. It has been replaced with the ConfigurationManager class, used in Example 18-11.

Configuration settings are read by an application using the static AppSettings property of the ConfigurationManager class. This class provides methods and properties for reading configuration settings in an application's configuration files. It is part of the System.Configuration namespace, which is automatically imported into every ASP.NET application.

The AppSettings property of the ConfigurationManager class is of type NameValueCollection. It takes a key as a parameter and returns the value associated with that key.

Custom errors

Custom errors allow you to control what the user sees when an error occurs. The Custom Errors configuration page is shown in Figure 18-8, with the Custom error mode and Default redirect properties set and two custom errors.

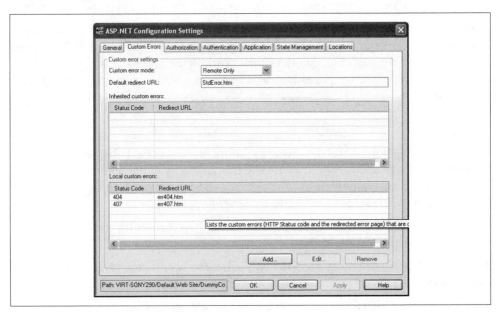

Figure 18-8. Custom error configuration

Setting the custom errors, as shown in Figure 18-8, will result in a <customErrors> configuration section in a *web.config* file listed in Example 18-12.

Example 18-12. <customErrors> configuration section

```
<customErrors defaultRedirect="StdError.htm">
   <error statusCode="404" redirect="err404.htm" />
   <error statusCode="407" redirect="err407.htm" />
</customErrors>
```

When custom errors are enabled, if an error occurs, the web page specified in defaultRedirect is presented to the client rather than the standard ASP.NET error page.

The Custom error mode drop-down sets the mode attribute that specifies how custom errors are enabled. There are three possible values for this mode, which are shown in Table 18-2.

Table 18-2. Values for the mode attribute of the <customErrors> tag

Value	Description
On	Custom errors are enabled for all users.
Off	Custom errors are disabled for all users.
RemoteOnly	Custom errors are shown only to remote clients, not to local clients. This setting allows developers to see the full error message provided by ASP.NET while showing end users the error page you wish them to see.

You can add multiple <error> tags to present specific error pages for specific errors.

In Example 18-12, error 404 will result in *err404.htm* being presented to the client, error 407 will result in *err407.htm*, and all other errors will result in *StdError.htm* being presented. In any case, the developer working on the local machine will see none of these custom error pages but rather will see the standard error page put up by ASP.NET.

Authorization

Authorization is how ASP.NET security controls access to URL resources. The Authorization page allows you to configure this access by either allowing or denying access based on any combination of user, role, and HTTP verb. This information is saved in an <authorization> element in *web.config*.

Clicking on the Add button on the Authorization page brings up the Edit Rule dialog box, as shown in Figure 18-9.

The <authorization> element supports two sub-elements, <allow> and <deny>, which correspond to the Rule Type radio buttons in Figure 18-9.

Both sub-elements have the same set of three attributes, controlling the Verb, the User, and the Roles. Each of these attributes, listed in Table 18-3 and accessible in

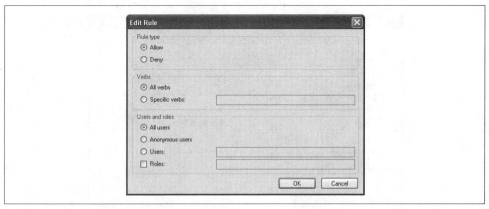

Figure 18-9. Authorization Edit Rule dialog box

the Edit Rule dialog, are used to define access rules that are iterated at runtime. Access for a particular user is allowed or denied based on the first rule found that fits that user.

Table 18-3. Attributes of the <allow> and <deny> subtags

Attribute	Description
users	Comma-separated list of users either allowed or denied access. Question mark (?) allows anonymous users. Asterisk (*) allows all users.
roles	Comma-separated list of roles that are allowed or denied access.
verbs	Comma-separated list of HTTP verbs that are allowed or denied access. Registered verbs are GET, HEAD, POST, and DEBUG.

The default <authorization> tag in *machine.config* is shown here. It allows all users:

```
<authorization>
    <allow users="*" />
</authorization>
```

Security is covered thoroughly in Chapter 12.

Authentication

As is described fully in Chapter 12, authentication is the process whereby ASP.NET security verifies that clients making a request are who they say they are. The Authentication settings page, shown in Figure 18-10, exposes the <authentication> element saved in *web.config*.

The <authentication> element has one attribute, mode, which specifies the default authentication mode for the application. There are four legal values for mode, available in the Authentication mode drop-down and shown in Table 18-4.

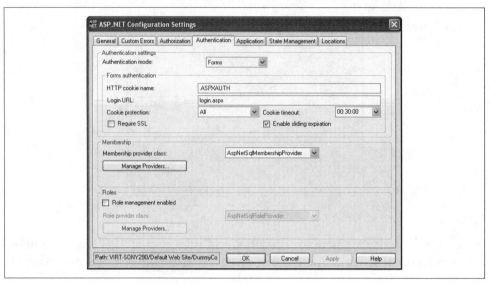

Figure 18-10. Authentication configuration page

Table 18-4. Values of the <authentication> tag's mode attribute

Mode value	Description
Windows	Sets the default authentication mode to Windows. Using this mode allows IIS to perform authentication. This is the default value of the mode attribute.
Forms	Sets the default authentication mode to Forms. Using this mode, your application controls authentication through a login form created as part of the application.
Passport	Sets the default authentication mode to Passport. Passport is a centralized authentication service offered by Microsoft.
None	No authentication will be performed. This means only anonymous users will access the site, or the application will provide its own authentication.

The <authentication> element also has two possible sub-elements. They are <forms> and <passport>. Here is a typical <authentication> element with a <forms> sub-element, as populated by the Authentication page of the configuration tool:

```
<authentication mode="Forms">
    <forms protection="Encryption" timeout="60" requireSSL="true" />
</authentication>
```

The <forms> element has seven attributes, which are set in the Authentication page with the controls in the Forms Authentication panel and listed in Table 18-5.

Table 18-5. Attributes of the <forms> tag

Attribute	Description
name	Specifies the name of the HTTP cookie used for authentication. The default name is *.ASPXAUTH.*
loginUrl	Will specify the URL to which the request is redirected if there is no valid authentication.
protection	Four legal values. All, the default and recommended value, specifies that the application use both data validation and encryption to protect the authentication cookie. None specifies that the cookies will be neither validated nor encrypted but will be available for personalization. Encryption specifies that the authentication cookie is encrypted but not validated. Validation specifies that the authentication cookie is validated (that is, it is verified as not having been altered in transit between the client and the server).
timeout	The integer number of minutes after the last request that the cookie expires. Does not apply to persistent cookies. If the cookie expires, then the user must re-authenticate. Default value is 30.
path	Specifies the path for cookies. Default value is / (backslash). Most browsers are case-sensitive and will not return a cookie if there is a path/case mismatch.
requireSSL	If true, then the page requires Secure Sockets Layer (SSL) be implemented to be viewed. The default is false.
slidingExpiration	If true, the default, the expiration time for a cookie, is reset every time a request is made involving that cookie.

The <forms> element also has one sub-element, <credentials>. This subtag allows you to specify the type of password encryption used and also to define name/password pairs within the <user> subtag.

The <credentials> element has a several attributes, the most important of which is passwordFormat (which cannot be set via the configuration pages). This attribute has three legal values, shown in Table 18-6.

Table 18-6. Values of the <credentials> tag's passwordFormat attribute

passwordFormat values	Description
Clear	Passwords are not encrypted.
MD5	Passwords are encrypted using the MD5 hash algorithm.
SHA1	Passwords are encrypted using the SHA1 hash algorithm.

The <credentials> element enables you to specify user/password pairs using the <user> sub-element. The <user> sub-element has two attributes: name and password. Their values are the username and password, respectively.

The <passport> sub-element of the <authentication> element has a single attribute, redirectUrl. The value of this attribute is the URL to redirect to if the page requires authentication and the user has not signed on with Passport.

The Membership and Roles panels on the Authentication page allow for adding, removing, and otherwise managing membership and role providers. The myriad details involved in doing so are beyond the scope of this book.

One useful set of attributes is available to providers of type `SqlMembershipProvider`, added within the `<membership>` element, that allows control over password requirements. These attributes must be manually added to the configuration file, as shown in the highlighted lines of code in the following snippet (which shows the default values from *machine.config*):

```
<membership>
  <providers>
    <add name="AspNetSqlMembershipProvider"
         type="System.Web.Security.SqlMembershipProvider"
         enablePasswordRetrieval="false"
         enablePasswordReset="true"
         requiresQuestionAndAnswer="true"
         requiresUniqueEmail="false"
         passwordFormat="Hashed"
         maxInvalidPasswordAttempts="5"
         passwordAttemptWindow="10"
         passwordStrengthRegularExpression="" />
  </providers>
</membership>
```

The attributes (properties of the `SqlMembershipProvider` class) available for this purpose are listed in Table 18-7.

Table 18-7. SqlMembershipProvider properties relating to password security

Value	Description
EnablePasswordReset	If `true` (the default), users will be allowed to reset their password.
EnablePasswordRetrieval	If `true`, users will be allowed to retrieve their password. The default is `false`.
MaxInvalidPasswordAttempts	Integer number of attempts allowed. Default is 5.
MinRequiredNonAlphanumericCharacters	Integer number of non-alphanumeric characters required in a password. Default is 1.
MinRequiredPasswordLength	Integer minimum number of characters required in a password. Default is 7.
PasswordAttemptWindow	Integer number of minutes in which a maximum number of failed login attempts may be made before the user is locked out. Default is 10.
PasswordFormat	The type of format used for storing passwords. Default is `Hashed`. Other values are `Clear` and `Encrypted`.
PasswordStrengthRegularExpression	Default is an empty string.
RequiresQuestionAndAnswer	If `true` (the default), the user will be required to answer a question for password reset and retrieval.
RequiresUniqueEmail	If `true`, each user name will have to have a unique email address. The default is `false`.

Security is covered thoroughly in Chapter 12.

Application

The Application configuration page, shown in Figure 18-11, allows you to set a number of parameters.

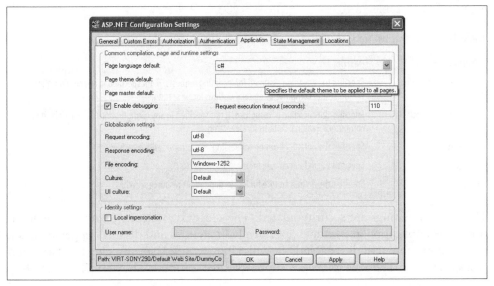

Figure 18-11. Application configuration page

The Page language default drop-down provides a choice of programming languages. The available choices are c#, vb, js, vj#, and c++. The selected value is saved in *web. config* as the defaultLanguage attribute of the <compilation> element. The default is vb (believe it or not).

The Page theme default and Page master default text boxes allow you to specify the default theme and master page, respectively. Themes are covered in Chapter 13 and master pages are covered in Chapter 11.

Both of these settings are saved in *web.config* as attributes of the <pages> element. The default theme is saved as the theme attribute and the default master page is saved as the masterPageFile attribute.

The Enable debugging checkbox dictates if debugging is enabled. The default is unchecked, (false). This is saved as the debug attribute of the <compilation> element.

The Request execution timeout textbox allows you to enter the number of seconds allowed before a request times out and is shut down. This is saved as the executionTimeout attribute of the <httpRuntime> element.

The following code snippet from a *web.config* file demonstrates all of these settings:

```
<pages masterPageFile="MyMaster.master" theme="MyTheme" />
<httpRuntime executionTimeout="99" />
<compilation language="c#" debug="true" />
```

The Globalization panel includes the attributes contained in the `<globalization>` element, listed in Table 18-8.

Table 18-8. <globalization> attributes

Attribute	Description
requestEncoding	Specifies the encoding assumed for incoming requests. If not specified in any configuration file, will default to computer's Regional Options locale setting.
responseEncoding	Specifies the encoding of responses. If not specified in any configuration file, will default to computer's Regional Options locale setting.
fileEncoding	Specifies the default encoding for parsing *.aspx*, *.asmx*, and *.asax* files.
culture	Specifies the default culture for incoming requests.
uiCulture	Specifies the default culture for locale-dependent resource searches.

The Identity settings are security-related. The `<identity>` element controls the identity of the application at runtime. Specifically, it enables and disables impersonation, and if impersonation is enabled, it will allow you to specify the `userName` and `password` to use. The `<identity>` tag supports three attributes shown in Table 18-9.

Table 18-9. <identity> attributes

Attribute	Description
impersonate	Set to `true` to enable impersonation or `false` to disable impersonation.
userName	If impersonation is enabled, will specify the username to use.
password	If impersonation is enabled, will specify the password to use.

<compilation>. In addition to the `defaultLanguage` and `debug` attributes mentioned above, the `<compilation>` element has a number of other attributes and sub-elements. Some of the more commonly used attributes are described in Table 18-10.

Table 18-10. <compilation> attributes

Attribute	Description
explicit	Available if the default language is VB2005. If set to `true`, this will be the equivalent of including the `Option Explicit On` statement in your page or web service.
batch	If `true`, will cause all the uncompiled files in a web site to be precompiled. This increases the execution delay when the app is started but eliminates any compilation delay after that. The default is `false`.
batchTimeout	The time-out period, in seconds, for batch compilation.
defaultLanguage	Programming language for the web site. Default is `vb`.
explicit	If the language is VB2005, will be equivalent to setting Option Explicit to on.

Table 18-10. <compilation> attributes (continued)

Attribute	Description
maxBatchSize	Specifies maximum number of pages per batched compilation.
maxBatchGeneratedFileSize	Specifies maximum size (in KB) of generated files per batched compilation.
tempDirectory	Specifies a directory to use for temporary file storage during compilation.

In addition to setting the language and debug mode, the <compilation> element can include several other child elements, listed in Table 18-11.

Table 18-11. <compliation> elements

Child element	Description
<compiler>	Used to specify compilers and what language extension maps with what compiler. It also specifies the class containing the code provider and version information.
<assemblies>	Specifies which assembly files are to be included when the project is compiled.
<codeSubDirectories>	Specifies subdirectories containing files to be compiled at runtime. The default value is App_Code though this value is not contained in any configuration file. Multiple directories can be specified. The order in which they are listed dictates the order in which the code is compiled.
<buildProviders>	Specifies build providers used to compile custom resource files.

<pages>. In addition to the master page and theme settings mentioned above, the <pages> element specifies many page options, such as buffering, session state, view state, and master page file path, for the pages under the control of the configuration file. The most important are listed in Table 18-12.

Table 18-12. <pages> attributes

Attribute	Description
autoEventWireup	If true (the default), the .NET Framework will call page events (Page_Init and Page_Load) automatically with no code necessary to explicitly add an event handler to an event delegate. If autoEventWireup is false, you will have to explicitly add event handler methods to the event delegates.
buffer	If true, response buffering will be used.
compilationMode	Valid values are Always (the default), Auto (ASP.NET will only compile if necessary), and Never.
enableSessionState	Specifies if session state is used for the page. Valid values are true (the default), false, and ReadOnly.
enableViewState	Specifies if view state is used for the page. Valid values are true (the default) and false.
enableViewStateMac	If true, an encrypted version of the view state called the message authentication code is included on postback to verify that the view state has not been tampered with. Default is false.

Table 18-12. <pages> attributes (continued)

Attribute	Description
maintainScrollPositionOnPostBack	If true, the position of the page will be maintained between postbacks to the server. Default is false.
masterPageFile	Specifies the name of the master page file for this page.
maxPageStateFieldLength	Specifies the maximum length of the view state hidden field, in bytes. If this value is exceeded, the field will be broken into chunks and sent separately. Default value is -1, which indicates no maximum size.
pageBaseType	Specifies a code-behind class inherited by the page.
smartNavigation	If true, Smart Navigation will be enabled. Requires IE 5.5 or higher. Default is false.
theme	Specifies the name of the page theme.
userControlBaseType	Specifies a code-behind class inherited by user controls.
validateRequest	If true (the default), ASP.NET will examine all browser input for potentially dangerous data. If found, an HttpRequestValidationException will be raised.

The <pages> element also provides two child elements, <namespaces> and <controls>, which cannot be edited through the configuration UI. The <namespaces> child element specifies namespaces referenced by default by the page. Namespaces added via the <namespaces> child element need not be explicitly referenced at compile time but are still accessible to the code. The default global *web.config* file includes the following <namespaces> child element:

```
<namespaces>
    <add namespace="System" />
    <add namespace="System.Collections" />
    <add namespace="System.Collections.Specialized" />
    <add namespace="System.Configuration" />
    <add namespace="System.Text" />
    <add namespace="System.Text.RegularExpressions" />
    <add namespace="System.Web" />
    <add namespace="System.Web.Caching" />
    <add namespace="System.Web.SessionState" />
    <add namespace="System.Web.Security" />
    <add namespace="System.Web.Profile" />
    <add namespace="System.Web.UI" />
    <add namespace="System.Web.UI.WebControls" />
    <add namespace="System.Web.UI.WebControls.WebParts" />
    <add namespace="System.Web.UI.HtmlControls" />
</namespaces>
```

The <controls> child element associates tagPrefixes with a namespace and assembly. The default global *web.config* file contains the following <controls> child element:

```
<controls>
    <add tagPrefix="asp"
        namespace="System.Web.UI.WebControls.WebParts"
```

```
                    assembly="System.Web, Version=2.0.0.0,
                    Culture=neutral, PublicKeyToken=b03f5f7f11d50a3a" />
    </controls>
```

httpRuntime. The <httpRuntime> element configures the ASP.NET HTTP runtime settings. There are many attributes available in this element, in addition to the executionTimeout attribute mentioned above. The most important are listed in Table 18-13.

Table 18-13. <httpRuntime> attributes

Attribute	Description
appRequestQueueLimit	Maximum number of requests queued waiting for a free thread. If an incoming request is rejected, then a "503 Server too busy" error will be returned.
enable	If true (the default), the AppDomain will accept requests. If false, the application is effectively turned off.
executionTimeout	Maximum number of seconds a request is allowed to execute before being shut down by ASP.NET.
maxRequestLength	Maximum file size for upload, in bytes. This can help prevent denial of service attacks by preventing clients from posting large files. The default is 4096 KB.
minFreeThreads	Minimum number of free threads for execution of new requests. These threads are available for requests that require additional threads.
minLocalRequestFreeThreads	Minimum number of free threads available for requests to localhost.
shutdownTimeOut	Idle time, in minutes, before the application is shut down. Default is 20 minutes.
useFullyQualifiedRedirectUrl	Specifies if client-side redirects are fully qualified, which is necessary for some mobile controls. Legal values are true, for fully qualified URLs, and false, for relative URLs.

State Management

The State Management configuration page, shown in Figure 18-12, allows you to configure session state. For a complete discussion of session state, see Chapter 6.

If the Session state mode is set to StateServer, then the State server settings panel will be enabled. If the Session state mode is set to SQLServer, the SQL Server settings panel will be enabled.

All of the properties on this page are saved in the <sessionState> element of *web.config*. This element supports the attributes listed in Table 18-14.

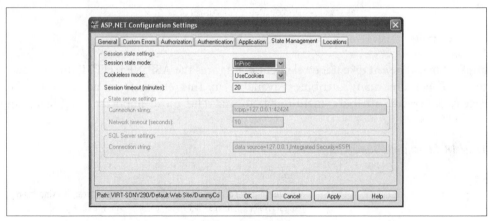

Figure 18-12. State Management configuration page

Table 18-14. <sessionState> attributes

Attribute	Description
mode	Specifies where the session state is stored. It has four legal values. Off disables session state. InProc, the default value, stores session state on the local server. StateServer stores session state in a remote process, which may be hosted either on the same computer or a remote server. SQLServer stores session state in a SQL Server database. One of the latter two values are required when running a web farm.
cookieless	Specifies whether cookieless sessions should be used. A value of true indicates that cookieless sessions should be used, in which case the session information will be munged as part of the URL. A value of false, the default, indicates that cookies will be used to maintain session state.
timeout	The number of minutes a session is idle before it is abandoned. The default is 20.
stateConnectionString	Specifies the connection string to the server where session is to be stored if mode is set to StateServer.
sqlConnectionString	Specifies the connection string to the SQL Server where session is to be stored if mode is set to SQLServer.

Locations

The Location configuration page, shown in Figure 18-13, is used to apply configuration settings to specific resources, such as individual web pages or contained subdirectories. After clicking on the Add button, you can add files or paths to the <location> element, which saves the information.

The <location> tag has several attributes, the most important of which is path. The path attribute specifies a file or child directory (relative to the location of the current *web.config* file) to which specific configuration settings apply.

Suppose you have an application with custom error pages specified in the *web.config* file in the application root directory. These custom error pages would apply to the entire application, including all child directories. Suppose further that two subdirectories are

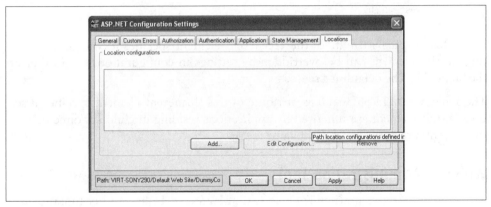

Figure 18-13. Location configuration page

under the application root directory, called *sub1* and *sub2*. *sub1* is to have the application-wide custom error handling, but *sub2* is to have its own specific error handling.

You could put another copy of *web.config* in *sub2* to override the custom error handling, but an alternative would be to use the <location> element. You would add the following lines to the *web.config* file in the application root:

```
<location path="sub2"
         allowOverride="true"
         inheritInChildApplications="true" >
   <system.web>
      <customErrors defaultRedirect="Sub2Error.htm" mode="RemoteOnly" >
         <error statusCode="404" redirect="err404-sub2.htm" />
         <error statusCode="407" redirect="err407-sub2.htm" />
      </customErrors >
   </system.web>
</location>
```

The <system.web> tag must be reproduced within the <location> element.

The configuration settings contained in a <location> element will apply to the directory specified in the path attribute and also to any child directories of that directory, unless they are further overridden either by another *web.config* file or another <location> element.

If you want to apply specific configuration settings to a single file, that too can be done using a <location> element. Suppose the application root had a web page that requires special error handling. The following <location> element will accomplish that:

```
<location path="SpecialPage.aspx" allowOverride="false">
    <system.web>
       <customErrors defaultRedirect="SpecialError.htm"
                    mode="RemoteOnly" >
          <error statusCode="404" redirect="err404-spcl.htm" />
       </customErrors >
```

```
        </system.web>
    </location>
```

The `allowOverride` attribute of the `<location>` element specifies if configuration settings in this element can be overridden by settings in configuration files further up the hierarchy. The default is `true`.

The `inheritInChildApplications` attribute of the `<location>` element specifies if settings in this element are inherited by applications residing in child subdirectories of the current directory. The default value is `true`.

Web Site Administration Tool

The Web Site Administration Tool, shown in Figure 18-14, is another tool provided to ease common configuration chores. As with the Configuration UI covered in the previous sections, this tool edits the *web.config* file. However, unlike the Configuration UI, the Web Site Administration Tool only edits the *web.config* file in the *current* application.

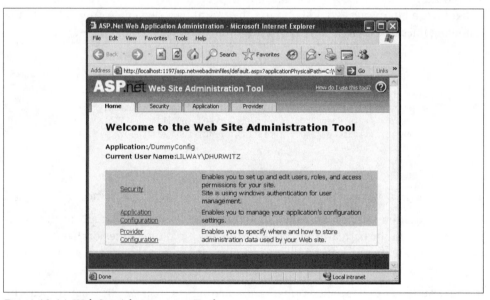

Figure 18-14. Web Site Administration Tool

In addition, some of the configuration data is stored in a SQL Server database file. As you will see, the type and location of that database file is configurable.

The Web Site Administration Tool is accessed from within VS2005 in two different ways: from the Website → ASP.NET Configuration menu item or from the ASP.NET Configuration icon (![icon]) at the top of the Solution Explorer.

In Figure 18-14, there are three tabs available in the Web Site Administration Tool: Security, Application, and Provider. Each will be covered in the following sections.

 When VS2005 is first installed on a machine, the Security tab will be available but will report a problem accessing the data store. You must first configure the SQL Server database file, which is used to store much of the security configuration information. Do this by going to the Provider tab in this tool, clicking on either of the links, and then clicking on the Test link for the provider you wish to initialize.

You can also configure this data file by running the *aspnet_regsql.exe* program from a command prompt.

Security

Clicking on either the Security tab or the Security link in the Web Site Administration Tool brings you to the Security page, as shown in Figure 18-15.

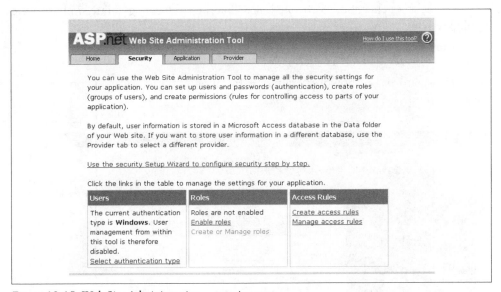

Figure 18-15. Web Site Administration—security page

The Security page offers two ways to configure security: a wizard and individual links. The wizard will walk you through setting up individual users, assigning roles or groups to those users, and defining access rules either for specific users or roles. Alternatively, you can perform all of these steps with the individual links on the page. Or you can use the wizard to get started and then maintain the settings with the individual links. You can also always manually edit the appropriate *web.config* file to configure the application.

The first page of the application is an introductory welcome page. The next page offers a choice of access method: "From the Internet" or "From a local area network."

These radio buttons have the effect of setting the Authentication mode, as was set in the IIS Configuration page, shown in Figure 18-10 with the values listed in Table 18-4. It adds a line similar to the highlighted line below to *web.config*:

```
<system.web>
    <authentication mode="Forms" />
```

The next page addresses the data store used to store users and roles. By default, this is a SQL Server database located in the *App_Data* directory under the application root. This wizard page does not actually give you the opportunity to change or configure the data store but suggests you exit the wizard and use the Provider Configuration tab to configure the data store.

The next wizard page offers a checkbox to enable roles for this web site. Roles are groups of users who share a common level of functionality. Some predefined roles include Administrators, Guests, Users, and Power Users. You can also define your own roles, such as Management, Developers, Sales, and so on.

If the Enable roles checkbox is checked, it will add to *web.config*: a line similar to the highlighted line below:

```
<system.web>
    <roleManager enabled="true" />
```

The next wizard page, shown in Figure 18-16, allows you to add your own roles to the application.

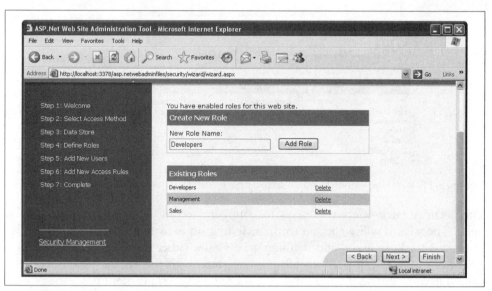

Figure 18-16. Security wizard—adding roles

The three roles shown in Figure 18-16 would not result in any lines being added to *web.config* since this configuration data is stored in the application data store, by default in the App_Data folder.

The next page, shown in Figure 18-17, allows you to create users for the application. For each user, you must fill in all the text boxes. After filling in the information and clicking on Create User, you will be able to cycle back through this page as many times as necessary to add additional users.

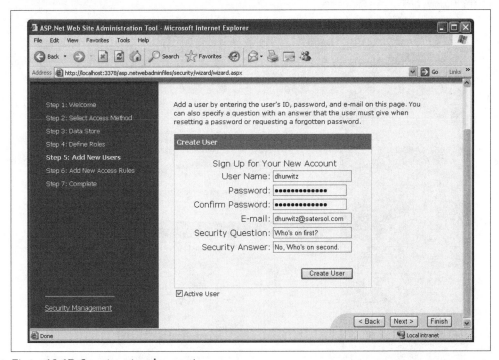

Figure 18-17. Security wizard—creating a user

You can only add users to the configuration if the Authentication mode is set to Forms, i.e., "From the internet," not if it is the default value of Windows, i.e., "From a local area network."

The default is to require *strong passwords* that conform to the following requirements (these requirements are configurable in *web.config*, as described above in the section on Authentication):

- At least seven characters
- Can contain alpha, numeric, or punctuation characters
- Case sensitive with at least one uppercase and one lowercase alpha character
- At least one punctuation mark

The wizard does not verify that the email is a valid email address, but it does require that it at least be in a valid email address format. The security question and answer is used to prompt the users if they forget their password.

The next page, shown in Figure 18-18, allows you to create access rules, exactly as described previously for the Authorization tab in the IIS configuration tool in Figure 18-9 and with the attributes listed in Table 18-3. In this screen shot, all users who are members of the Developers role will be allowed access to the root directory of the DummyConfig application.

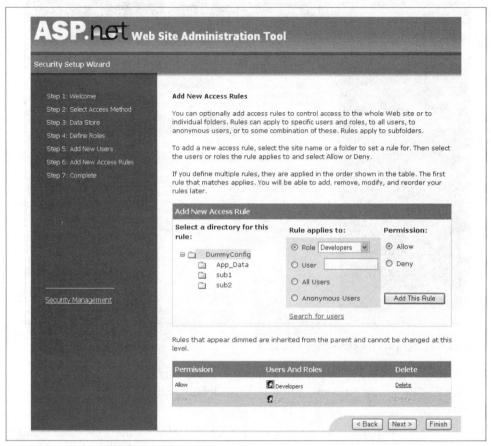

Figure 18-18. Security wizard—adding access rules

This would result in the following highlighted lines being added to *web.config*:

```
<system.web>
    <authorization>
        <allow roles="Developers" />
    </authorization>
```

The bottom half of the page shown in Figure 18-18 shows both the rules defined for this application, which you can delete, and the rules inherited from a parent configuration file, which cannot be edited or deleted from this page.

That completes the wizard. As you perform each step in the Security wizard, any necessary changes to the application database or to *web.config* are made immediately.

Clicking on the Security Management link at the bottom of the menu panel on the left of the wizard takes you back to the Security page shown in Figure 18-15.

The individual links on the Security page allow you to perform the same steps as the wizard in any sequence you prefer. In addition, by clicking on the Manage Users link, you can edit any user or role, as well as delete any user.

The two links under the Roles column allow you to enable or disable roles and to create or manage roles, i.e., to delete roles or add and remove users from roles.

Application

The Application tab of the Web Site Administration Tool brings up a page that looks like that shown in Figure 18-19.

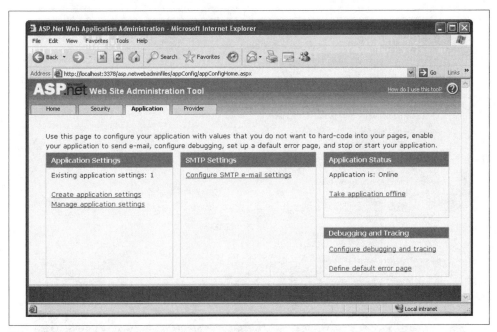

Figure 18-19. Web Site Administration—application page

The Application Settings column has two links for creating and managing application settings, described previously for the General page of the IIS configuration page and shown in Figure 18-7, with an example *web.config* listed in Example 18-10 and some lines of code that use the appSettings in Example 18-11.

The Configure SMTP e-mail settings link allows you to configure the SMTP mail server on the web server.

 In the Beta 2 version of VS2005, clicking on the Configure SMTP e-mail settings link displays an error page.

The link under Application Status allows you to toggle the online status of the application. Taking the application offline hides the web site from browser requests by adding the following highlighted line to *web.config*:

```
<system.web>
    <httpRuntime enable="false" />
```

The "Configure debugging and tracing" link brings up the page shown in Figure 18-20, which allows you to set various debugging and tracing parameters. This page adds the <trace> element to *web.config*.

Figure 18-20. Web site administration—debugging and tracing

The <trace> element configures the ASP.NET trace service. Chapter 7 describes tracing fully. The <trace> element supports the attributes shown in Table 18-15.

Table 18-15. <trace> attributes

Attribute	Description
enabled	Enables or disables tracing. Legal values are `true` or `false`. The default is `false`.
requestLimit	The number of trace requests to store on the server.
pageOutput	`true` specifies that trace output is appended to each page. `false` (the default) specifies that trace output is accessible only through the trace utility.
traceMode	Specifies the sort order of the trace display. `SortByTime`, the default value, specifies that trace information is sorted in the order processed. `SortByCategory` specifies that trace information is displayed alphabetically by user-defined category.
localOnly	If `true` (the default), will specify the trace viewer is available only on the host web server. `false` specifies that the trace viewer is available remotely.

The typical <trace> element might look something like the following:

```
<trace
    enabled="false"
    localOnly="true"
    pageOutput="false"
    requestLimit="10"
    traceMode="SortByTime"
/>
```

The "Define custom error pages" link duplicates the functionality described previously on the Custom Errors page of the IIS configuration tool, shown in Figure 18-8.

Provider

A provider is a class that manages data storage for the different features of ASP.NET, such as users and roles. The Provider tab provides two links: one for selecting a single provider for all site management data and one for selecting a different provider for each feature.

The provider classes available are specified in one of the configuration files. The providers provided as part of ASP.NET for all applications are specified in the following lines of *machine.config* (wrapped and truncated to enhance readability):

```
<system.web>
  <membership>
    <providers>
      <add name="AspNetSqlMembershipProvider"
          type="System.Web.Security.SqlMembershipProvider, ..."
          connectionStringName="LocalSqlServer"
          enablePasswordRetrieval="false" enablePasswordReset="true"
          requiresQuestionAndAnswer="true" applicationName="/"
          requiresUniqueEmail="false" passwordFormat="Hashed"
          maxInvalidPasswordAttempts="5" passwordAttemptWindow="10"
          passwordStrengthRegularExpression="" />
    </providers>
  </membership>
  <profile>
```

```
        <providers>
          <add name="AspNetSqlProfileProvider"
               connectionStringName="LocalSqlServer" applicationName="/"
               type="System.Web.Profile.SqlProfileProvider, ... />
        </providers>
      </profile>
      <roleManager>
        <providers>
          <add name="AspNetSqlRoleProvider"
               connectionStringName="LocalSqlServer"
               applicationName="/"
               type="System.Web.Security.SqlRoleProvider, ... />
          <add name="AspNetWindowsTokenRoleProvider"
               applicationName="/"
               type="System.Web.Security.WindowsTokenRoleProvider, ... />
        </providers>
      </roleManager>
    </system.web>
```

Other Configuration Settings

In addition to all the configuration settings described so far in this chapter, many other configuration sections are available in the configuration files. To use these settings, you must manually edit the relevant file, either *machine.config* or the appropriate *web.config*, as described in the section on Hierarchical Configuration. These configuration sections are described next.

system.net

The system.net configuration section, defined in *machine.config*, contains subsections that deal with networking. These subsections include authenticationModules, defaultProxy, connectionManagement, and webRequestModules. These subsections are not used by ASP.NET developers and are outside the scope of this book.

system.web

The system.web configuration section contains subsections that configure ASP.NET. Each of these subsections, not covered elsewhere in this chapter, will be described briefly in the following sections.

browserCaps. This subsection contains information about the capabilities of all the web browsers and operating systems your clients are likely to use. This information includes such items as the name of the browser; its major and minor version numbers; whether it supports frames, tables, cookies, cascading style sheets, VBScript, JavaScript, Java applets; and so on.

As new browser versions come on the market, you can update the information contained in this section by visiting *www.cyscape.com/browsercaps/*.

---

httpHandlers. This subsection maps incoming requests to a class that implements the `IHttpHandler` or `IHttpHandlerFactory` interfaces. There is a fairly extensive mapping in the default machine level *web.config* file, which maps standard file types to a specific class (for example, all *.aspx* requests are mapped to the `PageHandlerFactory` class).

The `<httpHandlers>` tag has several sub-elements:

`<add>`

Specifies the mapping. A typical `<add>` sub-element looks like this:

```
<add verb="*"
     path="*.cs"
     type="System.Web.HttpForbiddenHandler"
     validate="True"/>
```

The `verb` attribute can contain a comma-separated list of HTTP verbs, such as `GET`, `PUT`, or `POST`, or contain the wildcard character (*). The `path` attribute can contain either a single URL path or a wildcard string. The `type` attribute is a class name. ASP.NET first searches for the specified class in the *bin* directory, then in the global assembly cache. (See the next chapter for a description of the global assembly cache.)

`<remove>`

Removes a previously added mapping. It has the same syntax as the `<add>` sub-element, except there is no type attribute.

`<clear>`

Clears all currently configured or inherited mappings. It has no attributes.

httpModules. This subsection configures the HTTP modules within an application. Each `<add>` sub-element within the subsection assigns a class to a module. The default machine level *web.config* file includes the modules and their classes shown in Table 18-16.

Table 18-16. Modules and classes defined in the httpModules subsection

Module	Class
OutputCache	System.Web.Caching.OutputCacheModule
Session	System.Web.SessionState.SessionStateModule
WindowsAuthentication	System.Web.Security.WindowsAuthenticationModule
FormsAuthentication	System.Web.Security.FormsAuthenticationModule
PassportAuthentication	System.Web.Security.PassportAuthenticationModule
UrlAuthorization	System.Web.Security.UrlAuthorizationModule
FileAuthorization	System.Web.Security.FileAuthorizationModule
AnonymousIdentification	System.Web.Security.AnonymousIdentificationModule
Profile	System.Web.Profile.ProfileModule

processModel. This element configures the process model settings on an IIS web server. The most commonly used attributes of the `<processModel>` element are listed in Table 18-17. Many of these attributes are related to improving the robustness of the ASP.NET run-time environment, hardware utilization, or security.

Table 18-17. <processModel> attributes

Attribute	Description
comAuthenticationLevel	Specifies level of authentication for DCOM security.
comImpersonationLevel	Specifies type of impersonation for DCOM security.
cpuMask	Specifies which processors on a multiprocessor machine can run ASP.NET processes. Works in conjunction with the webGarden attribute.
enable	If true (the default), the process model will be enabled.
idleTimeout	Specifies a time period of inactivity, in the format hr:min:sec, after which the worker process is ended. The default is Infinite.
logLevel	Specifies whether to log All events, None, or Errors.
maxWorkerThreads	Integer between 5 and 100 specifying the maximum number of worker threads per process per CPU. The default is 20.
maxIoThreads	Integer between 5 and 100 specifying the maximum number of I/O threads per process per CPU. The default is 20.
memoryLimit	Maximum amount of memory, as a percentage of total system memory, that can be consumed by a worker process before a new process is spawned. The default is 60 percent.
password	Specifies, in conjunction with the userName attribute, the credentials used to run the worker process.
pingFrequency	Specifies the time interval, in the format hr:min:sec, between pings to the worker process. If the process does not return the ping, it will be restarted. The default is 30 seconds.
pingTimeout	Specifies the time interval of process inactivity after a ping, in the format hr:min:sec,. If the process does respond within the specified time, it will be restarted. The default is 5 seconds.
requestLimit	Number of requests before a new worker process is automatically launched to replace the current process. The default is Infinite.
requestQueueLimit	Number of requests allowed in the queue before the server returns 503-Server Too Busy. The default is 5000.
responseDeadlockInterval	Specifies the time interval, in the format hr:min:sec, after which the process will be restarted if there are queued requests and there have been no responses. The default is 3 minutes.
timeout	Specifies the number of minutes after which a new worker process is started to replace the current process. The default is Infinite.
userName	Specifies, in conjunction with the password attribute, the credentials used to run the worker process.
webGarden	If true, the cpuMask attribute will be used to specify which CPUs are available. The default is false.

For a detailed description of each of these attributes, consult the SDK documentation. These settings are ignored if you are using IIS 6, which has its own process model settings.

webControls. The `<webControls>` element specifies the location of the script that is generated to be run client-side. It supports a single attribute, `clientScriptsLocation`.

The default `<webControls>` element in the machine level *web.config* is shown here:

```
<webControls
    clientScriptsLocation="/aspnet_client/{0}/{1}/"
/>
```

machineKey. The `<machineKey>` element configures keys used for encryption and decryption of view state and authentication cookies. This section can be declared at the server level or in *web.config* files at the application root level. The `<machineKey>` tag supports three attributes, which are shown in Table 18-18. It is particularly useful in web farm environments, where every server in the farm must use the same key value for state to be properly retrieved.

Table 18-18. <machineKey> attributes

Attribute	Description
validationKey	Specifies the key used for validation. Supports two types of values: AutoGenerate, the default value, specifies that ASP.NET will generate a random key. The other type of value can be manually set to allow operation across a web farm. This value must be between 40 and 128 hexadecimal characters long (between 20 and 64 bytes).
decryptionKey	Specifies the key used for decrypting the cookie. Uses the same values as the validationKey.
validation	Specifies the type of encryption used for data validation. There are three legal values: SHA1 specifies SHA1 encryption, MD5 specifies MD5 encryption, and 3DES specifies Triple-DES encryption.

securityPolicy. The `<securityPolicy>` element maps named security levels to policy files. This section can be declared at the server level or in *web.config* files at the application root level.

The `<securityPolicy>` tag supports one child element, `<trustLevel>`. This child element is used to specify one security-level name and an associated policy level. There is a separate `<trustLevel>` tag for each named security level.

The `<trustLevel>` tag supports the two attributes shown in Table 18-19.

Table 18-19. <trustLevel> attributes

Attribute	Description
name	Defines a name to associate with the specified level of trust. Legal values are Full, High, Low, and None. If set to None, will indicate file mapping for the Full security level.
policyFile	Specifies the policy level, relative to the directory containing *machine.config*, associated with the specified level of trust.

The default <securityPolicy> in the machine level *web.config* is shown here:

```
<securityPolicy>
  <trustLevel name="Full" policyFile="internal" />
  <trustLevel name="High" policyFile="web_hightrust.config" />
  <trustLevel name="Medium" policyFile="web_mediumtrust.config" />
  <trustLevel name="Low"  policyFile="web_lowtrust.config" />
  <trustLevel name="Minimal" policyFile="web_minimaltrust.config" />
</securityPolicy>
```

trust. The <trust> tag configures the code access security permissions for an application. This section can be declared at the server level or in *web.config* files at the application root level.

The <trust> tag supports the two attributes shown in Table 18-20.

Table 18-20. <trust> attributes

Attribute	Description
level	Specifies the security level under which the application will be run. Legal values are Full, High, Low, and None. Required.
originalUrl	Specifies an application's URL of origin. Optional.

The default <trust> in the machine level *web.config* is shown here:

```
<trust level="Full" originUrl="" />
```

Custom Configuration Sections

In addition to all the predefined configuration sections, you can also add your own custom configuration sections. You might wish to add two different types of custom configuration sections:

- Sections that provide access to a collection of name/value pairs, similar to appSettings
- Sections that return any type of object

Both will be demonstrated here.

Name/value pairs

Back in Example 18-10, you added an <appSettings> element to store strings containing an ISBN number and a title. Suppose you wanted to store connection strings for multiple databases, say one called Test (for testing purposes) and one called Content (to hold the production content). A custom configuration section returning a name/value pair would be one way to handle this situation.

The finished version of lines of code inserted into *web.config* is shown in Example 18-13. There are three steps to adding a custom configuration section that returns a name/value pair:

1. Determine which specific configuration file to add the custom section to. This will determine the scope, or visibility, of the custom section, as described in the section on Hierarchical Configuration.

   Adding the section to *machine.config* or the machine-level *web.config* will make it available to every application on that machine. Adding it to a *web.config* file in the Default Web Site, *c:\inetpub\wwwroot*, will make it available to every web site under the default web site. Adding it to a *web.config* file in the application root will make the section visible to that entire application but to no other applications. Adding it to a *web.config* file in an application subdirectory will make it visible only to that subdirectory and its child subdirectories.

2. Declare the section handler by adding a line to the `<configSections>` section of the designated configuration file. This tells ASP.NET to expect a configuration section with the specified name and which class and assembly file to use to process the section.

   Add the highlighted lines between the `<configSections>` tags in Example 18-13 to the designated configuration file. If the file you are editing does not have a pair of `<configSections>` tags, you will need to add those as well. The `<configSections>` element should be the first child of the root `<configuration>` element.

3. Add the custom section itself to the configuration file. This consists of the highlighted lines in Example 18-13 between the `<altDB>` tags. This custom configuration section contains two entries, one named Test and the other named Content, each with its own value attribute.

Example 18-13. Custom sections in web.config

```
<configSections>
   <section name="altDB"
            type="System.Configuration.DictionarySectionHandler,
                 System, Version=2.0.0.0, Culture=neutral,
                 PublicKeyToken=b77a5c561934e089" />
</configSections>

<altDB>
   <add key="Test"
        value=" SERVER=Zeus;DATABASE=Test;UID=sa;PWD=secret;" />
   <add key="Content"
        value=" SERVER=Zeus;DATABASE=Content;UID=sa;PWD=secret;" />
</altDB>
```

The type in the <section> element specifies the DictionarySectionHandler class in the *System.dll* assembly file. For further documentation, check SDK documentation, search on "Custom Elements" and choose "Custom Element for NameValueSectionHandler."

To read the contents of this custom configuration section, you again use a method from the ConfigurationManager class, this time the GetSection method. The code for doing this is highlighted in Example 18-14, which assumes that the content page has two labels named lblTest and lblContent. Notice the using statement referencing the System.Collections namespace at the top of the code-behind file. This is necessary to allow use of the Hashtable object without having to code a fully qualified name.

Example 18-14. Reading custom configuration values

```
using System.Collections;      // necessary for Hashtable

    protected void Page_Load(object sender, EventArgs e)
    {
       if (!IsPostBack)
       {
          string strTest;
          strTest = ((Hashtable)ConfigurationManager.
                            GetSection("altDB"))["Test"].ToString( );
          lblTest.Text = strTest;

          lblContent.Text = ((Hashtable)ConfigurationManager.
                            GetSection("altDB"))["Content"].ToString( );
       }
    }
```

The code in Example 18-14 shows two equivalent ways of displaying the contents of the key value. One way is to assign the value to a string and then assign the string to the Text property of a label. The other way is to assign the value directly to the Text property. Though the latter technique is more concise, the former is often easier to debug.

The GetSection method takes a configuration section name as a parameter and returns an object of type Hashtable. The desired value in the collection is retrieved by using the key as an offset into the collection, using the get property syntax. In C#, the property is retrieved using square brackets.

The C# code first casts, or converts, the value returned by GetSection to type Hashtable since C# does not support late binding. In addition, the value returned is of type object, so it must be converted to a string using the static ToString method.

Objects

appSettings and custom configuration sections are very useful. However, they suffer from the same limitation of only being able to return a name/value pair. Sometimes, it would be useful to return an object.

For example, suppose you have a standard query into a database. You could store the query string in an appSettings tag and then open a database connection after retrieving the string. However, it would be more convenient to store the query string in *web.config* and then have the configuration system return a DataSet directly.

To do this, you must add a <section> tag and a configuration section to the designated configuration file as with the custom section returning name/value pairs, described in the previous section.

Edit the *web.config* file used in the previous example and shown in Example 18-14, adding the lines of code highlighted in Example 18-15.

Example 18-15. Custom sections returning objects in web.config

```
<?xml version="1.0" encoding="utf-8" ?>
<configuration>

   <configSections>
      <section name="altDB"
            type="System.Configuration.NameValueSectionHandler, System" />
      <sectionGroup name="system.web">
         <section name="DataSetSectionHandler"
                  type="DataSetSectionHandler,SectionHandlers" />
         </section>
      </sectionGroup>
   </configSections>

   <altDB>
      <add key="Test"
           value=" SERVER=Zeus;DATABASE=Test;UID=sa;PWD=secret;" />
      <add key="Content"
           value=" SERVER=Zeus;DATABASE=Content;UID=sa;PWD=secret;" />
   </altDB>

  <system.web>
  .
  .
  .

     <!-- Custom config section returning an object -->
     <DataSetSectionHandler
         str="Select CompanyName,ContactName,City from Customers"  />
  .
  .
  .

  </system.web>
</configuration>
```

In the <sectionGroup> child element within the <configSections> element, a handler declaration is created for the DataSetSectionHandler within the system.web group. This specifies that elsewhere within the file, there will be a custom configuration section called DataSetSectionHandler within the system.web element. Furthermore, it specifies that the class that will handle the configuration section is called DataSetSectionHandler, and the class will be found in an assembly file called *SectionHandlers.dll* located in the *bin* directory.

Further down in the file, within the `<system.web>` section, there is a section called `DataSetSectionHandler`. It has a single attribute, `str`. This is a string containing the SQL statement you wish to pass to the database.

Next you must create the `DataSetSectionHandler` class and place it in a file called *SectionHandler.cs*. To do this in VS2005, right-click on the application root in the Solution Explorer. Select Add New Item. Select a new Class and name the file *SectionHandlers.cs*. Add the highlighted code from Example 18-16.

Example 18-16. SectionHandler.cs

```
using System;
using System.Data;
using System.Data.SqlClient;        //  necessary for data access
using System.Configuration;
using System.Web;
using System.Web.Security;
using System.Web.UI;
using System.Web.UI.WebControls;
using System.Web.UI.WebControls.WebParts;
using System.Web.UI.HtmlControls;

public class DataSetSectionHandler : IConfigurationSectionHandler
{
   public Object Create(Object parent,
                        Object configContext,
                        System.Xml.XmlNode section)
   {
      string strSql;
      strSql = section.Attributes.Item(0).Value;

      string connectionString = "server=MyServer; uid=MyID; " +
                  "pwd=secret; database=Northwind";

      // create the data set command object and the DataSet
      SqlDataAdapter da = new SqlDataAdapter(strSql,
                        connectionString);

      DataSet dsData = new DataSet( );

      // fill the data set object
      da.Fill(dsData, "Customers");

      return dsData;
   }
}
```

The name of the class has been changed to `DataSetSectionHandler` to match the class name used in the *web.config* listed in Example 18-15. This class inherits from `IConfigurationSectionHandler`.

Set the connection string to match your specific database. The server name and password are certainly different than that shown in Example 18-16.

The database aspects of the code in this example are covered thoroughly in Chapters 9 and 10.

For a class to be used as a configuration section handler, it must be derived from the `IConfigurationSectionHandler` interface. In C#, this is indicated by a colon between the class or method name and the class or interface being inherited.

A full discussion of object-oriented concepts such as inheritance, base classes, and interfaces is beyond the scope of this book. For now, you should just know that an interface acts as a contract that the implementing class must fulfill. The interface may, for example, dictate the signature of methods that the implementing class must implement, or it may dictate which properties the class must provide.

The `IConfigurationSectionHandler` interface has only one method, `Create`. Therefore, our implementing class must implement the `Create` method with the specified signature. The three parameters are dictated by the interface. The first two parameters are rarely used and will not be further discussed here. The third parameter is the XML data from the configuration file.

The XML node is parsed, and the value of the first item in the Attributes collection is assigned to a string variable in this line:

```
strSql = section.Attributes.Item(0).Value
```

Once the SQL string is in hand, the connection string is hard-coded, a `SqlDataAdapter` object is instantiated and executed, and the `DataSet` is filled and then returned.

Before this class can be used, it must be compiled and placed in the application assembly cache located in the *bin* directory under the application root.

The assembly referenced in the type attribute of the <section> tag must be precompiled and available to the application. You cannot just put the source code for the class into the *App_Code* directory and have it automatically compiled at runtime, as is the normal practice, since the name of the assembly is required at compile time and not just its contents.

Open a command prompt by clicking Start → Microsoft Visual Studio 2005 → Visual Studio Tools → Visual Studio 2005 Command Prompt. Use the cd command to make the application root the current directory. This assumes that the application root directory already has a child directory called *bin*. If not, you'll have to make one. Then enter the following command line (all on one line):

```
csc /t:library /out:bin\SectionHandlers.dll
        /r:system.dll,System.data.dll,System.xml.dll SectionHandlers.cs
```

The target type of output is set to be library, i.e., a *dll*. The name of the output file to be placed in the *bin* directory will be *SectionHandlers.dll*. Three *dll* files are referenced. The input source file is *SectionHandler.cs*. When the source file is compiled, you will have the output *dll* in the *bin* directory, where the classes it contains will automatically be available to the application.

A typical way to utilize this custom configuration section would be to have a GridView on a page which databinds to the dataset returned by this section. Assuming the GridView control was named gv, the code listed in Example 18-17 would retrieve the dataset and bind the control.

Example 18-17. Code-behind for retrieving custom configuration object

```
protected void Page_Load(object sender, EventArgs e)
{
   if (!IsPostBack)
   {
      CreateGrid();
   }
}

private void CreateGrid()
{
   DataSet dsGrid = new DataSet();
   dsGrid = (DataSet)ConfigurationManager.
                      GetSection("system.web/DataSetSectionHandler");
   gv.DataSource = dsGrid.Tables[0];
   gv.DataBind();
}
```

The interesting work in Example 18-17 is done in the CreateGrid method. Rather than supply connection information and a SQL query string, a call is made to the GetSection method of the ConfigurationManager class, which returns a DataSet object directly. Then the DataSet object is set as the DataSource of the GridView control, and the control is data bound. The parameter of the GetSection method is a string containing the name of the section containing the configuration settings. The syntax with the section name (system.web) is separated from the subsection name (DataSetSectionHandler) by a slash.

CHAPTER 19

Deployment

Perhaps the single greatest improvement that .NET has made over previous generations of development environments, especially compared to classic ASP, is in the area of deployment, for the following reasons:

- Source code files need only be located in a specific directory (*App_Code*) to be automatically compiled and available.

- Precompiled *dll* files only have to be located in a specific directory (*bin*) to be visible to an application.

- You don't need to register objects, either in the Registry or elsewhere, for an application to use the contents of a *dll*. Installation does not require any registering of components with *regsrvr32* or any other utility, though globally available components may be placed in the Global Assembly Cache.

- Web sites can be deployed with installer files (*.msi*) or using XCOPY.

- Web sites can be updated without stopping the web server or the application.

- There are no versioning issues with conflicting *dll* files.

All of this will be described in this chapter. In the meantime, shout it from the rooftops: *No more DLL hell!*

ASP.NET derives all this deployment bliss by virtue of being part of the .NET Framework. These deployment features are common to all applications developed under the .NET Framework.

Understand that with all the different deployment scenarios, the fundamental requirement is that you are deploying the web application to a web server (or to servers in the case of a web farm,) which is running IIS, as described in the previous chapter. Even if you developed the app in VS2005 using a File System location on a machine without IIS installed, you must deploy to a virtual directory on a server running IIS if you want your site to be visible to other users.

There are two broad categories of deployment: local and global. With local deployment, the entire application is self-contained within a virtual directory. All of the content and assemblies (described shortly) that make up the application are contained within the virtual directory and are available to this single application. With global deployment, assemblies are made available to every application running on the server.

Within the category of local deployment, there are several scenarios available:

Automatic runtime compilation of all content and code
This provides the most convenience and flexibility but provides the least security and slowest performance on first load. It is the default model used by VS2005.

Manual pre-compilation of assemblies
Assemblies are compiled and then placed in the application assembly cache, described below. This was the method used with ASP.NET Version 1.x and is still fully supported. It provides better performance the first time the assembly is called than automatic runtime compilation.

Full pre-compilation of all content and code
This provides the best performance and security at the expense of convenience and flexibility.

Pre-compilation of all code only
The content files are not pre-compiled, and remain available for update after deployment. This provides nearly the performance of full pre-compilation, but retains the ability to modify the content files after deployment, without a full redeploy.

Finally, two different techniques are available for deployment: XCOPY and Microsoft Installer. Your choice of which method to use will be driven by the requirements of your situation. All of this will be described, with pros and cons of each, later in this chapter. First, we will digress a bit to discuss assemblies, which are fundamental to the whole issue of deployment.

Assemblies

An *assembly* is the .NET unit of versioning and deploying code modules. An assembly consists of Portable Executable (PE) files. PE files can be either dynamic link library (*dll*) files or *exe* files. These PE files are in the same format as normal Windows PE files.

Assemblies contain versioning information. An assembly is the minimum unit for a single version of a piece of code. Multiple versions of the same code can run side-by-side in different applications, with no conflicts, by packaging the different versions into separate assemblies, and specifying in the configuration files which version is current.

Assemblies are *self-describing* because they contain *metadata* that fully describes the assembly and the classes, methods, and types it contains. One of the files in the assembly contains a *manifest* as part of the metadata, which details exactly what is in the assembly. This includes identification information (e.g., name, version), a list of the types and resources in the assembly, a map to connect public types with the implementing code, and a list of other assemblies referenced by this assembly.

A web application consists of all the files and resources in an application's virtual root directory and its subdirectories. One standard subdirectory is the *bin* directory, sometimes called the *application assembly cache*. Any assemblies placed in this directory are considered *private assemblies,* and are automatically made available to the application.

Another standard subdirectory is *App_Code*. Any source code placed in this folder is automatically compiled at runtime, and the resulting private assembly is added to the application assembly cache (though it is not physically copied to the *bin* directory). The physical location of the assembly files is unimportant since the CLR handles all aspects of managing these assemblies. It just works.

If an assembly file is placed in the application assembly cache, then all the classes contained in that assembly are automatically registered with the application. There is no developer or user action required for this registration to occur. Any class, method, or type defined in any assembly cache, either application or global (described below), is available to the rest of the application, subject to the access modifiers: private, protected, internal, and internal protected.

ASP.NET is configured to prohibit access to the *bin* and *App_Code* subdirectories. This prevents anyone from examining or tampering with your source code or assemblies.

Assemblies are not loaded into memory unless and until they are needed. When an assembly is needed, the CLR does not load the assembly itself into memory. If it did, that assembly would be locked until the application was stopped. This would require the application to be stopped and restarted every time a new version of the assembly was to be installed. Instead, a *shadow copy* of the *dll* is created in memory. This shadow copy is then locked, leaving the original assembly file unlocked.

The CLR constantly monitors the assembly cache to see if any new assemblies have been added or if any of the existing assemblies have changed. If a new or updated assembly is detected, the classes it contains are automatically registered with the application. In either case, all pending requests to the old version of the assembly are allowed to complete, but all new requests are handled by the new version. When the last request to the old version is finished, the shadow copy of that version is allowed to expire and the transition is complete.

Microsoft Intermediate Language (MSIL)

When a .NET application is compiled into an executable file, that file does not contain machine code (unless it was compiled with the Managed C++ compiler), as is the case with most other language compilers. Instead, the compiler output is a language known as Microsoft Intermediate Language (MSIL), or IL for short. When the program is run, the .NET Framework calls a Just-In-Time (JIT) compiler to compile the IL code into machine code, which is then executed. The JIT'ed machine code is cached on the server, so there is no need to recompile with every execution.

In theory, a program will produce the same IL code if written with any .NET compliant language. Though this is not always precisely true in practice, it is fair to say that for all practical purposes, all the .NET languages are equivalent.

> In theory, theory and practice are the same; but in practice, they never are.
> —Pat Johnson, 1992

The use of IL offers several advantages. First, it allows the JIT compiler to optimize the output for the platform. As of this writing, the .NET platform is supported on Windows environments running on Intel Pentium-compatible processors, and an open source work-alike is available on some flavors of Linux. It is not a stretch to imagine the Framework being ported to other operating environments, such as other flavors of Linux or Unix, the Mac OS, or other hardware platforms. Even more likely, as new generations of processor chips become available, Microsoft could release new JIT compilers that detect the specific target processor and optimize the output accordingly.

The second major advantage of an IL architecture is that it enables the Framework to be language neutral. To a large degree, language choice is no longer dictated by the capabilities of one language over another but rather by the preferences of the developer or the team. You can even mix languages in a single application. A class written in C# can be derived from a VB2005 class, and an exception thrown in a C# method can be caught in a VB2005 method.

A third advantage is that the code can be analyzed by the CLR to determine compliance with requirements such as type safety. Things like buffer overflows and unsafe casts can be caught *at compile time*, greatly reducing maintenance headaches.

ILDASM

You can examine the contents of a compiled .NET EXE or DLL using Intermediate Language Disassembler (ILDASM), a tool provided as part of the .NET SDK. ILDASM parses the contents of the file, displaying its contents in human-readable format. It shows the IL code, as well as namespaces, classes, methods, and interfaces.

For details on IL programming, we recommend *CIL Programming: Under the Hood of .NET* by Jason Bock, published by APress.

This extremely useful tool is accessible from the Start menu by clicking on Start → All Programs → Microsoft .NET Framework SDK → Tools → MSIL Disassembler. Alternatively, you can run it from a command prompt, which you can open by clicking on Start → Programs → Microsoft Visual Studio 2005 → Visual Studio Tools → Visual Studio 2005 Command Prompt. At the command prompt, enter:

```
ildasm
```

to open the program.

Once the program is open, click on File → Open to open the file you wish to look at, or drag the file from Windows Explorer onto the ILDASM window.

Alternatively, at the command prompt enter:

```
ildasm <full path>\<appname.exe>
```

where the full path (optional if the *exe* or *dll* is in the current directory) and name of the *exe* or *dll* will be given as an argument. In either case, you will get something similar to that shown in Figure 19-1. You can click on the plus sign next to each node in the tree to expand that node and so drill down through the file.

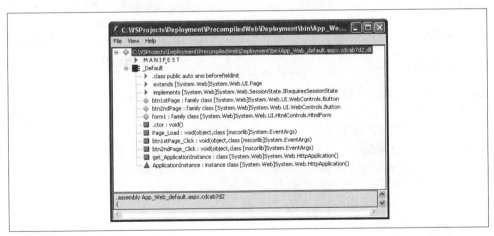

Figure 19-1. ILDASM

In Figure 19-1, the file being examined is called *App_Web_default.aspx.cdcab7d2.dll*, which was created as part of a pre-compiled web site. You can see that it has a manifest (which will be described below), and it contains a class called _Default. The class _Default contains several properties, fields, and methods.

The icons used in ILDASM are listed in Table 19-1. Since this is a monochrome book, the colors in which the icons are displayed are mentioned.

Table 19-1. ILDASM icons

Icon	Description
▼	Namespace (blue icon with red top edge)
▣	Class (blue icon)
I▣	Interface (blue icon w/ yellow letter I)
▣	Value class (brown icon)
E▣	Enum (brown icon w/ purple letter E)
■	Method (pink icon)
S	Static method (pink icon with yellow letter S)
◇	Field (aqua icon)
◈	Static field (aqua icon with dark blue letter S)
▽	Event (green icon)
▲	Property (red icon)
▶	Manifest or class info item (red icon)

Manifests

Assemblies in .NET are self-describing: they contain *metadata*, which describes the files contained in the assembly and how they relate to each other (references to types, for example), version and security information relevant to the assembly, and dependencies on other assemblies. This metadata is contained in the *assembly manifest*. Each assembly must have exactly one assembly manifest.

Looking back at Figure 19-1, you can see a manifest is in the file. Double-clicking on the manifest in ILDASM will bring up a window that displays the contents of the manifest, as shown in Figure 19-2.

Looking at the manifest displayed in Figure 19-2, you can see two external assemblies are referenced: System.Web and mscorlib. Both are part of the .NET Framework. This assembly itself is referred to with the following section:

```
.assembly App_Web_default.aspx.cdcab7d2
```

All of these assemblies have version attributes, and the Framework assemblies also have public key token attributes. Both of these attributes will be discussed shortly.

Versioning

Every assembly can have a four-part version number assigned to it, of the following form:

```
<major version>.<minor version>.<build number>.<revision number>
```

```
 MANIFEST                                                            _ □ ×
 Find  Find Next
// Metadata version: v2.0.50215
.assembly extern System.Web
{
  .publickeytoken = (B0 3F 5F 7F 11 D5 0A 3A )                       // .?_....:
  .ver 2:0:0:0
}
.assembly extern mscorlib
{
  .publickeytoken = (B7 7A 5C 56 19 34 E0 89 )                       // .z\U.4..
  .ver 2:0:0:0
}
.assembly App_Web_default.aspx.cdcab7d2
{
  .custom instance void [System.Web]System.Web.Compilation.AspNetGeneratedCodeAttribu
  .custom instance void [mscorlib]System.Runtime.CompilerServices.CompilationRelaxati
  .hash algorithm 0x00008004
  .ver 0:0:0:0
}
.module App_Web_default.aspx.cdcab7d2.dll
// MVID: {0E6B204F-0F3D-44C1-B087-33EE6133F696}
.imagebase 0x00400000
.file alignment 0x00000200
.stackreserve 0x00100000
.subsystem 0x0003       // WINDOWS_CUI
.corflags 0x00000001    // ILONLY
// Image base: 0x02F30000
```

Figure 19-2. Manifest

Each part of the version can have any meaning you wish to assign. There is no enforced meaning to the first number as opposed to the second, for example. The generally recommended meanings are that the major version represents a distinctly new release that may not be backward compatible with previous versions, the minor version represents a significant feature enhancement that probably is backward compatible, the build number represents a bug fix or patch level, and the revision number represents a specific compilation. Of course, your marketing department may have other ideas, and you are free to assign any versioning meaning you wish to the parts of the version number.

> Though there is no enforced meaning to the four parts of the version number, the fact that they are ordered from most significant to least significant is used in the assembly binding process if you specify a range of versions to redirect.

Looking back at the manifest shown in Figure 19-2, every assembly has a version associated with it. For example, in that figure System.Web has the following version attribute:

    .ver 2:0:0:0

This corresponds to a major version of 2, a minor version of 0, a build number of 0, and a revision number of 0.

Version numbers are part of the identity of an assembly. The CLR considers two assemblies that differ only in version number to be two distinctly different assemblies.

This allows for multiple versions of the same assembly to reside side by side in the same application, not to mention on the same machine.

 Though it is possible to have side-by-side versions of the same assembly in the same application, this is rarely a good idea as a practical matter. You must go out of your way to make this work and it can be a maintenance headache.

As you will see shortly, the CLR differentiates between two different types of assemblies: *private* (those assemblies located in the application assembly cache, described above) and *shared*. The CLR ignores the version number of private assemblies. Adding a version number to a private assembly is a form of self-documentation, for the benefit of people examining the source code or the manifest. However, if an assembly is shared, which will be explained in detail below, the CLR will be cognizant of the version and can use it to allow or disallow the assembly to load, depending on which version is called for.

You assign versions to an assembly with assembly attributes, either at the top of your main source file or at the top of a separate source file compiled into the assembly.

 Versions of Visual Studio prior to 2005 automatically included a file called *AssemblyInfo.cs* (or *AssemblyInfo.vb*) with every web project. This file provided a convenient means of adding or modifying attributes.

Any source file that is going to include attributes must make reference to the System. Reflection namespace (unless you type in fully qualified attribute names). In C#, include the following using statement:

```
using System.Reflection;
```

The attribute, or attributes, must be at the top of the source file, after the using statements but before any class definitions. In C#, it looks something like this:

```
[assembly: AssemblyVersion("1.1.*")]
```

 Version syntax in manifests use colons to separate the numbers, and attributes in source code use periods.

The argument provided to the attribute is a string. Though the four parts of the version number have the meanings described above (major, minor, build, and revision), you can use any values you want. To the extent that the CLR checks the version number, it does not enforce any meaning other than to compare if the total version number is equal to, greater than, or less than a specified value or falls within a specified range.

That said, the Framework does impose some rules and it also provides some short-cuts for automatically generating meaningful version numbers.

- If you specify the version, you must specify at least the major revision number. That is, specifying "1" will result in Version 1.0.0.0.

- You can specify all four parts of the version. If you specify fewer than four parts, the remaining parts will default to zero. For example, specifying "1.2" will result in Version 1.2.0.0.

- You can specify the major and minor numbers plus an asterisk for the build. The build will then be equal to the number of days since January 1, 2000, and the revision will be equal to the number of seconds since midnight local time, divided by 2 and truncated to the nearest integer. For example, specifying "1.2.*" will result in Version 1.2.1963.28933 if the file was compiled on May 17, 2005 at 4:04:27 P.M.

- You can specify the major, minor, and build numbers plus an asterisk for the revision. The revision will then be equal to the number of seconds since midnight local time, divided by 2 and truncated to the nearest integer. For example, "1.2.3.*" will result in Version 1.2.3.28933 if the file was compiled at 4:04:27 P.M.

Private Versus Shared Assemblies

Broadly speaking, there are two types of assemblies: *private* and *shared*. A private assembly is one that is used only by a single application; a shared assembly is one which can be used by more than one application.

A private assembly is located in one of two locations. If you are using full runtime compilation, where source files are located in the *App_Code* directory, then the assemblies compiled from that source code and the content files will be located in a system folder somewhere on the machine, managed by the CLR. In addition, any assembly files located in the *bin* directory will be private assemblies.

Any public member, (such as a method, field, or property) contained in a private assembly will be available to any application in that directory by virtue of its presence in the directory. There is no need to register the assembly with the Registry, for example, as is the case with COM.

Private assemblies make no provision for versioning. The CLR does not check the version of private assemblies and cannot make load decisions based on version number. From this, it follows that it is not possible to have multiple versions of the same assembly in the same directory. However, it also follows that different directories can each have its own copy of a given assembly regardless of their respective versions. Be careful with this: it is easy to find yourself with inexplicable results when more than one version of an assembly is in use at the same time.

COM only allows a single copy of a given DLL on a machine, to be used by all the applications requiring that DLL. (Support for side-by-side COM DLLs has been added to Windows XP, but this is a relatively new feature.) Back in the days when hard disk space was a precious commodity, single copies of each DLL was a laudable, if imperfectly implemented, goal. Now, with large hard drives, it makes more sense to allow multiple copies of DLLs, one for each application that needs it. The benefit of this approach is the elimination of DLL Hell, and simplified installation and management. The deployment ramifications of private assemblies will be discussed in the section on XCOPY deployment.

DLL Hell is the following phenomenon: the user installs a new program (A) and suddenly a different program (B) stops working. As far as the user is concerned, A has nothing to do with B, but unbeknownst to the user, A and B share a DLL. Unfortunately, they require different versions of that same DLL. This problem goes away with .NET; each application can have its own private version of the DLL, or the application can specify which version of the DLL it requires.

In contrast, a shared assembly is one that can be made available to multiple applications on the machine. Typically shared assemblies are located in a special area of the drive called the Global Assembly Cache (GAC). The GAC will be discussed in more detail shortly.

Technically, you don't need to put shared assemblies in the GAC since you can specify an alternative location with a <CodeBase> element in a configuration file.

There are often reasons for creating a shared assembly other than to share an assembly between applications. For example, to take advantage of Code Access Security (CAS), an assembly must have a strong name (described below), which effectively makes it shared.

Shared assemblies also eliminate DLL Hell because the version of the assembly is part of its identity. An application will use the version of the assembly it was originally compiled with, or the version specified by the version policy contained in a controlling configuration file.

Of course, nothing prevents a developer from releasing a new assembly with the same version numbers as a previous release. In this circumstance, you will have replaced DLL Hell with Assembly Hell.

Shared assemblies in the GAC offer some benefits over shared assemblies not in the GAC, and shared assemblies in general offer several benefits over private assemblies though they are more of a bother to prepare, install, and administer. These benefits include the following:

Performance

- The CLR first looks for an assembly in the GAC and then in the application assembly cache.

- Assemblies stored in the GAC do not need to have their public key signature verified every time they are loaded, but shared assemblies not in the GAC do. However, private assemblies never have their signature verified because they do not have a strong name (described below).

- The files in a shared assembly in the GAC are verified to be present and neither tampered with nor corrupted when the assembly is installed in the GAC. For shared assemblies not in the GAC, this verification step is performed every time the assembly is loaded.

Versioning

- Side-by-side execution, where an application, or different applications, can use different versions of the same assembly. Private assemblies in different application directories can be different versions.

- An application will use the same version of an assembly that it was originally compiled with unless overridden by a binding policy specified in a configuration policy.

- Applications can be redirected to use a different version of an assembly (allowing for easy updating).

Robustness

- Files cannot be deleted except by an administrator.

- All the files in a shared assembly are verified to be present and neither tampered with nor corrupted.

- The shared assembly, whether in the GAC or another location, is signed with a public key to ensure that it has not been tampered with.

Strong Names

For an assembly to be shared, it must have a *strong name*. A strong name uniquely identifies a particular assembly. It is composed of a concatenation of the following:

- The text name of the assembly (without any file extension)
- The version
- The culture
- A public key token

A typical fully qualified name might look something like this:

```
myAssembly,Version=1.0.0.1,Culture=en-US,PublicKeyToken=9e9ddef18d355781
```

A strong name with all four parts is *fully qualified*, while one with fewer than all four components is *partially qualified*. If the culture is omitted, it can be specified as neutral. If the public key token is omitted, it can be specified as null.

The public key identifies the developer or organization responsible for the assembly. Functionally, it replaces the role of GUIDs in COM, guaranteeing the uniqueness of the name. It is the public half of a public key encryption scheme. The token listed as part of the strong name is a hash of the public key.

A public key encryption scheme, also called *asymmetric encryption*, relies on two numbers: a public key and a private key. They are mathematically related in such a way that if one key is used to encrypt a message, that message can only be decrypted by the other key, and vice versa. Furthermore, it is computationally infeasible, though possible, to determine one key given only the other. (Given enough time with a supercomputer, any encryption scheme can be broken.)

Many algorithms are available for calculating hashes. The only two directly supported by the .NET Framework at this time are the MD5 and SHA1 algorithms. The algorithm used for an assembly is indicated in the manifest by the key words .hash algorithm, followed by 0x00008003 for MD5 or 0x00008004 for SHA1.

The general principle is this: you generate a pair of keys, one of which you designate as private and one as public. You keep your private key very safe and very secret.

A hash code is generated for the assembly using the specified encryption algorithm, commonly SHA1. That hash code is then encrypted using RSA encryption and the private key. The encrypted hash code is embedded in the assembly manifest along with the public key. (The spaces where the encrypted hash code and the public key will go in the manifest are set to zeros before the encryption and taken into account by the encryption program.)

The CLR decrypts the hash code included in the manifest using the public key. The CLR also uses the algorithm indicated in the manifest, again typically SHA1, to hash the assembly. The decrypted hash code is compared to the just-generated hash code. If they match, the CLR can be sure the assembly has not been altered since it was signed.

Creating a strong name

There are two steps required to generate a strong name for an assembly.

The first step is to create the public/private pair of keys. The .NET Framework provides a command line tool for this purpose, *sn.exe*. Generate a pair of keys by executing *sn* with the -k option and the name of the file to hold the keys.

```
sn -k KeyPair.snk
```

The options passed to *sn.exe* are case-sensitive.

Save this file and guard it carefully if you are going to use the keys for providing proof of origin. Make a copy (on diskette or CD) and put it in a secure place, such as a safe deposit box. (If you are using the keys for testing purposes or as a guaranteed unique identifier, then there is no need for this level of security.) This file contains the private key which you should use for all the assemblies created by your organization.

In a large organization where it is not feasible for all the developers to have access to the private key, you can use a procedure known as delayed signing. This will be explained in the next section.

The second step is to compile the source code, including the key file, into an assembly. The specifics of doing so will be covered in the section on Local Deployment. For now, note the name and location of the key file for use in that process.

Delayed signing

As we mentioned, the private key must be a closely guarded item. However, this presents a quandary: access to the private key is necessary to create a strong name for an assembly. Creating a strong name is necessary to develop and test a shared assembly. Yet it may be imprudent to provide the firm's private key to all the developers working on the project who legitimately need to create strong names.

To get around this quandary, you can use *delayed signing*, sometimes called *partial signing*. In this scenario, you create the strong-named assembly using only the public key, which is safe to disseminate to anybody who wants it. You do all your development and testing. Then when you are ready to do the final build, you sign it properly with both the private and public keys.

The first step in delayed signing is to extract the public key from the key file, which contains both the private and public key. This is done from the command line using the *sn* tool again, passing it the -p option, the name of the key file, and the name of a file to hold the public key. In the following command, only the public key is contained in *PublicKey.snk*.

```
sn -p KeyPair.snk PublicKey.snk
```

During the publish process, described below, you can check the Delay Signing checkbox and include the key file with only the public key.

Local Deployment

All that is strictly necessary to deploy most ASP.NET applications—to deploy most .NET applications—is to copy the new files to the proper directories on the proper machine, overwriting any previous versions of files if they exist. This is referred to as *XCOPY deployment*.

XCOPY deployment is so simple as to cause experienced developers to ask, "Is that all there is to it?" It provides all the deployment benefits of .NET except for the ability to deploy assemblies globally (i.e., to use application code modules for multiple applications) and to pre-compile the application. To implement globally available code modules, you will use *global deployment*, described later in this section. Precompilation scenarios of local deployment will be covered shortly.

XCOPY is a command-prompt command that originated in the DOS days and has been enhanced for use in modern networks. It is used to copy files and directories from one location to another. The basic syntax is:

    XCOPY source destination switches

Both source and destination can be either filenames or directories. There is full support for wildcards. There are a multitude of switches available that control such things as resetting (or not) the archive bit, copying (or not) any empty subdirectories, controlling the screen display during copying, and copying (or not) security information about the files. For a full list of the switches available, go to a command prompt and enter:

    XCOPY /?

All command-prompt commands (known colloquially as DOS commands though DOS is no more) are case-insensitive, unless otherwise noted.

You can, of course, copy the files in any manner you wish, including dragging and dropping in Windows Explorer or FTP over the Internet. It is called XCOPY deployment to convey the essential fact that all that is required for deployment is to copy the application virtual root and all its subdirectories.

The CLR automatically handles any changes to application files seamlessly and invisibly to the user. If the *global.asax* or *web.config* file changes, the application will be automatically restarted. If a page, web service, or custom or user control file changes, the next request to come in to the application will get the new version. If an assembly file changes, the CLR will handle the transition from old version to the new one for any pending requests. It doesn't get much easier than this.

Since all the files necessary to the application are contained within the application virtual root and its child directories, this implies that if two different applications on a server use a *dll* of the same name, they will be two independent copies of the file. They may be identical copies, but they don't have to be. It is possible to have two or more different versions of a *dll* on the same machine, each in its own application directory structure, with no conflict between applications. This relegates DLL Hell to something that old programmers will tell war stories about, like 64KB boundaries or running out of conventional memory in DOS.

Within the category of local deployment, several scenarios are available, as discussed in the next several sections. You can use .NET's full compilation of all content and code at runtime, you can compile the assemblies manually, you can completely pre-compile all the content and code, or just the code.

Full Runtime Compilation

Compiling all the content and code at runtime is the easiest and most convenient way to compile applications, since no work is required on the part of the developer other than to place any source code files requiring compilation in the *App_Code* directory under the application root. You have seen this approach used in building the web service proxy in Chapter 16.

This is the preferred way for VS2005 to operate. Right-clicking on a web app root directory in the Solution Explorer, there is a menu item for adding a folder. One of the choices is *App_Code*. Further, if you attempt to add a class file to a web application, you will be prompted to place it in the *App_Code* directory. You can decline and place it wherever you wish, but VS2005 tries to guide you to this approach.

If a source file is located outside the *App_Code* directory, then you will have to take active steps to compile the file and make the resulting assembly available to the app, using one of other three scenarios described here.

Full runtime compilation is independent of VS2005. Even if you create all the application files in Notepad, as long as the source files are in the *App_Code* directory under the application virtual root, they will be compiled by the CLR at runtime.

The big advantage to this technique is convenience and automatic synchronicity between content and code files. If you have to remember to do a complete recompile before deploying, it is possible for deployment errors to slip in.

There are two downsides to this compilation scenario: performance and security. A page or class is not compiled until it is first called.

The lag time on first call is noticeable, sometimes significant, but it only occurs the first time a page or class is called. There is no performance penalty after the first hit because the compiled assemblies are cached on the server and immediately available on subsequent calls.

The other issue is security. Deploying an app in this manner means the source code and content files are all present on the server as plain text files. Though ASP.NET and IIS are configured to prohibit access to these files, there is always the possibility that a hacker might penetrate security and gain access to the server's file system (or that a disgruntled or unscrupulous employee will steal or corrupt the code). In a hosting scenario, where your web site is hosted by a commercial hosting service, your source files will be available for any prying eyes with sufficient access rights.

Manual Compilation of Assemblies

As mentioned above, another reserved subdirectory of the application root is *bin*, which is part of the application assembly cache. Any compiled assemblies located in this folder will automatically be made available to the application. The key here is that you must manually compile the assemblies, using the command-line compiler, as described shortly.

This was the normal method of operation in ASP.NET Version 1.x, and is still supported. Aside from the inconvenience of manual compilation (which can be automated with batch files or a *make* system), it provides good performance and security (at least for the compiled source code files; the content files are still present in plain text). In some cases, such as when using custom configuration sections (covered in the previous chapter), having a manually compiled assembly is a requirement.

To compile a class file manually, open a command prompt by going to Start → All Programs → Microsoft Visual Studio 2005 → Visual Studio Tools → Visual Studio 2005 Command Prompt, to open a command prompt window what used to be known as a DOS prompt, for you old-timers.

Change the current directory of the command window to be the directory containing the source file. The command to do this is something like this:

```
cd \websites\MyWebApp
```

The generic syntax for the C# compiler is:

```
csc [parameters] inputFile.ext
```

For example, the following command (the command is wrapped here for readability; in reality, it would be on a single line) will output an assembly file called *MyClasses.dll* in the *bin* directory, using *\websites\MyWebApp\MyClasses.cs* as the input source code file:

```
csc /out:bin\MyClasses.dll /t:library /r:system.dll,system.web.dll,
    MyClasses.cs
```

The command-line compiler has a large number of parameters available to it, three of which are used here. To see the complete list of parameters available, enter the following command at the command prompt:

```
csc /?
```

Table 19-2 lists the parameters used in the preceding command lines.

Table 19-2. Compiler parameters

Parameter	Short form	Description
`/out:<filename>`		Output filename. If not specified, then the output filename will be derived from the first source file.
`/target:library`	`/t: library`	Build a library file. Alternative values for target are `exe`, `winexe`, and `module`.
`/reference:<file list>`	`/r:`	Reference the specified assembly files. If more than one file, either include multiple reference parameters or separate filenames with commas within a single reference parameter. Do not include any spaces between filenames.

Full Pre-Compilation

If you do not want to subject the web site users to any compilation delay the first time a page or class is hit, you can pre-compile the entire application, including the content files. This allows you to deploy only compiled assembly files, which will have no delay the first time they are called and will keep them resistant to prying eyes. There will be no plain text source code files deployed.

 For greater security, you can obfuscate the compiled assemblies to make them more difficult to decompile and reverse-engineer. An obfuscator, called the Dotfuscator Community Edition, is included with VS2005 under the Tools menu.

This full pre-compile can be accomplished from the command line using the *aspnet_compiler.exe* utility. However, the easier way to do it is by using the Build → Publish command in VS2005, which integrates in the MSBuild build engine.

After clicking that command, you will get the dialog box shown in Figure 19-3. The default target location, if you're using a File System location, will be a folder called *PrecompiledWeb* under the VS2005 project file location. You can enter an FTP or HTTP URL to deploy to a remote server.

For a full pre-compile with maximum security, i.e., including the content files, uncheck the checkbox labeled "Allow this precompiled site to be updateable."

To use strong names with a key file, as described previously, check the checkbox labeled "Ename strong naming on precompiled assemblies" ("Ename" must be a typo in the Beta 2 checkbox label, it should be "Enable"), and enter or browse to the key file location. There is a checkbox to implement Delay signing as described above. The Key container controls allow you to use RSA Key Containers (a topic beyond the scope of this book) rather than a key file.

The result of this pre-compile will be a directory structure, suitable for XCOPY deployment to a production server, in the location specified in the dialog box. In that directory structure will be a *bin* directory containing all the compiled *dll*s, plus compiled

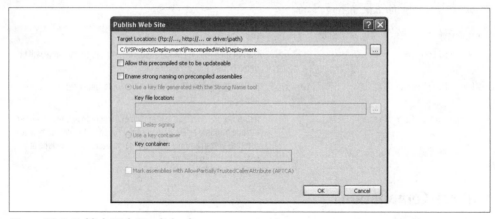

Figure 19-3. Publish Web Site dialog box

versions of the content files. The content files will not be present, although stub files named identically as the original content files will be there. These stub files provide a target for browser requests but are used only to redirect the request to the compiled version in the *bin* directory.

If you want to make any changes to any file, you must do so in VS2005 and recompile.

Pre-Compilation of Code Only

Often times, the full re-compile is what you need, but you want the flexibility to make minor modifications to the content files after they have been deployed, without the hassle of a full recompile and redeploy. In this case, check the checkbox in Figure 19-3 labeled "Allow this precompiled site to be updateable."

The result will be the same as with a full pre-compile, except that the content files will be the original version rather than stub versions. These content files can be edited after deployment and those changes will take effect with any subsequent requests, transparently to any users of the site.

Global Deployment

In the previous section, we stated that most applications are deployed by copying files to the proper directory. The exception occurs when you wish to use the same assembly in more than one application. In this case, you use *global deployment*.

There are many scenarios in which you might want to have a common assembly file accessible to multiple applications. A firm might have two different web sites on a server, both providing access to the same database. One web site is free of charge and open to the public but of limited functionality, but the other is fully functional, requiring a paid subscription. Since both sites access the same database, they will have common database query routines. They might also have common login routines. Using the same assembly to contain those common routines will enhance maintainability. Another scenario might be a web-hosting firm that has many web sites running on a server. It might want to offer some functionality to all its client web sites. Encapsulating this functionality in a globally available assembly would make this easy to offer and maintain.

Another consideration is versioning. When assemblies are local to an application, then each application can have its own version of common assemblies. The .NET Framework allows for global assemblies to have multiple versions. Each application making use of the global assembly can either specify the version it wants to use or take the latest version. By specifying the version, an application will not break if a newer version of the assembly introduces signature changes or bugs.

To provide global availability of an assembly, it must be installed to the GAC. The GAC is a machine-wide location for code to be shared among multiple applications on that machine. Typically, it is physically located at *c:\windows\assembly*. However, you cannot just copy an assembly file to that directory and have it be made available to all the applications. The assembly needs to be registered with the GAC, using the .NET command-line utility *GacUtil.exe*.

To make an assembly file suitable for inclusion in the GAC, it must have assembly information compiled into it. This is done using `Assembly` attributes. These `Assembly` attributes can either be included in the same source code file as the class or classes being compiled into the assembly or can be in a separate source code file that is compiled into the assembly along with the class source code file(s). The format of the `Assembly` attributes look like this:

```
[Assembly:attributeName(attributeValue)]
```

`attributeName` is the name of the `Assembly` attribute, and `attributeValue` is the string value assigned to the attribute. So, for example, if you're assigning the `AssemblyVersionAttribute`, it would look like the following:

```
[Assembly: AssemblyVersionAttribute ("1.0.3.101")]
```

Table 19-3 lists the available `Assembly` attributes with a brief description.

Table 19-3. Assembly attributes

Attribute	Description
AssemblyCompanyAttribute	String containing company name.
AssemblyConfigurationAttribute	String configuration, such as Retail or Debug. Not used by CLR.
AssemblyCopyrightAttribute	String containing copyright information.
AssemblyCultureAttribute	Field indicating culture supported by the assembly.
AssemblyDefaultAliasAttribute	String containing default alias for the assembly. Can contain a friendly name.
AssemblyDelaySignAttribute	Boolean indicating delayed application of digital signature.

Table 19-3. Assembly attributes (continued)

Attribute	Description
AssemblyDescriptionAttribute	String containing short description of the assembly.
AssemblyFileVersionAttribute	String containing Win32 file version number. Defaults to assembly version.
AssemblyFlagsAttribute	Flag indicating the kind of side-by-side execution allowed.
AssemblyInformationalVersionAttribute	String containing version information not used by the CLR.
AssemblyKeyFileAttribute	String containing name of file with either public key signature if using delayed signing, or both public and private keys. Filename is relative to output file path and not source file path.
AssemblyKeyNameAttribute	String containing key container.
AssemblyName	String containing an assembly's unique name.
AssemblyProductAttribute	String containing product information.
AssemblyTitleAttribute	String containing friendly name for the assembly.
AssemblyTrademarkAttribute	String containing trademark information.
AssemblyVersionAttribute	A numeric version representation, in the form *major.minor. build.revision*.

If you are using Assembly attributes in a source file, you must reference the System. Reflection namespace with the using keyword in C#.

For an assembly to be included in the GAC, it must have a *strong name*.

Once all this is in place, you can use *GacUtil.exe* to add the assembly to the GAC. The syntax is:

```
gacutil /i pathToDLL\myDLL.DLL
```

where pathToDLL is the path to the directory containing the assembly file, and *myDLL.DLL* is the name of the assembly file.

The *GacUtil.exe* utility has several command-line switches. For a complete list, enter the following at a command prompt:

```
gacutil /?
```

Some of the more commonly used switches are described in Table 19-4.

Table 19-4. Some common switches to GacUtil.exe

Switch	Description
/i	Installs an assembly to the GAC.
/u	Uninstalls an assembly from the GAC. If the name of the assembly to be uninstalled has no qualifying information, such as version, then all assemblies of that name will be uninstalled.
/l	Lists all the assemblies installed in the GAC.

To use a global assembly in applications, it must be registered in the *machine.config* file or the machine level *web.config* file. To add the above assembly to the configuration file, add the following line to the `<configuration><system.web><compilation>` `<assemblies>` section:

```
<add assembly="myDLL, Version=1.0.3.101, Culture=neutral,
    PublicKeyToken=nnnnnnnn"/ >
```

where nnnnnnnn is obtained from *GacUtil* by running:

```
gacutil /l
```

from the command line, finding `myDLL` in the listing, and copying the public key token into place.

Windows Installer

XCOPY deployment works well for many web sites. However, there are some situations where it falls short. For example, XCOPY does not automate the installation of assemblies into the GAC, nor does it make Registry edits. Further, if you need to install to multiple servers, such as a web farm, or have a precisely scripted and repeatable installation process, then XCOPY may get tedious and error-prone. For all of these scenarios, you need an installation tool with more robust capabilities. There are several third-party installation tools available, such as InstallShield, InstallAnywhere, and ActiveInstall.

Windows has its own installation technology, known as *Windows Installer*, which has been included with all the Windows operating systems starting with Windows 2000.

Windows Installer provides installation, removal, and management of applications. It also supports features such as automatic repair of existing installations, transactional operations (a set of operations performed by the installer can all be undone if installation does not complete successfully), installation on demand (application features are not installed until the first time a user tries to use that feature), and installation in locked-down environments if an administrator approves an installation package by means of group policy.

The Windows Installer is based on a database. Each application to be installed has a file associated with it, with an extension of *.msi*, which contains the data for that application, including rules for controlling the installation.

There are several ways of opening an *.msi* file. Double-clicking on the file will open the Windows Installer for that application. If the application is not currently installed on the machine, you will be presented with a series of dialog boxes for installing the application. Depending upon how the installation package was customized (described below), these dialogs will allow the user to select a target destination, offer installation for the current user or all users, present software license information, and so on.

If the application is already installed on the machine, you will be presented with a dialog box offering the choice to repair or remove the installation.

If you right-click on an *.msi* file in Windows Explorer, the context menu will include three relevant menu items: Install, Repair, and Uninstall. These options perform the same operations you might access by double-clicking on the file.

 You can execute the Windows Installer from a command prompt. To install an application, use the following command:

```
msiexec /i MyApp.msi
```

To uninstall the app, use the following command:

```
msiexec /x MyApp.msi
```

To repair an installation, use this line:

```
msiexec /f MyApp.msi
```

Interestingly, *msiexec.exe* is one of the few command line tools provided by Microsoft that does not display a list of parameters when executed with the /? switch. However, executing the command with no command-line switches will bring up a dialog box with a list of all the command-line switches.

Probably the easiest way to run the Installer is to execute *setup.exe*, the Installer Bootstrapper which is created by VS2005 in a process that will be described below. Do so by double-clicking on the file in Windows Explorer.

The Windows Installer automatically logs installations and removals in the Application Log of the Event Viewer found in Control Panel → Administrative Tools. Each entry in the log will have the MsiInstaller as the value for Source.

The Windows Installer is integrated into VS2005. You create installation packages for your application by adding one or more setup projects to the web application. By having more than one setup project as part of an application, you can easily deploy the same application with different configurations.

 VS2005 uses MSBuild, the Microsoft build engine, to perform the builds that get packaged into the *.msi* files. You can create powerful and flexible MSBuild projects. MSBuild is also available outside VS2005, from the command line, with the *MSBuild.exe* utility. Going into all the detail of MSBuild is beyond the scope of this book.

To demonstrate using VS2005 to build deployment packages, you will first create a three-page web site called *Deployment*, with the pages named *Default.aspx*, *FirstPage.aspx*, and *SecondPage.aspx*. Each page will consist of two buttons to navigate to the other two pages. In addition, you will create a class file, *Class1.cs* in the *App_Code* directory, which will have a single static public method called GetTime that returns a string representing the current time.

All three content files, along with their associated code-behind files and the class file, are listed in Examples 19-1 through 19-7. (You might want to download these code examples from *www.LibertyAssociates.com*, since the code itself is not the focus of this section but rather how to deploy the code.)

Example 19-1. Default.aspx for Deployment

```
<%@ Page Language="C#" AutoEventWireup="true"  CodeFile="Default.aspx.cs"
   Inherits="_Default" %>

<!DOCTYPE html PUBLIC "-//W3C//DTD XHTML 1.1//EN"
   "http://www.w3.org/TR/xhtml11/DTD/xhtml11.dtd">

<html xmlns="http://www.w3.org/1999/xhtml" >
<head runat="server">
    <title>Deployment Example</title>
</head>
<body>
    <form id="form1" runat="server">
    <div>
      <h1>Deployment Example</h1>
      <h2>Home Page</h2>
      <asp:Label ID="lblTime" runat="server" />
      <br />
      <asp:Button ID="btn1stPage" runat="server"
                  Text="Go To First Page"
                  OnClick="btn1stPage_Click" />
      <asp:Button ID="btn2ndPage" runat="server"
                  Text="Go To Second Page"
                  OnClick="btn2ndPage_Click" />
    </div>
    </form>
</body>
</html>
```

Example 19-2. Default.aspx.cs for Deployment

```
using System;
using System.Data;
using System.Configuration;
using System.Web;
using System.Web.Security;
using System.Web.UI;
using System.Web.UI.WebControls;
using System.Web.UI.WebControls.WebParts;
using System.Web.UI.HtmlControls;

public partial class _Default : System.Web.UI.Page
{
    protected void Page_Load(object sender, EventArgs e)
    {
        lblTime.Text = Class1.GetTime( );
    }
```

Example 19-2. Default.aspx.cs for Deployment (continued)

```csharp
    protected void btn1stPage_Click(object sender, EventArgs e)
    {
        Response.Redirect("FirstPage.aspx");
    }

    protected void btn2ndPage_Click(object sender, EventArgs e)
    {
        Response.Redirect("SecondPage.aspx");
    }
}
```

Example 19-3. FirstPage.aspx for Deployment

```
<%@ Page Language="C#" AutoEventWireup="true" CodeFile="FirstPage.aspx.cs"
    Inherits="FirstPage" %>

<!DOCTYPE html PUBLIC "-//W3C//DTD XHTML 1.1//EN"
    "http://www.w3.org/TR/xhtml11/DTD/xhtml11.dtd">

<html xmlns="http://www.w3.org/1999/xhtml" >
<head runat="server">
    <title>Deployment Example</title>
</head>
<body>
    <form id="form1" runat="server">
    <div>
      <h1>Deployment Example</h1>
      <h2>First Page</h2>
       <asp:Button ID="btnHomePage" runat="server"
                   Text="Go To Home Page"
                   OnClick="btnHomePage_Click" />
       <asp:Button ID="btn2ndPage" runat="server"
                   Text="Go To Second Page"
                   OnClick="btn2ndPage_Click" />
    </div>
    </form>
</body>
</html>
```

Example 19-4. FirstPage.aspx.cs for deployment

```csharp
using System;
using System.Data;
using System.Configuration;
using System.Collections;
using System.Web;
using System.Web.Security;
using System.Web.UI;
using System.Web.UI.WebControls;
using System.Web.UI.WebControls.WebParts;
using System.Web.UI.HtmlControls;
```

Example 19-4. FirstPage.aspx.cs for deployment (continued)

```
public partial class FirstPage : System.Web.UI.Page
{
    protected void btnHomePage_Click(object sender, EventArgs e)
    {
        Response.Redirect("Default.aspx");
    }

    protected void btn2ndPage_Click(object sender, EventArgs e)
    {
        Response.Redirect("SecondPage.aspx");
    }
}
```

Example 19-5. SecondPage.aspx for Deployment

```
<%@ Page Language="C#" AutoEventWireup="true"
    CodeFile="SecondPage.aspx.cs" Inherits="SecondPage" %>

<!DOCTYPE html PUBLIC "-//W3C//DTD XHTML 1.1//EN"
    "http://www.w3.org/TR/xhtml11/DTD/xhtml11.dtd">

<html xmlns="http://www.w3.org/1999/xhtml" >
<head runat="server">
    <title>Deployment Example</title>
</head>
<body>
    <form id="form1" runat="server">
    <div>
      <h1>Deployment Example</h1>
      <h2>Second Page</h2>
       <asp:Button ID="btnHomePage" runat="server"
                   Text="Go To Home Page"
                   OnClick="btnHomePage_Click" />
       <asp:Button ID="btn1stPage" runat="server"
                   Text="Go To First Page"
                   OnClick="btn1stPage_Click" />
    </div>
    </form>
</body>
</html>
```

Example 19-6. SecondPage.aspx.cs for deployment

```
using System;
using System.Data;
using System.Configuration;
using System.Collections;
using System.Web;
using System.Web.Security;
using System.Web.UI;
using System.Web.UI.WebControls;
using System.Web.UI.WebControls.WebParts;
using System.Web.UI.HtmlControls;
```

Example 19-6. SecondPage.aspx.cs for deployment (continued)

```
public partial class SecondPage : System.Web.UI.Page
{
    protected void btnHomePage_Click(object sender, EventArgs e)
    {
        Response.Redirect("default.aspx");
    }

    protected void btn1stPage_Click(object sender, EventArgs e)
    {
        Response.Redirect("FirstPage.aspx");
    }
}
```

Example 19-7. App_Code\Class1.cs for Deployment

```
using System;
using System.Data;
using System.Configuration;
using System.Web;
using System.Web.Security;
using System.Web.UI;
using System.Web.UI.WebControls;
using System.Web.UI.WebControls.WebParts;
using System.Web.UI.HtmlControls;

public class Class1
{
    public static string GetTime()
    {
        return DateTime.Now.ToLongTimeString();
    }
}
```

Build Configurations

By default, web sites created in VS2005 are configured to enable debugging and to be run in debug mode within VS2005. If any unhandled errors occur, the user will automatically be brought into the debugger. The price for being in debug mode is reduced performance.

A web site can be configured to disable debugging. In this mode, all breakpoints will be ignored and any unhandled errors will result in an error page being displayed to the user. The non-debug (release) mode is more performant than debug mode and is typically used when a web application is deployed.

You can select debug or non-debug mode with an entry in the <compilation> element in *web.config*. (Configuration is covered in Chapter 18.) You can configure this by manually editing *web.config* or by running the Web Site Administration Tool.

To edit the file manually, set the debug attribute of the <compilation> tag to true or false as in the following code snippet:

```
<compilation debug="true" />
```

To use the Web Site Administration Tool, click on the Website → ASP.NET Configuration menu item. When the tool opens, click on the Application tab, then the "Configure debugging and tracing" link. On that page, check or uncheck the "Enable debugging" checkbox. Doing so will automatically make the correct entry in *web.config*.

In versions of ASP.NET prior to 2.0, and still the case when creating .NET Windows applications (as distinct from ASP.NET applications), Visual Studio provides two default build configurations: Debug and Release. In VS2005 with ASP.NET, there is no longer a Release build configuration. (You can add your own build configurations, a topic beyond the scope of this book.)

Even if you have configured the web site to run in non-debug mode, the Active configuration will still be called Debug. This might cause some confusion, especially when building setup projects, as will be discussed shortly.

Adding a Setup Project with the Setup Wizard

You are now ready to add a project to the web site that will take advantage of the Setup Wizard to walk you through the steps of creating an installation package. This installation package will install a version of the application with the debug mode set to the value currently indicated in *web.config*, as described in the section above. For this example, verify that debug mode is set to true.

With the web site root directory highlighted in the Solution Explorer, click on the File → Add → New Project menu item. (This menu item is unavailable by right-clicking on the Solution Explorer.) From the tree view on the left, select Setup and Deployment under Other Project Types. From the list on the right, select Setup Wizard. Name the project *Setup-Debug* and leave the default location. The dialog box will look something like that shown in Figure 19-4.

By using the default location, the setup project will be located in its own folder under the root location for all your project files (set using Tools → Options). You might want to consider changing the location of this setup project to be in a subdirectory of the project it is setting up.

The wizard will take you through five screens. The first is a splash screen. The second screen asks you to choose a Project Type. Select "Create a setup for a web application."

The third screen asks you to select the outputs from all the projects in the solution. Check the only checkbox available, next to "Content Files from c:\websites\

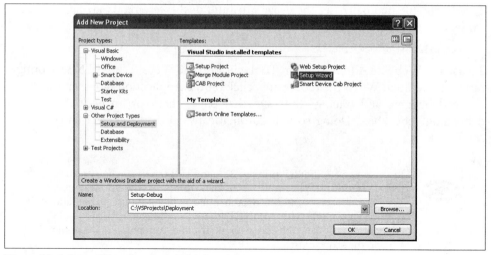

Figure 19-4. Setup Wizard project dialog box

Deployment." (Your directory structure may be different from those shown here.) Click the Next button.

The next screen allows you to include other files, such as READMEs, of which there are none. The final screen displays a summary of all the settings for this setup project. Click Finish.

A project will be added to the Solution Explorer and the main design window will now show a File System editor for the setup project, similar to the screenshot shown in Figure 19-5.

Build the setup project by right-clicking on the project name in the Solution Explorer and selecting the Build menu item.

Build will build the application, taking all dependencies into account but not building any components that are up to date. In a large solution where current development work is only being done on one or two projects, it makes for a faster build process.

The Rebuild menu item first deletes all intermediary files and previous build outputs and then builds the entire app from scratch. It may take longer, but it is smart to do a Rebuild before testing the final build.

You can open the Output window to view a log of the build process by clicking on View → Other Windows → Output. At the end of the build process, it should say:

```
Build: 2 succeeded or up-to-date, 0 failed, 0 skipped
```

The number 2 refers to the two projects in this application, i.e., the web site and the setup project.

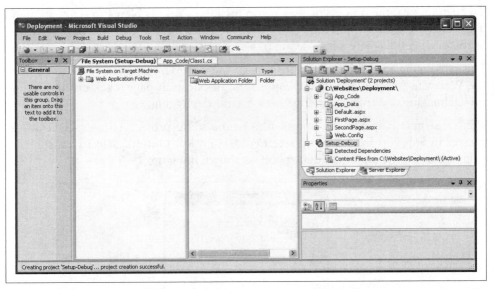

Figure 19-5. Setup project added to web site

Two files are created by this build process that actually need to be deployed: *setup.exe* and *Setup-Debug.msi*. Copying these files to the deployment target, (the server), and double-clicking on the setup file will cause the contents of the *.msi* file to be installed on the local machine.

The output files from the build process will be located in a directory called *Setup-Debug* (which is the name of the setup project) under the directory where the projects are stored, in this case in *c:\VSProjects*. *Setup-Debug* will contain a *.vdproj* file which contains information used by VS2005 to properly handle the project.

The *Setup-Debug* folder will contain two other subdirectories: *Debug* and *Release*. These folder names are a consequence of the warning in the previous section. The deployment output files, *setup.exe* and *Setup-Debug.msi*, will be contained in the folder called *Debug* because that is the name of the current active build configuration. Even if the web site is configured to run in non-debug mode, the output files will still be placed in a folder called *Debug*.

Adding a Setup Project Manually

You can create a setup project manually without using the setup wizard. This gets you to the same place as using the wizard, trading convenience for greater control.

 You can manually or automatically create either debug or release versions by editing *web.config* prior to building the setup project.

To begin, repeat the process of clicking on the File → Add → New Project menu item. This time select the Web Setup Project template, and name the project *Setup-Release*, as this time you'll create a non-debug (release) version.

Edit *web.config* to set the debug attribute of the `<compilation>` tag to `false` or open the Web Site Administration Tool, go to the Application page, click on the Configure Debugging and tracing, and uncheck Enable debugging.

You must manually add the output files to the setup project, so right-click on the project in Solution Explorer and select Add → Project Output. Select Content Files from the list at the top of the dialog box, as shown in Figure 19-6.

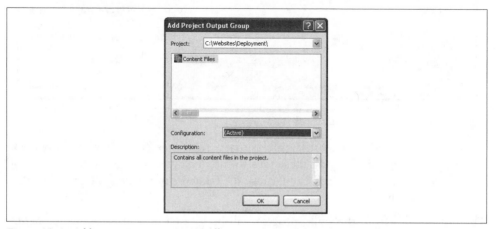

Figure 19-6. Adding project output manually

 You can select multiple outputs using standard Windows techniques with the Ctrl or Shift keys.

As soon as the output is added, any dependencies are detected and the class `library` is automatically included in the build.

The new project with that name will display in Solution Explorer with the primary outputs, similar to that shown in Figure 19-7.

Further Customizations

Whether the setup project came from the wizard or not, a number of customizations are available to you. Specifically, right-clicking on a setup project in Solution Explorer and selecting View or clicking on the View → Editor menu item will bring up six different editor choices.

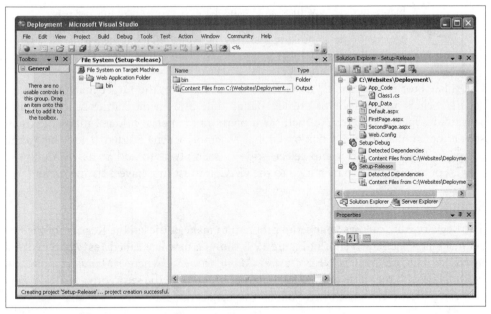

Figure 19-7. Adding output manually to a setup project

Clicking on any of these editors will display that editor for that project in the main pane. (When you first added a setup project, the File System editor is what you are looking at.)

File System

This editor, displayed in Figure 19-7, allows you to control where files are added to the end user's machine. The items in the leftmost pane are named folders on the target machine, such as the Web Application folder, the directory where the application is installed. Clicking on any of the named folders displays its contents in the right pane.

 You created this example project using the Web Setup Project, for which the only named folder displayed on the left side is Web Application Folder. If you had instead based this on the more generic Setup Project, there would be, instead, three named folders: Application Folder, User's Desktop, and User's Program Menu.

Right-clicking on an item displays a context menu. Select Add to add a folder, a file, an assembly, or a project output. You can add shortcuts to the desktop or to the Start → Programs menu by right-clicking on the appropriate item.

Before adding any files to a named folder, you must first set the AlwaysCreate property of that folder to true before building the setup project. To do so, click on the relevant named folder in the left pane, and set the AlwaysCreate property in the Properties window.

Use this editor to add shared assemblies to the GAC on the target machine. To do so, right-click on the root of the left pane, "File System on Target Machine" and select Add Special Folder. You will see a plethora of special folders, many of which should be familiar to you. Click on Global Assembly Cache Folder to add this to the left pane. Right-click on it and select Add → Assembly... to add an assembly to the GAC. For an assembly to be added to the GAC, it must first have a strong name.

Registry

The Registry editor allows your setup program to make entries in the Registry of the target machine. The screen shot in Figure 19-8 shows a new key called TestValue inserted in *HKEY_LOCAL_MACHINE\Software\<Manufacturer>*, where *<Manufacturer>* will be replaced with the value of the Manufacturer property of the setup project. (It defaults to the organization entered when VS2005 was installed.)

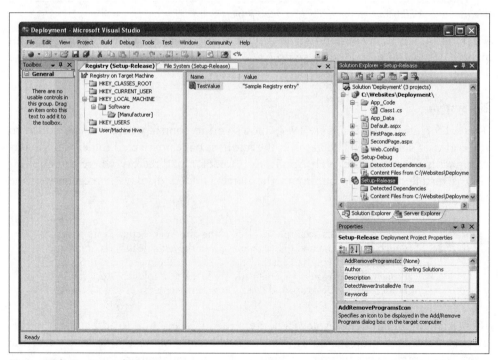

Figure 19-8. Registry editor

You can add new keys to the Registry by right-clicking on a node in the left pane and selecting New → Key. If you want to add a value to a key, right-click on that key and select New. Then select one of the following:

- String Value
- Environment String Value
- Binary Value
- DWORD Value

You can name the new value in the right pane or in the Properties window. The value is set in the Properties window.

File Types

The File Types editor allows you to associate file extensions with the application. If an associated file type has been double-clicked in Windows Explorer, the application will open with that file name passed in as an argument.

To add a file type to the project, right-click on "File Types on Target Machine" and select Add File Type. A default document type will appear with the &Open command below it. In the Properties window, change the name to something meaningful, say, *MyApp Data File*, and enter the extension in the Extensions property, say, *abc*, as shown in Figure 19-9.

Now if a file on the target machine with an extension of *.abc*, say *SomeData.abc*, has been double-clicked in Windows Explorer, the application will open with that file.

User Interface

The User Interface editor allows you to customize the dialog boxes that are displayed during the installation process. The process is divided into two categories: Install and Administrative Install. The first is for normal installation by users on their local machine, and the latter is for installation to a network for use by members of a workgroup.

Within each category, it is further divided into three phases: Start, Progress, and End. The default configuration looks like that shown in Figure 19-10.

Right-clicking on any item in the window and selecting the Add Dialog menu item brings up a selection of standard dialog boxes which can be added and further customized, such as dialogs with radio buttons, checkboxes, or text boxes, a customer information screen, a splash screen, a license agreement, and so on.

Again, since this example is based on a Web Setup Project, the middle node under Start is Installation Address. If you had based the project on Setup Project, those nodes would be Installation Folder.

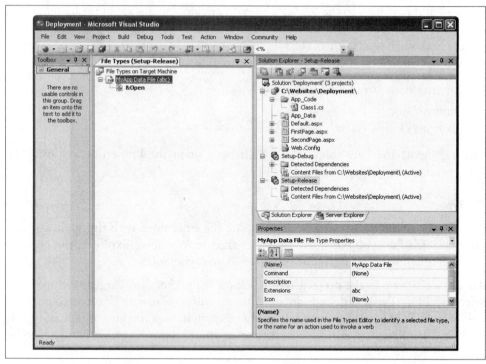

Figure 19-9. File Types editor

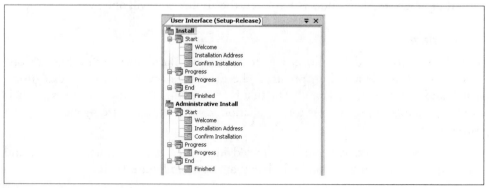

Figure 19-10. UI editor

Any dialog box added this way will have properties for text files or bitmaps to display, executables to run, and so on.

Custom Actions

The Custom Actions editor displays the four phases of the installation process: Install, Commit, Rollback, and Uninstall. You can assign an executable or script file to execute at the conclusion of any of these phases.

Launch Conditions

The Launch Conditions editor allows you to create conditional installs. For example, you can specify that a certain version of Windows be installed, a certain file is present, or a certain Registry entry has the correct value.

By default, Web Setup Projects verify that IIS has been installed with a version greater than or equal to 4.

Deploying the Web Site

To deploy the web site created by building a setup project, copy the two output files, *setup.exe* and *.msi*, to the target machine and double-click on *setup.exe* in Windows Explorer. The installation program will run, opening up the Setup Wizard, as shown in Figure 19-11.

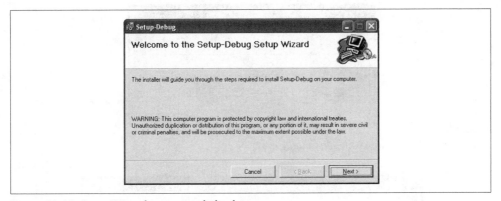

Figure 19-11. Setup Wizard—opening dialog box

Clicking on the Next button will bring up the dialog box shown in Figure 19-12. All the web sites available on that machine will be listed in the Site drop-down. You can enter the name of the virtual directory you wish to use.

Clicking on the Disk Cost button will bring up a dialog box, shown in Figure 19-13, which details the drive space required and available on the local machine.

After looking at the drive space, click the Next button on the setup wizard dialog box to go to a confirmation page. Click Next one more time to start the installation.

Assuming that the installation succeeds, you will see the new virtual directory created under Default Web Site in Computer Management, as shown in Figure 19-14. (See Chapter 18 for a description of using Computer Management.)

You can then run the web site by opening a browser and navigating to the new URL, with a web address similar to the following:

```
localhost/setup-debug/default.aspx
```

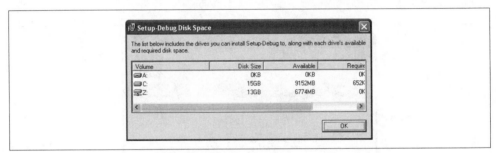

Figure 19-12. Selecting an installation address

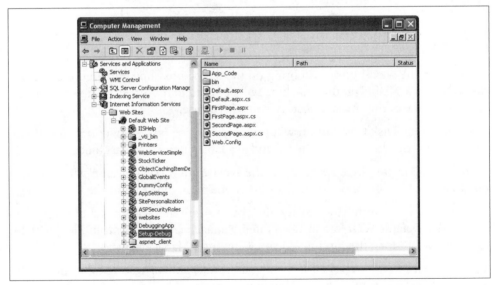

Figure 19-13. Disk space availability dialog box

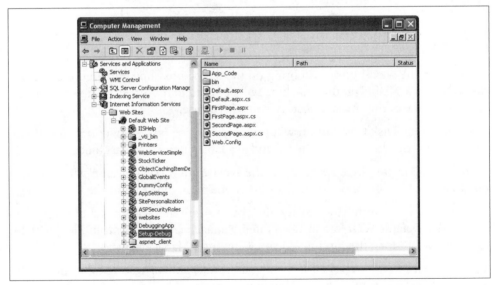

Figure 19-14. New virtual directory created

Keyboard Shortcuts

Shortcut	Command
Ctrl-Shift-B	Build → Build Solution
Ctrl-Alt-Break	Debug → Break All
F5	Debug → Continue
Ctrl-Shift-F9	Debug → Delete All Breakpoints
Ctrl-Alt-E	Debug → Exceptions…
Ctrl-B	Debug → New Breakpoint → Break At Function…
Ctrl-Alt-Q	Debug → Quick Watch
Ctrl-Shift-F5	Debug → Restart
F5	Debug → Start
Ctrl-F5	Debug → Start Without Debugging
F11	Debug → Step Into
Shift-F11	Debug → Step Out
F10	Debug → Step Over
Shift-F5	Debug → Stop Debugging
F9	Debug → Toggle Breakpoint
Ctrl-Alt-V, A	Debug → Windows → Autos
Ctrl-Alt-B	Debug → Windows → Breakpoints
Ctrl-Alt-C	Debug → Windows → Call Stack
Ctrl-Alt-D	Debug → Windows → Disassembly
Ctrl-Alt-I	Debug → Windows → Immediate
Ctrl-Alt-V, L	Debug → Windows → Locals
Ctrl-Alt-U	Debug → Windows → Modules
Ctrl-Alt-Z	Debug → Windows → Processes
Ctrl-Alt-G	Debug → Windows → Registers
Ctrl-Alt-N	Debug → Windows → Script Explorer
Ctrl-Alt-H	Debug → Windows → Threads

Shortcut	Command
Ctrl-Alt-M, 1	Debug → Windows → Watch → Memory 1
Ctrl-Alt-M, 2	Debug → Windows → Watch → Memory 2
Ctrl-Alt-M, 3	Debug → Windows → Watch → Memory 3
Ctrl-Alt-M, 4	Debug → Windows → Watch → Memory 4
Ctrl-Alt-W, 1	Debug → Windows → Watch → Watch 1
Ctrl-Alt-W, 2	Debug → Windows → Watch → Watch 2
Ctrl-Alt-W, 3	Debug → Windows → Watch → Watch 3
Ctrl-Alt-W, 4	Debug → Windows → Watch → Watch 4
Ctrl-K, Ctrl-C	Edit → Advanced → Comment Selection
Ctrl-K, Ctrl-\	Edit → Advanced → Delete Horizontal White Space
Ctrl-I	Edit → Advanced → Incremental Search
Ctrl-U	Edit → Advanced → Make Lowercase
Ctrl-Shift-U	Edit → Advanced → Make Uppercase
Ctrl-K, Ctrl-U	Edit → Advanced → Uncomment Selection
Ctrl-R, Ctrl-W	Edit → Advanced → View White Space
Ctrl-E, Ctrl-W	Edit → Advanced → Word Wrap
Ctrl-K, Ctrl-H	Edit → Bookmarks → Add Task List Shortcut
Ctrl-K, Ctrl-L	Edit → Bookmarks → Clear Bookmarks
Ctrl-K, Ctrl-N	Edit → Bookmarks → Next Bookmark
Ctrl-B, N	Edit → Bookmarks → Next Bookmark (Source view)
Ctrl-Shift-K, Ctrl-Shift-N	Edit → Bookmarks → Next Bookmark in Folder
Ctrl-K, Ctrl-P	Previous Bookmark
Ctrl-B, P	Edit → Bookmarks → Previous Bookmark (Source view)
Ctrl-Shift-K, Ctrl-Shift-P	Edit → Bookmarks → Previous Bookmark in Folder
Ctrl-K, Ctrl-K	Edit → Bookmarks → Toggle Bookmark
Ctrl-C	Edit → Copy
Ctrl-X	Edit → Cut
Ctrl-Shift-V	Edit → Cycle Clipboard Ring
Del	Edit → Delete
Ctrl-R, F	Edit → Find All References
Ctrl-Shift-F	Edit → Find and Replace → Find in Files
Alt-F12	Edit → Find and Replace → Find Symbol
Ctrl-Shift-H	Edit → Find and Replace → Replace in Files
Ctrl-F	Edit → Find and Replace → Quick Find
Ctrl-H	Edit → Find and Replace → Quick Replace
Ctrl-K, Ctrl-D	Edit → Advanced → Format Document
Ctrl-K, Ctrl-F	Edit → Advanced → Format Selection

Shortcut	Command
Ctrl-G	Edit → Go To…
Alt-Right Arrow	Edit → Intellisense → Complete Word
Ctrl-K, Ctrl-M	Edit → Intellisense → Generate Method Stub
Ctrl-K, Ctrl-T	Edit → Intellisense → Implement Abstract Class
Ctrl-K, Ctrl-E	Edit → Intellisense → Implement Interface → Explicitly
Ctrl-K, Ctrl-I	Edit → Intellisense → Implement Interface → Implicitly
Ctrl-K, Ctrl-X	Edit → Intellisense → Insert Snippet…
Ctrl-J	Edit → Intellisense → List Members
Ctrl-Shift-Space	Edit → Intellisense → Parameter Info
Ctrl-K, Ctrl-I	Edit → Intellisense → Quick Info
Ctrl-K, Ctrl-S	Edit → Intellisense → Surround With…
Ctrl-M, Ctrl-O	Edit → Outlining → Collapse to Definitions
Ctrl-M, Ctrl-H	Edit → Outlining → Hide Selection
Ctrl-M, Ctrl-U	Edit → Outlining → Stop Hiding Current
Ctrl-M, Ctrl-P	Edit → Outlining → Stop Outlining
Ctrl-M, Ctrl-L	Edit → Outlining → Toggle All Outlining
Ctrl-M, Ctrl-M	Edit → Outlining → Toggle Outlining Expansion
Ctrl-V	Edit → Paste
Ctrl-K, Ctrl-P	Edit → Previous Bookmark (Design view)
Ctrl-Y	Edit → Redo
Ctrl-A	Edit → Select All
Ctrl-Z	Edit → Undo
Ctrl+N	File → New → File…
Ctrl-Shift-N	File → New → New Project…
Ctrtl+O	File → Open → File…
Ctrl-Shift-O	File → Open → Open Project…
Ctrl-P	File → Print…
Ctrl-S	File → Save
Ctrl-Shift-S	File → Save All
Ctrl-L	Format → Convert to Hyperlink…
Ctrl-B	Format → Font → Bold
Ctrl-I	Format → Font → Italic
Ctrl-U	Format → Font → Underline
Ctrl-Shift-L	Format → Insert Bookmark…
Ctrl-Alt-F1	Help → Contents
Ctrl-Alt-F4	Help → Dynamic Help
Ctrl-Alt-F	Help → Help Favorites

Shortcut	Command
Ctrl-F1, H	Help → How Do I
Ctrl-Alt-F2	Help → Index
Shift-Alt-F2	Help → Index Results
Ctrl-Alt-F3	Help → Search
Ctrl-Alt-Left Arrow	Layout → Insert → Column to the Left
Ctrl-Alt-Right Arrow	Layout → Insert → Column to the Right
Ctrl-Alt-Up Arrow	Layout → Insert → Row Above
Ctrl-Alt-Down Arrow	Layout → Insert → Row Below
Ctrl-R, Ctrl-F	Refactor → Encapsulate Field
Ctrl-R, Ctrl-M	Refactor → Extract Method
Ctrl-R, Ctrl-P	Refactor → Promote Local Variable to Parameter
Ctrl-R, Ctrl-V	Refactor → Remove Parameters
Ctrl-R, Ctrl-R	Refactor → Rename
Ctrl-R, Ctrl-O	Refactor → Reorder Parameters
Ctrl-Alt-P	Tools → Attach to Process…
Ctrl-K, Ctrl-B	Tools → Code Snippets Manager…
Alt-F8	Tools → Macros → Macro Explorer
Alt-F11	Tools → Macros → Macro IDE
Ctrl-Shift-R	Tools → Macros → Record TemporaryMacro
Ctrl-Shift-P	Tools → Macros → Run TemporaryMacro
Ctrl-Alt-A	View → Other Windows → Command Window
Ctrl-Shift-Q	View → Details
Ctrl-Alt-T	View → Other Windows → Document Outline
Ctrl-\, Ctrl-E	View → Error List
Shift-Alt-Enter	View → Show Full Screen
Ctrl--	View → Navigate Backward
Ctrl-Shift--	View → Navigate Forward
Ctrl-Shift-N	View → Non Visual Controls
Ctrl-Alt-J	View → Other Windows → Object Browser
Ctrl-K, Ctrl-W	View → Other Windows → Bookmark Window
Ctrl-Shift-C	View → Other Windows → Class View
Ctrl-Alt-F12	View → Other Windows → Find Symbol Results
Alt-F8	View → Other Windows → Macro Explorer
Ctrl-Alt-O	View → Other Windows → Output
Ctrl-Shift-E	View → Other Windows → Resource View
Ctrl-Alt-R	View → Other Windows → Show Browser
F4	View → Properties Window

Shortcut	Command
Shift-F4	View → Property Pages
Ctrl-Alt-S	View → Other Windows → Server Explorer
Ctrl-Alt-L	View → Solution Explorer
Ctrl-\, Ctrl-T	View → Task List
Shift-Alt-T	View → Team Explorer
Ctrl-Alt-X	View → Toolbox
Ctrl-Q	View → Visible Borders
Shift-Alt-A	Website → Add Existing Item…
Ctrl-Shift-A	Website → Add New Item…

Relational Database Technology: A Crash Course

You can use ADO.NET to access data from any data source: relational databases, object databases, flat files, and text files. The vast majority of web applications, however, will access data from a relational database such as SQL Server. Though we could certainly write an entire book on relational databases and another on SQL, the essentials of these technologies are not hard to understand.

 All of the examples in this appendix assume you are working with SQL Server or SQL Server Express. Users of other relational databases will find that the lessons learned here transfer well to their environment, but be careful with applications like Access that use a different variation of SQL.

A *database* is a repository of data. A *relational database* organizes your data into tables that are "related" to one another. For example, one table might contain a customer's information and a second table might contain information about orders. The tables are related to one another because each customer has certain orders, and each order is owned by an individual customer.

Similarly, you might have a table of cars and a second table of car parts. Each part can be in one or more cars, and each car is made up of many parts. Or, you might have a table for bugs and a table for developers. Each bug is owned by one developer, and each developer has a list of bugs he owns.

Tables, Records, and Columns

The principal division of a database is into *tables*. Tables, like classes, typically describe one logical entity and all of what you know about that entity.

Every table in a relational database is organized into rows, where each row represents a single record. The rows are organized into columns. All the rows in a table have the same column structure. For example, the Bugs table used in Chapter 10 might have columns for the `bugID`, the ID of the person reporting the bug, the date the bug was reported, the status of the bug, and so forth.

It is common to make an analogy between tables and classes and between rows and objects. The `Bugs` table, for example, tells you a great deal about the contents of a `Bug`, just as a `Bug` class tells you about the state and structure of a `Bug`. Each row in the `Bug` table describes a particular `Bug`, much as an object does.

This analogy is compelling but limited. There is only an imperfect match between relational databases and objects, and one of the challenges facing an object-oriented programmer is overcoming the design differences between the object model, on the one hand, and the database model, on the other.

Relational databases are very good at defining the relationship among objects, but they are not good at capturing the behavior of the types described in the table. The "impedance mismatch" between relational databases and object-oriented programs has led some developers to try to create object databases. While this has met with some success, the vast majority of data is still stored in relational databases because of their great flexibility, performance, and ability to be searched quickly and easily.

 Typically, the interface between the back-end relational database and the objects in the application is managed by creating a database interface layer of objects that negotiate between the creation of objects and the storage of information in the database tables.

Table Design

To understand the issues in table design, consider the `Bug` database described in Chapter 10. You need to know who reported each bug, and it would be useful to know the email address, phone number, and other identifying information about each person as well.

You can imagine a form in which you display details about a given bug, and in that detail page you offer the email address and phone number of the "reporter" so the developer working on the bug can contact that person.

You could store the identifying information with each bug, but that would be inefficient. If John Doe reported 50 bugs, you'd rather not repeat John Doe's email address and phone number in 50 records. It's also a data maintenance nightmare. If John Doe changes his email address and phone number, you'd have to make the change in 50 places.

Instead, you'll create a second table called `People`, in which each row represents a single person. In the `People` table there will be a column for the `PersonID`. Each person will have a unique ID, and that field will be marked as the *primary key* for the

Person table. A primary key is the column or combination of columns that uniquely identifies a record in a given table.

The Bugs table will use the PersonID as a *foreign key*. A foreign key is a column (or combination of columns) that is a primary (or otherwise unique) key from a different table. The Bug table uses the PersonID, which is the primary key in People, to identify which person reported the bug. If you need to determine the email address for that person, you can use the PersonID to look up the Person record in the People table and that will give you all the detailed information about that person.

By "factoring out" the details of the person's address into a Person table, you reduce the redundant information in each Bug record. This process of taking out redundant information from your tables is called *normalization*.

Normalization

Normalization makes your use of the database more efficient, and it reduces the likelihood of data corruption. If you kept the person's email address in the People table and in the Bug table, you would run the risk that a change in one table might not be reflected in the other. Thus, if you changed the person's email address in the Person table, that change might not be reflected in every row in the Bugs table (or it would be a lot of work to make sure that it was reflected). By keeping only the PersonID in Bugs, you are free to change the email address or other personal information in People, and the change will automatically be reflected for each bug.

Just as VB and C# programmers want the compiler to catch bugs at compile time rather than at runtime, database programmers want the database to help them avoid data corruption. A compiler helps avoid bugs by enforcing the rules of the language. For example, in C# you can't use a variable you've not defined. SQL Server and other modern relational databases help you avoid bugs by enforcing constraints that you create. For example, the People database marks the PersonID as a primary key. This creates a primary key constraint in the database, which ensures that each PersonID is unique. If you were to enter a person named Jesse Liberty with the PersonID of LIBE, and then you were to try to add Stacey Liberty with a PersonID of LIBE, the database would reject the second record because of the primary key constraint. You would need to give one of these people a different, and unique, personID.

Declarative Referential Integrity

Relational databases use *Declarative Referential Integrity* (DRI) to establish constraints on the relationships among the various tables. For example, you might declare a constraint on the Bug table that dictates that no Bug may have a PersonID unless that PersonID represents a valid record in People. This helps you avoid two types of mistakes. First, you cannot enter a record with an invalid PersonID. Second, you cannot delete a `Person` record if that `PersonID` is used in any `Bug`. The integrity of your data and the relationships among records is thus protected.

SQL

The language of choice for querying and manipulating databases is *Structured Query Language*, often referred to as SQL. SQL is often pronounced "sequel". SQL is a declarative language, as opposed to a procedural language, and it can take a while to get used to working with a declarative language if you are used to languages like VB or C#.

Most programmers tend to think in terms of a sequence of steps: "Find me all the bugs, then get the reporter's ID, then use that ID to look up that user's records in People, then get me the email address". In a declarative language, such as SQL, you declare the entire query, and the query engine returns a set of results. You are not thinking about a set of steps; rather, you are thinking about designing and "shaping" a set of data. Your goal is to make a single declaration that will return the right records. You do that by creating temporary "wide" tables that include all the fields you need and then filtering for only those records you want. "Widen the `Bugs` table with the `People` table, joining the two on the `PersonID`, then filter for only those that meet my criteria".

The heart of SQL is the *query*. A query is a statement that returns a set of records from the database. Typically, queries are in this form:

```
Select <column,column,column> from <table> where <column> = <value>
```

For example, you might like to see information about your customers in the United States. To do so you would write:

```
Select CompanyName, ContactName  from Customers where Country = 'USA'
```

Joining Tables

SQL is capable of much more powerful queries (see the sidebar for the full syntax as provided by Microsoft).

For example, suppose you'd like to know about all the orders by all the customers in the United States after January 1 of 1997. You might create this query:

```
Select CompanyName, ContactName, city, orderDate, shippedDate,
productID, unitprice, quantity   from Customers c
join Orders o on o.customerID = c.customerID
join [order details] od on od.orderid = o.orderid
where c.Country = 'USA' and orderDate > '1/1/97'
```

SQL Select Statement

```
SELECT statement ::=
    < query_expression >
    [ ORDER BY { order_by_expression | column_position [ ASC | DESC ] }
        [ ,...n ]    ]
    [ COMPUTE
        { { AVG | COUNT | MAX | MIN | SUM } ( expression ) } [ ,...n ]
        [ BY expression [ ,...n ] ]
    ]
    [ FOR { BROWSE | XML { RAW | AUTO | EXPLICIT }
            [ , XMLDATA ]
            [ , ELEMENTS ]
            [ , BINARY base64 ]
        }
]
    [ OPTION ( < query_hint > [ ,...n ]) ]
< query expression > ::=
    { < query specification > | ( < query expression > ) }
    [ UNION [ ALL ] < query specification | ( < query expression > ) [...n ] ]
< query specification > ::=
    SELECT [ ALL | DISTINCT ]
        [ { TOP integer | TOP integer PERCENT } [ WITH TIES ] ]
        < select_list >
    [ INTO new_table ]
    [ FROM { < table_source > } [ ,...n ] ]
    [ WHERE < search_condition > ]
    [ GROUP BY [ ALL ] group_by_expression [ ,...n ]
        [ WITH { CUBE | ROLLUP } ]
    ]
    [ HAVING < search_condition > ]
```

At first glance, you appear to be selecting orderDate from the Customers table, but that is not possible because the Customers table does not have an orderDate. The key phrase is:

```
join Orders o on o.customerID = c.customerID
```

It is as if the join phrase creates a temporary table that is the width of the Customers table and the Orders table joined together. The on keyword dictates how the tables are joined. In this case, the tables are joined on the CustomerID column in Customers and in Orders.

Each record in Customers (represented by the alias c) is joined to the appropriate record in Orders (represented by the alias o) when the CustomerID fields match in both records. Similarly, each record in the Order Details record is joined to the Orders table by matching the OrderID column in both tables.

When you join two tables you can say "get every record that exists in either" (this is called an *outer join*) or you can say, as we've done here, "get only those records that exist in both tables" (called an *inner join*).

 Inner joins are the default, so writing `join` is the same as writing `inner join`.

The inner join shown above says: get only the records in Orders that match the records in Customers by having the same value in the CustomerID field (*on o.customerID = c.customerID*).

The `where` clause further constrains the search to those records where the Country field in Customers is an exact match for the string USA and where the orderDate in the orders table is greater than January 1, 1997.

```
where c.Country = 'USA' and orderDate > '1/1/97'
```

I did not specify the table for the orderDate. I could have written:

```
where c.Country = 'USA' and o.orderDate > '1/1/97'
```

but since Orders is the only table with an orderDate column, there is no ambiguity if I just use the column name. SQL is able to translate the string "1/1/97" into a DateTime representing January 1, 1997.

Using SQL to Manipulate the Database

SQL can be used for searching for and retrieving data and for creating, updating, and deleting tables and generally managing and manipulating the content and the structure of the database. For example, you can update the ContactName of a specific company:

```
Update Customers set ContactName = 'Jesse Liberty' where CompanyName = 'Save-a-lot
Markets'
```

 For a full explanation of SQL and details on using it well, see *Transact-SQL Programming*, by Kevin Kline, Lee Gould, and Andrew Zanevsky (O'Reilly).

Index

We'd like to hear your suggestions for improving our indexes. Send email to *index@oreilly.com*.

machine.config file (*continued*)
    configuring applications, 801–804, 806, 809
    global assemblies and, 865
    name/value pairs, 839
    OutputCache directive and, 735
    provider classes, 833
    purpose, 776
    session state, 271
    system.net configuration section, 834
    view state, 275
machineKey subsection, 837
Macro Explorer window (View), 46, 55
macros, 46
    breakpoints and, 312
    icon for, 37
    Macros command, 54–56
Macros command (Tools), 54–56
maintainScrollPositionOnPostBack attribute (<pages>), 822
MaintainScrollPositionOnPostback property (Page), 245
managed code, 773
manifests, 847
    hash calculations, 856
    overview, 850
    versioning and, 852
<map> tag, 176
maps, 37
Master directive, 291, 530
.master file extension, 19, 247
master pages
    configuration settings, 819
    content pages, 526–528
    controls and, 60
    creating, 537–539
    editing, 531–534
    nested, 528–531
    new features, 6
    overview, 521–526
    purpose, 61
Master property
    MasterType directive, 291
    Page class, 245
masterPageFile attribute (<pages>), 822
MasterPageFile property
    Master directive and, 530
    Page class, 245
MasterType directive, 291
MaximumValue property (RangeValidator), 339

MaxInvalidPasswordAttempts property, 818
maxIoThreads attribute (processModel), 836
MaxLength property
    setting constraints, 443
    TextBox control, 101, 237
maxPageStateFieldLength attribute (<pages>), 822
maxRequestLength attribute (<httpRuntime>), 823
maxWorkerThreads attribute (processModel), 836
MD5 algorithm, 856
MDI (Multiple Document Interface), 24
member lists, 36
member variables, 799
<membership> element, 818
membership, enabling, 548
MembershipUser object, 511
memory
    assemblies and, 847
    caching and, 735, 745, 749
    performance and, 775
    scavenging, 760
    session state and, 266, 271
    web applications and, 284, 794
    web pages and, 285
Memory windows (Debug), 314, 318
memoryLimit attribute (processModel), 836
menus
    Build menu, 25, 52
    customizing, 23
    Data menu, 26, 52
    Debug menu, 52
    Edit menu, 29–38
    File menu, 26–28
    Format menu, 26, 52
    Help menu, 58–59
    keyboard shortcuts, 26
    Layout menu, 26
    navigating via, 544
    overview, 26
    Project menu, 51
    Refactor menu, 46–49
    Tools menu, 53–57
    View menu, 38–46
    Website menu, 49–51
    Window menu, 57
Merge method, 410, 412
MessageName property (WebMethod), 656, 659–663
metacharacters, 340

OnClick attribute
    BulletedList control, 144, 148
    HTML and, 87
    image maps and, 181
onclick event, 91
OnClick method, 628
OnClientClick property, 91
OnFinishedEditRecord event, 606
onfocus event, 91
onInit event handler, 153, 156
onkeydown event, 91
onkeypress event, 91
onkeyup event, 91
OnLoad method, 287
OnLoadComplete method, 287
onmouseover event, 91
OnPreInit method, 287
OnPreLoad method, 287
OnPreRender method, 287
OnSelectedIndexChanged attribute, 133,
        139, 156
OnSelectionChanged event, 226
onServerClick event, 87, 91
OnTextChanged attribute, 102–104
OnUnload method, 287
Open menu (File), 28
Operator property (CompareValidator), 337,
        339
operators, 37
optimistic concurrency, 361–365
Options command (Tools), 57
OracleDataReader class, 414, 774
ordered lists, 143
Orientation property, 545
originalUrl attribute (<trust>), 838
OtherMonthDayStyle property
        (Calendar), 222
/out: parameter (disco), 684
outer joins, 891
outlining commands, 34
output caching, 721, 730–744, 793, 835
Output window (View), 46
OutputCache directive, 291, 730–737, 766
OutputCache module (httpModules), 835
Overline subproperty, 100

P

Page attribute (Reference), 293
Page class
    application-wide logic, 782
    callback support, 764

    Control class and, 244
    cross-page posting and, 260
    IsPostBack property, 66
    postback properties, 264
    PreviousPage property, 255
    properties, 244
    web page process, 243
    web services and, 649
Page directive
    child pages and, 527
    class names in, 249
    control tree and, 285
    EnableSessionState attribute, 271
    nested pages and, 530
    overview, 292
    page-level tracing, 297, 303
    page-specific error pages, 323
    session state, 768
    single-file model and, 247
    themes and, 573, 577
    validation and, 325
    view state and, 769
    WebService directive and, 649
page files (see .aspx file extension)
pageBaseType attribute (<pages>), 822
PageCount property
    DetailsView control, 392
    GridView control, 353
PageHandlerFactory class, 835
PageIndex property
    DetailsView control, 392
    GridView control, 353
PageIndexChanged event, 406
PageIndexChanging event, 406
pagelets (see user controls)
page-level tracing, 297–299
Page_Load event handler, 137
Page_Load method
    code-behind file, 236
    master pages and, 534
    Panel control example, 169, 171
    round trips and, 770
    site map nodes and, 546
    table rows and, 160
    user controls and, 607
pageOutput property (<trace>), 304, 833
PagerSettings property
    DetailsView control, 392
    GridView control, 353, 355
PagerStyle property
    DetailsView control, 392
    GridView control, 353

About the Authors

Jesse Liberty is the bestselling author of *Programming C#*, *Programming Visual Basic 2005*, *Learning C#*, and a dozen other books on web and object-oriented programming. He is the president of Liberty Associates, Inc., where he provides contract programming, consulting, and on-site training in ASP.NET, C#, C++, and related topics. He is a former vice president of Citibank and a former Distinguished Software Engineer and Software Architect for AT&T, Ziff Davis, Xerox, and PBS.

Dan Hurwitz is the president of Sterling Solutions, Inc., where for nearly two decades, he has provided contract programming and database development to a wide variety of clients.

Colophon

Our look is the result of reader comments, our own experimentation, and feedback from distribution channels. Distinctive covers complement our distinctive approach to technical topics, breathing personality and life into potentially dry subjects.

The animal on the cover of *Programming ASP.NET*, Third Edition, is a guitarfish (*Rhinobatos*). Members of the guitarfish family are considered rays, but they look like a combination of rays and sharks, with flat bodies like rays and two dorsal fins on the tail, similar to most sharks. The pectoral fins of the guitarfish are fused to its head, creating a triangle-shaped body, and it swims by moving its thick tail side to side, much like a shark. The five species of guitarfish are found in coastal waters around the world, from Asia to South Africa to Greenland to the East Coast of the United States, where they have also been known to inhabit rivers. Their habitat ranges anywhere from the shoreline to as far out as nearly 100 feet out, and they are believed to tolerate fresh, brackish, and marine water.

Guitarfish are bottom-dwellers and often bury themselves in sand, mud, or weeds near reefs. There they feed on a variety of mollusks and small fish. While catching prey, the guitarfish uses its rostrum (snout) to hold the prey against the sea floor to block its escape route. Guitarfish reproduce via internal fertilization and give birth to live young, which are fully developed at birth. The males are considered mature at 19–20 inches. Guitarfish pose no threat to humans and are of no interest to fisheries or anglers, though at times they do get caught in shrimp trawls.

Matt Hutchinson was the production editor for *Programming ASP.NET*, Third Edition. GEX, Inc. provided production services. Darren Kelly, Reba Libby, and Marlowe Shaeffer provided quality control.

Emma Colby designed the cover of this book, based on a series design by Edie Freedman. The cover image is a 19th-century engraving from the Dover Pictorial Archive. Karen Montgomery produced the cover layout with Adobe InDesign CS using Adobe's ITC Garamond font.

David Futato designed the interior layout. This book was converted from Microsoft Word to Adobe FrameMaker 5.5.6 by Keith Fahlgren with a format conversion tool created by Erik Ray, Jason McIntosh, Neil Walls, and Mike Sierra that uses Perl and XML technologies. The text font is Linotype Birka; the heading font is Adobe Myriad Condensed; and the code font is LucasFont's TheSans Mono Condensed. The illustrations that appear in the book were produced by Robert Romano, Jessamyn Read, and Lesley Borash using Macromedia FreeHand MX and Adobe Photoshop CS. The tip and warning icons were drawn by Christopher Bing. This colophon was written by Lydia Onofrei.

Better than e-books

Buy *Programming ASP.NET,* 3rd Edition, and access the digital edition FREE on Safari for 45 days.

Go to www.oreilly.com/go/safarienabled
and type in coupon code Y1D1-FJCD-AHAX-FCE9-F296

Search thousands of top tech books

Download whole chapters

Cut and Paste code examples

Find answers fast

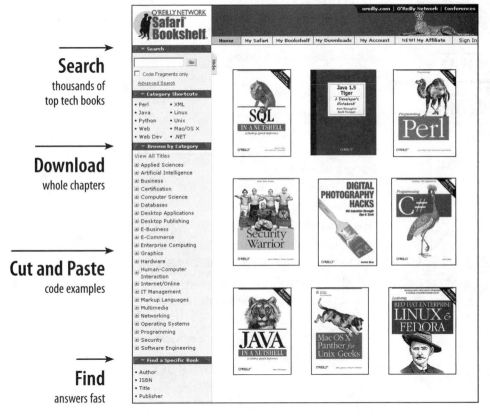

Search Safari! The premier electronic reference library for programmers and IT professionals.

Related Titles from O'Reilly

.NET

.NET and XML

.NET Framework Essentials, *3rd Edition*

ADO.NET in a Nutshell

ADO.NET Cookbook

ASP.NET 2.0: A Developer's Notebook

C# Cookbook

C# Essentials, *2nd Edition*

C# in a Nutshell, *2nd Edition*

C# Language Pocket Guide

Learning C#

Learning Visual Basic.NET

Mastering Visual Studio.NET

Mono: A Developer's Notebook

Programming .NET Components, *2nd Edition*

Programming .NET Security

Programming .NET Web Services

Programming ASP.NET, *3rd Edition*

Programming C#, *4th Edition*

Programming Visual Basic 2005

VB.NET Language in a Nutshell, *2nd Edition*

VB.NET Language Pocket Reference

Visual Basic 2005: A Developer's Notebook

Visual Basic 2005 Jumpstart

Visual C# 2005: A Developer's Notebook

Visual Studio Hacks

O'REILLY®

Our books are available at most retail and online bookstores.

To order direct: 1-800-998-9938 • *order@oreilly.com* • *www.oreilly.com*

Online editions of most O'Reilly titles are available by subscription at *safari.oreilly.com*

Keep in touch with O'Reilly

Download examples from our books

To find example files from a book, go to: *www.oreilly.com/catalog* select the book, and follow the "Examples" link.

Register your O'Reilly books

Register your book at *register.oreilly.com* Why register your books? Once you've registered your O'Reilly books you can:

- Win O'Reilly books, T-shirts or discount coupons in our monthly drawing.
- Get special offers available only to registered O'Reilly customers.
- Get catalogs announcing new books (US and UK only).
- Get email notification of new editions of the O'Reilly books you own.

Join our email lists

Sign up to get topic-specific email announcements of new books and conferences, special offers, and O'Reilly Network technology newsletters at:

elists.oreilly.com

It's easy to customize your free elists subscription so you'll get exactly the O'Reilly news you want.

Get the latest news, tips, and tools

www.oreilly.com

- "Top 100 Sites on the Web"—PC Magazine
- CIO Magazine's Web Business 50 Awards

Our web site contains a library of comprehensive product information (including book excerpts and tables of contents), downloadable software, background articles, interviews with technology leaders, links to relevant sites, book cover art, and more.

Work for O'Reilly

Check out our web site for current employment opportunities:

jobs.oreilly.com

Contact us

O'Reilly Media, Inc.
1005 Gravenstein Hwy North
Sebastopol, CA 95472 USA
Tel: 707-827-7000 or 800-998-9938
    (6am to 5pm PST)
Fax: 707-829-0104

Contact us by email

For answers to problems regarding your order or our products:
order@oreilly.com

To request a copy of our latest catalog:
catalog@oreilly.com

For book content technical questions or corrections: **booktech@oreilly.com**

For educational, library, government, and corporate sales: **corporate@oreilly.com**

To submit new book proposals to our editors and product managers:
proposals@oreilly.com

For information about our international distributors or translation queries:
international@oreilly.com

For information about academic use of O'Reilly books:
adoption@oreilly.com
or visit:
academic.oreilly.com

For a list of our distributors outside of North America check out:
international.oreilly.com/distributors.html

Order a book online

www.oreilly.com/order_new